STUDIES IN SEMANTICS

VOLUMES I AND II

INTRODUCTION TO SEMANTICS
and
FORMALIZATION OF LOGIC

By RUDOLF CARNAP

Two Volumes in One

CAMBRIDGE · MASSACHUSETTS
HARVARD UNIVERSITY PRESS
1961

DISTRIBUTED IN GREAT BRITAIN BY
OXFORD UNIVERSITY PRESS
LONDON

Second printing of the two volumes in one

LIBRARY OF CONGRESS CATALOGUE CARD NUMBER 58–13846
PRINTED IN THE UNITED STATES OF AMERICA

PREFACE TO THE ONE-VOLUME EDITION

The two volumes of my Studies in Semantics, both of which deal with semantical concepts and their relations to syntactical concepts, are here combined in one book. Except for minor corrections the text of both volumes is unchanged; the original pagination has been preserved, in order to facilitate references. Both bibliographies have been brought up to date.

In the original preface to volume II, I indicated my intention of writing another volume in this series, which was to deal with the logic of modalities. My book *Meaning and Necessity* (1947) may be regarded as a partial fulfillment of the promise. It does not give the actual construction of systems of modal logic, but it lays the groundwork for this task through philosophical discussions and semantical analyses of modalities with the help of the semantical concepts of extension and intension. Since then I have studied various more comprehensive modal systems with variables of all finite levels; but these investigations are not yet finished.

RUDOLF CARNAP

UNIVERSITY OF CALIFORNIA AT LOS ANGELES
JULY 1958

VOLUME I

INTRODUCTION TO SEMANTICS

(*Fifth Printing*)

PREFACE

The purpose of this book

In recent years many philosophers and scientists interested in the logical analysis of science have become aware that we need, in addition to a purely formal analysis of language, an analysis of the signifying function of language — in other words, a theory of meaning and interpretation. It is the purpose of this book to furnish a theory of this kind, called semantics. It will be seen that this theory, if sufficiently developed, contains not only a theory of designation, i.e. the relation between expressions and their meaning, but also a theory of truth and a theory of logical deduction.

Semantical concepts are often used, not only in science but in everyday life. When, for example, a person says that a certain word is used by him in a different sense than by somebody else, or that a certain assertion is true or that it is false, that a particular statement is analytic, i.e. true for purely logical reasons, that another statement follows from the first, or is compatible with it or contradicts it, — then in all these cases he applies semantical concepts. Thus some of the problems of semantics deal with familiar concepts and are by no means new. The task of a systematic construction of semantics is to find adequate, exact definitions for the customary semantical concepts and for new concepts related to them, and to supply a theory based on these definitions.

The development of semantics

Semantical concepts, especially the concept of truth, have been discussed by philosophers since ancient times. But a systematic development with the help of the exact instruments of modern logic has been undertaken only in recent years. This development originated with the Warsaw school of logicians. This group has made many contributions of great value to contemporary logic and the logical foundations of mathematics; their work has, for the time being, been interrupted by the invasion of Warsaw. There S. Lesniewski, in lectures from 1919 on, analyzed semantical concepts, especially the concept of truth and the semantical antinomies; and T. Kotarbinski, likewise in lectures and later (1926) in his book, made an elaborate analysis of certain semantical and related pragmatical concepts. (For a summary in German of his book see R. Rand, *Erkenntnis* 7, 1938–39.) On the basis of these preliminary analyses, Alfred Tarski (who is now in this country) laid the foundation of a systematic construction. In his book on the concept of truth (Polish, 1933; German translation, 1936), he set forth a method for defining the semantical concept of truth with respect to deductive systems and arrived at very important results, among them an answer to the question under what conditions a language of semantics is rich enough for the construction of an adequate definition of truth for a given system. Unfortunately, the whole development of semantical investigations in Poland remained unknown to the outside world until 1936 because the pertinent publications were in Polish only. This fact, incidentally, confirms once more the urgent need for an international auxiliary language, especially for scientific purposes.

Tarski, both through his book and in conversation, first called my attention to the fact that the formal method of syntax must be supplemented by semantical concepts, showing at the same time that these concepts can be defined by means not less exact than those of syntax. Thus the present book owes very much to Tarski, more indeed than to any other single influence. On the other hand, our conceptions of semantics seem to diverge at certain points. First — as will be seen by a look at the Table of Contents of this book — I emphasize the distinction between semantics and syntax, i.e. between semantical systems as interpreted language systems and purely formal, uninterpreted calculi, while for Tarski there seems to be no sharp demarcation. Second, within semantics, I stress the distinction between factual truth, dependent upon the contingency of facts, and logical truth, independent of facts and dependent merely on meaning as determined by semantical rules. I believe that this distinction is indispensable for the logical analysis of science; and one of the chief problems discussed in this book is that of representing this distinction, which has been made in some form or other by most philosophers since ancient times, by exact semantical definitions. Here again, Tarski seems to doubt whether there is an objective difference or whether the choice of a boundary line is not more or less arbitrary. (The two points of divergence mentioned seem, incidentally, to go back to a common root, namely to the distinction between logical and descriptive signs.) At present, it is not quite clear to me whether the divergence is a genuine difference of opinion or perhaps merely a difference in emphasis, direction of attention, and preference in procedure.

Arguments con and pro semantics

While many philosophers today urge the construction of a system of semantics, others, especially among my fellow empiricists, are rather sceptical. They seem to think that pragmatics — as a theory of the use of language — is unobjectionable, along with syntax as a purely formal analysis; but semantics arouses their suspicions. They are afraid that a discussion of propositions — as distinguished from sentences expressing them — and of truth — as distinguished from confirmation by observations — will open the back door to speculative metaphysics, which was put out at the front door. Some metaphysicians have indeed raised futile issues concerning truth, or rather the Truth, and I certainly should not like to help in reviving them. The same, however, holds for many other concepts, e.g. number, space, time, quality, structure, physical law, etc. Should we then refrain from talking about them in a non-metaphysical, scientific way? It seems to me that the only question that matters for our decision in accepting or rejecting a certain concept is whether or not we expect fruitful results from the use of that concept, irrespective of any earlier metaphysical or theological doctrines concerning it.

Will the semantical method lead to fruitful results? Since the development of semantics is still in its very beginning, it is too early to give a well-founded answer. But the use of this method for the construction of a theory of truth by Tarski and its use in the present book for the construction of a theory of logical deduction and a theory of interpretations of formal systems seem to justify the expectation that semantics will not only be of accidental help to pure logic but will supply the very basis for it. In addition, I believe, semantics will be of great importance for the so-called theory of knowledge and the methodology of mathematics and of empirical science. However, the form in which semantics is constructed in this book need not necessarily be the most appropriate for this purpose. This form is only a first attempt; its particular features, e.g. the contrast between semantics and syntax, and that between logical and factual truth, not to mention all the minor features, may possibly undergo fundamental changes in their further development. But it seems plausible to assume that both pure logic and the methodology of science will continue to require a method which — like that of semantics and syntax at present — sacrifices through abstraction some of the features which a full, pragmatical investigation of language would take into account, and thereby gains an exactness not attainable by the empirical concepts of pragmatics.

Plan of a series of books

The present book is the first of a series of small books which will appear under the common title *Studies in Semantics*. The further units of this series will in general be independent of one another, but each of them presupposes this first volume, which gives a general introduction to the field and an explanation of the most important concepts, many of which will be used in later studies. The second volume (Formalization) will deal with the problem of whether a full formalization of logic is possible and how such a formalization can be made. Logic will then be regarded as represented by a semantical system, and a formalization of logic will consist in the construction of a corresponding calculus (syntactical system). A full formalization would be a calculus which mirrors all essential properties of the system of logic in a formal way such that the intended interpretation is the only one possible. It will be shown that the customary forms of the calculus of logic (propositional and functional calculus) do not fulfil this condition. With the help of new basic concepts, to be used both in syntax and in semantics, a new calculus will be constructed which represents a full formalization of logic.

Use of symbols

In the present book, symbols of symbolic logic are used chiefly in examples and seldom for the systematic construction of semantics. Nevertheless, a knowledge of the elements of symbolic logic will generally be of great help in understanding, because the general viewpoint of modern symbolic logic, if not its technical details, is essential for our conception of semantics. A survey of those symbols and terms of symbolic logic which are used in this book is given in §6.

While the first chapter contains explanations that are easily comprehensible, the remainder of the book is on a more technical level. Some devices are used to facilitate reading. Material not absolutely necessary for an understanding of the main text is printed in small type, e.g. digressions into more technical problems, examples, proofs, references to other authors, etc. Among the numbered definitions and theorems, the more important are marked by ' + '. Each chapter and each section is preceded by a brief summary. This will enable the reader to look back over what has been covered and to anticipate the path immediately ahead, so that he will not feel lost in the jungle.

Acknowledgments

I wish to express my gratitude to the Department of Philosophy at Harvard University and to the American Council of Learned Societies for grants in aid of publication. I am indebted to Dr. C. G. Hempel, Dr. J. C. C. McKinsey, and Professor W. V. Quine for many valuable critical remarks on an earlier version of the manuscript. I want to thank Mr. A. Kaplan for expert help in the preparation of the manuscript and Mr. W. Pitts for assisting me in reading the proofs.

R. C.

CHICAGO, DECEMBER 1941

CONTENTS

A. SEMIOTIC AND ITS PARTS

1. Object Language and Metalanguage 3
2. Signs and Expressions 4
3. Sign-Events and Sign-Designs 5
4. The Parts of Semiotic: Pragmatics, Semantics, and Syntax 8
5. Descriptive and Pure Semantics 11
6. Survey of Some Symbols and Terms of Symbolic Logic 15

B. SEMANTICS

7. Semantical Systems 22
8. Truth-Tables as Semantical Rules 30
9. Radical Concepts 33
10. Further Radical Concepts 41
11. Variables 44
12. The Relation of Designation 49

C. L–SEMANTICS

13. Logical and Descriptive Signs 56
14. L-Concepts 60
15. L-Concepts in Special Semantics 78
16. L-Concepts in General Semantics 83
17. Correspondence between Semantical and Absolute Concepts 88
18. L-Range 95
19. The Concept of L-Range in an Extensional Metalanguage 118
20. General Semantics Based upon the Concept of L-Range 134
21. F-Concepts 140
22. Characteristic Sentences 145
23. L-Content 148

CONTENTS

D. SYNTAX

24. Calculi 155
25. Proofs and Derivations 159
26. The Null Sentential Class in Syntax 161
27. Examples of Calculi 164
28. C-Concepts (1) 167
29. Theorems Concerning C-Concepts 173
30. C-Concepts (2) 178
31. C-Concepts (3) 186
32. C-Content and C-Range 197

E. RELATIONS BETWEEN SEMANTICS AND SYNTAX

33. True and False Interpretations 202
34. L-True and L-False Interpretations 207
35. Examples of Interpretations 212
36. Exhaustive and L-Exhaustive Calculi 216

APPENDIX

37. Terminological Remarks 229
38. Outline of Further Semantical Problems 242
39. Remarks on "Logical Syntax of Language" 246

BIBLIOGRAPHY 253

INDEX 255

INTRODUCTION TO SEMANTICS

A. SEMIOTIC AND ITS PARTS

Semiotic, the theory of signs and languages, is divided into three parts: pragmatics, semantics, and syntax. Semantics is divided into descriptive and pure semantics; syntax is divided analogously into descriptive and pure syntax. The present book deals with pure semantics, pure syntax, and their relations.

§ 1. Object Language and Metalanguage

The language spoken about in some context is called the *object language*; the language in which we speak about the first is called the *metalanguage*.

A **language**, as it is usually understood, is a system of sounds, or rather of the habits of producing them by the speaking organs, for the purpose of communicating with other persons, i.e. of influencing their actions, decisions, thoughts, etc. Instead of speech sounds other movements or things are sometimes produced for the same purpose, e.g. gestures, written marks, signals by drums, flags, trumpets, rockets, etc. It seems convenient to take the term 'language' in such a wide sense as to cover all these kinds of systems of means of communication, no matter what material they use. Thus we will distinguish between speech language (or spoken language), language of writing (or written language), gesture language, etc. Of course, speech language is the most important practically, and is, moreover, in most cases the basis of any other language, in the sense that this other language is learned with the help of the speech language. But this fact is accidental; any of the other kinds of language could be learned and used in a way independent of the speech language.

If we investigate, analyze, and describe a language L_1, we need a language L_2 for formulating the results of our investigation of L_1 or the rules for the use of L_1. In this case we call L_1 the **object language**, L_2 the **metalanguage**. The sum total of what can be known about L_1 and said in L_2 may be called the *metatheory* of L_1 (in L_2). If we describe in English the grammatical structure of modern German and French or describe the historical development of speech forms or analyze literary works in these languages, then German and French are our object languages and English is our metalanguage. Any language whatever can be taken as an object language; any language containing expressions suitable for describing the features of languages may be taken as a metalanguage. Object language and metalanguage may also be identical, e.g. when we are speaking in English about English grammar, literature, etc.

§ 2. Signs and Expressions

> The smallest units of a language are called *signs*; sequences of signs are called *expressions*.

A continuous utterance in a language, e.g. a speech, a book, or a flag message, may be analyzed into smaller and smaller parts. Thus a speech may be divided into sentences, each sentence into words, each word into phonemes. A book or letter may be divided into (written) sentences, each sentence into (written) words, each word into letters of the alphabet, each letter into the simple strokes of which it consists. Where we stop the analysis is to some extent arbitrary, depending upon the purpose of our investigation. When interested in grammar, we may take (spoken or written) words or certain parts of words as ultimate units; when interested in spelling, letters; when interested in the historical development of letter forms, the single form elements of the letters. When we speak *in abstracto* about analysis of language, we use the term 'sign' to designate the ultimate units of the expressions of the languages. Thereby it remains undecided whether words or letters or whatever else are taken as signs; this may be specified as soon as we go over from the general discussion to a special investigation of some one language.

By an **expression** in a language we mean any finite sequence of signs in that language, no matter whether meaningful or not. Thus we treat all utterances in language as being of linear form. This is convenient because it enables us to specify the positions of signs in an expression by enumeration. A spoken utterance in one of the ordinary languages is a temporal series of sounds; a written utterance consists of marks ordered in lines; either of them can therefore easily be taken as linear, i.e. as one sequence. Where in practice a second dimension is used — as e.g. in written accents or similar discriminating marks, in a statistical table of figures, or in a diagram of a configuration in chess — it is always possible by some device to regard the whole expression as linear (e.g. by counting the accent in 'très' as the fourth sign, the 's' as the fifth).

§ 3. Sign-Events and Sign-Designs

The word 'sign' is ambiguous. It means sometimes a single object or event, sometimes a kind to which many objects belong. Whenever necessary, we shall use 'sign-*event*' in the first case, 'sign-*design*' in the second.

In the ordinary way of speaking about signs and expressions, e.g. letters of the alphabet, words, phrases, and sentences in English, certain ambiguities often occur. Thus, for instance, the word 'letter' — and analogously the words 'word', 'sentence', etc. — is used in two different ways, as exhibited by the following two sets of examples: 1. "There are two letters 's' in the eighth word of this paragraph"; "The second letter 's' in that word is a plural ending". 2. "The letter 's' occurs twice in the word 'signs' "; "The letter 's' is in many cases used as a plural ending in English". In (1) we say "many letters 's' ", in (2) "the letter 's' ", thus indicating that there is only one; hence the phrase "letter 's' " has two different meanings. In (1), a letter is a single thing or event, e.g. a body consisting of printer's ink or a sound event; therefore, it is at a certain time-moment or during a certain time-interval, and at each time-moment within its duration it occupies a certain place. In (2), on the other hand, a letter is not a single thing but a class of things to which many things may belong, e.g. the letter 's' is that class of written or printed marks to which all lower case S's belong. Although, in most cases, the context leaves no doubt as to which of the two meanings is intended, it will sometimes be advisable to distinguish them explicitly. In cases of this kind we shall use the term '**event**' — or 'letter-event', and analogously 'word-event', 'expression-event', 'sentence-event', etc. — for meaning (1), and the term '**design**' — or 'letter-design', and analogously 'word-design', 'expression-design', 'sentence-design', etc. — for meaning (2).

In historical descriptions of particular acts of speaking or writing, expression-events are often dealt with. But they are usually characterized by the designs to which they belong. When we say "Caesar wrote 'vici' ", then we are speaking about a certain word-event produced by Caesar's hand; but we describe it by its design; the sentence is meant to say: "Caesar wrote a word-event of the design 'vici' ". When we are not concerned with the history of single acts but with the linguistic description of a certain language or the logical (syntactical or semantical) analysis of a certain language system, then the features which we study are common to all events of a design. Therefore, in this kind of investigation, it is convenient to drop reference to expression-events entirely and to speak only about designs. Instead of saying, "Every event of the word-design 'Hund' is a noun-event (in German)", we may simply say, "The word-design 'Hund' is a noun-design". Since in these fields we are dealing with designs only, we may establish the convention that, in texts belonging to these fields, e.g. in this treatise, 'word' is to be understood as 'word-design', 'noun' as 'noun-design', and analogously with 'sign', 'expression', 'sentence', etc. Thus we come to the ordinary formulation, "The word 'Hund' is a noun". In the same way, if we say in syntax that a certain sentence is provable in a certain calculus, or in semantics that a certain sentence is true, then we mean to attribute these properties to sentence-designs, because they are shared by all sentence-events of a design; the same holds for all other concepts of syntax and semantics.

An expression-event consists of (one or more) sign-events, and an expression-design consists of sign-designs. However, the relation is not the same in the two cases. In an expression-event all elements are different (i.e. non-identical); there is no repetition of sign-events, because an event (e.g. a physical object) can only be at one place at a time. On the other hand, in an expression-design a certain sign-design may occupy several positions; in this case we speak of the several *occurrences* of the sign (-design) within the expression (-design).

Examples. The first and the last letter-event in the eighth word-event of § 3 in your copy (-event) of this book (-design) are two bodies of ink. They are different (i.e. non-identical), although similar (i.e. of similar geometrical shape); their similarity enables you to recognize them as belonging to the same design. Thus that word-event contains two letter-events 's'. On the other hand, the word-design 'signs' cannot contain two letter-designs 's' because there is only one letter-design 's'; but this design 's' occurs at two positions in the design 'signs' just as one and the same color or kind of substance or disease or architectural style may occur at different places, i.e. be exhibited by different things.

In an exact exhibition, an expression-event may be represented either as a (discrete, finite) series of sign-events or as a sequence without repetitions. But an expression-design has to be represented as a (finite) sequence of sign-designs because the same sign-design may occur in it several times. (Concerning the difference between series and sequences, see § 6.)

Whether in the metalanguage names of sign-events or names of sign-designs are assigned to the zero-level, i.e. taken as individual constants, depends upon the purpose of the investigation. If sign-events are dealt with at all (as in descriptive semiotic), they will in general be taken as individuals and hence be designated by individual constants. In this case, a sign-design is a property or class of sign-events and hence to be designated by a predicate (level 1, degree 1; see § 6). If, however, only designs and not events are referred to — as is mostly the case in pure semiotic, especially in pure syntax and pure semantics — then sign-designs may be taken as individuals.

Another ambiguity of the word 'word' may be mentioned, although it is of less importance for our subsequent discussions. 'Speak', 'speaks', 'speaking', 'spoken' are sometimes, e.g. in grammar books, called four forms of the same word, but at other times four different words (of the same word group). We prefer the second use of the phrase 'the same word (-design)', hence applying it only in cases of literal similarity, i.e. where the word-events consist of letter-events of the same designs.

§ 4. The Parts of Semiotic: Pragmatics, Semantics, and Syntax

> In an application of language, we may distinguish three chief factors: the speaker, the expression uttered, and the designatum of the expression, i.e. that to which the speaker intends to refer by the expression. In *semiotic*†, the general theory of signs and languages, three fields are distinguished. An investigation of a language belongs to *pragmatics* if explicit reference to a speaker is made; it belongs to *semantics*† if designata but not speakers are referred to; it belongs to *syntax*† if neither speakers nor designata but only expressions are dealt with.
>
> † For *terminological remarks* concerning the terms marked by an obelisk, see § 37.

When we observe an application of language, we observe an organism, usually a human being, producing a sound, mark, gesture, or the like as an expression in order to refer by it to something, e.g. an object. Thus we may distinguish three factors involved: the speaker, the expression, and what is referred to, which we shall call the **designatum** of the expression. (We say e.g. that in German 'Rhein' designates the Rhine, and that the Rhine is the designatum of 'Rhein'; likewise, the designatum of 'rot' is a certain property, namely the color red; the designatum of 'kleiner' is a certain relation, that of 'Temperatur' a certain physical function, etc.)

If we are analyzing a language, then we are concerned, of course, with expressions. But we need not necessarily also deal with speakers and designata. Although these factors are present whenever language is used, we may abstract from one or both of them in what we intend to say about the language in question. Accordingly, we distinguish three fields of investigation of languages. If in an investigation explicit reference is made to the speaker, or, to put it in more general terms, to the user of a language, then we assign it to the field of **pragmatics**. (Whether in this case reference to designata is made or not makes no difference for this classification.) If we abstract from the user of the language and analyze only the expressions and their designata, we are in the field of **semantics**†. And if, finally, we abstract from the designata also and analyze only the relations between the expressions, we are in (logical) **syntax**†. The whole science of language, consisting of the three parts mentioned, is called **semiotic**†.

The distinction between the three parts of semiotic has been made by C. W. Morris [Foundations] (see bibliography at the end of this book) on the basis of earlier distinctions of the three factors mentioned. There is a slight difference in the use of the term 'pragmatics', which is defined by Morris as the field dealing with the relations between speakers (or certain processes in them) and expressions. In practice, however, there does not seem to be a sharp line between investigations of this kind and those which refer also to designata.

Examples of *pragmatical* investigations are: a physiological analysis of the processes in the speaking organs and in the nervous system connected with speaking activities; a psychological analysis of the relations between speaking behavior and other behavior; a psychological study of the different connotations of one and the same word for different individuals; ethnological and sociological studies of the speaking habits and their differences in different tribes, different age groups, social strata; a study of the procedures applied by scientists in recording the results of experiments, etc. *Semantics* contains the theory of what is usually called the meaning of expressions, and hence the studies leading to the construction of a dictionary translating the object language into the metalanguage. But we shall see that theories of an apparently quite different subject-matter also belong to semantics, e.g. the theory of truth and the theory of logical deduction. It turns out that truth and logical consequence are concepts based on the relation of designation, and hence semantical concepts.

An investigation, a method, a concept concerning expressions of a language are called **formal**† if in their application reference is made not to the designata of the expressions but only to their form, i.e. to the kinds of signs occurring in an expression and the order in which they occur. Hence anything represented in a formal way belongs to *syntax*. It can easily be seen that it is possible to formulate rules for the construction of sentences, so-called *rules of formation*, in a strictly formal way (see e.g. the rules for S_3 in § 8). One might perhaps think at first that syntax would be restricted to a formulation and investigation of rules of this kind and hence would be a rather poor field. But it turns out that, in addition, *rules of deduction* can be formulated in a formal way and hence within syntax. This can, among other possibilities, be done in such a way that these rules lead to the same results as the semantical rules of logical deduction. In this way it is possible to represent logic in syntax.

The representation of certain concepts or procedures in a formal way and hence within syntax is sometimes called *formalization*. The formalization of semantical systems, i.e. the construction of corresponding syntactical systems, will be explained in § 36.

The result that logical deduction can be represented in a formal way — in other words, the possibility of a *formalization of logic* — is one of the most important results of the development of modern logic. The trend in this direction is as old as logic itself; but in different periods of its development the formal side has been emphasized sometimes more and sometimes less (comp. Scholz, *Geschichte der Logik*, 1931). The problem of the possibility of a full formalization of logic will be the chief subject-matter of Volume II.

For terminological remarks concerning the terms 'syntax' and 'formal', see § 37.

§ 5. Descriptive and Pure Semantics

> *Descriptive semantics* is the empirical investigation of the semantical features of historically given languages. *Pure semantics* is the analysis of semantical systems, i.e. systems of semantical rules. Syntax is divided analogously. The present book is concerned with semantical and syntactical systems and their relations, hence only with pure semantics and syntax.

Semantical investigations are of two different kinds; we shall distinguish them as descriptive and pure semantics. By **descriptive semantics** we mean the description and analysis of the semantical features either of some particular historically given language, e.g. French, or of all historically given languages in general. The first would be *special* descriptive semantics; the second, *general* descriptive semantics. Thus, descriptive semantics describes facts; it is an empirical science. On the other hand, we may set up a system of semantical rules, whether in close connection with a historically given language or freely invented; we call this a *semantical system*. The construction and analysis of semantical systems is called **pure semantics**. The rules of a semantical system S constitute, as we shall see, nothing else than a definition of certain semantical concepts with respect to S, e.g. 'designation in S' or 'true in S'. Pure semantics consists of definitions of this kind and their consequences; therefore, in contradistinction to descriptive semantics, it is entirely analytic and without factual content.

We make an analogous distinction between **descriptive** and **pure syntax** (compare [Syntax] §§ 2 and 24), and divide these fields into two parts, *special* and *general syntax* (compare [Syntax] § 46). Descriptive syntax is an empirical investigation of the syntactical features of given languages. Pure syntax deals with syntactical systems. A syntactical system (or calculus) K consists of rules which define syntactical concepts, e.g. 'sentence in K', 'provable in K', 'derivable in K'. Pure syntax contains the analytic sentences of the metalanguage which follow from these definitions. Both in semantics and in syntax the relation between the pure and the descriptive field is perfectly analogous to the relation between pure or mathematical geometry, which is a part of mathematics and hence analytic, and physical geometry, which is a part of physics and hence empirical (compare [Syntax] § 25; [Foundations] § 22).

Sometimes the question is discussed whether semantics and syntax are dependent upon pragmatics or not. The answer is that in one sense they are but in another they are not. Descriptive semantics and syntax are indeed based on pragmatics. Suppose we wish to study the semantical and syntactical properties of a certain Eskimo language not previously investigated. Obviously, there is no other way than first to observe the speaking habits of the people who use it. Only after finding by observation the pragmatical fact that those people have the habit of using the word 'igloo' when they intend to refer to a house are we in a position to make the semantical statement "'igloo' means (designates) house" and the syntactical statement "'igloo' is a predicate". In this way all knowledge in the field of descriptive semantics and descriptive syntax is based upon previous knowledge in pragmatics. *Linguistics*, in the widest sense, is that branch of science which contains all empirical investigation concerning languages. It is the descriptive, empirical part of semiotic (of spoken or written languages); hence it consists of pragmatics, descriptive semantics, and descriptive syntax. But these three parts are not on the same level; *pragmatics is the basis for all of linguistics*. However, this does not mean that, within linguistics, we must always explicitly refer to the users of the language in question. Once the semantical and syntactical features of a language have been found by way of pragmatics, we may turn our attention away from the users and restrict it to those semantical and syntactical features. Thus e.g. the two statements mentioned before no longer contain explicit pragmatical references. In this way, descriptive semantics and syntax are, strictly speaking, parts of pragmatics.

With respect to pure semantics and syntax the situation is different. These fields are independent of pragmatics. Here we lay down definitions for certain concepts, usually in the form of rules, and study the analytic consequences of these definitions. In choosing the rules we are entirely free. Sometimes we may be guided in our choice by the consideration of a given language, that is, by pragmatical facts. But this concerns only the motivation of our choice and has no bearing upon the correctness of the results of our analysis of the rules. (Analogy: the fact that somebody's garden has the shape of a pentagon may induce him to direct his studies in mathematical geometry to pentagons, or rather to certain abstract structures which correspond in a certain way to bodies of pentagonal shape; the shape of his garden guides his interests but does not constitute a basis for the results of his study.)

This treatise is devoted to *pure semantics* and *pure syntax*, or rather to the field in which semantical systems and syntactical systems, and in addition their relations, are analyzed. (There is so far no suitable name for this field; see terminological remarks, § 37, 'Theory of Systems'.) There will occasionally also occur examples referring to semantical or syntactical features of historical languages, say English or French, apparently belonging to descriptive semantics or syntax. But these examples are in fact meant as referring to semantical or syntactical systems which either are actually constructed or could be constructed in close connection with those languages.

Examples. Suppose that we make the statement, "The sentences 'Napoleon was born in Corsica' and 'Napoleon was not born in Corsica' are logically exclusive (incompatible) in English". This is meant as based upon a system E of semantical rules, especially a rule for 'not', constructed in consideration of the English language. The system E is tacitly or explicitly presupposed in this statement; it might be that a rule for 'not' has really been given previously, or it might be that it has not but easily could be given. In any case, concepts of logical analysis like 'logically exclusive', 'logically equivalent', etc., can only be applied on the basis of a system of rules.

The subject-matter of this treatise is restricted in still another direction, as compared with that of semiotic in general. Our discussions apply *only to declarative sentences*, leaving aside all sentences of other kinds, e.g. questions, imperatives, etc.; and hence only to language systems (semantical systems) consisting of declarative sentences. Our terminology is to be understood in this restricted sense; 'sentence' is short for 'declarative sentence', 'language' for 'language (system) consisting of declarative sentences', 'English' for 'that part of English which consists of declarative sentences', 'interpretation of a sentence of a calculus' for 'interpretation of the sentence as a declarative sentence', etc.

Not much has been done so far in the logical analysis of other than declarative sentences. Concerning *imperatives* and ought-sentences see: E. Mally, *Grundgesetze des Sollens; Elemente der Logik des Willens*, 1926; W. Dubislav, "Zur Unbegründbarkeit der Forderungssätze", *Theoria* 3, 1937; J. Jørgensen, "Imperatives and Logic", *Erkenntnis* 7, 1938; K. Menger, "A Logic of the Doubtful: On Optative and Imperative Logic", *Reports of a Math. Colloquium*, 2nd ser., no. 1, pp. 53–64; R. Rand, "Logik der Forderungssätze", *Zeitschr. f. Theorie d. Rechtes*, 1939; A. Hofstadter and J. C. C. McKinsey, "On the Logic of Imperatives", *Phil. of Sc.* 6, pp. 446–457, 1939. Concerning *questions* see short remarks in [Syntax] § 76, and in Hofstadter and McKinsey, *loc. cit.*, p. 454.

§ 6. Survey of Some Symbols and Terms of Symbolic Logic

Symbols and technical terms are listed here for later use in this book. Features deviating from other authors are chiefly found in the following paragraphs: use of letters; terminology of designata; (series and sequences); German letters; metalanguage.

† For terminological remarks concerning the terms marked by an obelisk, see § 37.

In the subsequent discussions we shall often make use of symbolic logic, especially its elementary parts. Therefore a brief survey of the symbols, letters, and terms used will be given here. We shall later apply these symbols chiefly in examples of sentences in object languages, but occasionally also in a metalanguage. While we usually take the ordinary English word-language as metalanguage, it will sometimes be convenient, for greater clarity and precision, to use a few symbols in the metalanguage, either in combination with English words or alone.

	SYMBOL	TRANSLATION
1. *Propositional*† *calculus*†	*connectives*	
one-place { negation†	'∼ . . .'	'not . . .'
⎧ disjunction†	'. . . ∨ - - -'	' . . . or - - -'
two-place ⎨ conjunction†	'. . . . - - -'	'. . . and - - -'
connections ⎨ implication†	'. . . ⊃ - - -'	'not . . . or - - -' (or: 'if . . . then - - -')
⎩ equivalence†	'. . . ≡ - - -'	'. . . if and only if - - -'
2. *Functional*† *calculus*†		
universality	$\left\{\begin{array}{l}\text{'. . } x \text{ . .'} \\ \text{'}(x)\ (\text{. . } x \text{ . .})\text{'}\end{array}\right\}$	'for every x, . . x . .'
existence	'(∃x) (. . x . .)'	'for some (i.e. at least one) x, . . x . .' (or: 'there is an x such that . . x . .')
abstraction	'(λx) (. . x . .)'	'the class of all x such that . . x . .'
	'(λx,y) (. . x . . y . .)'	'the relation between x and y such that . . x . . y . .'
identity	'$x = y$'	'x is identical with (i.e. the same object as) y'

Use of *letters* for the different types.

	CONSTANTS	VARIABLES
individual signs	'a', 'b', etc.	'x', 'y', 'z', etc.
predicates (level 1), degree 1	'P', 'Q'	'F', 'G'
predicates (level 1), degree 2	'R', 'S'	'H', 'L'
functors	'k', 'l'	'f', 'g'
propositional signs†	'A', 'B', etc.	'p', 'q', etc.
signs without types		'u', 'v', etc.

Examples of sentences. 'P(a)' means "a is P (i.e. has the property P)"; 'R(a,b)' "a has the relation R to b"; 'M(P)' "P is M (i.e. the property P has the property of second level M)".

Individual signs designate the individuals of the realm in question (objects); they belong to the zero **level**. Their properties and relations, and the **predicates** by which these are designated, belong to the first level. An **attribute** (i.e. a property or a relation) attributed to something of the level n, and the predicate designating it, belong to the level $n + 1$. A predicate of **degree** 1 (also called one-place predicate) designates a property; a predicate of degree n (n-place predicate) designates an n-adic relation, i.e. a relation holding between n members.

Examples of **functors**: 'prod', 'temp'; 'prod(m,n)' designates the product of the numbers m and n, 'temp(x)' the temperature of the body x.

A **definition** has the form '... $=_{Df}$ - - -'; this means: " '...' is to be interchangeable with '- - -' " (see § 24). Sometimes, instead of ' $=_{Df}$ ', ' $\equiv$ ' (between sentences) or ' $=$ ' (between other expressions) is used. '...' is called the **definiendum**, '- - -' the **definiens**.

Classification of forms of sentences. **Atomic sentences** are those which contain neither connectives nor variables (e.g. 'R(a,b)', 'b = c'); a **molecular** sentence is one not containing variables but consisting of atomic sentences (called its **components**) and connectives (e.g. ' $\sim$P(a)', 'A $\vee$ B'); a **general** sentence is one containing a variable (e.g. '$(\exists x)$P(x)').

In a sentence of the form '$(x)(...)$' or '$(\exists x)(...)$' or an expression of the form '$(\lambda x)(.. x ..)$', '(x)', '$(\exists x)$', and '(λx)' are called **operators** (universal, existential, and lambda- operator, respectively); '...' is called the **operand** belonging to the operator. A variable at a certain place in an expression is called **bound** if it stands at that place in an operator or in an operand whose operator contains the same variable; otherwise it is called **free**. An expression is called **open**, if it contains a free variable; otherwise **closed**. (A class of sentences is called closed if all its sentences are closed; this concept must be distinguished from that of a class closed with respect to a certain relation.) An open expression will also be called an **expressional function**†; and, moreover, an expressional function of degree n, if the number of (different) variables occurring in it as free variables is n. An expressional function such that it or the closed expressions constructed out of it by substitution are sentences is called a **sentential function**†.

Terminology of designata. In this treatise, the following terms for designata will be used. (Some of them do not seem to me quite satisfactory; they will be changed as soon as better ones have been proposed.)

Signs or Expressions	Designata			
individual constants	**individuals**			
predicates of degree 1	**properties** (classes) ⎱ **attri-**	⎱ **functions**		
predicates of degree 2 and higher	**relations** ⎰ **butes**	⎰ (†II) or		
functors	**functions** (†IIB)	**concepts**†	**entities**	
sentences	**propositions**†			

Series and sequences. There are two different ways of ordering objects in a linear order; it can be done by a series or by a sequence. A **series** of n objects is a transitive, irreflexive, and connected relation ('x precedes y'). A **sequence** with n members is, so to speak, an enumeration of the objects (at most n); it can be represented in two different ways: (1) by a predicate of degree 2 which designates a one-many relation between the objects and the ordinal numbers up to n, (2) by an argument expression containing n terms (in this case, the argument expression and the sequence designated are said to be of degree n). [*Example:* Suppose we want to order the objects b, c, d in such a way that we take first b, then c, then d, then c again. Thus we have a sequence with $n = 4$ but only three objects. This sequence may be represented in either of the following ways: (1) by '{b;1, c;2, d;3, c;4}' i.e. as the relation which correlates the object b to the number 1, c to 2 and also to 4, and d to 3; (2) by 'b;c;d;c'. If the objects are individuals, the expression in (1) is of the first level, that in (2) of the zero level. Thus method (2) leads to simpler formulations; we shall apply it in this book. The sentence 'T(b,c,d,c)' is usually paraphrased in about this way: "The relation T (of degree 4) holds for the objects b, c, d and c in this order"; on the basis of method (2), we shall permit, in addition, the following formulation: "The relation T (of degree 4) holds for the sequence (of degree 4) b;c;d;c."] In a sequence, repetitions are possible, i.e. the same member may occur at several places (e.g., c in the example given). In a series, this is impossible because of its irreflexivity. Therefore, in many cases we cannot use series but have to use sequences (e.g. in the representation of expression-designs, § 3 at the end).

German letters are used as signs of the metalanguage designating kinds of signs or expressions of the object language. '$\mathfrak{i}$' designates (the class of) individual variables, '$\mathfrak{in}$' individual signs (including variables), '$\mathfrak{p}$' predicate variables, '$\mathfrak{pr}$' predicates (including variables), '$\mathfrak{f}$' functor variables, '$\mathfrak{fu}$' functors (including variables), '$\mathfrak{f}$' propositional variables†, '$\mathfrak{fe}$' propositional signs (including variables), '$\mathfrak{S}$' sentences (including propositional signs); '$\mathfrak{v}$' variables (of any kind), '$\mathfrak{c}$' constants, '$\mathfrak{a}$' signs, '$\mathfrak{A}$' expressions; '$\mathfrak{K}$' classes of expressions (in most cases classes of sentences); '$\mathfrak{T}$' sentences and classes of sentences (see § 9). '$\mathfrak{pr}^n$' designates predicates of degree n, '$^m\mathfrak{pr}$' predicates of level m, e.g. '$^2\mathfrak{pr}^1$' predicates of first degree and second level; analogously with '$\mathfrak{p}$', '$\mathfrak{fu}$', and '$\mathfrak{f}$'. A constant of the metalanguage designating a particular sign (-design) or expression (-design) of one of the kinds mentioned is formed with the help of a figure as subscript; a corresponding variable of the metalanguage with the help of a letter 'i', 'j', etc., as subscript. Thus '$\mathfrak{in}_1$' is the name (in the metalanguage) of a particular individual constant (of the object language), e.g. 'a'; '$\mathfrak{in}_2$' of another one, e.g. 'b', etc.; '$^1\mathfrak{pr}_1^2$' of a predicate of first level and second degree, e.g. 'R'; '$\mathfrak{S}_3$' of a particular sentence, e.g. 'Q(b)'. "If $\mathfrak{pr}_i$ occurs in $\mathfrak{S}_j$, then ..." is short for "if a predicate $\mathfrak{pr}_i$ occurs in a sentence $\mathfrak{S}_j$, then . . .". '$\mathfrak{A}_j\left(\begin{smallmatrix}\mathfrak{v}_k\\\mathfrak{A}_i\end{smallmatrix}\right)$' designates that expression which is constructed out of $\mathfrak{A}_j$ by substituting $\mathfrak{A}_i$ for $\mathfrak{v}_k$ (i.e. by replacing $\mathfrak{v}_k$ at every place where it occurs as a free variable in $\mathfrak{A}_j$ by $\mathfrak{A}_i$). The designation of a compound expression is formed by putting the designations of its parts one after the other in the order in which the parts occur in the expression; signs which are not letters (e.g. brackets, comma, connectives, etc.) are in this procedure designated by themselves. Thus e.g. '$\mathfrak{pr}_1\,(\mathfrak{in}_2,\,\mathfrak{in}_1)$' (with the above examples) designates the expression 'R(b,a)'; $\mathfrak{S}_3 \vee \mathfrak{S}_2$ is the sentence which consists of $\mathfrak{S}_3$ (this may be 'Q(b)') followed by '$\vee$' followed by $\mathfrak{S}_2$.

As *metalanguage* we shall usually employ the English word-language, but supplemented by symbols, for the sake of brevity and precision. In this way, we shall use the German letter symbols just explained, and occasionally also certain symbols of symbolic logic, among them variables (e.g. 'x', 'F', etc.), operators (e.g. '(x)', '$(\exists F)$', '(λx)', etc.), the signs of identity ('$=$') and of definition ('$=_{\mathrm{Df}}$'). '$=_{\mathrm{Df}}$' is to mean 'is (hereby defined to be) the same as' or 'if and only if'. Further, with respect to classes, especially $\mathfrak{K}$, we use the customary symbols of the theory of sets: '$x\,\epsilon\,\mathfrak{K}_j$' means "$x$ is an element of $\mathfrak{K}_j$"; '$\mathfrak{K}_i \subset \mathfrak{K}_j$' means "$\mathfrak{K}_i$ is a sub-class of $\mathfrak{K}_j$"; $-\mathfrak{K}_i$ is the complement of $\mathfrak{K}_i$, i.e. the class of all elements (of the type in question) not belonging to $\mathfrak{K}_i$; $\mathfrak{K}_i + \mathfrak{K}_j$ is the sum of $\mathfrak{K}_i$ and $\mathfrak{K}_j$, i.e. the class containing all elements of $\mathfrak{K}_i$ and all elements of $\mathfrak{K}_j$; $\mathfrak{K}_i \times \mathfrak{K}_j$ is the product of $\mathfrak{K}_i$ and $\mathfrak{K}_j$, i.e. the class of all elements belonging to both classes. (If in $\mathfrak{T}_i + \mathfrak{T}_j$, $\mathfrak{T}_i$ or $\mathfrak{T}_j$ is not a class but a sentence $\mathfrak{S}_k$, then its unit class $\{\mathfrak{S}_k\}$ is meant as component of the sum.) $\{x\}$ is the class whose only element is x; $\{x_1,\,x_2,\,..\,x_n\}$ is the class whose elements are $x_1,\,x_2,\,..\,x_n$. If $\mathfrak{M}_i$ is a class of classes, $pr(\mathfrak{M}_i)$ is the product of the classes of $\mathfrak{M}_i$ (if $\mathfrak{M}_i$ is null, $pr(\mathfrak{M}_i)$ is the universal class).

As first introductions into *symbolic logic* for beginners see Cooley [Logic] and Tarski [Logic]. On a higher technical level see Whitehead and Russell [Princ. Math.], Quine [Math. Logic], Church [Logic], Carnap [Logic].

B. SEMANTICS

The construction of semantical systems is explained. Semantical concepts are introduced, especially truth, designation, and other concepts defined with their help.

§ 7. Semantical Systems

A *semantical system* is a system of rules which state *truth-conditions* for the sentences of an object language and thereby determine the meaning of these sentences. A semantical system S may consist of *rules of formation*, defining 'sentence in S', *rules of designation*, defining 'designation in S', and *rules of truth*, defining 'true in S'. The sentence in the metalanguage '$\mathfrak{S}_i$ is true in S' means the same as the sentence $\mathfrak{S}_i$ itself. This characteristic constitutes a condition for the *adequacy* of definitions of truth.

By a **semantical system** (or interpreted system) we understand a system of rules, formulated in a metalanguage and referring to an object language, of such a kind that the rules determine a **truth-condition** for every sentence of the object language, i.e. a sufficient and necessary condition for its truth. In this way the sentences are *interpreted* by the rules, i.e. made understandable, because to understand a sentence, to know what is asserted by it, is the same as to know under what conditions it would be true. To formulate it in still another way: the rules determine the *meaning* or *sense* of the sentences. Truth and falsity are called the **truth-values** of sentences. To know the truth-condition of a sentence is (in most cases) much less than to know its truth-value, but it is the necessary starting point for finding out its truth-value.

Example. Suppose that Pierre says: "Mon crayon est noir" ($\mathfrak{S}_1$). Then, if we know French, we understand the sentence $\mathfrak{S}_1$ although we may not know its truth-value. Our understanding of $\mathfrak{S}_1$ consists in our knowledge of its truth-condition; we know that $\mathfrak{S}_1$ is true if and only if a certain object, Pierre's pencil, has a certain color, black. This knowledge of the truth-condition for $\mathfrak{S}_1$ tells us what we must do in order to determine the truth-value of $\mathfrak{S}_1$, i.e. to find out whether $\mathfrak{S}_1$ is true or false; what we must do in this case is to observe the color of Pierre's pencil.

In what way can the truth-conditions for the sentences of a system be stated? If the system contains only a finite number of sentences, then we may give a full list of the truth-conditions, one for each sentence. This is done, for instance, in the ordinary cable codes. A code translates each sentence separately and thereby interprets it. Hence a code is a semantical system, but one of a primitive kind. We may thus distinguish two chief kinds of semantical systems, *code systems* and *language systems*. A code system lists the truth-conditions separately for each sentence, while a language system gives general rules for partial expressions of sentences in such a way that the truth-condition for every sentence is determined by the rules for the expressions of which it consists. In the case of the ordinary cable codes, flag codes, and the like, only the first form, that of particular rules, is possible. In the case of a language system containing an infinite number of sentences, only the second form, that of general rules, is possible, because we cannot formulate an infinite number of rules. There are cases of languages with a finite number of sentences where either form is applicable.

Examples. 1. We construct a semantical system S_1 in the following way. S_1 (that is to say, the object language of S_1) contains seven signs: three individual constants, in_1, in_2, in_3, two predicates, pr_1 and pr_2, and the two parentheses '(' and ')'. [In order to be able to write down actual examples of sentences of S_1, we may choose some letters as the first five signs, e.g. 'a', 'b', 'c', 'P', 'Q'. But this choice is obviously irrelevant for the semantical properties of S_1 and is therefore, strictly speaking, outside of pure semantics. Its role is the same as that of diagrams in geometry; they facilitate the operations practically but have no theoretical bearing on the proofs.] Sentences of S_1 are the expressions of the form $\mathfrak{pr}$ ($\mathfrak{in}$). The truth-conditions are given separately for each sentence by the following rules:

1. $\mathfrak{pr}_1$ ($\mathfrak{in}_1$) is true if and only if Chicago is large.
2. $\mathfrak{pr}_1$ ($\mathfrak{in}_2$) is true if and only if New York is large.
3. $\mathfrak{pr}_1$ ($\mathfrak{in}_3$) is true if and only if Carmel is large.
4. $\mathfrak{pr}_2$ ($\mathfrak{in}_1$) is true if and only if Chicago has a harbor.
5. $\mathfrak{pr}_2$ ($\mathfrak{in}_2$) is true if and only if New York has a harbor.
6. $\mathfrak{pr}_2$ ($\mathfrak{in}_3$) is true if and only if Carmel has a harbor.

2. We construct the semantical system S_2 in the following way. S_2 contains the same signs and sentences as S_1. We give five particular rules each specifying the designatum of one of the five chief signs, and one general rule for the truth-conditions of the sentences:

1. $\mathfrak{in}_1$ designates Chicago.
2. $\mathfrak{in}_2$ designates New York.
3. $\mathfrak{in}_3$ designates Carmel.
4. $\mathfrak{pr}_1$ designates the property of being large.
5. $\mathfrak{pr}_2$ designates the property of having a harbor.
6. A sentence $\mathfrak{pr}_i$ ($\mathfrak{in}_j$) is true if and only if the designatum of $\mathfrak{in}_j$ has the designatum of $\mathfrak{pr}_i$ (i.e. the object designated by $\mathfrak{in}_j$ has the property designated by $\mathfrak{pr}_i$). The systems S_1 and S_2 contain the same sentences, and every sentence has the same truth-condition (interpretation, meaning) in both systems. Hence they are essentially alike, but differ with respect to the kinds of rules applied; S_1 is a code system, S_2 a language system.

As the previous and the following examples show, a *semantical system* may be constructed in this way: first a *classification of the signs* is given, then **rules of formation** are laid down, then **rules of designation**, and finally **rules of truth**. By the rules of formation of a system S the term 'sentence of S' is defined; by the rules of designation 'designation in S'; by the rules of truth 'true in S'. The definition of 'true in S' is the real aim of the whole system S; the other definitions serve as preparatory steps for this one, making its formulation simpler. On the basis of 'true in S', other semantical concepts with respect to S can be defined, as we shall see later. (The simplest one is the definition of falsity: a sentence $\mathfrak{S}_i$ of S is *false* in S $=_{\text{Df}}$ $\mathfrak{S}_i$ is not true in S.) It is especially important to be aware of the fact that the rules of designation do not make factual assertions as to what are the designata of certain signs. There are no factual assertions in pure semantics. The rules merely lay down conventions in the form of a definition of 'designation in S'; this is done by an enumeration of the cases in which the relation of designation is to hold. Sometimes the term 'designation' is also used for compound expressions and even for sentences; this will be discussed later (§ 12). In this case, the rules of designation define by enumeration the preliminary term 'direct designation'; and with its help the more general term 'designation' is defined recursively.

In the case of the very simple system S_2 it can easily be shown that the rules of designation define 'designation' by enumeration. We can transform those rules into an explicit definition:

> *x designates t* in S_2 $=_{\text{Df}}$ ($x = \text{in}_1$ and $t =$ Chicago) or ($x = \text{in}_2$ and $t =$ New York) or ($x = \text{in}_3$ and $t =$ Carmel) or ($x = \text{pr}_1$ and $t =$ the property of being large) or ($x = \text{pr}_2$ and $t =$ the property of having a harbor).

('t' is here a variable not satisfying the ordinary rule of types; its range of values comprehends both individuals and properties. The problem involved here will be discussed later; see § 12.)

It will now be shown that the whole set of rules of formation, rules of designation and rules of truth for S_2 can be brought into the form of a definition for 'true in S_2', based upon a classification of the signs of S_2. (The classes $\mathfrak{K}_1$ to $\mathfrak{K}_4$ are meant as in, pr, {'('}, and {')'} respectively; but this need not be mentioned in the formulation of the system.)

1. Classification. S_2 contains four (mutually exclusive) classes of signs, $\mathfrak{K}_1$, $\mathfrak{K}_2$, $\mathfrak{K}_3$, and $\mathfrak{K}_4$; $\mathfrak{K}_1$ contains (only) the signs $\mathfrak{a}_1$, $\mathfrak{a}_2$, $\mathfrak{a}_3$; $\mathfrak{K}_2$, $\mathfrak{a}_4$ and $\mathfrak{a}_5$; $\mathfrak{K}_3$, $\mathfrak{a}_6$; $\mathfrak{K}_4$, $\mathfrak{a}_7$.

2. $\mathfrak{A}_i$ is true in S_2 $=_{\text{Df}}$ $(\exists x)\ (\exists y)\ (\exists z)\ (\exists F)$ $[\mathfrak{A}_i$ consists of x, $\mathfrak{a}_6$, y, $\mathfrak{a}_7$ in this order and $x \in \mathfrak{K}_2$ and $y \in \mathfrak{K}_1$ and $[(y = \mathfrak{a}_1$ and $z =$ Chicago) or $(y = \mathfrak{a}_2$ and $z =$ New York) or $(y = \mathfrak{a}_3$ and $z =$ Carmel)] and $[(x = \mathfrak{a}_4$

and $F = $ the property of being large) or $(x = a_5$ and $F = $ the property of having a harbor)] and $F(z)$].

By this definition, the system S_2 is established.

A remark may be added as to the way in which the term *'true'* is used in these discussions. We apply this term chiefly to sentences (and later to classes of sentences also). [The term may also be applied in an analogous way to propositions as designata of sentences (see D_{17}–I); but this use will not occur often in the following discussions; compare the terminological remarks in § 37.] We use the term here in such a sense that *to assert that a sentence is true means the same as to assert the sentence itself*; e.g. the two statements "The sentence 'The moon is round' is true" and "The moon is round" are merely two different formulations of the same assertion. (The two statements mean the same in a logical or semantical sense; from the point of view of pragmatics, in this as in nearly every case, two different formulations have different features and different conditions of application; from this point of view we may e.g. point to the difference between these two statements in emphasis and emotional function.)

The decision just mentioned concerning the use of the term 'true' is itself not a definition for 'true'. It is rather a standard by which we judge whether a definition for truth is adequate, i.e. in accordance with our intention. If a definition of a predicate pr_i — e.g. the word 'true' or 'valid' or any sign arbitrarily chosen — is proposed as a definition of truth, then we shall accept it as an adequate definition of truth if and only if, on the basis of this definition, pr_i fulfills the condition mentioned above, namely that it yields sentences like " 'The moon is round' is . . . if and only if the moon is round", where pr_i (e.g. 'true') is to be put at the place of '. . .'. This leads to the following definition D7–A.

D7-A. A predicate pr_i is an *adequate* predicate (and its definition an adequate definition) for the concept of *truth* within a certain class of sentences $\Re_j =_{Df}$ every sentence which is constructed out of the sentential function '*x* is *F* if and only if *p*' by substituting $\mathfrak{pr}_i$ for '*F*', any sentence $\mathfrak{S}_k$ of $\Re_j$ for '*p*', and any name (syntactical description) of $\mathfrak{S}_k$ for '*x*', follows from the definition of $\mathfrak{pr}_i$.

Example. Let $\Re_j$ contain the sentence 'Chicago is a city'. Let '$\mathfrak{S}_1$' be a name of this sentence. Suppose that somebody introduces the word 'verum' into English by a certain definition D. In order to apply D7–A, we have to examine all sentences constructed in the way described in D7–A. By putting 'verum' for '*F*', 'Chicago is a city' for '*p*', and '$\mathfrak{S}_1$' for '*x*', we obtain '$\mathfrak{S}_1$ is verum if and only if Chicago is a city'. If our examination comes to the result that D is of such a kind that this and all analogous sentences follow from D, then, according to D7–A, we shall call 'verum' an adequate predicate for truth and the proposed definition D an adequate definition for truth. This is practically justified by the fact that the result mentioned shows that the new word 'verum' as introduced by D is used in the same way as the ordinary word 'true' according to the decision mentioned above.

D7–A is the simplest form of the definition of adequacy; it refers only to the special case where the sentences to which the predicate for the concept of truth is applied belong to the same language as this predicate — in other words, where the object language is the same as (or part of) the metalanguage. In general, object language *S* and metalanguage *M* are different. In this case, the following more general definition of adequacy applies. (This definition is due to Tarski; see below.)

D7-B. A predicate $\mathfrak{pr}_i$ in *M* is an *adequate* predicate (and its definition an adequate definition) for the concept of *truth* with respect to an object language $S =_{Df}$ from the definition of $\mathfrak{pr}_i$ every sentence in *M* follows which is constructed out of the sentential function '*x* is *F* if and only if *p*' by substituting $\mathfrak{pr}_i$ for '*F*', a translation of any sentence $\mathfrak{S}_k$ of *S* into M for 'p', and any name (syntactical description) of $\mathfrak{S}_k$ for 'x'.

Example. Let S be a certain part of the German language, containing among others the sentence 'Der Mond ist rund'. Let '$\mathfrak{S}_2$' be the name of this sentence. We take English as metalanguage M. The translation of $\mathfrak{S}_2$ in M is 'The moon is round'. Suppose that a definition D_2 for the sign 'T' is proposed and that we wish to find out whether D_2 is an adequate definition for truth with respect to the part S of the German language. According to D7–B, one of the sentences to be examined is constructed by substituting 'T' for 'F', the translation 'The moon is round' for 'p', and '$\mathfrak{S}_2$' for 'x'. Thus we obtain the sentence '$\mathfrak{S}_2$ is T if and only if the moon is round'. If this and all analogous sentences are found to follow from the definition D_2 of 'T', then D_2 is an adequate definition and 'T' an adequate predicate for truth in S.

It can easily be shown that two predicates each of which is an adequate predicate for truth with respect to the same object language S have the same extension (they are equivalent, D10–11b, and even L-equivalent, T22–13).

It is especially to be noticed that the concept of truth in the sense just explained — we may call it the *semantical concept of truth* — is fundamentally different from concepts like 'believed', 'verified', 'highly confirmed', etc. The latter concepts belong to pragmatics and require a reference to a person.

In order to make clearer the distinction just mentioned, let us consider the following example. 'The moon has no atmosphere' ($\mathfrak{S}_1$); '$\mathfrak{S}_1$ is true' ($\mathfrak{S}_2$); '$\mathfrak{S}_1$ is confirmed to a very high degree by scientists at the present time' ($\mathfrak{S}_3$). $\mathfrak{S}_2$ says the same as $\mathfrak{S}_1$; $\mathfrak{S}_2$ is, like $\mathfrak{S}_1$, an astronomical statement and is, like $\mathfrak{S}_1$, to be tested by astronomical observations of the moon. On the other hand, $\mathfrak{S}_3$ is a historical statement; it is to be tested by historical, psychological observations of the behavior of astronomers.

Wittgenstein ([Tractatus] 4.024, 4.46) has emphasized the point of view that the truth-conditions of a sentence constitute its meaning, and that understanding consists in knowing these conditions. This view is also connected with his conception of logical truth (compare quotations given at the end of § 18A).

According to Tarski ([Wahrheitsbegriff] p. 267), S. Lesniewski was the first to formulate an exact requirement of adequacy for the definition of truth, in the simple form of D7-A above (in unpublished lectures since 1919); and similar formulations are found in a Polish book on the theory of knowledge by T. Kotarbinski (1926). F. P. Ramsey, in his review (1923) of Wittgenstein's book, gives a related formulation: "If a thought or proposition token 'p' says p, then it is called true if p, and false if $\sim p$" ("Foundations of Mathematics", p. 275). Tarski himself gave the more general form (like D7-B above) of the definition of adequacy (his "Konvention $\mathfrak{W}$", [Wahrheitsbegriff] p. 305). Further, he gave the first exact definition for truth with respect to certain formalized languages; his definition fulfills the requirement of adequacy and simultaneously avoids the antinomies connected with an unrestricted use of the concept of truth as e.g. in everyday language. In the same work [Wahrheitsbegriff], Tarski comes to very valuable results by his analysis of the concept of truth and related semantical concepts. These results are of a highly technical nature and therefore cannot be explained in this introductory Volume I.

The requirement mentioned is not meant as a new theory or conception of truth. Kotarbinski has already remarked that it is the old classical conception which dates back to Aristotle. The new feature is only the more precise formulation of the requirement. Tarski says further that the characterization given is also in agreement with the ordinary use of the word 'true'. It seems to me that he is right in this assertion, at least as far as the use in science, in judicial proceedings, in discussions of everyday life on theoretical questions is concerned. But I will not stress this point; it may be remarked that Arne Ness has expressed some doubts about the assertion, based on systematic questioning of people. At any rate, this question is of a pragmatical (historical, psychological) nature and has not much bearing on the questions of the method and results of semantics.

§ 8. Truth-Tables as Semantical Rules

> The customary truth-tables are semantical truth-rules in the form of diagrams. The rules of formation, and likewise the rules of truth, for molecular sentences may be stated in the form of a recursive definition, specifying the condition first for atomic sentences and then for molecular sentences with reference to their components.

The semantical systems considered so far contain only atomic sentences. Now we come to systems possessing connectives and molecular sentences constructed with their help. The number of sentences in a system of this kind is infinite. This is the case with nearly all symbolic systems usually dealt with, and also with the natural languages. [In English, for instance, for any given sentence, however long, we can construct a longer sentence by adding 'and the moon is round'; therefore the number of sentences is infinite.]

The connectives are often introduced with the help of **truth-tables**. It is easily seen that a truth-table is nothing but a semantical rule in the form of a diagram. Take e.g. the table of disjunction (usually written in a less correct way with variables 'p', etc., of the object language instead of signs '$\mathfrak{S}_i$', etc., of the metalanguage):

	$\mathfrak{S}_i$	$\mathfrak{S}_j$	$\mathfrak{S}_i \lor \mathfrak{S}_j$
1.	T	T	T
2.	T	F	T
3.	F	T	T
4.	F	F	F

The four lines of the table are meant to say this: 1. If $\mathfrak{S}_i$ is true and $\mathfrak{S}_j$ is true, $\mathfrak{S}_i \lor \mathfrak{S}_j$ is true; 2. if $\mathfrak{S}_i$ is true and $\mathfrak{S}_j$ is false, $\mathfrak{S}_i \lor \mathfrak{S}_j$ is true; 3. if $\mathfrak{S}_i$ is false and $\mathfrak{S}_j$ is true, $\mathfrak{S}_i \lor \mathfrak{S}_j$ is true; 4. if $\mathfrak{S}_i$ is false and $\mathfrak{S}_j$ is false, $\mathfrak{S}_i \lor \mathfrak{S}_j$ is false. Hence the whole table says: $\mathfrak{S}_i \lor \mathfrak{S}_j$ is true if and only if $\mathfrak{S}_i$ is true or $\mathfrak{S}_j$ is true or both. Thus the table states a truth-condition for the sentences of the form $\mathfrak{S}_i \lor \mathfrak{S}_j$; it says the same as rule (4c) in the example S_3 below.

The customary truth-table for negation is this:

	$\mathfrak{S}_i$	$\sim\mathfrak{S}_i$
1.	T	F
2.	F	T

It says: 1. If $\mathfrak{S}_i$ is true, $\sim\mathfrak{S}_i$ is false; 2. if $\mathfrak{S}_i$ is false, $\sim\mathfrak{S}_i$ is true. In other words, $\sim\mathfrak{S}_i$ is true if and only if $\mathfrak{S}_i$ is false, i.e. not true. Hence it says the same as rule (4b) in the example S_3 below.

In the same way, the customary truth-tables for the other connectives are truth-rules in the form of diagrams. Some of them are reformulated in words in the rules of the example S_4 below.

The rules of formation for a system S in which the number of components in a sentence is not limited may be formulated in the following way. First, the form or forms of atomic sentences of S are stated, and, second, the operations are described by which compound sentences of S may be constructed out of sentences (and sometimes other expressions) of atomic form. Thus the definition of 'sentence in S' is not an explicit but a recursive definition. The term defined occurs also in the definiens (see e.g. rules (2) for S_3 below, where '$\mathfrak{S}$' occurs in the definiens). This fact, however, does not make the definition circular. If we wish to determine whether a given expression $\mathfrak{A}_k$ is a sentence, the definition refers us back to the question whether another expression $\mathfrak{A}_i$ is a sentence. But it does so in such a way that $\mathfrak{A}_i$ is a proper part of $\mathfrak{A}_k$. Therefore, after a finite number of applications of the second part of the recursive definition we come to an expression of atomic form and hence to a solution with the help of the first part of the definition. The situation with the rules of truth is similar. They give a recursive definition for 'true in S' in strict analogy to the definition for 'sentence in S'. Therefore, for any given sentence $\mathfrak{S}_i$ of S, the rules of truth determine a truth-condition, although in general they do not determine the truth-value of $\mathfrak{S}_i$.

Examples of semantical systems. To facilitate understanding, we formulate the rules in the following systems by using signs and expressions of the object language in quotes. The exact method using names of the signs (German letters) has been shown in § 7.

Semantical System S_3

1. Classification of signs. Three in ('a', 'b', 'c'), two pr ('P', 'Q'); further single signs: '$\sim$', '$\vee$', '(', ')'.

2. Rules of formation. An expression $\mathfrak{A}_k$ in S_3 is a *sentence* ($\mathfrak{S}$) in $S_3 =_{\text{Df}} \mathfrak{A}_k$ has one of the following forms:

  a. pr(in); b. $\sim(\mathfrak{S}_i)$; c. $(\mathfrak{S}_i) \vee (\mathfrak{S}_j)$.

3. Rules of designation. $\mathfrak{a}_i$ *designates* (an entity) u in $S_3 =_{\text{Df}} \mathfrak{a}_i$ is the first and u the second member in one of the following pairs: a. 'a', Chicago; b. 'b', New York; c. 'c', Carmel; d. 'P', the property of being large; e. 'Q', the property of having a harbor.

4. Rules of truth. $\mathfrak{S}_k$ is *true* in $S_3 =_{\text{Df}}$ one of the following three conditions is fulfilled:

  a. $\mathfrak{S}_k$ has the form $\mathfrak{pr}_i(\mathfrak{in}_j)$, and the object designated by $\mathfrak{in}_j$ has the property designated by $\mathfrak{pr}_i$.
  b. $\mathfrak{S}_k$ has the form $\sim(\mathfrak{S}_i)$, and $\mathfrak{S}_i$ is not true.
  c. $\mathfrak{S}_k$ has the form $(\mathfrak{S}_i) \vee (\mathfrak{S}_j)$, and at least one of the sentences $\mathfrak{S}_i$ and $\mathfrak{S}_j$ is true.

Examples of application of the rules. (While the rules require every component of a connection to be included in parentheses, we shall omit the parentheses here and in later examples under the customary conditions.) Let us examine the expression 'P(c) $\vee \sim$Q(a)' ($\mathfrak{A}_1$) on the basis of the rules of S_3. By applying rules (2c) and (2b), and rule (2a) twice, we find that $\mathfrak{A}_1$ is a sentence in S_3. Now we apply rules (4) in order to construct a truth-condition for $\mathfrak{A}_1$ in S_3. According to rule

(4c), $\mathfrak{A}_1$ is true in S_3 if and only if 'P(c)' is true or '$\sim$Q(a)' is true or both. According to (4b), '$\sim$Q(a)' is true if and only if 'Q(a)' is not true. Hence, $\mathfrak{A}_1$ is true if and only if 'P(c)' is true or 'Q(a)' is not true or both. According to (4a) and (3), 'P(c)' is true if and only if Carmel is large, and 'Q(a)' is true if and only if Chicago has a harbor. Therefore, $\mathfrak{A}_1$ is true in S_3 if and only if either Carmel is large or Chicago does not have a harbor or both. Thus we have found a truth-condition for $\mathfrak{A}_1$ in S_3 as determined by the rules of S_3. But these rules do not suffice to determine the truth-value of $\mathfrak{A}_1$. In order to find this we must know certain facts in addition to the rules. This would lead us outside of semantics into empirical science, in this case into geography.

Semantical System S_4

1. Classification of signs. The same signs as in S_3, and in addition '$\bullet$', '$\supset$', '$\equiv$'.

2. Rules of formation. (a),(b), and (c) as in S_3; further: d. $(\mathfrak{S}_i) \bullet (\mathfrak{S}_j)$; e. $(\mathfrak{S}_i) \supset (\mathfrak{S}_j)$; f. $(\mathfrak{S}_i) \equiv (\mathfrak{S}_j)$.

3. Rules of designation. The same as in S_3.

4. Rules of truth. (a), (b), and (c) as in S_3; further:

   d. $\mathfrak{S}_k$ has the form $(\mathfrak{S}_i) \bullet (\mathfrak{S}_j)$, and both $\mathfrak{S}_i$ and $\mathfrak{S}_j$ are true.

   e. $\mathfrak{S}_k$ has the form $(\mathfrak{S}_i) \supset (\mathfrak{S}_j)$, and $\mathfrak{S}_i$ is not true or $\mathfrak{S}_j$ is true or both.

   f. $\mathfrak{S}_k$ has the form $(\mathfrak{S}_i) \equiv (\mathfrak{S}_j)$, and $\mathfrak{S}_i$ and $\mathfrak{S}_j$ are either both true or both not true.

§ 9. Radical Concepts

On the basis of the concept of truth, the following concepts, called radical semantical concepts, are defined: 'false', 'implicate', 'equivalent', 'disjunct', 'exclusive', 'comprehensive'. Theorems for these concepts are stated.

By the rules of a semantical system S the concept of truth in S (for sentences) is defined, as we have seen. We shall now define other semantical concepts on this basis. These concepts are called *radical concepts* and their terms *radical terms*, in distinction to terms formed with prefixes ('L-' and 'F-', §§ 14 and 21). We add some theorems; these are based merely on the definitions, not on any postulates; hence they are analytic. In the definitions and theorems we make no special assumptions concerning any particular features of S. Hence these definitions and theorems belong to general semantics. For the sake of brevity, we often omit the phrase 'in S' in connection with a semantical term; but it must be kept in mind that every semantical term has a meaning only with respect to a semantical system and therefore, in a complete formulation, must be accompanied by a reference to a semantical system.

Most of the theorems in this section are not of great importance in themselves but are lemmas to other theorems or serve for later reference. Here and later, the more important definitions, theorems, postulates, etc., are marked by a *plus symbol* ' $+$ '. In referring to a definition, a theorem, a postulate, etc., of the same section, we omit the section number (e.g. a reference 'D3' in this section refers to D9-3).

We shall apply the semantical concepts not only to sentences but also to *classes of sentences* (including the null class and transfinite classes). Thus we may e.g. regard a book or a paper as a (finite) class of sentences; and a theory may be regarded as the class (in general transfinite) of all those sentences which are deducible from a given finite set of sentences, e.g. physical laws. Now a book or a paper or a theory is meant as the joint assertion of all sentences belonging to it; hence it seems natural to call it true if and only if those sentences are true (D1).

$+$**D9-1.** $\mathfrak{R}_i$ is *true* (in S) $=_{\mathrm{Df}}$ every sentence of $\mathfrak{R}_i$ is true.

One possible way of defining the semantical terms for both sentences and sentential classes would be to define them for classes and then to add the general convention that a term may be applied to a sentence $\mathfrak{S}_i$ if and only if it applies to its unit class $\{\mathfrak{S}_i\}$. Instead, we formulate the definitions with the help of '$\mathfrak{T}$' (§ 6); '$\mathfrak{T}_i$' is a variable of the metalanguage whose range of values comprehends both sentences and sentential classes of the object language.

+**D9-2.** $\mathfrak{T}_i$ is **false** (in S) $=_{\mathrm{Df}}$ $\mathfrak{T}_i$ belongs to S and is not true in S.

+**T9-1.** $\mathfrak{R}_i$ is false if and only if at least one sentence of $\mathfrak{R}_i$ is false. (From D2 and 1.)

T9-2. $\mathfrak{T}_i$ is not both true and false. (From D2.)

T9-3. $\mathfrak{T}_i$ is either true or false. (From D2.)

T9-4. If $\mathfrak{R}_j \subset \mathfrak{R}_i$ and $\mathfrak{R}_i$ is true, then $\mathfrak{R}_j$ is true. (From D1.)

T9-5. If $\mathfrak{R}_j \subset \mathfrak{R}_i$ and $\mathfrak{R}_j$ is false, then $\mathfrak{R}_i$ is false. (From T1.)

T9-6. The class of all true sentences of S is true. (From D1.)

T9-7. There is a false sentential class in S if and only if there is a false sentence in S. (From T1; if $\mathfrak{S}_i$ is false, $\{\mathfrak{S}_i\}$ is false.)

T9-8. $\mathfrak{R}_i + \mathfrak{R}_j$ is false if and only if $\mathfrak{R}_i$ is false or $\mathfrak{R}_j$ is false. (From T1.)

The relation of *implication*, to be defined now (D3), must be clearly distinguished from logical implication, to be defined later ('L-implication', §14). [In order to stress the difference, the first is sometimes called material implication; see terminological remarks, §37, Connections (1).] Analogously, *equivalence* (D9-4) must be distinguished from logical equivalence ('L-equivalence', §14). Implication and equivalence as defined here are not logical relations; they do not require any connection between the subject-matter of $\mathfrak{T}_i$ and that of $\mathfrak{T}_j$, but merely certain conditions with respect to the truth-values of $\mathfrak{T}_i$ and $\mathfrak{T}_j$. Therefore, these relations are much less important than the corresponding L-concepts and the corresponding concepts in syntax (C-concepts, §28); they serve chiefly as a basis for these other concepts. The same holds for the terms 'disjunct', 'exclusive', and 'comprehensive' in relation to the corresponding L-terms and C-terms. For the sake of brevity, we shall often write '$\mathfrak{T}_i \rightarrow \mathfrak{T}_j$' instead of '$\mathfrak{T}_j$ is an implicate of $\mathfrak{T}_i$' (or '$\mathfrak{T}_i$ implies $\mathfrak{T}_j$', a formulation we usually avoid). (Thus the arrow '$\rightarrow$' is here not, as in Hilbert's notation, a connective (of implication) but a predicate of the metalanguage designating a certain relation between sentences, not between propositions.)

+D9-3. $\mathfrak{T}_j$ is an **implicate** of $\mathfrak{T}_i$ ($\mathfrak{T}_i$ implies $\mathfrak{T}_j$, $\mathfrak{T}_i \rightarrow \mathfrak{T}_j$) (in S) $=_{Df}$ $\mathfrak{T}_i$ and $\mathfrak{T}_j$ belong to S, and either $\mathfrak{T}_i$ is false or $\mathfrak{T}_j$ is true (or both).

+T9-10. If $\mathfrak{T}_i \rightarrow \mathfrak{T}_j$ and $\mathfrak{T}_i$ is true, $\mathfrak{T}_j$ is true. (From D3 and 2.)

+T9-11. If $\mathfrak{T}_i \rightarrow \mathfrak{T}_j$ and $\mathfrak{T}_j$ is false, $\mathfrak{T}_i$ is false. (From D3 and 2.)

T9-12. If $\mathfrak{T}_i$ is false, $\mathfrak{T}_i \rightarrow$ every $\mathfrak{T}_j$. (From D3.)

T9-13. If $\mathfrak{T}_j$ is true, every $\mathfrak{T}_i \rightarrow \mathfrak{T}_j$. (From D3.)

T9-14. The relation of implication is
    a) reflexive (i.e. $\mathfrak{T}_i \rightarrow \mathfrak{T}_i$),
    b) transitive (i.e., if $\mathfrak{T}_i \rightarrow \mathfrak{T}_j$ and $\mathfrak{T}_j \rightarrow \mathfrak{T}_k$, then $\mathfrak{T}_i \rightarrow \mathfrak{T}_k$). (From T3, D3; T10, T13, T12.)

T9-15. If $\mathfrak{S}_j \in \mathfrak{R}_i$, then $\mathfrak{R}_i \rightarrow \mathfrak{S}_j$. (From D3, D1.)

T9-16. If $\mathfrak{R}_j \subset \mathfrak{R}_i$, then $\mathfrak{R}_i \rightarrow \mathfrak{R}_j$. (From D3, D1.)

T9-17. $\mathfrak{T}_i \rightarrow \mathfrak{R}_j$ if and only if $\mathfrak{T}_i \rightarrow$ every sentence of $\mathfrak{R}_j$. (From D3, D1, T13, T12; T15, T14b.)

T9-18. $\mathfrak{T}_j$ is not an implicate of $\mathfrak{T}_i$ if and only if $\mathfrak{T}_i$ is true and $\mathfrak{T}_j$ is false. (From D3.)

+D9-4. $\mathfrak{T}_i$ is **equivalent** to $\mathfrak{T}_j$ (in S) $=_{Df}$ $\mathfrak{T}_i$ and $\mathfrak{T}_j$ belong to S, and either both are true or neither of them is true.

T9-20. Each of the following conditions is a sufficient and necessary condition for $\mathfrak{T}_i$ and $\mathfrak{T}_j$ to be equivalent (to one another):

+**a.** $\mathfrak{T}_i$ and $\mathfrak{T}_j$ are both true or both false. (From D4, D2.)

+**b.** $\mathfrak{T}_i \rightarrow \mathfrak{T}_j$ and $\mathfrak{T}_j \rightarrow \mathfrak{T}_i$. (From D4, D3.)

T9-21. Each of the following conditions is a sufficient and necessary condition for $\mathfrak{T}_i$ and $\mathfrak{T}_j$ not to be equivalent:

a. Exactly one of them is true.

b. Exactly one of them is false. (From T20a.)

T9-22. $\mathfrak{S}_i$ and $\{\mathfrak{S}_i\}$ are equivalent. (From T20a, D1, T1.)

It is important to notice the difference (1) between a negation sentence, whether in a symbolic language (example $\mathfrak{S}_1$ below) or in English ($\mathfrak{S}_2$), and a sentence about falsity ($\mathfrak{S}_3$); and likewise (2) between an equivalence sentence ($\mathfrak{S}_4$ and $\mathfrak{S}_5$) and a sentence about equivalence ($\mathfrak{S}_6$), and (3) between an implication sentence ($\mathfrak{S}_7$ and $\mathfrak{S}_8$) and a sentence about implication ($\mathfrak{S}_9$).

Examples:

1. $\mathfrak{S}_1$: ' $\sim Q(c)$ '.
   $\mathfrak{S}_2$: 'Carmel does not have a harbor'.
   $\mathfrak{S}_3$: ' '$Q(c)$' is false'.

2. $\mathfrak{S}_4$: '$P(a) \equiv Q(b)$'.
   $\mathfrak{S}_5$: 'Chicago is large if and only if New York has a harbor'.
   $\mathfrak{S}_6$: ' '$P(a)$' is equivalent to '$Q(b)$' '.

3. $\mathfrak{S}_7$: '$Q(c) \supset P(b)$'.
   $\mathfrak{S}_8$: 'If Carmel has a harbor, New York is large'.
   $\mathfrak{S}_9$: ' '$Q(c)$' implies '$P(b)$' ' $\big($or ' '$P(b)$' is an implicate of '$Q(c)$' ' or ' '$Q(c)$'$\rightarrow$'$P(b)$' '$\big)$.

$\mathfrak{S}_2$, not $\mathfrak{S}_3$, is the direct translation of $\mathfrak{S}_1$ into English; likewise, $\mathfrak{S}_5$, not $\mathfrak{S}_6$, of $\mathfrak{S}_4$; and $\mathfrak{S}_8$, not $\mathfrak{S}_9$, of $\mathfrak{S}_7$. Here, for the sake of simplicity, we have translated ' ... $\equiv$ - - - ' into ' ... if and only if - - - ', and ' ... $\supset$ - - - ' into 'if ... then - - - '. These translations are often appropriate; but in these examples they deviate somewhat from the customary use of the word 'if' and the phrase 'if and only if' in English, because these expressions are usually restricted to cases where there is a logical or causal or motivational connection between the two

members. A more precise but somewhat lengthy translation of 'A ⊃ B'
is 'not A, or B', and of 'A ≡ B' 'A and B, or, not A and not B'. The
chief distinction is between $\mathfrak{S}_1$ and $\mathfrak{S}_2$ on the one hand and $\mathfrak{S}_3$ on the
other. $\mathfrak{S}_1$ belongs to a symbolic object language. $\mathfrak{S}_2$ may be regarded
as belonging either to English as an object language or, so to speak,
to the object part of the Englih metalanguage, i.e. to that part which
does not contain semiotical terms. On the other hand, $\mathfrak{S}_3$ belongs to
the metalanguage and, moreover, to its semantical part. In the cases
(2) and (3), the situation is analogous.

D9-5. $\mathfrak{T}_i$ is **disjunct** with $\mathfrak{T}_j$ (in S) $=_{Df}$ at least one of
them is true (and hence, not both of them false).

T9-25. If $\mathfrak{T}_i$ is disjunct with $\mathfrak{T}_j$, then $\mathfrak{T}_j$ is disjunct with
$\mathfrak{T}_i$. (From D5.)

D9-6. $\mathfrak{T}_i$ is **exclusive** of $\mathfrak{T}_j$ (in S) $=_{Df}$ not both of them
are true (and hence, at least one is false).

T9-27. $\mathfrak{T}_i$ and $\mathfrak{T}_j$ are exclusive (of one another) if and
only if $\mathfrak{T}_i + \mathfrak{T}_j$ is false. (From D6, T8, T1.)

We shall designate the **null class of sentences** in S, i.e.
that class of the type of sentential classes which has no elements, by 'Λ_S' or simply 'Λ' (D7) and the **universal sentential class** in S, i.e. the class of all sentences of S by 'V_S' or
simply 'V' (D8). Then Λ is true (T32); it fulfills the condition of D1 that every sentence of it is true, because there
is no such sentence. There is no analogous theorem for V.
Although in most semantical systems V is false, we cannot
state it as a general theorem that V is false, but only that V
is false if there is a false $\mathfrak{T}_i$ at all in S (T43b). There are
systems in which every sentence and hence every $\mathfrak{R}_i$ and
every $\mathfrak{T}_i$ is true, including V (e.g. in the system S$_5$, which is
like S$_2$, § 7, except that in$_3$ designates San Francisco instead
of Carmel). The fact that every system contains a true $\mathfrak{R}_i$,
namely Λ, but not every system a false $\mathfrak{R}_i$, reveals an aston-
ishing *lack of symmetry* in the edifice of semantics. We shall
find in the discussion in [II] (see Bibliography) that this is

due to a lack of symmetry in the customary way of dealing with sentential classes. By employing new concepts, which are not definable by the concepts ordinarily used, it will be possible to gain symmetry for semantics and simultaneously for syntax.

+D9-7. Λ (Λ_S) $=_{\mathrm{Df}}$ the null sentential class.

T9-30. For every $\mathfrak{R}_i$, $\Lambda \subset \mathfrak{R}_i$. (From D7.)

+T9-32. Λ is true. (From D7, D1; can also be seen with the help of T30, 6, and 4.)

T9-33. Every $\mathfrak{T}_i \to \Lambda$. (From T32 and 13.)

T9-34 (lemma). If $\Lambda \to \mathfrak{T}_j$, then $\mathfrak{T}_j$ is true. (From T32 and 10.)

T9-35. $\mathfrak{T}_i$ is true if and only if $\Lambda \to \mathfrak{T}_i$. (From T34; T13.)

+D9-8. V (V_S) $=_{\mathrm{Df}}$ the universal sentential class.

T9-37 (lemma). Every $\mathfrak{S}_i \in V$.

T9-38 (lemma). Every $\mathfrak{R}_i \subset V$.

T9-39 (lemma). V $\to$ every $\mathfrak{S}_i$. (From T37 and 15.)

T9-40 (lemma). V $\to$ every $\mathfrak{R}_i$. (From T38 and 16.)

+T9-41. V $\to$ every $\mathfrak{T}_i$. (From T39 and 40.)

T9-42. Each of the following conditions is a sufficient and necessary condition for V to be true in S:

    a. Every $\mathfrak{S}_i$ in S is true.

    b. Every $\mathfrak{R}_i$ in S is true.

    c. Every $\mathfrak{T}_i$ in S is true. (From D8, D1.)

T9-43. Each of the following conditions is a sufficient and necessary condition for V to be false in S:

    a. At least one sentence in S is false.

    b. At least one sentential class in S is false

    c. At least one $\mathfrak{T}_i$ in S is false.

    (From T42.)

The term 'comprehensive' (D9) is introduced only for the sake of corresponding L- and C- terms (D14–5, D30–6).

D9-9. $\mathfrak{T}_i$ is *comprehensive* (in S) $=_{Df} \mathfrak{T}_i \rightarrow$ every sentence in S.

T9-50. Each of the following conditions is a sufficient and necessary condition for $\mathfrak{T}_i$ to be comprehensive:

    a. $\mathfrak{T}_i \rightarrow$ V. (From D9, T17.)

    b. $\mathfrak{T}_i$ is equivalent to V. (From (a), T41.)

    c. $\mathfrak{T}_i \rightarrow$ every $\mathfrak{R}_j$. (From (a), T40, T14b.)

    d. $\mathfrak{T}_i \rightarrow$ every $\mathfrak{T}_j$. (From D9, (c).)

We shall now define the concept of equivalence of semantical systems; it must clearly be distinguished from the concept of equivalence of sentences or sentential classes (D9-4).

D9-11. The *semantical system* S_m is *equivalent* to the semantical system S_n $=_{Df}$ the following two conditions are fulfilled:

    a. S_m and S_n contain the same sentences.

    b. For every $\mathfrak{S}_i$, $\mathfrak{S}_i$ is true in S_m if and only if $\mathfrak{S}_i$ is true in S_n.

T9-70. The systems S_m and S_n are equivalent if and only if the following three conditions are fulfilled:

    a. S_m and S_n contain the same sentences.

    b. For every $\mathfrak{S}_i$, if $\mathfrak{S}_i$ is true in S_m, it is true in S_n.

    c. For every $\mathfrak{S}_i$, if $\mathfrak{S}_i$ is false in S_m, it is false in S_n.
(From D11.)

T9-71. If S_m and S_n are equivalent systems, then each of the following concepts (applied to sentences and sentential classes) has the same extension in S_m as in S_n: **a.** truth, **b.** falsity, **c.** implication, **d.** equivalence, **e.** disjunctness, **f.** exclusion, **g.** comprehensiveness. ((a), from D11, D1; (b) to (g), from D11 and the definitions of these concepts, which are all based on the concept of truth.)

§ 10. Further Radical Concepts

Some concepts applicable to attributes are defined, among them 'universal', 'empty', 'implicate', 'equivalent'. These concepts are absolute, i.e. not dependent upon language. With their help, corresponding semantical concepts ('universal in S', etc.), applicable to predicates, are defined. Further, the terms 'interchangeable', 'extensional sentence', and 'extensional system' are defined. Theorems for the concepts defined are stated.

There are some semantical properties and relations of predicates analogous to some of the properties and relations of sentences defined in § 9. As a preliminary step to the introduction of these semantical terms we shall first define some terms which may belong to any suitable object language rather than to the metalanguage. (They are, however, not descriptive but logical in the sense to be explained in § 13.) Therefore these terms are not accompanied by a reference to a language, but — as we shall say later (§ 17) — they are used in an absolute way. The concepts designated by these terms are thus not dependent upon language; we call them *absolute concepts* (§ 17).

In the following definitions, M and N are attributes of any degree, say n. '$M(u)$' means 'M holds for the argument u' or 'u possesses the attribute M', where u is a sequence of n members belonging to types suitable for M. H is a relation of degree two; '$H(x,y)$' means 'H holds between x and y'

D10-1. M is **universal** $=_{\mathrm{Df}}$ for every u, $M(u)$.

D10-2. M is **empty** $=_{\mathrm{Df}}$ for every u, not $M(u)$ (in other words, there is no u such that $M(u)$).

D10-3. M is **non-empty** $=_{\mathrm{Df}}$ M is not empty (in other words, there is at least one u such that $M(u)$).

D10-4. N is an **implicate** of M (or, M implies N) $=_{\mathrm{Df}}$ for every u, if $M(u)$ then $N(u)$ (in other words, the extension of M is contained in that of N).

D10-5. M is **equivalent** to N $=_{Df}$ for every u, $M(u)$ if and only if $N(u)$ (in other words, M and N imply one another, they coincide, they have the same extension).

D10-6. M is **exclusive** of N $=_{Df}$ there is no u such that $M(u)$ and $N(u)$.

Further, the familiar concepts of the theory of relations belong to this kind of absolute concept, e.g. 'symmetric', 'non-symmetric', 'asymmetric', 'reflexive', 'non-reflexive', 'irreflexive', 'transitive', 'non-transitive', 'intransitive', 'connected', 'one-many', 'many-one', 'one-one', etc. We shall give only one example here:

D10-7. H is *symmetric* $=_{Df}$ for every x and y, if $H(x,y)$ then $H(y,x)$.

Now we decide to use the same terms as semantical terms also, hence for different but closely corresponding concepts. While the terms in their absolute use defined above are applied to attributes, in their semantical use they will be applied to those predicates which designate attributes of the kind specified. For these concepts, the dependence upon a language system is essential. Thus e.g. (the property of being) large is non-empty independently of any language, just because of the fact that there are some large things. On the other hand, the predicate 'P' is non-empty *in* S_3 (§ 8) because of the same fact; the same predicate 'P' may be empty in some other system because there it may designate some other property which happens to be empty.

D10-10. A *predicate* $\mathfrak{pr}_i$ is **a. universal** (**b. empty, c. non-empty**) in S $=_{Df}$ the attribute designated by $\mathfrak{pr}_i$ in S is **a.** universal (**b.** empty, **c.** non-empty, respectively).

D10-11. $\mathfrak{pr}_i$ is **a.** an **implicate** of (**b. equivalent** to, **c. exclusive** of) $\mathfrak{pr}_j$ in S $=_{Df}$ the designatum of $\mathfrak{pr}_i$ in S is **a.** an implicate of (**b.** equivalent to, **c.** exclusive of, respectively) the designatum of $\mathfrak{pr}_j$.

D10-12. A *predicate* $\mathfrak{pr}_i$ of degree two is *symmetric* in S $=$ $_{\text{Df}}$ the relation designated by $\mathfrak{pr}_i$ in S is symmetric.

Analogous definitions may be laid down for the other terms of the theory of relations.

The following concept is of interest chiefly because of the corresponding L- and C- concepts (D14–6, D31–6).

D10-15. $\mathfrak{A}_i$ is **interchangeable** with $\mathfrak{A}_j$ (in S) $=$ $_{\text{Df}}$ any closed sentence $\mathfrak{S}_i$ is equivalent to every sentence $\mathfrak{S}_j$ constructed out of $\mathfrak{S}_i$ by either replacing $\mathfrak{A}_i$ at some place in $\mathfrak{S}_i$ by $\mathfrak{A}_j$ or $\mathfrak{A}_j$ by $\mathfrak{A}_i$, and there is at least one pair of sentences $\mathfrak{S}_i$ and $\mathfrak{S}_j$ of this kind. (The last condition is added in order to exclude trivial cases.)

If a sentence $\mathfrak{S}_i$ is constructed out of other sentences as components with the help of some of the ordinary sentential connectives (as e.g. in S_3 and S_4, § 8) then the truth-value of $\mathfrak{S}_i$ depends merely upon the truth-values of its components. Therefore, a sentence of this kind is sometimes called a truth-function of its components; we shall call it *extensional* with respect to its partial sentences. This concept is defined in a general way in D20.

D10-20. $\mathfrak{S}_i$ is **extensional** (in S) in relation to a partial sentence $\mathfrak{S}_j$ occurring at a certain place in $\mathfrak{S}_i$ $=$ $_{\text{Df}}$ for every closed (§ 6) $\mathfrak{S}_k$, if $\mathfrak{S}_j$ is equivalent to $\mathfrak{S}_k$, then $\mathfrak{S}_i$ is equivalent to the sentence constructed out of $\mathfrak{S}_i$ by replacing $\mathfrak{S}_j$ at the place in question by $\mathfrak{S}_k$.

D10-21. The *system S* is **extensional** in relation to partial sentences $=$ $_{\text{Df}}$ for every $\mathfrak{S}_i$ in S, if $\mathfrak{S}_i$ contains a closed sentence $\mathfrak{S}_j$ at some place, then $\mathfrak{S}_i$ is extensional in relation to $\mathfrak{S}_j$ at that place.

T10-20. If S is extensional in relation to partial sentences, then any two closed equivalent sentences in S are interchangeable. (From D21, D20, D15.)

§ 11. Variables

If a system S contains variables, then, on the basis of the rules of designation and as basis for the rules of truth, we lay down first *rules of values*, and then either *rules of determination* or *rules of fulfillment*. The rules of values specify which entities are the values of the variables of the kinds occurring in S; the rules of determination specify which attributes are determined by the sentential functions in S; the rules of fulfillment specify which entities fulfill the sentential functions in S.

The examples of semantical systems discussed so far (S_1 to S_4, §§ 7 and 8) are constructed in a very simple way. They lack one important feature, variables. The chief application of variables is in expressing universal and existential propositions.

If a system S is to contain variables, the classification of signs, which precedes the formulation of rules, has to specify the kinds of variables. The rules of formation refer to these kinds in describing the forms of sentences. Then, in a **rule of values** related to the rules of designation, it is stated for each kind of variable which entities are to be **values** of the variables of that kind. Their class is sometimes called the **range of values** of the variables in question. If an expression $\mathfrak{A}_i$ or a sign $\mathfrak{a}_i$ designates a value of a variable $\mathfrak{v}_j$, we call $\mathfrak{A}_i$ a **value expression** and $\mathfrak{a}_i$ a value sign of $\mathfrak{v}_j$. A rule of values might e.g. state that the range of values of the individual variables $\mathfrak{i}$ in the system S comprehends all space-time points, or all physical things, or all events, or all human beings in general, or all human beings living at a certain time, etc. The values of the $\mathfrak{i}$ are then called the individuals in S. A rule for another kind of variables, say $\mathfrak{p}$, might state that all properties of individuals are their values, or all second-degree relations of individuals, or all attributes of any degree of individuals, or all properties of any finite level, or all attributes of any finite level, etc. A rule for still another kind of variables, say $\mathfrak{i}$, might state that the propositions (designata of sentences) are their values.

Further, for a system S containing variables, rules have to be given specifying which entities are **determined** *by the expressional functions* (i.e. expressions with free variables; see § 6) of various forms, and especially which attributes are determined by sentential functions. These rules which define 'determination in S' are called **rules of determination**.

Then, with the help of the concepts defined by the preceding rules, especially the range of values of a variable and the attribute determined by a sentential function, truth rules for general sentences have to be laid down.

Example of a semantical system containing variables. We construct the system S_6 out of S_3 (§ 8) by adding new signs and rules. (S_6 contains only individual variables; all sentences are closed; all operands have molecular form, i.e. they do not contain operators.) Here again, to facilitate understanding, we sometimes use expressions of the object language included in quotes.

Semantical system S_6

1. Classification of signs. In addition to the signs of S_3, S_6 contains '$\mathfrak{I}$' and an infinite number of $\mathfrak{i}$ ('x', 'y', etc.).

2. Rules of formation. An expression $\mathfrak{A}_k$ in S_6 is a *sentential function* in S_6 $=_{\mathrm{Df}}$ $\mathfrak{A}_k$ has one of the following forms: $\alpha.$ $\mathfrak{pr}(\mathfrak{i})$; $\beta.$ $\sim(\mathfrak{A}_i)$, where $\mathfrak{A}_i$ is a sentential function; $\gamma.$ $(\mathfrak{A}_i)$ V $(\mathfrak{A}_j)$, where $\mathfrak{A}_i$ and $\mathfrak{A}_j$ are sentential functions containing the same variable.

An expression $\mathfrak{A}_k$ in S_6 is a *sentence* ($\mathfrak{S}$) in S_6 $=_{\mathrm{Df}}$ $\mathfrak{A}_k$ has one of the following forms: a. $\mathfrak{pr}_i(\mathfrak{in}_j)$, where $\mathfrak{in}_j$ is a constant; b. $\sim(\mathfrak{S}_i)$; c. $(\mathfrak{S}_i)$ V $(\mathfrak{S}_j)$; d. $(\mathfrak{i}_j)$ $(\mathfrak{A}_i)$, where $\mathfrak{A}_i$ is a sentential function containing $\mathfrak{i}_j$; e. $(\mathfrak{I}\mathfrak{i}_j)$ $(\mathfrak{A}_i)$, where $\mathfrak{A}_i$ is a sentential function containing $\mathfrak{i}_j$.

3A. Rules of designation. The same as in S_3. (We might, of course, add in S_6 more $\mathfrak{pr}$ and $\mathfrak{in}$ and then specify here the designatum of each of these signs.)

3B. Rules of determination. A sentential function $\mathfrak{A}_k$ *determines* in S_6 the property F $=_{\mathrm{Df}}$ one of the following three conditions is fulfilled:

a. $\mathfrak{A}_k$ has the form $\mathfrak{pr}_i(\mathfrak{i}_j)$, and $\mathfrak{pr}_i$ designates F;

b. $\mathfrak{A}_k$ has the form $\sim(\mathfrak{A}_i)$, and F is the property of not having the property determined by $\mathfrak{A}_i$;

c. $\mathfrak{A}_k$ has the form $(\mathfrak{A}_i) \vee (\mathfrak{A}_j)$, and F is the property of having either the property determined by $\mathfrak{A}_i$ or that determined by $\mathfrak{A}_j$ or both.

3C. Rule of values. *Values* of the $\mathfrak{i}$ in S_6 are the towns in the United States.

4. Rules of truth. $\mathfrak{S}_k$ is *true* in S_6 =$_{\text{Df}}$ one of the following conditions is fulfilled:

(a), (b), and (c) as in S_3.

d. $\mathfrak{S}_k$ has the form $(\mathfrak{i}_j)(\mathfrak{A}_i)$ and every value of $\mathfrak{i}_j$ (i.e. every town in the United States) has the property determined by $\mathfrak{A}_i$.

e. $\mathfrak{S}_k$ has the form $(\exists \mathfrak{i}_j)(\mathfrak{A}_i)$ and at least one value of $\mathfrak{i}_j$ has the property determined by $\mathfrak{A}_i$.

The rules, especially those of determination, become more complicated in a system where operators within operands and therefore sentential functions of higher degree occur (e.g. '$(x)(\exists y)(..x..y..)$'). Here, an order of the variables must be specified, an alphabetical order, so to speak. It is very convenient for many purposes, and especially for the formulation of rules for systems containing variables, to supplement the English word language (as metalanguage) by adding variables and the operators '(x)', '$(\exists x)$', and '(λx)'.

Examples of *rules of determination* ('M' is used as a $^1\mathfrak{p}^n$).

1. If (the sentential function) $\mathfrak{A}_i$ determines (the attribute of degree n) M and if $\mathfrak{i}_k$ is the mth in alphabetical order among the n variables occurring freely in $\mathfrak{A}_i$, then the sentential function (of degree $n\text{--}1$) $(\mathfrak{i}_k)(\mathfrak{A}_i)$ determines $(\lambda x_1, x_2, .. x_{m-1}, x_{m+1}, ... x_n)[(x_m)M(x_1, x_2, .. x_m, .. x_n)]$ (this is an attribute of degree $n\text{--}1$). (Formulated in words and variables but without symbolic operators, it would run like this: "$(\mathfrak{i}_k)(\mathfrak{A}_i)$ determines that relation which holds between x_1, $x_2, .. x_{m-1}, x_{m+1}, .. x_n$ if and only if for every individual x_m, M holds between $x_1, x_2, ... x_m, .. x_n$".)

2. Under the same conditions $(\exists \mathfrak{i}_k)(\mathfrak{A}_i)$ determines $(\lambda x_1, x_2, .. x_{m-1}, x_{m+1}, .. x_n)[(\exists x_m)M(x_1, x_2, .. x_n)]$.

If S contains other kinds of variables, then the rules of values for these kinds are of course different from the examples given here (as shown by the examples given at the beginning of this section). But the form of rules of determination is in all essential respects similar to that of the examples just given.

The concept of fulfillment (or satisfaction) to be defined now is closely related to that of determination.

D11-1. *u* **fulfills** $\mathfrak{A}_i$ in S $=_{Df}$ there is an M such that $\mathfrak{A}_i$ determines M, and that $M(u)$ (i.e. there is an attribute M of degree n such that the sentential function $\mathfrak{A}_i$ of degree n determines M and that M holds for u, which is a sequence of degree n).

Examples. 1. The ordered pair (i.e. sequence of two members) Castor, Pollux (a pair of objects, not of names!) fulfills the sentential function '*x* ist ein Bruder von *y*' in German. 2. Chicago fulfills 'P(x)' in S_6. 3. Suppose that the system S_7 contains S_6 and, in addition, predicate variables ('F' etc.). The simple formulation "Chicago, large fulfills '$F(x)$' in S_7" is, unfortunately, not permitted by the traditional English grammar; therefore we have to replace it by the following clumsy formulation: "The pair consisting of Chicago and the property of being large fulfills '$F(x)$' in S_7".

D1 defines 'fulfillment' on the basis of 'determination'; the latter term is hereby supposed to be defined by rules of determination. The inverse procedure is also possible; 'determination' can be defined on the basis of 'fulfillment' (DA). $\mathfrak{A}_i$ is here a sentential function of degree n, M an attribute of degree n, u a sequence of degree n.

D11-A. $\mathfrak{A}_i$ *determines* M in S $=_{Df}$ for every u, $M(u)$ if and only if u fulfills $\mathfrak{A}_i$.

Thus fulfillment may serve as the basic concept in the construction of a semantical system, defined by rules of fulfillment instead of rules of determination. (For the formulation of rules of fulfillment, as for those of determination, it is convenient but not necessary to make use of the concept of designation to be defined by rules of designation.) Then determination would be defined on the basis of fulfillment as in DA, and truth on the basis of determination, as e.g. in the truth rules of S_6.

There is another way of defining truth directly on the basis of fulfillment without the use of the concept of determination. The definition can be given an especially simple form (DB below) if we make use of the concept of the null sequence (i.e. the sequence which has no members, analogous to the null class) and regard a sentence as a sentential function of degree zero. Analogously, we may regard a proposition as an attribute of degree zero. [This widening out of the concepts would of course involve certain modifications in previous explanations and definitions, especially with respect to the concept of fulfillment.]

D11-B. $\mathfrak{S}_i$ is *true* in S $=_{Df}$ the null sequence fulfills $\mathfrak{S}_i$.

Tarski [Wahrheitsbegriff] bases his definition of truth on the concept of fulfillment or satisfying (but in a way technically different from that indicated here). This procedure seems to have certain advantages in those cases where it can be applied, namely for languages containing variables.

In a later volume of these studies it is planned to make a systematic comparison of the different forms of bases for semantical systems.

Previously we defined 'universal', etc., for attributes (D10–1, etc.) and 'universal in S', etc., for predicates designating those attributes (D10–10, etc.). We now define the same terms for sentential functions determining those attributes.

D11-2. A *sentential function* $\mathfrak{A}_i$ is **a. universal** (**b. empty, c. non-empty**) in S $=_{Df}$ the attribute determined by $\mathfrak{A}_i$ in S is **a.** universal (**b.** empty, **c.** non-empty, respectively).

D11-3. A sentential function $\mathfrak{A}_i$ is **a.** an **implicate** of (**b. equivalent** to, **c. exclusive** of) a sentential function $\mathfrak{A}_j$ in S $=_{Df}$ the attribute determined by $\mathfrak{A}_i$ in S is **a.** an implicate of (**b.** equivalent to, **c.** exclusive of, respectively) the attribute determined by $\mathfrak{A}_j$ in S.

§ 12. The Relation of Designation

> It is convenient to adopt for semantical discussions a use of the term 'designation' which is wider than the ordinary use, so that we may speak of the designata not only of individual constants and predicates but also of functors and sentences. A general convention for this wider use is laid down (D12–B).

To which signs and expressions of a semantical system S (i.e. of its object language) is it possible and advisable to apply the relation of designation? So far we have applied it to individual constants and predicates of different levels and degrees. In a similar way it may of course be applied to functors of any type occurring in S. But it is possible to enlarge the domain of application to a considerable extent, and it seems convenient to do so for the signs and expressions of S of all those types for which variables occur in the metalanguage, even if this includes the type of sentences and the types of sentential connectives. We use as metalanguage in this section the English language supplemented by variables, including propositional variables. Instead of 'u designates v in S' we write '$\mathrm{Des}_S(u,v)$' or simply '$\mathrm{Des}(u,v)$' where the context makes clear which system is meant.

Instead of, and in analogy to, the rules of truth based on the narrower concept of designation in the previous form of a semantical system (e.g. S_3 in § 8) we should have here rules of designation for sentences and, in addition, a general explicit definition for truth; the latter has the same form in all systems and may therefore be stated once for all in general semantics (D1).

D12-1. $\mathfrak{S}_i$ is *true* in S $=_{Df}$ there is a (proposition) p such that $\mathrm{Des}(\mathfrak{S}_i,p)$ and p.

In order to satisfy the ordinary rule of types, we should have to use different terms for the relation of designation as applied to individuals, attributes (of different types), and propositions, e.g. 'DesInd', 'DesAttr', 'DesProp'. It is, however, much more convenient to use only one term 'Des'. This does not lead to ambiguities because the type of the second argument makes clear which kind of designation is meant. But this use presupposes a suitable structure of the metalanguage so as to avoid the restrictions by the ordinary rule of types in this point (see remark below).

Example. In order to reformulate the *system* S₃ (§ 8) in the way described, we replace (3) by (3A) and (3B), and (4) (§ 8) by (3C) and (4) (here). (3A) and (3B) are explicit definitions; (3C) is recursive, like (4) in § 8. 3A, B, and C could be combined into one recursive definition for 'Des$_{S_3}$'.

3. Rules of designation.

    A. For individuals.

      DesInd$_{S_3}$ $(\mathfrak{in}_i,x)$ $=_{Df}$ one of the following three conditions is fulfilled:

        a. $\mathfrak{in}_i =$ 'a', and $x =$ Chicago,
        b. $\mathfrak{in}_i =$ 'b', and $x =$ New York,
        c. $\mathfrak{in}_i =$ 'c', and $x =$ Carmel.

    B. For attributes.

      DesAttr$_{S_3}$ $(\mathfrak{pr}_i,F)$ $=_{Df}$ one of the following two conditions is fulfilled:

        a. $\mathfrak{pr}_i =$ 'P', and $F =$ (the property of being) large,
        b. $\mathfrak{pr}_i =$ 'Q', and $F =$ having a harbor.

    C. For propositions.

      DesProp$_{S_3}$ $(\mathfrak{S}_k,p)$ $=_{Df}$ one of the following three conditions is fulfilled:

    a. $\mathfrak{S}_k$ has the form $\mathfrak{pr}_i$ ($\mathfrak{in}_j$), and there is an F and an x such that $\text{DesAttr}(\mathfrak{pr}_i, F)$ and $\text{DesInd}(\mathfrak{in}_j, x)$, and $p =$ (the proposition that) x is F.

    b. $\mathfrak{S}_k$ has the form $\sim\mathfrak{S}_i$, and there is a q such that $\text{DesProp}(\mathfrak{S}_i, q)$, and $p =$ not q.

    c. $\mathfrak{S}_k$ has the form $\mathfrak{S}_i \vee \mathfrak{S}_j$, and there is a q and an r such that $\text{DesProp}(\mathfrak{S}_i, q)$ and $\text{DesProp}(\mathfrak{S}_j, r)$, and $p = q$ or r.

4. Rule of truth.

    $\mathfrak{S}_k$ is *true* in S_3 $=_{\text{Df}}$ there is a (proposition) p such that $\text{DesProp}(\mathfrak{S}_k, p)$ and p.

Application of the rules. It follows from (3Aa), (3Ba), (3Ca), that $\text{DesProp}('P(a)'$, Chicago is large); and hence with (4), that '$P(a)$' is true in S_3 if and only if Chicago is large. A similar result holds for each of the other sentences of S_3. Therefore, the definition of 'true in S_3' given by the rules stated above fulfills the requirement of adequacy (§ 7); it is merely another formulation for the same system S_3.

According to the ordinary *rule of types*, usually called the simple theory of types, a particular argument-place beside a particular predicate may be filled only by expressions which all have the same type and hence the same level and the same degree. Therefore, on the basis of this rule, we could not have 'x', 'F', and 'p' as second arguments to the same predicate 'Des', as we had above. [The same holds for 'Chicago' and 'the property - - -' as second arguments for 'designates' in the formulation of rule (3) for S_3 in § 8; that already was a violation of the rule of types.] We may, however, modify the rule of types by admitting transfinite levels; a predicate of level ω is allowed to take as arguments expressions of any finite level, including sentences, which we assign to the zero level. If we assign 'Des' to this level ω, then its use instead of 'DesInd', 'DesAttr', and 'DesProp' in the examples mentioned, and likewise its use with arguments of still other types, is correct. Another way of accommodating 'Des' as here used would be to use as metalanguage a language system without distinctions of types or levels; systems of this kind have recently been constructed especially by Quine [Math. Logic] and Bernays (*Journ. Symb. Logic*, vol. 2 (1937) and subsequent volumes).

Concerning the simple theory of types see [Syntax] § 27, [Logic] §§ 21b and 29b. Concerning transfinite levels see [Syntax] § 53 with references to Hilbert and Gödel, Tarski [Wahrheitsbegriff] § 7, Carnap [Logic] § 29b.

Sometimes objections are raised, especially by empiricists, against the wider use of the relation of designation and especially against its application as a relation between sentences and propositions. It is said that, while object names (individual constants) and predicates do designate something, namely objects and properties or relations, a sentence does not designate anything; it rather describes or states that something is the case. This may indeed be true with respect to the customary use of the words 'designation', 'to designate', etc., in English. It is obviously not in accordance with ordinary usage to say " 'P(a)' designates Chicago is large"; and the same holds for corresponding sentences in languages of similar structure. First, English grammar does not admit a sentence in the position of grammatical object. This difficulty, however, can easily be overcome by inserting 'that' after 'designates'. Second, 'to designate' would ordinarily not be used in this case. But this does not seem to me to be a sufficient reason against its wider use as a technical term. Very often, in transferring a word from the ordinary language into the language of science, we enlarge its domain of application. The only question in such a case seems to be a question of expediency; and the decision will depend chiefly upon whether the similarity between the cases of ordinary application and the new cases is strong enough for the enlargement to seem natural. In the case under discussion there seems to be a strong analogy between the different cases, in spite of the difference in types; this will soon become clear.

This analogy will also help us to remove from our path some other stumblingblocks. With respect to some of the types to which the relation of designation is here applied, the puzzling question is sometimes raised, what exactly is the kind of designata of the expressions of the one type or the other? Thus it is e.g. discussed whether the designatum of a thing-name (e.g. 'Chicago') is the corresponding thing or its unit-class (e.g. whether it is Chicago or {Chicago}). Further, the question is discussed whether the designatum of a predicate of first degree is a property or a class. In both cases it is said as an argument in favor of the second answer that a designatum should always be a class. If designata of sentences are admitted at all, the question is raised whether they are states of affairs (or possible facts, conditions, etc., which seems chiefly a terminological difference) or rather thoughts.

Let us suppose for the moment that we understand a given object language S, say German or S_3 (§ 8), in such a way that we are able to translate its expressions and sentences into the metalanguage M used, say English (including some variables and symbols). It does not matter whether this understanding is based on the knowledge of semantical rules or is intuitive; it is merely supposed that, if an expression is given (say e.g. 'Pferd', 'drei' in German, 'P', 'P(a)' in S_3), for all practical purposes we know an English expression corresponding to it as its "literal translation" (e.g. 'horse', 'three'; 'large', 'Chicago is large'). Then we will lay down a definition of adequacy for the concept of designation, which is not itself a definition for a term 'Des_S' (or 'to designate in S') but a standard with which to compare proposed definitions. In a similar way, we had before a definition of adequacy for truth (D7–B), and later we shall have one for L-truth (D16–1). 'Adequacy' means here simply agreement with our intention for the use of the term.

D12-B. A predicate of second degree $\mathfrak{pr}_i$ in M is an *adequate* predicate for *designation* in S $=_{Df}$ every sentence in M of the form $\mathfrak{pr}_i (\mathfrak{A}_j, \mathfrak{A}_k)$ where $\mathfrak{A}_j$ is a name (or a syntactical description) in M of an expression $\mathfrak{A}_m$ of S (belonging to one of the kinds of expressions for which pr_i is defined) and $\mathfrak{A}_k$ is a translation of $\mathfrak{A}_m$ into M, is true in M.

If pr_i is adequate then we also call its definition and its designatum, i.e. the relation defined as designation, adequate. This definition of adequacy leaves open the question of which types are admitted as arguments for pr_i; it determines only *how* a predicate for designation is to be used for certain types *if* we choose to use it for these types. Hence we may, for instance, restrict its use, in the sense of the objection mentioned, to in and pr. But it is proposed here to use it for all types for which there are variables in M, i.e. to admit as a second argument $\mathfrak{A}_k$ any value expression of any variable in M. The practical justification for the given definition of adequacy lies in these two facts: 1. It supplies a general rule for all the different types, in a simple way; 2. it seems to be in agreement with the ordinary use of 'designation' as far as this use goes.

On the basis of an adequate relation of designation, the question of the designatum of an object name is to be answered in favor of the object (see example 2a below) as against its unit class.

Examples. 1. If 'DesG' is an adequate predicate (in M, i.e. English) for designation in German, then the following sentences are true: a. 'DesG('Pferd', horse)'; b. 'DesG('drei', three)'. 2. If 'Des$_{S_3}$' is defined as indicated above (taking the place of 'DesInd$_{S_3}$', 'DesAttr$_{S_3}$', and 'DesProp$_{S_3}$' simultaneously), then it is an adequate predicate for designation in S_3. Among other sentences, the following must become true: a. 'Des$_{S_3}$('a', Chicago)'; b. 'Des$_{S_3}$('P', large)'; c. 'Des$_{S_3}$('P(a)', Chicago is large)'; and they are indeed true, as we have seen before. We see that adequacy requires us to write in the argument-place of 'Des' 'large' instead of 'largeness' (as English grammar would demand after the word 'designates') or 'the property of being large' (as we formulated it previously) or 'the class of large things'; and likewise 'horse' instead of 'the property of being a horse' or 'the class of horses'. This shows that we can assign designata to predicates without using either the term 'property' or 'class'. [The question whether a designatum, e.g. large, is a property or a class will thus not disturb us in using the relation of designation, but it, too, must finally, of course, be answered. The answer will depend upon the structure of the languages used, especially with respect to extensionality. The same holds for the question whether sentential designata are truth-values or whatever else. It is planned to discuss these questions in a later volume of these studies in connection with the discussion of extensional and non-extensional language systems.]

We define 'synonymous' on the basis of 'designation' (D2). Thus the term 'synonymous' may be applied in a narrower or wider way according to the narrower or wider domain of application chosen for 'designation'.

D12-2. $\mathfrak{A}_i$ in S_m is **synonymous** with $\mathfrak{A}_j$ in S_n $=_{Df}$ $\mathfrak{A}_i$ designates in S_m the same entity as $\mathfrak{A}_j$ in S_n.

Thus the relation of synonymity is in general not restricted to the expressions of one system. Most of the semantical relations can be applied to expressions of *different systems*, even those which, for the sake of simplicity and in consideration of their most frequent use, we have defined with respect to one system.

Example. 'Gross' in German is synonymous with 'P' in S_3 because Des_G('gross', large) and Des_{S3}('P', large).

Examples of other semantical relations for two systems. Instead of D9–4, we might take the following definition:

D12-C. $\mathfrak{T}_i$ in S_m is *equivalent* to $\mathfrak{T}_j$ in S_n $=_{Df}$ either $\mathfrak{T}_i$ is true in S_m and $\mathfrak{T}_j$ is true in S_n, or $\mathfrak{T}_i$ is false in S_m and $\mathfrak{T}_j$ is false in S_n.

The same could be done with 'implicate', 'exclusive', 'disjunct', and also with the corresponding L-terms (§ 14ff; see remark at the end of § 16), but not with the corresponding C-terms in syntax (§ 28).

C. L-SEMANTICS

This chapter is concerned with the problems of *logical truth* ('L-true'), logical deducibility ('L-implicate'), and related concepts (L-concepts). It will become clear that logic, in the sense of a theory of logical deduction and thereby of logical truth, is a special part of semantics. The task of defining the L-concepts not only for particular systems (special L-semantics) but for systems in general (general L-semantics) involves peculiar difficulties. At present, no complete solution of this problem is known.

§ 13. Logical and Descriptive Signs

In preparation for the later discussion of L-concepts, the distinction between logical and descriptive signs is explained. By descriptive signs we mean those designating things or events, their properties or relations, etc. The two kinds of signs can easily be defined with respect to any given system (special semantics), but a definition for systems in general (general semantics) is not yet known.

The problem of the nature of logical deduction and logical truth is one of the most important problems in the foundations of logic and perhaps in the whole of theoretical philosophy. Although in the development of modern logic much has been done to throw more light on this problem, especially by Frege, Russell, and Wittgenstein, it can still not be regarded as completely solved.

In this chapter, we shall look at the old problem from a new standpoint. The view will here be explained that logic is a special branch of semantics, that logical deducibility and logical truth are semantical concepts. They belong to a special kind of semantical concepts which we shall call L-concepts. (For logical truth we shall use the term 'L-true', for logical deducibility 'L-implicate'.) It will be shown that the L-concepts differ in a peculiar way from the radical semantical concepts which we have discussed above. If the rules of a semantical system S and thereby the concept of truth in S are given, then the L-concepts are thereby also determined in a certain sense; nevertheless, the task of defining them on the basis of the radical concepts (e.g. 'designation' and 'true') involves some peculiar difficulties. Thus this chapter is, even more than the others, of a preliminary nature; it contains more open questions than answers.

The discussion of the L-concepts will begin in the next section. At present, we shall deal with a distinction between two kinds of expressions; we call them *descriptive* and *logical* expressions. We shall see later (§ 16 at the end) that there is a close relation between the concepts 'descriptive' and 'logical' and the L-concepts. The former concepts are, like the L-concepts, of great practical importance in the logical analysis of languages; but for them also no satisfactory precise definition in general semantics is known. As **descriptive** are classified names of single items in the world, i.e. of single things or parts of things or events (e.g. 'Napoleon', 'Lake Michigan', 'the sun', 'the French revolution'), signs designating empirical properties, including kinds of substances, and relations of things, places, events, etc. (e.g. 'black', 'hot', 'dog', 'silver', 'father', 'citizen'), empirical functions of things, points, etc. (e.g. 'weight', 'age', 'temperature', 'I.Q.', 'price'). Examples of signs which are regarded as **logical** are the sentential connectives ('$\sim$', '$\vee$', etc.), the sign of the universal operator ('for every'), the sign of the element-class relation ('ϵ', 'is a'), auxiliary signs (e.g. parentheses and comma as ordinarily used in symbolic logic, punctuation marks in the written word languages), the sign of logical necessity in a (non-extensional) system of modalities ('N'). Further, all those signs are regarded as logical which are definable by those mentioned; hence e.g. the sign of the existential operator ('Ǝ', or 'for some'), signs for universal and null classes of all types, the sign of identity (' = ', 'is the same as'), all signs of the system of [Princ. Math.] by Whitehead and Russell and of nearly all other systems of symbolic logic, all signs of mathematics (including arithmetic, analysis of real numbers, infinitesimal calculus, but not geometry) with the meaning they have when applied in science, all logical modalities (e.g. Lewis' 'strict implication'). A defined sign is descriptive if its definiens contains a descriptive sign; otherwise logical. An expression is called descriptive if it contains a descriptive sign; otherwise logical. (Descriptivity is, so to speak, a dominant property, logicality a recessive one.)

When we are constructing a semantical system S we usually have in mind a specific meaning for each sign; and then we lay down the rules in accordance with this intention. In a case like this it is not difficult to define 'logical sign in S' and 'descriptive sign in S' in such a way that the distinction is in accordance on the one hand with our general conception of the distinction as explained above and, on the other hand, with the meanings intended for the signs and formulated by the rules. The distinction will usually be made in the simple form of an enumeration either of the logical or of the descriptive (primitive) signs or of kinds of signs as listed in the classification of signs with which the construction of the system begins.

Examples. With respect to each of the systems S_1 and S_2 (§ 7), S_3 and S_4 (§ 8), and S_6 (§ 11), the distinction with respect to constants can be made in the following simple way (concerning variables, see below). The individual constants and predicates are descriptive, the other constants logical. With respect to languages I and II in [Syntax] the distinction for the primitive signs is likewise simple: the primitive predicates and functors are descriptive; all other primitive signs, including the variables, are logical ([Syntax] §§ 8 and 29).

As to *variables*, it might seem at first glance as if they must be regarded as logical signs. A closer analysis shows, however, that with respect to some languages this would not be in agreement with the intended distinction. This is the case for a variable whose range of values is specified by a descriptive expression of the metalanguage. It seems that a variable of this kind should be regarded as a descriptive variable. However, the whole question is in need of further study. (The question is not merely a terminological one; which terminological decision in this point leads to simpler general theorems about logical and descriptive signs and their relation to L-concepts is an objective question.)

Example. The range of values of the variables in the system S_6 (§ 11) is the class of the towns in the United States. The English translation of a sentence of the form '$(x)(\ldots)$' is: 'For every town x in the United States, . . .', which is clearly descriptive. Hence it seems natural to call 'x' descriptive.

So far we have discussed the distinction between logical and descriptive expressions only in the form in which it appears when we have to do with a particular semantical system, in other words, as a question of special semantics. The problem is more difficult in the form it takes in *general semantics*. Here it is the question whether and how 'logical' and 'descriptive' can be defined on the basis of other semantical terms, e.g. 'designation' and 'true', so that the application of the general definition to any particular system will lead to a result which is in accordance with the intended distinction. A satisfactory solution is not yet known.

The possibility and the method of solution depend upon the kind of metalanguage M chosen. A solution seems possible if we presuppose that M is constructed in such a way that its rules, as formulated in the metametalanguage MM, involve a corresponding distinction of the signs of M. From another point of view, some light will be thrown on the question by the results of a discussion of the sentential connectives in [II]. It is planned to discuss the general question in a later volume of these studies.

§ 14. L-Concepts

An L-term (e.g. 'L-true') is to apply whenever the corresponding radical term (e.g. 'true') applies on the basis of merely logical reasons, in contradistinction to factual reasons. Later, our problem will be to transform this vague characterization into a precise definition. In this section, five L-terms are taken as primitive terms for a set of postulates (P1 to 15). On the basis of these postulates, theorems are stated. Then definitions for further L-terms are laid down.

Logic, in the sense of the theory of logical deduction, will here be shown to be a part of semantics. This, however, does not contradict the possibility of dealing with logical deduction in syntax also. We shall see later (in Chapter E and, more in detail, in [II]) that what is usually called formal logic is the construction of a formal procedure in syntax corresponding to the semantical procedure.

We begin with a discussion in general semantics. We have previously defined the concepts of equivalence and implication (§ 10). They, however, are not logical concepts; as was emphasized, they must be distinguished respectively from logical equivalence, in the sense of agreement in meaning or content, and logical implication, in the sense of logical deducibility or entailment. For these latter concepts, we shall use the terms '*L-equivalence*' and '*L-implication*' (for terminological remarks, see § 37: Prefixes, and Connections). If we had a definition for L-implication we could easily define L-equivalence as mutual L-implication; the problem will be how to define L-implication.

Further, there are other logical concepts very much used in the logical analysis of science and closely connected with those just mentioned. Above all, there is the concept of logical truth, truth for logical reasons in contradistinction to empirical, factual reasons. The traditional term for this concept is 'analytic'; we shall use the term '*L-true*,' for the sake of analogy. As a correlate to logical truth we have the concept of logical falsity, falsity for merely logical reasons, logical self-contradiction; for it, the term 'contradictory' is often used; we shall use here the term '*L-false*'. The terms constructed with the prefix 'L-' out of the original semantical terms are called L-terms; the concepts designated by them, L-concepts. Later we shall introduce the prefix 'F-', and in syntax the prefix 'C-'. The unprefixed semantical terms (e.g. 'designation', 'true', 'implicate', etc.) are called *radical terms*; the designated concepts, radical concepts. For other radical concepts we shall also introduce corresponding L-concepts; e.g. if two sentences are disjunct (D9–5) for logical reasons, we shall call them L-disjunct; if they are exclusive (D9–6) for logical reasons, we shall call them L-exclusive.

The L-concepts — irrespective of the terminology used for them — are of the greatest importance for the logical analysis of science. Suppose that a certain physical theory, formulated as a class of laws $\Re_1$, is investigated and compared with another theory $\Re_2$. There are many questions which are beyond the scope of a merely logical analysis and require factual observation; e.g. the questions to what degree the particular laws belonging to $\Re_1$ or their combination are confirmed by the available evidence, whether $\Re_2$ is confirmed to a higher or lower degree than $\Re_1$, etc. On the other hand, there are questions of another kind, usually called logical questions, whose answers are not dependent upon the result of observations and therefore can be given before any relevant observations are made. These questions involve L-concepts.

Examples of answers which might be given to logical questions concerning two theories $\Re_1$ and $\Re_2$, as results of logical analysis (formulations in our L-terminology are added in parentheses). 1. The law

$\mathfrak{S}_1$ in $\mathfrak{K}_1$ does not have any factual content but is merely analytic ("$\mathfrak{S}_1$ is L-true"); hence it is unnecessary to look for a confirmation of $\mathfrak{S}_1$ by the observation of facts, since $\mathfrak{S}_1$ is in accordance with all possible facts; it follows that the simplified theory $\mathfrak{K}_1{}'$ obtained from $\mathfrak{K}_1$ by omitting $\mathfrak{S}_1$ asserts just as much as the original theory $\mathfrak{K}_1$ ("$\mathfrak{K}_1{}'$ is L-equivalent to $\mathfrak{K}_1$"). 2. The law $\mathfrak{S}_2$ in $\mathfrak{K}_1$, although it has factual content ("$\mathfrak{S}_2$ is not L-true"), follows from another law $\mathfrak{S}_3$ in $\mathfrak{K}_1$ ("$\mathfrak{S}_2$ is an L-implicate of $\mathfrak{S}_3$"); hence the omission of $\mathfrak{S}_2$ in addition to $\mathfrak{S}_1$ leads to a theory $\mathfrak{K}_1{}''$ which is likewise not weaker than $\mathfrak{K}_1$ ("$\mathfrak{K}_1{}''$ is also L-equivalent to $\mathfrak{K}_1$"). 3. The laws $\mathfrak{S}_4$ and $\mathfrak{S}_5$ in $\mathfrak{K}_2$ contradict each other, are logically incompatible with each other ("$\mathfrak{S}_4$ and $\mathfrak{S}_5$ are L-exclusive"); hence $\mathfrak{K}_2$ contains a contradiction, is inconsistent ("$\mathfrak{K}_2$ is L-false"); therefore there is no purpose in looking for a confirmation of $\mathfrak{K}_2$ by observation, because such a confirmation is impossible. 4. The three theories $\mathfrak{K}_3$, $\mathfrak{K}_4$, and $\mathfrak{K}_5$ constitute an exhaustive set of competitive theories; that is to say, for merely logical reasons at least one of them must hold ("$\mathfrak{K}_3$, $\mathfrak{K}_4$, and $\mathfrak{K}_5$ are L-disjunct with one another").

The above explanation of the meaning which we intend for the L-terms, i.e. of the way in which we intend to use these terms, is obviously rather vague. We have not said what, exactly, we mean by "logical reasons" for truth as against factual reasons, or by "logical deduction" as against other kinds of deduction. A precise account of the meaning of the L-terms has to be given by definitions for them; and the chief aim of the following discussions will be to look for suitable ways of arriving at these definitions. The explanations merely circumscribe what it is we are looking for. In order to make this circumscription more precise we shall now formulate some *postulates*. They are in agreement with our intention with respect to the L-terms, and they will guide our search for definitions. Not every definition compatible with these postulates will necessarily be acceptable to us, i.e. agree with our intention. But no definition will be accepted unless it is in accordance with each of these postulates (with the possible exception of P14 and 15; see below). We do not try to make the number of these postulates as small as possible, nor to make the set complete. This set is to serve only a provisional purpose. We shall later (§ 20) come to a system of general semantics using a new concept; it will be shown that the present postulates P14–1 to 15 are all provable as theorems in that later system on the basis of definitions without use of postulates. And it is planned to construct in a later volume of these studies a set of postulates for general semantics on a still different basis of concepts which are not available at the present stage of our discussions.

Primitive terms for the postulates:

1. 'True'. (We make further use of the radical terms defined in § 9 on the basis of 'true'.)

2. a. 'L-true', b. 'L-false', c. 'L-implicate', d. 'L-equivalent', e. 'L-disjunct'. (Later we shall see that (a) and (d) are definable by the other ones.)

The postulates may be divided into four groups.

1. P1 to 4 state the relation of inclusion between L-concepts and the corresponding radical concepts.

2. P5 to 10 state general properties of L-concepts.

3. P11 to 13 concern relations between sentences and sentential classes.

4. P14 and 15 state a particular property of L-truth and L-falsity which will be discussed later.

In this postulate system, we take the sentences in S as individuals; hence, the values of the variables '$\mathfrak{S}_i$', etc., are the individuals, of '$\mathfrak{K}_i$', etc., the classes of individuals, of '$\mathfrak{T}_i$', etc., both. The L-terms are applied, as the radical terms were earlier, both to sentences and sentential classes. We write 'L-true' instead of 'L-true in S', and likewise with the other semantical terms. Instead of '$\mathfrak{T}_j$ is an L-implicate of $\mathfrak{T}_i$' (or '$\mathfrak{T}_i$ L-implies $\mathfrak{T}_j$'), we often write '$\mathfrak{T}_i \; \overset{\mathbf{L}}{\mathbf{r}} \; \mathfrak{T}_j$'.

+**P14-1.** If $\mathfrak{T}_i$ is L-true, it is true.

+**P14-2.** If $\mathfrak{T}_i$ is L-false, it is false.

+**P14-3.** If $\mathfrak{T}_i \vec{\mathrm{L}} \mathfrak{T}_j$, then $\mathfrak{T}_i \rightarrow \mathfrak{T}_j$.

P14-4. If $\mathfrak{T}_i$ and $\mathfrak{T}_j$ are L-disjunct (with one another), they are disjunct.

+**P14-5.** L-implication is transitive (i.e. if $\mathfrak{T}_i \vec{\mathrm{L}} \mathfrak{T}_j$, and $\mathfrak{T}_j \vec{\mathrm{L}} \mathfrak{T}_k$, then $\mathfrak{T}_i \vec{\mathrm{L}} \mathfrak{T}_k$).

+**P14-6.** If $\mathfrak{T}_i \vec{\mathrm{L}} \mathfrak{T}_j$ and $\mathfrak{T}_i$ is L-true, $\mathfrak{T}_j$ is L-true.

+**P14-7.** If $\mathfrak{T}_i \vec{\mathrm{L}} \mathfrak{T}_j$ and $\mathfrak{T}_j$ is L-false, $\mathfrak{T}_i$ is L-false.

P14-8. For every $\mathfrak{S}_i$, $\mathfrak{S}_i \vec{\mathrm{L}} \mathfrak{S}_i$.

+**P14-9.** $\mathfrak{T}_i$ is L-equivalent to $\mathfrak{T}_j$ if and only if $\mathfrak{T}_i \vec{\mathrm{L}} \mathfrak{T}_j$ and $\mathfrak{T}_j \vec{\mathrm{L}} \mathfrak{T}_i$.

P14-10. If $\mathfrak{T}_i$ is L-true, $\mathfrak{T}_i$ and $\mathfrak{T}_j$ are L-disjunct (with one another).

P14-11. If $\mathfrak{S}_j \in \mathfrak{R}_i$, then $\mathfrak{R}_i \vec{\mathrm{L}} \mathfrak{S}_j$.

P14-12. If $\mathfrak{T}_i \vec{\mathrm{L}}$ every element of $\mathfrak{R}_j$, then $\mathfrak{T}_i \vec{\mathrm{L}} \mathfrak{R}_j$.

P14-13. If every element of $\mathfrak{R}_i$ is L-true, $\mathfrak{R}_i$ is L-true.

+**P14-14.** If $\mathfrak{T}_j$ is L-true, then every $\mathfrak{T}_i \vec{\mathrm{L}} \mathfrak{T}_j$.

+**P14-15.** If $\mathfrak{T}_i$ is L-false, then $\mathfrak{T}_i \vec{\mathrm{L}}$ every $\mathfrak{T}_j$.

Now we shall show that these postulates are in agreement with the previous explanations. (These considerations are necessarily as vague as those explanations.) P1, 2, and 4 are obvious on the basis of the explanations. P3 si in agreement with the conception generally held that logical implication (deducibility, logical entailment) is narrower than (material) implication; P3 states nothing more than this: if $\mathfrak{T}_i \vec{\mathrm{L}} \mathfrak{T}_j$ and $\mathfrak{T}_i$ is true, $\mathfrak{T}_j$ is also true. The transitivity stated by P5 is obviously in agreement with the conception of deducibility, no matter whether "by logical means" or otherwise. P6 is easily seen to fulfill our intention; if something is true for logical reasons and something else follows from it for logical reasons, then that is also true for logical reasons. P7 is justified by an analogous remark: if by logical

means (whatever that may be) we can show that $\mathfrak{T}_j$ is false
and also that $\mathfrak{T}_j$ follows from $\mathfrak{T}_i$, then we have shown by
the same logical means that $\mathfrak{T}_i$ is false. P8 is trivial. P9
states, in accord with the previous explanation, that L-
equivalence is mutual L-implication. P10 is in accordance
with the explanations; if $\mathfrak{T}_i$ is true for logical reasons, then
for logical reasons at least one of $\mathfrak{T}_i$ and $\mathfrak{T}_j$ is true. P11 to
13 are simply based on our convention to regard the asser-
tion of a sentential class as the joint assertion of its sentences.
Therefore we have called $\mathfrak{R}_i$ true if and only if all its sentences are true (D9–1). On the basis of this definition, if
$\mathfrak{R}_i$ is true any of its sentences is necessarily also true (P11).
And if every sentence of $\mathfrak{R}_j$ follows logically from certain
premisses, then $\mathfrak{R}_j$ itself follows from these premisses (P12).
And if every sentence of $\mathfrak{R}_i$ is true for some reasons, then $\mathfrak{R}_i$
is true for just the same reasons; if the reasons for the first
are logical (whatever that may mean), those for the second
are logical as well (P13). The status of the last postulates,
P14 and 15, is controversial. Some logicians would not accept these postulates. But they are in accordance with our
conception of L-implication. This can best be seen if we formulate the explanation of our use of the term 'L-implica-
tion' in this way: $\mathfrak{T}_i \, \overrightarrow{\text{L}} \, \mathfrak{T}_j$ if and only if it is impossible for
logical reasons that $\mathfrak{T}_i$ be true and $\mathfrak{T}_j$ be false. Now this is
obviously the case if $\mathfrak{T}_j$ is true for logical reasons (P14); and
likewise if $\mathfrak{T}_i$ is false for logical reasons (P15).

Fundamentally, it is not a question of truth but a question of convention whether we want to take the term 'L-implication' in such a
wide sense as to include the cases referred to in P14 and 15 or in a
narrower sense. As always in questions of this kind concerning extreme
cases, which frequently occur in logic and mathematics, the guiding
principle is the simplicity of the resulting theorems. The question here
is of the same nature as the following ones: "What shall we understand
by '$x + \mathrm{o}$', '$x \cdot \mathrm{o}$', 'x^{o}', etc.?", "Shall we take the concept of sub-class
in such a wide sense as to include the cases $\Lambda \subset F$ and $F \subset V$ for any

class F or not?" The latter question is not a mere analogy to our problem. Regarded from a certain point of view the question of P14 and 15 is just a special case of application of the question just mentioned; this will be shown in § 18. It is well known that the acceptance of the wider concept of sub-class leads to a considerable simplification in the theory of sets, although most beginners at first raise objections against it. There can be no doubt that the theory of logical deduction also becomes much simpler if framed so as to include P14 and 15 than otherwise, although the feelings against both, and especially against P15, are psychologically well understandable.

The wider concept of logical implication here accepted is in agreement with that of C. I. Lewis, which he took as a basis for his system of "strict implication" and defended against several objections ([Logic] pp. 174f, 248ff). (Strict implication is a relation between propositions, while L-implication is the corresponding relation between sentences (see § 17); this difference, however, is irrelevant for the question discussed here.)

The following *theorems* are based on the postulates P1 to 15. As far as radical concepts are concerned, the proofs of the following theorems make use also of the definitions in § 9 and the theorems based on these definitions (without postulates) in § 9.

T14-1. $\mathfrak{T}_i$ is not both L-true and L-false. (From P1, P2, T9–2.)

+T14-2. If $\mathfrak{T}_i$ and $\mathfrak{T}_j$ are L-equivalent, they are equivalent. (From P9, P3, T9–20b.)

+T14-3.

    a. If $\mathfrak{T}_i$ and $\mathfrak{T}_j$ are L-equivalent and $\mathfrak{T}_i$ is true, $\mathfrak{T}_j$ is also true. (From T2 and T9–20a.)

    b. Analogously with 'false' instead of 'true'.

    c. With 'L-true'. (From P9, P6.)

    d. With 'L-false'. (From P9, P7.)

T14-4. For every $\mathfrak{R}_i$, $\mathfrak{R}_i \overset{\mathrm{L}}{\Longrightarrow} \mathfrak{R}_i$. (From P11, P12.)

T14-5. L-implication is reflexive (i.e. for every $\mathfrak{T}_i$, $\mathfrak{T}_i \overset{\mathrm{L}}{\Longrightarrow} \mathfrak{T}_i$). (From P8, T4.)

+T14-6. L-equivalence is **a.** reflexive, **b.** symmetric, **c.** transitive. (From P9, T5; P5.)

T14-7 (lemma). $\mathfrak{S}_i \; \rightrightarrows \{\mathfrak{S}_i\}$. (From P8, P12.)

T14-8 (lemma). $\{\mathfrak{S}_i\} \; \rightrightarrows \mathfrak{S}_i$. (From P11.)

T14-9. $\{\mathfrak{S}_i\}$ and $\mathfrak{S}_i$ are L-equivalent. (From T7, T8, P9.)

T14-10. If $\mathfrak{K}_j \subset \mathfrak{K}_i$, then $\mathfrak{K}_i \; \rightrightarrows \mathfrak{K}_j$. (From P11, P12.)

T14-11. If an element of $\mathfrak{K}_i$ is L-false, $\mathfrak{K}_i$ is L-false. (From P11, P7.)

T14-12. If $\mathfrak{K}_j \subset \mathfrak{K}_i$ and $\mathfrak{K}_i$ is L-true, $\mathfrak{K}_j$ is L-true. (From T10, P6.)

T14-13. If $\mathfrak{K}_j \subset \mathfrak{K}_i$ and $\mathfrak{K}_j$ is L-false, $\mathfrak{K}_i$ is L-false. (From T10, P7.)

+T14-14. If $\mathfrak{T}_i$ is true and $\mathfrak{T}_i \; \rightrightarrows \mathfrak{T}_j$, then $\mathfrak{T}_j$ is true. (From P14–3, T9–10.)

T14-18. The class of the L-true individuals (i.e. sentences in S) is L-true. (From P13.)

T14-19 (lemma). If $\mathfrak{K}_i$ is L-true, every element of $\mathfrak{K}_i$ is L-true. (From P11, P6.)

+T14-20. $\mathfrak{K}_i$ is L-true if and only if every element of $\mathfrak{K}_i$ is L-true. (From T19, P13.)

T14-21 (lemma). If $\mathfrak{T}_i \; \rightrightarrows \mathfrak{K}_j$, then $\mathfrak{T}_i \; \rightrightarrows$ every element of $\mathfrak{K}_j$. (From P11, P5.)

T14-22. $\mathfrak{T}_i \; \rightrightarrows \mathfrak{K}_j$ if and only if $\mathfrak{T}_i \; \rightrightarrows$ every element of $\mathfrak{K}_j$. (From T21, P12.)

T14-23. If $\mathfrak{T}_i \; \rightrightarrows \mathfrak{K}_j$ and $\mathfrak{T}_i \; \rightrightarrows \mathfrak{K}_k$, then $\mathfrak{T}_i \; \rightrightarrows \mathfrak{K}_j + \mathfrak{K}_k$. (From T22.)

T14-24 (lemma). If $\mathfrak{K}_i \; \rightrightarrows \mathfrak{K}_j$, then $\mathfrak{K}_i \; \rightrightarrows \mathfrak{K}_i + \mathfrak{K}_j$. (From T4, T23.)

T14-25 (lemma). If $\mathfrak{K}_i \; \rightrightarrows \mathfrak{K}_j$ and $\mathfrak{K}_i + \mathfrak{K}_j$ is L-false, then $\mathfrak{K}_i$ is L-false. (From T24, P7.)

Theorems concerning Λ and V.

T14-30 (lemma). Every $\mathfrak{K}_i \; \rightrightarrows \Lambda$. (From P12.)

T14-31 (lemma). Every $\mathfrak{S}_i$ T Λ. (From T7, T30, P5.)

+**T14-32.** Every $\mathfrak{T}_i$ T Λ. (From T30, T31; also directly from P12.)

+**T14-33.** Λ is L-true. (From P13; or from T18, T30, P6.)

T14-34. If Λ T $\mathfrak{T}_j$, $\mathfrak{T}_j$ is L-true. (From T33, P6.)

T14-40 (lemma). V T every $\mathfrak{R}_j$. (From T10.)

T14-41 (lemma). V T every $\mathfrak{S}_j$. (From P11.)

+**T14-42.** V T every $\mathfrak{T}_j$. (From T40, T41.)

T14-43. The following conditions for a system S coincide (i.e. if one is fulfilled, any other one is fulfilled):

    a. V is L-false in S.

    b. There is an L-false $\mathfrak{R}_i$ (but not necessarily an L-false $\mathfrak{S}_i$) in S.

    c. There is an L-false $\mathfrak{T}_i$ in S.

(From T40, P7; T42.)

The following theorems depend upon the controversial postulates 14 and 15.

T14-50 (lemma). If $\mathfrak{T}_j$ is L-true, then Λ T $\mathfrak{T}_j$. (From P14.)

+**T14-51.**

    a. $\mathfrak{T}_j$ is L-true if and only if Λ T $\mathfrak{T}_j$.

    b. $\mathfrak{T}_j$ is L-true if and only if $\mathfrak{T}_j$ is L-equivalent to Λ. (From T50, T34; T32, P9.)

T14-52. If $\mathfrak{T}_i$ and $\mathfrak{T}_j$ are both L-true, they are L-equivalent to one another. (From P9, P14.)

T14-53. If $\mathfrak{T}_i$ and $\mathfrak{T}_j$ are both L-false, they are L-equivalent to one another. (From P9, P15.)

T14-54 (lemma). If $\mathfrak{T}_i$ is L-false, $\mathfrak{T}_i$ T V. (From P15.)

T14-55. If $\mathfrak{T}_i$ is L-false, $\mathfrak{T}_i$ is L-equivalent to V. (From P9, T54, T42.)

T14-56. If $\Re_j$ is L-true, then $\Re_i \, \text{L}^\flat \, \Re_i + \Re_j$. (From T4, P14, T23.)

T14-57. If $\Re_i + \Re_j$ is L-false and $\Re_j$ is L-true, then $\Re_i$ is L-false. (From T56, P7.)

T14-58. If $\mathfrak{T}_j$ is L-false, then $\mathfrak{T}_i$ is L-false if and only if $\mathfrak{T}_i \, \text{L}^\flat \, \mathfrak{T}_j$. (From P7, P15.)

T14-59. If $\{\mathfrak{S}_i, \mathfrak{S}_j\} \, \text{L}^\flat \, \mathfrak{T}_k$ and $\mathfrak{S}_j$ is L-true, then $\mathfrak{S}_i \, \text{L}^\flat$ $\mathfrak{T}_k$. (From P8, P14, P12, P5.)

If T50 is taken as postulate P14A instead of P14, and T54 as P15A instead of P15, then the resulting postulate set P1 to 13, 14A, 15A yields the same theorems as P1 to 15. In the new system, P14 as theorem can easily be proved on the basis of P14A (= T50), T32, and P5; and likewise P15 on the basis of P15A (= T54), T42, and P5.

We have taken five L-terms among the primitive terms for the postulates. Are all of them necessary? With respect to the corresponding radical terms we have seen (§ 9) that 'false' and 'implicate' can be defined on the basis of 'true'. However, an analogous procedure is not possible for the L-concepts in general semantics. Neither is 'L-false' definable by 'L-true', nor 'L-implicate' by 'L-true' and 'L-false'.

In the special semantics of some systems, an analogous order of definitions is possible, but only with the additional help of some other concepts, e.g. negation and conjunction. Let us consider a system S of such a kind that, first, for any open sentence $\mathfrak{S}_i$, if such occur at all in S (e.g. 'R(x,y)'), there is a corresponding closed sentence, designated by '$(\ )\mathfrak{S}_i$' (e.g. '$(x)\,(y)$R(x,y)'); second, for any closed sentence $\mathfrak{S}_j$ there is another sentence which is its negation, designated by '$\sim\mathfrak{S}_j$'; and third, that for any sentential class $\Re_i$ there is a sentence which is the conjunction of $\Re_i$, designated by 'conj$(\Re_i)$', i.e. such that conj$(\Re_i)$ is L-equivalent to $\Re_i$. (The systems S_3 and S_4 in § 8 fulfill these conditions.)

If 'L-true in S' for sentences is given, we may lay down the following definitions:

D14-A1. $\Re_i$ is L-true $=_{\text{Df}}$ conj$(\Re_i)$ is L-true.

D14-A2. $\mathfrak{S}_i$ is L-false $=_{\mathrm{Df}} \sim (\ )\mathfrak{S}_i$ is L-true.

D14-A3. $\mathfrak{K}_i$ is L-false $=_{\mathrm{Df}} \mathrm{conj}(\mathfrak{K}_i)$ is L-false.

D14-A4. $\mathfrak{K}_i \overset{\rightarrow}{\mathrm{L}} \mathfrak{S}_j =_{\mathrm{Df}} \mathfrak{K}_i + \{\sim(\ )\mathfrak{S}_j\}$ is L-false. (Compare [*Syntax*] § 34f, definition of 'consequence in II'.)

D14-A5. $\mathfrak{S}_i \overset{\rightarrow}{\mathrm{L}} \mathfrak{S}_j =_{\mathrm{Df}} \{\mathfrak{S}_i\} \overset{\rightarrow}{\mathrm{L}} \mathfrak{S}_j$.

D14-A6. $\mathfrak{T}_i \overset{\rightarrow}{\mathrm{L}} \mathfrak{K}_j =_{\mathrm{Df}} \mathfrak{T}_i \overset{\rightarrow}{\mathrm{L}}$ every sentence of $\mathfrak{K}_j$.

It is, however, easily possible to define 'L-true' and 'L-equivalent' in the following way, in accordance with T51a and P9.

D14-B1. $\mathfrak{T}_i$ is *L-true* $=_{\mathrm{Df}} \Lambda \overset{\rightarrow}{\mathrm{L}} \mathfrak{T}_i$.

D14-B2. $\mathfrak{T}_i$ is *L-equivalent* to $\mathfrak{T}_j =_{\mathrm{Df}} \mathfrak{T}_i \overset{\rightarrow}{\mathrm{L}} \mathfrak{T}_j$ and $\mathfrak{T}_j \overset{\rightarrow}{\mathrm{L}} \mathfrak{T}_i$.

If we adopt DB1, we may omit P6, 13 and 14; if we adopt DB2, we may omit P9. Hence an *alternative system* could take 'L-false', 'L-implicate', and 'L-disjunct' as primitive L-terms and would consist of P1 to 5, 7, 8, 10, 11, 12, 15, DB1, and DB2. This system yields the same theorems as the original.

We shall now lay down definitions for *more L-concepts*, on the basis of the five concepts occurring in the postulates P1 to 15. These new L-concepts are not as important as those five. They will, however, occasionally be applied in later sections, especially those defined by D1, 4, and 5; and the remarks preceding D5 have some bearing on later discussions.

+D14-1. $\mathfrak{T}_i$ is **L-determinate** (in S) $=_{\mathrm{Df}} \mathfrak{T}_i$ is either L-true or L-false.

T14-64. If every $\mathfrak{S}_i$ in S is L-determinate, then every $\mathfrak{T}_i$ in S is L-determinate. (From P13, T11.)

D14-2. $\mathfrak{T}_i$ is **L-exclusive** of $\mathfrak{T}_j$ (in S) $=_{\mathrm{Df}} \mathfrak{T}_i + \mathfrak{T}_j$ is L-false. (If $\mathfrak{T}_i$ or $\mathfrak{T}_j$ is a sentence $\mathfrak{S}_k$, then $\{\mathfrak{S}_k\}$ is to be taken as component of the sum.)

T14-70. If $\mathfrak{T}_i$ and $\mathfrak{T}_j$ are L-exclusive (of one another), they are exclusive. (From P2, T9-1, D9-6.)

T14-71. If $\mathfrak{T}_j$ is L-false, $\mathfrak{T}_j$ is L-exclusive of every $\mathfrak{T}_i$. (From T13.)

T14-72. If $\mathfrak{T}_i$ and $\mathfrak{T}_j$ are L-exclusive and $\mathfrak{T}_j$ is L-true, then $\mathfrak{T}_i$ is L-false. (From D2, T57.)

T14-73 (lemma). If $\mathfrak{T}_i$ is L-exclusive of Λ, $\mathfrak{T}_i$ is L-false. (From T72, T33.)

T14-74 (lemma). If $\mathfrak{T}_i$ is L-false, $\mathfrak{T}_i$ is L-exclusive of Λ. (From D2, T9; also from T71.)

T14-75. $\mathfrak{T}_i$ is L-false if and only if $\mathfrak{T}_i$ is L-exclusive of Λ. (From T73 and 74.)

T14-76. If $\mathfrak{T}_j$ is L-exclusive of $\mathfrak{T}_k$ and $\mathfrak{T}_i \ \overrightarrow{\text{L}} \ \mathfrak{T}_k$, then $\mathfrak{T}_j + \mathfrak{T}_i$ is L-false, and hence $\mathfrak{T}_j$ is L-exclusive of $\mathfrak{T}_i$. [Proof. If the condition is fulfilled, $\mathfrak{T}_j + \mathfrak{T}_k$ is L-false (D2); hence also $\mathfrak{T}_j + \mathfrak{T}_k + \mathfrak{T}_i$ (T13); hence also $\mathfrak{T}_j + \mathfrak{T}_i$ (T25).]

D14-3. $\mathfrak{T}_j$ is **L-dependent** upon $\mathfrak{T}_i$ (in S) $=_{Df}$ $\mathfrak{T}_j$ is either an L-implicate of $\mathfrak{T}_i$ or L-exclusive of $\mathfrak{T}_i$. [Explanation. If $\mathfrak{T}_j$ is L-dependent upon $\mathfrak{T}_i$, then either the truth or the falsity of $\mathfrak{T}_j$ can be logically inferred from the truth of $\mathfrak{T}_i$.]

T14-80. If $\mathfrak{T}_i$ is L-false, every $\mathfrak{T}_j$ is L-dependent upon $\mathfrak{T}_i$. (From P15.)

T14-81. If $\mathfrak{T}_i$ is L-true and $\mathfrak{T}_j$ is L-dependent upon $\mathfrak{T}_i$, then $\mathfrak{T}_j$ is L-determinate. (From P6, T72.)

T14-82. If $\mathfrak{T}_j$ is L-determinate, then $\mathfrak{T}_j$ is L-dependent upon every $\mathfrak{T}_i$. (From P14, T71.)

T14-83. $\mathfrak{T}_j$ is L-determinate if and only if $\mathfrak{T}_j$ is L-dependent upon Λ. (From D1, T51, T75, D3.)

T14-84. If $\mathfrak{T}_j$ is L-dependent upon $\mathfrak{T}_k$ and $\mathfrak{T}_i \ \overrightarrow{\text{L}} \ \mathfrak{T}_k$, then $\mathfrak{T}_j$ is L-dependent upon $\mathfrak{T}_i$. (From D3, P5, T76.)

D14-4. $\mathfrak{T}_i$ is **L-complete** (in S) $=_{Df}$ every sentence $\mathfrak{S}_j$ (in S) is L-dependent upon $\mathfrak{T}_i$. [Explanation. If $\mathfrak{T}_i$ is L-complete, then from its truth the truth or falsity of every other sentence and sentential class is logically deducible;

in other words, the assumption of $\mathfrak{T}_i$ decides about all questions expressible in S.]

T14-88. $\mathfrak{T}_i$ is L-complete in S if and only if every $\mathfrak{T}_j$ (in S) is L-dependent upon $\mathfrak{T}_i$. (From P12, T76, P11.)

T14-90. If $\mathfrak{T}_i$ is L-false, $\mathfrak{T}_i$ is L-complete. (From T80.)

T14-91. V is L-complete. (From T41.)

T14-92. If $\mathfrak{T}_i$ ⊥' $\mathfrak{T}_j$ and $\mathfrak{T}_j$ is L-complete, $\mathfrak{T}_i$ is L-complete. (From T84.)

T14-93 (lemma). If there is a $\mathfrak{T}_i$ in S which is L-true and L-complete, then every $\mathfrak{T}_j$ in S is L-determinate. (From T81, T88.)

T14-94. The following conditions for a system S coincide:
  a. Λ is L-complete in S.
  b. Every $\mathfrak{T}_i$ in S is L-complete.
  c. Every $\mathfrak{T}_i$ in S is L-determinate.
  d. Every $\mathfrak{S}_i$ in S is L-determinate.
  e. There is a $\mathfrak{T}_i$ in S which is L-true and L-complete.
(From T32, T92; T83; T33, T81; T64; T93.)

On the basis of L-implication, L-truth is definable in general semantics (DB1) but it turns out that L-falsity is not. The reason for this is that there is a $\mathfrak{T}_i$ which is L-true in every system, namely, Λ; but there is no $\mathfrak{T}_i$ which is L-false in every system, and there is not even in every system an L-false $\mathfrak{T}_j$. This reveals again the lack of symmetry in the customary foundations of logic. We found it earlier with respect to the radical concepts (see remarks before D9–7) and now with respect to the L-concepts. If we take 'L-implicate', 'L-true', and 'L-false' as basis, then 'L-exclusive' is definable (D2) but 'L-disjunct' is not and has therefore to be taken as primitive in the present system, although the two concepts show some sort of analogy (compare D20–9 and 10). This fact is another symptom of the asymmetry mentioned. (This asymmetry will be analyzed and over-come in [II].)

One might perhaps feel inclined to consider the following definition, in analogy to DB1.

D14-C1. $\mathfrak{T}_i$ is L-false (in S) $=_{Df}$ $\mathfrak{T}_i$ $\mathfrak{r}$ every sentence in S (and hence V).

(An analogous definition has sometimes been taken for the corresponding syntactical concept 'C-false'; see § 29.) How-ever, the definiens of DC1 cannot be taken as a definiens for 'L-false'; it is rather the definiens for 'L-comprehensive' (D5). The two concepts 'L-false' and 'L-comprehensive' are closely related to one another and even coincide in most systems (see T107b and examples); in the special semantics of systems of this kind the definition DC1 would therefore be adequate. But since there are other systems, although not frequently used, in which there are L-comprehensive but no L-false classes, DC1 would be inadequate with respect to those systems and hence inadequate in general semantics.

If $\mathfrak{T}_i$ L-implies all sentences of S, and hence, so to speak, comprehends all their contents, we shall call it *L-compre-hensive*:

D14-5. $\mathfrak{T}_i$ is **L-comprehensive** (in S) $=_{Df}$ $\mathfrak{T}_i$ $\mathfrak{r}$ every sentence in S.

T14-100. V is L-comprehensive. (From T41.)

T14-101. If $\mathfrak{T}_i$ is L-false, $\mathfrak{T}_i$ is L-comprehensive. (From P15.) The converse does not hold generally but only under certain conditions; compare T107b.

T14-102. Each of the following conditions is a sufficient and necessary condition for $\mathfrak{T}_i$ to be L-comprehensive:

    a. $\mathfrak{T}_i$ $\mathfrak{r}$ V.

    b. $\mathfrak{T}_i$ is L-equivalent to V.

    c. $\mathfrak{T}_i$ $\mathfrak{r}$ every $\mathfrak{R}_i$ (in S).

    d. $\mathfrak{T}_i$ $\mathfrak{r}$ every $\mathfrak{T}_j$ (in S).

    (From T22; (a), T42; T22; (c).)

T14-103. If $\mathfrak{T}_i$ is L-comprehensive, $\mathfrak{T}_i$ is L-complete. (From T102d.)

T14-104. If $\mathfrak{T}_i$ is L-comprehensive, it is comprehensive. (From P3, D9–9.)

T14-105. The following conditions for S coincide:

    a. Every L-comprehensive $\mathfrak{T}_i$ in S is L-false.

    b. V is L-false in S.

    c. There is an L-false $\mathfrak{R}_i$ in S.

    d. There is an L-false $\mathfrak{T}_i$ in S.

    (From T100, T102a, P7; T43.)

T14-106. If $\mathfrak{T}_i \mathrel{\overrightarrow{\mathrm{L}}} \mathfrak{T}_j$, and $\mathfrak{T}_j$ is L-comprehensive, then $\mathfrak{T}_i$ is L-comprehensive. (From D5, P5.)

T14-107. If S contains an L-false $\mathfrak{T}_i$, the following holds:

    a. V is L-false in S.

    b. 'L-false in S' and 'L-comprehensive in S' coincide.

    (From T105 and 101.)

The condition in T107 is fulfilled by most of the language systems practically used. If (but not only if) S contains a sign of negation, say ' $\sim$ ', then it contains an L-false class, e.g. $\{\mathfrak{S}_i, \sim\mathfrak{S}_i\}$, even if it does not contain an L-false sentence. (Hence the condition is fulfilled e.g. by the systems S_3, S_4 (§ 8), and S_6 (§ 11). On the other hand, the systems S_1 and S_2 (§ 7), which contain atomic sentences only, fulfill the condition of T108.)

T14-108. If S does not contain an L-false $\mathfrak{R}_i$, the following holds:

    a. No $\mathfrak{S}_i$ is L-false in S.

    b. No $\mathfrak{T}_i$ is L-false in S.

    c. V is not L-false, but L-comprehensive in S.

    (From T9, T100.)

D14-6. $\mathfrak{A}_i$ is **L-interchangeable** with $\mathfrak{A}_j$ (in S) $=_{Df}$ any closed sentence $\mathfrak{S}_i$ is L-equivalent to every sentence $\mathfrak{S}_j$ constructed out of $\mathfrak{S}_i$ by either replacing $\mathfrak{A}_i$ at some place in S by $\mathfrak{A}_j$ or $\mathfrak{A}_j$ by $\mathfrak{A}_i$, and there is at least one pair of sentences $\mathfrak{S}_i$ and $\mathfrak{S}_j$ of this kind.

The difference between this L-concept and the corresponding radical concept (D10–15) is this. If two expressions are interchangeable, then the exchange of one for the other in a closed sentence does not change its truth-value but might change its logical content. Both remain unchanged if the expressions are not only interchangeable but L-interchangeable.

T14-112. If $\mathfrak{A}_i$ and $\mathfrak{A}_j$ are L-interchangeable, they are interchangeable. (From T2.)

In many systems, 'interchangeable' and 'synonymous' coincide, and also 'L-interchangeable' and 'L-synonymous'. But, in general, the first concept in each pair is weaker than the second. If $\mathfrak{A}_i$ and $\mathfrak{A}_j$ are interchangeable in S, then their designata have all properties in common which can be expressed (by closed sentences) in S but are not necessarily identical. If they are L-interchangeable, then this is the case for logical reasons, i.e. on the basis of the semantical rules, but the designata may still be different. If, however, $\mathfrak{A}_i$ and $\mathfrak{A}_j$ are synonymous, then their designata are identical; therefore they have all properties in common whether expressible in S or not. And if $\mathfrak{A}_i$ and $\mathfrak{A}_j$ are, moreover, L-synonymous, then the semantical rules show us that the designata are identical; hence the expressions have, so to speak, the same meaning.

D14-7. $\mathfrak{K}_i$ is **L-perfect** (in S) $=_{Df}$ for every $\mathfrak{S}_j$, if $\mathfrak{K}_i \mathrel{\text{L}'} \mathfrak{S}_j$ then $\mathfrak{S}_j \in \mathfrak{K}_i$.

The defining condition means that any logical deduction starting from any sentences of $\mathfrak{K}_i$ leads always again to a sentence of $\mathfrak{K}_i$.

Tarski's Theory of Systems (see remark on D30–7) can also be applied to the L-perfect classes.

T14-116. $\Re_i$ is L-perfect if and only if for every $\Re_j$, if $\Re_i \sqsubset' \Re_j$ then $\Re_j \subset \Re_i$. (From D7, P11, P5; P12.)

T14-117. The following classes are L-perfect:
  a. The class of the L-true sentences (in S). (From D7, P13, P6.)
  b. The class of the true sentences (in S). (From D9–1, T14.)
  c. V. (From D7.)

T14-118 (lemma). For every $\mathfrak{T}_i$, the class of the sentences which are L-implicates of $\mathfrak{T}_i$ is L-perfect. (From D7, P12, P5.)

T14-120. If $\Re_i$ and $\Re_j$ are L-perfect and L-equivalent to one another, then $\Re_i = \Re_j$. (From T116.)

If $\mathfrak{M}_i$ is a class of sentential classes, 'pr($\mathfrak{M}_i$)' designates the product of the classes in $\mathfrak{M}_i$. (If $\mathfrak{M}_i$ is null, then pr($\mathfrak{M}_i$) = V.)

T14-121. If the classes in $\mathfrak{M}_i$ are L-perfect, then pr($\mathfrak{M}_i$) is L-perfect.

Proof. Let pr($\mathfrak{M}_i$) $\sqsubset' \mathfrak{S}_k$, and $\Re_i \in \mathfrak{M}_i$. Then pr($\mathfrak{M}_i$) $\subset \Re_i$, hence $\Re_i \sqsubset' $ pr($\mathfrak{M}_i$) (T10), hence $\Re_i \sqsubset' \mathfrak{S}_k$ (P5), hence $\mathfrak{S}_k \in \Re_i$ (D7). Since this holds for every $\Re_i$ in $\mathfrak{M}_i$, $\mathfrak{S}_k \in $ pr($\mathfrak{M}_i$). Therefore, pr($\mathfrak{M}_i$) is L-perfect.

T14-122. If $\Re_i$ and $\Re_j$ are L-perfect, then $\Re_i \times \Re_j$ is L-perfect.

If $\Re_i$ and $\Re_j$ are L-perfect, $\Re_i + \Re_j$ is not necessarily also L-perfect; but Lc($\Re_i + \Re_j$) (as defined by D23–F1) is L-perfect (T23–F21) and is L-equivalent to $\Re_i + \Re_j$ (T23–F13). Compare remark on T30–84.

T14-123. Let $\mathfrak{M}_i$ be a class of L-perfect classes. If $\Re_j$ is an L-implicate of every class in $\mathfrak{M}_i$, then $\Re_j \subset $ pr($\mathfrak{M}_i$) and pr($\mathfrak{M}_i$) $\sqsubset' \Re_j$. (From T116, T10.)

T14-124. If $\Re_i$ is L-false and L-perfect, then $\Re_i = $ V. (From P15.)

D14-8. S is an **L-determinate system** $=_{Df}$ every sentence in S is L-determinate.

A system of this kind does not contain any factual sentences (D21–1), only L-true and L-false sentences. Expressed in terms of L-ranges (§ 18): there are only the two extreme L-ranges (Λ_s and V_s). Many of the systems dealt with in symbolic logic are L-determinate. Systems of this kind often contain a large number and even an infinite number of sentences; but they are, nevertheless, in a certain sense poor in means of expression. Only two propositions (§ 17) can be asserted or represented. For all L-true $\mathfrak{T}$ are L-equivalent to one another (T52), and likewise all L-false $\mathfrak{T}$ (T53).

T14-130. Each of the following conditions is a sufficient and necessary condition for S to be an L-determinate system:

    a. Λ is L-complete in S.
    b. Every $\mathfrak{T}_i$ is L-complete in S.
    c. There is a $\mathfrak{T}_i$ in S which is both L-true and L-complete.
    d. Every $\mathfrak{T}_i$ in S is L-determinate.
    (From T94.)

The system P1 to 15 is far from complete. Especially with respect to '*L-disjunct*', hardly anything is determined. We shall mention here three fundamental assumptions PE1 to 3 concerning this concept without trying to analyze them into simpler postulates. The concept 'L-disjunct' is here applied not only to two sentences or sentential classes but to any (possibly infinite) number of sentences or sentential classes, in the sense that for purely logical reasons at least one of them must be true. Thus we must speak here of a class of classes $\mathfrak{M}_i$. [The reason why a procedure of this kind is necessary for this concept but not for the other L-concepts is not any special nature of this concept but rather the lack of symmetry mentioned above (see remark preceding DC1).] We will not add to the previous system P1 to 15 either PE1 to 3 nor other postulates on the basis of which these could be proved. We shall later (in § 20) construct a much simpler system of L-concepts in which P1 to 15 and also PE1 to 3 will be provable. The concept 'L-disjunct' will be used very seldom in this book. Only once (in the proofs for T19–E20 and 21) shall we refer to PE2 and 3.

P14-E1. If $\mathfrak{T}_i$ is L-exclusive of $\mathfrak{T}_j$ and $\mathfrak{T}_j$ is L-disjunct with $\mathfrak{T}_k$, then $\mathfrak{T}_i \overset{\rightarrow}{\cdot} \mathfrak{T}_k$.

P14-E2. Let $\mathfrak{M}_i$ be a class of classes each of which contains only two sentences which are L-disjunct and L-exclusive of one another. Let $\mathfrak{M}_j$ be the class of all classes which contain exactly one sentence out of each class in $\mathfrak{M}_i$. Then the classes in $\mathfrak{M}_j$ are L-disjunct with one another.

P14-E3. If the sentential classes of $\mathfrak{M}_j$ are L-disjunct with one another and $\mathfrak{K}_i$ and $\mathfrak{S}_k$ are such that, for every $\mathfrak{K}_j$ in $\mathfrak{M}_j$, $\mathfrak{K}_i + \mathfrak{K}_j \overset{\rightarrow}{\cdot} \mathfrak{S}_k$, then $\mathfrak{K}_i \overset{\rightarrow}{\text{L}} \mathfrak{S}_k$.

We can easily see that these postulates are in agreement with the previous intuitive explanations of the L-concepts. If, for logical reasons, $\mathfrak{T}_i + \mathfrak{T}_j$ is false and hence at least one of them is false and either $\mathfrak{T}_j$ or $\mathfrak{T}_k$ is true, then, likewise for logical reasons, if $\mathfrak{T}_i$ is true, $\mathfrak{T}_j$ must be false and hence $\mathfrak{T}_k$ must be true (PE1). If, for logical reasons, exactly one sentence in each pair in $\mathfrak{M}_i$ is true, then there must be a class in $\mathfrak{M}_j$ which is true, namely the class which picks the true sentence out of each pair (PE2). If, for logical reasons, there is a class $\mathfrak{K}_l$ in $\mathfrak{M}_j$ which is true, and if, furthermore, for every class $\mathfrak{K}_j$ in $\mathfrak{M}_j$, $\mathfrak{K}_i + \mathfrak{K}_j \overset{\rightarrow}{\text{L}} \mathfrak{S}_k$, then $\mathfrak{K}_i + \mathfrak{K}_l \overset{\rightarrow}{\text{L}} \mathfrak{S}_k$; that is to say, if all sentences of $\mathfrak{K}_i$ and of $\mathfrak{K}_l$ are true, then $\mathfrak{S}_k$ is also true. Since all sentences of $\mathfrak{K}_l$ are true, it follows that, if all sentences of $\mathfrak{K}_i$ are true, $\mathfrak{S}_k$ is true (PE3).

§ 15. L-Concepts in Special Semantics

We lay down *L-rules* for the system S_3 (§ 8) in the following way. We decide to apply an L-term (e.g. 'L-true in S_3') if and only if the corresponding radical term (e.g. 'true in S_3') can be shown to hold by making use of the semantical rules of S_3 only, without referring to facts. This decision is in agreement with the previous characterization of the L-concepts if the phrase 'on the basis of logical reasons alone' is understood as 'on the basis of the semantical rules of the system in question'.

So far we have discussed the L-concepts in general semantics, i.e. without reference to any particular semantical system. We will now interrupt this general discussion and turn to special semantics. The examples studied here may furnish some helpful suggestions for the general analysis, to which we shall return later.

Let us consider the semantical system S_3 given earlier (§ 8) and the following examples of sentences of this system (written here with the customary omission of parentheses):

$\mathfrak{S}_1$: 'P(a) ∨ ∼P(a)'.
$\mathfrak{S}_2$: ' ∼(P(a) ∨ ∼P(a))'.
$\mathfrak{S}_3$: 'P(a)'.
$\mathfrak{S}_4$: 'P(a) ∨ Q(b)'.
$\mathfrak{S}_5$: 'Q(b) ∨ P(a)'.

$\mathfrak{S}_1$ is a famous example (principle of excluded middle) of the kind of sentence called analytic in traditional terminology. How can we define the term 'L-true in S_3' in such a way that it will be applicable to this and similar examples? Are we to lay down primitive sentences and rules of inference as is customary in the systems of symbolic logic? We shall apply this method later within syntax; but here it is not necessary. We need no special rules in addition to those of S_3 in order to show that $\mathfrak{S}_1$ is true. If 'P(a)' is true, then, according to rule (4c) of S_3 (§ 8), $\mathfrak{S}_1$ is true; and if 'P(a)' is not true, then, according to (4b), ' ∼P(a)' is true, and hence, according to (4c), $\mathfrak{S}_1$ is true again. Hence $\mathfrak{S}_1$ is true in any case, no matter what is the case with 'P(a)'. From the semantical rules alone it does not follow whether 'P(a)' is true or not. In order to decide this question we have to observe facts. But we found that $\mathfrak{S}_1$ is true without making use of any factual knowledge, by using merely the semantical rules. We previously characterized L-true sentences as those which are true on logical grounds, without, however, specifying what are logical as against factual grounds. Now we see how that characterization can be made more precise. The logical grounds on which L-truth is based are the semantical rules. A sentence of S_3 is *L-true* in S_3 if and only if it is true

in S_3 in such a way that its truth follows from the semantical
rules of S_3 alone.

In the same way it is characteristic of an *L-false* sentence
that it is false in such a way that its falsity can be shown by
using merely the semantical rules. We found that $\mathfrak{S}_1$ is
true in any case. Therefore, according to rule (4b), $\mathfrak{S}_2$ is not
true, and hence, according to the definition of 'false in S_3',
is false. Therefore, we call $\mathfrak{S}_2$ L-false. Next we consider $\mathfrak{S}_3$
and $\mathfrak{S}_4$. On the basis of the interpretations of these sentences
previously given we see that $\mathfrak{S}_4$ follows logically from $\mathfrak{S}_3$;
therefore we should wish to call $\mathfrak{S}_4$ an *L-implicate* of $\mathfrak{S}_3$.
But we need no procedure of deduction leading from $\mathfrak{S}_3$ as
a premiss to $\mathfrak{S}_4$ as a conclusion. We merely show that, on
the basis of the rules of the system S_3, if $\mathfrak{S}_3$ is true, $\mathfrak{S}_4$ cannot be other than true. In this case it is very simple to show
this, because one application of rule (4c) is sufficient; in other
cases it would be more complicated. The result of the application of (4c) in this case may also be formulated in this
way: either $\mathfrak{S}_3$ is false or (i.e. if $\mathfrak{S}_3$ is not false but true) $\mathfrak{S}_4$
is true; in other words $\mathfrak{S}_4$ is an implicate of $\mathfrak{S}_3$. Generally,
$\mathfrak{S}_j$ is an L-implicate of $\mathfrak{S}_i$ in S_3 if the semantical rules of S_3
suffice to show that $\mathfrak{S}_j$ is an implicate of $\mathfrak{S}_i$ in S_3.

In the case of *L-equivalence* the situation is quite analogous.
When we understand the sentences $\mathfrak{S}_4$ and $\mathfrak{S}_5$ on the basis
of the rules of S_3, we see that they assert the same although
we may not know whether what they assert is the case or not.
Therefore we want to call them L-equivalent. By merely
applying rule (4c) we can show that, if $\mathfrak{S}_4$ is true, $\mathfrak{S}_5$ is true
and vice versa; in other words, that $\mathfrak{S}_4$ and $\mathfrak{S}_5$ are equivalent.
To put it in general terms, $\mathfrak{S}_i$ and $\mathfrak{S}_j$ are L-equivalent in S_3
if and only if the semantical rules of S_3 suffice to show that
they are equivalent in S_3.

The result found with respect to the system S_3 may be
generalized. We shall be in accordance with our original in-

tention with respect to the L-concepts and with the essential features of the traditional use of these concepts if we adopt the following convention: we shall apply the concept of L-truth to a sentence $\mathfrak{S}_i$ in a semantical system S if and only if $\mathfrak{S}_i$ is true in S in such a way that its truth follows from the semantical rules of S alone without the use of any factual knowledge. And likewise we shall use an L-term corresponding to another radical term if and only if the semantical rules suffice to show that the radical term applies. This convention applies not only to the L-terms mentioned before (besides 'L-true': 'L-false', 'L-implication', 'L-equivalence', and 'L-disjunct') but also to others ('L-exclusive', 'L-comprehensive', 'L-designation', 'L-fulfillment', 'L-determination' (of an attribute by a sentential function), 'L-synonymous', 'L-universal', 'L-empty', etc.).

The given characterizations of L-concepts are not definitions of these concepts, but rather requirements which the definitions to be constructed either in general or in special semantics should fulfill. The nature of these requirements and the problem of definitions for the L-concepts in general semantics in accordance with the requirements will be discussed in the next section. Here we turn back to system S_3; we shall lay down definitions for L-terms with respect to S_3, hence in special semantics.

Semantical system S_3 (§ 8)

5. **L-rules.** If in a sentence $\mathfrak{S}_i$ n different atomic sentences occur as components, then there are 2^n distributions of the two truth-values among these components. As long as we do not apply rule (4a), each of these distributions may be regarded as a possible case. For each of these distributions, the rules (4b) and (4c) determine a truth-value for $\mathfrak{S}_i$. In the truth-table of $\mathfrak{S}_i$, constructed in the customary way (see § 8), each distribution is represented by a line.

    a. $\mathfrak{S}_i$ is *L-true* in $S_3 =_{Df} \mathfrak{S}_i$ is true by virtue of rules (4b) and (4c) for every distribution of the truth-values among the components; in other words, the truth-table of $\mathfrak{S}_i$ shows 'T' on each line.

b. $\mathfrak{S}_i$ is *L-false* in S_3 $=_{\mathrm{Df}}$ $\sim\mathfrak{S}_i$ is L-true; in other words, the truth-table of $\mathfrak{S}_i$ shows 'F' on each line.

Since S_3 contains 6 atomic sentences, a truth-table containing all of them as arguments has 2^6 lines. In what now follows, by the truth-table of a sentence $\mathfrak{S}_i$, we understand its truth-table with respect to all 6 atomic sentences as arguments whether they occur in $\mathfrak{S}_i$ or not. The truth-table of a class of sentences $\mathfrak{R}_i$ is (in accordance with D9–1) constructed by putting 'T' on just those lines on which the truth-tables of all sentences of $\mathfrak{R}_i$ bear 'T'.

c. $\mathfrak{R}_i$ is *L-true* in S_3 $=_{\mathrm{Df}}$ the truth-table of $\mathfrak{R}_i$ bears 'T' on each line.
d. $\mathfrak{R}_i$ is *L-false* in S_3 $=_{\mathrm{Df}}$ the truth-table of $\mathfrak{R}_i$ has 'T' on no line.
e. $\mathfrak{T}_i$ $\overrightarrow{\mathbf{L}}$ $\mathfrak{T}_j$ in S_3 $=_{\mathrm{Df}}$ the truth-table of $\mathfrak{T}_j$ has 'T' on every line on which the truth-table of $\mathfrak{T}_i$ has 'T'.
f. $\mathfrak{T}_i$ is *L-equivalent* to $\mathfrak{T}_j$ in S_3 $=_{\mathrm{Df}}$ the truth-tables of $\mathfrak{T}_i$ and $\mathfrak{T}_j$ have 'T' on the same lines.
g. $\mathfrak{T}_i$ is *L-exclusive* of $\mathfrak{T}_j$ in S_3 $=_{\mathrm{Df}}$ on no line of their truth-tables do both have a 'T'.
h. $\mathfrak{T}_i$ is *L-disjunct* with $\mathfrak{T}_j$ in S_3 $=_{\mathrm{Df}}$ on every line of their truth-tables at least one of them has a 'T'.

It is easily seen that $\mathfrak{S}_i$ is L-true in S_3 if and only if the rules of S_3, and, moreover, only the rules (4b) and (4c), suffice to show that $\mathfrak{S}_i$ is true. Hence the given definition of 'L-true in S_3' is in accordance with the characterization given earlier and fulfills the requirement of adequacy to be formulated later (§ 16). The same holds for the other definitions of L-terms in S_3. Further, it can be shown that the postulates for L-concepts P14–1 to 15 are fulfilled, including the two controversial ones (P14–14 and 15).

The definitions of *L-concepts for the system S_4* (§ 8) are perfectly analogous, i.e. they may be formulated in exactly the same words. The same holds for similar language systems containing only molecular sentences and a finite number of atomic sentences logically independent of one another, but not containing variables.

§ 16. L-Concepts in General Semantics

Generalizing the result found in § 15 for S_3, a predicate or concept is called adequate for L-truth if it holds for a sentence $\mathfrak{S}_i$ if and only if the sentence of the metalanguage M saying that $\mathfrak{S}_i$ is true is L-true in M (D1). No complete solution of the problem of defining an adequate concept of L-truth in general semantics is given, but several ways believed to lead to such a solution are outlined. One of these ways presupposes M to contain logical modalities and hence to be non-extensional (1a). In another one, M is split up into M_1 and M_2 where M_2 contains the L-semantics or the syntax of M_1 (1b). In the two last cases (2a and b), M is supposed to contain the concepts 'descriptive' and 'logical'.

In our previous discussion we found a characteristic feature of the L-true sentences of a semantical system S; their truth follows from the rules of S alone. This characterization as it stands cannot be taken as a definition of 'L-true in S'. If we expand the phrase 'the truth of $\mathfrak{S}_i$ follows from the semantical rules of S', we see that it does not belong to the metalanguage M, in which the definition of 'L-true in S' has to be formulated, but to the metametalanguage MM, i.e. the language in which the rules for M are formulated. '. . . follows from . . . alone' means '. . . follows logically from . . .', or in our terminology, '. . . is an L-implicate of . . .'. Hence, the full formulation of the above phrase is like this: "The sentence (in M) '$\mathfrak{S}_i$ is true in S' is an L-implicate in M of the rules of S". Now, the rules of S are nothing else than a definition of 'true in S'; and if a definition is incorporated in a system (here in M), any sentence which is an L-implicate of it is L-true in that system. Therefore we may reformulate the above phrase in this way: "The sentence '$\mathfrak{S}_i$ is true in S' is L-true in M". This phrase, however, speaks about M and hence belongs to MM but not to M. Therefore it cannot be taken as a definiens for '$\mathfrak{S}_i$ is L-true in S'. It rather expresses a requirement which must be fulfilled for all sentences of S if the term 'L-true in S' is to be in agreement with our intention and traditional use, or, as we may say briefly, if the definition of 'L-true in S' is to be accepted as adequate. Therefore we shall formulate the requirement as a definition (in MM) of adequacy (in M).

D16-1. A predicate $\mathfrak{pr}_i$ in the metalanguage M of a semantical system S is an *adequate predicate for L-truth* in $S =_{\mathrm{Df}}$ if $\mathfrak{pr}_j$ is an adequate predicate for truth in S (§ 7) and $\mathfrak{A}_k$ is a name (or a syntactical description) in M of a sentence $\mathfrak{S}_k$ of S, then $\mathfrak{pr}_i(\mathfrak{A}_k)$ is true in M if and only if $\mathfrak{pr}_j(\mathfrak{A}_k)$ is L-true in M.

If $\mathfrak{pr}_i$ fulfills this condition, we call its definition an adequate definition for L-truth in S, and we call the property designated by $\mathfrak{pr}_i$ an adequate concept of L-truth in S. The definition D1 uses the term 'L-true in M' and thus presupposes that M has been constructed as a semantical system and that, in addition to a definition for 'true in M', a definition for 'L-true in M' has been given in MM. In analogy to the definition of adequacy with respect to L-truth, adequacy with respect to each of the other L-concepts can be defined.

So far we do not have a definition for 'L-true in S' in general semantics but only a definition of adequacy which may serve as a standard for the examination of any definition of L-truth proposed either in general or in special semantics. As far as special semantics is concerned, the task of defining L-truth does not involve great difficulties. For each particular semantical system S we can lay down a definition for 'L-true in S' besides that for 'true in S', and likewise definitions for the other L-concepts in such a way that they are adequate. Only in general semantics do serious difficulties arise. Here the problem is how to define L-concepts on the basis of other semantical concepts in a general way such that the application to any particular semantical system furnishes adequate L-concepts.

There seem to be different ways of solving this problem. For two of them we shall give some brief indications below; a third one will be discussed later (in § 20). Further investigations are needed in order to find out the particular features, advantages, and disadvantages of each of these and possibly other ways.

Two ways (1) and (2) are here indicated, and in each of them two alternatives (a) and (b). For each of these ways, the metalanguage M must fulfill certain conditions.

1. M is constructed in such a way that M *itself*, and not only MM, *contains concepts describing logical deduction in M or in a part of M.* Then the characterization given earlier can be turned into a definition of L-concepts in M.

1a. M is constructed as a non-extensional language (see D10–21 and § 17) containing signs for logical modalities, e.g. 'N' for logical necessity. Then the definitions could be stated in the following way (leaving aside here certain complications).

D16-A1. $\mathfrak{T}_i$ is L-true in $S =_{Df} N(\mathfrak{T}_i$ is true in $S)$.

D16-A2. $\mathfrak{T}_i \mathrel{\underline{\mathbf{L}}} \mathfrak{T}_j$ in $S =_{Df} N(\mathfrak{T}_i \rightarrow \mathfrak{T}_j$ in $S)$.

The definitions for the other L-terms are analogous. If M contains a relation of designation for S applied also to propositions, then, instead of DA1, DB1 might be taken into consideration.

D16-B1. $\mathfrak{T}_i$ is L-true in $S =_{Df} \mathrm{Des}_S(\mathfrak{T}_i, A \vee \sim A)$.

Here, instead of 'A $\vee \sim$A', any other sentence which is L-true in M may be written. 'Des$_S$' is here a modal, non-extensional term. In order to make this method (1a) feasible, the task must first be solved of constructing a non-extensional logic of modalities containing not only (like Lewis' system) the logic of propositions but, in addition, the logic of functions up to a level higher than any level occurring in any of the object languages to be covered by that system of general semantics.

1b. M consists of two parts M_1 and M_2, where M_1 contains the radical terms of general semantics ('designation', 'true', etc.) and M_2 contains the means of logical deduction in M_1 either in a syntactical or in an L-semantical form. (Here it is necessary to split up M into these two parts because a language cannot contain the whole syntax or the whole L-semantics of itself.) Thus, in M_2, we should define either C-concepts (§ 28) with respect to M_1 or L-concepts with respect to M_1. In the first case it would have to be done in such a way that the C-concepts represent a formalization of logical deduction in M_1 (in other words, that 'C-true in M_1' is an adequate predicate for L-truth in M_1). In the second case, it would be a task of special semantics to be solved by the means explained in § 15. Then we lay down the definition DC1, form (a) for the first case, (b) for the second; and analogous definitions for the other L-concepts.

D16-C1. $\mathfrak{S}_i$ is L-true in $S =_{Df}$ the sentence of M_1 '$\mathfrak{S}_i$ is true in S' is **a.** C-true (**b.** L-true) in M_1. (More precisely, without the use of quotes: There is a predicate $\mathfrak{pr}_j$ and an expression $\mathfrak{A}_k$ in M_1 such that the following holds: $\mathfrak{pr}_j$ is an adequate predicate for truth in S (§ 7), $\mathfrak{A}_k$ designates $\mathfrak{S}_i$ in M_1 (i.e., it is a syntactical description of $\mathfrak{S}_i$ in M_1), and the full sentence of $\mathfrak{pr}_j$ with the argument $\mathfrak{A}_k$ is C-true in M_1.)

This definition is itself in M_2 and hence in M. (It will have to be examined whether an extensional language system M would do for this method.)

2. Let us suppose that the system of general semantics formulated in M already *contains* the concept '*descriptive*', and hence also its correlate '*logical*'. (Here it does not matter whether 'descriptive' is defined on the basis of radical semantical terms, e.g. 'designation' and 'true', or is taken as an additional primitive term of the system of general semantics; compare § 13.)

2a. We restrict ourselves to those object languages which contain, for any descriptive constant $\mathfrak{a}_i$ occurring, a corresponding (logical) variable $\mathfrak{v}_i$ (i.e. such that $\mathfrak{a}_i$ is a value-sign of $\mathfrak{v}_i$; see § 11). (This restriction is the disadvantage of this method.)

D16-E1. A sentential function $\mathfrak{A}_j$ is a *logical sentential function* corresponding to a sentence $\mathfrak{S}_i =_{Df} \mathfrak{A}_j$ is constructed out of $\mathfrak{S}_i$ by replacing all descriptive signs occurring in $\mathfrak{S}_i$ by corresponding (logical) variables. (Example. $\mathfrak{S}_i$: '$R(a,b) \lor R(b,c)$'; $\mathfrak{A}_j$: '$H(x,y) \lor H(y,z)$'.)

D16-E2. $\mathfrak{S}_i$ is *L-true* in $S =_{Df}$ a (and hence any) logical sentential function corresponding to $\mathfrak{S}_i$ is universal in S (D11–2) (in other words, everything fulfills this sentential function).

The definitions of the other L-terms would be analogous. Let $\mathfrak{S}_j$ be a logical sentence (i.e. a sentence not containing descriptive signs). It follows from the definition that $\mathfrak{S}_j$ is L-true if and only if it is true, because a sentential function of degree zero is universal if and only if it is fulfilled by the null sequence.

The method of basing the definition of the L-concepts on the distinction between logical and descriptive signs with the help of the concept of the logical sentential function corresponding to a sentence was first applied in [Syntax] § 34d, in the definition of 'analytic in language II', rule DA 1Cb. This definition represents a formalization of the concept of L-truth in the special syntax of a particular language system. Tarski [Folgerung] has utilized this method for definitions of L-concepts in general *semantics*; the definitions E1 and 2 above show the essential features of his procedure. This change of the definition from a syntactical to a semantical one is an essential improvement. In semantics we can say "for every object . . .", but in syntax only "for every descriptive sign"; the latter formulation is often not adequate because not all values of the variables in S are necessarily designated by signs in S. Tarski expresses, however, some doubt whether the distinction between logical and descriptive signs and hence also between L- and F-truth is objective or perhaps more or less arbitrary.

The formulations given here show only the chief features of the definitions. The actual definitions will be more complicated because of the fact that logical relations may hold between the designata of the descriptive signs. [Suppose e.g. that the rules of designation state that 'a' designates Chicago and 'b' also designates Chicago. Then the sentence 'a = b' should be regarded as L-true because its truth can be established by the use of the semantical rules alone. But the sentential function '$x = y$' is obviously not universal. Suppose, further, that the rules state that 'Q' designates horse and 'P' designates white horse; then '$(x)(P(x) \supset Q(x))$' should be regarded as L-true although '$(x)(F(x) \supset G(x))$' is not universal.]

2b. The restriction involved in method 2a can be avoided with the help of the concept of the *logical attribute determined by a sentence*. In special semantics, this concept is to be defined by a recursive definition analogous to the definition of 'the attribute determined by a sentential function' (§ 11), but making use of the term 'descriptive' also. In general semantics that concept could be taken as primitive, in addition to designation with respect to descriptive signs. On this basis, truth and L-truth could be defined in about the following way.

D16-F1. $\mathfrak{S}_i$ is *true* $=_{\text{Df}}$ the logical attribute determined by $\mathfrak{S}_i$ holds for the sequence of the designata of the descriptive signs of $\mathfrak{S}_i$.

D16-F2. $\mathfrak{S}_i$ is *L-true* $=_{Df}$ the logical attribute determined by $\mathfrak{S}_i$ is universal.

Examples. W_1 is the logical attribute determined by the sentence $\mathfrak{S}_1$; likewise W_2 for $\mathfrak{S}_2$. $\mathfrak{S}_1$: '$(\exists x)R(x,a)$', W_1: $(\lambda y, H)\big[(\exists x)H(x,y)\big]$; $\mathfrak{S}_2$: '$P(a) \lor \sim P(a)$', W_2: $(\lambda x, F)(F(x) \lor \sim F(x))$. W_2 is universal, W_1 is not; therefore $\mathfrak{S}_2$ is L-true, $\mathfrak{S}_1$ is not.

It was remarked earlier (at the end of § 12) that the radical semantical relations, e.g. synonymity and equivalence, can also be applied as holding between members in *different semantical systems*. The same holds for L-relations, e.g. L-implication and L-equivalence. A definition for an L-relation used in this wider way is adequate if it holds in just those cases where the sentence of *M* which says that the corresponding radical concept holds follows from the rules of the two systems and hence is L-true in *M*. Thus e.g. we may find that we can show by merely referring to the rules of S_m and S_n that $\mathfrak{T}_i$ in S_m is equivalent to $\mathfrak{T}_j$ in S_n (D12–C); then $\mathfrak{T}_i$ in S_m is L-equivalent to $\mathfrak{T}_j$ in S_n.

§ 17. Correspondence between Semantical and Absolute Concepts

We decide to apply some radical terms (e.g. 'true') not only to expressions (e.g. 'the sentence 'P(a)' is true in *S*') but also to the designata of those expressions (e.g. 'the proposition P(a) is true'). In the second case, no reference to a language system is made; the concept is not a semantical but an *absolute* concept. An analogous procedure is carried out for L-terms. A non-extensional metalanguage is needed for this purpose. Modalities, including Lewis' concept of strict implication, are absolute L-concepts, applied to propositions, not to sentences.

All semantical concepts are based on relations between expressions of a language system *S* and entities in the realm of designata of expressions of *S*. Some semantical concepts are themselves relations of this kind, e.g. designation (§§ 7 and 12), determination of an attribute by a sentential function (§ 11), fulfillment of a sentential function by a sequence of entities (D11–1). Semantical concepts of a second kind, although based on relations of the kind just mentioned, are themselves attributed only to expressions, not to designata, e.g. truth and the other radical concepts defined by it, and the corresponding L-concepts. Now, for any semantical concept M_s of this kind of degree n there is a corresponding concept M_a of degree n such that, whenever M_s holds for n expressions, then M_a holds for the designata of these expressions. (Here the wider use of the concept of designatum is applied, as explained in § 12.) M_a is not a semantical concept, although related to a semantical concept. M_a belongs to the non-semiotical part of the metalanguage (or to the object language). In contradistinction to the concepts in any of the fields of semiotic, M_a is not dependent upon language. Therefore, we call M_a the **absolute concept** *corresponding to the semantical concept M*ₛ. It seems convenient to use the same term for the corresponding absolute concept as for the semantical concept. Or, rather, the same word; the terms are nevertheless different because the semantical term contains a reference to a semantical system (e.g. 'equivalent in S') while the absolute term ('equivalent') does not. Hence there is no ambiguity in the double use of the words, at least not in full formulations. [*Example.* If two sentences 'A' and 'B' are equivalent in S, we shall say that their designata, i.e. the propositions A and B, are equivalent (not with respect to any system, but absolutely).] This consideration leads to the following convention.

Convention 17-1. A term used for a radical semantical property of expressions will be applied in an absolute way (i.e. without reference to a language system) to an entity u if and only if every expression $\mathfrak{A}_i$ which designates u in any semantical system S has that semantical property in S. Analogously with a semantical relation between two or more expressions.

The transference of semantical terms to the corresponding absolute concepts can be carried out quite easily as far as radical semantical concepts are concerned. The convention is not itself a definition for the absolute terms in question; it merely states under what conditions we will accept such definitions. Hence it is of a similar nature to the requirements of adequacy for definitions of semantical terms as discussed previously (§§ 7 and 16). To give an example, the definition of 'true proposition' must be such that the following theorem is provable on its basis:

T17-A. (A proposition) p is true if and only if the following holds: for every S and every $\mathfrak{S}_i$, if $\mathfrak{S}_i$ designates p in S, then $\mathfrak{S}_i$ is true in S.

The following definition would obviously fulfill this requirement:

D17-B. p is true $=_{\mathrm{Df}}$ for every S and every $\mathfrak{S}_i$, if $\mathfrak{S}_i$ designates p in S, then $\mathfrak{S}_i$ is true in S.

Since, however, the absolute concepts do not belong to semantics, their definitions need not take the roundabout way through semantics that DB does. They can be stated in a straightforward and rather simple way (see D1 instead of DB). We shall first give definitions for those absolute concepts which apply to propositions while the corresponding semantical concepts apply to sentences. These absolute terms are merely different formulations for the sentential connectives (e.g. 'false' for ' $\sim$ '), convenient because of their analogy to semantical terms. In the following we use the ordinary connectives (see § 6). For terminological remarks concerning the semantical and the absolute uses of the same terms, see § 37, Radical Terms (2); for the term 'true', see § 37, 'True' (2).

D17-1. (A proposition) p is **true** $=_{\mathrm{Df}} p$.

D17-2. p is **false** $=_{\mathrm{Df}} \sim p$.

D17-3. q is an **implicate** of p $=_{\mathrm{Df}} p \supset q$.

D17-4. p is **equivalent** to q $=_{Df}$ $p \equiv q$.
D17-5. p is **disjunct** with q $=_{Df}$ $p \vee q$.
D17-6. p is **exclusive** of q $=_{Df}$ $\sim (p \cdot q)$.

With respect to the absolute use of the terms 'universal', 'empty', 'equivalent', 'symmetric', etc., the definitions given earlier (D10–1 to 7) are in accordance with Convention 1. For these terms, we defined the absolute use first, and then took it as a basis for the definition of their use for semantical concepts (D10–10 to 12).

The same method could also be applied to the terms 'true', etc. In this case, we first define the absolute use of these terms by D1 to 6, and then define their semantical use with the help either of the absolute terms or of their definientia (as in DC1 and 2). Two examples may be given:

D17-C1. $\mathfrak{S}_i$ is *true* in S $=_{Df}$ there is a (proposition) p such that $\mathfrak{S}_i$ designates p in S, and p.
D17-C2. $\mathfrak{S}_i$ is *false* in S $=_{Df}$ there is a p such that $\mathfrak{S}_i$ designates p in S, and $\sim p$.

In order to apply these definitions, S must contain rules of designation in the wider sense, including propositions, as explained in § 12. DC1 is the same as D12–1.

In the case of the term 'synonymous' it seems advisable not to apply Convention 1. The corresponding absolute concept is identity. It would seem strange to use the word 'synonymous' for this concept (e.g. "The morning star and the evening star are synonymous"); it seems natural to use instead 'identical' or 'the same'.

We apply Convention 1 also for the *absolute use of L-terms* (and F-terms, § 21). Thus a proposition p will be called L-true if and only if every sentence designating p in some system S is L-true in S. However, these absolute L-concepts are non-extensional (i.e. not truth-functions, see D10–20). [*Example.* According to the convention, we shall not only say, "The sentence 'P(a) $\vee \sim$ P(a)' is L-true in S_4", but also, "The proposition that P(a) $\vee \sim$ P(a) is L-true". But if in this latter sentence we replace the sentence 'P(a) ∨ ∼ P(a)' by the equivalent (D9–4) sentence 'P(a)', the whole statement becomes false.] Hence, for the absolute use of the L-terms, we need a non-extensional language (D10–21), and, more specifically, a system of logical modalities. We shall not enter here into a detailed investigation of modalities and of non-extensional language-systems in general; a discussion of these problems is planned for a later volume of these studies. Here we shall only briefly outline the use of absolute L-concepts. These concepts will be used in the next section, but will seldom be referred to in the remainder of this book. In general, in this book, we have tried to frame definitions and theorems in a neutral way, so as not to require the language used — especially the metalanguage used for semantics and syntax — either to be non-extensional or to be extensional.

Absolute L-concepts apply to *propositions*, not merely to truth-values. We construe propositions in such a way that L-equivalent sentences designate the same proposition. Hence, the absolute concept of L-equivalence is the same as identity among propositions (D13). [*Example.* The sentences 𝔖₄ and 𝔖₅ in S₃ (see § 15) are not identical but L-equivalent; therefore we say that the proposition that Chicago is large or New York is large is identical with (i.e. is the same proposition as) the proposition that New York is large or Chicago is large.] For the sake of brevity, we supplement the word-language in the following by the customary connectives and by variables, especially propositional variables '*p*', '*q*', etc., and variables for properties (or classes) of propositions '*F*', '*G*', etc. These variables are used also in operators; '(*p*)' is short for 'for every proposition *p*', '(∃*p*)' is short for 'there is a proposition *p* such that'. We shall speak of the disjunction of (the propositions of) a class *F* even if *F* is infinite. This disjunction is the proposition that at least one of the propositions of *F* is true; it is symbolized by 'dj(*F*)'

(D20). Analogously, the conjunction of F, symbolized by 'cj(F)', is the proposition that every proposition of F is true.

As an example, take an infinite realm of individuals a_1, a_2, etc. The proposition $(\exists x)P(x)$ is the disjunction of the infinitely many propositions $P(a_1)$, $P(a_2)$, etc. Likewise, the proposition $(x)P(x)$ is the conjunction of the same propositions. It is to be noticed that we are not speaking of infinite disjunctions or conjunctions of *sentences*. This is sometimes done but seems hardly admissible (if, as is customary, the language in question is restricted to expressions of finite length). There seems, however, no objection against infinite disjunctions and conjunctions of propositions once infinite classes of propositions are admitted.

The absolute terms 'L-true' and 'L-false' mean the same as the customary terms 'necessary' and 'impossible' in systems of modalities. The absolute term 'L-implication', for which we use here the same symbol ' $\underset{\tiny{\mathbb{L}}}{\to}$ ' as for the semantical term, means the same as 'strict implication' in Lewis' system. For the following definitions, we presuppose the absolute term 'L-true'. In a modal logic, suitable rules would have to be laid down for this term. We shall not construct them here. With respect to the formulation of the following definitions, the difference between "the *sentence* $\mathfrak{S}_i$ is L-true *in S*" and "the *proposition p* is L-true" should be kept in mind. Because of the analogy between the absolute and the semantical L-terms, if $\mathfrak{T}_i$ designates p in S, then p is L-true if and only if $\mathfrak{T}_i$ is L-true in S; and analogously for the other L-terms. Therefore, theorems analogous to the postulates and theorems in § 14 hold here. There are, however, two points of difference which make the present theory simpler than L-semantics. First, there are no different L-equivalent propositions; hence there is only one L-true and only one L-false proposition. Second, negation, disjunction, and conjunction of given propositions always exist, while the analogue for sentences or sentential classes does not generally hold.

D17-10. p is **L-false** $=_{Df} \sim p$ is L-true.

D17-11. p is **L-determinate** $=_{Df} p$ is L-true or L-false.

D17-12. p **L-implies** q $(p \overset{\rightarrow}{\text{L}} q)$ $=_{Df} p \supset q$ is L-true.

D17-13. p is **identical** with q (p is **L-equivalent** to q; $p = q$) $=_{Df} p \equiv q$ is L-true.

D17-14. p is **L-exclusive** of q $=_{Df} \sim (p \cdot q)$ is L-true (hence $p \cdot q$ is L-false, hence $p \overset{\rightarrow}{\text{L}} \sim q$).

D17-15. p is **L-disjunct** with q $=_{Df} p \vee q$ is L-true.

D17-16. q is **L-dependent** upon p $=_{Df}$ either $p \overset{\rightarrow}{\text{L}} q$ or $p \overset{\rightarrow}{\text{L}} \sim q$.

D17-17. p is **L-complete** with respect to the class F of propositions $=_{Df}$ every proposition of F is L-dependent upon p.

D17-20. The **disjunction** of the class F of propositions $\big(\text{dj}(F)\big)$ $=_{Df}$ (the proposition that) $(\exists q)\big(F(q) \cdot q\big)$.

D17-21. The **conjunction** of the class F of propositions $\big(\text{cj}(F)\big)$ $=_{Df}$ (the proposition that) $(q)\big(F(q) \supset q\big)$.

T17-5. If $p \overset{\rightarrow}{\text{L}} q$ and $q \overset{\rightarrow}{\text{L}} p$, then $p = q$.

T17-8. If $p \, \epsilon \, F$, then $p \overset{\rightarrow}{\text{L}} \text{dj}(F)$.

T17-9. If F and G are classes of propositions and $F \subset G$, then $\text{dj}(F) \overset{\rightarrow}{\text{L}} \text{dj}(G)$.

T17-11. If F is the null class, $\text{dj}(F)$ is L-false.

T17-12. If every proposition in F L-implies q, then $\text{dj}(F) \overset{\rightarrow}{\text{L}} q$.

The application of *C-terms* (to be introduced later, in § 28) to designata is also possible but perhaps not very useful because they would not become absolute but would even depend upon two language systems, a semantical and a syntactical one. Example:

D17-F. A property F is *C-universal* with respect to a calculus K and a semantical system $S =_{Df}$ there is a sentence $\mathfrak{S}_i$ which is C-true in K and true in S and which designates in S the proposition that every individual has the property F.

It might be possible to make the concept dependent upon a calculus only, perhaps in the following way.

D17-G. F is *C-universal* in $K =_{Df}$ there is a sentence $\mathfrak{S}_i$ such that

$\mathfrak{S}_i$ is C-true in K and that for every true interpretation (D33–2) S of K, $\mathfrak{S}_i$ designates in S the proposition that every individual has the property F.

But it seems impossible to avoid the reference to a calculus and thereby come to an absolute C-concept.

§ 18. L-Range

A possible state of affairs of all objects dealt with in a system S with respect to all properties and relations dealt with in S is called an *L-state* with respect to S. A sentence or sentential class designating an L-state is called a *state-description*. A given L-state leaves no question in S open; every sentence in S either admits or excludes that L-state. The class of the L-states admitted by $\mathfrak{S}_i$ is called the *L-range* of $\mathfrak{S}_i$ (Lr$\mathfrak{S}_i$). Two postulates for L-ranges are laid down (P1 and 2). L-states are propositions. Therefore, with the help of some absolute concepts defined in § 17, some concepts of a general theory of propositions are here defined (D1 to 5). With their help, three procedures A, B, and C are explained for defining concepts of L-state and L-range in such a way that the postulates P1 and 2 are fulfilled. For this purpose, a non-extensional metalanguage is used. The procedure A deals with a system containing only molecular sentences on the basis of a finite number of atomic sentences (S_4, § 8). Here the L-states correspond to the lines in the truth-table for the atomic sentences. The procedure B applies to semantical systems in general. It is shown that if S contains negation, every L-state is designated by a state-description (TB43). The procedure C is based on the concept of atomic proposition.

A semantical system will, in general, contain not only true but also false sentences. If a false sentence is not L-false, hence not self-contradictory, it describes a situation which is possible though not real. Let us compare the following sentences: "My pencil is blue" ($\mathfrak{S}_1$), "My pencil is blue or red" ($\mathfrak{S}_2$), "My pencil is blue or green" ($\mathfrak{S}_3$). None of them specifies precisely the color of my pencil; each admits a plurality of colors as possible. Even $\mathfrak{S}_1$ still admits all the various shades of blue. But the range of possible colors admitted by $\mathfrak{S}_1$ is narrower than those admitted by $\mathfrak{S}_2$ and by $\mathfrak{S}_3$; $\mathfrak{S}_1$ is therefore more precise. Between $\mathfrak{S}_2$ and $\mathfrak{S}_3$, there is no simple way of comparing preciseness. Their ranges overlap, but none of them is contained in the other.

The concept of the range of possible cases admitted by a sentence is only vaguely indicated by the foregoing explanation. We shall try several ways of making it more exact in subsequent discussions. We shall use for it the term '**L-range**' because it turns out to be an L-concept. Whenever we understand a sentence we know what possibilities it admits. The semantical rules determine under what conditions the sentence is true; and that is just the same as determining what possible cases are admitted by it. Therefore, the L-range of a sentence is known if we understand it — in other words, if the semantical rules are given; factual knowledge is not required. Thus, in the above example, we found certain relations between the L-ranges without knowing which color the pencil really had. Like the other semantical concepts, the concept L-range will be applied to sentential classes as well as to sentences. As an abbreviation for 'the L-range of $\mathfrak{T}_i$ in S', we write '$\mathrm{Lr}_S\mathfrak{T}_i$' or, briefly, '$\mathrm{Lr}\mathfrak{T}_i$'. Later we shall introduce a corresponding syntactical concept under the term 'C-range' (§ 32).

The sentence $\mathfrak{S}_2$ is true if my pencil has one of the blue or one of the red colors. Generally speaking, a sentence $\mathfrak{S}_i$ is true if and only if one of the possible states of affairs in $\mathrm{Lr}\mathfrak{S}_i$ is the real one.

The concept of L-range is useful for various purposes. It may be taken as basis for the whole of L-semantics; all the L-concepts which we have taken as primitive or defined in § 14 can be defined with its help. This procedure will be shown in § 20 and practically applied in [II]. The concept is also useful in the logical analysis of science in order to characterize sentences and theories with respect to what they say and what they leave undetermined. Furthermore, the concept of L-range may be taken as a basis for a theory of probability (Wittgenstein, Waismann) or of the degree of confirmation.

We shall now lay down two postulates for the concept of L-range, which seem to be in accordance with the above intuitive explanations. When we later discuss different ways of defining a concept of L-range, we shall show that each of them fulfills these postulates. The following considerations leading to the postulates start from the concept vaguely explained above and hence are necessarily likewise vague. They are to give merely the practical motivation for the choice of the two postulates.

1. Suppose that $\mathfrak{T}_i \; \overrightarrow{\mathfrak{r}} \; \mathfrak{T}_j$. Then every possibility admitted by $\mathfrak{T}_i$ must also be admitted by $\mathfrak{T}_j$; hence, $\mathrm{Lr}\mathfrak{T}_i$ must be a sub-class of $\mathrm{Lr}\mathfrak{T}_j$. For, if a possibility is admitted by $\mathfrak{T}_i$ but not by $\mathfrak{T}_j$, then, in case this possibility were real, $\mathfrak{T}_i$ would be true and $\mathfrak{T}_j$ false. Since, however, $\mathfrak{T}_i \; \overrightarrow{\mathfrak{r}} \; \mathfrak{T}_j$, this cannot occur in any possible case. This suggests P1.

2. Suppose that $\mathrm{Lr}\mathfrak{T}_i \subset \mathrm{Lr}\mathfrak{T}_j$. Then we know, merely on the basis of the semantical rules, that every possibility admitted by $\mathfrak{T}_i$ is admitted by $\mathfrak{T}_j$. If, now, $\mathfrak{T}_i$ were true, one of the possibilities admitted by $\mathfrak{T}_i$ would be real; since this same possibility is also admitted by $\mathfrak{T}_j$, $\mathfrak{T}_j$ would likewise be true. Thus we know, merely on the basis of the semantical rules, that, if $\mathfrak{T}_i$ is true, $\mathfrak{T}_j$ is also true. Hence $\mathfrak{T}_i \; \overrightarrow{\mathfrak{r}} \; \mathfrak{T}_j$. This leads to P2.

Postulates for L-range

+**P18-1.** If $\mathfrak{T}_i \; \overrightarrow{\mathfrak{r}} \; \mathfrak{T}_j$ (in S), then $\mathrm{Lr}\mathfrak{T}_i \subset \mathrm{Lr}\mathfrak{T}_j$.

+**P18-2.** If $\mathrm{Lr}\mathfrak{T}_i \subset \mathrm{Lr}\mathfrak{T}_j$ (in S), then $\mathfrak{T}_i \; \overrightarrow{\mathfrak{r}} \; \mathfrak{T}_j$.

The following theorems T1 to 9 are based on these two postulates in addition to the earlier postulates, definitions, and theorems concerning L-concepts (§ 14). L-equivalence coincides with identity of L-ranges (T2). The L-range of V is the maximum L-range, in which every other L-range is contained (T5). It is that of all the L-true $\mathfrak{T}$, and only these (T7). The L-range of V is the minimum L-range, which is contained in every other L-range (T6). It is the L-range of all the L-comprehensive $\mathfrak{T}$, and only these (T8), and of all the L-false $\mathfrak{T}$, and only these, if there are any such (T9).

T18-1. $\mathrm{Lr}\mathfrak{T}_i \subset \mathrm{Lr}\mathfrak{T}_j$ (in S) if and only if $\mathfrak{T}_i \; \overline{\mathfrak{T}} \; \mathfrak{T}_j$. (From P1 and 2.)

+**T18-2.** $\mathrm{Lr}\mathfrak{T}_i = \mathrm{Lr}\mathfrak{T}_j$ (in S) if and only if $\mathfrak{T}_i$ and $\mathfrak{T}_j$ are L-equivalent. (From T1, P14–9.)

T18-5. For every $\mathfrak{T}_i$ (in S), $\mathrm{Lr}\mathfrak{T}_i \subset \mathrm{Lr}\Lambda$. (From T14–32, P1.)

T18-6. For every $\mathfrak{T}_i$ (in S), $\mathrm{Lr}V \subset \mathrm{Lr}\mathfrak{T}_i$. (From T14–42, P1.)

T18-7. $\mathrm{Lr}\mathfrak{T}_i = \mathrm{Lr}\Lambda$ (in S) if and only if $\mathfrak{T}_i$ is L-true. (From T2, T14–51b.)

T18-8. $\mathrm{Lr}\mathfrak{T}_i = \mathrm{Lr}V$ if and only if $\mathfrak{T}_i$ is L-comprehensive. (From T14–102b, T2.)

T18-9. If S contains an L-false $\mathfrak{T}_j$, then, for every $\mathfrak{T}_i$, $\mathrm{Lr}\mathfrak{T}_i = \mathrm{Lr}V$ if and only if $\mathfrak{T}_i$ is L-false. (From T8, T14–107b.)

We shall later explain several ways of defining concepts which may be taken as concepts of L-range and which fulfill the postulates P1 and 2. The ways discussed in this section (A, B, and C) take L-ranges as classes of propositions. In preparation for them we shall now introduce some concepts based both on the absolute concepts concerning propositions explained in § 17 and on semantical concepts, and hence requiring a reference to a semantical system S. The metalanguage M, in which we speak about S and propositions and L-ranges with respect to S, must be non-extensional as explained in § 17. We shall also give some theorems. They presuppose general theorems concerning propositions which are listed neither here nor in § 17 and could be fully developed only in an elaborate non-extensional system of propositions (logic of modalities) as indicated in § 17; many of the theorems used but not stated here are analogues to theorems in § 14 concerning semantical L-concepts.

We say that p is *based upon* a class F of propositions $(p \, \epsilon \, \mathrm{bas}(F), \mathrm{D}18\text{–}1)$, if p can be obtained by starting from propositions in F and applying the operations of negation and disjunction (also to an infinite class of propositions, $\mathrm{D}17$–20) any finite number of times.

+**D18-1.** $\mathrm{bas}(F)$ (the class of the **propositions based upon** F) $=_{\mathrm{Df}}$ the product of all classes G such that $F \subset G$ and G is closed with respect to negation and disjunction (i.e. if $q \, \epsilon \, G$, then $(\sim q) \, \epsilon \, G$, and if $H \subset G$, then $\mathrm{dj}(H) \, \epsilon \, G$).

T18-15. For every F, $\mathrm{bas}(F)$ is closed with respect to negation, disjunction, and conjunction.

T18-16. For every F, $\mathrm{bas}(\mathrm{bas}(F)) \subset \mathrm{bas}(F)$.

T18-17. If $p \, \epsilon \, \mathrm{bas}(F)$, then p is a disjunction of conjunctions of propositions in F and their negations.

This theorem is analogous to the known theorem of the disjunctive normal form for molecular sentences (see e.g. Hilbert and Ackermann, *Logik*). It can be proved by induction with respect to the number of times the operations of negation and disjunction are applied; this number is finite, although the classes involved may be infinite.

T18-18. If a proposition is L-complete with respect to F ($\mathrm{D}17$–17), it is also L-complete with respect to $\mathrm{bas}(F)$; and vice versa.

Proof. Let p be L-complete with respect to F. Then every proposition in F is L-dependent upon p. If q is L-dependent upon p, $\sim q$ is likewise; if every proposition in G is L-dependent upon p, then $\mathrm{dj}(G)$ is likewise. It follows by induction that every proposition based upon F is L-dependent upon p. Hence p is L-complete with respect to $\mathrm{bas}(F)$.

We say that p is *designated in* S ($p \, \epsilon \, \mathrm{des}(S)$, $\mathrm{D}2$) if p is designated by a sentence (not only by a sentential class) in S.

D18-2. des(S) (the class of the **propositions designated in S**) $=_{Df}$ the class of the propositions designated by sentences in S.

D18-3. p is **L-complete with respect to the semantical system** $S =_{Df} p$ is L-complete (D17–17) with respect to des(S).

T18-19. Each of the following conditions is sufficient and necessary for p to be L-complete with respect to S.

> **a.** p is L-complete with respect to bas(des(S)). (From T18.)
> **b.** For every q in des(S), either $p \; \mathfrak{L}^{\flat} \; q$ or $p \; \mathfrak{L}^{\flat} \sim q$.
> **c.** For every q designated by a $\mathfrak{T}_i$ in S, either $p \; \mathfrak{L}^{\flat} \; q$ or $p \; \mathfrak{L}^{\flat} \sim q$. (From (b).)
> **d.** For every q in bas(des(S)), either $p \; \mathfrak{L}^{\flat} \; q$ or $p \; \mathfrak{L}^{\flat} \sim q$. (From (a).)

The realm of those propositions, in connection with a system S, which we take into consideration in the following discussions (including A and B) is bas(des(S)). It comprehends all propositions obtainable from those designated in S by applying any of the ordinary connections (T15). (Later, in C, we shall consider a still wider realm.)

D18-4. F is a **selection class of propositions** with respect to $S =_{Df} F$ is a class of propositions containing for every p in bas(des(S)) either p or $\sim p$ but not both and no other propositions.

D18-5. p is a **selection proposition** with respect to $S =_{Df} p$ is the conjunction of a selection class of propositions with respect to S.

T18-20. Every selection proposition with respect to S is L-complete with respect to S.

T18-22. If F is the class of all selection propositions with respect to S, then dj(F) is L-true.

T18-24. If $p \in$ bas(des(S)) and is not L-false, there is at least one selection proposition q such that q is not L-false and $q \; \overline{\mathrm{L}} \; p$.

Proof. Let d be the disjunction of all selection propositions. Then d is L-true (T22). Hence $p \cdot d = p$; hence $p \cdot d$ is not L-false. For every selection proposition r, consider the conjunction $p \cdot r$. These conjunctions cannot all be L-false because otherwise their disjunction would be L-false; this disjunction, however, is $p \cdot d$ and hence not L-false. Therefore, there is a selection proposition q such that $p \cdot q$ is not L-false. Hence, q is not L-false and does not L-imply $\sim p$. Therefore, since q is L-complete with respect to S (T20), $q \; \overline{\mathrm{L}} \; p$.

Now we are going to outline several procedures for defining L-ranges as classes of propositions in a non-extensional metalanguage. Since, however, the nature of propositions and of non-extensional concepts is still controversial and some logicians even reject non-extensional language systems, we shall, in the next section, explain concepts which are in a certain way analogous to the concepts of L-state and L-range as here explained and which, therefore, may be taken as substitutes for them, although they are definable in an extensional metalanguage.

A. *Systems with molecular sentences only*

In the example at the beginning of this section, we spoke of possible cases admitted by a sentence. We considered the possible cases with respect to one object only, viz. my pencil. But, in general, a system S has to do with many objects, and hence we have to consider the possible states of affairs of all the objects dealt with in S and with respect to all properties, relations, etc., dealt with in S, while in the earlier example we considered only colors. For brevity, we shall use the term '**L-state**' for these possible states of affairs with respect to a system S. Then $\mathrm{Lr}\mathfrak{S}_i$ (i.e. the L-range of the sentence $\mathfrak{S}_i$) will be a class of certain L-states; roughly speaking, the class of the L-states admitted by $\mathfrak{S}_i$. The linguistic expression for an L-state, as the earlier example shows, is a sentence or a sentential class; we shall call it later a **state-description**. Therefore, L-states are propositions of a certain kind. Hence the need of concepts concerning propositions and of a non-extensional metalanguage, as explained previously, for the discussion of L-states and L-ranges.

As an example for the application of the concepts to be introduced, let us consider the system S_4 (§ 8). S_4 contains two predicates 'P' and 'Q' designating the properties of being large and of having a harbor respectively, and three individual constants 'a', 'b', and 'c' designating Chicago, New York, and Carmel respectively; S_4 contains further the customary (extensional) connectives. Thus, S_4 possesses six atomic sentences. Let us construct their truth-table (§ 8) as shown (partly) in the subsequent diagram.

	'P(a)'	'P(b)'	'P(c)'	'Q(a)'	'Q(b)'	'Q(c)'
s_1	T	T	T	T	T	T
s_2	T	T	T	T	T	F
s_3	T	T	T	T	F	T
s_4	T	T	T	T	F	F
s_5	T	T	T	F	T	T
•	•	•	•	•	•	•
•	•	•	•	•	•	•
s_{10}	T	T	F	T	T	F
•	•	•	•	•	•	•
•	•	•	•	•	•	•
s_{64}	F	F	F	F	F	F

Each line of the table represents one of the possible distributions of the two truth-values among the six atomic sentences. Hence, there are 64 ($= 2^6$) lines. Each line corresponds to one of the possible states of affairs of the three objects with respect to the two properties involved; this is what we call an *L-state* with respect to S_4. We designate them with 's_1', 's_2', . . . 's_{64}'. A class of six sentences, containing for each atomic sentence $\mathfrak{S}_i$ either $\mathfrak{S}_i$ itself or $\sim\mathfrak{S}_i$ but not both, is called an *atomic sentential selection* in S_4

(DA1). It is easily seen that there are 64 atomic sentential selections in S_4, and that each of them is a *state-description*. The state-description $\Re_r$ for any state s_r ($r = 1$ to 64) is that atomic sentential selection which contains those atomic sentences which have the value T for s_r, and the negations of those which have F. Here, since the number of atomic sentences in S_4 is finite and S_4 possesses a sign of conjunction, there is even a sentence $\mathfrak{S}_r$ as a state-description for any s_r, namely the conjunction of the sentences of $\Re_r$. Thus, for instance, $\mathfrak{S}_{10}$ is the sentence 'P(a).P(b).~P(c).Q(a) .Q(b).~Q(c)'; it is a state-description for s_{10}. For any two conjunctions $\mathfrak{S}_r$ and $\mathfrak{S}_q$ of the kind described, for different L-states s_r and s_q, there is at least one atomic sentence $\mathfrak{S}_i$ such that $\mathfrak{S}_i$ occurs in the one and ~$\mathfrak{S}_i$ in the other; hence $\mathfrak{S}_r$ and $\mathfrak{S}_q$ are L-exclusive (TA1d, TA2d). Exactly one of the 64 state-descriptions $\mathfrak{S}_r$ must be true; hence the disjunction of those 64 conjunctions is L-true (this leads to TA11). Which of the state-descriptions is the true one cannot be determined by logical analysis alone. Factual knowledge, based on geographical observations, is required. These observations show that Chicago and New York are both large and provided with harbors, while Carmel is neither. Thus, of the atomic sentences as listed in the table, the third and the sixth are false, the others true. Hence, the conjunction $\mathfrak{S}_{10}$ mentioned above is true; all the others are false. Therefore we call s_{10} the real L-state (DA8); the other L-states, although possible, are not real; their state-descriptions are false.

If a sentence $\mathfrak{S}_i$ in S_4 is given, then, without knowledge of the relevant facts, we cannot know whether $\mathfrak{S}_i$ is true or not, except in the case that $\mathfrak{S}_i$ is L-determinate. Nevertheless, we can know, for any L-state s_r ($r = 1$ to 64), whether or not $\mathfrak{S}_i$ would be true within this L-state; that is to say, whether or not $\mathfrak{S}_i$ would be true if s_r were the real L-state.

For, the semantical rules for the connectives suffice to determine in the customary way the truth-value of any molecular sentence for any line of the truth-table. Thus, for instance, 'P(a).P(b).P(c).Q(a)' is true within the first four L-states s_1 to s_4 and false within the others. Now we take as **L-range** of $\mathfrak{S}_i$ the class of those L-states which make $\mathfrak{S}_i$ true; in other words, those which L-imply the proposition designated by $\mathfrak{S}_i$ (DA6). Thus, for every sentence, we can find its L-range with the help of the semantical rules alone without referring to facts. Hence, the concepts of L-state and L-range are both L-concepts; that is the reason why we form their terms with the prefix 'L'.

Every sentence in S_4 is a molecular sentence constructed out of certain atomic sentences which are logically completely independent of each other. Therefore, on the basis of well-known theorems for the ordinary (extensional) propositional connections, the following holds for S_4. Let $\mathfrak{S}_r$ ($r = 1$ to 64) again be the state-description in conjunctive form for s_r, as described above. For every not L-false sentence $\mathfrak{S}_i$ in S_4 there is exactly one (non-null) class $\mathfrak{K}_i$ of certain of these conjunctions $\mathfrak{S}_r$ such that the disjunction $\mathfrak{D}_i$ of the sentences of $\mathfrak{K}_i$ is L-equivalent to $\mathfrak{S}_i$ (this leads to TA10). ($\mathfrak{D}_i$ is the so-called complete disjunctive normal form for $\mathfrak{S}_i$; for the procedure of its construction see, for instance, Hilbert-Bernays, *Grundlagen der Mathematik*, I, 57.) $\mathfrak{S}_r \in \mathfrak{K}_i$ if and only if $\mathfrak{S}_r \, \overrightarrow{L} \, \mathfrak{S}_i$. Hence, $Lr\mathfrak{S}_i$ is the class of the propositions designated by the sentences of $\mathfrak{K}_i$. If not $\mathfrak{S}_r \in \mathfrak{K}_i$, $\mathfrak{S}_r \, \overrightarrow{L} \sim \mathfrak{S}_i$. Hence, for any sentence $\mathfrak{S}_j$ in S_4, either $\mathfrak{S}_r \, \overrightarrow{L} \, \mathfrak{S}_j$ or $\mathfrak{S}_r \, \overrightarrow{L} \sim \mathfrak{S}_j$; hence, $\mathfrak{S}_r$ is L-complete with respect to S_4 (TA1c, TA2c, TA3c). Let $\mathfrak{S}_i$ and $\mathfrak{S}_j$ be any sentences in S_4, and $\mathfrak{K}_i$ and $\mathfrak{K}_j$ the classes corresponding to them as described. Then $\mathfrak{S}_i \, \overrightarrow{L} \, \mathfrak{S}_j$ if and only if $\mathfrak{K}_i \subset \mathfrak{K}_j$, hence if and only if $Lr\mathfrak{S}_i \subset Lr\mathfrak{S}_j$ (TA5). Thus the concept of L-range here defined (DA6) fulfills the postulates P1 and 2. On the basis of these considerations, we lay down the following definitions. We add some theorems, based on these definitions and on the earlier definitions and theorems in this section and in § 17 (absolute concepts) and § 14 (L-concepts, based on postulates P14–1 to 15) and on the known theorems of propositional logic referred to above. The following definitions and theorems concern the system S_4; but they can be laid down in the same way for any semantical system containing only molecular sentences. [If the atomic sentences of a system do not possess complete logical independence — in other words, if some atomic sentential selections are L-false — then some slight modifications are required; for instance, DA2 and 3 must be restricted to not L-false selections.]

D18-A1. $\Re_i$ is an *atomic sentential selection* in S_4 $=_{Df}$ $\Re_i$ contains, for every atomic sentence $\mathfrak{S}_i$ in S_4, either $\mathfrak{S}_i$ or $\sim \mathfrak{S}_i$ but not both, and no other sentences.

D18-A2. $\mathfrak{T}_i$ is (an L-state-description or briefly) a *state-description* in S_4 $=_{Df}$ $\mathfrak{T}_i$ is L-equivalent to an atomic sentential selection in S_4.

D18-A3. s_r is an *L-state* with respect to S_4 $=_{Df}$ s_r is a proposition designated by an atomic sentential selection in S_4. (Hence every state-description designates an L-state.)

D18-A6. $\mathrm{Lr}\mathfrak{T}_i$ (the *L-range* of $\mathfrak{T}_i$ with respect to S_4) $=_{Df}$ the class of the L-states which L-imply the proposition designated by $\mathfrak{T}_i$.

D18-A8. rs (the *real L-state* with respect to S_4) $=_{Df}$ the p such that p is an L-state and true.

D18-A9. V_s (the *universal L-range* with respect to S_4) $=_{Df}$ the class of all (64) L-states with respect to S_4.

D18-A10. Λ_s (the *null L-range* with respect to S_4) $=_{Df}$ the null class (of L-states with respect to S_4).

The L-ranges V_s and Λ_s must not be confused with the sentential classes V and Λ.

T18-A1. For any atomic sentential selections $\mathfrak{K}_i$ and $\mathfrak{K}_j$ (in S_4) the following holds.

    a. $\mathfrak{K}_i$ is not L-true.

    b. $\mathfrak{K}_i$ is not L-false.

    c. $\mathfrak{K}_i$ is L-complete.

    d. If $\mathfrak{K}_i$ and $\mathfrak{K}_j$ are different, they are L-exclusive.

T18-A2. For any state-descriptions $\mathfrak{T}_i$ and $\mathfrak{T}_j$ (in S_4) the following holds.

    a. $\mathfrak{T}_i$ is not L-true.

    b. $\mathfrak{T}_i$ is not L-false.

    c. $\mathfrak{T}_i$ is L-complete.

    d. $\mathfrak{T}_i$ and $\mathfrak{T}_j$ are either L-equivalent or L-exclusive. (From TA1.)

T18-A3. For any L-states p and q (with respect to S_4) the following holds.

    a. p is not L-true.

    b. p is not L-false.

    c. p is L-complete (with respect to S_4).

    d. If p and q are different, they are L-exclusive.

T18-A5. $\mathfrak{T}_i \overrightarrow{\text{L}} \mathfrak{T}_j$ (in S_4) if and only if $\text{Lr}\,\mathfrak{T}_i \subset \text{Lr}\,\mathfrak{T}_j$.

Thus the postulates P1 and 2 are fulfilled. Hence the theorems based on those postulates hold here too.

T18-A7. $\mathfrak{T}_i$ is true (in S_4) if and only if $\text{rs} \in \text{Lr}\,\mathfrak{T}_i$.

T18-A8. $\mathfrak{T}_i$ is L-true (in S_4) if and only if $\text{Lr}\,\mathfrak{T}_i = V_s$.

T18-A9. $\mathfrak{T}_i$ is L-false (in S_4) if and only if $\text{Lr}\,\mathfrak{T}_i = \Lambda_s$.

T18-A10. If $\mathfrak{T}_i$ designates p (in S_4), then $\text{dj}(\text{Lr}\,\mathfrak{T}_i) = p$.

T18-A11. $\text{dj}(V_s)$ is L-true.

T18-A14. $\text{Lr}(\sim \mathfrak{S}_i) = V_s - \text{Lr}\,\mathfrak{S}_i$.

T18-A15. $\text{Lr}(\mathfrak{S}_i \cdot \mathfrak{S}_j) = \text{Lr}\,\mathfrak{S}_i \times \text{Lr}\,\mathfrak{S}_j$.

T18-A16. $\text{Lr}(\mathfrak{S}_i \lor \mathfrak{S}_j) = \text{Lr}\,\mathfrak{S}_i + \text{Lr}\,\mathfrak{S}_j$.

T18-A17. $\text{Lr}\,\mathfrak{K}_i$ is the product of the L-ranges of the sentences of $\mathfrak{K}_i$.

T18-A18. $\text{Lr}(\mathfrak{K}_i + \mathfrak{K}_j) = \text{Lr}\,\mathfrak{K}_i \times \text{Lr}\,\mathfrak{K}_j$.

Wittgenstein uses the concept of the range of a proposition for informal, intuitive explanations; he shows that L-truth (tautology), L-falsity (contradiction), and L-implication are determined by the ranges. "The truth-conditions determine the range which is left to the facts by the proposition. Tautology leaves to reality the whole infinite logical space; contradiction fills the whole logical space and leaves no point to reality. Neither of them, therefore, can in any way determine reality" ([Tractatus] 4.463). Wittgenstein explains the concept of range for molecular sentences only. Our preceding discussion is an attempt to define the concept in an exact way, likewise for molecular sentences only. In the following we shall try to define it in a general way.

B. *Systems in general*

Now we come back to *general semantics*. We shall try to define concepts of L-state and L-range in such a way that they become applicable to semantical systems of any kind, including those containing variables and hence general sentences. The aim is to define those concepts in such a way that they are analogous, as far as possible, to the concepts defined above for the molecular sentences of system S_4 and that they satisfy the postulates P1 and 2

The chief difficulty to be overcome in constructing a general definition for L-state consists in the fact that what we mean by an L-state with respect to a system S is not always designated by a $\mathfrak{T}_i$, a state-description in S (see the example below, at the end of B). Hence we cannot apply here a procedure analogous to DA3. Instead, we require in the definition (DB1) two of the properties of L-states which we found in the earlier discussion of S_4 (TA3b and c): first, every L-state is logically possible, i.e. not L-false (D17–10); and second, an L-state does not leave open any question within the system, i.e. it is L-complete with respect to the system (D3).

+**D18-B1.** p is an **L-state** with respect to S $=_{Df}$ p fulfills the following three conditions. **a.** $p \in \mathrm{bas}(\mathrm{des}(S))$. **b.** p is not L-false. **c.** p is L-complete with respect to S.

D18-B3. The **L-range of the proposition** p with respect to S $\left(\mathrm{Lr}(p)\right)$ $=_{\mathrm{Df}}$ the class of the L-states with respect to S which L-imply p.

+**D18-B4.** The **L-range of the sentence** $\mathfrak{S}_i$ with respect to S $(\mathrm{Lr}\mathfrak{S}_i)$ $=_{\mathrm{Df}}$ the L-range of the proposition designated by $\mathfrak{S}_i$ in S.

For DB5, compare TA17.

+**D18-B5.** The **L-range of the sentential class** $\mathfrak{R}_i$ with respect to S $(\mathrm{Lr}\mathfrak{R}_i)$ $=_{\mathrm{Df}}$ the product of the L-ranges of the sentences of $\mathfrak{R}_i$.

D18-B7. $\mathrm{V_s}$ (the **universal L-range** with respect to S) $=_{\mathrm{Df}}$ the class of all L-states with respect to S.

D18-B8. Λ_s (the **null L-range** with respect to S) $=_{\mathrm{Df}}$ the null class (of propositions).

D18-B9. rs (the **real L-state** with respect to S) $=_{\mathrm{Df}}$ the conjunction of the class which contains, for every p in des(S), either p, if p is true, or $\sim p$, if p is false.

The adequacy of DB9 will be shown by TB33 and 34.

+**T18-B1.** If p is an L-state with respect to S and $q \in \mathrm{bas}(\mathrm{des}(S))$, then either $p \overset{\rightarrow}{\mathrm{L}} q$ or $p \overset{\rightarrow}{\mathrm{L}} \sim q$. (From DB1c, T19d.)

+**T18-B2.** If p is a selection proposition with respect to S and not L-false, then p is an L-state with respect to S; and vice versa.

Proof. a. From T20. — b. Let p be an L-state. Let F be the class of all propositions in bas(des(S)) L-implied by p. For every q in bas(des(S)), either $p \overset{\rightarrow}{\mathrm{L}} q$ or $p \overset{\rightarrow}{\mathrm{L}} \sim q$ (TB1) but not both (DB1b). Therefore, F is a selection class of propositions (D4). p L-implies every element of F, hence $p \overset{\rightarrow}{\mathrm{L}} \mathrm{cj}(F)$. $p \in F$, hence $\mathrm{cj}(F) \overset{\rightarrow}{\mathrm{L}} p$. Therefore, $p = \mathrm{cj}(F)$ (T17–5). Hence, p is a selection proposition (D5) and not L-false (DB1b).

TB5 says in effect that the L-states are the strongest not L-false propositions.

+**T18-B5.** If $q \in \mathrm{bas}(\mathrm{des}(S))$ and q is not L-false and L-implies an L-state p, then $q = p$.

Proof. Either $p \; \mathsf{Ľ} \; q$ or $p \; \mathsf{Ľ} \sim q$ (TB1). The second case is not possible, because otherwise q would L-imply $\sim q$ and hence be L-false. Therefore, $p \; \mathsf{Ľ} \; q$, and hence, $q = p$ (T17–5).

T18-B6. If p and q are L-states with respect to S and $q \; \mathsf{Ľ} \; p$, then $q = p$. (From TB5.)

+T18-B7. Different L-states with respect to S are L-exclusive.

Proof. Let p and q be different L-states. Then either $p \; \mathsf{Ľ} \; q$ or $p \; \mathsf{Ľ} \sim q$ (TB1). The first case is not possible (TB6). Hence $p \; \mathsf{Ľ} \sim q$; hence p and q are L-exclusive (D17–14).

The value of TB10 lies in the fact that it refers to des(S), not merely to bas(des(S)). Thus it shows a close connection between the L-states and the sentences in S and thereby prepares the way for the important theorem of state-descriptions (TB43).

T18-B10. Every L-state with respect to S is the conjunction of a class of propositions every one of which is either itself designated in S or is the negation of a proposition designated in S.

Proof. Let p be an L-state with respect to S. Then $p \; \epsilon \; \mathrm{bas(des}(S))$ (DB1a). Therefore, there is a class G (T17) such that $p = \mathrm{dj}(G)$ and that every proposition in G is a conjunction of the kind described. If all propositions in G were L-false, then p would be L-false, which is not the case (DB1b). Therefore, there is a q in G which is not L-false and is a conjunction of the kind described. $q \; \epsilon \; G$; hence $q \; \mathsf{Ľ} \; \mathrm{dj}(G)$ (T17–8); hence $q \; \mathsf{Ľ} \; p$; hence $q = p$ (TB5). Thus, p itself is a conjunction of the kind described.

+T18-B12. If $p \; \epsilon \; \mathrm{bas(des}(S))$ and is not L-false, then there is at least one L-state (with respect to S) which L-implies p. (From T24, TB2.)

T18-B14 (lemma). If F and G are different classes of L-states (with respect to S), then $\mathrm{dj}(F)$ and $\mathrm{dj}(G)$ are different.

Proof. There must be an L-state r which belongs to the one of the two classes, say F, but not to the other, G. Therefore, for every p in G,

$p \; \overrightarrow{\mathrm{L}} \; \sim r$ (TB7). Hence, $\mathrm{dj}(G) \; \overrightarrow{\mathrm{L}} \; \sim r$ (T17–12). On the other hand, $\sim r$ is not L-implied by $\mathrm{dj}(F)$ (because otherwise, since $r \; \overrightarrow{\mathrm{L}} \; \mathrm{dj}(F)$ (T17–8), $r \; \overrightarrow{\mathrm{L}} \; \sim r$; hence r would be L-false, which it is not (DB1b)). Thus, $\mathrm{dj}(F)$ and $\mathrm{dj}(G)$ are different.

+**T18-B15.** Let $p \in \mathrm{bas}(\mathrm{des}(S))$.
    a. $\mathrm{dj}(\mathrm{Lr}(p)) = p$.
    b. $\mathrm{Lr}(p)$ is the only class of L-states with respect to S which satisfies (a).

Proof. a. Every proposition in $\mathrm{Lr}(p)$ L-implies p; hence $\mathrm{dj}(\mathrm{Lr}(p)) \; \overrightarrow{\mathrm{L}} \; p$ (T17–12). Let q be $p \cdot \sim \mathrm{dj}(\mathrm{Lr}(p))$. We will show that q is L-false. Let us assume that this is not the case. Then there is an L-state r such that $r \; \overrightarrow{\mathrm{L}} \; q$ (TB12) and, since $q \; \overrightarrow{\mathrm{L}} \; p$, $r \; \overrightarrow{\mathrm{L}} \; p$; hence $r \in \mathrm{Lr}(p)$, hence $r \; \overrightarrow{\mathrm{L}} \; \mathrm{dj}(\mathrm{Lr}(p))$ (T17–8). On the other hand, $\sim \mathrm{dj}(\mathrm{Lr}(p))$ is an L-implicate of q and hence of r. Thus r is L-false and hence not an L-state. Thus our assumption leads to a contradiction. Therefore, q must be L-false. Hence, $p \; \overrightarrow{\mathrm{L}} \; \mathrm{dj}(\mathrm{Lr})(p))$ and $\mathrm{dj}(\mathrm{Lr}(p)) = p$. — b. From TB14.

Now we shall show that the concept of L-range as defined here (DB4 and 5) satisfies the postulates P1 and 2 (TB18 and 19).

+**T18-B18.** If $\mathfrak{T}_i \; \overrightarrow{\mathrm{L}} \; \mathfrak{T}_j$, then $\mathrm{Lr}\mathfrak{T}_i \subset \mathrm{Lr}\mathfrak{T}_j$. — This is P1.

Proof. Let $\mathfrak{T}_i \; \overrightarrow{\mathrm{L}} \; \mathfrak{T}_j$; let p and q be the propositions designated by $\mathfrak{T}_i$ and $\mathfrak{T}_j$ respectively; hence $p \; \overrightarrow{\mathrm{L}} \; q$. Let r be an arbitrary element of $\mathrm{Lr}\mathfrak{T}_i$. Then r is an L-state, and $r \; \overrightarrow{\mathrm{L}} \; p$. Hence, $r \; \overrightarrow{\mathrm{L}} \; q$, and $r \in \mathrm{Lr}\mathfrak{T}_j$. This holds for every element of $\mathrm{Lr}\mathfrak{T}_i$. Therefore, $\mathrm{Lr}\mathfrak{T}_i \subset \mathrm{Lr}\mathfrak{T}_j$.

+**T18-B19.** If $\mathrm{Lr}\mathfrak{T}_i \subset \mathrm{Lr}\mathfrak{T}_j$, then $\mathfrak{T}_i \; \overrightarrow{\mathrm{L}} \; \mathfrak{T}_j$. — This is P2.

Proof. Let $\mathrm{Lr}\mathfrak{T}_i \subset \mathrm{Lr}\mathfrak{T}_j$; let p and q be the propositions designated by $\mathfrak{T}_i$ and $\mathfrak{T}_j$ respectively. Then $\mathrm{dj}(\mathrm{Lr}\mathfrak{T}_i) \; \overrightarrow{\mathrm{L}} \; \mathrm{dj}(\mathrm{Lr}\mathfrak{T}_j)$ (T17–9). $\mathrm{Lr}\mathfrak{T}_i = \mathrm{Lr}(p)$; hence $\mathrm{dj}(\mathrm{Lr}\mathfrak{T}_i) = \mathrm{dj}(\mathrm{Lr}(p)) = p$ (TB15a). Likewise $\mathrm{dj}(\mathrm{Lr}\mathfrak{T}_j) = q$. Therefore, $p \; \overrightarrow{\mathrm{L}} \; q$, hence $\mathfrak{T}_i \; \overrightarrow{\mathrm{L}} \; \mathfrak{T}_j$.

T18-B22. If p is L-true, then $\mathrm{Lr}(p) = \mathrm{V_s}$.

Proof. If p is L-true, then every L-state L-implies p; hence $\mathrm{Lr}(p) = \mathrm{V_s}$.

T18-B23. $\mathrm{dj}(\mathrm{V_s})$ is L-true.

Proof. Let p be L-true. Then $\mathrm{Lr}(p) = \mathrm{V_s}$ (TB22). Hence $\mathrm{dj}(\mathrm{V_s}) = p$ (TB15a); hence $\mathrm{dj}(\mathrm{V_s})$ is L-true.

+T18-B24. $\mathrm{Lr}(p) = \mathrm{V_s}$ if and only if p is L-true.

Proof. a. From TB22. — b. Let $\mathrm{Lr}(p)$ be $\mathrm{V_s}$. Then $p = \mathrm{dj}(\mathrm{V_s})$ (TB15a); hence p is L-true (TB23).

T18-B25. If p is L-false, then $\mathrm{Lr}(p) = \Lambda_\mathrm{s}$.

Proof. Let p be L-false. If there were an element q of $\mathrm{Lr}(p)$, then q would be an L-state and $q \mathrel{\overset{\text{L}}{\supset}} p$; hence q would be L-false, which is not possible (DB1b).

+T18-B26. $\mathrm{Lr}(p) = \Lambda_\mathrm{s}$ if and only if p is L-false.

Proof. a. From TB25. — b. Let $\mathrm{Lr}(p) = \Lambda_\mathrm{s}$. Then $p = \mathrm{dj}(\Lambda_\mathrm{s})$ (TB15a); hence p is L-false (T17–11).

TB29 and 30 are analogous to TB24 and 26 but deal with $\mathfrak{T}$ instead of propositions.

+T18-B29. $\mathrm{Lr}\mathfrak{T}_i = \mathrm{V_s}$ if and only if $\mathfrak{T}_i$ is L-true. (From TB24.)

+T18-B30. $\mathrm{Lr}\mathfrak{T}_i = \Lambda_\mathrm{s}$ if and only if $\mathfrak{T}_i$ is L-false. (From TB26.)

T18-B33. rs is an L-state (with respect to S).

Proof. We have to show that rs satisfies the three conditions in DB1. — a. rs ϵ bas(des(S)) (T15). — b. rs is true, hence not L-false. — c. Let p be an arbitrary proposition in des(S). If p is true, p is a conjunctive component of rs, and hence an L-implicate of rs. If p is false, that holds for $\sim p$. Thus rs is L-complete with respect to S (D18–2, D17–17).

T18-B34. rs is the only true L-state with respect to S.

Proof. If p is an L-state different from rs, then rs and p are L-exclusive (TB33, TB7). Hence, rs $\supset \sim p$ is L-true. Since rs is true, p is false.

T18-B35. Let $p \,\epsilon\, \mathrm{bas}(\mathrm{des}(S))$. rs $\epsilon\, \mathrm{Lr}(p)$ if and only if p is true.

Proof. a. Let p be true. Then $\mathrm{dj}(\mathrm{Lr}(p))$ is true (TB15a); hence at least one L-state in $\mathrm{Lr}(p)$ is true. Therefore, rs $\epsilon\, \mathrm{Lr}(p)$ (TB34). — b. Let rs $\epsilon\, \mathrm{Lr}(p)$. Hence, rs $\mathrel{\overset{\text{L}}{\supset}} p$. Since rs is true, p must be true.

+T18-B36. Let $\mathfrak{T}_i$ be in S. rs $\epsilon\, \mathrm{Lr}\mathfrak{T}_i$ if and only if $\mathfrak{T}_i$ is true. (From TB35.)

A $\mathfrak{T}_i$ which designates an L-state with respect to S is called an L-state-description or simply a **state-description** in S. However, we shall not take this condition as a definition because it refers to L-states, i.e. to propositions of a certain kind, and thereby it presupposes a non-extensional metalanguage M. We shall rather formulate the following definitions in such a way that they are independent of M's being extensional or non-extensional; this is done by using no absolute concepts but only (L-)semantical concepts. This is essential for the purposes of the next section, where the concept of state-description will be used in one of the procedures of defining L-range in an extensional language (§ 19E). For the comparison of that procedure with the one used here, the following theorems will be of special importance. DB12 is analogous to the previous definition of L-state (DB1). The analogy between state-descriptions and L-states is of great importance; however, it holds only as far as there are state-descriptions. While it easily follows from DB12 and DB1 that every state-description designates an L-state, the question arises whether also every L-state is designated by a state-description. We shall see that this is not always the case; it holds, however, under a certain condition, which is fulfilled by the majority of the customary systems (TB43).

+**D18-B12.** $\mathfrak{T}_i$ is a **state-description** in S $=_{Df}$ $\mathfrak{T}_i$ is (a) in S, (b) not L-false, (c) L-complete in S.

+**D18-B13.** $\mathfrak{R}_i$ is a **maximum state-description** in S $=_{Df}$ $\mathfrak{R}_i$ is (a) a state description in S, and (b) L-perfect (i.e. $\mathfrak{R}_i$ contains every sentence in S L-implied by $\mathfrak{R}_i$, D14–7).

T18-B40. L-equivalent maximum state-descriptions are identical. (From T14–120.)

T18-B41. For any L-state p with respect to S, there is at most one maximum state-description in S designating p.

Proof. If $\mathfrak{R}_i$ and $\mathfrak{R}_j$ designate p, they are L-equivalent. If they are maximum state-descriptions, they are identical (TB40).

In TB43 (and in several theorems in § 19E), we refer to a *system S containing negation*. By this is meant a system S such that all sentences in S are closed (i.e. without free variables) and that to every sentence $\mathfrak{S}_i$ in S there is a negation $\sim\mathfrak{S}_i$ in S, constructed with a normal sign of negation (i.e. one fulfilling the normal truth-table for negation). However, the theorems referring to a system containing negation hold likewise for any system S which, for any sentence $\mathfrak{S}_i$ in S, contains also another sentence $\mathfrak{S}_j$, whether constructed with a sign of negation or not, such that $\mathfrak{S}_i$ and $\mathfrak{S}_j$ are L-exclusive and L-disjunct with one another (hence L-non-equivalent, D20–11; compare T20–22). (These are the characteristic features of the relation between a sentence and its negation. The concepts of negation and of the other propositional connections will be discussed in detail in [II].)

+T18-B43. *Theorem of state-descriptions.* Let S contain negation. Then every L-state with respect to S is designated by exactly one maximum state-description in S.

Proof. Let p be an L-state. Then there is a class F of propositions such that $p = \mathrm{cj}(F)$ and $F \subset \mathrm{des}(S)$ (TB10), since S contains negation. Let $\mathfrak{R}_i$ be the class of the sentences designating the propositions in F. Then $\mathfrak{R}_i$ designates $\mathrm{cj}(F)$ and hence p, and is a state-description. Let $\mathfrak{R}_j$ be constructed out of $\mathfrak{R}_i$ by adding all sentences L-implied by $\mathfrak{R}_i$. Then $\mathfrak{R}_j$ is a maximum state-description, and, being L-equivalent to $\mathfrak{R}_i$, $\mathfrak{R}_j$ designates the same proposition p. $\mathfrak{R}_j$ is the only maximum state-description designating p (TB41).

Further theorems concerning state-descriptions will be proved in § 19E.

If in the theorem of state-descriptions TB43 the condition that S contains negation were omitted, then the theorem would no longer hold generally. This is shown by the example of a system S′ of the following kind. Let S′ contain a descriptive predicate 'P' and individual constants 'a₁', 'a₂', etc., one for each individual of a denumerable realm. Let S′ contain only the following sentences; first, $\mathfrak{S}_0$: "The class P is finite", further the full sentences of 'P' with one individual constant each: 'P(a₁)', 'P(a₂)', etc. Although $\mathfrak{S}_0$ is a factual sentence and not L-false, there is no maximum state-description and hence no state-description at all in S′ containing or L-implying $\mathfrak{S}_0$. This is shown as follows. If $\mathfrak{R}_i$ contains, in addition to $\mathfrak{S}_0$, only a finite number or none of the full sentences of 'P', then every other full sentence is not L-dependent upon $\mathfrak{R}_i$, and hence $\mathfrak{R}_i$ is not L-complete. If $\mathfrak{R}_i$, on the other hand, contains an infinite number of the full sentences in addition to $\mathfrak{S}_0$, then $\mathfrak{R}_i$ is L-false. Thus, for any $\mathfrak{R}_i$ in S′, if $\mathfrak{S}_0 \,\epsilon\, \mathfrak{R}_i$, $\mathfrak{R}_i$ cannot be a state-description (DB12c and b). Moreover, $\mathfrak{S}_0$ is an L-implicate of $\mathfrak{R}_i$ only if $\mathfrak{S}_0 \,\epsilon\, \mathfrak{R}_i$. — Let S″ contain the sentences of S′ and, in addition, the negations of the full sentences of 'P'. Let $\mathfrak{R}_j$ be any class containing a finite number of the full sentences and the negations of the remaining full sentences. Then $\mathfrak{R}_j$ is a state-description in S″ and $\mathfrak{R}_j \:\overline{\mathsf{L}}\: \mathfrak{S}_0$; $\mathfrak{R}_j + \{\mathfrak{S}_0\}$ is a maximum state-description containing $\mathfrak{S}_0$.

C. *Systems in general; atomic propositions*

We shall here take into consideration a more comprehensive realm of propositions in connection with a system S than that considered in B. For certain purposes, this extension seems to be useful and interesting. In B, we started from the propositions designated in S $(\mathrm{des}(S))$ and applied to them the operations of negation and disjunction; thus we obtained the realm of propositions bas(des(S)). Here we shall start from certain propositions which we call the *atomic propositions* with respect to S $(\mathrm{atom}(S))$, and we apply to them the same operations. Thus we obtain the realm bas(atom(S)). This realm is, in general, wider than the previous one because an atomic proposition with respect to S is, in general, neither designated in S nor even based upon propositions designated in S.

The way which will lead us to the concept of atomic proposition starts from a consideration of the fact that the sentences of a system S which contains variables speak not only about those entities which are designated by expressions in S but also about those to which the variables refer. This suggests the following definition.

D18-C1. The semantical system S *covers* the entity $u \;=_{\mathrm{Df}} u$ is designated (or determined, § 11) by an expression in S or is a value of a variable in S.

Let us take as an example the system S_6 (§ 11). According to the rule of values (3C) for S_6, all towns in the United States are covered by S_6, but only three of them are designated in S_6. S_6 contains an atomic sentence 'P(a)' for the proposition that Chicago is large, but none for the proposition that Philadelphia is large. Although this proposition is not designated in S_6, we shall call it an atomic proposition with respect to S_6 because Philadelphia belongs to the objects covered by S_6. Thus any proposition which attributes a property covered by S_6 (both of them are designated by predicates in S_6) to an individual covered by S_6 will be called an atomic proposition with respect to S_6. With other systems we proceed analogously. For any descriptive attribute (i.e. property or relation) H, we regard as its atomic propositions those which attribute H to some descriptive entity (or sequence of entities) covered by S; this entity is called the argument entity in the atomic proposition in question. Which entities covered by S may be taken as argument entities for a given attribute H covered by S is determined by the rules of formation of S. These rules state which constants or variables may be used as argument expressions in connection with the predicate expression whose designatum or value H is; the designata of these constants and the values of these variables are then the argument entities admitted for H. The rules of formation vary widely for different systems. [S may, for instance, contain a predicate 'R', and the rules of formation of S may require that an argument expression for 'R' consist of three signs (say, 'a,b,c' in the sentence 'R(a,b,c)'); the rules may, moreover, require that these three signs belong to certain specified types with respect to a hierarchy of types. Again, it may be that an expression consisting of any finite number of such signs is admitted as argument expression for 'R'; or perhaps signs of all types on a certain level are admitted, or even signs of many levels. It may be that there are no restrictions at all with respect to degree, type, or level.] In an analogous way we find the atomic propositions for the functions covered by S (i.e. the designata of functors or values of functor variables).

For the following definitions we presuppose that the concept of atomic proposition has been defined in a suitable way for the system S in question. This involves that every proposition p designated in S is analyzed into atomic propositions in such a way that p is constructible out of these atomic propositions by iterated application of negation and disjunction (which includes also conjunction, see T15); in other words, that p is based upon atomic propositions. [This takes care also of universal and existential propositions because disjunction and conjunction may be applied to infinite classes; see explanations to D17–20.] This requirement is laid down as postulate PC1 below. The subsequent definitions presuppose PC1 in the sense that they are intended to be applied only to a concept of atomic proposition fulfilling this postulate.

P18-C1. $\mathrm{des}(S) \subset \mathrm{bas}(\mathrm{atom}(S))$.

The following theorem TC1 shows that the realm of propositions previously considered is a part of the new realm of propositions. In general, it is a proper part; that is to say, some propositions in bas(atom (S))), and frequently (e.g. for S_6) a vast majority of them, do not belong to bas(des(S)).

T18-C1. $\mathrm{bas}(\mathrm{des}(S)) \subset \mathrm{bas}(\mathrm{atom}(S))$. (From PC1, T16.)

The definition of L-state (DC2) is analogous to the previous one (DB1) but refers to the wider realm of propositions.

D18-C2. p is an *L-state* with respect to $S =_{\mathrm{Df}} p$ fulfills the following three conditions. **a.** $p \in \mathrm{bas}(\mathrm{atom}(S))$. **b.** p is not L-false. **c.** p is L-complete (D17–17) with respect to atom(S).

T18-C3. If p is an L-state with respect to S and $q \in \mathrm{bas}(\mathrm{atom}(S))$ or $q \in \mathrm{bas}(\mathrm{des}(S))$, then either $p \overrightarrow{\mathrm{L}} q$ or $p \overrightarrow{\mathrm{L}} \sim q$. (From DC2c, T18–18; TC1.)

The terms 'Lr(p)', 'Lr$\mathfrak{S}_i$', 'Lr$\mathfrak{R}_i$', 'V_s', 'Λ_s', and 'rs' may here be defined on the basis of 'L-state' in the same way as in DB3 to 9, except that 'des(S)' is here replaced by 'atom(S)'. Likewise all theorems in B concerning those concepts (TB1 to 36) together with their proofs have exact analogues here in C. The necessary modification consists again in referring to atom(S) instead of des(S); accordingly, 'L-complete with respect to S' must be replaced by 'L-complete with respect to atom(S)' (see D3); further, 'p is a selection proposition' (in TB2) is to be replaced by 'p is an atomic selection proposition' (i.e. a conjunction of a class of propositions which contains, for every atomic proposition $\mathfrak{S}_i$ with respect to S, either $\mathfrak{S}_i$ or $\sim\mathfrak{S}_i$ but not both and no other propositions). In analogy to TB18 and 19, the result is obtained that the concept of L-range as here defined fulfills the postulates P1 and 2.

An L-state leaves no atomic propositions undetermined (DC2c). In other words, if p is an L-state, then p determines for any attribute H covered by S and every entity u covered by S and admitted as argument entity for H, whether or not H is attributed to u in p. In this way, an L-state determines the extension of every concept (attribute or function) covered by S. These considerations will later be taken as basis for other procedures (§ 19K and L).

The definitions for '*state-description*' (DC 12) and 'maximum state-description' (DC13) are analogous to the previous ones (DB12 and 13).

D18-C12. $\mathfrak{T}_i$ is a *state-description* in $S =_{Df} \mathfrak{T}_i$ is (a) in S, (b) not L-false; (c) the proposition designated by $\mathfrak{T}_i$ is L-complete with respect to atom(S).

D18-C13. $\mathfrak{R}_i$ is a *maximum state-description* in $S =_{Df} \mathfrak{R}_i$ is a state-description in S containing every sentence in S L-implied by $\mathfrak{R}_i$.

While the analogues to TB40 and 41 hold here in C, the same is not the case for the theorem of state-descriptions (TB43). In the proof of this theorem the fact was used that for every proposition in des(S) there is a sentence designating it. On the other hand, for a proposition in the corresponding class atom(S), there is, in general, no sentence designating it. Therefore, an L-state (DC2) with respect to S is, in general, not designated by a $\mathfrak{T}_i$, a state-description, in S; and in many systems, an overwhelming majority of L-states or even all of them are without state-descriptions. [Take S_6 (§ 11) as an example. Let n be the number of the towns in the United States. There are 2n atomic propositions and hence 2^{2n} L-states with respect to S_6. Only six of the atomic propositions are designated in S_6. And only four of the L-states have state-descriptions in S_6, namely these: (a) the proposition that all individuals have the properties P and Q, (b) all have P and $\sim$Q, (c) all have $\sim$P and Q, (d) all have $\sim$P and $\sim$Q.] This is a disadvantage of the present procedure C. On the other hand, an advantage of C in comparison with B consists in the fact that the concept of L-state as here defined (DC2) seems perhaps to be in better agreement with the original intuitive concept (vaguely explained at the beginning of § 18), especially if we pay more attention to the concepts and entities covered by S and less to the sentences in S. [Consider S_6 again. Let A_1 be the true proposition that Chicago, New York, etc. (referring here specifically to each town in the United States which actually is large) are large, while the other ones are not, and that Chicago, Boston, etc. (referring here specifically to each one which actually has a harbor) have harbors, while the other ones have not. Here in C, A_1 is called an L-state and, since it is true, the real L-state rs with respect to S_6 although there is no state-description for it; in B, however, A_1 is not even regarded as an L-state with respect to S_6, because A_1 not ϵ bas(des(S_6)). Although we can (falsely) say in S_6 that Chicago, New York, and Carmel are large and have harbors, the (likewise false) proposition A_2 that this is the case and that all other towns are neither large nor provided with harbors is not designated in S_6

(because S_6 lacks a sign of identity). This proposition A_2 is not re-garded as an L-state in B; but it is so regarded in C, and, from a certain point of view, this seems perhaps more natural.]

§ 19. The Concept of L-Range in an Extensional Meta-language

Several alternative procedures are explained for defining a concept of *L-range* fulfilling the postulates P18–1 and 2. In order to make possible the use of an extensional metalanguage, here not propositions, as in § 18, but other entities are taken as elements of L-ranges; namely, in procedure E state-descriptions; in F and G sentences; in K and L certain relations, called state-relations, corresponding to L-states. It is shown that the semantical rules of a system *S* determining the meaning of the sentences in *S*, which previously were formulated as rules of truth, may instead be formulated as *rules of L-ranges* determining the L-range of every sentence in *S*.

In the previous section we construed L-ranges as classes of propositions of a certain kind, namely the L-states. This required the use of a non-extensional metalanguage *M*. On the question whether in general the use of an extensional (truth-functional) or a non-extensional (so-called intensional) metalanguage is preferable, logicians are at present far from an agreement. The structure of an extensional language is simpler, and some logicians go so far as to regard it as the only acceptable form. On the other hand, a non-extensional language seems to express certain things, e.g. modalities, in a more direct and thereby technically simpler way; and many logicians even believe that this form of a language is not only preferable but necessary for certain purposes, e.g. for dealing with modalities and semantical concepts like designation. Much more investigation of languages of both kinds applied to different purposes will have to be made before this controversy is settled. The two preceding sections contain tentative contributions to this problem from the one side, while this section will attempt approaches from the other side.

Here we shall discuss definitions for the concept of L-range which make use of extensional concepts only. Therefore these definitions, and the theorems based upon them, may be formulated in an extensional metalanguage M. They do not require, however, that M be extensional; they can be used in an M of either kind; they are, so to speak, neutral in this respect.

The aim of the following discussions is to find definitions for concepts of L-range, which are in agreement with the intuitive concept for which some vague explanations were given at the beginning of § 18; in particular, the concepts defined are to fulfill the postulates P18–1 and 2 for L-range. Therefore, the concepts looked for, although extensional, must show a close analogy to the non-extensional concepts defined in § 18. The change must consist in replacing the propositions as elements of L-ranges by something else that corresponds to those propositions in some way. The procedures to be explained here are of two different kinds. Those of the first kind take as elements of L-ranges something within the object language in question, e.g. sentences or sentential classes. The procedures of the second kind take instead something belonging to the realm of entities spoken about in the object language, e.g. relations between such entities.

Procedures of the first kind: the elements of L-ranges are intra-linguistic

E. *State-descriptions as elements of L-ranges*

If we wish to avoid L-states because they are propositions, the most natural way seems to be to take state-descriptions instead. We take here the concepts of state-description and maximum state-description in the sense of D18–B12 and 13. Then T18–B40, based on these definitions, holds here too. However, we will repeat those definitions and that theorem here with new numbers (DE1 and 2, TE8) in order to emphasize the fact that here we are in a new framework of an extensional M. Then it will be possible for the proofs in this section to avoid any reference to definitions or theorems in §§ 17 and 18. Such references will be made only for purposes of comparison, be it contrast or analogy, outside of the systematic construction. For the L-concepts here used, we refer in the proofs to the postulates in § 14 (including the additional postulates P14–C2 and 3 concerning L-disjunctness; see the remark on TE20, below) and to the theorems in § 14 based upon them.

+D19-E1. $\mathfrak{T}_i$ is a **state-description** in S $=_{Df}$ $\mathfrak{T}_i$ is **(a)** in S, **(b)** not L-false, **(c)** L-complete (in S).

+D19-E2. $\mathfrak{R}_i$ is a **maximum state-description** in S $=_{Df}$ $\mathfrak{R}_i$ is **(a)** a state-description in S and **(b)** L-perfect (D14–7).

T19-E1. If $\mathfrak{T}_i$ is a state-description in S and $\mathfrak{T}_j$ is in S, then either $\mathfrak{T}_i$ $\overrightarrow{L}$ $\mathfrak{T}_j$ or $\mathfrak{T}_i$ and $\mathfrak{T}_j$ are L-exclusive. (From DE1c, T14–88, D14–3.)

TE2 says that the state-descriptions are the strongest not L-false $\mathfrak{T}$ in S (in analogy to T18–B5).

T19-E2. If $\mathfrak{T}_k$ is a state-description and $\mathfrak{T}_i$ is not L-false and $\mathfrak{T}_i$ $\overrightarrow{L}$ $\mathfrak{T}_k$, then $\mathfrak{T}_i$ and $\mathfrak{T}_k$ are L-equivalent.

Proof. Either $\mathfrak{T}_k$ $\overrightarrow{L}$ $\mathfrak{T}_i$ or $\mathfrak{T}_i$ and $\mathfrak{T}_k$ are L-exclusive (TE1). The second case is not possible, because otherwise $\mathfrak{T}_i$ would be L-false (T14–76). Hence, $\mathfrak{T}_k$ $\overrightarrow{L}$ $\mathfrak{T}_i$, and $\mathfrak{T}_i$ and $\mathfrak{T}_k$ are L-equivalent.

T19-E3. If $\mathfrak{T}_i$ and $\mathfrak{T}_j$ are state-descriptions in S and $\mathfrak{T}_i$ $\overrightarrow{L}$ $\mathfrak{T}_j$, then $\mathfrak{T}_i$ and $\mathfrak{T}_j$ are L-equivalent. (From TE2.)

T19-E4. Two state-descriptions in S are either L-equivalent or L-exclusive of one another. (From TE1, TE3.)

T19-E7. Let $\mathfrak{R}_k$ be a maximum state-description.
  a. If $\mathfrak{R}_k$ $\overrightarrow{L}$ $\mathfrak{R}_j$, then $\mathfrak{R}_j \subset \mathfrak{R}_k$. (From DE2b, T14–116.)
  b. If $\mathfrak{R}_k$ $\overrightarrow{L}$ $\mathfrak{S}_j$, then $\mathfrak{S}_j \in \mathfrak{R}_k$. (From (a).)

T19-E8. L-equivalent maximum state-descriptions are identical. (From DE2b, T14–120.)

T19-E9. Two different maximum state-descriptions in S are L-exclusive. (From TE4, TE8.)

The following concepts are applied only to systems S which contain negation (see explanation to T18–B43). DE5 has some analogy with D18–4 and 5.

D19-E4. $\Re_i$ is a **sentential selection in the class** $\Re_j$ in S $=_{Df}$ S contains negation, $\Re_i$ is closed with respect to negation; $\Re_i \subset \Re_j$, and for every $\mathfrak{S}_j$ in $\Re_j$, $\Re_i$ contains either $\mathfrak{S}_j$ or $\sim\mathfrak{S}_j$ but not both.

D19-E5. $\Re_i$ is a **sentential selection in the system** S $=_{Df}$ $\Re_i$ is a sentential selection (DE4) in V in S.

T19-E13. Let S contain negation. $\Re_i$ is a sentential selection in S if and only if, for every $\mathfrak{S}_j$ in S, either $\mathfrak{S}_j \in \Re_i$ or $\sim\mathfrak{S}_j \in \Re_i$ but not both. (From DE5, DE4.)

T19-E14. Let S contain negation. Then every sentential selection in S is L-complete (in S).

Proof. Let $\Re_i$ be a sentential selection in S. Then (TE13), for every $\mathfrak{S}_j$ in S, either $\Re_i \overrightarrow{\text{L}} \mathfrak{S}_j$ (P14–11), or $\Re_i \overrightarrow{\text{L}} \sim\mathfrak{S}_j$ and hence $\Re_i$ and $\mathfrak{S}_j$ are L-exclusive. Therefore, $\Re_i$ is L-complete (D14–4).

T19-E16. Let S contain negation. If $\Re_i$ is a sentential selection in S and not L-false, then $\Re_i$ is L-perfect.

Proof. Let $\mathfrak{S}_j$ be an arbitrary L-implicate of $\Re_i$. Then either $\mathfrak{S}_j \in \Re_i$ or $\sim\mathfrak{S}_j \in \Re_i$ (TE13). The second case is impossible, because $\Re_i$ would L-imply $\sim\mathfrak{S}_j$ and hence be L-false. Therefore, $\mathfrak{S}_j \in \Re_i$. Hence, $\Re_i$ is L-perfect (D14–7).

T19-E17. Let S contain negation. $\Re_i$ is a maximum state-description in S if and only if $\Re_i$ is a sentential selection in S and not L-false.

Proof. a. Let $\Re_i$ be a sentential selection and not L-false. $\Re_i$ is a state-description (TE14) and L-perfect (TE16), hence a maximum state-description. — b. Let $\Re_i$ be a maximum state-description. For every $\mathfrak{S}_j$ in S, either $\Re_i \overrightarrow{\text{L}} \mathfrak{S}_j$ or $\Re_i \overrightarrow{\text{L}} \sim\mathfrak{S}_j$ (TE1); hence either

$\mathfrak{S}_j \in \mathfrak{R}_i$ or $\sim\mathfrak{S}_j \in \mathfrak{R}_i$ (TE7b). $\mathfrak{R}_i$ is not L-false (DE1b); hence it cannot contain both sentences. Thus $\mathfrak{R}_i$ is a sentential selection in S (TE13).

T19-E18. Let S contain negation. The class $\mathfrak{R}_T$ of the true sentences in S is a sentential selection and hence a maximum state-description in S. (From TE17.)

In our earlier discussion of L-states in a non-extensional metalanguage, we found that if a proposition is not impossible there must be a possible state of affairs in which it would hold; this is formulated in technical terms in T18–B12 (based on T18–24). The question arises whether the analogue to T18–B12 holds with respect to state-descriptions. An affirmative answer under the condition that S contains negation will be given by TE23. Before we try to construct a proof for this theorem let us do some inexact reasoning in order to show its plausibility. Applied to a true $\mathfrak{R}_i$, the theorem is even trivial, because in this case $\mathfrak{R}_T$ (see TE18) is a maximum state-description of the kind described. Now let us assume that the theorem does not hold generally. This would mean that there was a $\mathfrak{R}_i$, false but not L-false, hence not such that its falsity could be discovered by logical analysis alone, and such that $\mathfrak{R}_i$ was not contained in any maximum state-description in S. The latter circumstance, however, is of a purely logical nature, because no factual knowledge is involved in finding out whether or not a given class $\mathfrak{R}_j$ is a maximum state-description in S and whether or not $\mathfrak{R}_i \subset \mathfrak{R}_j$, where both are syntactically described. Thus the non-existence of maximum state-descriptions for a given $\mathfrak{R}_i$ could be ascertained, if at all, by purely logical means. Let us assume we had found this result for a given $\mathfrak{R}_i$. Then it would follow that $\mathfrak{R}_i$ could not be true. Thus we should have found by merely logical means that $\mathfrak{R}_i$ was false, although $\mathfrak{R}_i$ was not L-false. This seems hardly conceivable. Thus it seems plausible that the theorem should hold not only for any true $\Re_i$ but also for any false, and not L-false, $\Re_i$. — TE23 can be proved in a rather simple way in a non-extensional metalanguage; it follows directly from T18–B12 and T18–B43. Here, however, in an extensional metalanguage, the proof is not so simple. It is based on some rather complicated, though plausible, additional postulates concerning L-disjunctness. The following theorems prepare the way for TE23.

For TE20 and 21, we make use of the fact that $\mathfrak{S}_i$ and $\sim\mathfrak{S}_i$ are L-disjunct and L-exclusive of one another (see explanation to T18–B43 concerning negation). For the concept of L-disjunctness, the system of the postulates P14–1 to 15 is not strong enough; the additional postulates P14–E2 and 3 are necessary for T20 and 21.

T19-E20. Let S contain negation.
   a. If $\Re_i$ is closed with respect to negation, the sentential selections in $\Re_i$ are L-disjunct with one another. (From P14–E2.)
   b. The sentential selections in S are L-disjunct with one another. (From (a).)

T19-E21. Let S contain negation. If every sentential selection $\Re_j$ in S, such that $\Re_i \subset \Re_j$, L-implies $\mathfrak{S}_k$, then $\Re_i \;\overrightarrow{\text{L}}\; \mathfrak{S}_k$.

Proof. Let the conditions be fulfilled. Let $\Re_i$ be not L-false; otherwise the assertion follows simply from P14–15. Let us call (for the moment) two sentences related to one another if the one is constructed out of the other by the addition of some number n of signs of negation (including $n = 0$, i.e. identity); we call the sentences evenly or oddly related according to whether n is even or odd. Let $\Re_i'$ be the class of all sentences in S oddly related to the sentences of $\Re_i$; likewise $\Re_i''$ for the sentences evenly related; hence $\Re_i \subset \Re_i''$. Let $\Re_j$ be an arbitrary sentential selection in S such that $\Re_i \subset \Re_j$. Then $\Re_i'' \subset \Re_j$ and $\Re_i' \subset -\Re_j$ (DE4). Let $\Re_j'$ be $\Re_j - \Re_i''$; hence $\Re_j = \Re_i'' + \Re_j'$. Evenly related sentences are L-equivalent. Therefore, $\Re_i \;\overrightarrow{\text{L}}\; \Re_i''$; hence $\Re_i + \Re_j' \;\overrightarrow{\text{L}}\; \Re_i'' + \Re_j'$ which is $\Re_j$. $\Re_j \;\overrightarrow{\text{L}}\; \mathfrak{S}_k$; therefore, $\Re_i + \Re_j' \;\overrightarrow{\text{L}}\; \mathfrak{S}_k$. Let the classes in $\mathfrak{M}_j'$ be the classes $\Re_j'$ constructed in the way described, i.e. $\Re_i - \Re_i''$ for every sentential selection $\Re_j$ such that $\Re_i \subset \Re_j$. Then these classes are the sentential selections in the class $V - \Re_i' - \Re_i''$, which is closed with respect to negation. Therefore, the classes in $\mathfrak{M}_i'$ are L-disjunct with one another (TE20a). For every $\Re_i'$ in $\mathfrak{M}_i'$, $\Re_i + \Re_i' \; \overrightarrow{\mathrm{L}} \; \mathfrak{S}_k$; hence $\Re_i \; \overrightarrow{\mathrm{L}} \; \mathfrak{S}_k$ (P14–E3).

T19-E22. Let S contain negation. If every sentential selection $\Re_j$ such that $\Re_i \subset \Re_j$ is L-false, then $\Re_i$ is L-false.

Proof. If every $\Re_j$ as described is L-false, it L-implies both $\mathfrak{S}_k$ and $\sim\mathfrak{S}_k$. Therefore, $\Re_i$ does the same (TE21) and hence is L-false.

+T19-E23. Let S contain negation. If $\Re_i$ is not L-false, then there is at least one maximum state-description $\Re_j$ such that $\Re_i \subset \Re_j$ and hence $\Re_j \; \overrightarrow{\mathrm{L}} \; \Re_i$.

Proof. Let the conditions be fulfilled. There must be a sentential selection $\Re_j$ in S such that $\Re_i \subset \Re_j$ and that $\Re_j$ is not L-false, because otherwise $\Re_i$ would be L-false (TE22). $\Re_j$ is a maximum state-description (TE17).

The concept of *L-range* is now defined in analogy to D18–B3 to 5, replacing the reference to L-states by that to state-descriptions. We take as elements of L-ranges only maximum state-descriptions because, under certain conditions, they correspond uniquely to L-states (T18–B43).

+D19-E7. $\mathrm{Lr}\,\mathfrak{T}_i$ (the **L-range** of $\mathfrak{T}_i$ in S) $=_{\mathrm{Df}}$ the class of the maximum state-descriptions $\mathfrak{T}_k$ in S such that $\mathfrak{T}_k \; \overrightarrow{\mathrm{L}} \; \mathfrak{T}_i$.

We shall now examine whether the concept of L-range defined by DE7 fulfills the postulates P18–1 and 2. TE27 shows that P18–1 is always fulfilled; TE36 shows that for systems containing negation also P18–2 is fulfilled.

+T19-E27. If $\mathfrak{T}_i \; \overrightarrow{\mathrm{L}} \; \mathfrak{T}_j$, then $\mathrm{Lr}\,\mathfrak{T}_i \subset \mathrm{Lr}\,\mathfrak{T}_j$. — This is P18–1.

Proof. Let $\mathfrak{T}_i \; \overrightarrow{\mathrm{L}} \; \mathfrak{T}_j$, and let $\mathfrak{T}_k$ be an arbitrary element of $\mathrm{Lr}\,\mathfrak{T}_i$. Then $\mathfrak{T}_k$ is a maximum state-description such that $\mathfrak{T}_k \; \overrightarrow{\mathrm{L}} \; \mathfrak{T}_i$. Hence $\mathfrak{T}_k \; \overrightarrow{\mathrm{L}} \; \mathfrak{T}_j$, hence $\mathfrak{T}_k \in \mathrm{Lr}\,\mathfrak{T}_j$. Thus $\mathrm{Lr}\,\mathfrak{T}_i \subset \mathrm{Lr}\,\mathfrak{T}_j$.

T19-E28. If $\mathfrak{T}_i$ and $\mathfrak{T}_j$ are L-equivalent, then $\mathrm{Lr}\,\mathfrak{T}_i = \mathrm{Lr}\,\mathfrak{T}_j$. (From TE27.)

T19-E31. Let S contain negation. For every $\mathfrak{T}_i$ in S, $\mathfrak{T}_i \ \overrightarrow{\text{L}} \ \mathrm{pr}(\mathrm{Lr}\mathfrak{T}_i)$. [$\mathrm{pr}(\mathfrak{M}_i)$ is the product of the classes in $\mathfrak{M}_i$.]

Proof. Let $\mathfrak{K}_i$ be $\mathfrak{T}_i$ or, if $\mathfrak{T}_i$ is a sentence, $\{\mathfrak{T}_i\}$. Let $\mathfrak{S}_k$ be an arbitrary element of $\mathrm{pr}(\mathrm{Lr}\mathfrak{K}_i)$. Let $\mathfrak{K}_j$ be an arbitrary sentential selection in S such that $\mathfrak{K}_i \subset \mathfrak{K}_j$. We will show that $\mathfrak{K}_j \ \overrightarrow{\text{L}} \ \mathfrak{S}_k$. If $\mathfrak{K}_j$ is L-false, this is obvious (P14–15). If $\mathfrak{K}_j$ is not L-false, it is a maximum state-description (TE17) and hence belongs to $\mathrm{Lr}\mathfrak{K}_i$, since $\mathfrak{K}_j \ \overrightarrow{\text{L}} \ \mathfrak{K}_i$. Therefore, $\mathfrak{S}_k \in \mathfrak{K}_j$ and hence $\mathfrak{K}_j \ \overrightarrow{\text{L}} \ \mathfrak{S}_k$. Since this holds for every $\mathfrak{K}_j$ as described, $\mathfrak{K}_i \ \overrightarrow{\text{L}} \ \mathfrak{S}_k$ (TE21). This holds for every element of $\mathrm{pr}(\mathrm{Lr}\mathfrak{K}_i)$; hence $\mathfrak{K}_i \ \overrightarrow{\text{L}} \ \mathrm{pr}(\mathrm{Lr}\mathfrak{K}_i)$.

T19-E32. Let S contain negation. For every $\mathfrak{K}_i$ in S, $\mathfrak{K}_i \subset \mathrm{pr}(\mathrm{Lr}\mathfrak{K}_i)$, and hence $\mathrm{pr}(\mathrm{Lr}\mathfrak{K}_i) \ \overrightarrow{\text{L}} \ \mathfrak{K}_i$.

Proof. For every $\mathfrak{K}_j$ in $\mathrm{Lr}\mathfrak{K}_i$, $\mathfrak{K}_j \ \overrightarrow{\text{L}} \ \mathfrak{K}_i$ and hence $\mathfrak{K}_i \subset \mathfrak{K}_j$ (TE7a). Hence, $\mathfrak{K}_i \subset \mathrm{pr}(\mathrm{Lr}\mathfrak{K}_i)$.

T19-E33. Let S contain negation. $\mathfrak{S}_j \in \mathrm{pr}(\mathrm{Lr}\mathfrak{T}_i)$ if and only if $\mathfrak{T}_i \ \overrightarrow{\text{L}} \ \mathfrak{S}_j$.

Proof. a. For every $\mathfrak{K}_k$ in $\mathrm{Lr}\mathfrak{T}_i$, $\mathfrak{K}_k \ \overrightarrow{\text{L}} \ \mathfrak{T}_i$ and hence $\mathfrak{K}_k \ \overrightarrow{\text{L}} \ \mathfrak{S}_j$, and hence $\mathfrak{S}_j \in \mathfrak{K}_k$ (TE7b). Therefore, $\mathfrak{S}_j \in \mathrm{pr}(\mathrm{Lr}\mathfrak{T}_i)$. — b. From TE31, T14–21.

+T19-E34. Let S contain negation. Let $\mathfrak{K}_j$ be the class of all sentences in S L-implied by $\mathfrak{T}_i$.

      a. $\mathfrak{T}_i$ is L-equivalent to $\mathrm{pr}(\mathrm{Lr}\mathfrak{T}_i)$. (From TE31 and 32.)

      b. $\mathfrak{K}_j = \mathrm{pr}(\mathrm{Lr}\mathfrak{T}_i)$. (From TE33.)

+T19-E36. Let S contain negation. If $\mathrm{Lr}\mathfrak{T}_i \subset \mathrm{Lr}\mathfrak{T}_j$, then $\mathfrak{T}_i \ \overrightarrow{\text{L}} \ \mathfrak{T}_j$. — This is P18–2.

Proof. Let the conditions be fulfilled. Let $\mathfrak{S}_k$ be an arbitrary element of $\mathrm{pr}(\mathrm{Lr}\mathfrak{T}_j)$. Then $\mathfrak{S}_k$ belongs to every class in $\mathrm{Lr}\mathfrak{T}_j$ and hence to every class in $\mathrm{Lr}\mathfrak{T}_i$ and hence to $\mathrm{pr}(\mathrm{Lr}\mathfrak{T}_i)$. Thus $\mathrm{pr}(\mathrm{Lr}\mathfrak{T}_j) \subset \mathrm{pr}(\mathrm{Lr}\mathfrak{T}_i)$, hence $\mathrm{pr}(\mathrm{Lr}\mathfrak{T}_i) \ \overrightarrow{\text{L}} \ \mathrm{pr}(\mathrm{Lr}\mathfrak{T}_j)$. $\mathfrak{T}_i$ is L-equivalent to $\mathrm{pr}(\mathrm{Lr}\mathfrak{T}_i)$ (TE34a), likewise $\mathfrak{T}_j$ to $\mathrm{pr}(\mathrm{Lr}\mathfrak{T}_j)$. Therefore, $\mathfrak{T}_i \ \overrightarrow{\text{L}} \ \mathfrak{T}_j$.

For a system which does not contain negation, TE36 does in general not hold. As an example, consider the system S' described at the end of § 18B. Let $\mathfrak{K}_i$ be any of the L-false classes described. As previously shown, there is no state-description in S' L-implying $\mathfrak{S}_0$. Therefore,

$Lr\mathfrak{S}_0$ is null and hence $Lr\mathfrak{S}_0 \subset Lr\mathfrak{R}_i$. However, in contradistinction to TE36, $\mathfrak{S}_0$ does not L-imply $\mathfrak{R}_i$ because otherwise $\mathfrak{S}_0$ would be L-false (P14–7), which it is not.

T19-E37. Let S contain negation. If $Lr\mathfrak{T}_i = Lr\mathfrak{T}_j$, then $\mathfrak{T}_i$ and $\mathfrak{T}_j$ are L-equivalent. (From TE36.)

T19-E39. If $\mathfrak{T}_i$ is L-false, $Lr\mathfrak{T}_i$ is the null L-range (i.e. the null class of sentential classes). (From DE7, DE1b, P14–7.)

+T19-E40. Let S contain negation. $Lr\mathfrak{T}_i$ is the null L-range if and only if $\mathfrak{T}_i$ is L-false. (From TE39; TE23.)

T19-E42. If $\mathfrak{T}_i$ is L-true, $Lr\mathfrak{T}_i$ is the universal L-range (i.e. the class of all maximum state-descriptions in S). (From P14–14.)

T19-E43. $Lr\Lambda$ is the universal L-range. (From T14–33, TE42.)

+T19-E44. Let S contain negation. $Lr\mathfrak{T}_i$ is the universal L-range if and only if $\mathfrak{T}_i$ is L-true.

Proof. a. From TE42. — b. Let $Lr\mathfrak{T}_i$ be the universal L-range; hence $Lr\Lambda \subset Lr\mathfrak{T}_i$. Therefore, $\Lambda \mathbin{\overrightarrow{\mathsf{L}}} \mathfrak{T}_i$ (TE36); hence $\mathfrak{T}_i$ is L-true (T14–34).

F *and* G. *Sentences as elements of L-ranges*

The procedures F and G are ways of defining L-ranges as certain classes of sentences. However, this is not done in such a way that some or all of those sentences or anything else could be regarded as corresponding to L-states. Nevertheless, the L-ranges as defined here correspond in a certain way to the L-ranges as explained earlier (at the beginning of § 18); and the essential requirements, formulated in P18–1 and 2, are fulfilled. The considerations leading to the procedures F and G will be explained at the end of § 23.

D19-F1. $Lr\mathfrak{T}_i$ (in S) $=_{Df}$ the class of the sentences in S not L-implied by $\mathfrak{T}_i$.

T19-F1. $\mathrm{Lr}\Lambda$ = the class of the sentences in S which are not L-true. (From DF1, T14–51a.)

T19-F2. $\mathrm{Lr}V = \Lambda$. (From DF1, T14–41.)

T19-F5. If $\mathfrak{T}_i \; \mathbb{L}^\flat \; \mathfrak{T}_j$, then $\mathrm{Lr}\mathfrak{T}_i \subset \mathrm{Lr}\mathfrak{T}_j$. — This is P18–1.

Proof. Let the condition be fulfilled, and $\mathfrak{S}_k \, \epsilon \, \mathrm{Lr}\mathfrak{T}_i$. Then $\mathfrak{S}_k$ is not an L-implicate of $\mathfrak{T}_i$ (DF1), and hence not of $\mathfrak{T}_j$ (P14–5). Therefore, $\mathfrak{S}_k \, \epsilon \, \mathrm{Lr}\mathfrak{T}_j$.

T19-F6. If $\mathrm{Lr}\mathfrak{T}_i \subset \mathrm{Lr}\mathfrak{T}_j$, then $\mathfrak{T}_i \; \mathbb{L}^\flat \; \mathfrak{T}_j$. — This is P18–2.

Proof. Let the condition be fulfilled. Then (DF1) every sentence L-implied by $\mathfrak{T}_j$ is L-implied by $\mathfrak{T}_i$. Therefore, every sentence identical with or an element of $\mathfrak{T}_j$ is L-implied by $\mathfrak{T}_i$ (P14–11); and hence $\mathfrak{T}_j$ itself (P14–12).

The procedure G is merely a modification of F, leading to analogous results. DG1 is not quite as simple as DF1. The reason for stating DG1 is chiefly its analogy to a certain definition for 'L-content' to be explained later (D23–C1).

D19-G1. $\mathrm{Lr}\mathfrak{T}_i$ (in S) $=_{\mathrm{Df}}$ the class of the sentences $\mathfrak{S}_j$ in S such that $\mathfrak{S}_j$ is L-true or $\mathfrak{S}_j$ is not L-implied by $\mathfrak{T}_i$.

T19-G1. $\mathrm{Lr}\Lambda = V$. (From DG1, T14–51a.)

T19-G2. $\mathrm{Lr}V$ = the class of the L-true sentences in S. (From DG1, T14–41.)

Theorems corresponding to P18–1 and 2 can here be proved in analogy to F (T19–F5 and 6).

In comparison with E, the procedures F and G have two advantages. First, the L-ranges are classes of sentences, not classes of classes of sentences. Second, for the applicability of these procedures there is no restricting condition like that of the occurrence of negation (TE36). On the other hand, if S contains negation and if further, for every state-description in S (in the sense of DE1), there is an L-equivalent sentence in S, then the procedure E could be slightly modified by taking these sentences as the elements of L-ranges; this procedure would then perhaps be preferable to F and G.

Procedures of the second kind: the elements of L-ranges are extra-linguistic

K. *Relations of predication as elements of L-ranges*

We take as example the system S_4 as in § 18A. This system covers three objects a, b, c, and two properties P and Q. As explained earlier, an L-state with respect to S_4 is a possible distribution of those properties among those objects. To every distribution of this kind, there is a corresponding relation relating each of the properties to those objects of which it is predicated. Thus there is a one-one correlation between the L-states s_r ($r = 1$ to 64) and the corresponding relations R_r, which we call *state-relations* (DK1). The procedure K consists in taking state-relations instead of L-states as elements of L-ranges. The subsequent diagram shows —

OBJECTS TO WHICH P AND Q BEAR THE STATE-RELATIONS R_r

r	P	Q
1	a,b,c	a,b,c
2	a,b,c	a,b
3	a,b,c	a,c
4	a,b,c	a
5	a,b,c	b,c
.	.	.
.	.	.
10	a,b	a,b
.	.	.
.	.	.
64	—	—

for (some of) the L-states s_r — of which objects P and Q are predicated in s_r (compare the diagram in § 18A), and thus to which objects P and Q bear the state-relation R_r. For instance, the L-state s_4 was the proposition that the property P holds for a, b, and c, and Q only for a. Therefore, the corresponding state-relation R_4 is that relation which holds between P and each of the objects a, b, and c, and between

Q and a; hence it may be regarded as the class of the following four ordered pairs: P;a, P;b, P;c, Q;a. Thus we may define: $R_4 =_{Df} \{P;a, P;b, P;c, Q;a\}$. (Here it is to be kept in mind that we are speaking in an extensional language M; therefore, no distinction is made between properties and classes, or between relations and relation-extensions; coextensive properties or relations are here identical.) In this way, each of the 64 state-relations R_r can be defined. Each of them is a possible relation of predication; but only one, namely the state-relation R_{10} corresponding to the real L-state s_{10}, is the relation of true predication, that is to say, the relation which holds between a property F and an object x if and only if F can truly be predicated of x — in other words, if x has the property F. This consideration leads to the subsequent definition of 'rs' (DK2).

D19-K1. H is a *state-relation* with respect to $S_4 =_{Df} H$ is a relation such that every first member of it is P or Q, and every second member is a, b, or c.

D19-K2. rs (with respect to S_4) $=_{Df}$ the state-relation H such that $H(F,x)$ if and only if $F(x)$.

D19-K3. V_s (the universal L-range with respect to S_4) $=_{Df}$ the class of the state-relations with respect to S_4.

D19-K4. $\Lambda_s =_{Df}$ the null class (of state-relations).

The rules of a semantical system S have the purpose of stating the meaning of the sentences of S. So far, we have formulated the rules of S as rules of truth, i.e. as rules stating for each sentence of S a sufficient and necessary condition for its truth. To know the L-range of a sentence $\mathfrak{S}_i$ means to know what possibilities are admitted and what are excluded by $\mathfrak{S}_i$. This, however, is the same as knowing under what conditions $\mathfrak{S}_i$ would be true and under what conditions it would be false. Thus, stating the L-ranges of sentences is in effect the same as stating their truth-conditions. Therefore, instead of laying down rules of truth we may lay down rules which determine the L-ranges of the sentences of S; we call them **rules of L-ranges**. This procedure is of especial importance if we intend to take the concept of L-range as basis for the definitions of the other L-concepts (L-implication, L-truth, etc.), as will be done in § 20; in this case, obviously, any procedure defining L-range with the help of the other L-concepts (as in all procedures previously explained: A, B, C, E, F, and G) is inapplicable. The rules of L-ranges here, like the rules of truth previously, presuppose rules of designation. The procedure may be illustrated by the following rules for S_4; the previous rules of designation for S_4 (§ 8) are here presupposed.

Rules of L-ranges for S_4

4a. Let $\mathfrak{S}_i$ be an atomic sentence $\mathfrak{pr}_k(\mathfrak{in}_j)$, where $\mathfrak{pr}_k$ designates the property F and $\mathfrak{in}_j$ the individual x; $\mathrm{Lr}\mathfrak{S}_i$ is the class of the state-relations H with respect to S_4 (DK1) such that $H(F,x)$.

4b. $\mathrm{Lr}(\sim\mathfrak{S}_i) = -\mathrm{Lr}\mathfrak{S}_i$ (i.e. the class of those state-relations which do not belong to $\mathrm{Lr}\mathfrak{S}_i$).

4c. $\mathrm{Lr}(\mathfrak{S}_i \vee \mathfrak{S}_j) = \mathrm{Lr}\mathfrak{S}_i + \mathrm{Lr}\mathfrak{S}_j$.

4d. $\mathrm{Lr}(\mathfrak{S}_i \bullet \mathfrak{S}_{j}) = \mathrm{Lr}\mathfrak{S}_i \times \mathrm{Lr}\mathfrak{S}_j$.

4e. $\mathrm{Lr}(\mathfrak{S}_i \supset \mathfrak{S}_j) = -\mathrm{Lr}\mathfrak{S}_i + \mathrm{Lr}\mathfrak{S}_j$.

4f. $\mathrm{Lr}(\mathfrak{S}_i \equiv \mathfrak{S}_j) = (\mathrm{Lr}\mathfrak{S}_i \times \mathrm{Lr}\mathfrak{S}_j) + (-\mathrm{Lr}\mathfrak{S}_i \times -\mathrm{Lr}\mathfrak{S}_j)$. $\mathrm{Lr}\mathfrak{K}_i =$ the product of the L-ranges of the sentences of $\mathfrak{K}_i$.

Quine (*A System of Logistic*, 1934) has construed the proposition that x has the property F (or, in other words, that x is an element of the class F) as the ordered pair F; x. In his system, all propositions have this simple predicative form. Here, we apply this device only to the propositions designated by atomic sentences. Then it seems natural to construe an L-state as a class of ordered pairs of the form F; x. This yields the state-relations described above.

If we have to do with a system S different in structure from S_4, an analysis on the basis of the rules of formation of S has to be made as described in § 18C in order to find the atomic propositions for the descriptive concepts covered by S. Then every atomic proposition is construed as an ordered pair, and the state-relations are the sub-classes of the class of all these pairs. [Let S, for instance, contain a descriptive predicate 'R' of degree three such that R(a,b,c) is an atomic proposition. Then the corresponding ordered pair consists of the relation R and the ordered triad a;b;c; hence it is R;(a;b;c). Like-wise for higher levels; if, for instance, 'M' is a descriptive predicate of second level and M(P) an atomic proposition, then the corresponding pair is M;P. Let k(a,b) = c be an atomic proposition for the descriptive functor 'k'; then we may take as total argument entity the pair (a;b);c, and hence as corresponding to the atomic proposition, the pair k;((a;b);c).] If S contains variables, then as argument entities for atomic propositions not only entities designated in S but also those covered by S have to be taken. However, with respect to the concepts (attributes and functions) different procedures are possible. The analysis, and thereby the construction of state-relations, may either be restricted to the atomic propositions for those descriptive concepts which are designated in S, or it may be extended to all descriptive concepts covered by S. [Let S, for instance, contain a predicate variable 'F' which, according to the rules of values for 'F' in S (§ 11), has certain colors as values; then we may either take all those colors as first members of the state-relations, or only those for which there are predicates in S. The rules of formation of S will then determine what entities are to be taken as second members.] The real L-state rs is to be construed as that state-relation whose pairs correspond to the true atomic propositions with respect to S.

L. *Correlations of extension as elements of L-ranges*

The procedure L is a simple modification of K. It may be illustrated again for the system S_4. In K, a state-relation R_r holds between the properties P and Q and certain individuals, in correspondence to the atomic sentences of the L-state s_r. Here in L, a state-relation $R_r{}'$ is a relation between those properties and certain classes of individuals, namely the classes of the relata of P and Q with respect to R_r (see the subsequent diagram). In K, for instance, R_4 holds between P and each of the individuals a, b, and c; thus, here in L, R_4' holds between P and the class $\{a,b,c\}$; furthermore, R_4 holds between Q and a; hence R_4' holds between Q and $\{a\}$. Therefore we define: $R_4' =_{Df} \{P;\{a,b,c\}, Q;\{a\}\}$. The same procedure may be described as follows. Accord-

CLASSES TO WHICH P AND Q BEAR THE STATE-RELATIONS R_r'

r	P	Q
1	$\{a,b,c\}$	$\{a,b,c\}$
2	$\{a,b,c\}$	$\{a,b\}$
3	$\{a,b,c\}$	$\{a,c\}$
4	$\{a,b,c\}$	$\{a\}$
5	$\{a,b,c\}$	$\{b,c\}$
.	.	.
.	.	.
10	$\{a,b\}$	$\{a,b\}$
.	.	.
.	.	.
64	Λ	Λ

ing to the earlier explanations (see § 18A, also the diagram), in the L-state s_4, the property P holds for the individuals a, b, and c, and Q holds for a; thus in s_4, P has the extension $\{a,b,c\}$ and Q the extension $\{a\}$. Here in L, we take as the state-relation R_r' corresponding to the L-state s_r the relation which holds between P and Q and the extensions which they have in s_r. Therefore we may define: a state-relation is a relation correlating with each of the properties P and Q exactly one class of individuals (DL1). rs is here construed as that state-relation which correlates with P and Q their actual extensions. Both these extensions are $\{a,b\}$ (this is factual knowledge obtained by observations, see § 18A; therefore it is not used in framing the definition for 'rs'). Since *M* is extensional, the coextensive properties P and $\{a,b\}$ are here regarded as identical, as the same class. Thus rs is that state-relation which is a sub-relation of identity. This consideration leads to DL2.

D19-L1. *H* is a *state-relation* with respect to S_4 $=_{Df}$ *H* is a many-one relation which correlates to each of the properties P and Q as first members exactly one sub-class of $\{a,b,c\}$ as second member.

D19-L2. rs (with respect to S_4) $=_{Df}$ the state-relation *H* such that $H(F,G)$ if and only if $F = G$.

D19-L3. V_s $=_{Df}$ the class of the state-relations with respect to S_4.

D19-L4. Λ_s $=_{Df}$ the null class (of state-relations).

It seems convenient here, as in K, to lay down **rules of L-ranges** for S_4 instead of rules of truth.

4a. Let $\mathfrak{S}_i$ be an atomic sentence $\mathfrak{pr}_k(\mathfrak{in}_j)$, where $\mathfrak{pr}_k$ designates the property F and $\mathfrak{in}_j$ the individual x; $\mathrm{Lr}\mathfrak{S}_i$ is the class of those state-relations H (with respect to S_4) which hold between F and a class to which x belongs.

The rules 4b to f are here the same as in K.

The procedure L, here explained for S_4, can likewise be applied to any other system S. First, on the basis of the rules of formation of S, the atomic propositions for the descriptive concepts designated in S — or for all those covered by S — are determined, as described in C and K. In other words, it is determined which entities (including sequences of entities) are admitted as argument entities for each of the concepts. Then, for any concept u, every sub-class of the class of entities admitted as argument entities for u is admitted as a possible extension for u. And a state-relation with respect to S is a relation correlating with every one of the concepts exactly one possible extension. If S contains a hierarchy of types, then the possible extensions for a concept u are simply all those concepts (which means here the same as concept-extensions, since M is extensional) which are of the same type as u. Thus the state-relations are here homogeneous (i.e. their first and second members belong to the same type).

§ 20. General Semantics Based upon the Concept of L-Range

A system of general semantics, containing both L-concepts and radical concepts, is constructed on the basis of the concepts of L-range (for sentences) and of the real L-state rs as primitives. Theorems are based on the definitions without the use of postulates, among them theorems corresponding to all the previous postulates P14–1 to 15 for L-concepts.

In §§ 18 and 19, several procedures have been explained for defining concepts of L-range. Now we shall construct a system of definitions in general semantics of a fundamentally different kind. Here, we take the concept of L-range as primitive and define the other L-concepts on its basis; we add the concept of the real L-state (rs) as primitive, and construct definitions also for the radical semantical concepts. If these definitions in general semantics are to be applied to a particular semantical system S, the concept 'L-range in S' which here is primitive must then be defined. However, it cannot of course be defined with the help of L-implication or other L-concepts as was done in most of the procedures in §§ 18 and 19. Instead we have to introduce the concept of L-range in S by laying down rules of L-ranges for S, instead of rules of truth, based on rules of designation. [This may, for instance, be done in a way similar to those explained for S_4 in § 19K and L.]

The following inexact considerations based on earlier explanations (§ 18) suggest ways for making the subsequent definitions. $\mathfrak{S}_i$ is *true* if and only if the real L-state rs is admitted by $\mathfrak{S}_i$ and hence belongs to $Lr\mathfrak{S}_i$; this suggests D13 (in agreement with earlier considerations for the procedures A and B, see T18–A7 and T18–B36). In order to fulfill the requirement of adequacy (§ 16) we must define the term '*L-true*' in such a way that it applies to a sentence $\mathfrak{S}_i$ if and only if the truth of $\mathfrak{S}_i$ follows from the semantical rules which are here supposed to have the form of rules of L-ranges. If we know the rules but not the relevant facts, then we know the L-range for any given sentence $\mathfrak{S}_i$, but we do not know which of the L-states is the real L-state. There is only one case in which we nevertheless shall be able to ascertain that $\mathfrak{S}_i$ is true, and that is the case in which $\mathrm{Lr}\mathfrak{S}_i$ is V_s, i.e. the class of all L-states (D3). Only in the case in which $\mathrm{Lr}\mathfrak{S}_i$ is Λ_s, i.e. the null L-range (D4), are we in a position to find out that $\mathfrak{S}_i$ is false by making use merely of the semantical rules (which tell us that $\mathrm{Lr}\mathfrak{S}_i = \Lambda_s$) but not of any factual knowledge (which would tell us which is the real L-state). Thus we can characterize the L-true sentences as those with the L-range V_s (D5) and the L-false sentences as those with Λ_s (D6) (in agreement with T18–A8 and 9, and T18–B29 and 30). For the definition of *L-implicaion* we have to consider the question of the conditions under which it would be possible to find out with the help of the semantical rules alone that if $\mathfrak{S}_i$ is true $\mathfrak{S}_j$ must also be true. In other words, if we know the L-ranges $\mathrm{Lr}\mathfrak{S}_i$ and $\mathrm{Lr}\mathfrak{S}_j$ but do not know which L-state is the real L-state rs, under what condition can we nevertheless know that, if rs $\epsilon\ \mathrm{Lr}\mathfrak{S}_i$, then rs $\epsilon\ \mathrm{Lr}\mathfrak{S}_j$? This is possible only if $\mathrm{Lr}\mathfrak{S}_i \subset \mathrm{Lr}\mathfrak{S}_j$; and therefore this condition is an adequate definiens for L-implication (D7) (in agreement with T18–1, based on P18–1 and 2; T18–A5 and T18–B18 and 19). L-equivalence is mutual L-implication (P14–9) and hence characterized by the identity of L-ranges (D8) (in agreement with T18–2). Here, as earlier, the concept of L-range will be applied to sentential classes also. We regard $\mathfrak{R}_i$ as true if and only if every sentence of $\mathfrak{R}_i$ is true (D9–1). Therefore an L-state makes $\mathfrak{R}_i$ true if and only if it makes every sentence of $\mathfrak{R}_i$ true. Hence we take as $\mathrm{Lr}\mathfrak{R}_i$ the class of all those L-states which belong to the L-range of every sentence of $\mathfrak{R}_i$, or, in other words, the product of the L-ranges of the sentences of $\Re_i$ (D1b) (in agreement with T18–A17).

Examples. In § 15 we analyzed five examples of sentences $\mathfrak{S}_1$ to $\mathfrak{S}_5$, belonging to S_3 and hence also to S_4. 'P(a)' was designated by '$\mathfrak{S}_3$'; we now designate '$\sim$P(a)' by '$\mathfrak{S}_6$' and 'Q(b)' by '$\mathfrak{S}_7$'. The application of the rules of L-ranges for S_4 stated in § 19K yields the following results. According to rule (4b), $\mathrm{Lr}\mathfrak{S}_6 = -\mathrm{Lr}\mathfrak{S}_3$. Hence, according to (4c), $\mathrm{Lr}\mathfrak{S}_1 = \mathrm{Lr}\mathfrak{S}_3 + (-\mathrm{Lr}\mathfrak{S}_3) = V_s$; and $\mathrm{Lr}\mathfrak{S}_2 = -\mathrm{Lr}\mathfrak{S}_1 = -V_s = \Lambda_s$. Therefore, according to the preceding considerations and the subsequent definitions, $\mathfrak{S}_1$ is L-true and $\mathfrak{S}_2$ L-false, in agreement with the results in § 15. Further, $\mathrm{Lr}\mathfrak{S}_4 = \mathrm{Lr}\mathfrak{S}_3 + \mathrm{Lr}\mathfrak{S}_7$; hence $\mathrm{Lr}\mathfrak{S}_3 \subset \mathrm{Lr}\mathfrak{S}_4$; hence $\mathfrak{S}_3 \overrightarrow{\mathrm{L}} \mathfrak{S}_4$. $\mathrm{Lr}\mathfrak{S}_5 = \mathrm{Lr}\mathfrak{S}_7 + \mathrm{Lr}\mathfrak{S}_3 = \mathrm{Lr}\mathfrak{S}_4$; hence $\mathfrak{S}_5$ and $\mathfrak{S}_4$ are L-equivalent.

In the following system we have two types of individuals. The sentences $\mathfrak{S}$ are the individuals of the first type; the L-states are the individuals of the second type (for the sake of simplicity we write 'sentence' instead of 'individual of the first type' and 'L-state' instead of 'individual of the second type'). As primitive terms we take 'LrSent' (L-range for sentences) and 'rs' as explained before. We might lay down some postulates; but they would not be of great importance. We shall see that all theorems wanted can be proved merely on the basis of the definitions. Among these theorems we shall find all the postulates of the previous system for L-concepts (P14–1 to 15, occurring here as T20–25, 27, 29, 33, 11, 12, 13, 14, 19, 20, 15, 16, 9, 17, 18). Therefore, all the theorems based on these postulates (T14–1 to 59) also hold in the present system of definitions. [The sometimes disputed postulates P14–14 and 15 also result here from definitions which seem simple and natural. This fact seems to lend additional support to the choice of those postulates. The same holds for P14–E1 to 3; see below D9'.]

The rules of formation of the metalanguage in which this system is formulated are supposed to specify the types for the two primitive signs in the following way. 'LrSent' is a functor whose argument entities are individuals of the first type and whose values are classes of individuals of the second type; 'rs' is an individual constant of the second type. Hence, the L-ranges are classes of L-states, and rs is an L-state.

'LrSent' is used only in the definition D1 for 'Lr' (L-range for sentences and sentential classes); further on, only 'Lr' is used. (It would also be possible to take 'Lr' as primitive instead of 'LrSent', and lay down a postulate instead of D1.) We begin with definitions and theorems on the basis of 'Lr' alone. This includes the L-concepts. Then we shall add 'rs' and thereby come to the radical concepts. Thus, from a certain point of view, the L-concepts appear simpler than the radical concepts.

D20-1.

    a. $\mathrm{Lr}\mathfrak{S}_i$ (in S) $=_{\mathrm{Df}} \mathrm{LrSent}\mathfrak{S}_i$.

    b. $\mathrm{Lr}\mathfrak{K}_i$ (in S) $=_{\mathrm{Df}}$ the product of the classes $\mathrm{LrSent}\mathfrak{S}_j$ for all sentences $\mathfrak{S}_j$ of $\mathfrak{K}_i$.

T20-1 (lemma). If $\mathfrak{S}_j \in \mathfrak{K}_i$, $\mathrm{Lr}\mathfrak{K}_i \subset \mathrm{Lr}\mathfrak{S}_j$. (From D1.)

T20-2 (lemma). If $\mathrm{Lr}\mathfrak{T}_i \subset \mathrm{Lr}\mathfrak{S}_j$ for every sentence $\mathfrak{S}_j$ of $\mathfrak{K}_j$, then $\mathrm{Lr}\mathfrak{T}_i \subset \mathrm{Lr}\mathfrak{K}_j$. (From D1.)

T20-3. $\mathrm{Lr}(\mathfrak{K}_i + \mathfrak{K}_j) = \mathrm{Lr}\mathfrak{K}_i \times \mathrm{Lr}\mathfrak{K}_j$. (From D1b.)

D20-3. V_s (the **universal L-range** in S) $=_{\mathrm{Df}}$ the class of all L-states (i.e. the universal class of the second type of individuals).

T20-5 (lemma). For every $\mathfrak{T}_i$, $\mathrm{Lr}\mathfrak{T}_i \subset V_s$. (From D3.)

D20-4. Λ_s (the **null L-range** in S) $=_{\mathrm{Df}}$ the null class (of L-states).

T20-6 (lemma). For every $\mathfrak{T}_i$, $\Lambda_s \subset \mathrm{Lr}\mathfrak{T}_i$. (From D4.)

+D20-5. $\mathfrak{T}_i$ is **L-true** (in S) $=_{\mathrm{Df}} \mathrm{Lr}\mathfrak{T}_i = V_s$.

T20-9. If every sentence of $\mathfrak{K}_i$ is L-true, $\mathfrak{K}_i$ is L-true. (From D5, D1.)

+D20-6. $\mathfrak{T}_i$ is **L-false** (in S) $=_{\mathrm{Df}} \mathrm{Lr}\mathfrak{T}_i = \Lambda_\mathrm{s}$.

+D20-7. $\mathfrak{T}_i \; \overrightarrow{\mathrm{L}} \; \mathfrak{T}_j$ (in S) $=_{\mathrm{Df}} \mathrm{Lr}\mathfrak{T}_i \subset \mathrm{Lr}\mathfrak{T}_j$.

T20-10 (lemma). $\mathfrak{T}_i \; \overrightarrow{\mathrm{L}} \; \mathfrak{T}_j$ if and only if $-\mathrm{Lr}\mathfrak{T}_i + \mathrm{Lr}\mathfrak{T}_j = V_\mathrm{s}$. (From D7, D3.)

T20-11. L-implication is transitive. (From D7.)

T20-12. If $\mathfrak{T}_i \; \overrightarrow{\mathrm{L}} \; \mathfrak{T}_j$ and $\mathfrak{T}_i$ is L-true, $\mathfrak{T}_j$ is L-true. (From D7, D5.)

T20-13. If $\mathfrak{T}_i \; \overrightarrow{\mathrm{L}} \; \mathfrak{T}_j$ and $\mathfrak{T}_j$ is L-false, $\mathfrak{T}_i$ is L-false. (From D7, D6.)

T20-14. For every $\mathfrak{S}_i$, $\mathfrak{S}_i \; \overrightarrow{\mathrm{L}} \; \mathfrak{S}_i$. (From D7.)

T20-15. If $\mathfrak{S}_j \, \epsilon \, \mathfrak{R}_i$ then $\mathfrak{R}_i \; \overrightarrow{\mathrm{L}} \; \mathfrak{S}_j$. (From T1, D7.)

T20-16. If $\mathfrak{T}_i \; \overrightarrow{\mathrm{L}}$ every sentence of $\mathfrak{R}_j$, then $\mathfrak{T}_i \; \overrightarrow{\mathrm{L}} \; \mathfrak{R}_j$. (From T2, D7.)

+T20-17. If $\mathfrak{T}_j$ is L-true, then every $\mathfrak{T}_i \; \overrightarrow{\mathrm{L}} \; \mathfrak{T}_j$. (From D5, D7.)

+T20-18. If $\mathfrak{T}_i$ is L-false, then $\mathfrak{T}_i \; \overrightarrow{\mathrm{L}}$ every $\mathfrak{T}_j$. (From D6, D7.)

+D20-8. $\mathfrak{T}_i$ is **L-equivalent** to $\mathfrak{T}_j$ (in S) $=_{\mathrm{Df}}$ $\mathrm{Lr}\mathfrak{T}_i = \mathrm{Lr}\mathfrak{T}_j$.

T20-19. $\mathfrak{T}_i$ is L-equivalent to $\mathfrak{T}_j$ if and only if $\mathfrak{T}_i \; \overrightarrow{\mathrm{L}} \; \mathfrak{T}_j$ and $\mathfrak{T}_j \; \overrightarrow{\mathrm{L}} \; \mathfrak{T}_i$. (From D8, D7.)

D20-9. $\mathfrak{T}_i$ is **L-disjunct** with $\mathfrak{T}_j$ (in S) $=_{\mathrm{Df}}$ $\mathrm{Lr}\mathfrak{T}_i + \mathrm{Lr}\mathfrak{T}_j = V_\mathrm{s}$.

T20-20. If $\mathfrak{T}_i$ is L-true, $\mathfrak{T}_i$ and $\mathfrak{T}_j$ are L-disjunct (with one another). (From D5, D9.)

D20-10. $\mathfrak{T}_i$ is **L-exclusive** of $\mathfrak{T}_j$ (in S) $=_{\mathrm{Df}}$ $\mathrm{Lr}\mathfrak{T}_i \times \mathrm{Lr}\mathfrak{T}_j = \Lambda_\mathrm{s}$.

D20-11. $\mathfrak{T}_i$ is **L-non-equivalent** to $\mathfrak{T}_j$ $=_{\mathrm{Df}}$ $\mathrm{Lr}\mathfrak{T}_i = -\mathrm{Lr}\mathfrak{T}_j$.

T20-22. $\mathfrak{T}_i$ is L-non-equivalent to $\mathfrak{T}_j$ if and only if $\mathfrak{T}_i$ is both L-disjunct and L-exclusive of $\mathfrak{T}_j$. (From D11, 9 and 10.)

T20-23. If $\mathfrak{T}_i$ is L-non-equivalent both to $\mathfrak{T}_j$ and to $\mathfrak{T}_k$, then $\mathfrak{T}_j$ is L-equivalent to $\mathfrak{T}_k$. (From D11, D8.)

If the concept 'L-disjunct' is applied not only to two members but to the sentences or sentential classes of any, possibly infinite, class $\mathfrak{M}_i$ (see remarks to P14–E1 to 3), then D20–9 is to be replaced by the following definition.

D20-9'. The elements (sentences or sentential classes) of $\mathfrak{M}_i$ are *L-disjunct* with one another $=_{Df}$ the sum of the L-ranges of the elements of $\mathfrak{M}_i$ is V_s.

On the basis of D9' together with the other definitions stated above, the postulates P14–E1 to 3 can easily be proved.

The following definitions of *radical concepts* make use of 'rs' also.

+D20-13. $\mathfrak{T}_i$ is **true** (in S) $=_{Df}$ rs ϵ Lr$\mathfrak{T}_i$.
  T20-25. If $\mathfrak{T}_i$ is L-true, $\mathfrak{T}_i$ is true. (From D5, D13.)

D20-14. $\mathfrak{T}_i$ is **false** (in S) $=_{Df}$ $\mathfrak{T}_i$ is not true.
  T20-26. $\mathfrak{T}_i$ is false if and only if not rs ϵ Lr$\mathfrak{T}_i$, hence if and only if rs ϵ $-$Lr$\mathfrak{T}_i$. (From D14, D13.)
  T20-27. If $\mathfrak{T}_i$ is L-false, $\mathfrak{T}_i$ is false. (From D6, T26.)

D20-15. $\mathfrak{T}_j$ is an **implicate** of $\mathfrak{T}_i$ ($\mathfrak{T}_i \rightarrow \mathfrak{T}_j$) (in S) $=_{Df}$ $\mathfrak{T}_i$ is false or $\mathfrak{T}_j$ is true (or both).
  T20-28. $\mathfrak{T}_i \rightarrow \mathfrak{T}_j$ if and only if rs ϵ ($-$Lr$\mathfrak{T}_i$ $+$ Lr$\mathfrak{T}_j$). (From D15, T26, D13.)
  T20-29. If $\mathfrak{T}_i \overrightarrow{\text{L}} \mathfrak{T}_j$, then $\mathfrak{T}_i \rightarrow \mathfrak{T}_j$. (From T10, T28.)

D20-16. $\mathfrak{T}_i$ is **equivalent** to $\mathfrak{T}_j$ (in S) $=_{Df}$ both are true or both are false.
  T20-30. $\mathfrak{T}_i$ and $\mathfrak{T}_j$ are equivalent (to one another) if and only if $\mathfrak{T}_i \rightarrow \mathfrak{T}_j$ and $\mathfrak{T}_j \rightarrow \mathfrak{T}_i$. (From D16, D15.)
  T20-31. If $\mathfrak{T}_i$ and $\mathfrak{T}_j$ are L-equivalent, they are equivalent. (From T19, T29, T30.)

D20-17. $\mathfrak{T}_i$ is **disjunct** with $\mathfrak{T}_j$ (in S) $=_{Df}$ at least one of them is true.

T20-32. $\mathfrak{T}_i$ and $\mathfrak{T}_j$ are disjunct (with one another) if and only if rs ϵ Lr$\mathfrak{T}_i$ + Lr$\mathfrak{T}_j$. (From D13, D17.)

T20-33. If $\mathfrak{T}_i$ and $\mathfrak{T}_j$ are L-disjunct, they are disjunct. (From D9, T32.)

D20-18. $\mathfrak{T}_i$ is **exclusive** of $\mathfrak{T}_j$ (in S) $=_{Df}$ at least one of them is false.

T20-35. If $\mathfrak{T}_i$ and $\mathfrak{T}_j$ are L-exclusive, they are exclusive. (From D10, 18, 14, 13.)

T20-36. If $\mathfrak{T}_i$ and $\mathfrak{T}_j$ are L-non-equivalent, then one of them is true and one is false; hence they are not equivalent. (From D11, 13, 14, 16.)

The definitions of radical terms on the basis of 'true' in the present system (D14 to 18) are in accordance with the definitions of the same terms in § 9. There we defined more terms; their definitions (D9–7 to 9) may be added to the present system also. Then all theorems of the former system (T9–1 to 50) hold here too, because they are based only on the definitions without postulates. Furthermore, the definitions in § 14 of other L-terms may here be added. Then the present system contains those of § 9 and § 14; it may be further supplemented by the definitions and theorems of the next section.

§ 21. F-Concepts

If a sentence is neither L-true nor L-false, then we cannot determine its truth-value by the help of the semantical rules alone but we need some knowledge of relevant facts. Therefore, the sentences of this kind are called *factual* ('synthetic', in traditional terminology). An F-term (e.g. 'F-true', for 'factually true') is applied if the corresponding radical term ('true') holds but the corresponding L-term ('L-true') does not. Some F-terms are defined in accordance with this convention, and theorems are stated for them.

If the L-terms with respect to a semantical system S are defined in such a way that the requirement of adequacy

(§ 16) is fulfilled, then the L-determinate sentences (D14–1) are those whose truth-values can be determined on the basis of the semantical rules alone. For the other sentences, the rules do not suffice; we must use some knowledge about something outside of language, which we may call knowledge of facts. Therefore the sentences which are not L-determinate have factual content, i.e. they assert something about facts, namely those facts upon which their truth-values depend. Therefore we shall call these sentences F-determinate (i.e. factually determinate) or simply *factual* (D1; compare the terminological remarks in § 37). In traditional terminology they are called synthetic (in the sense of being neither analytic nor contradictory). If a factual sentence is true, it is true by reasons of fact (as against merely logical reasons represented by the semantical rules); it may therefore be called factually true or *F-true* (D2). If a factual sentence is false, we call it *F-false* (D3). On the basis of these considerations we lay down the following definitions for **F-concepts**.

+**D21-1.** $\mathfrak{T}_i$ is (L-indeterminate or F-determinate or) **factual** (in S) $=_{Df}$ $\mathfrak{T}_i$ is not L-determinate.

+**D21-2.** $\mathfrak{T}_i$ is **F-true** (in S) $=_{Df}$ $\mathfrak{T}_i$ is true but not L-true.

T21-5. $\mathfrak{T}_i$ is F-true if and only if $\mathfrak{T}_i$ is factual and true. (From D1 and 2.)

T21-6. $\mathfrak{K}_i$ is F-true if and only if every sentence of $\mathfrak{K}_i$ is true and at least one of them F-true. (From D2, D9–1, T14–20.)

+**D21-3.** $\mathfrak{T}_i$ is **F-false** (in S) $=_{Df}$ $\mathfrak{T}_i$ is false but not L-false.

T21-9. $\mathfrak{T}_i$ is F-false if and only if $\mathfrak{T}_i$ is factual and false. (From D1 and 3.)

T21-10. $\mathfrak{T}_i$ is factual if and only if $\mathfrak{T}_i$ is F-true or F-false. (From D1, 2, 3.)

T21-11. $\mathfrak{T}_i$ is not both F-true and F-false. (From D2 and 3, T9–2.)

T21-12. If $\mathfrak{R}_i$ is F-false, then

   a. At least one sentence of $\mathfrak{R}_i$ is false.

   b. No sentence of $\mathfrak{R}_i$ is L-false.

   c. No sub-class of $\mathfrak{R}_i$ is L-false.

   (From T9–1; T14–11; T14–13.)

In an analogous way, we may introduce, for any L-term, a corresponding F-term. If there is a radical term corresponding to the L-term, then the F-term applies if the corresponding radical term applies but the L-term does not. Hence in this case the definition for the F-term may be stated in the form 'F- . . . =$_{\mathrm{Df}}$ . . . and not L- . . .'. We shall later define a few more F-terms.

On the basis of the definitions given, we have in general the following *classification of the sentences* of a semantical system S:

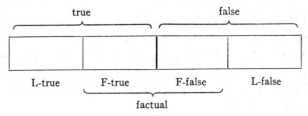

This schema, however, often degenerates. In a particular system, any one or two or three of the four kinds shown in the schema may be empty.

The diagram also represents in general the classification of sentential classes. Here, any one or two or three of the four fields may be empty, except that of L-true classes, because in any system S Λ is L-true (T14–33) even if S does not contain any L-true sentences. And in still another point the diagrams for sentences and for classes (in S) may differ.

There may be an L-false class in S even if there is no L-false sentence in S.

Example. Let us construct the system S_8 out of S_3 (§§ 8 and 15) by dropping the sign of disjunction 'V' and the rules referring to it (2c and 4c). Then all sentences of S_8 are factual. But besides the L-true class Λ there are L-false classes, e.g. any class of the form $\{\mathfrak{S}_i, \sim\mathfrak{S}_i\}$.

D21-5. $\mathfrak{T}_j$ is an **F-implicate** of $\mathfrak{T}_i$ ($\mathfrak{T}_i$ F-implies $\mathfrak{T}_j$; $\mathfrak{T}_i \overrightarrow{\text{F}} \mathfrak{T}_j$) (in S) $=_{\text{Df}} \mathfrak{T}_i \rightarrow \mathfrak{T}_j$ but not $\mathfrak{T}_i \overrightarrow{\text{L}} \mathfrak{T}_j$.

T21-20. If $\mathfrak{T}_i \overrightarrow{\text{F}} \mathfrak{T}_j$, then the following holds:

a (lemma). $\mathfrak{T}_i$ is false, or $\mathfrak{T}_j$ is true.

b. $\mathfrak{T}_i$ is not L-false.

c. $\mathfrak{T}_j$ is not L-true.

d. $\mathfrak{T}_i$ is F-false or $\mathfrak{T}_j$ is F-true.

(From D5, D9–3; P14–15; P14–14; a, b, c.)

D21-6. $\mathfrak{T}_i$ is **F-equivalent** to $\mathfrak{T}_j$ (in S) $=_{\text{Df}} \mathfrak{T}_i$ is equivalent, but not L-equivalent, to $\mathfrak{T}_j$.

T21-25.

a. If $\mathfrak{T}_i \overrightarrow{\text{F}} \mathfrak{T}_j$ and $\mathfrak{T}_j \overrightarrow{\text{F}} \mathfrak{T}_i$, then $\mathfrak{T}_i$ and $\mathfrak{T}_j$ are F-equivalent to one another.

b. If $\mathfrak{T}_i$ and $\mathfrak{T}_j$ are F-equivalent to one another, each of them is an L- or an F-implicate of the other, and at least one of them an F-implicate.

(From T9–20b, P14–9, D5.)

The converse of (a) does not hold generally, but only the weaker theorem (b). While equivalence is the same as mutual implication and L-equivalence is the same as mutual L-implication, F-equivalence is a weaker concept than mutual F-implication. F-equivalence holds also in the case where F-implication holds in one direction and L-implication in the other.

T21-26. If $\mathfrak{T}_i$ and $\mathfrak{T}_j$ are F-equivalent (to one another), then the following holds:

    a (lemma). Both are true or both are false.

    b. Not both are L-true.

    c. Not both are L-false.

    d. Both are true and at least one F-true, or both are false and at least one F-false.

    (From D9–4; T14–52; T14–53; (a). (b), (c).)

D21-7. $\mathfrak{T}_i$ is **F-disjunct** with $\mathfrak{T}_j$ (in S) $=_{Df}$ $\mathfrak{T}_i$ is disjunct but not L-disjunct with $\mathfrak{T}_j$.

T21-31. If $\mathfrak{T}_i$ and $\mathfrak{T}_j$ are F-disjunct (with one another), then the following holds:

    a (lemma). At least one of them is true.

    b. Neither is L-true.

    c. At least one is F-true.

    (From D9–5; P14–10; (a), (b).)

D21-8. $\mathfrak{T}_i$ is **F-exclusive** of $\mathfrak{T}_j$ (in S) $=_{Df}$ $\mathfrak{T}_i$ is exclusive but not L-exclusive of $\mathfrak{T}_j$.

T21-36. If $\mathfrak{T}_i$ and $\mathfrak{T}_j$ are F-exclusive (of one another), then:

    a (lemma). At least one of them is false.

    b. Neither is L-false.

    c. At least one is F-false.

    (From D9–6; T14–71; (a), (b).)

D21-10. $\mathfrak{A}_i$ is *F-interchangeable* with $\mathfrak{A}_j$ (in S) $=_{Df}$ $\mathfrak{A}_i$ is interchangeable but not L-interchangeable with $\mathfrak{A}_j$.

In analogy to the definitions given here, definitions for other F-terms can be laid down corresponding to L-terms and in most cases also to radical terms previously explained [e.g. 'F-designation', 'F-fulfillment', 'F-determination' (of an attribute by a sentential function), 'F-synonymous', 'F-universal', 'F-empty', 'F-non-empty', etc.; for the corresponding L-terms, see § 15.] (In those cases where only the L-concept is important, while the radical concept is trivial, the F-concept would not have much interest; this seems to be the case e.g. with 'F-dependent' and 'F-complete', perhaps also with 'F-comprehensive'.)

§22. Characteristic Sentences

For some quadruples of concepts (radical, L-, F-, and C-concepts, the last belonging to syntax) characteristic sentences are given. The radical, L-, F-, or C-concept holds in a certain case if the characteristic sentence constructed for that case is true, L-true, F-true, or C-true respectively.

The theorems of this section state sufficient and necessary conditions for some radical concepts and the corresponding F-, L-, and C-concepts. (The C-concepts will be explained later; they belong to syntax.) These conditions are not applicable in all systems but only in those containing certain signs (propositional connectives, universal or existential operator, sign of identity); these signs occur in most of the language systems dealt with in modern logic.

Every one of the theorems containing the prefix variable 'X-' is an abbreviated combination for four theorems; these are found by substituting for 'X-' the following four prefixes in turn: the null prefix (yielding e.g. 'true' from 'X-true'), the prefixes 'L-', 'F-', and 'C-'. We use the customary signs of symbolic logic (see § 6). For each of the four sets of conditions there is one basic term, namely 'X-true' (i.e. 'true' for the radical terms, 'L-true' for the L-terms, etc.), applied to sentences only.

The combined condition for each quadruple of concepts can be formulated in this way: 'The sentence . . . is X-true'. Thus, there is for the quadruple of concepts in question, with respect to any case of application, a certain sentence — we call it the **characteristic sentence** for these concepts (with respect to that case) — such that the radical concept holds in the case in question if (and only if) the characteristic sentence is true, the L-concept if it is L-true, the F-concept if it is F-true (and in syntax the C-concept if it is C-true). For the sake of brevity we omit the reference to the semantical or syntactical system (i.e. the phrase 'in S' or 'in K' respectively).

The subsequent table does not contain the full formulation of the theorems, but it gives the characteristic sentences for the quadruples of concepts. The theorems can easily be constructed in analogy to the full formulation given for T1 and 2. To simplify matters, the table does not use German letters but signs of the object language in quotes. These are examples, but the theorems are meant as general; hence in the place of 'A' or 'B' any closed sentence (i.e. one not containing a free variable) may be taken; instead of the examples with 'P' and 'Q' analogous cases with predicates of any degree; instead of 'R' any predicate of degree two; instead of 'a' and 'b' any individual constants.

Proofs for the theorems are not given here. They would have to be based on the rules of the system in question with respect to the signs referred to in the condition and on an adequate definition for the concept for which the condition is stated. The practical value of these theorems is that they show a convenient way to find out whether or not in a given case the concept in question applies. Each of the conditions may also be taken as a definiens for the concept in question; it could then be shown that the resulting definitions are adequate. (With respect to T1 to 5 taken as definitions, the disadvantage would be that the concepts would be defined only for (closed) sentences, not for sentential classes.)

Full formulation of the first two theorems:

T22-1. A closed sentence $\mathfrak{S}_i$ is *X-false* if and only if $\sim\mathfrak{S}_i$ is *X*-true.

T22-2. Two closed sentences $\mathfrak{S}_i$ and $\mathfrak{S}_j$ are *X-equivalent* if and only if $\mathfrak{S}_i \equiv \mathfrak{S}_j$ is *X*-true.

THEOREM NUMBER	CONCEPT	CHARACTERISTIC SENTENCE
	1. Concepts applicable to *sentences*.	
T22-1	'A' is *X-false*	'$\sim$A'
T22-2	'A' and 'B' are *X-equivalent* to one another	'A $\equiv$ B'
T22-3	'B' is an *X-implicate* of 'A'	$\begin{cases} \text{'A} \supset \text{B'} \\ \text{'}\sim\text{A} \vee \text{B'} \end{cases}$
T22-4	'A' and 'B' are *X-disjunct*	'A $\vee$ B'
T22-5	'A' and 'B' are *X-exclusive*	$\begin{cases} \text{'A} \mid \text{B'} \\ \text{'}\sim(\text{A} \bullet \text{B})\text{'} \\ \text{'}\sim\text{A} \vee \sim\text{B'} \end{cases}$
T22-6	'A' and 'B' are *X-non-equivalent*	'$\sim$(A $\equiv$ B)'
	2. Concepts applicable to *predicates* of any degree *n*.	
T22-10	'P' is *X-universal*	'$(x)P(x)$'
T22-11	'P' is *X-empty*	$\begin{cases} \text{'}(x)\,(\sim P(x))\text{'} \\ \text{'}\sim(\exists x)P(x)\text{'} \end{cases}$
T22-12	'P' is *X-non-empty*	'$(\exists x)P(x)$'
T22-13	'P' and 'Q' are *X-equivalent*	'$(x)\,(P(x) \equiv Q(x))$'
T22-14	'Q' is an *X-implicate* of 'P'	'$(x)\,(P(x) \supset Q(x))$'
T22-15	'P' and 'Q' are *X-disjunct*	'$(x)\,(P(x) \vee Q(x))$'
T22-16	'P' and 'Q' are *X-exclusive*	$\begin{cases} \text{'}(x)\,(P(x) \mid Q(x))\text{'} \\ \text{'}(x)\,(\sim(P(x) \bullet Q(x)))\text{'} \end{cases}$
	3. Concepts applicable to *predicates* of degree two.	
T22-20	'R' is *X-symmetric*	'$(x)\,(y)\,(R(x,y) \supset R(y,x))$'
T22-21	'R' is *X-non-symmetric*	'$\sim(x)\,(y)\,(R(x,y) \supset R(y,x))$'
T22-22	'R' is *X-asymmetric*	'$(x)\,(y)\,(R(x,y) \supset \sim R(y,x))$'
	In an analogous way, characteristic sentences for the other concepts of the theory of relations may be set up ('reflexive', 'transitive', 'one-many', etc.).	
	4. Concepts applicable to *individual constants*.	
T22-30	'a' and 'b' are *X-synonymous*	'$a = b$'

There are no characteristic sentences for 'X-determinate', 'X-dependent', 'X-complete', 'X-comprehensive', and 'X-perfect'. For the first three of these, the radical concept is of no interest since it is universal; hence, the F-concept is not of much interest either, since it coincides with the negation of the L-concept. Only the L- and the C-concepts have practical value here.

§ 23. L-Content

The concept of the L-content of a sentence $\mathfrak{S}_i$ (Lc$\mathfrak{S}_i$) is related to that of the L-range. Two postulates for L-content are laid down (P1 and 2). Several ways are shown for defining a concept of L-content which satisfies the postulates. According to these definitions, an L-content is a class whose elements are either in the realm of designata (namely, L-states; DB1) or in the realm of expressions (namely, sentences; DF1, DG1).

We shall explain here the problem of an L-concept which is in some respects closely related to the concept of L-range. We shall not try to give here a definitive solution of this problem any more than we did in the case of the concept of L-range.

The term 'content' is sometimes used in a loose way meaning something like the strength or assertive power of a sentence. We say sometimes that the content of a sentence includes that of another sentence but is larger than this, or that the first sentence is stronger than the second, meaning by this that the first asserts all that is asserted by the second and, in addition, something more. We shall now try to make this way of speaking more precise. We shall use the term '**L-content**', because it will turn out that it is an L-concept and that there is a corresponding syntactical concept for which we shall use the term 'C-content' (§ 32). Like the other semantical concepts, this concept will here be applied not only to sentences but also to sentential classes;

as an abbreviation for 'the L-content of $\mathfrak{T}_i$ in S' we write '$Lc_S\mathfrak{T}_i$' or simply '$Lc\mathfrak{T}_i$'.

Before explaining different possibilities of defining concepts of L-content, we shall lay down two *postulates* stating properties which any concept of L-content (with respect to a semantical system S) should have in order to be in accordance with our intention. These postulates still leave open not only different formulations of definitions but essentially different concepts to be defined. Since it is customary to speak of one content's being contained in another one, we shall construe the L-contents as classes; but we leave open the question of what kind of entities are to be taken as elements of these classes. The following considerations leading to the postulates are necessarily vague; they are not in any sense proofs for the postulates but give only practical justifications for them by making plausible that the postulates are in agreement with what we vaguely have in mind when speaking about contents.

1. If the content of $\mathfrak{T}_j$ is partly or totally outside that of $\mathfrak{T}_i$, then $\mathfrak{T}_j$ asserts, at least partly, something not asserted by $\mathfrak{T}_i$. This assertion might then be false even if $\mathfrak{T}_i$ is true. Therefore, in this case, $\mathfrak{T}_j$ is not logically deducible from $\mathfrak{T}_i$. To put it the other way round: if $\mathfrak{T}_j$ is logically deducible from $\mathfrak{T}_i$, the content of $\mathfrak{T}_j$ must be entirely within that of $\mathfrak{T}_i$. This, when expressed in our technical terms, is P1.

2. If the content of $\mathfrak{T}_j$ is contained in that of $\mathfrak{T}_i$, then $\mathfrak{T}_j$ does not assert anything that was not asserted by $\mathfrak{T}_i$. Hence it would be impossible that $\mathfrak{T}_i$ be true and $\mathfrak{T}_j$ false. And this impossibility is based on logical grounds, namely on the sense or content of $\mathfrak{T}_i$ and $\mathfrak{T}_j$, not on any facts. Therefore $\mathfrak{T}_j$ follows logically from $\mathfrak{T}_i$. This leads to P2.

Postulates for L-content

+**P23-1.** If $\mathfrak{T}_i \ \overrightarrow{\text{L}} \ \mathfrak{T}_j$ (in S), then $Lc\mathfrak{T}_j \subset Lc\mathfrak{T}_i$.

+**P23-2.** If $Lc\mathfrak{T}_j \subset Lc\mathfrak{T}_i$ (in S), then $\mathfrak{T}_i \ \overrightarrow{\text{L}} \ \mathfrak{T}_j$.

The following theorems are based on these two postulates in addition to the earlier postulates, definitions, and theorems concerning L-concepts (§ 14). L-equivalence coincides with identity of L-contents (T2). The L-content of Λ is the minimum L-content and is contained in any other L-content (T5). It is that of all and only the L-true $\mathfrak{T}$ (T7). The L-content of V is the maximum L-content, in which any other L-content is contained (T6). It is the L-content of all and only the L-comprehensive $\mathfrak{T}$ (T8) and of all the L-false $\mathfrak{T}$, and only these, if there are any such (T9). (For the sake of brevity we omit references to a system S in the theorems.)

T23-1. $\mathrm{Lc}\,\mathfrak{T}_j \subset \mathrm{Lc}\,\mathfrak{T}_i$ if and only if $\mathfrak{T}_i \,\overline{\mathrm{L}}\, \mathfrak{T}_j$. (From P1 and 2.)

+**T23-2.** $\mathrm{Lc}\,\mathfrak{T}_j = \mathrm{Lc}\,\mathfrak{T}_i$ if and only if $\mathfrak{T}_i$ and $\mathfrak{T}_j$ are L-equivalent. (From T1, P14–9.)

T23-5. For every $\mathfrak{T}_i$, $\mathrm{Lc}\,\Lambda \subset \mathrm{Lc}\,\mathfrak{T}_i$. (From T14–32, P1.)

T23-6. For every $\mathfrak{T}_i$, $\mathrm{Lc}\,\mathfrak{T}_i \subset \mathrm{Lc}\,\mathrm{V}$. (From T14–42, P1.)

T23-7. $\mathrm{Lc}\,\mathfrak{T}_i = \mathrm{Lc}\,\Lambda$ if and only if $\mathfrak{T}_i$ is L-true. (From T2, T14–51b.)

T23-8. $\mathrm{Lc}\,\mathfrak{T}_i = \mathrm{Lc}\,\mathrm{V}$ if and only if $\mathfrak{T}_i$ is L-comprehensive. (From T14–102b, T2.)

T23-9. If S contains an L-false $\mathfrak{T}_j$, then, for every $\mathfrak{T}_i$, $\mathrm{Lc}\,\mathfrak{T}_i = \mathrm{Lc}\,\mathrm{V}$ if and only if $\mathfrak{T}_i$ is L-false. (From T8, T14–107b.)

If we compare the concept of L-content with that of *L-range* (§§ 18, 19) we find a striking analogy or, rather, a duality, inasmuch as the relation of inclusion among L-contents is always inverse to that among L-ranges (T20), and hence identity of L-contents coincides with identity of L-ranges (T21).

+**T23-20.** $\mathrm{Lc}\,\mathfrak{T}_j \subset \mathrm{Lc}\,\mathfrak{T}_i$ if and only if $\mathrm{Lr}\,\mathfrak{T}_i \subset \mathrm{Lr}\,\mathfrak{T}_j$. (From T1, T18–1.)

+**T23-21.** $\mathrm{Lc}\,\mathfrak{T}_i = \mathrm{Lc}\,\mathfrak{T}_j$ if and only if $\mathrm{Lr}\,\mathfrak{T}_i = \mathrm{Lr}\,\mathfrak{T}_j$. (From T20.)

This result (T20) suggests a definition for 'L-content' which is in accordance with the postulates. If we suppose that the metalanguage M contains the concepts 'L-state' and 'L-range' as explained earlier (D18–B1, 4 and 5), then we may define $Lc\mathfrak{T}_i$ as the class of those L-states which do not L-imply $\mathfrak{T}_i$ or, in other words, the class of those L-states which do not belong to $Lr\mathfrak{T}_i$:

+**D23-B1.** $Lc\mathfrak{T}_i$ (in S) $=_{Df} -Lr\mathfrak{T}_i$.

This definition would accord well with our intention concerning the concept of L-content. For the assertive power of a sentence consists in its excluding certain states of affairs; the more it excludes, the more it asserts (Karl Popper). Hence the class of the L-states excluded by $\mathfrak{T}_i$ may well serve as a representation of the assertive power of $\mathfrak{T}_i$. The following theorems hold on the basis of DB1 and theorems in § 18B.

+**T23-B1.** $Lc\mathfrak{T}_j \subset Lc\mathfrak{T}_i$ if and only if $\mathfrak{T}_i \ \overrightarrow{L} \ \mathfrak{T}_j$. (From DB1, T18–B18 and 19.)

T23-B2. $Lc\mathfrak{T}_i = \Lambda_s$ if and only if $\mathfrak{T}_i$ is L-true. (From DB1, T18–B29.)

T23-B3. $Lc\mathfrak{T}_i = V$ if and only if $\mathfrak{T}_i$ is L-false. (From DB1, T18–B30.)

The concept defined by DB1 fulfills the postulates P1 and 2 (TB1). We need not base this concept of L-content on that of L-range (as is done in DB1). We may instead introduce it independently by rules of L-contents analogous to the rules of L-ranges. The other L-concepts can then be defined on the basis of L-content in analogy to the way in which we defined them previously on the basis of 'L-range' (§ 20). If we suppose that, in addition to 'L-content', the term 'rs', designating the real L-state, is given, we may define here the radical concepts too in analogy to D20–13ff. Thus e.g. $\mathfrak{T}_i$ is defined as true if the real L-state is not one of the L-states excluded by $\mathfrak{T}_i$ and hence does not belong to $Lc\mathfrak{T}_i$:

+**D23-B2.** $\mathfrak{T}_i$ is *true* (in S) $=_{Df}$ not rs $\epsilon\ Lc\mathfrak{T}_i$.

We have remarked previously that a concept 'L-range' based on the concept 'L-state' — where an L-state is something not on the side of the language but on the side of the designata — requires a non-extensional metalanguage (§ 18). The same holds for a concept 'L-content' defined on the same basis. Further, we have discussed possibilities of defining a concept 'L-range' in an extensional language (§ 19). An analogous procedure is possible with respect to 'L-content'.

In the following we shall show two ways for defining a concept 'L-content' within an extensional language (DF1 and DG1) on the basis of 'L-implicate' in such a way that our earlier postulates (P1 and 2) are fulfilled. It seems natural to characterize the assertive power of $\mathfrak{T}_i$ by stating which sentences follow from $\mathfrak{T}_i$. This leads to DF1.

+**D23-F1.** $\mathrm{Lc}\mathfrak{T}_i$ (in S) $=_{\mathrm{Df}}$ the class of those sentences (in S) which are L-implicates of $\mathfrak{T}_i$.

+**T23-F1.** If $\mathfrak{T}_i \overrightarrow{\mathrm{L}} \mathfrak{T}_j$, then $\mathrm{Lc}\mathfrak{T}_j \subset \mathrm{Lc}\mathfrak{T}_i$. (From DF1, P14–5.)

+**T23-F2.** If $\mathrm{Lc}\mathfrak{T}_j \subset \mathrm{Lc}\mathfrak{T}_i$, then $\mathfrak{T}_i \overrightarrow{\mathrm{L}} \mathfrak{T}_j$. (From DF1, P14–8, 11, and 12.)

TF1 and 2 show that the concept 'L-content' as defined by DF1 fulfills the postulates P1 and 2 and hence is in accordance with our intentions. Therefore, the theorems based above on P1 and 2 hold here, too. Since in DF1 $\mathrm{Lc}\mathfrak{T}_i$ is defined as a sentential class, it has the same status here as $\mathfrak{T}_i$ itself. The following theorems are based on this special feature.

T23-F3. $\mathrm{Lc}\Lambda =$ the class of the L-true sentences (of S). (From DF1, T14–34.)

+**T23-F4.** $\mathrm{Lc}\mathfrak{T}_i =$ the class of the L-true sentences (of S) if and only if $\mathfrak{T}_i$ is L-true. (From TF3, T14–51b, T2.)

T23-F5. $\mathrm{Lc}V = V$. (From DF1, T14–41.)

T23-F6. $\mathrm{Lc}\mathfrak{T}_i = V$ if and only if $\mathfrak{T}_i$ is L-comprehensive. (From TF5, D14–5, T2.)

T23-F7. If S contains an L-false $\mathfrak{T}_j$, then for every $\mathfrak{T}_i$, $\mathrm{Lc}\mathfrak{T}_i = V$ if and only if $\mathfrak{T}_i$ is L-false. (From TF6, T14–107b.)

T23-F11. $\mathfrak{S}_i \, \epsilon \, \mathrm{Lc}\mathfrak{S}_i$. (From DF1, P14–8.)

T23-F12. $\mathfrak{R}_i \subset \mathrm{Lc}\mathfrak{R}_i$. (From DF1, P14–11.)

T23-F13. $\mathfrak{T}_i$ and $\mathrm{Lc}\mathfrak{T}_i$ are L-equivalent. (From TF11 and 12, P14–11 and 12; P14–12.)

T23-F16. $\mathrm{Lc}(\mathrm{Lc}\mathfrak{T}_i) = \mathrm{Lc}\mathfrak{T}_i$. (From DF1, P14–5.)

The following theorems show the close connection between the concept 'L-content' as defined by DF1 and the concept 'L-perfect' (D14–7):

T23-F20. Each of the following conditions is a sufficient and necessary condition for $\Re_i$ to be L-perfect:

    a. $\mathrm{Lc}\Re_i \subset \Re_i$.

    b. $\mathrm{Lc}\Re_i = \Re_i$.

    (From D14–7, DF1; TF12, (a).)

T23-F21. For every $\mathfrak{T}_i$, $\mathrm{Lc}\mathfrak{T}_i$ is L-perfect. (From DF1, T14–118.)

The consideration that among the L-implicates of $\mathfrak{T}_i$ the L-true sentences are not characteristic for the content of $\mathfrak{T}_i$ because they are L-implicates of every $\mathfrak{T}_j$ may suggest the following definition DG1 as an alternative to DF1. The resulting theorem TG16 also speaks, perhaps, in favor of DG1; on the other hand, this definition is somewhat less simple than DF1.

+D23-G1. $\mathrm{Lc}\mathfrak{T}_i$ (in S) $=_{Df}$ the class of those sentences (of S) which are L-implicates of $\mathfrak{T}_i$ and not L-true.

The following theorems are based on this definition:

T23-G1 (lemma). If $\mathfrak{S}_i$ is not L-true, $\mathfrak{S}_i \in \mathrm{Lc}\mathfrak{S}_i$. (From DG1, P14–8.)

T23-G2 (lemma). If $\mathrm{Lc}\Re_j \subset \mathrm{Lc}\mathfrak{T}_i$, then $\mathfrak{T}_i \mathrel{\overrightarrow{\mathrm{L}}} \Re_j$.

Proof. Let $\Re_k$ be the class of the L-true sentences of $\Re_j$, and $\Re_l$ the class of the non-L-true sentences of $\Re_j$. Hence $\Re_j = \Re_k + \Re_l$. Then $\Re_k$ is L-true (P14–13); hence $\Re_l \mathrel{\overrightarrow{\mathrm{L}}} \Re_j$ (T14–56). $\Re_l \subset \mathrm{Lc}\Re_j$ (P14–11), hence $\Re_l \subset \mathrm{Lc}\mathfrak{T}_i$, $\mathfrak{T}_i \mathrel{\overrightarrow{\mathrm{L}}} \Re_l$ (P14–12), and $\mathfrak{T}_i \mathrel{\overrightarrow{\mathrm{L}}} \Re_j$ (P14–5).

T23-G3. If $\mathrm{Lc}\mathfrak{T}_j \subset \mathrm{Lc}\mathfrak{T}_i$, then $\mathfrak{T}_i \mathrel{\overrightarrow{\mathrm{L}}} \mathfrak{T}_j$. (For $\Re_j$ as $\mathfrak{T}_j$, this follows from TG2; for a non-L-true $\mathfrak{S}_j$, from TG1; for an L-true $\mathfrak{S}_j$, from DG1, P14–14.)

T23-G4. If $\mathfrak{T}_i \mathrel{\overrightarrow{\mathrm{L}}} \mathfrak{T}_j$, then $\mathrm{Lc}\mathfrak{T}_j \subset \mathrm{Lc}\mathfrak{T}_i$. (From DG1, P14–5.)

+T23-G5. $\mathrm{Lc}\mathfrak{T}_j \subset \mathrm{Lc}\mathfrak{T}_i$ if and only if $\mathfrak{T}_i \mathrel{\overrightarrow{\mathrm{L}}} \mathfrak{T}_j$. (From TG3, TG4.)

Hereby it is shown that the concept 'L-content' as defined here also fulfills the postulates P1 and 2. Therefore the theorems based on P1 and 2 hold here, too. Further, we have here the following theorems:

T23-G10 (lemma). If $\mathfrak{S}_i$ is not L-true and $\mathfrak{S}_i \in \Re_j$, then $\mathfrak{S}_i \in \mathrm{Lc}\Re_j$. (From DG1, P14–11.)

T23-G11. If no sentence of $\Re_i$ is L-true, then $\Re_i \subset \mathrm{Lc}\Re_i$. (From TG10.)

T23-G12 (lemma). If $\Re_i$ is not L-true, then there is an $\mathfrak{S}_j$ such that $\mathfrak{S}_j \in \Re_i$ and $\mathfrak{S}_j \in \mathrm{Lc}\Re_i$. (From P14–13, TG10.)

T23-G13. $\mathrm{Lc}\mathfrak{S}_i \mathrel{\overrightarrow{\mathrm{L}}} \mathfrak{S}_i$. (From DG1, P14–8, 11, 14.)

T23-G14. $\mathrm{Lc}\Lambda = \Lambda$. (From DG1, T14–34.)

T23-G15 (lemma). If $\mathfrak{T}_i$ is not L-true, then not $\mathrm{Lc}\mathfrak{T}_i = \Lambda$. (From DG1, P14–8, TG12.)

+**T23-G16.** $\mathrm{Lc}\mathfrak{T}_i = \Lambda$ if and only if $\mathfrak{T}_i$ is L-true. (From TG15, P14–6.)

+**T23-G20.** $\mathrm{Lc}V$ = the class of the non-L-true sentences. (From DG1, T14–41.)

T23-G25 (lemma). $\mathfrak{T}_i \; \mathbf{\mathtt{\Gamma}} \, \mathrm{Lc}\mathfrak{T}_i$. (From DG1, P14–12.)

T23-G26. If $\mathfrak{S}_j \,\epsilon\, \mathfrak{R}_i$, then $\mathrm{Lc}\mathfrak{R}_i \; \mathbf{\mathtt{\Gamma}} \, \mathfrak{S}_j$. (From DG1, P14–11, P14–14.)

T23-G27 (lemma). $\mathrm{Lc}\mathfrak{T}_i \; \mathbf{\mathtt{\Gamma}} \, \mathfrak{T}_i$. (From TG26, P14–12, TG13.)

+**T23-G28.** $\mathfrak{T}_i$ and $\mathrm{Lc}\mathfrak{T}_i$ are L-equivalent. (From TG25, 27.)

+**T23-G35.** $\mathrm{Lc}(\mathrm{Lc}\mathfrak{T}_i) = \mathrm{Lc}\mathfrak{T}_i$. (From DG1, P14–11; TG25, P14–5.)

A comparison of the theorems holding in each of the two ways just explained for defining 'L-content' (DF1 and DG1) shows the following. In the first case, the class of L-true sentences is contained in every L-content (TF3, T5); hence (provided there are L-true sentences in S) there is no null L-content, in contradistinction to the second case (TG14). There is a certain relationship between TF5 and TG14, and between TF3 and TG20. The two ways agree in certain features (e.g. TF13 and TG28; TF16 and TG35). On the other hand, TF11 and TF12 do not hold in the second case.

The possibility of simple definitions for 'L-content' (DF1, DG1) in combination with the relation between L-contents and L-ranges (T20) suggests equally simple ways for defining '*L-range*' in such a way that $\mathrm{Lr}\mathfrak{T}_i$ is a sentential class. Because of T20, we defined $\mathrm{Lc}\mathfrak{T}_i$ above as the complement of $\mathrm{Lr}\mathfrak{T}_i$ (DB1), both on the side of the designata. Now, on the side of the expressions of the object language, we may take the inverse procedure and define $\mathrm{Lr}\mathfrak{T}_i$ as the complement of $\mathrm{Lc}\mathfrak{T}_i$, the latter either defined by DF1 or by DG1. Thus we come to the two procedures F and G as explained in § 19.

Note on L-semantics (added 1958). The problems of the L-concepts are discussed in greater detail in [Meaning]; the L-concepts are defined by a method similar to, but simpler than procedure E in § 19. — If logical relations hold between the primitive descriptive constants (as discussed in the last paragraph in § 16, 2a), then these relations must be expressed by meaning postulates (see [Postulates]).

D. SYNTAX

This chapter deals with pure syntax, i.e. the theory of syntactical systems or calculi. The rules of a calculus determine the procedure of formal deduction, i.e. of the construction of proofs and derivations. We shall first use the ordinary terminology (§§ 25 to 27) and then introduce the C-terminology (§ 28, e.g. 'C-false' for 'refutable'), which shows the close analogy between syntax and semantics, especially L-semantics.

§ 24. Calculi

A syntactical system or *calculus K* is a system of formal rules. It consists of a classification of signs, the *rules of formation* (defining 'sentence in *K*'), and the *rules of deduction*. The rules of deduction usually consist of primitive sentences and rules of inference (defining 'directly derivable in *K*'). Sometimes, *K* contains also rules of refutation (defining 'directly refutable in *K*'). If *K* contains definitions they may be regarded as additional rules of deduction.

The last two chapters (B and C) dealt with semantics and, more precisely, with pure semantics, i.e. the analysis of semantical systems, systems of semantical rules, in contradistinction to descriptive semantics, i.e. the analysis of the semantical features of empirically given languages (§ 5). Now we come to the third branch of semiotic, to *syntax*, the field of investigation restricted to formal analysis without referring either to the users of the language or to the designata of the expressions (§ 4). And here, again, not empirically given languages but systems of rules will be studied; thus our field will be not descriptive syntax but *pure syntax* (§ 5). The system of rules may either be freely invented or constructed with regard to an empirically given language. The relation to this language is in this case analogous to the relation previously explained between a semantical system and an empirically given language.

A system of syntactical rules is called a *syntactical system* or a **calculus**. Systems of this kind have been studied much more than semantical systems. While the construction and investigation of semantical systems has begun only in recent years, calculi have been built and analyzed throughout the development of modern symbolic logic during the last hundred years, although the formulations have often not strictly satisfied the requirement of formality. And much older still is the method of postulate systems, dating back to Euclid, which prepared the way for the method of calculi. [For the distinction between a system of postulates or axioms and a calculus, see [Foundations] § 16; compare § 37, 'Primitive Sentence', and § 38 (f).] For these reasons we may be much briefer in the following exposition of the syntactical method than we could in the explanation of semantics.

We shall describe the construction of calculi first in ordinary terminology (in two formulations, formulation A without 'Λ' (§§ 24 and 25), formulation B with 'Λ' (§ 26)); later we shall introduce the C-terms (§ 28). The latter are convenient because of their analogy with semantical terms, especially in investigations dealing with both syntax and semantics. But we do not propose to abolish the ordinary terminology entirely. Since it is customary and many of its terms are well-established, it may be kept, at least for purely syntactical studies.

The first steps of the construction of a calculus K are similar to those of a semantical system. We must first give a *classification of the signs* of K, specifying as many classes of signs as are necessary for the formulation of the syntactical rules. Then we lay down the **rules of formation** for K, in other words, the definition of '**sentence** in K'. There is a difference between these rules and the rules of formation of a semantical system. In the latter rules we may refer to the designata of the signs, although it is not often done. But in the syntactical rules of formation this is not permitted; they must be formal. They specify which expressions are sentences by describing the kinds of signs occurring and the order in which they occur. And the definitions of these kinds, i.e. the classification of signs, must also be strictly formal. The definition of 'sentence in K' is often given in a recursive form; first some simple forms of sentences are described, and then certain operations for the construction of compound sentences out of the initial forms.

The essential part of a calculus consists of the **rules of deduction** (or transformation). They describe how proofs and derivations may be constructed; in other words, they constitute definitions for 'provable in K' and 'derivable in K' and sometimes other concepts. The customary procedure is this. First, **primitive sentences** are laid down, either by an enumeration, or by the stipulation that all sentences of certain forms are admitted as primitive sentences. In the latter case (primitive sentential schemata, see e.g. [Syntax] § 11) the number of primitive sentences may be transfinite. Secondly, **rules of inference** are laid down. They can be formulated in this way: " $\mathfrak{S}_j$ is directly derivable from $\mathfrak{R}_i$ if and only if one of the following conditions is fulfilled", and then each rule states a formal condition for $\mathfrak{R}_i$ and $\mathfrak{S}_j$. Thus, the rules of inference define '**directly derivable** in K'. Sometimes, but not often, **rules of refutation** are also laid down, defining '**directly refutable** in K'.

Further, a calculus K may contain **definitions**. The purpose of a definition is to introduce a new sign on the basis of the primitive signs of K and the signs defined by earlier definitions; thus the order of the definitions is essential. A definition may have the form either of a sentence (in the case of a recursive definition, several sentences), called a definition sentence (or defining sentence or definitory sentence) or

simply definition, or of a rule called a definition rule (or de
fining rule or definitory rule). A definition sentence in K may
be regarded as an additional primitive sentence in K, a
definition rule for K as an additional rule of inference for K.
A definition sentence may, for example, have the form
$\mathfrak{A}_1 =_{Df} \mathfrak{A}_2$, or $\mathfrak{A}_1 \equiv \mathfrak{A}_2$, or $\mathfrak{A}_1 = \mathfrak{A}_2$, a definition rule e.g.
' '. . .' for '- - -' ' where 'for' is short for 'is short for' or for
'is directly C-interchangeable with'. $\mathfrak{A}_1$ or '. . .' is called the
definiendum; it contains the sign defined. $\mathfrak{A}_2$ or '- - -' is called
the *definiens*; it contains only primitive signs and signs defined
by earlier definitions. In addition, the definiendum and the
definiens may and usually do contain free variables. If a definition is laid down, then it is permissible to replace the definiendum in any context by the definiens and vice versa, and to
do the same with any expressions constructed out of the definiendum and the definiens by the same substitutions for the
free variables. In other words, any two expressions of this
kind are C-interchangeable; i.e. any two sentences containing
them and being otherwise alike are directly derivable from
one another. Definitions must fulfill certain requirements
(see [Syntax] §§ 8 and 29) in order to assure (1) translatability in both directions, for introducing and for eliminating the
new sign; (2) the C-consistency of the calculus containing
the definition if the original calculus is C-consistent; (3) the
unique interpretation of the defined signs if the primitive
signs are interpreted. For the sake of simplicity, we will
leave aside definitions as parts of calculi in the following
discussions.

§ 25. Proofs and Derivations

We distinguish between two terminologies for syntax: the ordinary terminology, using the terms 'provable', 'derivable', 'refutable', etc., and the C-terminology, using instead 'C-true', 'C-implicate', 'C-false', etc. Within the ordinary terminology, we again distinguish two versions, called formulations A and B, B being characterized by the use of the null sentential class Λ. In this section, formulation A, which is more frequently used by other authors, is briefly explained. It will, however, not be used further on in this book.

On the basis of the rules of deduction for a calculus K, proofs and derivations in K are constructed. The explanations of the method for these constructions can be given in the form of definitions of the syntactical terms 'proof in K', and 'derivation in K'. These definitions can be stated uniformly for all calculi (of the customary kind). Therefore we may state them as definitions in *general syntax*, taking 'sentence', 'primitive sentence', 'directly derivable', and 'directly refutable' as basic terms. In special syntax, these four terms are defined separately for every single calculus, as indicated above (see the examples in § 27).

There are two ways of formulating syntax, differing in the use of the terms 'proof', 'provable,' 'derivation', 'derivable'. We call them formulations A and B. We regard both A and B as versions of the *ordinary terminology*, from which we shall distinguish the new C-terminology (§ 28). *Formulation A* is based on the following definitions DA1 to 4. Formulation B will be introduced in § 26. In § 27, some examples of calculi will be exhibited in both formulations. After that, only formulation B will occasionally be used, in addition to the prevailing C-terminology. (For terminological remarks concerning the terms 'syntax', 'formal', and 'derivable', see § 37.)

D25-A1. A sequence $\mathfrak{R}_k$ of sentences in K is a *proof* in

$K =_{Df}$ every sentence $\mathfrak{S}_l$ of $\mathfrak{R}_k$ is either a primitive sentence in K or directly derivable in K from a class $\mathfrak{R}_m$ of sentences which precede $\mathfrak{S}_l$ in $\mathfrak{R}_k$.

D25-A2. $\mathfrak{S}_j$ is *provable* in $K =_{Df} \mathfrak{S}_j$ is the last sentence of a proof in K.

D25-A3. A sequence $\mathfrak{R}_k$ of sentences in K is a *derivation with the premiss-class* $\mathfrak{R}_i$ in $K =_{Df}$ every sentence $\mathfrak{S}_l$ of $\mathfrak{R}_k$ is either an element of $\mathfrak{R}_i$ or a primitive sentence in K or directly derivable in K from a class $\mathfrak{R}_m$ of sentences which precede $\mathfrak{S}_l$ in $\mathfrak{R}_k$.

D25-A4. $\mathfrak{S}_j$ is *derivable* from $\mathfrak{R}_i$ in $K =_{Df} \mathfrak{S}_j$ is the last sentence of a derivation with the premiss-class $\mathfrak{R}_i$ in K.

The terms 'refutable', 'decidable', and 'undecidable' may be defined here on the basis of 'directly refutable' and the terms just defined, in the same way in which we shall define them later in formulation B (D26–6 to 8).

A sequence consisting of only one primitive sentence is, according to DA1, also a proof. This leads to TA1.

T25-A1. Every primitive sentence in K is provable in K.

Therefore, in analogy to the term 'directly derivable', we might use the term 'directly provable' instead of 'primitive sentence'.

When a rule of inference states that $\mathfrak{S}_j$ is directly derivable from $\mathfrak{R}_i$ if such and such a condition is fulfilled, the premiss-class $\mathfrak{R}_i$ may be either finite or transfinite. The rule is accordingly called a *finite* or a *transfinite rule*. Till recently, all rules applied in systems of modern logic have been finite; $\mathfrak{R}_i$ usually contains one or two sentences. In recent years, however, it has been found that transfinite rules can be applied, and that they are useful and even necessary for certain purposes. On the other hand, calculi containing transfinite rules are more complicated than other ones and have in some respects fundamentally different features (on transfinite rules see [Syntax] §§ 14 and 34a, [Foundations] § 10). It is planned for a later volume of these studies to explain and discuss the use of transfinite rules from the point of view of syntax and semantics. [Up to the present, the application of transfinite rules has not been made in the form of proofs and derivations, i.e. in sequences of sentences, but rather in a quite different form of deduction, e.g. in series of sentential classes (consequence-series, see e.g. [Syntax] § 14) or without any sequence or series, with the help of the concept 'sentential class closed with respect to direct derivability'. It will, however, be shown that the application of transfinite rules can also be made in the form of transfinite proofs or derivations. The definitions DA1 to 4 given above are then sufficient to cover the use of transfinite rules also; by a (finite or transfinite) sequence we understand a one-many correlation of sentences with the ordinal numbers of a (finite or transfinite) initial segment of the series of ordinal numbers. Hence a proof or derivation in which no repetition of sentences occurs may be regarded as a well-ordered series of sentences.]

§ 26. The Null Sentential Class in Syntax

In *formulation B*, the *null sentential class* Λ is used in the following way. Instead of (or besides) 'primitive sentence' we say 'directly derivable from Λ'; instead of 'provable', 'derivable from Λ'. In our subsequent discussions, formulation B will occasionally be used in addition to the C-terminology, which will be introduced later and then be used chiefly.

We cannot deal with syntax or, in other words, with formal logic, with deduction, by merely speaking about sentences; we have to speak about sentential classes also. (This fact is often not sufficiently noticed.) When this is done, there is no reason for not using the concept of the null class which has proved itself so very useful in the theory of classes and all its applications. We have seen the role of the *null sentential class* Λ in semantics (D9–7), especially in connection with L-concepts (see e.g. T14–30ff). In syntax likewise, the use of this concept leads to a simplification of definitions and theorems.

According to D25–A3, a derivation with the premiss-class Λ is a sequence $\Re_k$ of sentences such that every sentence of $\Re_k$ is either a primitive sentence or directly derivable from a class of preceding sentences; hence, according to D25-A1, it is the same as a proof (TA1).

T26-A1. $\mathfrak{R}_k$ is a proof in K if and only if $\mathfrak{R}_k$ is a derivation in K with the premiss-class Λ. (From D25-A1 and 3.)

T26-A2. $\mathfrak{S}_i$ is provable in K if and only if $\mathfrak{S}_i$ is derivable from Λ in K. (From TA1, D25-A2.)

On the basis of these results it will be possible in general syntax to define 'proof' and 'provable' by 'derivation' (D3 and 5).

T26-A3. Every primitive sentence (in K) is derivable from Λ. (From T25-A1 and T26-A2.)

Therefore we may use the term 'directly derivable from Λ' instead of 'primitive sentence'. This has the advantage that the two parts of the rules of deduction assume the same form. Seen from this point of view, a primitive sentence is nothing else than the special case of a rule of inference where $\mathfrak{R}_i$ is Λ. (As an example, see § 27, formulation IIIB of the rules of deduction for K_1.) In this way, we come to a slight modification of the formulation A, explained in § 25; we call it *formulation B* (of the ordinary terminology).

If we want to construct a system of *general syntax*, then the preceding considerations suggest that in formulation B we take '**directly derivable**' *as primitive term*, in addition to '*sentence*' and '**directly refutable**'. [Another concept for which we shall later introduce the term 'C-disjunct' would have to be taken as primitive also because it is not definable by those mentioned; but we shall not make use of it at present.] In special syntax, these terms are defined by the rules of a calculus (see the examples in § 27); here we take them as given. We take 'directly refutable $\mathfrak{R}_i$' as primitive because 'directly refutable $\mathfrak{S}_i$' is definable by it, but not vice versa. 'Directly derivable' is taken as a relation between a sentence and a class. We define 'primitive sentence' only in order to come into accordance with formulation A; it will not be used, however, in subsequent definitions.

D26-1. $\mathfrak{S}_j$ is a *primitive sentence* (in K) $=_{\mathrm{Df}}$ $\mathfrak{S}_j$ is directly derivable from Λ.

+**D26-2.** $\mathfrak{R}_k$ is a **derivation** *with the premiss-class* $\mathfrak{R}_i$ (in K) $=_{\mathrm{Df}}$ $\mathfrak{R}_k$ is a sequence of sentences such that every sentence $\mathfrak{S}_l$ of $\mathfrak{R}_k$ is either an element of $\mathfrak{R}_i$ or directly derivable from a class $\mathfrak{R}_m$ of sentences which precede $\mathfrak{S}_l$ in $\mathfrak{R}_k$.

+**D26-3.** $\mathfrak{R}_k$ is a **proof** (in K) $=_{\mathrm{Df}}$ $\mathfrak{R}_k$ is a derivation with the premiss-class Λ.

+**D26-4.**

    a. $\mathfrak{S}_j$ is **derivable** *from* $\mathfrak{R}_i$ (in K) $=_{\mathrm{Df}}$ $\mathfrak{S}_j$ is the last sentence in a derivation with the premiss-class $\mathfrak{R}_i$.

    b. $\mathfrak{R}_j$ is derivable from $\mathfrak{R}_i$ (in K) $=_{\mathrm{Df}}$ every sentence of $\mathfrak{R}_j$ is derivable from $\mathfrak{R}_i$.

    c. $\mathfrak{T}_j$ is derivable from $\mathfrak{S}_i$ (in K) $=_{\mathrm{Df}}$ $\mathfrak{T}_j$ is derivable from $\{\mathfrak{S}_i\}$.

+**D26-5.** $\mathfrak{T}_j$ is **provable** (in K) $=_{\mathrm{Df}}$ $\mathfrak{T}_j$ is derivable from Λ.
If $\mathfrak{S}_j$ has been laid down as directly refutable, then a derivation leading from $\mathfrak{R}_i$ to $\mathfrak{S}_j$ could be regarded as a refutation for $\mathfrak{R}_i$ (corresponding to the *modus tollens* in traditional logic). This suggests the following definition for refutable.

+**D26-6.** $\mathfrak{T}_i$ is **refutable** (in K) $=_{\mathrm{Df}}$ there is a $\mathfrak{T}_j$ which is directly refutable and derivable from $\mathfrak{T}_i$.

D26-7. $\mathfrak{T}_i$ is **decidable** (in K) $=_{\mathrm{Df}}$ $\mathfrak{T}_i$ is either provable or refutable.

D26-8. $\mathfrak{T}_i$ is **undecidable** (in K) $=_{\mathrm{Df}}$ $\mathfrak{T}_i$ is not decidable.

We shall mention a few very simple theorems which follow from the definitions given.

+**T26-1.** $\mathfrak{S}_j$ is provable if and only if $\mathfrak{S}_j$ is the last sentence of a proof. (From D5, 4, 3.)

+**T26-2.** Derivability is **a.** reflexive, **b.** transitive. (From D4 and 2.)

T26-3. If $\mathfrak{T}_i$ is provable and $\mathfrak{T}_j$ is derivable from $\mathfrak{T}_i$, then $\mathfrak{T}_j$ is also provable. (From D5, T2b.)

§ 27. Examples of Calculi

Two calculi, K_1 and K_2, are given as examples, in both formulations A and B. K_1 and K_2 are similar to the ordinary propositional calculus, but K_2 contains, in addition, a rule of refutation. A proof and two derivations in these calculi are constructed as examples.

We shall construct two calculi K_1 and K_2 similar to each other which possess the same signs and sentences as the semantical system S_3 (§§ 8 and 15) and have, in addition, a close relationship to S_3 in another respect that will be discussed later. Because of the accordance with S_3, we need not formulate the classification of signs and the rules of formation here again; they have already been formulated in a formal way for S_3. The rules of deduction are given in the two formulations A (§ 25) and B (with 'Λ', § 26). The rules of deduction are those of the *propositional calculus* in the form of Hilbert and Bernays (see Hilbert and Ackermann, *Grundzüge d. theor. Logik*). There is one rule of inference (IIIA2); it corresponds to the *modus ponens* of traditional logic. This rule is usually given in the form "From $\mathfrak{S}_k \supset \mathfrak{S}_j$ and $\mathfrak{S}_k$, $\mathfrak{S}_j$ follows", or, if there is no sign of implication but a sign of disjunction, as in K_1, "From $\sim\mathfrak{S}_k \vee \mathfrak{S}_j$ and $\mathfrak{S}_k$, $\mathfrak{S}_j$ follows". The formulation given below is the same, only brought into the form of a definition for 'directly derivable'. A practical justification of the rules of deduction of K_1 will be given later by a comparison of K_1 with S_3 (§ 35).

Rules of the calculus K_1

I. *Classification of signs of K_1:* the same as in S_3 (three individual constants, two predicates, parentheses, '$\sim$', '$\vee$ ').

II. *Rules of formation for K_1:* the same as in S_3 (three forms of sentences: atomic sentences, negations, disjunctions).

III. *Rules of deduction for K_1:*

    A. (Formulation A without 'Λ'.)

        1. A sentence $\mathfrak{S}_i$ in K_1 is a *primitive sentence* in $K_1 =_{Df} \mathfrak{S}_i$ has one of the following four forms:

    1a. $\sim(\mathfrak{S}_k \vee \mathfrak{S}_k) \vee \mathfrak{S}_k$.

    1b. $\sim\mathfrak{S}_k \vee (\mathfrak{S}_k \vee \mathfrak{S}_l)$.

    1c. $\sim(\mathfrak{S}_k \vee \mathfrak{S}_l) \vee (\mathfrak{S}_l \vee \mathfrak{S}_k)$.

    1d. $\sim(\sim\mathfrak{S}_k \vee \mathfrak{S}_l) \vee (\sim(\mathfrak{S}_m \vee \mathfrak{S}_k) \vee (\mathfrak{S}_m \vee \mathfrak{S}_l))$.

2. *One rule of inference.* $\mathfrak{S}_j$ is directly derivable from $\mathfrak{R}_i$ in $K_1 =_{Df}$ there is an $\mathfrak{S}_k$ such that $\mathfrak{R}_i = \{\sim\mathfrak{S}_k \vee \mathfrak{S}_j, \mathfrak{S}_k\}$.

4. Definitions of a. 'proof in K_1', b. 'provable in K_1', c. 'derivation in K_1', d. 'derivable in K_1' as in D25–A1 to 4 (D26–4).

B. (Formulation B with 'Λ'.)

    2. $\mathfrak{S}_j$ is directly derivable from $\mathfrak{R}_i$ in $K_1 =_{Df} \mathfrak{S}_j$ and $\mathfrak{R}_i$ fulfill one of the following five conditions.

	$\mathfrak{R}_i$ is:	$\mathfrak{S}_j$ is:
2a.	Λ	$\sim(\mathfrak{S}_k \vee \mathfrak{S}_k) \vee \mathfrak{S}_k$
2b.	Λ	$\sim\mathfrak{S}_k \vee (\mathfrak{S}_k \vee \mathfrak{S}_l)$
2c.	Λ	$\sim(\mathfrak{S}_k \vee \mathfrak{S}_l) \vee (\mathfrak{S}_l \vee \mathfrak{S}_k)$
2d.	Λ	$\sim(\sim\mathfrak{S}_k \vee \mathfrak{S}_l) \vee (\sim(\mathfrak{S}_m \vee \mathfrak{S}_k) \vee (\mathfrak{S}_m \vee \mathfrak{S}_l))$
2e.	$\{\sim\mathfrak{S}_k \vee \mathfrak{S}_j, \mathfrak{S}_k\}$	$\mathfrak{S}_j$

4. Definitions of a. 'derivation', b. 'proof', c. 'derivable', d. 'provable' as in D26–2 to 5 (and, if wanted, of e. 'primitive sentence' as in D26–1).

The *rules of the calculus K_2* consist of those of K_1, and, in addition, a rule of refutation. For the latter, there is no distinction between formulations A and B.

III. Rules of deduction for K_2.

    Either IIIA1 and 2 or IIIB2 as for K_1.

    3. *Rule of refutation* for K_2. The class $\{\text{'P(a)'}, \text{'}\sim\text{P(a)'}\}$ ($\mathfrak{R}_1$) alone is directly refutable in K_2.

    (Instead of (3), the simple rule "V is directly refutable" could be taken.)

    4. Definitions of 'derivation', 'proof', 'derivable', 'provable', 'refutable' as in D26–2 to 6.

The following sequence of sentences is a *proof* in K_1 and hence also in K_2, in accordance with IIIA4a or IIIB4b respectively, as is easily confirmed by applying the following rules for the formulations A and B:

sentence	A	B
i	1d	2d
ii	1a	2a
iii	i,ii,2	2e
iv	1b	2b
v	iii,iv,2	2e

That the first sentence has the form required by (1d) or (2d) is easily seen if we take 'P(a) V P(a)' as $\mathfrak{S}_k$, 'P(a)' as $\mathfrak{S}_l$, '$\sim$P(a)' as $\mathfrak{S}_m$.

$$\sim(\sim(P(a){\vee}P(a)){\vee}P(a)){\vee}(\sim(\sim P(a){\vee}(P(a){\vee}P(a))){\vee}(\sim P(a){\vee}P(a)))$$
$$\sim(P(a){\vee}P(a)){\vee}P(a)$$
$$\sim(\sim P(a){\vee}(P(a){\vee}P(a))){\vee}(\sim P(a){\vee}P(a))$$
$$\sim P(a){\vee}(P(a){\vee}P(a))$$
$$\sim P(a){\vee}P(a)$$

Hence, '$\sim$P(a)V P(a)' is provable in K_1 and in K_2. An analogous sequence of sentences with any other sentence $\mathfrak{S}_i$ in the place of 'P(a)' throughout would also be a proof, according to the same rules. Therefore, every sentence of the form $\sim\mathfrak{S}_i{\vee}\mathfrak{S}_i$ is provable in K_1 and in K_2.

The following sequence of sentences is a *derivation* in K_1 and in K_2 with the first sentence as premiss.

A	B		
premiss	premiss	P(b)V Q(c)	(i)
1c	2c	$\sim$(P(b)V Q(c))V (Q(c)V P(b))	(ii)
ii, i, 2	2e	Q(c)V P(b)	(iii)

Hence, 'Q(c) V P(b)' is derivable in K_1 and in K_2 from 'P(b) V Q(c)'; and generally for every $\mathfrak{S}_i$ and $\mathfrak{S}_j$, $\mathfrak{S}_j$ V $\mathfrak{S}_i$ is derivable in K_1 and in K_2 from $\mathfrak{S}_i$ V $\mathfrak{S}_j$.

The following sequence is a *derivation* in K_1 and in K_2 with the first two sentences as premisses.

A	B		
premisses	premisses {	P(c)	(i)
		$\sim$P(c)	(ii)
1b	2b	$\sim(\sim$P(c)) V ($\sim$P(c)V Q(a))	(iii)
iii, ii, 2	2e	$\sim$P(c) V Q(a)	(iv)
iv, i, 2	2e	Q(a)	(v)

Hence, 'Q(a)' is derivable in K_1 and in K_2 from $\{$'P(c)', '$\sim$P(c)'$\}$; and generally for every $\mathfrak{S}_i$ and $\mathfrak{S}_j$, $\mathfrak{S}_j$ is derivable from $\{\mathfrak{S}_i, \sim\mathfrak{S}_i\}$. Thus e.g. 'P(a)' and '$\sim$P(a)' are derivable from any class of the form $\{\mathfrak{S}_i, \sim\mathfrak{S}_i\}$; hence, according to D26–4b, $\{$'P(a)', '$\sim$P(a)'$\}$ is derivable from any such class. Therefore, according to the rule of refutation III3 for K_2 and D26–6, for every $\mathfrak{S}_i$, $\{\mathfrak{S}_i, \sim\mathfrak{S}_i\}$ is refutable in K_2.

The terms 'primitive sentence' and 'premiss' must not be confused. A primitive sentence is a feature of a calculus; when the calculus is interpreted (to be explained later), the primitive sentences are asserted as true. On the other hand, a premiss is a feature of a particular derivation in the calculus. Any sentence of the calculus occurs as a premiss in some derivation. A premiss is not asserted; it is only investigated with respect to its consequences. 'Q(c) ∨ P(b)' is derivable from the premiss 'P(b) ∨ Q(c)' (see example above) even if this premiss is false in a certain interpretation.

The use of the term 'derivable from Λ' in formulation B instead of 'provable' in formulation A is by no means a reduction of the number of primitive sentences to zero. (This misunderstanding has occasionally occurred and led to great confusion, see e.g. *Mind*, vol. 47, 1938, p. 357.) It is merely a change in terminology, which leaves the number of the primitive sentences and even these themselves unchanged. This becomes clear by a comparison of the two formulations A and B for K_1; the number of primitive sentences in both is four (for B, this follows from IIIB2 and 4e).

§ 28. C-Concepts (1)

On the basis of 'direct C-implicate' (in the ordinary terminology, 'directly derivable') and 'directly C-false' ('directly refutable') as primitive terms for a system of general syntax, other C-terms are defined, among them 'C-false', 'C-implicate', 'C-true', 'C-equivalent'.

We shall later discuss the procedure of interpreting a calculus K by assigning designata to the expressions in K (§ 33). This obviously leads outside of syntax, to the field of semantics. But, although interpretations cannot be taken into consideration within syntax, they may and often do influence our practical decisions in the choice of the structure of the calculus, in other words, in the choice of the rules of formation and of deduction. Thus e.g. in constructing the calculus K_1 (§ 27), we had in mind that interpretation of its signs and sentences which is represented by the semantical system S_3 (§§ 8 and 15). It can be shown that every $\mathfrak{T}_i$ provable in K_1 is true and, moreover, L-true in S_3. If somebody were to propose an interpretation for K_1 such that one of the provable sentences, e.g. ' $\sim P(a) \vee P(a)$ ' was false, we should not accept that interpretation as being in accordance with the calculus K_1 (or, as we shall say later, as a true interpretation for K_1). Although the rules of a calculus do not speak about interpretations, they are nevertheless practically meant in such a way as to restrict possible interpretations. The provable sentences are intended to become true *if* we go over from the pure calculus to interpretations. Therefore it seems convenient to apply the term '**C-true** in K' to them (for terminological remarks, see § 37, Prefixes). Further, the refutable sentences or sentential classes (e.g. {'P(c)', ' $\sim P(c)$'} in K_1) are meant to become false. Therefore we shall use for them the term '**C-false**'. And, if $\mathfrak{T}_j$ is derivable from $\mathfrak{T}_i$ in K, then we should not regard an interpretation as fitting for K unless it were such that if $\mathfrak{T}_i$ is true, $\mathfrak{T}_j$ is also true, or in other words, such that $\mathfrak{T}_j$ is an implicate of $\mathfrak{T}_i$. Therefore if $\mathfrak{T}_j$ is derivable from $\mathfrak{T}_i$, we will call $\mathfrak{T}_j$ a **C-implicate** of $\mathfrak{T}_i$. (The definition will differ slightly from this condition; see below.) In an analogous way we use other *C-terms* as syntactical terms corresponding to radical terms of semantics. This *C-terminology* will turn out to be very convenient in our later discussions of relations between calculi and semantical systems. The following table shows the correspondence (which, however, is not in all cases a strict synonymity). (The C-terms in parentheses will not be used in what follows.)

	ORDINARY TERMS	C-TERMS
1	derivable	C-implicate
2	directly derivable	direct C-implicate
3	provable	C-true
4 {A	primitive sentence (directly provable)	(directly C-true)
4 {B	directly derivable from Λ	direct C-implicate of Λ
5	refutable	C-false
6	directly refutable	directly C-false
7	equipollent	C-equivalent
8	decidable	C-determinate
9	undecidable	C-indeterminate
10	incompatible	C-exclusive
11	compatible	non-C-exclusive
12	—	(C-disjunct)

On the basis of the explanations given we shall now lay down definitions for syntactical concepts in C-terminology. As *primitive terms* for these definitions in general syntax we take, in addition to 'sentence', '**direct C-implicate**' *and* '**directly C-false**'. The first of these concepts covers the concept of primitive sentences also because they are construed here as direct C-implicates of Λ. (By making use of 'Λ', the C-terminology is more similar to formulation B of the ordinary terminology than to A.) We shall later give some theorems (§ 29). They are based merely on the definitions; postulates are not needed. This means that in general syntax we do not impose any restrictions upon the choice of the concepts of direct C-implication and direct C-falsity with respect to any calculus. In other words, in constructing a particular calculus *K*, we are entirely free in setting up our rules of formation and deduction, i.e. we may choose any expressions we want to as sentences, any relation between sentences and sentential classes (including Λ) as direct C-implication, any sentences or sentential classes as directly C-false. It is true that if these choices are made in a certain way the calculus will become C-inconsistent (D31–2), but it is nevertheless a calculus. And although from the point of view of practical application it is of course important that a calculus should not be C-inconsistent, not trivial, not too poor in means of expression and means of deduction, in short, should be suitable for the purposes intended, from the point of view of general syntax no discrimination is made. The different kinds of possible structures of calculi are distinguished and studied, but none of these kinds is excluded, not even that of the C-inconsistent calculi.

We begin with definitions (similar to D26–2, 4, and 6) of some terms of the ordinary terminology because they are convenient auxiliary terms for the later definitions of C-terms. For the sake of brevity, we often omit the phrase 'in K', especially in definientia and in theorems.

+**D28-1.** $\Re_k$ is a **derivation** with the premiss-class $\Re_i$ (in K) = $_{Df}$ $\Re_k$ is a sequence of sentences such that every sentence $\mathfrak{S}_l$ of $\Re_k$ is either an element of $\Re_i$ or a direct C-implicate of a class $\Re_m$ of sentences which precede $\mathfrak{S}_l$ in $\Re_k$.

+**D28-2.**

    a. $\mathfrak{S}_j$ is **derivable** from $\Re_i$ (in K) = $_{Df}$ $\mathfrak{S}_j$ is the last sentence in a derivation with the premiss-class $\Re_i$.

    b. $\Re_j$ is derivable from $\Re_i$ (in K) = $_{Df}$ every sentence of $\Re_j$ is derivable from $\Re_i$.

    c. $\mathfrak{T}_j$ is derivable from $\mathfrak{S}_i$ (in K) = $_{Df}$ $\mathfrak{T}_j$ is derivable from $\{\mathfrak{S}_i\}$.

+**D28-3.** $\mathfrak{T}_i$ is **C-false** (in K) = $_{Df}$ there is a $\mathfrak{T}_j$ which is directly C-false and derivable from $\mathfrak{T}_i$.

According to our previous explanations we shall define ' $\mathfrak{T}_j$ is a C-implicate of $\mathfrak{T}_i$ in K' in such a way that it holds whenever $\mathfrak{T}_j$ would become an implicate of $\mathfrak{T}_i$ in every true interpretation of K. This, however, is not only the case if $\mathfrak{T}_j$ is derivable from $\mathfrak{T}_i$, but also if $\mathfrak{T}_i$ is C-false irrespective of $\mathfrak{T}_j$, because in this case $\mathfrak{T}_i$ would become false and hence, according to T9–12, $\mathfrak{T}_j$ would be an implicate of $\mathfrak{T}_i$. This is the reason for adding 'or $\mathfrak{T}_i$ is C-false' in the definiens of D4 below. But this addition and hence the distinction between 'C-implicate' and 'derivable' seldom, if ever, comes into effect in practice, i.e. with respect to the calculi actually constructed so far in logic or mathematics. For, in most of these calculi, no rules of refutation are stated at all; hence in these calculi 'C-false' ('refutable') is empty (T29–54). And in nearly all or perhaps all of the few calculi where rules of refutation are given, 'directly C-false' ('directly refutable') applies only to sentences or sentential classes from which every sentence is derivable (e.g. in K_2, § 27). Therefore (according to T29–55) for these calculi too the new concept 'C-implicate' and the old one 'derivable' coincide.

We use '$\mathfrak{T}_i \overset{\rightharpoonup}{c} \mathfrak{T}_j$' as an abbreviation for '$\mathfrak{T}_j$ is a C-implicate of $\mathfrak{T}_i$', and '$\mathfrak{T}_i \overset{\rightharpoonup}{dc} \mathfrak{T}_j$' for '$\mathfrak{T}_j$ is a direct C-implicate of $\mathfrak{T}_i$'.

+D28-4. $\mathfrak{T}_i \overset{\rightharpoonup}{c} \mathfrak{T}_j$ ($\mathfrak{T}_i$ *C-implies* $\mathfrak{T}_j$; $\mathfrak{T}_j$ is a **C-implicate** of $\mathfrak{T}_i$) (in K) $=_{Df}$ $\mathfrak{T}_j$ is derivable from $\mathfrak{T}_i$ or $\mathfrak{T}_i$ is C-false.

+D28-5. $\mathfrak{T}_i$ is **C-true** (in K) $=_{Df}$ $\Lambda \overset{\rightharpoonup}{c} \mathfrak{T}_i$.

For all practical purposes, that is to say, for all C-consistent calculi (D31–3), 'C-true' as here defined coincides with 'derivable from Λ' and hence with 'provable' (T31–36).

+D28-6. $\mathfrak{T}_i$ is **C-equivalent** to $\mathfrak{T}_j$ (in K) $=_{Df}$ $\mathfrak{T}_i \overset{\rightharpoonup}{c} \mathfrak{T}_j$ and $\mathfrak{T}_j \overset{\rightharpoonup}{c} \mathfrak{T}_i$.

In order to show the connection between the C-terminology and the ordinary terminology, the terms 'primitive sentence', 'proof', and 'provable' can be defined in the following way; but in the subsequent discussions we shall seldom make use of these terms.

D28-10. $\mathfrak{S}_i$ is a *primitive sentence* (or *directly C-true*) (in K) $=_{Df}$ $\mathfrak{S}_i$ is a direct C-implicate of Λ.

D28-11. $\mathfrak{R}_k$ is a *proof* (in K) $=_{Df}$ $\mathfrak{R}_k$ is a derivation with the premiss-class Λ.

D28-12. $\mathfrak{T}_i$ is *provable* (in K) $=_{Df}$ $\mathfrak{T}_i$ is derivable from Λ.

It would be possible to formulate here a requirement of *adequacy*

for C-concepts in analogy to that given previously for L-concepts
(§ 16). The analogy would, however, not be a strict one. If we try to
define an L-concept, say 'L-true in S', then the corresponding radical
concept, i.e. 'true in S', is given by the rules of S. On the other hand,
if we try to define a C-concept, say 'C-true in K', then no corresponding radical concept is given. 'True in K' makes no sense because
'true' is a semantical concept and must therefore refer to a semantical
system, not to a calculus. And there is not one but many semantical
systems which we may connect with a given calculus as an interpretation for it. Therefore we have to refer to all true interpretations of K
in order to define adequacy. We might call a predicate $\mathfrak{pr}_i$ in M adequate for a certain C-concept (say, C-implication) if, with respect to a
calculus K, it holds for all those $\mathfrak{T}$ or pairs of $\mathfrak{T}$, and only those, for
which it follows from the rules of K that the corresponding radical con-
cept (in the example, implication) holds in every semantical system
S which is a true interpretation for K. A requirement of this kind,
although not formulated explicitly, has guided our previous discussions leading to the definitions of C-concepts D3 to 6.

We do not introduce here the concept '*C-disjunct*' (corresponding
to 'disjunct', D9–5). As was explained before, 'L-disjunct' is not
definable on the basis of 'L-implicate', 'L-true', and 'L-false' (§ 14).
Analogously, 'C-disjunct' is not definable by 'C-implicate', 'C-true',
and 'C-false'; in other words, not definable on the basis of primitive
sentences, rules of inference, and rules of refutation. If the concept
'C-disjunct' is to be introduced at all, a new kind of rule of deduction
must be laid down, defining 'directly C-disjunct'. It seems that this
has never been done; and it is doubtful whether it would have great
practical importance. But the fact that this syntactical concept is not
definable by those ordinarily used is, of course, theoretically important; it will be explained in [II], together with the other asymmetries
mentioned before. If rules of the kind mentioned are taken into consideration, 'directly C-disjunct' will be an additional primitive term
of general syntax. Then we might lay down the following definition.

D28-A. $\mathfrak{T}_i$ is *C-disjunct* with $\mathfrak{T}_j$ (in K) $=_{\mathrm{Df}}$ either there is a $\mathfrak{T}_k$
and a $\mathfrak{T}_l$ such that $\mathfrak{T}_k$ is directly C-disjunct with $\mathfrak{T}_l$ and that $\mathfrak{T}_i$ is
derivable from $\mathfrak{T}_k$ and $\mathfrak{T}_j$ is derivable from $\mathfrak{T}_l$, or $\mathfrak{T}_i$ is C-true, or $\mathfrak{T}_j$
is C-true.

Further, the definitions of some of the other C-concepts must be
modified by use of the term 'directly C-disjunct' in order to make
them adequate.

§ 29. Theorems Concerning C-Concepts

> Theorems are given which are based on the definitions of C-concepts in § 28 without using postulates. There is an analogy between C-concepts and L-concepts to a certain extent.

The following theorems are based merely on the definitions in § 28; postulates are not needed.

1. *Theorems concerning derivability.* These theorems serve as preliminary steps for those concerning C-implication.

+**T29-1.** Derivability is **a.** reflexive, **b.** transitive. (From D28–1 and 2.)

T29-2. If $\mathfrak{S}_j \,\epsilon\, \mathfrak{R}_i$, then $\mathfrak{S}_j$ is derivable from $\mathfrak{R}_i$. (From D28–2.)

T29-3. If $\mathfrak{R}_j \subset \mathfrak{R}_i$, then $\mathfrak{R}_j$ is derivable from $\mathfrak{R}_i$. (From T2, D28–2b.)

T29-5 (lemma). $\mathfrak{S}_j$ is derivable from $\{\mathfrak{S}_j\}$. (From T2.)

T29-6 (lemma). $\{\mathfrak{S}_j\}$ is derivable from $\mathfrak{S}_j$. (From D28–2b, T1a.)

T29-8. Λ is derivable from every $\mathfrak{T}_i$. (From D28–2b.)

T29-9. If every sentence of $\mathfrak{R}_j$ is derivable from $\mathfrak{T}_i$, then $\mathfrak{R}_j$ is derivable from $\mathfrak{T}_i$. (From D28–2b, c.)

T29-10. Every $\mathfrak{T}_j$ is derivable from V. (From T2, T3.)

T29-12. If every sentence (in K) is derivable from $\mathfrak{T}_i$, then every $\mathfrak{T}_j$ is derivable from $\mathfrak{T}_i$. (From T9.)

T29-13. If $\mathfrak{T}_i \overrightarrow{\mathrm{dC}} \mathfrak{T}_j$, then $\mathfrak{T}_j$ is derivable from $\mathfrak{T}_i$. (From D28–1 and 2.)

2. *Theorems concerning C-falsity*

T29-20. If $\mathfrak{T}_j$ is derivable from $\mathfrak{T}_i$ and $\mathfrak{T}_j$ is C-false, $\mathfrak{T}_i$ is C-false. (From D28–3, T1b.)

T29-21. If $\mathfrak{T}_i$ is directly C-false, $\mathfrak{T}_i$ is C-false. (From D28–3, T1a.)

T29-22. There is a C-false $\mathfrak{T}_i$ in K if and only if there is a directly C-false $\mathfrak{T}_j$ in K. (From D28–3, T21.)

T29-23. If $\mathfrak{S}_j \,\epsilon\, \mathfrak{R}_i$ and $\mathfrak{S}_j$ is C-false, $\mathfrak{R}_i$ is C-false. (From T2, T20.)

T29-24. If $\mathfrak{R}_j \subset \mathfrak{R}_i$ and $\mathfrak{R}_j$ is C-false, $\mathfrak{R}_i$ is C-false. (From T3, T20.)

T29-25. Each of the following conditions is a sufficient and necessary condition for V to be C-false in K :

    a. There is a C-false $\mathfrak{R}_i$ (but not necessarily a C-false $\mathfrak{S}_i$) in K.

    b. There is a C-false $\mathfrak{T}_i$ in K.

    (From T24; T23.)

T29-26 (lemma). If every directly C-false $\mathfrak{T}_k$ in K is such that every sentence in K is derivable from it, and if $\mathfrak{T}_i$ is C-false, then every $\mathfrak{T}_j$ is derivable from $\mathfrak{T}_i$. (Proof. Under the conditions specified, according to D28–3 and T1b, every sentence is derivable from $\mathfrak{T}_i$, and hence, according to T12, every $\mathfrak{T}_j$ is derivable from $\mathfrak{T}_i$.)

3. *Theorems concerning C-implication*

T29-30. If $\mathfrak{T}_j$ is derivable from $\mathfrak{T}_i$, then $\mathfrak{T}_i \,\overrightarrow{c}\, \mathfrak{T}_j$. (From D28–4.)

+**T29-31.** If $\mathfrak{T}_i$ is C-false, $\mathfrak{T}_i \,\overrightarrow{c}\,$ every $\mathfrak{T}_j$. (From D28–4.)

T29-32. C-implication is reflexive, i.e. $\mathfrak{T}_i \,\overrightarrow{c}\, \mathfrak{T}_i$. (From D28–4, T1a.)

T29-33. If $\mathfrak{S}_j \,\epsilon\, \mathfrak{R}_i$, then $\mathfrak{R}_i \,\overrightarrow{c}\, \mathfrak{S}_j$. (From T2, T30.)

T29-34. If $\mathfrak{R}_j \subset \mathfrak{R}_i$, then $\mathfrak{R}_i \,\overrightarrow{c}\, \mathfrak{R}_j$. (From T3, T30.)

T29-35. $\{\mathfrak{S}_j\} \,\overrightarrow{c}\, \mathfrak{S}_j$. (From T5, T30.)

T29-36. $\mathfrak{S}_j \,\overrightarrow{c}\, \{\mathfrak{S}_j\}$. (From T6, T30.)

T29-37. If $\mathfrak{T}_i \,\overrightarrow{dc}\, \mathfrak{T}_j$, then $\mathfrak{T}_i \,\overrightarrow{c}\, \mathfrak{T}_j$. (From T13, T30.)

T29-40 (lemma). If $\mathfrak{T}_i \,\overrightarrow{c}\,$ every sentence of $\mathfrak{R}_j$, then $\mathfrak{T}_i \,\overrightarrow{c}\, \mathfrak{R}_j$. (From D28–4, T9, T31.)

+**T29-43.** If $\mathfrak{T}_i \,\overrightarrow{c}\, \mathfrak{T}_j$ and $\mathfrak{T}_j$ is C-false, $\mathfrak{T}_i$ is C-false. (From D28–4, T20.)

+**T29-44.** C-implication is transitive. (From D28–4, T1b, T43, T31.)

T29-45 (lemma). If $\mathfrak{T}_i \vec{c} \mathfrak{K}_j$, then $\mathfrak{T}_i \vec{c}$ every sentence of $\mathfrak{K}_j$. (From T33, T44.)

+**T29-46.** $\mathfrak{T}_i \vec{c} \mathfrak{K}_j$ if and only if $\mathfrak{T}_i \vec{c}$ every sentence of $\mathfrak{K}_j$. (From T40, T45.)

T29-49. Every $\mathfrak{T}_i \vec{c} \Lambda$. (From T8, T1.)

T29-50. V $\vec{c}$ every $\mathfrak{T}_j$. (From T33, T34.)

T29-51 (lemma). If $\mathfrak{T}_i$ is C-false, $\mathfrak{T}_i \vec{c}$ V. (From T31.)

T29-54. If there is no rule of refutation, i.e. no directly C-false $\mathfrak{T}_i$ in K, then the following holds:

    a. 'C-implicate in K' and 'derivable in K' coincide.

    b. 'C-true in K' and 'provable in K' coincide.

    (From T22, D28–4; (a), D28–11 and 5.)

T29-55. If every directly C-false $\mathfrak{T}_i$ in K is such that every sentence in K is derivable from it, then the following holds:

    a. 'C-implicate in K' and 'derivable in K' coincide.

    b. 'C-true in K' and 'provable in K' coincide.

(From D28–4, T26; (a), D28–11 and 5.) (The condition of this theorem is fulfilled by most of the calculi which have rules of refutation.)

T29-56. If $\mathfrak{T}_i \vec{c} \mathfrak{T}_j$ and $\mathfrak{T}_i \vec{c} \mathfrak{T}_k$, then $\mathfrak{T}_i \vec{c} \mathfrak{T}_j + \mathfrak{T}_k$. (From T46.)

T29-57 (lemma). If $\mathfrak{K}_i \vec{c} \mathfrak{K}_j$, then $\mathfrak{K}_i \vec{c} \mathfrak{K}_i + \mathfrak{K}_j$. (From T32, T56.)

T29-58 (lemma). If $\mathfrak{K}_i \vec{c} \mathfrak{K}_j$ and $\mathfrak{K}_i + \mathfrak{K}_j$ is C-false, then $\mathfrak{K}_i$ is C-false. (From T57, T43.)

4. *Theorems concerning C-truth*

+**T29-70.** If $\mathfrak{T}_i \vec{c} \mathfrak{T}_j$ and $\mathfrak{T}_i$ is C-true, $\mathfrak{T}_j$ is C-true. (From D28–5, T44.)

T29-71. If $\mathfrak{K}_j \subset \mathfrak{K}_i$ and $\mathfrak{K}_i$ is C-true, $\mathfrak{K}_j$ is C-true. (From T34, T70.)

T29-72 (lemma). If every sentence of $\Re_i$ is C-true, $\Re_i$ is C-true. (From T40.)

+**T29-73.** $\Re_i$ is C-true if and only if every sentence of $\Re_i$ is C-true. (From T33, T44; T72.)

+**T29-74.** If $\mathfrak{T}_j$ is C-true, every $\mathfrak{T}_i \; \overrightarrow{c} \; \mathfrak{T}_j$. (From D28–5, T49, T44.)

T29-75 (lemma). If $\mathfrak{T}_i$ and $\mathfrak{T}_j$ are C-true, then $\mathfrak{T}_i \; \overrightarrow{c} \; \mathfrak{T}_j$. (From T74.)

+**T29-76.** Λ is C-true. (From T72.)

T29-77. If $\mathfrak{T}_i$ is derivable from Λ, then $\mathfrak{T}_i$ is C-true. (From D27–4 and 5.) [The converse does not hold generally; but it holds if K is C-consistent (see T31–36).]

T29-78. If $\Re_j$ is C-true, then $\Re_i \; \overrightarrow{c} \; \Re_i + \Re_j$. (From T32, T31, T56.)

T29-79. If $\Re_i + \Re_j$ is C-false, and $\Re_j$ is C-true, then $\Re_i$ is C-false. (From T78, T43.)

T29-80. If $\Re_i + \Re_j \; \overrightarrow{c} \; \mathfrak{S}_k$ and $\Re_j$ is C-true, then $\Re_i \; \overrightarrow{c} \; \mathfrak{S}_k$. [Proof. If the condition is fulfilled, then either $\mathfrak{S}_k$ is derivable from $\Re_i + \Re_j$ or $\Re_i + \Re_j$ is C-false (D28–4). In the first case, $\Re_i \; \overrightarrow{c} \; \Re_i + \Re_j$ (T78); hence $\Re_i \; \overrightarrow{c} \; \mathfrak{S}_k$ (T44). In the second case, $\Re_i$ is C-false (T79); hence $\Re_i \; \overrightarrow{c} \; \mathfrak{S}_k$ (D28–4).]

T29-81. If $\{\mathfrak{S}_i, \mathfrak{S}_j\} \; \overrightarrow{c} \; \mathfrak{S}_k$ and $\mathfrak{S}_j$ is C-true, then $\mathfrak{S}_i \; \overrightarrow{c} \; \mathfrak{S}_k$. (From T80.)

5. *Theorems concerning C-equivalence*

+**T29-85.** C-equivalence is **a.** reflexive, **b.** symmetric, **c.** transitive. (From D28–6, T32; T44.)

+**T29-86.** If both $\mathfrak{T}_i$ and $\mathfrak{T}_j$ are C-true, they are C-equivalent to one another. (From T74.)

+**T29-87.** If both $\mathfrak{T}_i$ and $\mathfrak{T}_j$ are C-false, they are C-equivalent to one another. (From T31.)

T29-88. $\mathfrak{S}_i$ and $\{\mathfrak{S}_i\}$ are C-equivalent to one another. (From T35, T36.)

T29-89. If $\mathfrak{T}_i$ is C-false, it is C-equivalent to V. (From T51, T50.)

+**T29-90.** $\mathfrak{T}_i$ is C-true if and only if $\mathfrak{T}_i$ is C-equivalent to Λ. (From D28–5, T49.)

6. *Theorems connecting the C-terms with the ordinary terms 'primitive sentence', 'proof', 'provable' (D28–10 to 12)*

T29-100. If $\mathfrak{T}_i$ is provable it is C-true. (From D28–12, T77.)

T29-101. Every primitive sentence in K is **a.** provable in K, and **b.** C-true in K. (From D28–10 and 12, T13; T100.)

The C-concepts show an analogy with the L-concepts to a considerable extent. (Concerning the limits of this analogy, see comment on D31–1.) If among the postulates concerning L-concepts (P14–1 to 15) we leave aside those which also refer to radical semantical concepts (because their relation to C-concepts cannot be dealt with here in syntax) or to 'L-disjunct' (because we did not define the corresponding C-concept, see § 28), then we find, for each of the remaining postulates, an analogous theorem concerning C-concepts: the analogues to P14–5 to 9, 11 to 15 are T29–44, 70, 43, 32, D28–8, T29–33, 40, 73, 74, 31. It is noteworthy that here, for the C-concepts, we needed no postulates; all the theorems in this section are based merely on the definitions.

Since analogues to the ten postulates mentioned hold for the C-concepts, analogues to all theorems based only on those ten postulates also hold for the C-concepts. Some of these are among the theorems listed in this section.

The point in which the analogy between C-concepts and L-concepts does not hold is this: any $\mathfrak{T}_i$ cannot be both L-true and L-false, but it might be both C-true and C-false. This will be discussed soon (see remarks to D30–6).

§ 30. C-Concepts (2)

> More definitions of C-concepts and theorems are added to
> those in §§ 28 and 29. Among the C-concepts are 'C-determi-
> nate', 'C-indeterminate', and 'C-comprehensive', which should
> not be identified with 'C-false'. Examples in K_1 and K_2 (§ 27)
> are given.

We shall now introduce more C-concepts, and state
theorems concerning them. This system of definitions and
theorems is a continuation of that in §§ 28 and 29. The definitions of some C-concepts in this section (D1 to 7) are
analogous to those of the corresponding L-concepts (D14–1,
D21–1, D14–2 to 5 and 7). Hence the analogues to previous
theorems also hold here, except those based on postulates
referring to radical concepts or to 'L-disjunct'. 'C-indeterminate' (D2) does not correspond to a radical concept
but is a convenient abbreviation for 'non-C-determinate'; it
corresponds to the L-concept 'non-L-determinate' (or 'L-
indeterminate') for which we have introduced the term
'factual' (D21–1). The C-concepts defined here are less
important than those defined in § 28; of more general interest are only D1 and 2 and the paragraph after T44.

+**D30-1.** $\mathfrak{T}_i$ is **C-determinate** (in K) $=_{Df} \mathfrak{T}_i$ is either
C-true or C-false.
T30-1. If K does not contain a directly C-false $\mathfrak{T}_i$,
then 'C-determinate in K' and 'C-true in K' coincide.
(From T29–22.)
T30-4. If every sentence of K is C-determinate, then
every $\mathfrak{T}_i$ of K is C-determinate. (From T29–73, T29–23.)

+**D30-2.** $\mathfrak{T}_i$ is **C-indeterminate** (in K) $=_{Df} \mathfrak{T}_i$ is not
C-determinate.
T30-6. $\mathfrak{T}_i$ is C-indeterminate if and only if $\mathfrak{T}_i$ is
neither C-true nor C-false. (From D1.)

T30-7. If K does not contain a directly C-false $\mathfrak{T}_j$, then $\mathfrak{T}_i$ is C-indeterminate if and only if $\mathfrak{T}_i$ is not C-true. (From T29–22, T6.)

D30-3. $\mathfrak{T}_i$ is **C-exclusive** of $\mathfrak{T}_j$ (in K) $=_{Df}$ $\mathfrak{T}_i + \mathfrak{T}_j$ is C-false. (If $\mathfrak{T}_i$ or $\mathfrak{T}_j$ is a sentence $\mathfrak{S}_k$, then $\{\mathfrak{S}_k\}$ is to be taken as component of the sum.)

T30-11. If $\mathfrak{T}_j$ is C-false, $\mathfrak{T}_j$ is C-exclusive of every $\mathfrak{T}_i$. (From T29–24.)

T30-12. If $\mathfrak{T}_i$ and $\mathfrak{T}_j$ are C-exclusive and $\mathfrak{T}_j$ is C-true, then $\mathfrak{T}_i$ is C-false. (From D3, T29–79.)

T30-13 (lemma). If $\mathfrak{T}_i$ is C-exclusive of Λ, $\mathfrak{T}_i$ is C-false. (From T12, T29–76.)

T30-15. $\mathfrak{T}_i$ is C-false if and only if $\mathfrak{T}_i$ is C-exclusive of Λ. (From T13, T11.)

T30-16. If $\mathfrak{T}_i \overrightarrow{c} \mathfrak{T}_k$ and $\mathfrak{T}_j$ is C-exclusive of $\mathfrak{T}_k$, $\mathfrak{T}_j$ is C-exclusive of $\mathfrak{T}_i$. [Proof. Under the conditions stated, $\mathfrak{T}_j + \mathfrak{T}_k$ is C-false (D3); hence also $\mathfrak{T}_j + \mathfrak{T}_k + \mathfrak{T}_i$ (T29–24); hence also $\mathfrak{T}_j + \mathfrak{T}_i$ (T29–58).]

T30-17. If K does not contain a directly C-false $\mathfrak{T}_i$, then 'C-exclusive in K' is empty. (From T29–22.)

D30-4. $\mathfrak{T}_j$ is **C-dependent** upon $\mathfrak{T}_i$ (in K) $=_{Df}$ either $\mathfrak{T}_i \overrightarrow{c} \mathfrak{T}_j$ or $\mathfrak{T}_i$ and $\mathfrak{T}_j$ are C-exclusive.

T30-25. If $\mathfrak{T}_i$ is C-false, every $\mathfrak{T}_j$ is C-dependent upon $\mathfrak{T}_i$. (From T29–31.)

T30-26. If $\mathfrak{T}_i$ is C-true and $\mathfrak{T}_j$ is C-dependent upon $\mathfrak{T}_i$, then $\mathfrak{T}_j$ is C-determinate. (From T29–70, T12.)

T30-27. If $\mathfrak{T}_j$ is C-determinate, then $\mathfrak{T}_j$ is C-dependent upon every $\mathfrak{T}_i$. (From T29–74, T11.)

T30-28. $\mathfrak{T}_j$ is C-determinate if and only if $\mathfrak{T}_j$ is C-dependent upon Λ. (From D1, D28–5, T15, D4.)

T30-29. If $\mathfrak{T}_i \overrightarrow{c} \mathfrak{T}_k$ and $\mathfrak{T}_j$ is C-dependent upon $\mathfrak{T}_k$, then $\mathfrak{T}_j$ is C-dependent upon $\mathfrak{T}_i$. (From D4, T29–44, T16.)

T30-30. If K does not contain a directly C-false $\mathfrak{T}_i$, then 'C-dependent in K' and 'C-implicate in K' coincide. (From T17.)

D30-5. $\mathfrak{T}_i$ is **C-complete** (in K) $=_{Df}$ every $\mathfrak{T}_j$ (in K) is C-dependent upon $\mathfrak{T}_i$.

T30-40. If $\mathfrak{T}_i$ is C-false, $\mathfrak{T}_i$ is C-complete. (From T25.)

T30-41. V is C-complete. (From T29–50.)

T30-42. If $\mathfrak{T}_i \stackrel{\rightarrow}{c} \mathfrak{T}_j$ and $\mathfrak{T}_j$ is C-complete, $\mathfrak{T}_i$ is C-complete. (From T29.)

T30-43. If there is a $\mathfrak{T}_i$ in K which is C-true and C-complete, then every $\mathfrak{T}_j$ in K is C-determinate. (From T26.)

T30-44. The following conditions for a calculus K coincide:

    a. Λ is C-complete in K.
    b. Every $\mathfrak{T}_i$ in K is C-complete.
    c. Every $\mathfrak{T}_i$ in K is C-determinate.
    d. There is a $\mathfrak{T}_i$ in K which is C-true and C-complete.

(From T29–46, T42; T28; T29–76, T43.)

The procedure most frequently chosen in general syntax is the following (expressed in ordinary terminology, formulation A, as in § 25). Only primitive sentences and rules of inference are laid down, but no rules of refutation; in other words, only 'directly provable' and 'directly derivable' are defined, but not 'directly refutable'. In order to reach, nevertheless, the concepts 'refutable' and '(C-)inconsistent calculus', the following definitions are often laid down in general syntax. *D30-A1.* $\mathfrak{T}_i$ is *refutable* (in K) $=_{Df}$ every sentence in K is derivable from $\mathfrak{T}_i$. *D30-A2.* A calculus K is *inconsistent* $=_{Df}$ K contains a $\mathfrak{T}_i$ which is both provable and refutable. This leads to the following theorem. *T30-A1.* K is inconsistent if and only if every sentence in K is provable in K. (E. L. Post, "Introduction to a General Theory of Elementary Propositions," *Am. J. Math.* 43,

1921; A. Tarski [Methodologie] p. 27f; Carnap [Syntax] §§ 48 and 59.) The corresponding definitions and theorem in C-terminology would be like this. *D30–B1*. $\mathfrak{T}_i$ is *C-false* in K $=_{Df}$ every sentence in K is a C-implicate of $\mathfrak{T}_i$. *D30–B2*. K is *C-inconsistent* $=_{Df}$ K contains a $\mathfrak{T}_i$ which is both C-true and C-false. *T30–B1*. K is C-inconsistent if and only if every sentence in K is C-true. DB2 seems natural; we shall adopt it later (D31–1 and 2). But in contrast to the customary view which I shared previously it seems to me at present that DB1 is not suitable in general syntax; in other words, it is not adequate in the sense explained above (§ 28). An adequate concept of 'C-false' ('refutable') cannot be defined on the basis of 'C-implicate' ('derivable') and 'C-true' ('provable'). In the special syntax of a particular calculus it is quite permissible to define 'directly C-false' as in DB1, or to define it in such a way that the condition of DB1 for 'C-false' follows. But to adopt DB1 in general syntax would sometimes lead to undesirable consequences.

Let us consider a semantical system S_m containing only true sentences, whether L- or F-true (as e.g. S_5 in § 9, containing only atomic sentences; but S_m may, in addition, contain signs of disjunction and conjunction), or a system S_n containing only L-true sentences. If then we construct a calculus K_m in accordance with S_m, i.e. such that S_m is a true interpretation for it, we may choose any sub-class of the true sentences of S_m as class of the C-true sentences of K_m; this will be discussed more in detail in § 36. And there is no objection to constructing K_m in such a way that every true sentence of S_m, that is, every sentence of S_m, becomes C-true in K_m. In the case of S_n it will perhaps seem more natural to construct a calculus K_n such that every sentence which is L-true in S_n becomes C-true in K_n. Thus both in K_m and in K_n every sentence is C-true. If we adopted DB1, which, in combination with DB2, leads to TB1, we should have to call both K_m and K_n C-inconsistent. This, however, seems quite inappropriate in view of the fact that there is a true interpretation for either of them.

On the basis of these considerations, we do not adopt DB1 as a definition for 'C-false'. Since, however, the concept defined by DB1 has some interest nevertheless, we shall introduce a term for it; we take the term '**C-comprehensive**' (D6) because this concept corresponds to 'comprehensive' and 'L-comprehensive' as defined earlier (D9–9, D14–5). Then, on the one hand, we distinguish between the two concepts 'C-comprehensive' and 'C-false', the latter based on 'directly C-false' to be defined by rules of refutation. On the other hand, we shall find conditions under which the two concepts coincide, namely if and only if the calculus contains a directly C-false $\mathfrak{T}_i$ (T30–62). Under the same condition the old concept of C-inconsistency (DB1 and 2) and the new one (D31–2) coincide (T31–17).

D30-6. $\mathfrak{T}_i$ is **C-comprehensive** (in K) $=_{\text{Df}}$ $\mathfrak{T}_i$ $\overrightarrow{c}$ every sentence in K.

T30-49. If $\mathfrak{T}_i$ $\overrightarrow{c}$ $\mathfrak{T}_j$ and $\mathfrak{T}_j$ is C-comprehensive, then $\mathfrak{T}_i$ is C-comprehensive. (From T29–44.)

T30-50. V is C-comprehensive. (From T29–50.)

T30-51.

    a. If $\mathfrak{T}_i$ is C-false, $\mathfrak{T}_i$ is C-comprehensive.

    b. If $\mathfrak{T}_i$ is directly C-false, $\mathfrak{T}_i$ is C-comprehensive. (From T29–31; T29–21.) [The converse of (a) does not hold generally but only under certain conditions (see T6ob).]

T30-52. Each of the following conditions is a sufficient and necessary condition for $\mathfrak{T}_i$ to be C-comprehensive:

    a. $\mathfrak{T}_i$ $\overrightarrow{c}$ V.

    b. $\mathfrak{T}_i$ is C-equivalent to V.

    c. $\mathfrak{T}_i$ $\overrightarrow{c}$ every $\mathfrak{R}_j$.

    d. $\mathfrak{T}_i$ $\overrightarrow{c}$ every $\mathfrak{T}_j$.

    (From T29–46; T29–50, (a); T29–46; (c).)

T30-53. If $\mathfrak{T}_i$ is C-comprehensive, $\mathfrak{T}_i$ is C-complete. (From T52d.)

T30-55. The following conditions for a calculus K coincide:

   a. Every C-comprehensive $\mathfrak{T}_i$ in K is C-false.
   b. V is C-false in K.
   c. There is a C-false $\mathfrak{R}_i$ in K.
   d. There is a C-false $\mathfrak{T}_i$ in K.
   (From T50, T52a, T29–43; T29–25.)

T30-60. If K contains a (non-empty) rule of refutation and hence a $\mathfrak{T}_i$ which is directly C-false, then the following holds:

   a. V is C-false in K.
   b. 'C-false in K' and 'C-comprehensive in K' coincide.
   (From T29–22, T55, T51.)

T30-61. If K does not contain a (non-empty) rule of refutation and hence there is no directly C-false $\mathfrak{T}_i$ in K, then the following holds:

   a. There is no C-false $\mathfrak{T}_j$ in K.
   b. V is not C-false but C-comprehensive in K.
   c. 'C-false in K' and 'C-comprehensive in K' do not coincide.
   d. 'C-comprehensive in K' and 'C-complete in K' coincide.
   (From T29–22; T50; (b); T30, T52d.)

T30-62. 'C-false in K' and 'C-comprehensive in K' coincide if and only if K contains a (non-empty) rule of refutation and hence a directly C-false $\mathfrak{T}_i$. (From T60b; T61c.)

T30-63. 'C-false in K' either is empty or coincides with 'C-comprehensive in K'. (From T61a, T60b.)

The following theorem refers to calculi which on the basis of older definitions, as discussed above (DB1 and 2), would be called (C-)inconsistent, but not in our terminology.

T30-65. If K contains a $\mathfrak{T}_i$ which is both C-true and C-comprehensive, then the following holds:

    a. V is C-true in K.
    b. Every $\mathfrak{T}_j$ is C-true in K.
    (From T52a and d, T29–70.)

D30-7. $\mathfrak{K}_i$ is **C-perfect** $=_{\mathrm{Df}}$ for every $\mathfrak{S}_j$, if $\mathfrak{K}_i \overset{\rightarrow}{\mathrm{c}} \mathfrak{S}_j$ then $\mathfrak{S}_j \in \mathfrak{K}_i$.

According to this definition, a C-perfect class $\mathfrak{K}_i$ is such that any formal deduction (i.e. C-implication) with sentences of $\mathfrak{K}_i$ as premises leads always again to a sentence of $\mathfrak{K}_i$.

A. Tarski [Systemenkalkül] has developed a detailed theory of the C-perfect classes, which he calls systems, with many interesting results. He has applied the device of using $\mathrm{Cc}(\mathfrak{K}_i + \mathfrak{K}_j)$ as one of the basic connections between perfect classes (see below, remarks on T84).

T30-80. $\mathfrak{K}_i$ is C-perfect if and only if for every $\mathfrak{K}_j$, if $\mathfrak{K}_i \overset{\rightarrow}{\mathrm{c}} \mathfrak{K}_j$ then $\mathfrak{K}_j \subset \mathfrak{K}_i$. (From D7, T29–33, T29–44, T29–40.)

T30-81. The following classes are C-perfect:
    a. The class of the C-true sentences (of K). (From D7, T29–73, T29–70.)
    b. V. (From D7.)

T30-83 (lemma). For every $\mathfrak{T}_i$, the class of the sentences which are C-implicates of $\mathfrak{T}_i$ is C-perfect. (From D7, T29–40, T29–44.)

T30-84. If $\mathfrak{K}_i$ and $\mathfrak{K}_j$ are C-perfect, $\mathfrak{K}_i \times \mathfrak{K}_j$ is C-perfect.
    Proof. If the condition is fulfilled and $\mathfrak{K}_i \times \mathfrak{K}_j \overset{\rightarrow}{\mathrm{c}} \mathfrak{S}_k$, then $\mathfrak{K}_i \overset{\rightarrow}{\mathrm{c}} \mathfrak{S}_k$ (T29–34, T29–44) and likewise $\mathfrak{K}_j \overset{\rightarrow}{\mathrm{c}} \mathfrak{S}_k$. Therefore, $\mathfrak{S}_k \in \mathfrak{K}_i$ and $\mathfrak{S}_k \in \mathfrak{K}_j$ (D7), hence $\mathfrak{S}_k \in \mathfrak{K}_i \times \mathfrak{K}_j$.

If $\mathfrak{K}_i$ and $\mathfrak{K}_j$ are C-perfect, $\mathfrak{K}_i + \mathfrak{K}_j$ is not necessarily also C-perfect. Therefore, if one wants to deal with C-perfect classes only, the class sum is not a suitable connection. But instead of $\mathfrak{K}_i + \mathfrak{K}_j$, $\mathrm{Cc}(\mathfrak{K}_i + \mathfrak{K}_j)$ (as defined by D32–B1) may be taken as a basic connection; this is C-perfect (T32–B21) and is C-equivalent to $\mathfrak{K}_i + \mathfrak{K}_j$ (T32–B13). (See above, reference to Tarski.)

D30-8. K is a **C-determinate calculus** $=_{\mathrm{Df}}$ every $\mathfrak{T}_i$ in K is C-determinate.

T30-90. If K does not contain a directly C-false $\mathfrak{T}_i$, then

K is a C-determinate calculus if and only if every $\mathfrak{T}_i$ in K is C-true. (From T1.)

T30-91. Each of the following conditions is a sufficient and necessary condition for K to be a C-determinate calculus:

    a. Λ is C-complete in K.

    b. Every $\mathfrak{T}_i$ in K is C-complete.

    c. There is a $\mathfrak{T}_i$ in K which is both C-true and C-complete.

    d. Every sentence in K is C-determinate.

    (From T44; for d: T4.)

Examples of application of C-concepts to the calculi K_1 and K_2 described earlier (§ 27).

The formulation of the *rules of deduction* for K_1 and K_2 is on the whole the same as before, except that C-terms are used. Here also, if we want to, we might distinguish formulation A without 'Λ' and B with 'Λ'. In formulation A, we simply have to replace 'primitive sentence' by 'directly C-true', and 'directly derivable' by 'direct C-implicate'; in formulation B only 'directly derivable' by 'direct C-implicate'. For the following, we presuppose formulation B because the definitions in § 28 are based on it. In K_1, there is no rule of refutation; hence 'directly C-false in K_1' is empty. In the rule of refutation for K_2, we replace 'directly refutable' by 'directly C-false'. Then we may apply the definitions and theorems of §§ 28 to 30 which take 'direct C-implicate' and 'directly C-false' as primitive.

According to D28-1, the three sequences of sentences given in § 27 as examples of a proof and two derivations are still called derivations here; the proof is a derivation with the premiss-class Λ. Hence the following holds for both K_1 and K_2. According to D28-2, 4, and 5, '$\sim$P(a) $\vee$ P(a)' is derivable from Λ and a C-implicate of Λ and C-true. 'Q(c) $\vee$ P(b)' is derivable from and a C-implicate of 'P(b) $\vee$ Q(c)'. The inverse holds, too, as can easily be shown by a derivation of the same form with components exchanged. Hence, according to D28-6, 'Q(c) $\vee$ P(b)' and 'P(b) $\vee$ Q(c)' are C-equivalent. Because of the third derivation, 'Q(a)' is derivable from and a C-implicate of {'P(c)', '$\sim$P(c)'} ($\mathfrak{R}_3$). By a derivation of the same form with any sentence $\mathfrak{S}_i$ in the place of 'Q(a)' it can be shown that $\mathfrak{R}_3 \mathrel{\overline{c}} \mathfrak{S}_i$. Hence, according to D6, $\Re_3$ is C-comprehensive and hence C-complete in a trivial way (T53). It can be shown in the same way that any other class of the form $\{\mathfrak{S}_j, \sim\mathfrak{S}_j\}$ is C-comprehensive (in K_1 and K_2).

In K_1, because of the lack of a rule of refutation, 'C-false' is empty (T29–22); 'C-determinate' and 'C-true' coincide (T1); 'C-exclusive' is empty (T17); 'C-dependent' and 'C-implicate' coincide (T30); 'C-comprehensive' and 'C-complete' coincide (T61d). On the other hand, in K_2, because of its rule of refutation, the following holds. 'C-false' coincides with 'C-comprehensive' (T60b); hence $\Re_3$ is C-false; 'P(c)' and '$\sim$P(c)' are C-exclusive of one another (D3); and likewise are $\{$'P(c)', 'Q(a)'$\}$ and $\{$'$\sim$P(c)', 'Q(b)'$\}$ (T29–24). K_2 contains sentential classes which are C-complete in a non-trivial way, i.e. without being C-comprehensive, like $\Re_3$. It can be shown that any class containing each of the atomic sentences or its negation is C-complete in K_2, e.g. $\{$'P(a)', 'P(b)', '$\sim$P(c)', '$\sim$Q(a)', 'Q(b)', '$\sim$Q(c)'$\}$.

§ 31. C-Concepts (3)

> Further C-concepts are introduced. Some of them are properties of calculi (e.g. 'C-inconsistent', 'C-consistent', 'C-extensional') or relations between calculi (e.g. 'sub-calculus', 'coincident', 'isomorphic').

We have previously found (§ 29) that the C-concepts are in many respects analogous to the L-concepts in such a way that corresponding theorems hold in both fields. This analogy, however, fails in one decisive point. Since every L-true $\mathfrak{T}_i$ is true (P14–1) and every L-false $\mathfrak{T}_i$ is false (P14–2), no $\mathfrak{T}_i$ can be both L-true and L-false (T14–1). On the other hand, K and $\mathfrak{T}_i$ may be such that $\mathfrak{T}_i$ is both C-true and C-false in K; in this case we shall call $\mathfrak{T}_i$ **C-ambivalent** in K (D1) and K a **C-inconsistent calculus** (D2). The L-concepts are intimately connected with the radical concepts. If e.g. 'true in S' is given, then there is no choice, except in matters of formulation, for the definition of 'L-true in S'; there is only one adequate concept of 'L-true in S'. The same does not hold for the C-concepts with respect to a calculus K. Their connection with the radical concepts is, to a certain extent, a matter of choice; it depends upon the interpretation chosen for K. And the analogues for P14–1 and 2, and hence also for T14–1 do not hold with respect to every interpretation but only with respect to a true interpretation (T33–8f and d, T33–12). But a calculus may be C-inconsistent, i.e. contain a C-ambivalent $\mathfrak{T}_i$; then it does not possess a true interpretation (T33–13).

For the reasons stated, not only the radical concepts but also the L-concepts corresponding to the C-concepts to be defined by D1 and 2 are empty; therefore they have not been introduced.

+**D31-1.** $\mathfrak{T}_i$ is **C-ambivalent** (in K) $=_{Df}$ $\mathfrak{T}_i$ is both C-true and C-false.

T31-1 (lemma). If $\mathfrak{T}_i$ is C-ambivalent, then the following holds:

    a. $\mathfrak{T}_i$ $\overline{c}$ every $\mathfrak{T}_j$.
    b. Every $\mathfrak{T}_j$ (in K) is C-true.
    c. Every $\mathfrak{T}_j$ $\overline{c}$ $\mathfrak{T}_i$.
    d. Every $\mathfrak{T}_j$ (in K) is C-false.

    (From T29–31; (a), T29–70; T29–74; (c), T29–43.)

+**T31-2.** If there is a C-ambivalent $\mathfrak{T}_i$ in K, then every $\mathfrak{T}_j$ in K is C-ambivalent. (From T1b and d.)

T31-5 (lemma). If K is such that Λ is C-false, then Λ is C-ambivalent. (From T29–76, D1.)

T31-6 (lemma). If K contains a $\mathfrak{T}_i$ which is both C-true and C-comprehensive and if $\mathfrak{T}_j$ is C-false, then $\mathfrak{T}_j$ is C-ambivalent. (From T30–65b.)

While the C-concepts defined so far are properties or relations of $\mathfrak{T}_i$ in a calculus K, the concepts to be defined now are *properties of calculi and relations between calculi.*

+**D31-2.** A calculus K is **C-inconsistent** $=_{Df}$ K contains a C-ambivalent $\mathfrak{T}_i$.

T31-15. If K is C-inconsistent, then:

    a. Every $\mathfrak{T}_i$ in K is C-ambivalent.

    b. Every $\mathfrak{T}_i$ in K is both C-true and C-false.

    c. There is a directly C-false $\mathfrak{T}_i$ in K.

(From D2, T2; (a); (b), T29–22.)

T31-16 (lemma). If Λ is C-false in K, then K is C-inconsistent. (From T5.)

+T31-17. If K contains a $\mathfrak{T}_i$ which is both C-true and C-comprehensive and a $\mathfrak{T}_j$ which is directly C-false, then K is C-inconsistent. (From T29–22, T6.)

T31-18 (lemma). If there is a directly C-false $\mathfrak{T}_j$ in K and if V is C-true, then K is C-inconsistent. (From T30–50, T17.)

T31-19. If K contains $\mathfrak{T}_i$ and $\mathfrak{T}_j$ such that $\mathfrak{T}_i \,\overrightarrow{c}\, \mathfrak{T}_j$ and $\mathfrak{T}_i$ is C-true and $\mathfrak{T}_j$ is C-false, then K is C-inconsistent. (From T29–70, D2.)

T31-23. Each of the following conditions is a sufficient and necessary condition for K to be C-inconsistent:

    a. There is a C-ambivalent $\mathfrak{T}_i$ in K.

    b. Every $\mathfrak{T}_i$ in K is C-ambivalent.

    c. Every $\mathfrak{T}_i$ in K is both C-true and C-false.

    d. Λ is C-false in K.

    e. There is a directly C-false $\mathfrak{T}_j$ in K and V is C-true.

(From D2; T15a; (b); T16, T15b; T18, T15c and b.)

+T31-24. If every directly C-false $\mathfrak{T}_i$ in K is such that every sentence in K is derivable from it, then each of the following conditions is a sufficient and necessary condition for K to be C-inconsistent:

    a. There is a $\mathfrak{T}_i$ in K which is both provable and C-false.

    b. Every $\mathfrak{T}_i$ in K is both provable and C-false.

    c. There is a directly C-false $\mathfrak{T}_i$ in K, and V is provable.

(From T23, T29–55.)

+**D31-3.** A calculus K is **C-consistent** $=_{Df}$ K is not C-inconsistent.

T31-30. If K contains a $\mathfrak{T}_i$ which is not C-true, K is C-consistent. (From T23c.)

+**T31-31.** If K does not contain a directly C-false $\mathfrak{T}_i$, K is C-consistent. (From T29–22, T23c.)

Hence any calculus of the ordinary kind, containing only primitive sentences and rules of inference but no rule of refutation, is C-consistent. But in many cases, in order to fulfill the intention of the author of a calculus, we have to add a rule of refutation tacitly assumed by the author, e.g. a rule of the form III3 for K_2 (§ 27) or the simple rule "V is directly refutable". By an addition of this kind, those calculi which usually are regarded as containing a contradiction become C-inconsistent.

T31-32. If every directly C-false $\mathfrak{T}_i$ in K is such that every sentence in K is derivable from $\mathfrak{T}_i$ and if there is a $\mathfrak{T}_j$ in K which is not provable, then K is C-consistent. (From T24b.)

T31-35. Each of the following conditions is a sufficient and necessary condition for K to be C-consistent:

 a. No $\mathfrak{T}_i$ in K is C-ambivalent.
 b. There is a $\mathfrak{T}_i$ in K which is not C-ambivalent.
 c. Λ is not C-false in K.
 d. There is a $\mathfrak{T}_i$ in K which is not C-false.
 (From T23a; T23b; T23d; T23c, (c).)

T31-36. If K is C-consistent, then 'C-true in K' coincides with 'derivable from Λ (in K)' (and hence with 'provable in K'). (From D28–5, D28–4, T35c; D28–12.)

Examples. We previously constructed the calculi K_1 and K_2 (§ 27; C-terminology: § 30 at the end). Both are C-consistent. For K_1, this follows simply from the lack of a rule of refutation (T31). For K_2, it is shown in the following way. The rules of K_1 are those of the ordinary propositional calculus; for this it is known that an atomic sentence, e.g. 'P(a)' ($\mathfrak{S}_1$), is not provable. (From the analysis which will be carried out in § 35, it follows that every sentence which is provable in K_1 is L-true in S_3 (§ 15); $\mathfrak{S}_1$ is not L-true in S_3, hence not provable in K_1.) Therefore, $\mathfrak{S}_1$ is also not provable in K_2. Only the class {'P(a)', '$\sim$P(a)'} ($\mathfrak{R}_1$) is directly C-false in K_2. In § 27 we saw that every sentence is derivable in K_1 from a class of the form {$\mathfrak{S}_j$, $\sim\mathfrak{S}_j$} and hence also from $\mathfrak{R}_1$; the same holds for K_2. Thus both conditions in T32 are fulfilled, and K_2 is C-consistent.

For an example of a C-inconsistent calculus see K_6 in § 35.

If a calculus K_m is given, and we take as sentences of another calculus K_n some (or all) of the sentences of K_m and as rules of deduction for K_n some (or all) of the rules of K_m, then we call K_n a **direct sub-calculus** of K_m. Here, the rules of K_n may be formulated in a way different from those of K_m; it is only required that direct C-implication in K_n is a sub-relation of the corresponding concept in K_m, and direct C-falsity in K_n a sub-class of the corresponding concept in K_m (D5). It is easy to see (T40 and 45) that in this case the extension of C-implication, C-falsity, and other C-concepts in K_n is also contained in that of the corresponding concepts in K_m, or, as we shall say, that K_n is also a **sub-calculus** of K_m (D6). Suppose that we construct K_n as a sub-calculus of K_m in the following way. As V_n (the class of the sentences of K_n) we take any sub-class of V_m (the class of the sentences of K_m), and we keep as C-implication and C-falsity in K_n the corresponding concepts in K_m as far as they hold within V_n. Then we shall call K_n a **conservative sub-calculus** of K_m (D7). If K_m and K_n are direct sub-calculi of each other, in other words, if the direct C-concepts in these two calculi coincide, we shall call them **directly coincident calculi** (D8). Although in this case the concepts defined by the rules of deduction for the two calculi have the same extension, the formulation of the rules may still differ. If K_m and K_n are sub-calculi of each other we shall call them **coincident calculi** (D9). In this case some

C-concepts coincide (T65 and 69), while the direct C-concepts may or may not coincide.

D31-5. K_n is a **direct sub-calculus** of K_m $=_{Df}$ the following three conditions are fulfilled:

    a. Every sentence in K_n is a sentence in K_m.

    b. If $\mathfrak{T}_i \overrightarrow{dc} \mathfrak{T}_j$ in K_n, then likewise in K_m.

    c. If $\mathfrak{T}_i$ is directly C-false in K_n, it is likewise in K_m.

T31-40. If K_n is a direct sub-calculus of K_m, then the following holds:

    a. If $\mathfrak{T}_i \overrightarrow{c} \mathfrak{T}_j$ in K_n, then likewise in K_m.

    b. If $\mathfrak{T}_i$ is C-false in K_n, then likewise in K_m.

(From D5, D28–1, 2, 3, and 4.)

+**D31-6.** K_n is a **sub-calculus** of K_m $=_{Df}$ the following two conditions are fulfilled:

    a. If $\mathfrak{T}_i \overrightarrow{c} \mathfrak{T}_j$ in K_n, then $\mathfrak{T}_i \overrightarrow{c} \mathfrak{T}_j$ in K_m.

    b. If $\mathfrak{T}_i$ is C-false in K_n, it is C-false in K_m.

T31-45. If K_n is a direct sub-calculus of K_m, it is a sub-calculus of K_m. (From T40, D6.)

T31-46. If K_n is a sub-calculus of K_m, then for any instance (i.e. $\mathfrak{T}_i$ or pair $\mathfrak{T}_i$, $\mathfrak{T}_j$) for which one of the following concepts holds in K_n the same concept holds in K_m:

    a. Sentence. (From T29–32.)

    b. C-true. (From D28–5.)

    c. C-equivalent. (From D28–6.)

    d. C-determinate. (From D30–1, (b), D6b.)

    e. C-exclusive. (From D30–3, D6b.)

    f. C-dependent. (From D30–4, D6a, (e).)

    g. C-ambivalent. (From D1, (b), D6b.)

T31-47. If K_n is a sub-calculus of K_m, then the following holds:

    a. If K_n is C-inconsistent, K_m is also. (From D2, (T46g.)

    b. If K_m is C-consistent, K_n is also. (From D3, (a).)

D31-7. K_n is a **conservative sub-calculus** of K_m $=_{Df}$ the following three conditions are fulfilled:

    a. K_n is a sub-calculus of K_m.

    b. If $\mathfrak{T}_i \mathrel{\overline{c}} \mathfrak{T}_j$ in K_m and $\mathfrak{T}_i$ and $\mathfrak{T}_j$ belong also to K_n, then $\mathfrak{T}_i \mathrel{\overline{c}} \mathfrak{T}_j$ in K_n.

    c. If $\mathfrak{T}_i$ is C-false in K_m and belongs also to K_n, it is C-false in K_n.

T31-50. If K_n is a conservative sub-calculus of K_m, then for any instance (i.e. $\mathfrak{T}_i$ or pair $\mathfrak{T}_i$, $\mathfrak{T}_j$) which belongs to K_n and for which one of the following concepts holds in K_m, the same concept holds in K_n:

    a. C-true. (From D28–5.)

    b. C-equivalent. (From D28–6.)

    c. C-determinate. (From D30–1, (a), D7c.)

    d. C-indeterminate. (From D30–2, T46d.)

    e. C-exclusive. (From D30–3, D7c.)

    f. C-dependent. (From D30–4, D7b, (e).)

    g. C-complete. (From D30–5, T46a, (f).)

    h. C-comprehensive. (From T30–52b, T46a, D7b.)

    i. C-perfect. (From D30–7, D7b.)

    j. C-ambivalent. (From D1, (a), D7c.)

T31-51. If K_n is a conservative sub-calculus of K_m, then for any instance (i.e. $\mathfrak{T}_i$ or pair $\mathfrak{T}_i$, $\mathfrak{T}_j$) which belongs to K_n, each of the following concepts holds in K_n if and only if the same concept holds in K_m:

    a. C-implication. (From D7a, D6a, D7b.)

    b. C-false. (From D6b, D7c.)

    c. C-true. (From T46b, T50a.)

    d. C-equivalent. (From T46c, T50b.)

    e. C-determinate. (From T46d, T50c.)

    f. C-exclusive. (From T46e, T50e.)

    g. C-dependent. (From T46f, T50f.)

    h. C-ambivalent. (From T46g, T50j.)

T31-52. If K_n is a conservative sub-calculus of K_m, then the following holds:

   a. If K_m is a C-determinate calculus, K_n is also. (From D30–8, T50c.)

   b. K_m is C-inconsistent if and only if K_n is. (From T23d, T51b.)

   c. K_m is C-consistent if and only if K_n is. (From D3, (b).)

   D31-8. K_m and K_n are **directly coincident calculi** $=_{Df}$ each of them is a direct sub-calculus of the other.

   T31-60. K_m and K_n are directly coincident calculi if and only if the following two conditions are fulfilled:

   a. $\mathfrak{T}_i \overrightarrow{dc} \mathfrak{T}_j$ in K_m if and only if the same holds in K_n.

   b. $\mathfrak{T}_i$ is directly C-false in K_m if and only if the same holds in K_n.

   (From D8, D5.)

   T31-61. If K_m and K_n are directly coincident calculi, then each of the C-concepts defined in §§ 28, 30, and 31 as properties or relations of $\mathfrak{T}$ has the same extension in K_m and in K_n. (This follows from T60, because each of these concepts is defined directly or indirectly on the basis of 'direct C-implicate' and 'directly C-false'.)

   D31-9. K_m and K_n are **coincident calculi** $=_{Df}$ each of them is a sub-calculus of the other.

   T31-65. K_m and K_n are coincident calculi if and only if the following two conditions are fulfilled:

   a. C-implication in K_m and in K_n coincide.

   b. C-falsity in K_m and in K_n coincide.

   (From D9, D6.)

   T31-66. If K_m and K_n are directly coincident calculi, they are coincident calculi. (From T61, T65.)

   T31-67. K_m and K_n are coincident calculi if and only if each of them is a conservative sub-calculus of the other. (From D7, T65.)

   T31-68. If K_m and K_n are coincident calculi, they contain the same sentences. (From T46a.)

T31-69. If K_m and K_n are coincident calculi, then each of the following concepts has the same extension in K_m as in K_n: **a.** C-true, **b.** C-equivalent, **c.** C-determinate, **d.** C-indeterminate, **e.** C-exclusive, **f.** C-dependent, **g.** C-complete, **h.** C-comprehensive, **i.** C-perfect, **j.** C-ambivalent. (This follows from T65, because all the concepts mentioned (D28-5 and 6, D30-1 to 7, D31-1) are defined on the basis of 'C-implicate' and 'C-false'.)

T31-70. If K_m and K_n are coincident calculi, the following holds:

> **a.** K_m is a C-determinate calculus if and only if K_n is. (From T68, T69c.)
> **b.** K_m is C-inconsistent if and only if K_n is. (From D2, T69j.)
> **c.** K_m is C-consistent if and only if K_n is. (From D3, (b).)

D31-10. K_m and K_n are **isomorphic calculi** $=_{Df}$ there is a one-one correlation H between the signs of K_m and those of K_n such that the following two conditions are fulfilled, where $\mathfrak{T}_i{}'$ and $\mathfrak{T}_j{}'$ are those sentences or sentential classes in K_n which correspond to $\mathfrak{T}_i$ and $\mathfrak{T}_j$ respectively in K_m on the basis of H:

> **a.** $\mathfrak{T}_i{}' \vec{c} \mathfrak{T}_j{}'$ in K_n if and only if $\mathfrak{T}_i \vec{c} \mathfrak{T}_j$ in K_m.
> **b.** $\mathfrak{T}_i{}'$ is C-false in K_n if and only if $\mathfrak{T}_i$ is C-false in K_m.

T31-80. Isomorphism of calculi is **a.** reflexive, **b.** symmetric, **c.** transitive. (From D10.)

T31-81. If K_m and K_n are isomorphic calculi with the correlation H, then each of the following concepts holds for an instance (i.e. $\mathfrak{T}_i$ or pair $\mathfrak{T}_i$, $\mathfrak{T}_j$) in K_m if and only if the same concept holds for the instance in K_n corresponding to the first on the basis of H: **a.** C-true, **b.** C-equivalent, **c.** C-determinate, **d.** C-indeterminate, **e.** C-exclusive, **f.** C-dependent, **g.** C-complete, **h.** C-comprehensive,

i. C-perfect, **j.** C-ambivalent. (This follows from D10, because all the concepts mentioned are defined on the basis of 'C-implicate' and 'C-false'.)

In some of the following definitions (D10 and 12) we make use of the concept 'closed sentence' which is based on the concept 'free variable' (§ 6). Thus it is assumed for these definitions that the latter concept is available in the system of general syntax, although we have not introduced it so far. It seems that this concept — or another suitable concept related to it — has to be taken as an additional primitive concept in general syntax.

+**D31-13.** $\mathfrak{A}_i$ is **C-interchangeable** with $\mathfrak{A}_j$ (in K) $=_{Df}$ any closed sentence $\mathfrak{S}_k$ is C-equivalent to every sentence $\mathfrak{S}_l$ constructed out of $\mathfrak{S}_k$ by replacing either $\mathfrak{A}_i$ at some place in $\mathfrak{S}_k$ by $\mathfrak{A}_j$ or $\mathfrak{A}_j$ by $\mathfrak{A}_i$, and there is at least one pair of sentences $\mathfrak{S}_k$ and $\mathfrak{S}_l$ of this kind.

We add a few definitions and theorems concerning *extensionality* because they are needed in later discussions (e.g. in [II]). (For explanations of these concepts see [Syntax] § 65; T31-100 here is Theorem 65-4b there.) We shall not go into further detail here because a discussion of extensional and non-extensional semantical and syntactical systems and their features is planned for a later volume. For the corresponding radical semantical concepts, see D10-20 and 21.

D31-16. $\mathfrak{T}_i$ is *C-equivalent to $\mathfrak{T}_j$ in relation to* $\mathfrak{T}_k =_{Df} \mathfrak{T}_k + \mathfrak{T}_i \mathrel{\overline{C}} \mathfrak{T}_j$ and $\mathfrak{T}_k + \mathfrak{T}_j \mathrel{\overline{C}} \mathfrak{T}_i$. (Compare remark on D30-3.)

T31-90. $\mathfrak{T}_i$ and $\mathfrak{T}_j$ are C-equivalent (to one another) if and only if they are C-equivalent in relation to Λ. (From D16, D28-6.)

D31-17. $\mathfrak{S}_i$ is *C-extensional* (in K) in relation to a partial sentence $\mathfrak{S}_j$ occurring at a certain place in $\mathfrak{S}_i =_{Df} \mathfrak{S}_j$ is closed, and for every closed $\mathfrak{S}_k$ and every $\mathfrak{T}_l$, if $\mathfrak{S}_j$ and $\mathfrak{S}_k$ are C-equivalent in relation to $\mathfrak{T}_l$, then $\mathfrak{S}_i$ and the sentence constructed out of $\mathfrak{S}_i$ by replacing $\mathfrak{S}_j$ at the place in question by $\mathfrak{S}_k$ are C-equivalent in relation to $\mathfrak{T}_l$.

D31-18. A **calculus** K is **C-extensional** in relation to partial sentences $=_{Df}$ for every $\mathfrak{S}_i$ in K, if $\mathfrak{S}_i$ contains a closed sentence $\mathfrak{S}_j$ at some place, then $\mathfrak{S}_i$ is C-extensional in relation to $\mathfrak{S}_j$ at that place.

T31-100. If K is C-extensional in relation to partial sentences and

$\mathfrak{S}_i$ and $\mathfrak{S}_j$ are closed and C-equivalent in K, then $\mathfrak{S}_i$ and $\mathfrak{S}_j$ are C-interchangeable in K. (From D18, D17, T90.)

This theorem also holds for those non-extensional calculi (as e.g. Lewis' system of Strict Implication with propositional constants added) in which every non-extensional connective $\mathfrak{a}_i$ fulfills the following condition: if every two corresponding arguments in two full sentences $\mathfrak{S}_i$ and $\mathfrak{S}_j$ of $\mathfrak{a}_i$ are C-equivalent, then $\mathfrak{S}_i$ and $\mathfrak{S}_j$ are C-equivalent.

We have previously (§ 22) stated conditions with the help of *characteristic sentences* which hold not only for semantical concepts but also for syntactical concepts if the prefix 'C-' is substituted for 'X-'. Besides some of the C-concepts explained and defined in this chapter, there were also mentioned some other C-concepts, e.g. 'C-universal', 'C-empty', etc., for predicates in general, 'C-symmetric', etc., for predicates of degree two, 'C-synonymous' for individual constants. The conditions given for these C-concepts may often suggest a way of defining them with respect to particular calculi. But the task of defining these concepts in general syntax and even the simpler task of formulating the conditions in a general form for those calculi which contain the signs required for the characteristic sentences involve some unsolved problems not occurring in the task of formulating conditions for the corresponding semantical concepts.

The difficulty consists in the specification of the signs whose occurrence is essential for the characteristic sentences. If e.g. T22–2 is applied to the L-concept, it says: "$\mathfrak{S}_i$ and $\mathfrak{S}_j$ are L-equivalent in S if and only if the sentence $\mathfrak{S}_i \equiv \mathfrak{S}_j$ is L-true in S". But this will obviously hold only if '$\equiv$' fulfills a certain condition. Thus we must add: "... provided '$\equiv$' is in S a sign of equivalence". The same condition has to be added for 'equivalent' and 'F-equivalent'. And analogous conditions have to be added in the case of other concepts with respect to other signs or expressions, e.g. in T22–10: "... provided '(x)' is a universal operator in S", and in T22–30: "... provided '$=$' is a sign of identity in S". Now it is easy to formulate these conditions in semantics, i.e. to define the concepts 'sign of equivalence', 'sign of negation', 'sign of identity', etc., in general semantics. For instance, 'a_i is a sign of equivalence (negation, disjunction, etc.) in $S =_{Df} a_i$ fulfills such and such a truth-table', 'a_i is a sign of identity in $S =_{Df} a_i$ designates identity' (or: '. . . $=_{Df} in_j a_i in_k$ is true in S if and only if in_j and in_k designate the same object'). But it is a problem how to formulate the corresponding conditions with respect to a calculus in general syntax. The question can be put in this way: what syntactical properties must a sign a_i of K have in order to make sure that in every true interpretation of K a_i will become, say, a sign of equivalence (or disjunction, or existence, or identity, etc.)? With respect to the sentential connectives, this problem will be discussed and solved in [II]. For other kinds of signs, a discussion is planned for a later volume.

§ 32. C-Content and C-Range

> Two postulates for 'C-content', in analogy to 'L-content', are laid down; and likewise for 'C-range', in analogy to 'L-range'. Several ways of defining 'C-content' and 'C-range' so as to fulfill those postulates are shown. Here, C-contents and C-ranges are classes of sentences.

We have previously introduced the L-concepts 'L-range' (§§ 18, 19) and 'L-content' (§ 23) as correlations by which to every $\mathfrak{T}_i$ (in a semantical system S) a class is correlated. Different ways of defining these concepts have been explained, the chief distinction being whether the elements of the classes taken as L-ranges and L-contents are on the side of the designata (namely L-states or state-relations, see § 18 and § 19K and L for L-ranges and D23–B1 for L-contents) or on the side of the object language (namely $\mathfrak{T}$, e.g. state-descriptions or sentences, see § 19E, F, and G for L-ranges and D23–F1 and D23–G1 for L-contents). We shall now introduce corresponding C-concepts: 'the **C-range** of $\mathfrak{T}_i$' or briefly '$Cr\mathfrak{T}_i$', and 'the **C-content** of $\mathfrak{T}_i$' or briefly '$Cc\mathfrak{T}_i$'. Since in syntax we cannot deal with designata, we can define these C-concepts only in analogy to the second kind of L-concepts just mentioned.

With respect to each of the concepts 'L-range' and 'L-content' we first laid down two postulates (P18–1 and 2, P23–1 and 2) and then looked for possible concepts to fulfill these postulates. We shall do the same here. We lay down the two postulates P32–A1 and 2 for 'C-content' in strict analogy to P23–1 and 2, and likewise the postulates P32–E1 and 2 for 'C-range' in analogy to P18–1 and 2. A duality analogous to that between 'L-content' and 'L-range' (see § 23) is then found here between 'C-content' and 'C-range'. In order to exhibit this duality more clearly, we put the corresponding postulates or theorems side by side.

C-Content	C-Range
P32-A1. If $\mathfrak{T}_i \vec{c} \mathfrak{T}_j$, then $Cc\mathfrak{T}_j \subset Cc\mathfrak{T}_i$.	**P32-E1.** If $\mathfrak{T}_i \vec{c} \mathfrak{T}_j$, then $Cr\mathfrak{T}_i \subset Cr\mathfrak{T}_j$.
P32-A2. If $Cc\mathfrak{T}_j \subset Cc\mathfrak{T}_i$, then $\mathfrak{T}_i \vec{c} \mathfrak{T}_j$.	**P32-E2.** If $Cr\mathfrak{T}_i \subset Cr\mathfrak{T}_j$, then $\mathfrak{T}_i \vec{c} \mathfrak{T}_j$.
T32-A1. $Cc\mathfrak{T}_j \subset Cc\mathfrak{T}_i$ if and only if $\mathfrak{T}_i \vec{c} \mathfrak{T}_j$. (From PA1 and 2.)	**T32-E1.** $Cr\mathfrak{T}_i \subset Cr\mathfrak{T}_j$ if and only if $\mathfrak{T}_i \vec{c} \mathfrak{T}_j$. (From PE1 and 2.)
T32-A2. $Cc\mathfrak{T}_i = Cc\mathfrak{T}_j$ if and only if $\mathfrak{T}_i$ and $\mathfrak{T}_j$ are C-equivalent. (From TA1, D28–6.)	**T32-E2.** $Cr\mathfrak{T}_i = Cr\mathfrak{T}_j$ if and only if $\mathfrak{T}_i$ and $\mathfrak{T}_j$ are C-equivalent. (From TE1, D28–6.)
T32-A5. For every $\mathfrak{T}_i$, $Cc\Lambda \subset Cc\mathfrak{T}_i$. (From T29–49, PA1.)	**T32-E5.** For every $\mathfrak{T}_i$, $Cr\mathfrak{T}_i \subset Cr\Lambda$. (From T29–49, PE1.)
T32-A6. For every $\mathfrak{T}_i$, $Cc\mathfrak{T}_i \subset CcV$. (From T29–50, PA1.)	**T32-E6.** For every $\mathfrak{T}_i$, $CrV \subset Cr\mathfrak{T}_i$. (From T29–50, PE1.)
T32-A7. $Cc\mathfrak{T}_i = Cc\Lambda$ if and only if $\mathfrak{T}_i$ is C-true. (From TA2, T29–90.)	**T32-E7.** $Cr\mathfrak{T}_i = Cr\Lambda$ if and only if $\mathfrak{T}_i$ is C-true. (From TE2, T29–90.)
T32-A8. $Cc\mathfrak{T}_i = CcV$ if and only if $\mathfrak{T}_i$ is C-comprehensive. (From D30–6, TA2.)	**T32-E8.** $Cr\mathfrak{T}_i = CrV$ if and only if $\mathfrak{T}_i$ is C-comprehensive. (From D30–6, TE2.)
T32-A9. If K contains a directly C-false $\mathfrak{T}_j$, then for every $\mathfrak{T}_i$, $Cc\mathfrak{T}_i = CcV$ if and only if $\mathfrak{T}_i$ is C-false. (From TA8, T30–6ob.)	**T32-E9.** If K contains a directly C-false $\mathfrak{T}_j$, then for every $\mathfrak{T}_i$, $Cr\mathfrak{T}_i = CrV$ if and only if $\mathfrak{T}_i$ is C-false. (From TE8, T30–6ob.)

Inclusion of C-contents coincides with the inverse of C-implication (TA1). Therefore, identity of C-contents coincides with C-equivalence (TA2). The C-content of Λ is the minimum C-content, which is contained in every other one (TA5). It is the C-content of all the C-true $\mathfrak{T}$ (TA7), and only these. The C-content of V is the maximum C-content, in which every other one is contained (TA6). It is the C-content of all the C-comprehensive $\mathfrak{T}$ (TA8), and only these; and also of all the C-false $\mathfrak{T}$, and only these, if there are any such, i.e. if K has a rule of refutation (TA9). The theorems concerning C-ranges are analogous.

Theorems concerning relations between C-contents and C-ranges (analogous to T23-20 and 21):

T32-1. $\mathrm{Cc}\mathfrak{T}_j \subset \mathrm{Cc}\mathfrak{T}_i$ if and only if $\mathrm{Cr}\mathfrak{T}_i \subset \mathrm{Cr}\mathfrak{T}_j$. (From TA1, TE1.)

T32-2. $\mathrm{Cc}\mathfrak{T}_i = \mathrm{Cc}\mathfrak{T}_j$ if and only if $\mathrm{Cr}\mathfrak{T}_i = \mathrm{Cr}\mathfrak{T}_j$. (From T1.)

In the following there are shown two possible ways of defining a concept 'C-content' which fulfills the postulates PA1 and 2. The first (DF1) is analogous to the definition D23-F1 for 'L-content', the second (DG1) to D23-G1.

D32-F1. $\mathrm{Cc}\mathfrak{T}_i =_{\mathrm{Df}}$ the class of those sentences (of K) which are C-implicates of $\mathfrak{T}_i$.

T32-F1. $\mathrm{Cc}\mathfrak{T}_j \subset \mathrm{Cc}\mathfrak{T}_i$ if and only if $\mathfrak{T}_i\ \overrightarrow{\mathrm{c}}\ \mathfrak{T}_j$. (From DF1, T29-44, 32, 33, 40.)

TF1 shows that the postulates are fulfilled. Therefore the theorems based on the postulates hold here too. Further, theorems hold here which are specific to this definition. A few examples will be given.

T32-F3. $\mathrm{Cc}\Lambda$ = the class of the C-true sentences (of K). (From DF1, D28-5.)

T32-F4. $\mathrm{Cc}\mathfrak{T}_i$ = the class of the C-true sentences (of K) if and only if $\mathfrak{T}_i$ is C-true. (From TF3, T29-90, TA2.)

T32-F5. $\mathrm{Cc}V = V$. (From DF1, T29-50.)

T32-F6. $\mathrm{Cc}\mathfrak{T}_i = V$ if and only if $\mathfrak{T}_i$ is C-comprehensive. (From TF5, D30-6, TA2.)

T32-F7. If K contains a directly C-false $\mathfrak{T}_j$, then for every $\mathfrak{T}_i$, $\mathrm{Cc}\mathfrak{T}_i = V$ if and only if $\mathfrak{T}_i$ is C-false. (From TB6, T30-6ob.)

T32-F11. $\mathfrak{S}_i \, \epsilon \, Cc\mathfrak{S}_i$. (From DF1, T29–32.)

T32-F12. $\mathfrak{R}_i \subset Cc\mathfrak{R}_i$. (From DF1, T29–33.)

T32-F13. $\mathfrak{T}_i$ and $Cc\mathfrak{T}_i$ are C-equivalent. (From TF11 and 12, T29–33, T29–40; T29–40.)

T32-F16. $Cc(Cc\mathfrak{T}_i) = Cc\mathfrak{T}_i$. (From DF1, T29–44.)

The following theorems show the close connection between the concept 'C-content' as defined by DF1 and the concept 'C-perfect' (D30–7).

T32-F20. Each of the following conditions is a sufficient and necessary condition for $\mathfrak{R}_i$ to be C-perfect:

    a. $Cc\mathfrak{R}_i \subset \mathfrak{R}_i$.

    b. $Cc\mathfrak{R}_i = \mathfrak{R}_i$.

    (From D30–7, DB1; TB12, (a).)

T32-F21. For every $\mathfrak{T}_i$, $Cc\mathfrak{T}_i$ is C-perfect. (From DF1, T30–83.)

DG1 gives an alternative definition for 'C-content'. It is also in accordance with the postulates (TG5).

D32-G1. $Cc\mathfrak{T}_i =_{\mathrm{Df}}$ the class of those sentences (of K) which are C-implicates of $\mathfrak{T}_i$ and not C-true.

The following theorems are based on this definition. (The proofs are analogous to those of the theorems with the same number in § 23.)

T32-G5. $Cc\mathfrak{T}_j \subset Cc\mathfrak{T}_i$ if and only if $\mathfrak{T}_i \, \vec{c} \, \mathfrak{T}_j$.

T32-G14. $Cc\Lambda = \Lambda$.

T32-G16. $Cc\mathfrak{T}_i = \Lambda$ if and only if $\mathfrak{T}_i$ is C-true.

T32-G20. $CcV =$ the class of the non-C-true sentences.

T32-G28. $\mathfrak{T}_i$ and $Cc\mathfrak{T}_i$ are C-equivalent.

T32-G35. $Cc(Cc\mathfrak{T}_i) = Cc\mathfrak{T}_i$.

If we have a concept 'C-content' fulfilling the postulates PA1 and 2, we can easily define a corresponding concept 'C-range' by taking $Cr\mathfrak{T}_i$ as the complement of $Cc\mathfrak{T}_i$. Then, according to T1, this concept 'C-range' will fulfill the postulates PE1 and 2. In this way, DF1 leads to DF'1, DG1 to DG'1. DF'1 and DG'1 correspond to the definitions D19–F1 and D19–G1 for 'L-range'.

D32-F'1. $Cr\mathfrak{T}_i =_{\mathrm{Df}}$ the class of those sentences (of K) which are not C-implicates of $\mathfrak{T}_i$.

T32-F'1. $Cr\Lambda$ = the class of the non-C-true sentences (of K). (From DF'1, D28–5.)

T32-F'2. $CrV = \Lambda$. (From DF'1, T29–50.)

D32-G'1. $Cr\mathfrak{T}_i =_{Df}$ the class of those sentences (of K) which are either C-true or not C-implicates of $\mathfrak{T}_i$.

T32-G'1. $Cr\Lambda = V$. (From DG'1, D28–5.)

T32-G'2. CrV = the class of the C-true sentences (of K). (From DG'1, T29–50.)

E. RELATIONS BETWEEN SEMANTICS AND SYNTAX

The sentences of a calculus K may be interpreted by the truth-conditions stated in the semantical rules of a system S, provided S contains all sentences of K. Therefore, if this condition is fulfilled, S is called an *interpretation* for K. Different kinds of interpretations are distinguished. If the direct C-concepts of K (and, hence, also the other C-concepts of K) are in agreement with the corresponding radical concepts in an interpretation S for K, then S is called a true interpretation for K; otherwise, a false interpretation. If there is a similar agreement with the L-concepts in S, S is called an L-true interpretation for K. In this case, the rules of K and S suffice to show that S is a true interpretation for K. Other kinds of interpretations: L-false, L-determinate, factual, F-true, F-false, logical, and descriptive interpretations. These concepts of different kinds of interpretations are useful for the logical analysis of science; for what is usually called the construction of a model for a set of postulates is the same as the semantical interpretation of a calculus.

§ 33. True and False Interpretations

S is called an interpretation for K if S contains all sentences of K. An interpretation S for K is called a true interpretation for K if in any case where a direct C-concept (e.g. direct C-implication) holds in K the corresponding radical concept (e.g. implication) holds in S; otherwise, S is called a false interpretation for K. If S is a true interpretation for K, then in any case where a C-concept (e.g. 'C-true') holds in K the corresponding radical concept (e.g. 'true') holds in S (T8).

In this chapter, certain relations between semantical systems and calculi will be investigated, especially relations of interpretation. Since these relations belong neither to semantics nor to syntax, we are here in a wider field, which comprehends both pure semantics and pure syntax but goes beyond them (for terminological remarks, see § 37, Theory of Systems).

A calculus K is constructed and analyzed within syntax in a formal way. As long as we stay in syntax there do not arise questions as to the meaning of the expressions and sentences occurring in K, i.e. as to the designata of the expressions and the truth-conditions of the sentences. But, if a calculus K is given, we may go over to semantics and assign designata to signs of K and truth-conditions to sentences of K by semantical rules. Hereby sentences of K become interpreted. And if we lay down a sufficient set of such rules or, in other words, a semantical system S containing all the sentences of K, then all these sentences become interpreted. In this case we call S an **interpretation** for K (D1). S may contain many more sentences than those of K, but it must not contain fewer. We will call S, moreover, a **true interpretation** for K if the semantical rules of S are in accordance with the syntactical rules of K in such a way that if, according to a rule of K, a direct C-concept holds in a certain case, then the corresponding radical semantical concept holds in this case in S (D2). This definition involves that every primitive sentence of K is true in S (T8a). It will be shown that if this condition is fulfilled an instance of any C-concept, whether direct or not, becomes an instance of the corresponding radical concept. That is to say, if S is a true interpretation for K, then every $\mathfrak{T}_i$ which is C-true in K becomes true in S; and likewise every C-false $\mathfrak{T}_i$ becomes false; when C-implication holds, implication holds, etc. (T8).

Interpretations of calculi play an important role in the method of science. In mathematics, geometry, and physics, systems or theories are frequently constructed in the form of postulate sets. And these are calculi of a special kind (see [Foundations] § 16). For the application of such systems in science it is necessary to leave the purely formal field and construct a bridge between the postulate set and the realm of objects. This is usually called constructing models for the postulate set or laying down correlative definitions for it ('Zuordnungsdefinitionen', Reichenbach). It is easily seen that this procedure, described in our terminology, leads from syntax to semantics and is what we call here constructing an interpretation for a calculus.

In the following, we lay down definitions but no postulates, and add a few theorems based on the definitions. We make use of the definitions and theorems concerning C-concepts (§§ 28 to 31) and radical concepts (§ 10), and later (in § 34) also of the postulates, definitions, and theorems concerning L- and F-concepts (§§ 14 and 21).

+D33-1. S is an **interpretation** for $K =_{Df} K$ is a calculus and S is a semantical system and every sentence of K is a sentence of S.

While Λ in $K = \Lambda$ in S, V in K and V in S may be different. Therefore we shall write simply 'Λ', but 'V_K' and 'V_S'.

T33-1. If S is an interpretation for K, then $V_K \subset V_S$. (From D1.)

+D33-2. S is a **true interpretation** for $K =_{Df} S$ is an interpretation for K such that the following two conditions are fulfilled:

    a. If $\mathfrak{T}_i \overrightarrow{dC} \mathfrak{T}_j$ in K, then $\mathfrak{T}_i \rightarrow \mathfrak{T}_j$ in S.
    b. If $\mathfrak{T}_i$ is directly C-false in K, $\mathfrak{T}_i$ is false in S.

As mentioned before (§ 27 at the end), here we leave aside the concept 'C-disjunct'. If it were to be used in a calculus K, then K would have to contain special rules defining 'directly-C-disjunct in K'. The calculi constructed in modern logic and mathematics do not contain rules of this kind. If, however, we also wanted to take into consideration calculi containing such rules, then D2 would have to be supplemented by the condition "c. If $\mathfrak{T}_i$ and $\mathfrak{T}_j$ are directly C-disjunct in K, then they are disjunct in S".

+**T33-6.** If S is a true interpretation for K and $\mathfrak{S}_j$ is derivable from $\mathfrak{K}_i$ in K, then $\mathfrak{K}_i \rightarrow \mathfrak{S}_j$ in S.

Proof. If the conditions are fulfilled, then there is in K a derivation $\mathfrak{R}_k$ with the premiss-class $\mathfrak{K}_i$ and $\mathfrak{S}_j$ as the last sentence (D28–2a). According to D28–1, every sentence $\mathfrak{S}_l$ of $\mathfrak{R}_k$ is either a sentence of $\mathfrak{K}_i$ or a direct C-implicate of a class $\mathfrak{K}_m$ of sentences which precede $\mathfrak{S}_l$ in $\mathfrak{R}_k$. Therefore the following holds. 1. The first sentence of $\mathfrak{R}_k$ is an implicate of $\mathfrak{K}_i$ in S (T10–15, D2a). 2. If every sentence which precedes $\mathfrak{S}_l$ in $\mathfrak{R}_k$ is an implicate of $\mathfrak{K}_i$, then $\mathfrak{S}_l$ is an implicate of $\mathfrak{K}_i$ (T10–17, T10–16, T10–14b). The assertion follows from (1) and (2) according to the principle of complete induction. (This proof holds also if K contains transfinite rules of deduction and $\mathfrak{R}_k$ is transfinite. In this case, transfinite induction can be applied for the last step in the proof, because $\mathfrak{R}_k$ is well-ordered; compare the remark at the end of § 25.)

+**T33-8.** If S is a true interpretation for K, then for any instance (i.e. $\mathfrak{T}_i$ or pair $\mathfrak{T}_i$, $\mathfrak{T}_j$) for which the concept (1) in one of the following pairs of concepts holds in K, concept (2) holds in S.

	(1) IN K	(2) IN S	FROM
a.	primitive sentence	true	D28–10, D2, T9–34.
b.	derivable	implicate	T6, D28–2b and c.
c.	provable	true	D28–12, (b), T9–34.
d.	C-false	false	D28–3, (b), T9–11.
e.	C-implicate	implicate	D28–4, (b), (d), T9–12.
f.	C-true	true	D28–5, (e), T9–34.
g.	C-equivalent	equivalent	D28–6, (e), T9–20c.
h.	C-exclusive	exclusive	D30–3, (d), T9–27.

(Thus e.g. T8b is meant to say: "If S is a true interpretation for K and $\mathfrak{T}_j$ is derivable from $\mathfrak{T}_i$ in K, then $\mathfrak{T}_j$ is an implicate of $\mathfrak{T}_i$ in S".)

T33-9. If S is a true interpretation for K and $\mathfrak{T}_i$ is C-comprehensive in K, then the following holds:

      a. $\mathfrak{T}_i$ is equivalent in S to V_K. (From D30–6, T8e.) ($\mathfrak{T}_i$ is not necessarily comprehensive in

S because that would mean: equivalent in S to V_S.)

b. $\mathfrak{T}_i$ is true in S if and only if every sentence of K is true in S. (From (a), D9–1.)

c. $\mathfrak{T}_i$ is false in S if and only if at least one sentence of K is false in S. (From (b).)

d. If K contains a directly C-false $\mathfrak{T}_j$, then $\mathfrak{T}_i$ is false in S. (From D2, (c).)

e. If $\mathfrak{T}_i$ is C-true in K, then every $\mathfrak{T}_j$ of K is true in S. (From T8f, (b).)

T33-12 (lemma). If S is a true interpretation for K, then K does not contain a C-ambivalent $\mathfrak{T}_i$. (From D31–1, T8f, T8d, T9–2.)

+**T33-13.** A C-inconsistent calculus has no true interpretation. (From D31–2, T12.)

+**D33-3.** S is a **false interpretation** for K $=_{Df}$ S is an interpretation for K but not a true interpretation for K.

+**T33-20.** S is a false interpretation for K if and only if at least one of the following two conditions is fulfilled. (If K does not contain a rule of refutation, then condition (b) drops out and hence condition (a) is sufficient and necessary.)

a. There is a $\mathfrak{T}_i$ and a $\mathfrak{T}_j$ such that $\mathfrak{T}_i \overrightarrow{dc} \mathfrak{T}_j$ in K, and $\mathfrak{T}_i$ is true in S and $\mathfrak{T}_j$ is false in S.

b. There is a $\mathfrak{T}_i$ such that $\mathfrak{T}_i$ is directly C-false in K and true in S.

(From D3, D2, T9–18.)

This means that S is a false interpretation for K if and only if at least one of the rules of deduction in K is not in accordance with S; that is to say, either a primitive sentence (of K) is false (in S), or the application of a rule of inference to true sentences leads to a false sentence, or a $\mathfrak{T}_i$ which is established as directly C-false by a rule of refutation is true.

+**T33-21.** If S is an interpretation for K and if there is an instance (i.e. a $\mathfrak{T}_i$ or a pair $\mathfrak{T}_i$, $\mathfrak{T}_j$) for which both concepts of one of the following pairs of concepts hold, then S is a false interpretation for K.

	Concept in K	Concept in S	From
a.	primitive sentence	false	T8a.
b.	$\mathfrak{T}_j$ derivable from $\mathfrak{T}_i$	$\mathfrak{T}_i$ true, $\mathfrak{T}_j$ false	T8b, T9–18.
c.	provable	false	T8c.
d.	C-false	true	T8d.
e.	$\mathfrak{T}_i \overrightarrow{c} \mathfrak{T}_j$	$\mathfrak{T}_i$ true, $\mathfrak{T}_j$ false	T8e, T9–18.
f.	C-true	false	T8f.
g.	C-equivalent	non-equivalent	T8g.
h.	C-exclusive	both true	T8h, D9–6.

§ 34. L-True and L-False Interpretations

An interpretation S for K is called an L-true interpretation for K if direct C-implication in K becomes L-implication in S and direct C-falsity in K L-falsity in S. Under these conditions, the rules of K and S suffice to show that S is a true interpretation for K. 'L-false interpretation' is defined analogously, and further L- and F-terms for other kinds of interpretations are defined.

In accordance with our previous intentions with L-concepts in general (§ 16), we shall define '*L-true interpretation*' in such a way that this concept holds for those cases where the definitions embodied in the rules of K and S without any reference to factual knowledge constitute a sufficient basis for establishing that S is a true interpretation for K. Thus in this case, according to D33–2a, if by virtue of the rules of K $\mathfrak{T}_i \overrightarrow{dC} \mathfrak{T}_j$, then the rules of S must suffice to show that $\mathfrak{T}_i \to \mathfrak{T}_j$ in S, and hence $\mathfrak{T}_i \overrightarrow{L} \mathfrak{T}_j$ in S. And likewise (D33–2b), if $\mathfrak{T}_i$ is directly false in K, it must follow from the rules of S that $\mathfrak{T}_i$ is false in S, and hence $\mathfrak{T}_i$ must be L-false in S. This consideration shows that D34–1 is in accordance with our intention.

+D34-1. S is an **L-true interpretation** for K $=_{\mathrm{Df}}$ S is an interpretation for K such that the following two conditions are fulfilled.

    a. If $\mathfrak{T}_i \overrightarrow{dc} \mathfrak{T}_j$ in K, then $\mathfrak{T}_i \overrightarrow{L}' \mathfrak{T}_j$ in S.

    b. If $\mathfrak{T}_i$ is directly C-false in K, then $\mathfrak{T}_i$ is L-false in S.

    T34-1. An L-true interpretation is a true interpretation. (From D1, P14–3, P14–2, D33–2.)

    +T34-6. If S is an L-true interpretation for K and $\mathfrak{S}_j$ is derivable from $\mathfrak{R}_i$ in K, then $\mathfrak{R}_i \overrightarrow{L}' \mathfrak{S}_j$ in S.

(The proof is analogous to that of T33–6, making use of P14–11, 12, and 5.)

    +T34-8. If S is an L-true interpretation for K, then for any instance (i.e. $\mathfrak{T}_i$ or pair $\mathfrak{T}_i$, $\mathfrak{T}_j$) for which the concept (1) in one of the following pairs of concepts holds in K, concept (2) holds in S.

	(1) IN K	(2) IN S	FROM
a.	primitive sentence	L-true	D28–10, D1, T14–34.
b.	derivable	L-implicate	T6, D28–2b and c.
c.	provable	L-true	D28–12, (b), T14–34.
d.	C-false	L-false	D28–3, (b), P14–7.
e.	C-implicate	L-implicate	D28–4, (b), (d), P14–15.
f.	C-true	L-true	D28–5, (e), T14–34.
g.	C-equivalent	L-equivalent	D28–6, (e), P14–9.
h.	C-determinate	L-determinate	D30–1, (f), (d), D14–1.
i.	C-exclusive	L-exclusive	D30–3, (d), D14–2.
j.	C-dependent	L-dependent	D30–4, (e), (i), D14–3.

    T34-9. If S is an L-true interpretation for K and $\mathfrak{T}_i$ is C-complete in K, then the following holds.

        a. Every $\mathfrak{T}_j$ in K is L-dependent upon $\mathfrak{T}_i$ in S. (From D30–4, T8j.)

        b. If $V_S = V_K$ (i.e. if S does not contain other sentences than K) $\mathfrak{T}_i$ is L-complete in S. (From (a), T14–64.)

    T34-10. If S is an L-true interpretation for K and $\mathfrak{T}_i$ is C-comprehensive in K, then the following holds.

    a. Every $\mathfrak{T}_j$ in K is an L-implicate of $\mathfrak{T}_i$ in S. (From T30–52d, T8e.)

    b. If K contains a $\mathfrak{T}_j$ which is L-complete in S, then $\mathfrak{T}_i$ is L-complete in S. (From (a), T14–92.)

    c. If K contains a $\mathfrak{T}_j$ which is L-comprehensive in S, then $\mathfrak{T}_i$ is L-comprehensive in S. (From (a), T14–106.)

T34-11. If S is an L-true interpretation for K and $\mathfrak{T}_i$ is factual in S and belongs to K, then $\mathfrak{T}_i$ is C-indeterminate in K. (From D20–1, T8h, D30–2.)

T34-12. If S is an L-true interpretation for K and $\mathfrak{R}_i$ is L-perfect in S and belongs to K, then $\mathfrak{T}_i$ is C-perfect in K. (From D30–7, T8e, D14–7.)

We shall define '**L-false interpretation**' in such a way that this concept holds for those cases where the rules of K and S, without reference to facts, suffice to show that S is a false interpretation for K. A consideration similar to that for 'L-true interpretation' leads here to the following definition.

+D34-2. S is an **L-false interpretation** for K $=_{\text{Df}}$ S is an interpretation for K and at least one of the following two conditions is fulfilled.

    a. There is a $\mathfrak{T}_i$ and a $\mathfrak{T}_j$ such that $\mathfrak{T}_i \mathrel{\overrightarrow{\mathsf{c}}} \mathfrak{T}_j$ in K and $\mathfrak{T}_i$ is L-true and $\mathfrak{T}_j$ L-false in S.

    b. There is a $\mathfrak{T}_i$ which is C-false in K and L-true in S.

It is noteworthy that the conditions for 'true interpretation' (D33–1), 'false interpretation' (T33–20), and 'L-true interpretation' (D1) need only refer to direct C-concepts, while that for 'L-false interpretation' (D2) must make use of general C-concepts ('C-implicate' and 'C-false'). In order to show that this is necessary, let us suppose, for instance, that K possesses two rules of inference R1 and R2 such that R1 leads e.g. from $\mathfrak{S}_1$ to $\mathfrak{S}_2$ and R2 from $\mathfrak{S}_2$ to $\mathfrak{S}_3$, and that in S $\mathfrak{S}_1$ is L-true, $\mathfrak{S}_3$ L-false, but $\mathfrak{S}_2$ factual. Then each of the two rules separately does not lead in these two instances — nor, let us suppose, in any other instance — from an L-true to an L-false sentence. Nevertheless, the two rules combined lead from the L-true $\mathfrak{S}_1$ to the L-false $\mathfrak{S}_3$, and therefore we want to call S an L-false interpretation for K.

Generally, if S is a false interpretation for K, then there must be a single rule of deduction in K for which S is a false interpretation (T33–20), while in the case of an L-false interpretation it is not necessarily a single rule which is responsible but sometimes only a combination of rules. This situation is analogous to the following: any false $\mathfrak{R}_i$ necessarily contains a false sentence; but an L-false $\mathfrak{R}_i$ need not necessarily contain an L-false sentence; it might be that every sentence of $\mathfrak{R}_i$ is factual and only their combination makes the whole of $\mathfrak{R}_i$ L-false (see example S_8 in § 21).

T34-20. An L-false interpretation is a false interpretation. (From P14–1 and 2, T33–21e and d.)

+T34-21. If S is an interpretation for K and if there is an instance (i.e. a $\mathfrak{T}_i$ or a pair $\mathfrak{T}_i$, $\mathfrak{T}_j$) for which both concepts of one of the following pairs of concepts hold, then S is an L-false interpretation for K.

	CONCEPT IN K	CONCEPT IN S	FROM
a.	$\mathfrak{T}_j$ derivable from $\mathfrak{T}_i$	$\mathfrak{T}_i$ L-true, $\mathfrak{T}_j$ L-false	D2a, T29–30.
b.	provable	L-false	D28–12, (a), T14–33.
c.	primitive sentence	L-false	(b).
d.	directly C-false	L-true	D2b, T29–21.
e.	C-true	L-false	D2a, T14–33.
f.	$\mathfrak{T}_i \overrightarrow{dC} \mathfrak{T}_j$	$\mathfrak{T}_i$ L-true, $\mathfrak{T}_j$ L-false	T29–37, D2a.

+T34-25. Every interpretation of a C-inconsistent calculus is an L-false interpretation. (From T31–23d, T14–33, D34–2b.)

The following definitions of L- and F-concepts for interpretations are analogous to the definitions of the corresponding L- and F-concepts for $\mathfrak{T}$ (§ 21).

+**D34-3.** S is an **L-determinate interpretation** for K $=_{Df}$ S is an L-true or an L-false interpretation for K.

+**D34-4.** S is an (L-indeterminate or) **factual interpretation** for K $=_{Df}$ S is an interpretation for K but not an L-determinate interpretation for K.

In the case of an L-determinate interpretation the rules of K and S suffice to find out whether it is a true or a false interpretation, while in the case of a factual interpretation knowledge about facts is necessary.

D34-5. S is an **F-true interpretation** for K $=_{Df}$ S is a true interpretation for K but not an L-true interpretation for K.

T34-40. S is an F-true interpretation for K if and only if S is a factual and a true interpretation for K. (From D5, D4, D3.)

D34-6. S is an **F-false interpretation** for K $=_{Df}$ S is a false interpretation for K but not an L-false interpretation for K.

T34-45. S is an F-false interpretation for K if and only if S is a factual and a false interpretation for K. (From D6, D4, D3.)

T34-46. S is a factual interpretation for K if and only if S is an F-true or an F-false interpretation for K. (From T40 and 45.)

The definitions given furnish a *classification of the interpretations* for any given calculus, which is perfectly analogous to the classification of the sentences of a given semantical system as exhibited by a diagram in § 21. There we found that for a particular system any one or two or three of the four kinds of sentences (1. L-true, 2. F-true, 3. F-false, 4. L-false) may be empty. As to the corresponding kinds of interpretations for a particular calculus K, we have seen that (1), (2), and (3) are empty if K is C-inconsistent (T34–25).

Whether in any other case any of the four kinds may be empty is not known. It seems doubtful whether there can be a C-consistent calculus for which any of the four kinds of interpretation is impossible (in a sufficiently rich metalanguage).

If the concepts 'logical sign' and 'descriptive sign' (§ 13) are available, either in general semantics or in the special semantics of a particular system S, we may distinguish between logical and descriptive interpretations in the following way.

D34-7. S is a **logical interpretation** for $K =_{Df} S$ is an interpretation for K and every sign of K is logical in S.

D34-8. S is a **descriptive interpretation** for $K =_{Df} S$ is an interpretation for K and at least one sign of K is descriptive in S.

T34-50. If K_m and K_n are coincident calculi and S is an interpretation for K_m of one of the kinds here defined (**a.** interpretation, **b.** true, **c.** false, **d.** L-true, **e.** L-false, **f.** L-determinate, **g.** factual, **h.** F-true, **i.** F-false, **j.** logical, **k.** descriptive interpretation), then S is an interpretation of the same kind for K_n. (From T31-68 and 69.)

§ 35. Examples of Interpretations

> Several calculi and semantical systems are outlined, as examples of the different kinds of interpretations defined in §§ 33 and 34.

Among the examples of systems constructed previously there were the semantical systems S_3 and S_4 (§§ 8 and 15) and the calculi K_1 and K_2 (§§ 27 and 30). We shall now examine the relation between K_1, K_2, and some similar calculi on the one hand and S_3, S_4, and some similar semantical systems on the other hand, in order to find out whether some of these systems are interpretations for those calculi, and, if so, to which of the kinds of interpretations defined above they belong.

K_1 represents the ordinary *propositional calculus*. S_3 shows a close relationship to K_1; but while K_1, as a calculus, applies primitive sentences and rules of inference, S_3 applies truth-tables. These two methods are sometimes regarded as on a par, as alternative methods for representing the ordinary propositional calculus. But in fact they are fundamentally different. The method of primitive sentences and rules of inference is formal and hence belongs to syntax. The method of truth-tables states truth-conditions for the sentences and hence gives an interpretation and belongs to semantics. [There is, however, a formal method of value-tables (sometimes called matrices) analogous to that of the truth-tables but not involving the concept of truth.] A system which, like S_3, applies truth-tables should therefore not be called propositional calculus; a term like 'propositional logic' would seem more suitable. (A more detailed discussion of the relation between propositional calculus and propositional logic will be given in [II].)

For reference in the subsequent discussion of interpretations some features of S_3, S_4, K_1, and K_2 are listed here.

A. S_3 (§ 8) contains some atomic sentences and molecular sentences with '$\sim$' and 'V '.

B. S_4 (§ 8) contains the same atomic sentences as S_3 but more connectives.

C. S_4 contains all sentences of S_3.

D. Truth rules for the atomic sentences of S_3, see § 8, rules (3) and (4a).

E. Truth rules for the atomic sentences of S_4 are the same as those for S_3.

F. Truth rules for the molecular sentences of S_3, see § 8, rules (4b) and (4c); they correspond to the ordinary truth-tables.

G. Truth rules for the molecular sentences of S_4, see § 8, rules (4b) to (4f); they correspond to the ordinary truth-tables. For the sentences which belong to S_3 also, the rules are in accordance with those of S_3.

H. The L-concepts for S_3 and S_4 are defined with the help of the ordinary truth-tables (§ 15 at the end, rules 5a to g).

M. K_1 and K_2 (§ 27; C-terminology: § 30 at the end) contain the same sentences as S_3.

N. K_1 and K_2 contain four forms of primitive sentences.

O. K_1 and K_2 contain only one rule of inference: "$\mathfrak{S}_j$ is directly derivable from (§ 30: a direct C-implicate of) $\{\sim\mathfrak{S}_k \vee \mathfrak{S}_j, \mathfrak{S}_k\}$".

P. K_1 contains no rule of refutation.

Q. Rule of refutation for K_2: "$\{$'P(a)', '$\sim$P(a)'$\}$ ($\mathfrak{R}_1$) is directly C-false".

S_3 is an *interpretation* both for K_1 and for K_2 (D33-1, M); likewise S_4 (C). It will be shown that they are true and, moreover, L-true interpretations.

It can easily be seen that any sentence of the four forms of primitive sentences (N) satisfies the ordinary truth-tables and hence is true in S_3 (F) and S_4 (G); and, moreover, L-true (H, rule (5a)). Therefore, for any sentence $\mathfrak{S}_k$ of this kind, $\Lambda \rightarrow \mathfrak{S}_k$ in S_3 and S_4; and, moreover, $\Lambda \stackrel{\mathrm{L}}{\rightarrow} \mathfrak{S}_k$. Now we examine the rule of inference (O). If $\sim\mathfrak{S}_k \vee \mathfrak{S}_j$ and $\mathfrak{S}_k$ are true in S_3, then $\sim\mathfrak{S}_k$ is false (F, rule (4b)); if in this case $\mathfrak{S}_j$ were false, $\sim\mathfrak{S}_k \vee \mathfrak{S}_j$ could not be true (rule (4c)); therefore $\mathfrak{S}_j$ is true. Hence $\mathfrak{S}_j$ is an implicate of $\{\sim\mathfrak{S}_k\vee\mathfrak{S}_j, \mathfrak{S}_k\}$ (D9-3). Thus S_3 is a *true interpretation* for K_1 (P, D33-2). Likewise S_4 (E, G). For K_2, the rule of refutation (Q) must also be examined. $\mathfrak{R}_1$ is false in S_3 (T9-1, F rule (4b)) and in S_4 (E, G). Therefore condition (b) in D33-2 is also fulfilled. Hence S_3 is a *true interpretation* for K_2; and likewise S_4.

If we construct the truth-table (§ 15) with the arguments $\mathfrak{S}_k$ and $\mathfrak{S}_j$, then we find 'T' for $\mathfrak{S}_k$ on lines (1) and (2), for $\mathfrak{S}_j$ on (1) and (3), hence for $\sim\mathfrak{S}_k$ on (3) and (4), for $\sim\mathfrak{S}_k \vee \mathfrak{S}_j$ on (1), (3), and (4), for $\{\sim\mathfrak{S}_k\vee\mathfrak{S}_j, \mathfrak{S}_k\}$ on (1) only. Thus $\mathfrak{S}_j$ has 'T' on every line on which the class mentioned has 'T'. Therefore $\mathfrak{S}_j$ is an L-implicate of this class in S_3 and S_4 (see rule (5e) for S_3, § 15). Previously we found that the primitive sentences of K_1 are L-true in S_3 and S_4. Therefore, S_3 is an *L-true interpretation* for K_1 (P, D34-1); and likewise S_4. For K_2, the rule of refutation (Q) must also be examined. The truth-table for $\mathfrak{R}_1$ has 'F' on each line. Therefore, $\mathfrak{R}_1$ is L-false in S_3 and S_4 (H). Thus condition (b) in D34-1 is also fulfilled. S_3 is an *L-true interpretation* for K_2; and likewise S_4.

We construct the calculus K_3 out of K_1 by adding 'P(a)' ($\mathfrak{S}_1$) as a primitive sentence. According to D, $\mathfrak{S}_1$ is true in S_3 if and only if Chicago is large. Hence, $\mathfrak{S}_1$ is true. However, $\mathfrak{S}_1$ does not fulfill the condition for L-truth in S_3 (H); hence $\mathfrak{S}_1$ is F-true in S_3 (D21-2). We know that $\mathfrak{S}_1$ is true in S_3 not by merely analyzing this sentence on the basis of the semantical rules of S_3 but by using, in addition, the result of certain geographical observations. The other rules of K_3, namely those of K_1, have already been examined. Thus S_3 is a true interpretation for K_3 as it is for K_1; but here, in contradistinction to K_1, it is not an L-true interpretation. Hence, S_3 is an *F-true interpretation* for K_3 (D34–5); and likewise S_4.

We construct K_4 out of K_1 by adding '$\sim P(a)$' ($\mathfrak{S}_2$) as a primitive sentence. By an analysis similar to that concerning $\mathfrak{S}_1$, we find that $\mathfrak{S}_2$ is false but not L-false and hence F-false in S_3. Hence, S_3 is a *false* interpretation for K_4 (T33–21a); and likewise S_4. S_3 is not an L-false interpretation for K_4 (D34–2). Therefore, S_3 is an *F-false interpretation* for K_4 (D34–6); and likewise S_4.

We construct K_5 out of K_1 by adding both $\mathfrak{S}_1$ and $\mathfrak{S}_2$ as primitive sentences. Then each of these sentences is C-true in K_5 (T29–101b). Hence $\mathfrak{K}_1$, the class of these two sentences, is also C-true in K_5 (T29–73); but it is L-false in S_3 (as found above in the analysis of K_2). Therefore, S_3 is an *L-false interpretation* for K_5 (T34–21e); and likewise S_4.

We construct K_6 out of K_2 by adding the same two sentences $\mathfrak{S}_1$ and $\mathfrak{S}_2$ as primitive sentences. Then $\mathfrak{K}_1$ is C-true in K_6 also. On the other hand, $\mathfrak{K}_1$ is directly C-false in K_2 (Q) and hence in K_6, and therefore also C-false in K_6 (T29–21). Thus, $\mathfrak{K}_1$ is *C-ambivalent* in K_6 (D31–1), and K_6 is a *C-inconsistent calculus* (D31–2). Therefore every interpretation for K_6 is an L-false interpretation (T34–25), e.g. S_3 and S_4 and any other semantical system containing the sentences of K_6. For S_3, this is easily seen by the same consideration as with K_5.

We have found L-false interpretations for K_5 and K_6. K_6 is C-inconsistent because it contains a C-ambivalent $\mathfrak{T}_i$. K_5 is, although C-consistent (P, T31–31), similar to C-inconsistent calculi, because $\mathfrak{K}_1$ is, although not C-ambivalent, i.e. both C-true and C-false, nevertheless both C-true and C-comprehensive in K_5 (because every class of the form $\{\mathfrak{S}_j, \sim\mathfrak{S}_j\}$ is C-comprehensive in K_1; see examples at the end of § 30). There are, however, L-false interpretations also for calculi of other, so to speak, quite normal kinds, e.g. for K_1 and K_2, as seen by the following example.

We construct the semantical system S_9 out of S_3 by taking the following rule instead of rule (4c) (F). A sentence of the form $\mathfrak{S}_i \lor \mathfrak{S}_j$ is true if and only if both $\mathfrak{S}_i$ and $\mathfrak{S}_j$ are true; in other words, we take as the truth-table for '$\lor$' in S_9 not the table of disjunction, as in S_3, but the table of conjunction (i.e. the table for '$\bullet$' in S_4). We change (H) in the same way for S_9. Then every sentence of the form $\mathfrak{S}_i \vee \sim\mathfrak{S}_i$ is L-false in S_9 (as $\mathfrak{S}_i \bullet \sim\mathfrak{S}_i$ is L-false in S_4). On the other hand, in K_1 and K_2, $\mathfrak{S}_i \vee \sim\mathfrak{S}_i$ is provable (the proof is similar to the example in § 27, with an additional step using a primitive sentence of the form (1c)) and hence C-true (T29–100). Therefore, S_9 is an L-false interpretation for K_1 and for K_2 (T34–21e). But K_1 and K_2 are C-consistent (see examples for D31–3).

§ 36. Exhaustive and L-Exhaustive Calculi

> K is said to be in accordance with S if S is a true interpretation for K. If, in addition, the C-concepts in K coincide with the radical concepts or with the L-concepts in S, K is called, respectively, an exhaustive or an L-exhaustive calculus for S.

In the last sections we regarded calculi as given and discussed the relations which semantical systems might have to them as interpretations of various kinds. Now let us look at the relation between calculi and semantical systems from the other direction: let us suppose that a semantical system S is given; under what conditions should we say of a calculus K that it is in accordance with S? If S is given and we try to construct K so as to fit to S, then that means that K is intended to be a syntactical representation of some features of S; these features must be such that they can be represented in a syntactical, that is to say, a formal, way. That a certain sign of S designates a certain object and that a certain sentence of S asserts a certain fact cannot be represented syntactically; these features are essentially semantical. But that a certain sentence $\mathfrak{S}_1$ of S is true, that $\mathfrak{S}_3$ is an implicate of $\mathfrak{S}_2$, that $\mathfrak{S}_4$ and $\mathfrak{S}_5$ are exclusive, can be represented syntactically. These and similar features of S, especially also those concerning L-relations, e.g. L-implication, can be mirrored in a calculus K and thereby *formalized*. The formalization of the features mentioned would e.g. consist in constructing K in such a way that $\mathfrak{S}_1$ becomes C-true, that $\mathfrak{S}_3$ becomes a C-implicate of $\mathfrak{S}_2$, and that $\mathfrak{S}_4$ and $\mathfrak{S}_5$ become C-exclusive.

We should obviously not accept K as being in accordance with S, i.e. as a correct syntactical representation of features of S, if some $\mathfrak{T}_i$ which is false in S were C-true in K, or if a $\mathfrak{T}_i$ which is true in S were C-false in K, or if $\mathfrak{T}_i$ were true in S and $\mathfrak{T}_j$ false in S but $\mathfrak{T}_j$ a C-implicate of $\mathfrak{T}_i$ in K. But we need not explicitly exclude these cases. If we exclude the corresponding cases for the direct C-concepts, as D1 does in combination with D33–2, then the cases mentioned for the general C-concepts are also excluded, as shown by T33–8.

D36-1. A calculus K is **in accordance with** a semantical system S $=_{\text{Df}}$ S is a true interpretation for K.

Since the relation here defined is simply the converse of the relation 'true interpretation for', we need not state special theorems here; the theorems in § 33 can immediately be applied. The concept defined does not involve that K covers the whole of S; conditions of this kind will constitute other concepts (D2 and 3). Here it is only required that K does not, so to speak, contradict any features of S; it may cover any part of S, however small. Therefore, for any semantical system S there is a calculus — and indeed many calculi — in accordance with it.

A simple though trivial way of constructing a calculus K such that it is in accordance with a given system S and even contains all sentences of S is to make 'direct C-implication' and 'directly C-false' empty — in other words, let K not possess any primitive sentences, rules of inference, or rules of refutation; then, nevertheless, there are derivations in K — though only trivial ones — and 'C-true in K' and 'C-implicate in K' are not empty (T29–76; T29–32, 49, and 50).

If we find out that certain sentences are true in S — either finding by a logical analysis that they are L-true or finding by empirical investigation that they are F-true — then we may select any number of them and construct K in such a way that they become C-true in K. This is done by taking a suitable sub-class of these sentences, or if necessary all of them, as primitive sentences (i.e. direct C-implicates of Λ) in K. And likewise, if we find instances of implication (other than with Λ), either L- or F-implication, in S, then we may select any part of them and represent them by C-implication in K. This is done by taking a suitable sub-class of the instances selected, and if necessary all of them, as cases of 'direct C-implication', to be represented by rules of inference in K. And finally, if we know instances of either L- or F-falsity in S, we may represent any selection of them (in customary practice: none) by C-falsity in K. This is done by taking a suitable sub-class of them, and if necessary all of them, as directly C-false in K, to be represented by rules of refutation. If we proceed in this way, then the resulting calculus K will be in accordance with S. The selection of the extension of C-implication (and thereby also of C-truth) and C-falsity is essential for the nature of the resulting calculus and its relation to S. Of a different nature is the problem of the choice of suitable sub-classes as extensions for direct C-implication (primitive sentences and rules of inference) and direct C-falsity (rules of refutation) in such a way as to yield (at least) the selected extensions of C-truth, C-implication, and C-falsity. Whether this problem is solved in one way or another may sometimes be of great practical importance; but it does not affect the essential features of the resulting calculus. If different ways are chosen, the resulting calculi will be coincident (D31-9), although not necessarily directly coincident (D31-8).

While in constructing a calculus we may choose the rules arbitrarily, in constructing a calculus K in accordance with a given semantical system S we are not entirely free. In some essential respects the features of S determine those of K, although, on the other hand, there is still a freedom of choice left with respect to some features. Thus logic — if taken as a system of formal deduction, in other words, a calculus — is in one way conventional, in another not. If, however, by logic we understand the rules of logical deduction expressed in the definitions of the L-concepts for a given semantical system, then logic is not essentially conventional because the L-concepts cannot be chosen freely if they are to fulfill the requirement of adequacy (§ 16).

For discussions of the question of the conventional character of logic see W. V. Quine, "Truth by Convention", *Phil. Essays for A. N. Whitehead*, 1936, and [Foundations] § 12.

+**T36-1.** If K is in accordance with S, then K is C-consistent. (From D1, T33–13.)

If a semantical system S is given, then among the calculi which are in accordance with S there are two cases of special interest: first, when the C-concepts in K coincide with the radical concepts in S, and, second, when they coincide with the L-concepts in S. In the first case, the C-concepts in K have the maximum extension possible in a calculus in accordance with S; in this case we call K an *exhaustive calculus* for S (D2); in the second case we call K an *L-exhaustive calculus* for S (D3).

D36-2. K is an **exhaustive calculus** for S $=_{Df}$ the following two conditions are fulfilled:

    a. 'C-implicate in K' and 'implicate in S' coincide.
    b. 'C-false in K' and 'false in S' coincide.

T36-13. If K is an exhaustive calculus for S, then in each of the following pairs of concepts concept (1) in K and concept (2) in S coincide.

	(1) IN K	(2) IN S	FROM
a.	sentence (V_K)	sentence (V_S)	D2a, T9–14a, T29–32.
b.	C-true	true	T9–35, D2a, D28–5.
c.	C-equivalent	equivalent	T9–20c, D2a, D28–6.
d.	C-exclusive	exclusive	T9–27, D2b, D30–3.
e.	C-comprehensive	comprehensive	D9–9, D2a, (a), D30–6.
f.	C-interchangeable	interchangeable	D10–15, (a), (c), D31–13.

T36-14. If K is an exhaustive calculus for S, then in each of the following pairs of concepts the extension of concept (1) in S is contained in that of concept (2) in K (i.e. for any instance, $\mathfrak{T}_i$ or pair $\mathfrak{T}_i$, $\mathfrak{T}_j$, for which concept (1) holds in S concept (2) holds in K).

	(1) IN S	(2) IN K	FROM
a.	L-implicate	C-implicate	P14-3, D2a.
b.	L-false	C-false	P14-2, D2b.
c.	L-true	C-true	P14-1, T13b.
d.	L-equivalent	C-equivalent	T14-2, T13c.
e.	L-determinate	C-determinate	D14-1, (c), (b), D30-1.
f.	L-exclusive	C-exclusive	D14-2, (b), D30-3.
g.	L-dependent	C-dependent	D14-3, (a), (f), D30-4.
h.	L-complete	C-complete	D14-4, (g), T13a, D30-5.
i.	L-comprehensive	C-comprehensive	D-14-5, (a), T13a, D30-6.

T36-15. If K is an exhaustive calculus for S and $\mathfrak{R}_i$ is C-perfect in K, then $\mathfrak{R}_i$ is L-perfect in S. (From D30-7, D14-7, T14a.)

T36-18. If K is an exhaustive calculus for S, then the following is the case:

> **a.** S is a true interpretation for K. (From D2, D33-2, T29-37 and 21.)
> **b.** K is in accordance with S. (From (a), D1.)
> **c.** K is C-consistent. (From (b), T1.)
> **d** (lemma). Every $\mathfrak{T}_i$ in K is C-determinate. (From T13b, D2b, D30-1.)
> **e.** K is a C-determinate calculus. (From (d), D30-8.)

T36-20. If K_m is an exhaustive calculus for S, then K_n is an exhaustive calculus for S if and only if K_m and K_n are coincident. (From D2, D31-9.)

T36-21 (lemma). If every sentence which is true in S is C-true in K and every sentence which is false is S is C-false in K, then the following is the case:

   a. Every $\mathfrak{T}_i$ which is true in S is C-true in K. (From D10–1, T29–73.)

   b. Every $\mathfrak{T}_i$ which is false in S is C-false in K. (From T10–1, T29–23.)

   c. If $\mathfrak{T}_i \rightarrow \mathfrak{T}_j$ in S, then $\mathfrak{T}_i \vec{c} \mathfrak{T}_j$ in K.

Proof. If the condition is fulfilled, then either $\mathfrak{T}_i$ is false or $\mathfrak{T}_j$ is true (D10–3). In the first case $\mathfrak{T}_i$ is C-false (a), and T29–31 applies; in the second $\mathfrak{T}_j$ is C-true (b), and T29–74 applies.

T36-22. K is an exhaustive calculus for S if and only if the following four conditions are fulfilled together:

   a. Every sentence which is true in S is C-true in K.

   b. Every sentence which is false in S is C-false in K.

   c. Every sentence of K belongs to S.

   d. K is C-consistent.

Proof. If the four conditions (a) to (d) are fulfilled, the following holds. 1. If $\mathfrak{T}_i \vec{c} \mathfrak{T}_j$ in K, then $\mathfrak{T}_i \rightarrow \mathfrak{T}_j$ in S. [Otherwise $\mathfrak{T}_i$ would be true and $\mathfrak{T}_j$ false (T9–18), hence $\mathfrak{T}_i$ C-true and $\mathfrak{T}_j$ C-false (T21a and b), hence K C-inconsistent (T31–19).] 2. 'C-implication in K' and 'implication in S' coincide. (From (1), T21c.) 3. If $\mathfrak{T}_i$ is C-false in K, it is false in S. [Otherwise $\mathfrak{T}_i$ would be true, and hence C-true (T21a), hence C-ambivalent; hence K would be C-inconsistent.] 4. 'C-false in K' and 'false in S' coincide. (From (3), T21b.) 5. K is an exhaustive calculus for S. (From D36–2, (2), (4).) The inverse follows from T13b, D2b, T13a, T18c.

T36-23. K is an exhaustive calculus for S if and only if the following three conditions are fulfilled together:

   a. Every sentence of S belongs to K.

   b. S is a true interpretation for K.

   c. K is C-determinate.

Proof. 1. Let K be an exhaustive calculus for S. Then the conditions (a) (from T13a), (b) (from T18a), and (c) (from T18e) are fulfilled. 2. Let the conditions (a), (b), and (c) be fulfilled. Then every sentence which is true in S is C-true in K; because it is C-determinate (c), and not C-false (b). Analogously, every sentence which is false in S is C-false in K. Every sentence of K belongs to S (b, D33–1).

K is C-consistent (b, T33–13). Therefore, K is an exhaustive calculus for S (T22).

T36-25. If K is an exhaustive calculus for S_m, and S_n is a true interpretation for K containing only sentences of K, then S_m and S_n are equivalent systems. (Compare D9–11.)

Proof. Let the conditions be fulfilled. Then S_m contains the same sentences as K (T13a) and hence the same as S_n. If $\mathfrak{S}_i$ is true in S_m, it is C-true in K (T13b) and hence true in S_n (T33–8f). If $\mathfrak{S}_i$ is false in S_m, it is C-false in K (D2b) and hence false in S_n (T33–8d). Therefore S_m and S_n are equivalent systems (T9–70).

If a system S is rich in singular factual sentences, then in most cases we do not have sufficient factual knowledge for determining the truth-values of all sentences in S. Under these conditions we are not in a position to construct an exhaustive calculus for S. Therefore, the construction of an exhaustive calculus is usually attempted only in the following two cases. 1. S contains no factual sentences. In this case the concept 'exhaustive calculus for S' coincides with the concept 'L-exhaustive calculus for S' to be defined soon. 2. S contains factual sentences also, but in such a way that all of them are L-implicates of a small number of sentences which are known (or assumed) to be F-true, e.g. a set of fundamental laws of a physical theory. In this case, in order to construct K_n as an exhaustive calculus for S, we first construct K_m as an L-exhaustive calculus for S (see below) and then build K_n out of K_m by adding those fundamental F-true sentences as primitive sentences.

Most of the calculi in practical use at the present time contain no rules of refutation and hence no C-false $\mathfrak{X}$. Therefore, a calculus K of this kind cannot be an exhaustive calculus for a system S (unless S were to contain only true sentences) in the general sense defined by D2. But K may be exhaustive for S in the more restricted sense that C-implication in K coincides with implication in S. If this is the case, then the following of the previous theorems still hold for K and S, because they are based only on condition (a) of D2: T13a, b, c, e, f; T14a, c, d, i; T15; T18a, b, c; T20.

+**D36-3.** K is an **L-exhaustive calculus** for S $=_{Df}$ the following two conditions are fulfilled:

    a. 'C-implicate in K' and 'L-implicate in S' coincide.

    b. 'C-false in K' and 'L-false in S' coincide.

+**T36-30.** If K is an L-exhaustive calculus for S, then in each of the following pairs of concepts concept (1) in K and concept (2) in S coincide.

	(1) IN K	(2) IN S	FROM
a.	sentence	sentence	D3a, T29–32, P14–8.
b.	C-true	L-true	D3a, D28–5, T14–51a.
c.	C-equivalent	L-equivalent	D3a, D28–6, T14–9.
d.	C-determinate	L-determinate	D30–1, D14–1, (a), D3b.
e.	C-exclusive	L-exclusive	D30–3, D14–2, D3b.
f.	C-dependent	L-dependent	D30–4, D14–3, D3a, (e).
g.	C-indeterminate	factual	D30–2, D21–1, (a), (d).
h.	C-complete	L-complete	D30–5, D14–4, (a), D3a, (e).
i.	C-comprehensive	L-comprehensive	D30–6, D14–5, (a), D3a.
j.	C-interchangeable	L-interchangeable	D31–13, D14–6, (a), (c).
k.	C-perfect	L-perfect	D30–7, D14–7, D3a, (a).

+**T36-34.** If K is an L-exhaustive calculus for S, then the following is the case:

    a. S is an L-true interpretation for K. (From D3, D34–1, T29–37 and 21.)

    b. K is in accordance with S. (From (a), T34–1, D1.)

    c. K is C-consistent. (From (b), T1.)

    d. K is a C-determinate calculus if and only if S is an L-determinate system. (From D30–8, D14–8, T30a and d.)

T36-36. If K_m is an L-exhaustive calculus for S, then K_n is an L-exhaustive calculus for S if and only if K_m and K_n are coincident. (From D3, D31–9.)

If a semantical system S is given, then it is often more important to construct an L-exhaustive calculus for S than an exhaustive one. An L-exhaustive calculus for S represents logical relations holding within S and especially logical deduction in S in a formal way. Thus it is a *formalization of the logic* of S (as far as this logic is represented by L-implication and L-falsity). (The problems of the formalization of logic will be discussed in detail in [II].)

Here again we have to take into consideration the fact that most calculi up to the present do not contain rules of refutation and hence cannot be L-exhaustive for S (unless S does not contain any L-false $\mathfrak{T}_i$). But we often find a calculus K which is in a restricted sense L-exhaustive for a certain S, such that C-implication in K coincides with L-implication in S. If this is the case, then the following of the theorems given above apply also to K and S, although K is not an L-exhaustive calculus in the strict sense for S: T30a, b, c, i, j, k; T34a, b, c; T36.

For certain semantical systems, L-exhaustive calculi cannot be constructed without using transfinite rules (§ 25, at the end). (See [Foundations] § 10, at the end.)

Examples of exhaustive and L-exhaustive calculi. We again use the systems S_3 and S_4 and the calculi K_1 and K_2 analyzed in § 35. We found that both S_3 and S_4 are true interpretations for K_1 and for K_2; therefore, both K_1 and K_2 are in accordance with S_3 and with S_4.

Now it will be shown that K_2 is an *L-exhaustive calculus* for S_3. The primitive sentences and the rule of inference in K_2 are those of the ordinary propositional calculus. It is known for this calculus 1. that all the tautological sentences, i.e. those whose truth-table has a 'T' on each line, and only these, are provable (and hence derivable from Λ) in it, and 2. that $\mathfrak{S}_j$ is derivable from a non-empty $\mathfrak{T}_i$ in this calculus if and only if the truth-table of $\mathfrak{S}_j$ has a 'T' on every line on which that of $\mathfrak{T}_i$ has a 'T'. Because of (1), 'L-true in S_3' coincides with 'provable in K_2' and hence with 'C-true in K_2' (T31–36; it was shown in § 31 that K_2 is C-consistent). In other words, 'L-implicate of Λ in S_3' coincides with 'C-implicate of Λ in K_2'. Because of (2), for a non-empty $\mathfrak{T}_i$ 'L-implicate of $\mathfrak{T}_i$ in S_3' coincides with 'derivable from $\mathfrak{T}_i$ in K_2' and hence with 'C-implicate of $\mathfrak{T}_i$ in K_2' (T29–55; that K_2 fulfills the condition in this theorem has been shown in § 30).

Therefore, generally, 'L-implicate in S_3' coincides with 'C-implicate in K_2'. Finally, the class $\Re_1$ which is directly C-false in K_2 has been shown in § 35 to be L-false in S_3. $\Im_i$ is C-false in K_2 if and only if $\Re_1$ is derivable from $\Im_i$ in K_2 (D28–3), hence if and only if $\Im_i \stackrel{\text{L}}{\rightarrow} \Re_1$ in S_3 (see above), hence if and only if $\Im_i$ is L-false in S_3 (T14–58). Therefore K_2 is an L-exhaustive calculus for S_3 (D3).

In order to get an example of an *exhaustive calculus* for S_3, let us construct K_9 out of K_2 by adding six factual sentences as primitive sentences. First, we have to find out by observations which of the six atomic sentences in K_2 are, on the basis of their interpretation in S_3, true and which false (as we did with one of them, $\Im_1$, in § 35). Then we take as additional primitive sentences in K_9 the true atomic sentences and the negations of the false ones, hence six F-true sentences. We give an abridged indication of the proof for the statement that K_9 is an exhaustive calculus for S_3. 1. With respect to the ordinary propositional calculus and hence K_2 the following can be shown. If a molecular sentence $\Im_j$ with n different components has 'T' on a certain line of its truth-table, then $\Im_j$ is derivable from the class $\Re_i$ of the following n sentences: if a component of $\Im_j$ has 'T' on the line in question, it belongs to $\Re_i$; otherwise its negation belongs to $\Re_i$. 2. If $\Im_j$ is true in S_3 it is provable and C-true in K_9. (This follows from (1). We take the line which ascribes to the components those truth-values which they have in S_3. Then all sentences of $\Re_i$ are additional primitive sentences in K_9. $\Im_j$ is derivable from $\Re_i$ in K_2 and hence provable in K_9.) 3. If $\Im_i$ is false in S_3, it is C-false in K_9. (If $\Im_i$ is false $\sim\Im_i$ is true in S_3 and hence C-true in K_9 (2). Hence $\Im_i \stackrel{\text{C}}{\rightarrow} \{\Im_i, \sim\Im_i\}$. $\Re_1$, the directly C-false class in K_2 and K_9, is a C-implicate of any class of the form just mentioned (§ 30). Therefore, $\Im_i \stackrel{\text{C}}{\rightarrow} \Re_1$; hence $\Im_i$ is C-false.) 4. K_9 is C-consistent. (K_2 is C-consistent; the class of the additional primitive sentences in K_9 is not C-false in K_2.) 5. K_9 is an exhaustive calculus for S_3 (T36–22).

APPENDIX

APPENDIX

§ 37. Terminological Remarks

These remarks concern either particular terms or general terminological questions with respect to the formation of terms (e.g. as names of calculi, for kinds of variables, etc.).

The new systematization of logic will make it necessary at some time in the future to construct a new, systematic terminology. The present stage is not yet ripe for such an enterprise. The terminology will certainly depend upon the structure of the whole theory. We cannot know whether the outlines of the structure as we see it today in its two parts, syntax and semantics (or three parts, if we divide semantics into radical semantics and L-semantics), will not undergo major changes even in the near future, since everything is still in the first stages of development. Thus, with respect to the choice of terms, we cannot do more at the present moment than look for terms which seem to fit into the framework as we see it today, paying due regard to terms which are in common use or used by outstanding authors.

In the terminological remarks in this section, reference will be made to the following books, in addition to the bibliography.

Baldwin, J. M. *Dictionary of Philosophy and Psychology.* New York and London, 3 vols., 1901–05.

Cohen, M. R., and Nagel, E. *An Introduction to Logic and Scientific Method.* New York, 1934.

Eisler, R. *Handwörterbuch der Philosophie.* Berlin, 1913.

Lalande, A. *Vocabulaire technique et critique de la philosophie.* Paris (1902–23), 4th ed., 3 vols., 1932.

Langer, S. *Introduction to Symbolic Logic.* Boston and New York, 1937.

Quine, W. V. *A System of Logistic.* Cambridge, Mass., 1934.

Russell, B. [Principles] *The Principles of Mathematics.* Cambridge (1903), 1938.

* If, in the following, different terms for a concept or different meanings for a term are discussed, then that marked by an asterisk is the one *used in these studies.*

Absolute Concepts, see: Connections; Radical Terms (2); 'True'.
C-, see: Prefixes.

Calculi (§ 24). Two possible ways of forming *names for particular calculi*: I. with reference to expressions or signs occurring (e.g. 'sentential calculus', 'calculus of predicates'). II*. with reference to designata (e.g. 'propositional calculus'* or 'calculus of propositions', 'functional calculus'* or 'calculus of functions', 'calculus of classes', 'calculus of relations', 'calculus of real numbers'). II seems much more usual, as the examples show. A name of this kind is given to a calculus with regard to its chief interpretation, i.e. that which the author chiefly has in mind. Although this is, strictly speaking, something outside of syntax and hence foreign to the calculus itself, the designation may be used within syntax also if taken merely as a conventional name for the calculus. If used with this caution, method II seems convenient for practical purposes.

'Concept'. The word is used chiefly in three meanings:
    I. Psychological meaning: a certain result or feature of a certain mental activity.
    II. Logical meaning:
        IIa, narrowest sense: property*.
        IIb, wider sense: property or relation (attribute*).
        IIc*, widest sense: property, relation, or function.
    III. As 'term' or 'expression'.

Connections (§ 6; [II] § 3). Terms for propositional connections of degree two. [They are relations between propositions, not sentences; absolute, not semantical concepts; in distinction to the corresponding radical relations (§ 9), see Radical Terms, 1.] Since there are no terms in ordinary language for these concepts, we take into consideration: a. the usage in symbolic logic; b. the suitability of a term as a root for the corresponding L-term (constructed by prefixing 'L-').
    1. *'Implication'*. Although the use of this term by Russell for the propositional connection has sometimes led to misunderstandings, we keep it because it is widely used and suitable as a root for the L-term†. Other terms: 'material implication' (Russell); 'conditional'‡ (Quine). We may take into consideration terms used for *L-implication* (either between propositions or between sentences) or its converse, to see whether they suggest a suitable term for the connection, to be used simultaneously as a root for the L-term. 'Strict implication' (Lewis),

'formal implication' (Cohen-Nagel), 'tautologous implication', 'logical implication', 'necessary implication' are themselves not suitable as roots, but suggest again the root 'implication'. 'Entailment' seems possible but not better than 'implication'. For the converse: 'consequence' and 'deducible' seem suitable as roots for an L-term but not acceptable for the connection ('consequent' seems possible for both purposes).

2. *'Disjunction'**. We keep the term because it is in general use. Disadvantage: it has the connotation of exclusion. Other terms: 'alternation' (Quine, following Johnson; the same disadvantage); 'logical sum'‡ (Russell).

3. *'Conjunction'**. Generally used. Other term: 'logical product'‡ (Russell).

4. *'Equivalence'**. Widely used; well in accordance with the meaning "the same truth-value"†.

5. *'Exclusion'**†. Other term: 'non-conjunction'‡ (Sheffer). Other terms for the corresponding L-concept: 'incompatibility', 'inconsistency'; they do not seem quite suitable for the connection (the second is used in a different sense; see D_{31-2}).

6. *'Bi-negation'*(*) might be considered for the neither-nor connection.

General remarks:

† The terms (1), (4), and (5) originally, in traditional logic and in everyday language, have the meaning of the corresponding L-concepts. This is sometimes confusing for the beginner. On the other hand, this fact makes the terms suitable as roots for the corresponding L-terms.

‡ This term, although suitable for the connection, does not seem suitable as a root for L- and C-terms.

'Consequence', see: 'Derivable'.

'Derivable'* (D_{25}–A_4). Other terms: 'consequence', 'deducible'. These terms are used in two different meanings (leaving aside their use in the sense of 'provable', which should certainly be avoided).

I: As "constructible (out of the premisses) with the help of the rules of inference (of the calculus in question)".

II*: As "constructible (out of the premisses) with the help of the rules of inference and the primitive sentences" (D_{25}–A_4, D_{26}–4).

[Accordingly, 'provable' is to be defined as follows. I: 'derivable from the primitive sentences'; II*: 'derivable from Λ', D_{26}–5.] Concept II is much more important than I, more characteristic for the calculus in question. If, in the construction of a calculus, we wish to make it possible to infer a certain sentence from certain other sentences, then we often have the choice of doing this by laying down either a primitive sentence or a rule of inference. This difference has no effect upon the deductive power of the calculus and is therefore unessential; but it changes concept I, while concept II is the same in both cases. Therefore, if we want a term for only one of the two concepts — otherwise we should have an unnecessary increase in the number of terms — it seems preferable to use it for II*.

F-, see: 'Factual'; Prefixes.

'Factual'* (§ 21). Leibniz 'vérités de fait'. Other terms: 'synthetic' (Kant), 'material', 'empirical', 'contingent' (Leibniz).

'Formal', 'formalization' (§§ 4, 24). Among the many meanings in which the term is used in modern logic, the following three seem especially important:

I. As 'general' (in distinction to 'singular').

II. As 'logical', 'necessary' (e.g. truth) (in distinction to 'factual', 'contingent').

III*. As 'in abstraction from meaning', 'without reference to designata' ('syntactical'*).

I is used e.g. by Russell in his distinction between 'material implication' (e.g. '$P(a) \supset Q(b)$') and 'formal implication' (e.g. '$(x)(P(x) \supset Q(x))$'). It is to be noticed, however, that a formal implication in this sense is merely a universal material implication (the truth of '$(x)(P(x) \supset Q(x))$' is in general not more of a formal or logical nature in the ordinary sense of these words than that of '$P(a) \supset Q(b)$'; it may likewise be contingent).

'Function'. This term is used for many different concepts.

I. As 'expression with free variables' (§ 6). [Other terms: 'open expression'*, 'functional', 'matrix', 'expressional function'*.] Here we may distinguish two kinds:

IA. As 'expression of sentential form with free variables'. [Other terms: 'open sentence'*, 'sentential function'*, 'propositional function', 'sentential (propositional, statement) matrix' (Quine), 'sentential (propositional) functional', 'sentential (propositional) form' (Sheffer, Langer).]

IB. As 'expression with free variables, not of sentential form'. [Other terms: 'nominal function', 'functional'.]

II. For the corresponding designatum (strictly speaking, the entity determined by the expression, § 11).

IIA. As 'attribute'* (§ 6). [Other terms: 'propositional function', 'attribute', 'concept'.]

IIB. [Other terms: 'object function' ('Gegenstandsfunktion'), 'correlation'*, 'descriptive function'.]

Frege used the term 'function' in [Begriffsschrift] for I, later in [Grundgesetze] for II. Russell mixes the two uses (perhaps following Frege without being aware that Frege changed the meaning) as with 'proposition' (which see). [For I: "... I shall call the expression a propositional function" [Principles] p. 13; "By a 'propositional function' we mean something which contains a variable x, and expresses a proposition as soon as ..." [Princ. Math.] p. 38; "A function is what ambiguously denotes ..." [Princ. Math.] p. 39. For II: "The propositional function 'x has the relation R to y' will be expressed by the notation xRy" [Princ. Math.] p. 26.] The term has been taken from mathematics. There it is in general use for II; its occasional use for I may be regarded as a loose way of speaking, i.e. as an abbreviation for 'function expression'. Therefore it seems advisable to use the term 'function' in logic also primarily for II* (or IIB), and to search for a new term for I. At present, no other satisfactory term for I is known; in this book, therefore, we use 'expressional function'* for I and 'sentential function'* for IA as long as no better term has been found; the adjectives 'expressional' and 'sentential' will make it clear that II is not meant.

Implication, see: Connections; Radical Terms.

L-, see: Connections; 'Formal'; Negation ...; Prefixes; 'Tautologous'.

Negation of L-terms. With respect to a given radical concept, we must distinguish between two negative L-concepts:

1. The L-concept corresponding to the negation of the radical concept ('L-non- ...');

2. the negation of the L-concept corresponding to the radical concept ('non-L- ...').

Examples. 1. 'A' and 'B' are L-non-equivalent if '$\sim(A \equiv B)$' is L-true and hence 'A ≡ B' L-false. 2. 'A' and 'B' are non-L-equivalent (i.e. they are not L-equivalent) if and only if 'A ≡ B' is not L-true; it need not be L-false but may be factual. In many cases the radical term and its negation have little use (e.g. 'exclusive') or none at all (e.g. 'determinate', 'dependent', 'complete'), while the corresponding L-term and its negation are useful. It might be convenient to use in these cases the simpler and more natural form 'L-in . . .' instead of 'non-L- . . .'. In this way we might use 'L-indeterminate' (instead of 'non-L-determinate') as negation for 'L-determinate' (D14–1; D21–1), 'L-independent' as negation for 'L-dependent' (D14–3), 'L-incomplete' as negation for 'L-complete' (D14–4), and perhaps 'L-inexclusive' as negation for 'L-exclusive' (D14–2) (hence in the sense of 'logically compatible'). The same convention might be made for the corresponding C-terms.

'*Postulate*', see: 'Primitive Sentence'.

Prefixes. 1. The *use of prefixes* for semantical and syntactical terms — quite aside from the question of which particular letters are chosen — leads to a considerable increase in simplicity and uniformity of theorems. Compare e.g. the following formulations. (As old terminology that of [Syntax] is taken; the result would be similar with the terminology of other authors.)

Old Terminology	*New Terminology*
"If an equivalence sentence is true, the two components have the same truth-value; if it is valid, they are equipollent; if it is analytic, they are L-equipollent."	"If an equivalence sentence is true, the two components are equivalent; if it is C-true, they are C-equivalent; if it is L-true, they are L-equivalent."

2. *Choice of letters as prefixes.* The prefixes are added to radical terms in order to construct terms for the corresponding syntactical concepts ('C-'), for the L-semantical concepts ('L-'), and for their counterparts ('F-'). They are added mostly to 'true' and 'implicate'; therefore it is chiefly these terms that we take into consideration.

   a. 'C-true'* (§ 28) for 'true in a calculus'. Other possibilities: 'F-true' for 'formally true' (but this might be mistaken for L-true); 'D-' for 'deductively'; 'S-' for 'syntactically' or 'in a (syntactical) system' (but 'S-' might be misunderstood as 'semantically' or 'in a semantical system').

   b. 'L-true'* (§ 14) for 'logically true'. Other possibilities: 'F-true' for 'formally true' (but this might be mistaken for C-true); 'S-implication' for 'strict implication'; 'N-true' for 'necessarily true'; 'A-true' for 'analytic' (Kant).

c. 'F-true'* (§ 21) for 'factually true'. For other possibilities, see 'Factual'.

'Primitive Sentence'* (§ 24). Other terms: 1. 'primitive proposition'; if, however, 'proposition' is used for meaning II*, it is a semantical term and cannot be used in the construction of a calculus; 2. 'postulate'; 3. 'axiom'. I prefer to make a distinction between 'primitive sentence' and terms (2) and (3), between a calculus and a postulate (or axiom) set. The latter consists of a basic calculus with a certain interpretation (both are usually tacitly presupposed) and a specific calculus consisting of the postulates (see § 38(f) and [Foundations] § 16).

'Proposition'. The term is used for two different concepts, namely for certain expressions (I) and for their designata (II).

I: As 'declarative sentence'. Other terms: 'sentence'*, 'statement' (Quine), 'formula' (Bernays).

II*: As "that which is expressed (signified, formulated, represented, designated) by a (declarative) sentence" (§§ 6 and 18). Other terms: 'Satz an sich' (Bolzano), 'Objectiv' (A. Meinong), 'state of affairs' (Wittgenstein), 'condition'.

The philosophical dictionaries give only meaning I for the term 'proposition'. Lalande: "énoncé verbal . . .", "l'énoncé d'un jugement", quoting Bosanquet: "the unit of language which represents a judgment". Baldwin: "a judgment expressed in words". Eisler: "Satz (πρότασις, propositio, enunciatio) ist . . . der sprachliche Ausdruck für einen Gedanken". *Concise Oxford Dictionary* (1931): "statement, assertion, especially (Logic) form of words. . .". Russell sometimes uses the term with meaning I ["An expression such as . . . is not a proposition, . . . the expression becomes a proposition" [Principles] p. 13; "the fact that propositions are 'incomplete symbols' . . ." [Princ. Math.] p. 44; "a form of words which must be either true or false I shall call a proposition", *Our Knowledge of the External World*, p. 52] and sometimes with meaning II [". . . symbolizes the proposition that . . ." [Princ. Math.] p. 15; "the symbol . . . denotes one definite proposition" [Princ. Math.] p. 16; ". . . what we call a 'proposition' (in the sense in which this is distinguished from the phrase expressing it) . . .", ". . . the phrase which expresses a proposition . . ." [Princ. Math.] p. 44; "the propositions in the written expression of which such symbols occur . . ." [Principles] Introd. to

2nd ed. (1938), p. ix.] This makes his explanations often difficult to understand.

Many authors, even in books and papers in the field of symbolic logic, use some terms in the ambiguous way just indicated for 'proposition', namely, sometimes for certain expressions and sometimes for their designata (besides 'proposition', e.g. 'function' (which see), 'propositional function', 'number', and others). Further, the distinction between speaking about a sign (e.g. "we substitute 'R' for . . .") and using a sign in order to speak about its designatum (e.g. "the relation R is symmetric") is often neglected and hence the quotes in the first case are omitted. Each of these two inaccuracies, the ambiguity of terms and the omission of quotes, would be harmless alone (the reader would understand both "the proposition 'P(a)' " and "the sentence P(a)" as "the sentence 'P(a)' "). But the two combined make many formulations ambiguous and even incomprehensible. (Does "the proposition P(a)" mean "the proposition P(a)" or "the sentence 'P(a)' "?)

It seems that at present many authors (perhaps the majority of those in modern, as distinguished from traditional, logic) use the term 'proposition' with meaning II*. [For example, Cohen and Nagel (p. 28): "We have distinguished the proposition (as the objective meaning) from the sentence which states it"; Lewis and Langford: "the proposition . . . is the same with the fact that . . ." (p. 472), "that sentence does name a fact . . ." (p. 475); Langer (p. 50): "any linguistic statement of a proposition . . .", "any symbolic structure, such as a sentence, expresses a proposition, if . . ."; Quine (p. 32): "propositions, not in the sense of sentences, but in the sense of what sentences may be taken to symbolize"; A. A. Bennett and C. A. Baylis, *Formal Logic* (p. 47): "Propositions are usually expressed by sentences".]

Some authors use the term 'proposition' for meaning I but with the qualification that it applies to sentences only insofar as these are not regarded from a merely formal point of view but as having a meaning — in our terminology, sentences in semantics, not in syntax. This use seems to go back to Aristotle. Following Schlick, I used the term in this way in [Foundations]. But it now seems to me preferable to use it in meaning II, and then to use only one term (namely 'sentence') for I both in calculi and in semantical systems.

'*Propositional Calculus*', see: Calculi.

'Propositional Function', see: 'Function'.
'Propositional Variable', see: Variables.

Quotes. I use quotes mainly in two ways.

1. By adding quotes to an expression (sign, word) of a language, a name for that expression is constructed in the metalanguage for that language. [*Examples.* a. In English as metalanguage for a symbolic object language: " '*x*' is a variable", " '*a*' designates Chicago"; b. In English as metametalanguage: " 'equivalent' is a semantical word", "we define 'implicate' . . .".] Concerning the necessity of distinguishing between an expression and its name, whether formed with the help of quotes or in some other way, compare: Frege [Grundgesetze] I, p. 4; [Syntax] § 42. The requirement of the distinction should of course not be pedantically exaggerated. There is no objection to all kinds of shorter and simpler formulations, provided the reader can have no practical doubt as to what is meant. For examples of the confusion caused by a lack of the distinction, see 'Proposition'.

2. In a few cases, I include an expression (English word or phrase) in quotes although I am not speaking about that expression but about its designatum. This is done where the omission of quotes would look strange because of the restrictions of English grammar. In these cases a word like 'concept', 'property', 'relation', etc., is always added; thereby it immediately becomes clear that it is not the expression but its designatum which is being talked about. [*Examples.* I write "the relation 'implicate' is . . ." instead of "the relation implicate is . . .", because the latter formulation looks strange and might even be misunderstood, and because for the relation meant here, namely the converse of implication, there is no simple noun in English; likewise "the concept 'logical'" instead of the ambiguous formulation "the concept logical" or the awkward "the concept logicality".]

Radical terms.

1. Choice of terms. For the chief radical properties of sentences there is practically no problem of the choice of terms; the terms 'true' and 'false' seem in accordance with general usage (see 'True'). But the *radical relations* between sentences (e.g. implication, exclusion, etc., § 9) are hardly ever referred to in everyday life or in traditional logic and only occasionally even in modern logic. Therefore, there are no terms for them in common use. It seems convenient to take for them the terms used for the corresponding relations between propositions

(§ 17), i.e. the propositional connections (see 'Connections'). Here, it sometimes seems convenient to use the adjectival form of the terms also, especially for the symmetric relations. Two sentences are then called (2) disjunct*, (3) conjunct (not used in this book), (4) equivalent*, (5) exclusive*, in relation to one another (§ 9). In the case of the non-symmetric relation (1) (implication) it seems convenient to have simple terms both for the relation and for its converse. We use: '$\mathfrak{S}_i$ implies $\mathfrak{S}_j$' (because it is customary in modern logic, although not in accordance with the ordinary meaning of the word) and (more frequently) '$\mathfrak{S}_j$ is an implicate of $\mathfrak{S}_i$' (D9–3); both these terms seem suitable as roots for L- and C-terms.

2. *Multiple use of the terms.* We use many radical terms in four different ways, namely, as designating relations between a. propositions (e.g. "A is equivalent to B", D17–4); b. sentences ("'A' is equivalent to 'B'", D9–4); c. attributes ("P is equivalent to Q", D10–5); d. predicates ("'P' is equivalent to 'Q'", D10–11b). Since the context always shows the nature of the members of the relation, no confusion can arise from this multiple use. The relations of the kinds (a) and (c) are absolute concepts, those of the kinds (b) and (d) are semantical. This multiple use makes the practical application of the terminology much easier; otherwise we should need four times as many terms. And it is sufficiently in accordance with general use.

'**Semantics**' (§§ 4, 7). The term was coined by Michel J. A. Bréal, *Essai de sémantique; science des significations*, Paris, 1897 (English translation, *Semantics: Studies in the Science of Meaning*, London, 1900). (Bréal used it from 1883 on; see Lalande.) Baldwin: "Semantics (or Semasiology): the doctrine of historical word meanings". The term is used by A. Korzybski (*Science and Sanity* and many papers) for a theory concerning the use of language, and especially the causes and effects of, and cures for, certain misuses of language; thus here the term corresponds more to our 'pragmatics'. For Chwistek's use of the term, see 'Syntax'. Other term with a similar meaning: 'semasiology' (used in linguistics, sometimes also in logic, e.g. by Ajdukiewicz, covering semantics in connection with pragmatics).

'**Semiotic**' (§ 4). (Original meaning: medical theory of symptoms.) Locke: '$\Sigma\eta\mu\epsilon\iota\omega\tau\iota\kappa\acute{\eta}$', a science of signs and significations. Other terms used with a similar meaning: 1. 'significs' (V. Welby, *What is Meaning?*, 1903; Baldwin: theory of signification, in all senses — verbal sense, intention, worth; also used by a group of Dutch mathematicians,

Brouwer, Mannoury, and others, with special emphasis on pragmatical questions); 2. 'sematology' (Bühler). On the history of the words 'semantics' and 'semiotic' see R. A. Walker in *Word* 4 (1948), 78–97.

'Sentence', see: 'Proposition'.

Signs, see: Variables.

'Syntax', *'Syntactics'* (§§ 4, 24). Sometimes used for the general abstract theory of order and combinations (e.g. Cournot, *Traité de l'enchaînement* . . . , chap. II, § 11 (Lalande); he mentions the German word 'Syntaktik' used with this meaning). Morris ([Foundations] p. 13ff) distinguishes between 'syntactics' (for the wider field of formal (which see, meaning III) analysis of signs of any kinds, not only in declarative sentences) and '(logical) syntax' (for the part of syntactics concerned with a formal analysis of declarative sentences only). Other terms used with a similar meaning: 1. 'Metamathematics', used by Hilbert for the syntax of mathematics, and sometimes, e.g. by the Polish logicians, used for the whole field of what we call syntax. 2. 'Morphology', used (besides 'metamathematics') by Tarski for syntax, but sometimes also in a wider sense, including semantics. 3. 'Semiotik', used by H. Hermes (*Semiotik: eine Theorie der Zeichengestalten als Grundlage für Untersuchungen von formalisierten Sprachen*, 1938) for what we call pure general syntax; he seems to understand the term 'syntax' only in the sense of 'descriptive syntax'. 4. 'Semantics', used by L. Chwistek (e.g. *Math. Zeitschr.* 14, 1922; *Erkenntnis* 3, 1933) for a theory which seems to correspond to what we call syntax; whether this theory also contains semantical concepts is difficult to see because of a fundamental and thoroughgoing ambiguity in his formulations (of the kind described above under 'Proposition'). — The reason for the choice of the *term 'syntax'* for the field of formal investigations is its close relationship to the branch of linguistics usually called syntax, i.e. the theory of the construction of sentences out of words. There is, however, this difference: the latter field is, on the one hand, narrower than the former because it does not include the theory of formal deduction, and, on the other hand, wider because it does not restrict itself to formal analysis but formulates rules which refer to designata. Whenever a misunderstanding seems possible, one might use the terms 'logical syntax' and 'grammatical syntax' for the two fields.

'Tautologous', 'tautology'. Two meanings: I: as 'analytic', 'L-true'; II: as "true for each truth-possibility of the components on the basis of the truth-tables for the connectives" (compare § 15; this corresponds to 'L-true by NTT' in [II] D11–30). Wittgenstein introduced the term into modern logic; he perhaps meant I, but he defined it only with the help of the truth-tables, so that the concept defined is really II. The former use of the term by the Vienna Circle in meaning I frequently led to misunderstandings. Therefore it seems preferable to use it for II, if at all.

Theory of Systems. It would be convenient to have a term for the field in which semantical and syntactical systems are investigated. This field contains pure semantics and pure syntax and, in addition, the study of the relations between syntactical and semantical systems (e.g. interpretation); the latter belongs neither to syntax nor to semantics. Terms which might be considered: 1. 'systematics' (but the adjective 'systematical' could hardly be used in this sense); 2. 'systemics' (suggested by K. R. Symon); 3. '(logical) grammar' (Wittgenstein seems to use this term and likewise '(logical) syntax' for an analysis which, in our terminology, combines syntactical and semantical questions but also covers what we call descriptive syntax and descriptive semantics, and perhaps even something of pragmatics). (If I had known a suitable term, I should have taken it instead of 'semantics' in the title of these studies.)

'True' (§ 7). 1. Some philosophers restrict the use of the term to what we call factual truth. But the wider use, including logical, necessary truth, is in accordance both with traditional use (e.g. Leibniz, Kant, and many others: 'necessary truths') and with the generally accepted use in modern logic. This wider use is also much more convenient because the formulation of rules and theorems becomes much simpler ([Foundations] p. 14).

2. In another respect, there are chiefly three possible domains of application of the term 'true' (and likewise of 'false'); it may be applied (I) to propositions (in traditional terminology, 'judgments' or 'content of judgments'); (II) to sentences (in traditional terminology, 'propositions'); (III*) to both. The concept I is non-semantical; it is absolute in the sense of § 17 (see D17–1). II is the semantical concept of truth (see § 7 or D20–13 or D17–C1). [The name 'the absolute concept of truth' has occasionally been given to II (e.g. by M. Kokoszynska); however, if this name is to be used at all, it seems to be more appropriate for I.] Our use III* is deliberately ambiguous; see

above: Radical terms, 2. Multiple use. In traditional philosophy and logic, all three uses seem to occur (Lalande: "en parlant des jugements ou des propositions qui les expriment"). In modern logic, also, the use is not uniform. Many authors speak of 'true propositions'; but because of the ambiguity of this term (see 'Proposition') it is not clear whether they mean I or II. Some accept I and reject II explicitly (e.g. Cohen and Nagel (p. 27): "sentences . . . are not true or false. Truth or falsity can be predicated only of the propositions they signify"). But there seems to be an increasing tendency to accept II or III. It seems that III* is also the one used in everyday language, although a clear decision on this question is hardly possible in view of the lack of precision in that language. We may perhaps construe phrases like 'true statement', 'true report', 'true enunciation', as instances of II, and formulations of the form "it is true that . . ." as instances of I.

Variables (§§ 6, 11). Two possible ways of forming *designations for kinds of variables* (and analogously for kinds of *constants*, and for kinds of *signs*, comprehending both): I, with reference to their value-expressions (e.g. 'sentential variable', 'predicate variable', 'functor variable'); II. with reference to their values (designata) (e.g. 'propositional variable'*, 'function variable', 'individual variable'*, 'numerical variable', 'real number variable', 'relation variable'). This question is related to that of names for calculi (see Calculi). II seems in general more usual; but in some cases the terms (formed with the terms for designata given in § 6) would be unusual (e.g. 'property variable', 'attribute variable'). The terms in II, when used in syntax, would be taken from the chief interpretation for the calculus in question; they would be used in this case as technical terms for certain syntactical classes of variables and not understood as saying something about designata (in the same way as terms like 'predicate', 'numerical expression', 'sign of negation', etc., are used in syntax). Disadvantage of II: strange combinations like "propositional variables and other sentences", "a predicate which is a variable is an attribute variable", etc. But II might, nevertheless, be preferable.

§ 38. Outline of Further Semantical Problems

Here are listed some problems of semiotic and, especially, semantics, which either could not be discussed sufficiently in the present treatise or have not been mentioned at all. It is planned to deal with some of them in subsequent volumes of these studies.

a. General semantics and general syntax. It seems desirable to construct general semantics and general syntax systematically. This might be done in the form of systems of postulates in such a way that first a system is constructed exhibiting the features which are common to radical semantics, L-semantics, and syntax. This system might then be branched out into three systems for the three theories mentioned. The use of the new concepts mentioned in (b) below may lead to a simplification of these systems.

b. The propositional calculus and its interpretations. The system of the ordinary truth-tables for the connectives is a semantical system which we may call propositional logic. It is known to be a true interpretation of the ordinary propositional calculus (see § 35) consisting of primitive sentences and rules of inference. It can easily be shown to be, moreover, an L-true interpretation. This interpretation will be called the normal interpretation of the propositional calculus. It can be shown that there are two kinds of true interpretations for the propositional calculus which are non-normal. Hence, the propositional calculus is not, as seems to be generally believed, a full formalization of propositional logic in the sense of not admitting further syntactical determinations. If certain new syntactical concepts are used, which are not definable on the basis of those ordinarily used, the propositional calculus can be supplemented in such a way that the normal interpretation is the only true interpretation for it.

The introduction of the new concepts into the common foundation of syntax and semantics will also have other consequences of a more general nature. It will eliminate the lack of symmetry in this foundation which we found at several places (e.g. §§ 9, 14, 28) and thereby simplify the structure of the whole edifice of syntax and semantics. (In [II], the propositional calculus and its interpretations will be analyzed and the new concepts will be introduced.)

c. L-semantics. The distinction between logical and descriptive signs and the distinction between logical and factual truth belong to the most important problems of logical analysis. Our previous discussion has shown the difficulties connected with the problem of a general formulation of these distinctions (§§ 13 and 16). This problem is very much in need of further investigation. The discussion might perhaps distinguish between the two cases of an extensional and a non-extensional metalanguage (see d).

d. Extensional and non-extensional languages. Besides extensional language systems, non-extensional (so-called intensional) ones should also be studied as object languages both in semantics and in syntax. (An extensional system contains only extensional connectives, i.e. such as possess truth-tables, compare D10–21 and 22.) Among non-extensional connectives different kinds are to be studied, especially those designating logical modalities (like those of Lewis' system of Strict Implication; compare §§ 17 and 18) and those designating physical or causal modalities. Today no satisfactory and sufficiently comprehensive system for the connectives of the first kind exists, and no system at all for those of the second kind, it seems.

If and when a satisfactory non-extensional system is constructed, it would be worth while to examine how it can be applied as metalanguage, especially for semantics, and whether this application would have advantages in comparison with an extensional metalanguage. Certain conditions, especially in L-semantics, seem to point in this direction (see § 16 at the end, §§ 17 and 18). But the situation is at present not yet clear enough for a judgment.

e. Antinomies. Some of the so-called logical antinomies or paradoxes belong to the field of semantics, e.g. the antinomy of the concept 'heterological' and that of the concept 'false', usually called "the Liar". The modern analysis of these antinomies and of their consequences for logic, especially by Russell, Ramsey, Gödel, and Tarski, has brought clarity concerning the nature of the antinomies, shown ways of avoiding them, and led to further important results. It seems that the problem and the results will gain clarity if looked at from the present semiotical point of view, especially by distinguishing between the semantical and the syntactical form of the antinomies. (For their syntactical representation, compare [Syntax] § 60a–d.)

f. Postulate systems. Postulate systems (or axiom systems), whose construction has been found so useful in mathematics, geometry, and physics, are, regarded from the point of view of semantics and syntax, combinations of two parts, a basic system and a specific addition. The basic system usually contains logical words like 'not', 'and', 'every', etc.; these are not dealt with in a formal way but taken in their ordinary meaning. Therefore this part of the system is semantical, though not explicitly. The specific part, however, is taken in a formal way; deductions are carried out without presupposing a particular interpretation. Therefore this part is syntactical. What is usually called the construction of a model for a postulate set is the construction of an interpretation for this syntactical part (compare [Foundations] § 16).

Hence, the general theory of postulate systems, dealing with the various kinds of such systems and with problems of consistency, independence, completeness, monomorphism, existence of models, etc., is a branch of general syntax and general semantics. Hence, when general syntax and general semantics has been developed sufficiently, the theory of postulate systems will be in a position to make use of the concepts and theorems of these fields.

g. Truth, probability, degree of confirmation. For certain concepts which are related to the concept of truth in some way it is first essential to see their difference from the concept of truth, with which they are sometimes identified erroneously, and second, to study their nature and their relation to the concept of truth. Because of the fact that strict verification for factual sentences is not possible, the concept of verification has to be replaced by the concept of confirmation and the concept 'verified' by 'confirmed to such and such a degree'. Sometimes the concept 'verified' is taken as being the same as 'true' — although the difference between these two concepts becomes obvious from a semiotical analysis, since the first is pragmatical and the second semantical. On the basis of this error, it is then believed that the concept of truth has to be replaced by the concept of degree of confirmation. Sometimes a second wrong identification is combined with the first, namely, that of the concepts of probability (in the statistical sense, as used in the mathematical calculus of probability and its applications) and of degree of confirmation. The second concept is pragmatical (although there are corresponding syntactical and semantical concepts), but the first is not. (Probability can be expressed either as a semantical concept, applied to sentences or predicates, or as an absolute, non-semiotical concept, expressible in the object language, applied to events, i.e. propositions or attributes.) On the basis of these two identifications, the view is sometimes held that the concept of truth has to be replaced by that of probability, while in fact these two concepts are to be used one beside the other. Finally, the concept of probability was identified in previous stages of the development of the theory of probability, and by some philosophers is still identified to-day, with the concept of the degree of belief. This concept is, however, a pragmatical, psychological concept.

It may be expected that the nature of these and related concepts and their relations to one another will become more clear by an analysis from the point of view of semiotic and its branches, making use of the concepts to be developed in pragmatics, semantics, and syntax.

h. Philosophical problems. It has turned out to be very fruitful to look at the problems of theoretical philosophy from the point of view of semiotic, i.e. to try to understand them as problems which have to do with signs and language in one way or another. Among problems of this kind we may first distinguish between those problems — or components in complex problems — which are of a factual, empirical, rather than logical nature. They occur especially in the theory of knowledge and the philosophy of science. If construed as problems of semiotic, they belong to pragmatics. They have to do, for instance, with the activities of perception, observation, comparison, registration, confirmation, etc., as far as these activities lead to or refer to knowledge formulated in language. On the other hand, we have the problems of logical analysis; they occur in what is known as logic and, combined with problems of the first kind, in the theory of knowledge and the philosophy of science. These problems belong either to semantics or to syntax. The first is the case if the logical analysis takes into consideration the meaning of the expressions (in our technical terminology, their designata); the second, if the analysis is carried out in a purely formal way.

Many sentences in philosophy are such that, in their customary formulation, they seem to deal not with language but merely with certain features of things or events or nature in general, while a closer analysis shows that they are translatable into sentences of L-semantics. Sentences of this kind might be called *quasi-logical* or crypto-logical. By translating quasi-logical sentences into L-terms, the philosophical problems involved will often become clearer and their treatment in terms of L-semantics more precise. The same problems can often also be formalized and then dealt with by syntactical methods if a suitable calculus corresponding to the semantical system in question and formalizing its L-concepts is constructed. This way of syntactical reformulation of philosophical problems has been dealt with in [Syntax] Chapter V. The method of semantical formulation of philosophical problems is to be developed in an analogous way; it may sometimes turn out to be more appropriate than the syntactical method (compare § 39 below).

i. Application of semiotic in empirical science. A great number of sentences in the books and papers in all branches of empirical science do not belong to the object language but to the metalanguage; in other words, they do not speak about the things and events of the field in question but about the laws or other sentences of the field, which in their turn deal with the events. The difference between these two kinds of sentences is often not manifest in the ordinary formulation, but can easily be exhibited by a simple analysis. (See the examples of sentences of a treatise in physics in [Syntax] § 85, and examples in psychology in S. S. Stevens, "Psychology and the Science of Science," *Psychological Bulletin*, vol. 36, 1939, Appendix I, p. 251.) If an author in any field of science is conscious of this distinction between metasentences and object sentences, and, within the first kind, of the distinction between pragmatical, semantical, and syntactical sentences, then many ambiguities and mutual misunderstandings in scientific discussions might be avoided.

§39. Remarks on "Logical Syntax of Language"

The modifications which the views explained in my earlier book [Syntax] have to undergo, especially in view of semantics, are here indicated. Most of the earlier results remain valid. But certain concepts, especially the L-concepts, are now regarded as semantical, not syntactical; hence, the earlier attempts at syntactical definitions for them are abandoned. Many of the earlier discussions and analyses are now seen to be incomplete, although correct; they have to be supplemented by corresponding semantical analyses. The field of theoretical philosophy is no longer restricted to syntax but is regarded as comprehending the whole analysis of language, including syntax and semantics and perhaps also pragmatics.

I wish to indicate how the views exhibited in my earlier book, *The Logical Syntax of Language*, have to be modified as a result, chiefly, of the new point of view of semantics. (The German original of the book appeared in 1934, the English translation with additions in 1937.)

Parts I, II, and III of [Syntax] belong to *special syntax*. They deal with two particular calculi called Language I and Language II. Here *no decisive modifications* have to be made. Today I should not call the rules in § 14 rules of I but rather rules of a different though related system, say I_t, containing transfinite rules; instead of 'analytic in I', I should say 'provable in I_t'. Analogously, §§ 34b to f give the rules for system II_t, defining 'provable in II_t', etc. By the way, the rules for II_t can be brought into a technically more simple but not essentially different form by a procedure analogous to the method (originated by Tarski) of defining 'true' in semantics.

The *principle of tolerance* (perhaps better called "principle of conventionality"), as explained in [Syntax] § 17, is still maintained. It states that the construction of a calculus and the choice of its particular features are a matter of convention. On the other hand, the construction of a system of logic, i.e. the definitions for the L-concepts, within a given semantical system is not a matter of mere convention; here the choice is essentially limited if the concepts are to be adequate (see above, § 16). And if a semantical system S is given, then the construction of a calculus K in accordance with S is also not purely conventional; in some respects the features of K may be chosen arbitrarily, in other respects they are predetermined by S (compare above § 36, and [Foundations] § 12).

[Syntax] *Part IV* gives an outline of *general syntax*, which "is to be regarded as no more than a first attempt" ([Syntax] § 46). Here, as was to be expected, *greater changes are necessary*. Some definitions (especially those for L-concepts) have to be abandoned. In general, the syntactical discussions remain valid; but in many cases, they should be supplemented by semantical discussions.

The most important change concerns the distinction between logical and descriptive signs, and the related distinction between *logical and factual truth*. It seems to me at present that these distinctions have to be made primarily in semantics, not in syntax. They can then also be formalized, i.e. represented by syntactical concepts with respect to a suitably constructed calculus. But even this procedure is not entirely independent of semantics, because the question whether or not a given syntactical concept, e.g. 'C-true in K' is the formal representation of the corresponding L-concept, say 'L-true in S', is a question which cannot be answered in syntax alone. Its answer depends not only upon the syntactical features of K but, in addition, upon the semantical features of S and its relation to K (K might, for instance, be an L-exhaustive calculus for S, see D36–3). The syntactical L-concepts defined in [Syntax] §§ 50 to 52 will in many cases be the formal representations of the corresponding semantical L-concepts, and the syntactical P-concepts of the semantical F-concepts. But this correspondence will not hold with respect to every calculus and every semantical system. And it does not seem possible to define in general syntax concepts which would correspond to semantical L-concepts with respect to every system. Therefore I abandon the definitions in §§ 50 to 52.

With respect to the concept of *range* ([Syntax] § 36) an analogous remark holds. It is primarily a semantical L-concept ('L-range'; see above, §§ 18 and 19). In this case, however, a certain analogous concept in general syntax is of some interest too ('C-range'; see above, § 32), although in general it will not coincide with the concept of L-range.

A second change is more one of emphasis and terminology than of content. In [Syntax] §§ 34a and 47, I emphasized very much the distinction between two procedures of deduction, called *derivation and consequence series,* the first using only definite rules; and the corresponding distinction between two kinds of concepts and terms based on these two kinds of procedure (called 'd-concepts' and 'c-concepts'; in the original, 'a-Begriffe' and 'f-Begriffe'). At present, I prefer to simplify the terminology by using the same terms for both kinds of concepts. The chief reason is that I found in the meantime that the same procedure, namely the construction of a sequence of sentences, can be applied with both kinds of rules. This has been briefly indicated above (see remark concerning transfinite rules at the end of § 25) and will be explained in a later volume. Thus, the previous term 'consequence in K' is now replaced by 'derivable in K'; and the previous term 'derivable in K' becomes 'derivable in the sub-calculus of K which contains only the finite rules of K' or simply 'derivable in K' if K contains only finite rules.

The syntactical characterization of the *propositional connections* ('junctions') as given in [Syntax] § 57 holds for many calculi but not for all; hence it is not adequate in general syntax. It is possible to define the connections not only in semantics but also in general syntax, but not on the basis of those concepts hitherto used by logicians. The new syntactical concepts and the syntactical characterization of the propositional connections with their help will be explained in vol. II of these studies (see above, § 38b). An analogous remark holds for the characterization of universal and existential operators in [Syntax] § 55. But with respect to these operators, it seems doubtful whether they can be defined at all in general syntax, with respect to all kinds of calculi.

I should prefer now to call the procedure called interpretation in [Syntax] § 62 a transformation of one calculus into another (or a translation or a correlation), in order to reserve the term "interpretation' for a relation between a semantical system and a calculus (see above, §§ 33ff).

I now regard *extensionality* as primarily a semantical concept (see above, D10–20 and 21); but there is a syntactical concept corresponding to it (see above, D31–12 and 13). Thus the discussion of extensionality in [Syntax] §§ 65ff remains valid in general; but it has to be supplemented by a semantical discussion. The thesis of extensionality is still held as a supposition ([Syntax] § 67); it can be applied to the semantical concept of extensionality: intensional (i.e. non-extensional) sentences are translatable into sentences of an extensional language; translatability is here meant in the strong sense of L-equivalence.

In [Syntax] § 71 (2) it was asserted that an analysis of language is either formal, and hence syntactical, or else psychological. Today I would say that, in addition to these two kinds of analysis (the second is what is now called pragmatical), there is the possibility of semantical analysis. Hence I no longer believe that "*a logic of meaning* is superfluous"; I now regard semantics as the fulfillment of the old search for a logic of meaning, which had not been fulfilled before in any precise and satisfactory way.

Instead of the prefix 'S-' in [Syntax] § 71b I should now use 'C-' (compare above, §§ 22 and 37).

The concept of *quasi-syntactical sentences* plays a large role in the discussions in [Syntax] §§ 63ff and Part V. It seems to me at present that the concept of quasi-logical sentences (see above, § 38h) is more important in connection with the same problems (non-extensional sentences, especially modalities; philosophical problems in general). But in many cases it will still be convenient to translate sentences of this kind not only into L-semantical sentences but, in addition or instead, into syntactical sentences with respect to a suitably constructed calculus, in other words, to construe them not only as quasi-logical but as quasi-syntactical. Therefore, the discussions in the sections mentioned remain valid; but they should be supplemented by corresponding semantical discussions.

In [Syntax] Part V, many examples of *philosophical sentences* are translated into syntactical ones. It follows from the preceding remarks that they may first be translated into semantical sentences and then, under suitable conditions, into syntactical sentences also. For some of these examples, chiefly those which have to do with designation and meaning ([Syntax] § 75, and examples 54, 55, and 56 in § 81), the semantical translation seems more natural. Some of the examples of this kind involve radical concepts (e.g. examples 7 and 9 in § 75); thus they are not quasi-logical. Some even refer to a speaker or his activity (e.g. examples 15 and 16 in § 75); therefore, they belong to pragmatics but involve semantical concepts also.

The explanation of the dangers of the *material mode* of speech — which is now to include the quasi-logical sentences in addition to the quasi-syntactical ones — in [Syntax] §§ 78–80 remains valid.

The *chief thesis* of Part V, if split up into two components, was like this:

a. "(Theoretical) *philosophy* is the logic of science."

b. "Logic of science is the syntax of the language of science." (a) remains valid. It is a terminological question whether to use the term 'philosophy' in a wider sense, including certain empirical problems. If we do so, then it seems that these empirical problems will turn out to belong mostly to pragmatics. Thesis (b), however, needs modification by adding semantics to syntax. Thus *the whole thesis is changed to the following: the task of philosophy is semiotical analysis;* the problems of philosophy concern — not the ultimate nature of being but — the semiotical structure of the language of science, including the theoretical part of everyday language. We may distinguish between those problems which deal with the activities of gaining and communicating knowledge and the problems of logical analysis. Those of the first kind belong to pragmatics, those of the second kind to semantics or syntax — to semantics, if designata ("meaning") are taken into consideration; to syntax, if the analysis is purely formal.

For the convenience of the readers of [Syntax], there is given below a list for the *translation of terms* of [Syntax] (here in italics; the terms of the German original are added in square brackets) into the present terminology. The translation is not always a strict one. When two new terms are given (as e.g. for 'demonstrable'), they are sometimes not synonymous but so closely related that both correspond practically to the same old term.

analytic [analytisch] — L-true[1]

axiom [Axiom] — postulate

compatible [verträglich] — non-C-exclusive, (C-inexclusive)

complete [vollständig] — C-complete

consequence [Folge] — derivable[2], C-implicate[2]

consistent [konsistent] — C-consistent

content [Gehalt] — C-content

contradictory sentence [kontradiktorisch] — L-false[1]

contradictory system [widerspruchsvoll] — C-inconsistent[2]

contravalid [widergültig] — refutable[2], C-false[2]

demonstrable [beweisbar] — provable[2], C-true[2]

dependent [abhängig] — C-dependent

derivable [ableitbar] — derivable[2], C-implicate[2]

determinate [determiniert] — decidable[2], C-determinate[2]

direct consequence [unmittelbare Folge] — directly derivable[2]

directly derivable [unmittelbar ableitbar] — directly derivable[2]

equipollent [gehaltgleich] — C-equivalent

extensional [extensional] — C-extensional

formation rules [Formbestimmungen] — rules of formation

genus [Gattung] — syntactical genus

Gothic (*symbols*) [Fraktur] —German

incompatible [unverträglich] — C-exclusive

indeterminate [indeterminiert] — undecidable[2], C-indeterminate[2]

independent [unabhängig] — C-independent

intensional [intensional] — non-extensional

interpretation [Deutung] — (translation, transformation, correlation)

irresoluble [unentscheidbar] — undecidable[2], C-indeterminate[2]

isogenous [gattungsgleich] — C-isogenous

junction [Verknüpfung] — connection

junction symbol [Verknüpfungszeichen] — connective

language [Sprache] — calculus, (language system)

L-compatible [L-verträglich]— non-L-exclusive[1], (L-inexclusive)

L-consequence [L-Folge] — L-implicate[:]

L-equipollent [L-gehaltgleich]—L-equivalent[1]

L-incompatible [L-unverträglich] — L-exclusive[1]

non-contradictory (system) [widerspruchsfrei] — C-consistent[2]

P-consequence [P-Folge] — F-implicate[1]

P-contravalid [P-widergültig] — F-false[1]

perfect [abgeschlossen] — C-perfect

P-valid [P-gültig] — F-true[1]

range [Spielraum] — C-range, (L-range[1])

refutable [widerlegbar] — refutable[2], C-false[2]

regressive (definition) [rekursiv] — recursive

resoluble [entscheidbar] — decidable[2], C-determinate[2]

resolution (method, problem of) [Entscheidung] — decision

rules of consequence [Folgebestimmungen] — (transfinite) rules of deduction

sentential calculus [Satzkalkül] — propositional calculus

S-symmetrical [S-symmetrisch] — C-symmetric

symbol [Zeichen] — sign

synonymous [synonym] — C-interchangeable

synthetic [synthetisch] — factual[1], (L-indeterminate[1])

transformation rules [Umformungsbestimmungen] — rules of deduction

truth-value table [Wahrheitswerttafel] — truth-table

valid [gültig] — provable[2], C-true[2]

Remarks:

[1] This term t_2 belongs to semantics and is therefore defined in a way quite different from the old syntactical term t_1 with which it is correlated here. The syntactical term t_1 was previously intended to represent a concept which is now seen to be semantical and hence is designated by the semantical term t_2. (This holds especially for the old L-terms; the correspondence between the old P-terms and the new F-terms is still less close.)

[2] This new term t_2 (e.g. 'derivable', and likewise 'C-implicate') corresponds to two old terms t_{1a} ('consequence') and t_{1b} ('derivable'), t_{1a} being a c-term and t_{1b} a d-term; the terminological distinction between c- and d-terms has been abandoned (see above remark on [Syntax] §§ 34a and 47).

Most of the *terms* of [Syntax] not listed above are *still used* in the same sense, or a similar one, as before; among them are 'atomic sentence', 'autonymous', 'bound variable', 'calculus', 'closed expression', 'conjunction', 'definite', 'derivation', 'descriptive', 'design', 'disjunction', 'equivalence', 'formal', 'formal mode of speech', 'free variable', 'full expression', 'functor', 'general syntax', 'implication', 'indefinite', 'L-content', 'L-determinate', 'level', 'logical sign', 'L-synonymous', 'material mode of speech', 'molecular sentence', 'negation', 'object language', 'open expression', 'operand', 'operator', 'predicate', 'premiss', 'primitive sentence', 'proof', 'sentence', 'sentential function', 'truth-value', 'type'.

BIBLIOGRAPHY

The abbreviated titles in square brackets are used in citations in this book. The titles marked by an asterisk have been added since the first printing.

Ajdukiewicz, K. [Sprache] "Sprache und Sinn", *Erkenntnis*, vol. 4 (1934).

Carnap, R. [Syntax] *Logical Syntax of Language*. (Orig., Vienna, 1934) London and New York, 1937.

—— [Foundations] "Foundations of Logic and Mathematics", *International Encyclopedia of Unified Science*, vol. I, no. 3, Chicago, 1939.

—— [II] *Formalization of Logic*. Studies in Semantics, vol. II. Cambridge, Mass., 1943. (Included in the present volume.)

—— *"Remarks on Induction and Truth", *Philosophy and Phenomenological Research*, 6 (1946), 590–602. (§ 3 of this paper was reprinted in Feigl and Sellars [Readings].)

—— *[Ontology] "Empiricism, Semantics, and Ontology", *Revue International de Philosophie*, vol. 4 (1950). Reprinted in [Meaning], in Feigl and Sellars [Readings], and in Linsky [Semantics].

—— *[Meaning] *Meaning and Necessity: A Study in Semantics and Modal Logic*. Chicago, 1947; 2nd ed. 1956 (with a Supplement containing [Ontology], [Postulates], and three other articles published in 1950–55).

—— *[Postulates] "Meaning Postulates", *Philosophical Studies*, vol. 3 (1952).

—— *[Logic] *Introduction to Symbolic Logic and Its Applications*. New York, 1958.

Church, A. *"Carnap's Introduction to Semantics", *Philosophical Review*, 52 (1943), 298–304.

—— *[Logic] *Introduction to Mathematical Logic*, vol. I. Princeton, 1956.

Cooley, J. *[Logic] *A Primer of Formal Logic*. New York, 1942.

Feigl, H., and W. Sellars. *[Readings] *Readings in Philosophical Analysis*. New York, 1949.

Lewis, C. I., and C. H. Langford. [Logic] *Symbolic Logic*. New York and London, 1932.

Linsky, L. *[Semantics] *Semantics, and the Philosophy of Language: A Collection of Readings*. Urbana, Ill., 1952.

Martin, R. M. *Truth and Denotation: A Study in Semantical Theory*. Chicago and London, 1958.

254 BIBLIOGRAPHY

Morris, C. W. [Foundations] "Foundations of the Theory of Signs", *International Encyclopedia of Unified Science*, vol. I, no. 2, Chicago, 1938.

—— *Signs, Language, and Behavior*. New York, 1946.

Ogden, C. K., and I. A. Richards. [Meaning] *The Meaning of Meaning*. New York and London (1922), 3rd ed. 1930.

Quine, W. V. [Math. Logic] *Mathematical Logic*. New York, 1940, 3rd ed., Cambridge, Mass., 1951.

—— *From a Logical Point of View: Nine Logico-Philosophical Essays*. Cambridge, Mass., 1953.

Stegmüller, W. *Das Wahrheitsproblem und die Idee der Semantik*. Eine Einführung in die Theorien von A. Tarski und R. Carnap. Vienna, 1957.

Tarski, A. [Methodologie] "Fundamentale Begriffe der Methodologie der deduktiven Wissenschaften. I", *Monatshefte für Mathematik und Physik*, vol. 37, 1930.

—— [Wahrheitsbegriff] "Der Wahrheitsbegriff in den formalisierten Sprachen" (orig. 1933), *Studia Philosophica*, vol. I, 1936.

—— [Systemenkalkül] "Grundzüge des Systemenkalküls", *Fundamenta Mathematicae*, vol. 25, 1935; vol. 26, 1936.

—— [Grundlegung] "Grundlegung der wissenschaftlichen Semantik", *Actes du Congrès international de philosophie scientifique*, fasc. III, Paris, 1936.

—— [Folgerung] "Ueber den Begriff der logischen Folgerung", *ibid.*, fasc. VII, Paris, 1936.

—— [Logic] *Introduction to Logic*. New York, 1941.

—— *"The semantic conception of truth and the foundations of semantics", *Philosophy and Phenomenological Research*, vol. 4 (1944). Reprinted in Linsky [Semantics] and in Feigl and Sellars [Readings].

—— *[Metamathematics] *Logic, Semantics, Metamathematics*. Oxford, 1956. (This book contains English translations of the first five articles listed above, in chapters V, VIII, XII, XV, and XVI, respectively.)

Whitehead, A. N., and Bertrand Russell. [Princ. Math.] *Principia Mathematica*. 3 vols. Cambridge (1910–13), 2nd ed. 1925–27.

Wittgenstein, L. [Tractatus] *Tractatus Logico-Philosophicus*. (German and English) With introduction by Russell. London, 1922.

INDEX

The numbers refer to pages. The most important passages are indicated by bold-face type.

The following signs are sometimes used in order to indicate to what entities the term in question applies: '𝔄', expressions; '𝔖', sentences; '𝔎', sentential classes; '𝔗', 𝔖 or 𝔎; '*S*', semantical systems; '*K*', calculi; '*p*', propositions; '*F*', properties (classes).

𝔄, **19**

α, **19**

Absolute concept, **41f.**, **89ff.**, 230, 238, **240**

Accordance, *K*, *S*, **217**

ACKERMANN, W., 21, 99, 164

Adequacy, for C-concepts, 172; for designation, **53**; for L-truth, **84**; for truth, **26f.**, 29

AJDUKIEWICZ, K., 238

Analytic, *see* L-true

Antinomies, 29, **243**

ARISTOTLE, 29, 236

Atomic, 𝔖, **17**, 31; *p* ('atom'), **114f.**

Atomic sentential selection, 102, 105

Attribute, **17f.**

Axiom, *see* Postulate system

BALDWIN, J. M., 229, 235, 238

bas, based, *p*, **99**

BAYLIS, C. A., 236

BENNETT, A. A., 236

BERNAYS, P., **51**, 104, 164, 235

Bi-negation, 231

BOLZANO, B., 235

Bound variable, **17**

BRÉAL, M. J. A., 238

BROUWER, L. E. J., 239

BUEHLER, K., 239

c, **19**

C-, **168**, 234

C-ambivalent, **186f.**, 215

C-complete, **180**

C-comprehensive, **182**

C-concept, 94, 145ff., **168f.**

C-consistent, **189**

C-content, **197ff.**

C-dependent, **179**

C-determinate, 𝔗, 169, **178** [*K*, **184**]

C-disjunct, 𝔗, 147, 162, 172 [𝔭r, 147]

C-empty, 𝔭r, 147

C-equivalence, 𝔗, 147, 169, **171** [𝔭r, 147]

C-exclusive, 𝔗, 147, 169, **179** [𝔭r, 147]

C-extensional, **195**

C-false, 147, **168f.**, 170, 181

C-implication, 𝔗, 147, **168f.**, **171** [𝔭r, 147]

C-in . . ., **234**

C-inconsistent, 170, 181, **186f.**, 215

C-indeterminate, 169, **178**

C-interchangeable, **195**

C-non-equivalent, 147

C-perfect, **184**, 200

C-range, **197ff.**

C-symmetric, 𝔭r, 147

C-synonymous, 147

C-true, **168f.**, **171**

C-universal, 𝔭r, 147

Calculus, 12, **156ff.**, **164ff.**, 230

Cc, **197**

Characteristic sentence, **145ff.**, **196**

CHWISTEK, L., 238, **239**

cj, 93, **94**

Class, 18, 55; of sentences, *see* Sentential class

Classification, of interpretations, **211**; of sentences, **142**; of signs, 24f., 156

Closed, 𝔄, **17**

Code system, 23

COHEN, M. R., 229, 236, **241**

Coincident, *K*, **190**, 193

Component, 17

Comprehensive, 36, **39f.**

Concept, 18, **230**

Confirmation, verification, 28, **244**
Conjunction, **231** [of class of proposi-
   tions, *see* cj]
Connections, **230**, 238, 248
Connectives, **16**, 30ff., 197
Conservative sub-calculus, **190, 192**
Constant, **16**
Content, *see* L-content, C-content
Conventional character of logic, **218f.,**
   247
COURNOT, A. A., 239
Cover, **114**
Cr, **197**

Decidable, **163**
Declarative, $\mathfrak{S}$, **14**
Definiendum, **17, 158**
Definiens, **17**, 158
Definition, **17, 157**
Degree, **16ff.**
Derivable, **157**, 160, 163, 170, 231
Derivation, 160, 163, 166, 170
Des, **49**
des, **99f.**
Descriptive, $\mathfrak{A}$, **57ff.**, 86f
Descriptive (semiotic, semantics, syn-
   tax), 8, **11ff.**
Descriptive interpretation, **212**
Design (sign-), **6**
Designated, *p*, **99f.**
Designation, **24f.**, 49ff., 53
Designatum, **9, 18**, 53
Determination by expr. function, **45ff.**
Different systems, relations between,
   55, 88
Direct C-implication, **169**
Direct designation, **25**
Direct sub-calculus, **190f.**
Directly C-false, **169**
Directly coincident, *K*, **190, 193**
Directly derivable, **157**, 162
Directly refutable, **157**, 162
Disjunct, $\mathfrak{T}$, 36, **38**, 139, 147, 238 [*p*, 91;
   $\mathfrak{pr}$, 147]
Disjunction, **30, 231** [of class of proposi-
   tions, *see* dj]
Distinction between expression and its
   name, **236, 237**
dj, **92, 94**
DUBISLAV, W., **15.**

EISLER, R., 229, 235
Empirical science, 246
Empty, *F*, **41**; $\mathfrak{pr}$, 42, 147; sent. func-
   tion, **48**
Entity, **18**
Equivalence, $\mathfrak{T}$, **35f.**, 55, 139, 147, 238
   [*S*, **40**; *F*, 42; $\mathfrak{pr}$, 42, 147; sent. func-
   tion, **49**; *p*, **91**, 231]
Event (sign-), **6**
Everyday language, 29, 241
Exclusion, 231
Exclusive, $\mathfrak{T}$, 36, **38**, 140, 147, 238 [*F*,
   42; $\mathfrak{pr}$, 42, 147; sent. function, **49**;
   p, **91**]
Exhaustive, *K*, **219**, 225
Expression, **5**
Expressional function, **18, 232f.**
Extension, correlation of, **131ff.**
Extensional, $\mathfrak{S}$, *S*, **43**, 55, 118, 152, **249**

$\mathfrak{f}$, **19**
F-, **141**, 235
F-concepts, **141ff.**
F-disjunct, **144**
F-equivalence, **143**
F-exclusive, **144**
F-false, **141**
F-false interpretation, 211, 215
F-implication, **143**
F-interchangeable, **144**
F-true, **141**
F-true interpretation, 211, 215
Factual, **141, 232**
Factual interpretation, **211**
Factual knowledge, 33, 81, **141**
False, $\mathfrak{T}$, 25, 35, 91, 139, 147 [*p*, **90**]
False interpretation, **206**, 215
Finite rule, **160**
Formal, **10, 232**
Formalization, 11, 216, **232**, 247; of
   logic, ix, **11**, 60, 224, 242
Free variable, **17**
FREGE, G., 56, 233, 237
$\mathfrak{fu}$, **19**
Fulfill, **47**
Function, **18, 232**
Functor, **16ff.**

General, $\mathfrak{S}$, **17**
General (semantics, syntax), **11f.**, 34,
   134, 159, **242, 247**

German letters, 19f.
GOEDEL, K., 52, 243

HERMES, H., 239
HILBERT, D., 21, 52, 99, 104, 164, 239
HOFSTADTER, A., 15

i, 19
Identity, 91 [p, 94]
Imperatives, logic of, 15
Implication, $\mathfrak{T}$, 35f., 139, 147, 238 [F, 41; $\mathfrak{pr}$, 42, 147; sent. function, 49; p, 90, 230]
in, 19
Individual, 16, 18, 44
Individual (sign, constant, variable), 16
Intensional, see Non-extensional
Interchangeable, 43, 75
Interpretation, 203f., 212ff.
Interpreted system, see Semantical system
Isomorphic, K, 194

JOERGENSEN, J., 15

$\Re$, 19
K_1, 164f., 185, 213f., 224; K_2, 165, 185, 213f., 224
KANT, I., 232, 240
KOKOSZYNSKA, M., 240
KORZYBSKI, A., 238
KOTARBINSKI, T., vi, 29

L-, 56, 61, 234
L-complete, $\mathfrak{T}$, 71 [p, 94, 100]
L-comprehensive, 73
L-concepts, 56f., 60ff., 81, 83ff., 230, 233
L-content, 148ff.
L-dependent, $\mathfrak{T}$, 71 [p, 94]
L-designation, 81
L-determinate, $\mathfrak{T}$, 70 [p, 94; S, 77]
L-determinate interpretation, 211
L-determination, 81
L-disjunct, $\mathfrak{T}$, 61, 63, 77f., 81f., 123, 138f., 147 [p, 94; $\mathfrak{pr}$, 147]
L-empty, 81, 147
L-equivalence, $\mathfrak{T}$, 35, 60, 63, 70, 80ff., 135, 138, 147 [p, 92, 94; $\mathfrak{pr}$, 147]
L-exclusive, 61, 70, 81f., 138, 147 [p, 94; $\mathfrak{pr}$, 147]

L-exhaustive, K, 219, 223f.
L-false, $\mathfrak{T}$, 61, 63, 73, 80ff., 135, 138, 147 [p, 94]
L-false interpretation, 209, 215
L-fulfillment, 81
L-implication, $\mathfrak{T}$, 35, 60, 63, 65, 80, 135, 138, 147 [p, 94; $\mathfrak{pr}$, 147]
L-incomplete, 234
L-independent, 234
L-inexclusive, 234
L-interchangeable, 74f.
L-non-equivalent, 138, 147
L-perfect, 75, 152
L-range, 96ff., 104f., 108, 116, 124 126f., 130, 133, 137, 150
L-rules, 81
L-state, 101, 105, 107, 116, 136
L-symmetric, 147
L-synonymous, 75, 81, 147
L-true, $\mathfrak{T}$, 61, 63, 70, 79, 81f., 83ff. 134f., 137 [p, 93]
L-true interpretation, 207, 214
L-universal, 81, 147
LALANDE, A., 229, 235, 239, 241
LANGER, S., 229, 232, 236
LANGFORD, C. H., 21, 236
Language, 3
Language system, 23
Lc, Lc$_S$, 149
LEIBNIZ, G. W., 232, 240
LESNIEWSKI, S., vi, 29
Level, 16f., 51
LEWIS, C. I., 21, 58, 66, 85, 196, 230, 236, 243
Linguistics, 13
LOCKE, J., 238
Logic, 56, 60, 245
Logical, $\mathfrak{A}$, 57ff., 86f.
Logical attribute, 87
Logical interpretation, 212
Logical truth, logical deduction, 56, 60, 85, 247. See also L-
Lr, Lr$_S$, 96

McKINSEY, J. C. C., 15
MALLY, E., 15
MANNOURY, G., 239
Material (implication, etc.), 35, 230, 232
Mathematics, 58
Matrix, 213

Maximum state-description, **112**, 117, **120**

Meaning, 10, 22, **249**

MEINONG, A., 235

MENGER, K., 15

Metalanguage, **4**, **20**

Metamathematics, **239**

Metametalanguage, 59, 83

Metaphysics, viif.

Metatheory, **4**

Modalities, 57f., 85, 92, **243**, 249

Model, 204, **244**

Modus ponens, 164

Molecular, ⊙, **17**

MORRIS, C. W., **9**, **239**

NAGEL, E., 229, 236, **241**

Necessary, *p*, **57**, 85

Negation, 31, **113**

NESS, A., **29**

Non-extensional, 85, **92**, 101, 118, 196, **243**. *See also* Extensional; Modalities; Strict implication

Null class of sentences, 38f., **161ff.**

Null L-range, 105, 108, 137

Object language, **4**

Occurrence, **7**

Open, 𝔄, **17**

Operand, **17**

Operator, **16f.**

𝔭, **19**

Philosophy, **245**, **250**

Possible, 95

POST, E. L., **180**

Postulate system, 156, 203, 235, **243f.**

Postulates for C-content, **198**; for C-range, **198**; for L-concepts, **63f.**; for L-content, 149; for L-disjunct, 78; for L-range, 97

pr, 21, 76

𝔭r, ᵐ𝔭rⁿ, **19**

Pragmatics, **9f.**, 13, 28f., **245**, 250

Predicate, **16**

Predication, 129

Prefixes, **234**

Premiss, **160**, 163, **167**, 170

Primitive sentence, **157**, 163, **167**, 171, **235**

Probability, 97, **244**

Proof, **159**, **163**, 165, 171

Property, **18**

Proposition, **18**, 52f., 89f., **92f.**, **235f.**, 240

Propositional (sign, constant, variable), **16**, 92, **241**

Propositional calculus, **164**, **213**, 230, **242**

Propositional function, 233. *See also* Attribute; Sentential function

Propositional logic, **213**, **242**

Provable, **157**, **160**, **163**, 171

Pure (semiotic, semantics, syntax), 8, **12ff.**, 155

Quantifier, *see* Operator

Quasi-logical, **245**, **249**

QUINE, W. V., 21, **51**, 130, 219, 229ff., 235f.

Quotes, **236f.**

Radical, 33, **237**

RAMSEY, F. P., **29**, 243

RAND, R., vi, 15

Range, *see* L-range; C-range

Real L-state, *see* rs

Recursive definition, 31f., 157

Refutable, **163**

REICHENBACH, H., 204

Relation, 17f.

rs, 103, 105, **108**, 116, 129, 137, 151

Rule, 13

Rules, (1) semantical: of designation, 24, 32; of determination, **45f.**; of formation, 10, **24**; of L-contents, 151; of L-ranges, **130**, **133**; of truth, **24**; of values, 44

(2) syntactical: of deduction, 10, **157**; of formation, **156f.**; of inference, **157**; of refutation, 157; of transformation, *see* rules of deduction

RUSSELL, B., 21, 56, 58, 229ff., 232f., **235**, 243

⊙, ∫, **19**

S_1, **23**; S_2, **24f.**; S_3, 32, 50, **79ff.**, 213f., 224; S_4, **33**, 82, 130, 213f., 224; S_5, **38**; S_6, **45**

Satisfy, *see* Fulfill
SCHLICK, M., 236
SCHOLZ, H., 11
ſe, 19
Selection class of propositions, 100
Selection proposition, 100
Semantical system, 12, 22ff.
Semantics, 9f., 238; objections against,
    vii, 52
Semasiology, 238
Semiotic, 9, 238
Sentence, 24, 31f., 156f., 235f.
Sentential class, 34, 65
Sentential function, 18, 232f.
Sentential selection, 121
Sequence, 8, 18, 161
Series, 18
SHEFFER, H. M., 231f.
Sign, 4
Signification, *see* Designation
Significs, 238
Special (semantics, syntax), 11f.
State of affairs, *see* L-state
State-description, 102f., 105, 112f., 117,
    119f.
State-relation, 128f., 131, 133
STEVENS, S. S., 246
Strict implication, 58, 66, 196, 230, 243
Sub-calculus, 190f.
Substitution, 20
Symbolic logic, ix, 16, 21
Symmetric relation, 42; pr, 43, 147
Symmetry, lack of, 38f., 72, 77, 172, 242
SYMON, K. R., 240
Synonymous, 55, 75, 147
Syntactical system, *see* Calculus
Syntax, 9f., 155, 239
Synthetic, *see* Factual

$\mathfrak{T}$, 19, 34f.
TARSKI, A., vi, vii, 21, 27, 29, 48, 52, 75,
    87, 181, 184, 239, 243, 247
Tautology, 239
Terminology, 229ff.
Theory of systems, 14, 240
Tolerance, principle of, 247

Transfinite proof, 161
Transfinite rule, 160f., 224, 247
True, $\mathfrak{T}$, vii, 22, 24f., 26ff., 48, 50, 87, 91,
    134, 139, 151, 240, 244 [$\mathfrak{R}$, 34; p, 90]
True interpretation, 203f., 214
Truth condition, 22
Truth-function, *see* Extensional
Truth-table, 30f., 82
Truth-value, 22
Type, 25, 50f.

Undecidable, 163
Understanding, 22
Universal, F, 41; pr, 42, 147; sent. func-
    tion, 48
Universal L-range, *see* V_s
Universal sentential class, 38f.

v, 19
V, V_s, 38f.
V_s, 105, 108, 137
Value of variable, value expression, 44
Variable, 16, 44ff., 59, 241
Verification, *see* Confirmation

WAISMANN, F., 97
Warsaw school, vi, 239
WELBY, V., 238
WHITEHEAD, A. N., 21, 58
WITTGENSTEIN, L., 28, 56, 97, 107, 235,
    240

X-, 145

SYMBOLS

$\sim$, $\vee$, $\cdot$, $\supset$, $\equiv$, 16
$=$, $\exists$, 16
λ, 16, 46
$=_{Df}$, 17, 20
$\mathfrak{A}_i \binom{v_k}{\mathfrak{A}_i}$, 19
ϵ, $\mathbf{C}$, $-$, $+$, $\times$, $\{\,\}$, 20
$\rightarrow$, 36; $\underset{L}{\rightarrow}$, 63; $\underset{F}{\rightarrow}$, 143; $\underset{C}{\rightarrow}$, 171; $\underset{dC}{\rightarrow}$, 171
V, V_s, Λ, Λ_s, 38f.
V_s, Λ_s, 105, 108, 137

VOLUME II

FORMALIZATION OF LOGIC

(Fourth Printing)

PREFACE

The purpose of this book

In this volume, an application will be made of the method of semantics developed in *Introduction to Semantics*, the first volume of this series, Studies in Semantics. Among the characteristic features of this method are the distinction between a calculus and its interpretation, in other words, between syntactical and semantical systems; and the use of L-concepts based on the concept of L-range. The problem to be dealt with is that of the possibility and the scope of the formalization of logic. This problem has long been discussed, especially during the last hundred years, the period of the development of modern logic. However, before the method of semantics became available, no precise answer could be given, and not even a clear and precise formulation of the question was possible.

The task of the formalization of any theory, i.e. of its representation by a formal system or calculus, belongs to syntax, not to semantics. On the other hand, the question of whether a proposed calculus formalizes a given theory adequately and completely is a matter of the relations between a calculus and an interpreted system, and hence requires semantics in addition to syntax. In this book, the theory to be formalized is logic. Calculi representing logic in a formal way have been constructed and thoroughly investigated by many logicians. The most important and best known of these logical calculi are the propositional calculus (called PC in this book), containing the propositional connectives 'not', 'or', 'and', etc.; and, constructed on its basis, the functional calculus (here called FC), containing general sentences with terms like 'every' and 'there is'. Our problem will be to determine to what extent these calculi fulfill the task of formalizing logic, and more generally, to what extent any calculus of the customary kind can fulfill this task. Contrary to the general belief, not all essential questions concerning PC have so far found their answer. For instance, the question whether PC completely formalizes all logical features of the part of logic covered by it, i.e. of the connectives, has not been answered by previous investigations. It seems to be the tacit assumption of many that this question is answerable in the affirmative. In this book, it will be shown that the answer is negative; and more generally, that no calculus of the customary kind can fulfill the task of a full formalization. However, a full formalization of propositional logic will be shown to be possible by making use of new concepts. A similar analysis of FC will be made, which leads to analogous negative results. And there likewise a full formalization of the logic of functions will be given by the construction of a new calculus. These results do not of course affect the value of the purely formal method of constructing calculi; they rather make the foundations of that method more secure.

The role of semantics in the development of logic

Semantics — more exactly, pure semantics as here conceived — is not a branch of empirical science; it does not furnish knowledge concerning facts of nature. It is rather to be regarded as a tool, as one among the logical instruments needed for the task of getting and systematizing knowledge. As a hammer helps a man do better and more efficiently what he did before with his unaided hand, so a logical tool helps a man do better and more efficiently what he did before with his unaided brain, that is, by means of instinctive habits rather than through deliberate acts guided by explicit rules.

Aristotle's logic was the first logical tool of this kind. It did not originate the human activity of drawing inferences; from the time when language developed to the point of containing compound and general sentences, man has deduced conclusions from premises without once mentioning the mood *Barbara*. What was new in Aristotle's logic was not the activity but its systematization, that is, the construction of explicit rules for it. This made it possible to replace instinctive acts of inference by deliberate, methodical acts, and to examine critically the inferences made either instinctively or methodically.

The task of modern logic, as it has been developed since the middle of the last century, is fundamentally the same. The difference is only one of degree with respect to technical development, especially the multiplicity and efficiency of the tools. As a result of this development it has become possible not only to increase the safety and precision of the deductive method in realms already known, but also to reach results which could not have been obtained at all without the new tools. Although modern logic has already made a great advance in the degree of systematization and explicitness, nevertheless it has been long in reaching a full methodological understanding of its own procedures. This development of modern logic towards greater methodological consciousness is still going on and provides many of the basic problems for contemporary logical research.

Among the methodological tendencies or points of view in logic and especially in modern logic, two are of special interest for our present considerations. The one tendency emphasizes form, the logical structure of sentences and deductions, relations between signs in abstraction from their meaning. The other emphasizes just the factors excluded by the first: viz., meaning, interpretation; relations of entailment, compatibility, incompatibility, etc., as based on meaning; the distinction between necessary and contingent truth, etc. The two tendencies are as old as logic itself and have appeared under many names. Using contemporary terms, we may call them the syntactical and the semantical tendencies respectively. Theoretically they are not incompatible, but rather complementary to each other; yet in the historical development we find that logicians have sometimes emphasized one of them at the sacrifice of the other. Usually, however, both points of view were combined without explicit distinction. It took many decades, even after modern logic was under way, before each of them was clearly recognized in its nature and represented by a pure method of its own. The formal, syntactical method was the first to be developed, and its emergence was stimulated by certain trends within mathematics, namely, the generalization of algebra, and the development of the postulational method especially in geometry. The elaboration of the formal method in logic is chiefly due to the works of Frege, Hilbert, and their followers. The main features of this method have often been described and discussed. The best description and analysis of its historical development has been given by Milton B. Singer in a study which will, I hope, soon be published. The development of the semantical method in a form clearly distinguished from the syntactical method is still in its first phases. Its origin in the Warsaw School of Logic and the first steps made by Tarski towards its systematization have been mentioned in the preface to Volume I of this series. Each of the two methods has the function of making systematic and explicit certain procedures which have been practically applied in traditional logic for the last two thousand years and, in a more elaborate and exact way, in modern logic for the last hundred years. Today it is generally recognized that the long-run tendency of gradually increasing formalization has found its necessary systematization in the modern syntactical method. In my opinion an analogous necessity prevails for a systematization of the long-run semantical tendency.

The decisive steps in the development of logic — e.g. Aristotle's syllogistic rules, Boole's creation of symbolical logical calculi, and the initiation of the syntactical method by Frege and Hilbert, to mention only a few outstanding phases — all consist essentially in the invention of the kind of tools described above, i.e. procedures guided by explicit rules come to replace certain more or less instinctive procedures in the activity of thinking and especially the activity of deductive inference. It is important to realize that this development did not reach its end in the construction of the syntactical method. Some essential features in the contemporary work of logicians are guided by instinct and common sense, although they could be guided by explicit rules. These rules, however, would be not syntactical but semantical. This will become clear if we give a few examples from contemporary logical investigations.

One of the important questions investigated in modern logic is that of the completeness of given logical systems. Sometimes this question is meant in a clearly syntactical way; it is the question whether a given calculus is such that every sentence belonging to it is either provable or refutable (i.e. its negation is provable). In other cases, the question of completeness is meant in another sense. Take for example Gödel's theorem of 1930 concerning the completeness of a certain calculus (the so-called lower functional calculus similar to FC, but containing predicate variables). He formulates it in the following two ways: (1) "Every formula (i.e. sentential function of the calculus in question) which is universally valid is provable"; (2) "Every formula is either refutable or satisfiable." We find two different kinds of terms occurring here. The terms 'provable' and 'refutable' are obviously syntactical. They are exactly defined on the basis of the rules of the calculus in question; and those rules are explicitly stated in the form of primitive sentences (axioms) and rules of inference. Thus we are given everything required for an exact understanding and use of these terms. Not so for the terms 'universally valid' ("allgemeingültig") and 'satisfiable' ("erfüllbar"). They are explained in the following way: a formula (a sentential function of the calculus in question) is called universally valid if it is true for all values of the free variables; it is called satisfiable if there are values of the free variables for which it is true. Clearly these two terms are not of a syntactical but of a semantical nature. In a theory of semantics they could be exactly defined on the basis of the concept of entities satisfying a sentential function (this is the basic concept in Tarski's semantics, see 'fulfillment', Volume I, § 11). Gödel's theorem is accordingly of a peculiar nature which is usually not recognized: it combines syntactical and semantical concepts; in a more exact formulation it would state a relation between a syntactical and a corresponding semantical system. The terms 'universally valid' and 'satisfiable' play an important role in contemporary logical investigations, especially in problems of completeness and in the so-called decision-problem ("Entscheidungs-problem"). Other terms of a semantical nature which are frequently used are 'true', 'false', 'truth-value', 'values of a variable', etc. The decisive point is this: while the syntactical terms used by logicians are exactly defined and belong to a well-constructed and recognized theory (namely syntax), the same is not true for the semantical terms. These are merely explained in an informal manner, without a theory as framework for them. No rules constituting semantical systems corresponding to the calculi in question are given; although such rules would serve as a basis for the semantical terms used. Thus the understanding and the use of these terms is left to common-sense and instinct. It is assumed that the reader knows how to interpret and use them on the basis of his knowledge of everyday language. This assumption is perhaps correct to some extent. Similarly, however, most people know how to use the terms 'all' and 'some' before a logician expounds Aristotle's rules to them. Once we concede that it is essential for the development of logic to give explicit rules for all terms which play a central role, then we see that the demand for such rules in the case of the semantical terms is at least as urgent as in the case of 'all' and 'some'. It should be noted that the semantical terms used in recent investigations do not merely serve for incidental explanations or illustrations outside of the theory dealt with, but are essential to that theory; this is shown by the fact that they occur in the very formulations of the problems and the theorems.

It should be clear that the foregoing remarks concerning customary formulations in contemporary logic are not meant as a criticism of the authors, but simply as a critical description of the present status of the metalanguage commonly used by logicians. I wish merely to call attention to the fact that this customary language contains both syntactical and semantical terms. Once we are aware of this fact, we can see that, in order to improve the method of logic, we need a systematically constructed semantics as urgently as we previously needed a systematically constructed syntax (theory of proof). [Hilbert and Bernays, in *Grundlagen der Mathematik*, vol. I, distinguish between two theories, called theory of proof ("Beweistheorie") and set-theoretic logic ("mengentheoretische Logik") respectively. From their explanations it becomes clear that, in our terminology, the first is syntax, the second is semantics. The explanations given for set-theoretic logic may indeed be regarded as the beginning of a systematization of semantics. The fundamental difference between those discussions in the book mentioned which are syntactical and those which are semantical would become clearer if the distinction between expressions and their designata were observed more strictly.]

The value of semantics for philosophy and science

In the course of these last few decades the importance of logical analysis — sometimes called analysis of language, sometimes analysis of knowledge — for theoretical philosophy and for the methodology of science has been more and more widely acknowledged. Many of us even hold the view — first emphasized by Russell, and substantiated by his work — that logic is the very foundation of philosophical and methodological investigation. Hence, if it is true that the progress of logic in its present phase requires the development of a systematic semantics, the indirect value of semantics for philosophy and science becomes clear. It is the purpose of these Studies to help in the construction of semantics — that was the special aim of the first volume — and then to show possibilities of its application. The present volume gives an example of an application to a fundamental problem in logic; an application to philosophical problems in the narrower sense is not here intended. Some very brief indications of the relevance of semantics for certain philosophical problems have been given in the appendix to Volume I (§ 38). That scientists in talking about theories and hypotheses continually use concepts which belong to L-semantics, has been shown by a few examples in Volume I, pp. 61 f. A few first steps, still rather elementary and tentative, towards an application of semantics to the methodology of empirical science have been made in my Encyclopedia monograph (see Bibliography). I am convinced that many other workers will soon recognize the value of semantics as an instrument of logical analysis, will help in developing and improving this instrument, and will then apply it to the clarification and solution of their special problems in various fields.

The next volume

In the next volume of these Studies in Semantics, I intend to deal with modal logic, i.e. the theory of such concepts as logical necessity, possibility, impossibility, etc. (see Volume I, § 38d). It is amazing that modal logic, having been originated in its modern form by C. I. Lewis in 1918, has not made any essential progress since then. There have been numerous publications in this field, some of them, especially in recent years, with interesting and fruitful results. However, all these investigations continue to confine themselves to the same field as Lewis' systems: they investigate the modalities in connection with the most elementary logical system, namely propositional logic. It seems that as yet the modalities have not been introduced into the more important logic of functions. The construction of this more interesting but also much more complex system, both in semantical and in syntactical form, will be the chief task of the next volume. Then, in addition to logical modalities, other kinds of modalities will be studied, among them the concepts of causal necessity, possibility, etc. Further, the question will be discussed whether modal concepts (in the widest sense, including all concepts which are not extensional or truth-functional, compare § 12) are useful or even necessary in certain special fields, e.g. in the metalanguage used for semantics and perhaps in psychology, in statements concerning believing, knowing, and similar propositional attitudes.

Acknowledgments

The first draft of the manuscript for this book, containing the chief results (the possibility of non-normal interpretations for PC, and a full formalization with the help of junctives), was written in the autumn of 1938. I wish to express my gratitude to the University of Chicago for releasing me from teaching duties during that quarter. (What is now Volume I was written later when it became clear during the writing of the present book that a separate, systematic explanation of the semantical concepts used was necessary.) As in the case of the first volume, I again am indebted to the Department of Philosophy at Harvard University and to the American Council of Learned Societies for grants in aid of publication. I want to thank Dr. Abraham Kaplan, who again helped me in the preparation of the manuscript.

R. C.

SANTE FE, NOVEMBER 1942.

CONTENTS

1. Introduction: The Problem of a Full Formalization of Logic 3

A. THE PROPOSITIONAL CALCULUS (PC)

2. The Calculus PC_1 7
3. Propositional Connections$_C$ in PC 10
4. Forms of PC 16
5. Elementary Theorems Concerning PC 19
6. Extensible Rules 22
7. General Theorems Concerning Disjunction$_C$ 27
8. General Theorems Concerning Negation$_C$ 30
9. General Theorems Concerning Other Connections$_C$ . . 33

B. PROPOSITIONAL LOGIC

10. The Normal Truth-Tables (NTT). 36
11. The Connections in NTT 41
12. Extensionality 52
13. Theorems Concerning Particular Connections. 62

C. INTERPRETATIONS OF PC

14. NTT as an L-true Interpretation for PC 69
15. Non-Normal Interpretations of Signs of Negation$_C$ and Disjunction$_C$ 73
16. Non-Normal Interpretations in General 81
17. Examples of Non-Normal Interpretations 89
18. PC is not a Full Formalization of Propositional Logic . 94

D. JUNCTIVES

19. Syntactical Concepts of a New Kind are Required . . 97
20. C-Falsity 101
21. Junctives in Semantics 104

CONTENTS

22. Application of L-Concepts to Junctives 108
23. Junctives in Syntax 113
24. Rules of Deduction for Junctives 122

E. FULL FORMALIZATION OF PROPOSITIONAL LOGIC
25. Junctives in Propositional Logic 127
26. The Calculus PC* 128
27. PC* is a Full Formalization of Propositional Logic . . . 130

F. FULL FORMALIZATION OF FUNCTIONAL LOGIC
28. The Functional Calculus (FC) 135
29. Transfinite Junctives 142
30. The Calculus FC* 144
31. FC$_1^*$ is a Full Formalization of Functional Logic . . . 148
32. Involution 151

BIBLIOGRAPHY 155

INDEX 157

FORMALIZATION OF LOGIC

§ 1. Introduction: The Problem of a Full Formalization of Logic

> The problem is whether — and in what way — it is possible to construct a calculus as a full formalization of propositional and functional logic, i.e. such that the principal logical signs can be interpreted only in the normal way. New basic concepts for syntax and semantics will be required for this purpose.

In Volume I of these Studies in Semantics, we have developed concepts of syntax referring to calculi and concepts of semantics referring to semantical systems. Further, there were concepts relating semantical systems and calculi, especially the concepts of the different kinds of interpretations — true, false, L-true, L-false interpretations, etc.

If we look at a calculus from the point of view of semantics, then we might say that it formalizes certain semantical features of expressions. Thus e.g. the fact that a certain sentence $\mathfrak{S}_1$ is true is itself of a semantical, not a syntactical, nature. But it can be formalized, i.e. mirrored in a syntactical way, if a calculus K is constructed in such a way that $\mathfrak{S}_1$ is C-true in K. Analogously, the equivalence of $\mathfrak{S}_2$ and $\mathfrak{S}_3$ may be mirrored by their C-equivalence in K. But L-concepts also may be mirrored formally, e.g. L-truth by C-truth, L-implication by C-implication. In general, we might define the concept of a formalization of a semantical property in the following way. A radical semantical property F of an expression $\mathfrak{A}_i$ is *formalized* in $K =_{Df} \mathfrak{A}_i$ has the property F in every semantical system which is a true interpretation for K. And an L-semantical property F of $\mathfrak{A}_i$ is formalized in $K =_{Df} \mathfrak{A}_i$ has F in every L-true interpretation for K. Analogously for semantical relations.

Having a certain designatum is also a semantical property

of an expression. It is easy to see that, in the case of a descriptive sign, a property of this kind cannot in general be formalized. Thus e.g. it is not possible to formalize the property of 'a' designating Chicago and the property of 'P' designating the property of being large — in other words, it is not possible to construct a calculus K in such a way that in every true interpretation for K 'a' and 'P' have the designata mentioned. If a true interpretation for K with these designata is given, another true interpretation for K with different designata can always be constructed.

Whether or not logic can be completely formalized is an important question for the foundations of logic. If the question is taken simply in the ordinary sense, as referring to a formalization of logical deduction — in other words, to a formalization of the relation of L-implication — then the answer is of course in the affirmative. L-implication can in general be formally represented by C-implication (concerning some difficulties and qualifications, see [Foundations] § 10, at the end). But we will take the question here in a stronger sense. If a calculus K containing the ordinary connectives of propositional logic could be constructed in such a way that it would formalize all essential properties of these connectives so that it would exclude the possibility of interpreting the connectives in any other than the ordinary way, then we should say that K was a *full formalization of propositional logic*. And if K should, in addition, impose the ordinary interpretation on the universal and existential operators, we should speak of a *full formalization of functional logic*. The principal problem to be dealt with in this book is the question whether, and how, a full formalization of logic is possible, in the sense just indicated, which will be made more precise later. It is well known — it was shown first by E. L. Post — that the concept of L-truth within propositional logic is formalized in the ordinary propositional calculus, which we call PC; the same holds for L-implication. Further, it is easy to see that some essential logical properties of the connectives reveal themselves in the L-truth of certain sentences and in the L-implication between certain sentences in which the connectives occur. [Thus, e.g., it is characteristic of the sign of negation ' $\sim$ ' and the sign of disjunction ' $\vee$ ' that every sentence is an L-implicate of $\{\mathfrak{S}_i, \sim\mathfrak{S}_i\}$, that $\mathfrak{S}_i \vee \mathfrak{S}_j$ is an L-implicate of $\mathfrak{S}_i$ and also of $\mathfrak{S}_j$, that $\mathfrak{S}_i \vee \sim\mathfrak{S}_i$ is L-true, etc.] Thus one might perhaps be led to the assumption that PC is a full formalization for propositional logic. The subsequent discussions (Chapter C), however, will come to the surprising conclusion that this is not the case. We shall find non-normal interpretations for PC — that is to say, true and even L-true interpretations for PC in which the connectives have an interpretation different from the normal one as given by the normal truth-tables (NTT). And this holds not only for PC but likewise for any other calculus constructed with the help of the customary syntactical concepts. In spite of this, a full formalization will be found to be possible by the construction of a new calculus PC* (Chapter E). This, however, requires entirely new basic concepts for syntax. These concepts will be applicable not only to the propositional calculus but to calculi in general, and likewise to semantical systems (Chapter D).

The investigation of propositional logic will take up the greater part of this book. The results can then easily be extended so as to apply to functional logic (Chapter F). The result is analogous. The ordinary functional calculus FC (taken here with individual variables for a denumerable field of individuals, without predicate variables) admits of non-normal interpretations for the universal and existential operators, as is well known. A new calculus FC* will be constructed on the basis of PC* such that it imposes the normal interpretation upon the operators.

At several places in [I] (i.e. Volume I of these Studies; see Bibliography) we found symptoms of a thoroughgoing lack of symmetry in the foundations of semantics and syntax (e.g. in [I] pp. 38f., 72, 77, and 172). We shall find that the introduction of the new concepts will remove these defects and thereby lead to a simpler and more uniform structure of the system of concepts both in syntax and in semantics.

The development toward a formalization of logic begins, in a certain way, with the very beginning of systematic logic, in Aristotle. Leibniz emphasized the formal method in his construction of various calculi. But his ideas were all but forgotten by his successors, until a new development began about the middle of the last century with the creation of symbolic logic. It was Frege (1893) above all who recognized the importance of the formal method and carried it through in an exact way, while simultaneously insisting that a logical system should not be regarded merely as a formal calculus but should, in addition, be understood as expressing thoughts.

It is to be noted that we use the term '*formal*' here always in the strict sense of "in abstraction from the meaning", hence as synonymous with 'syntactical' (see [I] § 37, 'Formal', meaning III, and [I] p. 10), in contradistinction to the weaker meanings: "general" (meaning I), and "logically valid" (meaning II). The difference between II and III might be described in this way: in using the term 'formal' in meaning II, abstraction is made from the meaning of the descriptive signs but not from that of the logical signs. [Thus, for instance, the sentence 'P(a) $\vee \sim$P(a)' is called formally true (II) because its truth is logically necessary on the basis of the meaning of ' $\vee$ ' and '$\sim$' (as given by the truth-tables), independent of the meaning of 'P' and 'a'.] On the other hand, in the method which we call formal (in meaning III) or syntactical, abstraction is made from the meaning of all signs, including the logical ones. [For instance, in a suitable calculus, the sentence 'P(a) $\vee \sim$P(a)' is shown to be C-true (provable) on the basis of rules which are formal in the strict sense III inasmuch as they do not refer to the meaning of any signs, not even of the connectives.]

A. THE PROPOSITIONAL CALCULUS (PC)

Chapter A contains an analysis of the ordinary propositional calculus PC. Different forms of PC are distinguished. The four singulary extensional connectives (e.g. negation) and the sixteen binary (e.g. disjunction) are syntactically characterized. Syntactical theorems concerning the connectives in PC are proved. This chapter serves chiefly to prepare for the later discussions in Chapters B and C.

§ 2. The Calculus PC₁

PC$_1$ is the Hilbert-Bernays form of PC, with signs of negation and disjunction as the only connectives.

In what follows, we shall use the C-terminology for syntax ([I] § 28). The following table shows the correspondence between the customary terms and the C-terms.

CUSTOMARY TERMS	C-TERMS
derivable	C-implicate
directly derivable	direct C-implicate
provable	C-true
primitive sentence	direct C-implicate of Λ
refutable	C-false
directly refutable	directly C-false
equipollent	C-equivalent
decidable	C-determinate
undecidable	C-indeterminate

The correspondence of terms in the table above is here, with respect to PC, a strict synonymity. Since PC does not contain a rule of refutation, 'refutable in PC' and 'C-false in PC' are both empty, 'C-implicate in PC' coincides with 'derivable in PC', and 'C-true in PC' coincides with 'provable in PC' ([I] T29-54). Sometimes, but not frequently, a rule of refutation has been added to PC. It seems that in every calculus of this kind which has been constructed so far, every directly C-false (directly refutable) $\mathfrak{T}_i$ is such that every sentence is derivable from it. Therefore, for these calculi as well, the coincidences mentioned hold ([I] T29-55).

We shall use 'PC' as a common name for the different forms of the ordinary propositional calculus. (We shall later explain more in detail which calculi are meant as forms of PC.) The different forms vary with respect to the choice of primitive signs, primitive sentences, and rules of inference, but they are known to agree with respect to possible results of proofs and derivations. Hence, if two forms contain the same sentences, they are coincident, although not directly coincident, calculi ([I] D31-9 and 8).

As an example of a form of PC, we shall take here the one constructed by Hilbert and Bernays (it is constructed out of Russell's form in [Princ. Math.] by a simplification due to Bernays). It uses as primitive signs those of negation$_C$ (' $\sim$ ') and disjunction$_C$ (' $\vee$ ') (the subscript 'C' will be explained in § 3). We call this form of PC the calculus PC_1. Another similar form will be called PC_1^D; it contains further connectives defined on the basis of the two primitives mentioned. PC_1 does not contain rules of refutation.

A general connective (D1) is a sign that can be applied to any closed sentences as components (arguments). A connective is said to be of **degree** n if it is applied to n components. Connectives of degree one are also called **singulary** connectives, those of degree two **binary**. (As in [I], the more important definitions and theorems are marked by ' + '.)

+**D2-1.** $\mathfrak{a}_i$ is a **general connective** of degree n in a calculus K (or in a semantical system S) $=_{Df} K$ (or S) contains closed sentences, and for every n-term sequence of closed sentences in K (or S respectively) there is a full sentence of $\mathfrak{a}_i$ in K (or S) with that sequence of components.

If $\mathfrak{a}_k$ is a singulary and $\mathfrak{a}_l$ a binary general connective, then we designate the full sentence of a_k with the component $\mathfrak{S}_i$ by '$a_k(\mathfrak{S}_i)$' and the full sentence of a_l with the components $\mathfrak{S}_i$ and $\mathfrak{S}_j$ by '$a_l(\mathfrak{S}_i,\mathfrak{S}_j)$'.

+D2-2. *K* **contains PC₁ with neg**$_C$ *as sign of negation*$_C$ and **dis**$_C$ *as sign of disjunction*$_C$ =$_{Df}$ the calculus *K* fulfills the following conditions:

    a. neg$_C$ is a singular and dis$_C$ a binary general connective in *K*.

    b. The relation of **direct C-implication** ($\underset{dC}{\rightarrow}$) holds in the following cases for any $\mathfrak{S}_i$, $\mathfrak{S}_j$, and $\mathfrak{S}_k$ (but not necessarily only in these cases):

        1. $\Lambda \underset{dC}{\rightarrow} \mathrm{dis}_C(\mathrm{neg}_C(\mathrm{dis}_C(\mathfrak{S}_i,\mathfrak{S}_i)),\mathfrak{S}_i)$.

        2. $\Lambda \underset{dC}{\rightarrow} \mathrm{dis}_C(\mathrm{neg}_C(\mathfrak{S}_i),\mathrm{dis}_C(\mathfrak{S}_i,\mathfrak{S}_j))$.

        3. $\Lambda \underset{dC}{\rightarrow} \mathrm{dis}_C(\mathrm{neg}_C(\mathrm{dis}_C(\mathfrak{S}_i,\mathfrak{S}_j)),\mathrm{dis}_C(\mathfrak{S}_j,\mathfrak{S}_i))$.

        4. $\Lambda \underset{dC}{\rightarrow} \mathrm{dis}_C(\mathrm{neg}_C(\mathrm{dis}_C(\mathrm{neg}_C(\mathfrak{S}_i),\mathfrak{S}_j)),\mathrm{dis}_C(\mathrm{neg}_C(\mathrm{dis}_C(\mathfrak{S}_k,\mathfrak{S}_i)),\mathrm{dis}_C(\mathfrak{S}_k,\mathfrak{S}_j)))$.

        5. $\{\mathfrak{S}_i,\ \mathrm{dis}_C(\mathrm{neg}_C(\mathfrak{S}_i),\mathfrak{S}_j)\} \underset{dC}{\rightarrow} \mathfrak{S}_j$.

By (1) to (4) all sentences of four specified forms are declared to be direct C-implicates of Λ, in other words, primitive sentences in *K* (see the customary formulation below). (5) is the rule of implication. The definition does not exclude the possibility that *K* contains still other rules of deduction, e.g. further cases for direct C-implication or rules of refutation.

The *customary formulation* of the rules of deduction for PC₁ with propositional variables is the following:

Primitive sentences of PC₁:

    a. '$\sim(p \vee p) \vee p$'.
    b. '$\sim p \vee (p \vee q)$'.
    c. '$\sim(p \vee q) \vee (q \vee p)$'
    d. '$\sim(\sim p \vee q) \vee (\sim(r \vee p) \vee (r \vee q))$'.

Rules of inference for PC₁:

    a. Rule of substitution. From $\mathfrak{S}_i$, $\mathfrak{S}_i\left(\begin{smallmatrix}i_k\\\mathfrak{S}_l\end{smallmatrix}\right)$ is directly derivable.

b. Rule of implication (in disjunctive form). From $\mathfrak{S}_i$ and $\sim \mathfrak{S}_i \vee \mathfrak{S}_j$, $\mathfrak{S}_j$ is directly derivable.

D2 is formulated in such a way — as is often done — that no propositional variables are required; such variables may or may not occur in K. But K cannot have only propositional variables as ultimate components for the connectives; it must also contain closed sentences (see D1). In D2, not merely four sentences but an infinite number of sentences are taken as primitive sentences (D2b, 1 to 4); these are the same sentences as those which, in the form just mentioned, are constructed out of the primitive sentences by any substitutions. Hence, in D2, no rule of substitution is necessary.

An example of a calculus containing PC_1 is K_1, described in [I] §§ 27 and 30.

§ 3. Propositional Connections$_C$ in PC

Syntactical concepts for the four singulary and the sixteen binary propositional connections$_C$ are introduced (see table). PC_1^D is a calculus containing primitive signs of negation$_C$ and disjunction$_C$ and defined signs for the other connections$_C$.

We shall summarize in this section some of the known features of the propositional connections occurring in PC. There are two customary ways of constructing a system for the propositional connectives, one by the use of primitive sentences and rules of inference, the other by the use of truth-tables. The second method, however, gives truth-conditions for the sentences and thereby interprets them. Hence, it does not belong to syntax but to semantics. Therefore the name 'Propositional Calculus' is appropriate only to a system of the first kind. For a system of truth-tables, that term, although customarily used, might better be replaced by a term like 'Propositional Logic'.

There is also a syntactical method analogous to that of the truth-tables. It uses tables with arbitrary values (e.g. numerical values) or unspecified values instead of truth-values. This method, in contradistinction to that of truth-tables proper, can also be used with any other number of values than two (so-called many-valued systems). Instead of the term 'truth-table', the wider term 'value-table', which does not prejudge the question of the interpretation of the values, should be used; often the term 'matrix' is used. A system based on formal tables of this kind is then a syntactical system, a calculus. [For explanations of the formal method of value-tables ("method of matrices"), see Lukasiewicz and Tarski [Untersuchungen], pp. 3, 4.]

In propositional logic there are four singulary and sixteen binary extensional connectives (see § 10). In a system of PC, corresponding connectives are used. In the interpretation of PC most frequently used (we shall call it the normal interpretation) the connectives are interpreted as the corresponding extensional connectives; this is the reason for their customary names (e.g. 'sign of negation', 'sign of disjunction', etc.) even in syntax. We shall use these names here, but with the subscript 'C' added (see D2-2 and 3 and the subsequent table, column (2)). It is, however, to be noted that we do not intend by this to decide on the interpretation of the connectives. If S is a true or even an L-true interpretation for K, then a sign of negation$_C$ in K is not necessarily a sign of negation in S. ['Sign of negation$_C$' is a syntactical term to be defined in this section; 'sign of negation' is a semantical term to be defined by D11-23. Sometimes we shall also write 'connections$_C$' in order to emphasize the syntactical nature of this concept.] In examples, we shall often make use of the customary signs ' $\sim$ ' and ' $\vee$ '; in more exact formulations in the syntax language, however, we make use not of these customary signs, enclosed in quotation marks, but of their syntactical names 'neg$_C$' and 'dis$_C$' (see D2-2), thus leaving the particular shapes of the signs undetermined.

The *table* contains syntactical expressions referring to the 4 + 16 propositional connections$_C$ and connectives, i.e. signs of connections$_C$, with the exception of the few examples of customary connectives in column (3), which belong, of course, to the object language. The reason for distinguishing just four singular and sixteen binary connections$_C$ is of a semantical rather than a syntactical nature; it will become clear in the later explanation of the semantical concepts of the corresponding connections (§ 10).

SYNTACTICAL CONCEPTS OF PROPOSITIONAL CONNECTIONS$_C$ AND CONNECTIVES IN PC

(1)	(2)	(3)	(4)	(5)
Connections$_C$		Connectives		
Abbreviation	Ordinary Name	Customary Symbol	Syntactical Name	Expression in PC$_1$
I. The four singular connections$_C$				
$_C\mathrm{Conn}_1^1$	tautology$_C$		$_C\mathfrak{b}_1$	$\mathfrak{S}_i \vee \sim\mathfrak{S}_i$
$_C\mathrm{Conn}_2^1$	(identity$_C$)		$_C\mathfrak{b}_2$	$\mathfrak{S}_i$
$_C\mathrm{Conn}_3^1$	negation$_C$	$\sim$	$_C\mathfrak{b}_3$ (neg$_C$)	$\sim\mathfrak{S}_i$
$_C\mathrm{Conn}_4^1$	contradiction$_C$		$_C\mathfrak{b}_4$	$\sim(\mathfrak{S}_i \vee \sim\mathfrak{S}_i)$
II. The sixteen binary connections$_C$				
$_C\mathrm{Conn}_1^2$	tautology$_C$		$_C\mathfrak{c}_1$	$\mathfrak{S}_i \vee \sim\mathfrak{S}_i$
$_C\mathrm{Conn}_2^2$	disjunction$_C$	$\vee$	$_C\mathfrak{c}_2$ (dis$_C$)	$\mathfrak{S}_i \vee \mathfrak{S}_j$
$_C\mathrm{Conn}_3^2$	(inverse implication$_C$)		$_C\mathfrak{c}_3$	$\mathfrak{S}_i \vee \sim\mathfrak{S}_j$
$_C\mathrm{Conn}_4^2$	(first component)		$_C\mathfrak{c}_4$	$\mathfrak{S}_i$
$_C\mathrm{Conn}_5^2$	implication$_C$	$\supset$	$_C\mathfrak{c}_5$ (imp$_C$)	$\sim\mathfrak{S}_i \vee \mathfrak{S}_j$
$_C\mathrm{Conn}_6^2$	(second component)		$_C\mathfrak{c}_6$	$\mathfrak{S}_j$
$_C\mathrm{Conn}_7^2$	equivalence$_C$	$\equiv$	$_C\mathfrak{c}_7$ (equ$_C$)	$\sim(\sim\mathfrak{S}_i \vee \sim\mathfrak{S}_j) \vee \sim(\mathfrak{S}_i \vee \mathfrak{S}_j)$
$_C\mathrm{Conn}_8^2$	conjunction$_C$	$\bullet$	$_C\mathfrak{c}_8$ (con$_C$)	$\sim(\sim\mathfrak{S}_i \vee \sim\mathfrak{S}_j)$
$_C\mathrm{Conn}_9^2$	exclusion$_C$	$\mid$	$_C\mathfrak{c}_9$	$\sim\mathfrak{S}_i \vee \sim\mathfrak{S}_j$
$_C\mathrm{Conn}_{10}^2$	(non-equivalence$_C$)		$_C\mathfrak{c}_{10}$	$\sim(\sim\mathfrak{S}_i \vee \mathfrak{S}_j) \vee \sim(\mathfrak{S}_i \vee \sim\mathfrak{S}_j)$
$_C\mathrm{Conn}_{11}^2$	(negation$_C$ of second)		$_C\mathfrak{c}_{11}$	$\sim\mathfrak{S}_j$
$_C\mathrm{Conn}_{12}^2$	(first alone)		$_C\mathfrak{c}_{12}$	$\sim(\sim\mathfrak{S}_i \vee \mathfrak{S}_j)$
$_C\mathrm{Conn}_{13}^2$	(negation$_C$ of first)		$_C\mathfrak{c}_{13}$	$\sim\mathfrak{S}_i$
$_C\mathrm{Conn}_{14}^2$	(second alone)		$_C\mathfrak{c}_{14}$	$\sim(\mathfrak{S}_i \vee \sim\mathfrak{S}_j)$
$_C\mathrm{Conn}_{15}^2$	bi-negation$_C$		$_C\mathfrak{c}_{15}$	$\sim(\mathfrak{S}_i \vee \mathfrak{S}_j)$
$_C\mathrm{Conn}_{16}^2$	contradiction$_C$		$_C\mathfrak{c}_{16}$	$\sim(\mathfrak{S}_i \vee \sim\mathfrak{S}_i)$

The terms 'sign of negation$_C$ in PC$_1$' and 'sign of disjunction$_C$ in PC$_1$' have been defined in D2-2; 'neg$_C$' and 'dis$_C$' are used as names of signs of these kinds. We shall now define syntactical terms for the other connections$_C$, listed in columns (1) and (2) of the table with respect to PC$_1$ (D1 and 2; see the later example for D2(5)). The more general concepts with respect to any other form of PC will be defined in § 4.

+**D3-1.** (1) $\mathfrak{S}_k$ is a *sentence of* $_c Conn_1^1$ (or a *tautology$_C$ sentence*) with $\mathfrak{S}_i$ (as component) in PC$_1$ in $K =_{Df} K$ contains PC$_1$ and $\mathfrak{S}_k$ is C-equivalent in K to dis$_C(\mathfrak{S}_i, neg_C(\mathfrak{S}_i))$.

(3) $\mathfrak{S}_k$ is a *sentence of* $_c Conn_3^1$ (or a *negation$_C$ sentence*) with $\mathfrak{S}_i$ (as component) in PC$_1$ in $K =_{Df} K$ contains PC$_1$ and $\mathfrak{S}_k$ is C-equivalent in K to neg$_C(\mathfrak{S}_i)$.

(2) and (4) are analogous; see explanation below.

+**D3-2.** (1) $\mathfrak{S}_k$ is a *sentence of* $_c Conn_1^2$ (or a *tautology$_C$ sentence*) with $\mathfrak{S}_i$ and $\mathfrak{S}_j$ (as components) in PC$_1$ in $K =_{Df} K$ contains PC$_1$ and $\mathfrak{S}_k$ is C-equivalent in K to dis$_C(\mathfrak{S}_i, neg_C(\mathfrak{S}_i))$.

(2) $\mathfrak{S}_k$ is a *sentence of* $_c Conn_2^2$ (or a *disjunction$_C$ sentence*) with $\mathfrak{S}_i$ and $\mathfrak{S}_j$ in PC$_1$ in $K =_{Df} K$ contains PC$_1$ and $\mathfrak{S}_k$ is C-equivalent in K to dis$_C(\mathfrak{S}_i, \mathfrak{S}_j)$.

.

.

(5) $\mathfrak{S}_k$ is a *sentence of* $_c Conn_5^2$ (or an *implication$_C$ sentence*) with $\mathfrak{S}_i$ and $\mathfrak{S}_j$ in PC$_1$ in $K =_{Df} K$ contains PC$_1$ and $\mathfrak{S}_k$ is C-equivalent in K to dis$_C(neg_C(\mathfrak{S}_i), \mathfrak{S}_j)$.

.

.

(8) $\mathfrak{S}_k$ is a *sentence of* $_c Conn_8^2$ (or a *conjunction$_C$ sentence*) with $\mathfrak{S}_i$ and $\mathfrak{S}_j$ in PC$_1$ in $K =_{Df} K$ contains PC$_1$ and $\mathfrak{S}_k$ is C-equivalent in K to neg$_C(dis_C(neg_C(\mathfrak{S}_i), neg_C(\mathfrak{S}_j)))$.

(3), (4), (6), (7), (9) to (16) are analogous. Each of the four definitions in D1 and the sixteen in D2 is constructed in the following way. The terms in the definiendum are those in columns (1) and (2) of the table; the sentence mentioned at the end of the definiens is that described in column (5) of the table on the line in question (where, for the sake of brevity, '$\sim \mathfrak{S}_m$' is written for 'neg$_C(\mathfrak{S}_m)$', and '$\mathfrak{S}_m \vee \mathfrak{S}_n$' for 'dis$_C(\mathfrak{S}_m, \mathfrak{S}_n)$').

D3 is a definition schema furnishing four definitions if the numerals '1' to '4' are taken as subscripts in the place of 'q'. Likewise, D4 furnishes sixteen definitions with '1' to '16' in the place or 'r'. Subsequent definitions, theorems, and explanations containing a subscript variable 'q' or 'r' are to be understood analogously.

+**D3-3.** $\mathfrak{a}_k$ is a *sign* (or *connective*) for $_C Conn_q^1$ (q = 1 to 4) in PC$_1$ in K =$_{Df}$ K contains PC$_1$, $\mathfrak{a}_k$ is a general connective in K, and, for any closed sentence $\mathfrak{S}_i$ in K, the full sentence $\mathfrak{a}_k(\mathfrak{S}_i)$ is a sentence for $_C Conn_q^1$ in PC$_1$ in K.

+**D3-4.** $\mathfrak{a}_k$ is a *sign* (or *connective*) for $_C Conn_r^2$ (r = 1 to 16) in PC$_1$ in K =$_{Df}$ K contains PC$_1$, $\mathfrak{a}_k$ is a general connective in K, and, for any closed sentences $\mathfrak{S}_i$ and $\mathfrak{S}_j$ in K, the full sentence $\mathfrak{a}_k(\mathfrak{S}_i, \mathfrak{S}_j)$ is a sentence for $_C Conn_r^2$ in PC$_1$ in K.

If there is a sign for $_C Conn_q^1$ (q = 1 to 4) in PC$_1$ in K, we shall use '$_C \mathfrak{b}_q$' as a syntactical name for it; analogously, '$_C \mathfrak{c}_r$' (r = 1 to 16) for a sign for $_C Conn_r^2$ (column (4) of the table). Instead of '$_C \mathfrak{b}_3$' we usually write '**neg**$_C$'. Instead of '$_C \mathfrak{c}_2$' we usually write '**dis**$_C$'; likewise, for r = 5, 7, or 8, we usually use '**imp**$_C$', '**equ**$_C$', and '**con**$_C$' respectively.

Examples, for r = 5. The sentence dis$_C$(neg$_C(\mathfrak{S}_i), \mathfrak{S}_j$), and likewise any other sentence which is C-equivalent to it, is called a sentence of $_C Conn_5^2$ or a sentence of implication$_C$ with $\mathfrak{S}_i$ and $\mathfrak{S}_j$ in PC$_1$ in K (D2(5)). Thus, if K contains PC$_1$, it always contains implication$_C$ sentences, even if the signs of negation$_C$ and disjunction$_C$ are the only connectives. If K contains a general connective $\mathfrak{a}_k$, such that its full sentence with any closed components $\mathfrak{S}_i$ and $\mathfrak{S}_j$ is always C-equivalent to the sentence $\mathrm{dis}_C(\mathrm{neg}_C(\mathfrak{S}_i),\mathfrak{S}_j)$, then $\mathfrak{a}_k$ is called a sign of $_C\mathrm{Conn}_5^2$ (D4(5)) or of implication$_C$, and '$c\mathfrak{c}_5$' or 'imp$_C$' is used as a name for it.

The expressions in column (5) of the table show how all singulary and binary connections$_C$ can be expressed in PC_1. Therefore, these expressions may be taken as definientia in definitions of signs for these connections$_C$, on the basis of the signs for negation$_C$ and disjunction$_C$ as primitives.

Example. A definition of a sign of conjunction$_C$ $c\mathfrak{c}_8$ may be formulated as follows: "$c\mathfrak{c}_8(\mathfrak{S}_i,\mathfrak{S}_j)$ for $\mathrm{neg}_C(\mathrm{dis}_C(\mathrm{neg}_C(\mathfrak{S}_i), \mathrm{neg}_C(\mathfrak{S}_j)))$". Compare [I] § 24 concerning definition sentences and definition rules. A definition rule is here regarded as an additional rule of inference, which states that two sentences (e.g. 'A ⊃ C . D' and 'A ⊃ ∼ (∼ C ∨ ∼D)' in the above example) which differ only in two expressions of the forms of the definiendum ('C . D') and the definiens ('∼ (∼ C ∨ ∼D)') are direct C-implicates of each other.

The form of PC containing all the definitions indicated by column (5) on the basis of PC_1 will be called PC_1^D (D6). Hence, PC_1^D contains a connective for each of the $4 + 16$ connections$_C$ listed.

+**D3-6.** *K* **contains PC$_1^D$** $=_{Df}$ *K* contains PC$_1$ and, in addition, definition rules on the basis of the signs of negation$_C$ and disjunction$_C$ for signs for all other singulary and binary connections$_C$, with definientia as given in column (5) of the above table.

'a [b]' in D7, and analogously in some of the subsequent definitions, theorems, and proofs, means that (a), i.e. here D3-7a, is to be read without the *insertions in square brackets*, while for (b), here D3-7b, these insertions are to be added (or sometimes to be taken instead of the preceding expression).

D3-7a [b]. $\mathfrak{T}_j$ is a **C-implicate** of $\mathfrak{T}_i$ in *K* **by PC$_1$** [PC$_1^D$] $=_{Df}$ *K* contains PC$_1$ [PC$_1^D$] and $\mathfrak{T}_i \underset{C}{\rightarrow} \mathfrak{T}_j$ in virtue of the rules of deduction as given in D2-2b [and, in addition, the definition rules of PC_1^D as described in D3-6]. Analogously for any other C-term defined on the basis of 'C-implication'.

§4. Forms of PC

> The general concept of a calculus containing any form of PC and the concepts of the propositional connections$_C$ in a calculus of this kind are defined.

Under what conditions shall we say that K contains a form of PC? K need not contain all the $4 + 16$ connectives of PC_1^D; it would suffice if K contained e.g. signs of negation$_C$ and disjunction$_C$ (the primitives in PC_1) or signs of negation$_C$ and conjunction$_C$ (the primitives in another form, PC_2; see below). Suppose that K_n is a sub-calculus of a calculus K_m containing PC_1^D, and that some of the connectives in PC_1^D occur in K_n. Then under suitable conditions we shall say that K_n contains a form of PC. First, we shall require that, if $\mathfrak{T}_i \underset{C}{\rightarrow} \mathfrak{T}_j$ in K_m and $\mathfrak{T}_i$ and $\mathfrak{T}_j$ belong to K_n too, then $\mathfrak{T}_i \underset{C}{\rightarrow} \mathfrak{T}_j$ in K_n; in other words, that K_n is a conservative sub-calculus of K_m ([I] D31-7; PC_1^D usually does not contain rules of refutation). Second, K_n must not be too poor a sub-calculus; if it contained e.g. a sign of conjunction$_C$ as the only connective we should not say that it contained a form of PC. K_n must contain a sufficient set of connectives for building sentences for all $4 + 16$ connections$_C$. This can be formulated in a syntactical way by requiring that K_n be a sub-calculus of K_m containing for every sentence $\mathfrak{S}_i$ in K_m a C-equivalent sentence. (Thus, e.g., if K_n contains PC_2, this requirement is fulfilled, because for any sentence containing any connectives of PC_1^D there is a C-equivalent sentence with the connectives of negation$_C$ and conjunction$_C$ only.) But we have to admit still other calculi. Suppose that the connectives used in K_p happen to be different from those in K_n but in such a way that they correspond strictly to those in K_n; in other words, that K_p is isomorphic to K_n (see [I] D31-10). In this case also we should say that K_p contained a form of PC. These considerations lead to D1. It is to be noticed that K_m and K_n may be identical; likewise K_n and K_p, and hence K_m and K_p.

D4-1. A calculus K_p **contains** (a form of) **PC** $=_{Df}$ there are calculi K_m and K_n such that the following conditions are fulfilled:

    a. K_m contains PC_1^D;

    b. K_n is a conservative sub-calculus of K_m;

    c. for every sentence $\mathfrak{S}_i$ in K_m there is a sentence $\mathfrak{S}_j$ in K_n (and K_m) which is C-equivalent to $\mathfrak{S}_i$ in K_m;

    d. K_p is isomorphic to K_n by a correlation H.

The following definition is analogous to D3-7.

D4-2. $\mathfrak{T}_j$ is a **C-implicate** of $\mathfrak{T}_i$ in K **by PC** $=_{Df}$ K contains PC by being isomorphic by a correlation H with a sub-calculus of a calculus K_m containing PC_1^D, and $\mathfrak{T}_i' \overset{\rightarrow}{\underset{C}{}} \mathfrak{T}_j'$ in K_m by PC_1^D, where $\mathfrak{T}_i'$ is the correlate in K_m of $\mathfrak{T}_i$ by H and $\mathfrak{T}_j'$ that of $\mathfrak{T}_j$. Analogously for any other C-term defined by 'C-implication'.

Now we can easily define the syntactical concepts 'sign of negation$_C$', etc., with respect to any form of PC.

D4-3. $\mathfrak{a}_i$ is a *sign (connective)* for $_cConn_q^1$ ($q = 1$ to 4) or $_cConn_r^2$ ($r = 1$ to 16) in PC in $K =_{Df}$ K contains PC by being isomorphic by a correlation H to a sub-calculus of a calculus K_m containing PC_1^D, and $\mathfrak{a}_i$ is correlated by H to a sign for the same connection$_C$ (i.e. $_cConn_q^1$ or $_cConn_r^2$ respectively) in PC_1 in K_m.

As previously in PC_1^D, now in general in PC, we shall designate a sign for $_cConn_q^1$ by '$_c\mathfrak{b}_q$' and a sign for $_cConn_r^2$ by '$_c\mathfrak{c}_r$'.

A number of other forms of PC besides PC_1 are known. Thus e.g. each of the following sets of primitive signs is a sufficient basis for expressing all connections$_C$: signs for negation$_C$ and conjunction$_C$ (PC_2); negation$_C$ and implication$_C$ (PC_3); exclusion$_C$ (PC_4, shown by Sheffer), bi-negation$_C$ (PC_5, Sheffer). Suitable rules of deduction for these forms have been constructed for PC_3 by Frege, for PC_4 by Nicod and Quine; for PC_5 by Quine.

The systems mentioned are only a few examples. For each of the bases mentioned, there is an infinite number of different forms. Further, there are other bases besides those mentioned. For instance, a sign of negation$_C$ together with c_3 or c_{12} or c_{14} yields a sufficient basis; each of these systems is similar to PC_3 and to PC_2 since implication$_C$ and conjunction$_C$ can easily be expressed or defined. [Definientia for imp$_C(\mathfrak{S}_i,\mathfrak{S}_j)$: $c_3(\mathfrak{S}_j,\mathfrak{S}_i)$, neg$_C(c_{12}(\mathfrak{S}_i,\mathfrak{S}_j))$, and neg$_C(c_{14}(\mathfrak{S}_j,\mathfrak{S}_i))$ respectively.]

The following sections (§§ 5 to 9) contain theorems concerning not PC in isolation but, rather, calculi containing PC. This difference seems slight, but it is essential for the later discussion of interpretation. Sometimes calculi are constructed in symbolic logic which do not contain PC as a part, but, so to speak, represent *PC* itself *in a pure form*, i.e. as a calculus containing propositional variables as the only ultimate components (see "the customary formulation", at the end of § 2). But in a calculus of this kind, every sentence is open and is either C-true or C-comprehensive (i.e. every sentence is a C-implicate of it, [I] D30-6). This is a disadvantage for a discussion of interpretations. The customary interpretation is L-true, and hence all sentences in a pure form of PC become here L-determinate; there are no factual sentences. Moreover, the most convenient and customary formulation of semantical rules for the normal interpretation, namely the truth-tables, cannot be directly used for such a form of PC, because the truth-tables apply only to closed sentences (see remarks on the rules of NTT, § 10). Therefore, for the discussion of interpretations we shall have to take into consideration not pure

forms but calculi containing PC with or without propositional variables, but in any case containing closed sentences
and hence other constants in addition to the connectives (in
the simplest case propositional constants). For this reason,
the syntactical discussions in the following sections will
likewise refer not to a pure form of PC but to calculi containing PC with closed sentences. It is true that this will make
the theorems more complicated. It turns out that the results also depend to some extent upon certain features of the
calculus K in question outside of PC, e.g. upon the additional
rules of deduction of K. But it seems that by means of this
the results formulated in the theorems of this chapter are
more generally applicable. In the practical work in symbolic
logic and in the logical foundations of mathematics, we deal
in most cases not with pure forms of PC but with calculi
containing PC. Therefore it is important to see in what respect the features of the more comprehensive calculus influence the properties of the propositional connections that
occur.

§ 5. Elementary Theorems Concerning PC

> Some well-known elementary syntactical theorems con-
> cerning the propositional connections$_C$ in PC are listed for
> later reference.

Before we come to the discussion of our chief problem,
namely the normal interpretation of PC (§§ 10 and 11) and
the question of the possibility of non-normal interpretations
(beginning in § 15), we must study the syntactical features
of PC, independent of any interpretation. This is the task
of the rest of this chapter (§§ 5 to 9). The present section
lists only some elementary and well-known theorems for
the convenience of later reference. These theorems state
some examples of C-truth, C-implication, and C-equivalence.

Proofs are not given because they are either known or easily constructed with the help of those known. [Derivations for the cases listed in T2 and 3 may be found by first constructing a proof for the corresponding implication$_C$ sentences with the help of the conjunctive normal form; see e.g. Hilbert [Logik], Kap. I, §§ 3 and 4.] It is essential that the theorems refer not only to the forms of PC but to any calculus K containing such a form; the theorems hold for any sentences of K no matter what other signs besides those of PC they may contain. This is especially important for theorems like T2l.

Here, and in the further discussions as well, for the sake of simplicity, we shall refer mostly to the special form PC_1. But, as can easily be seen on the basis of D4-1, the results hold likewise for any other sentences which are C-equivalent to those mentioned here by PC_1 or PC_1^D or any other form with different primitive signs but the same connectives; and they hold also for the correlated sentences in any other form of PC. [Thus, for instance, if something is said about $\mathrm{dis}_C(\mathrm{neg}_C(\mathfrak{S}_i),\mathfrak{S}_j)$, i.e. $\sim\mathfrak{S}_i \vee \mathfrak{S}_j$, in PC_1, then the same holds for $\mathfrak{S}_i \supset \mathfrak{S}_j$, for $\sim(\mathfrak{S}_i \cdot \sim\mathfrak{S}_j)$, etc., in PC_1^D, and for any corresponding sentences in any other form of PC.]

T5-1. If K contains PC_1, then any sentence of one of the following forms is *C-true* in K by PC_1:

    a. $\mathrm{dis}_C(\mathfrak{S}_i,\mathrm{neg}_C(\mathfrak{S}_i))$.
    b. $\mathrm{dis}_C(\mathrm{neg}_C(\mathfrak{S}_i),\mathfrak{S}_i)$.

T5-2. If K contains PC_1 or (for (h) and (q) to (t)) PC_1^D, then in each of the following cases $\mathfrak{S}_j$ is a *C-implicate* of $\mathfrak{T}_i$ in K by PC_1 or PC_1^D, respectively.

$\mathfrak{T}_i$ is:	$\mathfrak{S}_j$ is:
a. $\mathrm{dis}_C(\mathfrak{S}_m, \mathfrak{S}_m)$	$\mathfrak{S}_m$
b. $\mathfrak{S}_m$	$\mathrm{dis}_C(\mathfrak{S}_m, \mathfrak{S}_n)$
c. $\mathfrak{S}_n$	$\mathrm{dis}_C(\mathfrak{S}_m, \mathfrak{S}_n)$
e. $\{\mathrm{dis}_C(\mathfrak{S}_m, \mathfrak{S}_n), \mathrm{neg}_C(\mathfrak{S}_m)\}$	$\mathfrak{S}_n$
f. $\{\mathrm{dis}_C(\mathfrak{S}_m, \mathfrak{S}_n), \mathrm{neg}_C(\mathfrak{S}_n)\}$	$\mathfrak{S}_m$
g. $\{\mathrm{dis}_C(\mathfrak{S}_m, \mathrm{neg}_C(\mathfrak{S}_n)), \mathfrak{S}_n\}$	$\mathfrak{S}_m$
h. $\{\mathrm{dis}_C(\mathfrak{S}_m, \mathfrak{S}_n), \mathrm{imp}_C(\mathfrak{S}_m, \mathfrak{S}_n)\}$	$\mathfrak{S}_n$
i. $\{\mathrm{dis}_C(\mathfrak{S}_m, \mathfrak{S}_n), \mathrm{dis}_C(\mathfrak{S}_m, \mathrm{neg}_C(\mathfrak{S}_n))\}$	$\mathfrak{S}_m$
k. $\{\mathrm{dis}_C(\mathfrak{S}_k, \mathrm{dis}_C(\mathrm{neg}_C(\mathfrak{S}_m), \mathfrak{S}_n)), \mathrm{dis}_C(\mathfrak{S}_k, \mathfrak{S}_m)\}$	$\mathrm{dis}_C(\mathfrak{S}_k, \mathfrak{S}_n)$
l. $\{\mathfrak{S}_m, \mathrm{neg}_C(\mathfrak{S}_m)\}$	any sentence (in K)
m. $\mathrm{neg}_C(\mathrm{dis}_C(\mathrm{neg}_C(\mathfrak{S}_m), \mathrm{neg}_C(\mathfrak{S}_n)))$	$\mathfrak{S}_m$
n. $\mathrm{neg}_C(\mathrm{dis}_C(\mathrm{neg}_C(\mathfrak{S}_m), \mathrm{neg}_C(\mathfrak{S}_n)))$	$\mathfrak{S}_n$
q. $\mathrm{con}_C(\mathfrak{S}_m, \mathfrak{S}_n)$	$\mathfrak{S}_m$
r. $\mathrm{con}_C(\mathfrak{S}_m, \mathfrak{S}_n)$	$\mathfrak{S}_n$
t. $\{\mathrm{dis}_C(\mathfrak{S}_k, \mathrm{imp}_C(\mathfrak{S}_m, \mathfrak{S}_n)), \mathrm{dis}_C(\mathfrak{S}_k, \mathfrak{S}_m)\}$	$\mathrm{dis}_C(\mathfrak{S}_k, \mathfrak{S}_n)$

T5-3. If K contains PC_1 or (for (n) to (u)) PC_1^D, then in each of the following cases $\mathfrak{T}_i$ and $\mathfrak{T}_j$ are *C-equivalent* in K by PC_1 or PC_1^D, respectively.

$\mathfrak{T}_i$ is:	$\mathfrak{T}_j$ is:
a. $\mathfrak{S}_m$	$\mathrm{neg}_C(\mathrm{neg}_C(\mathfrak{S}_m))$
b. $\{\mathfrak{S}_m, \mathfrak{S}_n\}$	$\mathrm{neg}_C(\mathrm{dis}_C(\mathrm{neg}_C(\mathfrak{S}_m), \mathrm{neg}_C(\mathfrak{S}_n)))$
d. $\mathrm{dis}_C(\mathfrak{S}_m, \mathfrak{S}_n)$	$\mathrm{dis}_C(\mathfrak{S}_n, \mathfrak{S}_m)$
i. $\{\mathrm{dis}_C(\mathrm{neg}_C(\mathfrak{S}_m), \mathfrak{S}_l), \mathrm{dis}_C(\mathrm{neg}_C(\mathfrak{S}_n), \mathfrak{S}_l)\}$	$\mathrm{dis}_C(\mathrm{neg}_C(\mathrm{dis}_C(\mathfrak{S}_m, \mathfrak{S}_n)), \mathfrak{S}_l)$
j. $\mathrm{dis}_C(\mathfrak{S}_m, \mathrm{dis}_C(\mathfrak{S}_n, \mathfrak{S}_p))$	$\mathrm{dis}_C(\mathfrak{S}_n, \mathrm{dis}_C(\mathfrak{S}_m, \mathfrak{S}_p))$
k. $\mathrm{dis}_C(\mathrm{dis}_C(\mathfrak{S}_m, \mathfrak{S}_n), \mathfrak{S}_p)$	$\mathrm{dis}_C(\mathfrak{S}_m, \mathrm{dis}_C(\mathfrak{S}_n, \mathfrak{S}_p))$
l. $\mathrm{dis}_C(\mathfrak{S}_m, \mathfrak{S}_m)$	$\mathfrak{S}_m$
n. $\mathrm{con}_C(\mathfrak{S}_m, \mathfrak{S}_n)$	$\mathrm{neg}_C(\mathrm{dis}_C(\mathrm{neg}_C(\mathfrak{S}_m), \mathrm{neg}_C(\mathfrak{S}_n)))$
p. $\{\mathfrak{S}_m, \mathfrak{S}_n\}$	$\mathrm{con}_C(\mathfrak{S}_m, \mathfrak{S}_n)$
r. $\mathrm{con}_C(\mathfrak{S}_m, \mathfrak{S}_n)$	$\mathrm{con}_C(\mathfrak{S}_n, \mathfrak{S}_m)$
s. $\mathrm{imp}_C(\mathfrak{S}_m, \mathfrak{S}_n)$	$\mathrm{dis}_C(\mathrm{neg}_C(\mathfrak{S}_m), \mathfrak{S}_n)$
t. $\mathrm{dis}_C(\mathfrak{S}_m, \mathfrak{S}_n)$	$\mathrm{imp}_C(\mathrm{neg}_C(\mathfrak{S}_m), \mathfrak{S}_n)$
u. $\{\mathrm{imp}_C(\mathfrak{S}_m, \mathfrak{S}_l), \mathrm{imp}_C(\mathfrak{S}_n, \mathfrak{S}_l)\}$	$\mathrm{imp}_C(\mathrm{dis}_C(\mathfrak{S}_m, \mathfrak{S}_n), \mathfrak{S}_l)$

§ 6. Extensible Rules

> The concept 'extensible rule of inference' is defined. In it-
> self it is not important, but it is needed for some later theorems.
> In a first reading, *this section may be left out*.

If a calculus K contains PC and, in addition, other rules
of deduction, then it is not so much the additional primitive
sentences as the additional rules of inference which have an
influence upon the syntactical properties of the propositional
connections$_C$ in K. In the present section, the property of
extensibility which a rule of inference in a calculus containing PC may or may not have will be defined and studied.
The results will be used in the later discussion.

Let us regard as an example the rule of substitution for
propositional variables ($\mathfrak{f}$), as it often occurs in calculi con-
taining PC. According to it, $\mathfrak{S}_j\left(\begin{smallmatrix} \mathfrak{f}_m \\ \mathfrak{S}_n \end{smallmatrix}\right)$ is a direct C-implicate
of $\mathfrak{S}_j$ in K. If now we add any closed sentence in K, say $\mathfrak{S}_k$,
as a left-hand disjunctive component to each of those two
sentences, we get $\mathrm{dis}_C(\mathfrak{S}_k, \mathfrak{S}_j\left(\begin{smallmatrix} \mathfrak{f}_m \\ \mathfrak{S}_n \end{smallmatrix}\right))$ and $\mathrm{dis}_C(\mathfrak{S}_k, \mathfrak{S}_j)$. It can
easily be seen that for these two sentences the relation of
C-implication in K still holds. The same holds generally for
any application of the rule of substitution even if $\mathfrak{S}_k$ is not
closed, provided only that $\mathfrak{S}_k$ does not contain a free variable
which occurs freely in $\mathfrak{S}_j$ or $\mathfrak{S}_n$ (see below, proof for T3a). We
shall formulate this result by saying that the rule mentioned
is *extensible* (with respect to a left-hand disjunctive component).

We shall now define this concept in a general way. We
take '$\mathrm{dis}_C'(\mathfrak{S}_k, \mathfrak{R}_i)$' as designation of that sentential class
which we construct out of $\mathfrak{R}_i$ by adding $\mathfrak{S}_k$ as left-hand disjunctive component to every sentence of $\mathfrak{R}_i$ (thus e.g. trans-
forming $\{\mathfrak{S}_1, \mathfrak{S}_2, \mathfrak{S}_3, \ldots\}$ into $\{\mathfrak{S}_k \vee \mathfrak{S}_1, \mathfrak{S}_k \vee \mathfrak{S}_2, \mathfrak{S}_k \vee \mathfrak{S}_3,$
$\ldots\}$). The sentences of $\mathrm{dis}_C''(\mathfrak{R}_i, \mathfrak{S}_k)$ are constructed out of

those of $\Re_i$ by adding $\mathfrak{S}_k$ as right-hand disjunctive component. Analogous designations are formed for other connections$_C$ (and likewise for the normal connectives in a semantical system; see § 10).

D6-1. A **rule of inference** R in a calculus K is (extensible with respect to a disjunctive component, or briefly) **extensible** $=_{Df}$ K contains PC; and for any $\mathfrak{S}_j$, $\Re_i$, and $\mathfrak{S}_k$ in K, if $\mathfrak{S}_j$ is a direct C-implicate of $\Re_i$ in virtue of R, and $\mathfrak{S}_k$ is either closed (i.e. does not contain a free variable) or at least does not contain a free variable also occurring freely in $\mathfrak{S}_j$ or any sentence of $\Re_i$, then $\text{dis}'_C(\mathfrak{S}_k,\Re_i) \underset{C}{\rightarrow} \text{dis}_C(\mathfrak{S}_k,\mathfrak{S}_j)$ in K.

In an analogous way we may define 'extensible with respect to a left-hand implicative component' by the condition that $\text{imp}'_C(\mathfrak{S}_k,\Re_i) \underset{C}{\rightarrow} \text{imp}_C(\mathfrak{S}_k,\mathfrak{S}_j)$, and 'extensible with respect to a conjunctive component' by the condition that $\text{con}'_C(\mathfrak{S}_k,\Re_i) \underset{C}{\rightarrow} \text{con}_C(\mathfrak{S}_k,\mathfrak{S}_j)$. But these terms will be used only here in T1 and 2. [In the case of disjunction$_C$ and conjunction$_C$ we need not distinguish between extensibility with respect to left-hand and with respect to right-hand component, because these connections$_C$ are commutative (T5-3d and r).]

The reason for the restricting condition with respect to $\mathfrak{S}_k$ in D1 will be explained later (see remarks on T28-10).

T6-1. If a rule is extensible with respect to a disjunctive component, then it is also extensible with respect to a left-hand implicative component; and vice versa. (From T5-3s and t.)

We shall see later that certain theorems in general syntax hold only for those calculi whose rules are extensible with respect to a disjunctive component; and this is the reason for introducing this concept. But there is no need in any theorem for an analogous condition with respect to a conjunctive component, because every rule fulfills this condition (T2).

T6-2. If K contains PC, then any rule of inference of K (and hence also any instance of C-implication in K with a non-empty premiss class) is extensible with respect to a conjunctive component.

Proof. Let $\mathfrak{S}_j$ be a direct C-implicate or a C-implicate of a non-empty class $\mathfrak{K}_i$ in K, and $\mathfrak{S}_k$ any sentence in K. For every sentence $\mathfrak{S}_i$ of $\mathfrak{K}_i$, $\mathfrak{S}_i$ and $\mathfrak{S}_k$ are C-implicates of $\mathrm{conc}_C(\mathfrak{S}_k,\mathfrak{S}_i)$ (T5-2q and r) and hence of $\mathrm{conc}'_C(\mathfrak{S}_k,\mathfrak{K}_i)$ ([I] T29-33 and 44). Hence each of the following items is a C-implicate of $\mathrm{conc}'_C(\mathfrak{S}_k,\mathfrak{K}_i)$: a. $\mathfrak{K}_i$ ([I] T29-40); b. $\{\mathfrak{S}_k, \mathfrak{S}_j\}$ (the same); c. $\mathrm{conc}_C(\mathfrak{S}_k,\mathfrak{S}_j)$ ((b), T5-3p).

Many forms of PC contain the rule of implication (or separation or abruption): "$\mathfrak{S}_j$ is a direct C-implicate of $\mathfrak{S}_i$ and the implication$_C$ sentence of $\mathfrak{S}_i$ and $\mathfrak{S}_j$". In some forms the implication$_C$ sentence is formed with the help of a sign of implication$_C$; in other forms, as e.g. PC$_1$, it is formed as $\mathrm{dis}_C(\mathrm{neg}_C(\mathfrak{S}_i),\mathfrak{S}_j)$. Thus we distinguish rules of implication in implicative and in disjunctive form.

T6-3. In any calculus containing PC, each of the following rules, if it occurs, is extensible: **a.** the rule of substitution for propositional variables; **b.** the rule of implication in implicative form; **c.** the rule of implication in disjunctive form.

Proof. a. Suppose that $\mathfrak{S}_k$ does not contain $\mathfrak{f}_m$ as a free variable. Then $\mathrm{dis}_C(\mathfrak{S}_k,\mathfrak{S}_i\left(\begin{smallmatrix}\mathfrak{f}_m\\\mathfrak{S}_n\end{smallmatrix}\right))$ is the same as $(\mathrm{dis}_C(\mathfrak{S}_k,\mathfrak{S}_i))\left(\begin{smallmatrix}\mathfrak{f}_m\\\mathfrak{S}_n\end{smallmatrix}\right)$ and, hence, is a C-implicate of $\mathrm{dis}_C(\mathfrak{S}_k,\mathfrak{S}_i)$. — b. From T5-2t. — c. From T5-2k.

T6-4. In any calculus containing PC, any definition rule (of the customary form; see § 3) is extensible.

Proof. If an application of a definition rule leads from $\mathfrak{S}_i$ to $\mathfrak{S}_j$, then, for any $\mathfrak{S}_k$, an application of the same rule leads from $\mathrm{dis}_C(\mathfrak{S}_k,\mathfrak{S}_i)$ to $\mathrm{dis}_C(\mathfrak{S}_k,\mathfrak{S}_j)$.

T6-5. If K contains PC$_1$ (either in the form given in § 2 or in a form using propositional variables and a rule of substitution) or PC_1^D (§ 3), then all rules of inference of PC_1 or PC_1^D in K are extensible. (From T3a, c, and T4.)

It can moreover be shown that, if K contains any form of PC, then all rules of inference of PC in K are extensible. It will be shown later that the rules of inference in the Lower Functional Calculus FC_1 are also extensible (T28-10).

As remarked previously, the subsequent theorems in § 6 to 9 refer to PC_1 or PC_1^D, but they hold likewise for any other form of PC.

T6-10. Let K fulfill the following three conditions:

A. K contains PC_1,

B. all rules of inference in K are extensible,

C. K either contains no rule of refutation or, if it does, every directly C-false $\mathfrak{T}_i$ in K is such that every sentence in K is derivable from it.

For any non-empty $\mathfrak{R}_i$, $\mathfrak{S}_j$, and $\mathfrak{S}_k$ such that $\mathfrak{S}_k$ does not contain any free variable occurring freely in $\mathfrak{S}_j$ or in any sentence of $\mathfrak{R}_i$, if $\mathfrak{R}_i \underset{C}{\rightharpoondown} \mathfrak{S}_j$ in K, then $\mathrm{dis}_C'\,(\mathfrak{S}_k, \mathfrak{R}_i) \underset{C}{\rightharpoondown} \mathrm{dis}_C\,(\mathfrak{S}_k, \mathfrak{S}_j)$.

Proof. Because of (C), 'C-implicate in K' and 'derivable in K' coincide ([I] T29-54a and 55a). Hence, if $\mathfrak{R}_i \underset{C}{\rightharpoondown} \mathfrak{S}_j$, then there is a derivation D_1 leading from $\mathfrak{R}_i$ to $\mathfrak{S}_j$. We transform D_1 into the sequence of sentences D_2 by adding $\mathfrak{S}_k$ as a left-hand disjunctive component to every sentence. (D_2 is not necessarily itself a derivation but is the skeleton of a derivation D_3 which leads from $\mathrm{dis}_C'(\mathfrak{S}_k, \mathfrak{R}_i)$ to $\mathrm{dis}_C(\mathfrak{S}_k, \mathfrak{S}_j)$.) Every sentence $\mathfrak{S}_l$ in D_1 is either (a) a sentence of $\mathfrak{R}_i$ or (b) a primitive sentence of K or (c) a direct C-implicate of a class $\mathfrak{R}_p$ of preceding sentences in virtue of a rule of inference. In the case (a), $\mathrm{dis}_C(\mathfrak{S}_k, \mathfrak{S}_l)$ is a sentence of $\mathrm{dis}_C'(\mathfrak{S}_k, \mathfrak{R}_i)$. In the case (b), $\mathrm{dis}_C(\mathfrak{S}_k, \mathfrak{S}_l)$ is C-true in K (T5-2c). The first sentence of D_2 belongs either to (a) or to (b); therefore (α): it is a C-implicate of $\mathrm{dis}_C'(\mathfrak{S}_k, \mathfrak{R}_i)$ ([I] T29-33 and 74). In the case (c), because of condition (B), $\mathrm{dis}_C(\mathfrak{S}_k, \mathfrak{S}_l)$ is a C-implicate of $\mathrm{dis}_C'(\mathfrak{S}_k, \mathfrak{R}_i)$, which is a class of preceding sentences in D_2. Thus (β): for any sentence $\mathfrak{S}_m$ in D_2 the following holds: if every sentence preceding $\mathfrak{S}_m$ is a C-implicate of $\mathrm{dis}_C'(\mathfrak{S}_k, \mathfrak{R}_i)$, then the same holds for $\mathfrak{S}_m$ ([I] T29-40 and 44). According to the principle of induction (transfinite induction if D_1 is a transfinite derivation; see [I] § 25 at the end), it follows from (α) and (β) that every sentence of D_2, and hence also $\mathrm{dis_C}(\mathfrak{S}_k,\mathfrak{S}_j)$, is a C-implicate of $\mathrm{dis_C'}(\mathfrak{S}_k,\mathfrak{R}_i)$.

+**T6-12.** Let K fulfill the conditions (A), (B), and (C) in T10. If $\mathfrak{S}_i$ is closed and $\mathfrak{S}_i \underset{C}{\rightrightarrows} \mathfrak{S}_j$ in K, then any implication$_C$ sentence with $\mathfrak{S}_i$ and $\mathfrak{S}_j$, e.g. $\mathrm{dis_C}(\mathrm{neg_C}(\mathfrak{S}_i),\mathfrak{S}_j)$, is C-true in K.

Proof. Under the conditions stated, $\mathrm{dis_C}(\mathrm{neg_C}(\mathfrak{S}_i),\mathfrak{S}_i)$ is C-true in K (T5-1b). Further, $\mathrm{dis_C}(\mathrm{neg_C}(\mathfrak{S}_i),\mathfrak{S}_i) \underset{C}{\rightrightarrows} \mathrm{dis_C}(\mathrm{neg_C}(\mathfrak{S}_i),\mathfrak{S}_j)$ in K, because $\mathfrak{S}_i \underset{C}{\rightrightarrows} \mathfrak{S}_j$ and $\mathrm{neg_C}(\mathfrak{S}_i)$ is closed (T10). Therefore $\mathrm{dis_C}(\mathrm{neg_C}(\mathfrak{S}_i),\mathfrak{S}_j)$ is also C-true in K ([I] T29-70). Any other implication$_C$ sentence is C-equivalent to this sentence (D3-2 (5)) and hence also C-true.

The reason for the condition in T12 that $\mathfrak{S}_i$ be closed becomes clear by the following counter-examples. 1. In a calculus containing propositional variables, 'q' is a (direct) C-implicate of 'p' (by substitution), but '$\sim p \vee q$' is not C-true. 2. In the functional calculus (§ 28), 'P(x)' $\underset{C}{\rightrightarrows}$ 'P(a)', but '$\sim$P(x) $\vee$ P(a)' (or 'P(x) $\supset$ P(a)'), which is C-equivalent to '(x)(P(x) $\supset$ P(a))', is not C-true.

In T12, $\mathfrak{S}_i$ is required to be closed. It would not suffice to require that $\mathfrak{S}_i$ do not contain a free variable which does not occur as a free variable in $\mathfrak{S}_j$. This is shown by the following counter-example. 'p' $\underset{C}{\rightrightarrows}$ '$\sim p$' (by substitution); but '$\sim p \vee \sim p$', which is C-equivalent to '$\sim p$', is not C-true.

T12 is a theorem of general syntax. It may be called the *general deduction theorem*. T14b and T28-11 are special applications of this theorem for the propositional and the functional calculi respectively. A theorem similar to T28-11 has been called deduction theorem by Hilbert and Bernays [Grundl. Math. I] p. 155.

T6-14. If K contains PC_1 or PC_1^D and there are no other rules of inference in K than those of PC_1 or PC_1^D, then the following holds:

      a. For any non-empty $\mathfrak{R}_i$, $\mathfrak{S}_j$, and $\mathfrak{S}_k$ such that $\mathfrak{S}_k$ does not contain any free variable occurring freely in $\mathfrak{S}_j$ or in any sentence of $\mathfrak{R}_i$, if $\mathfrak{R}_i \underset{C}{\rightarrow} \mathfrak{S}_j$

in K, then $\operatorname{dis}'_C(\mathfrak{S}_k,\mathfrak{R}_i) \underset{C}{\rightrightarrows} \operatorname{dis}_C(\mathfrak{S}_k,\mathfrak{S}_j)$. (From T5 and 10.)

+**b.** If $\mathfrak{S}_i$ is closed and $\mathfrak{S}_i \underset{C}{\rightrightarrows} \mathfrak{S}_j$, then any implication$_C$ sentence with $\mathfrak{S}_i$ and $\mathfrak{S}_j$ is C-true in K. (From T5 and 12.)

The same holds also for the functional calculus (T28-11).

If, in constructing a calculus, one finds that some rule of inference is not extensible, there is reason to doubt whether the calculus fulfills the purpose for which it was intended. It is then easy to transform the calculus in the following way into a stronger one whose rules are extensible. A rule R saying "$\mathfrak{R}_i \underset{dC}{\rightrightarrows} \mathfrak{S}_j$ if such and such conditions are fulfilled" is replaced by a rule R': "$\operatorname{dis}'_C(\mathfrak{S}_l,\mathfrak{R}_i) \underset{dC}{\rightrightarrows} \operatorname{dis}_C(\mathfrak{S}_l,\mathfrak{S}_j)$ if $\mathfrak{S}_l$ does not contain a free variable occurring freely in $\mathfrak{S}_j$ or in any sentence of $\mathfrak{R}_i$ and if such and such other conditions are fulfilled".

It is easy to see that any rule of the form R' is extensible. If $\mathfrak{S}_k$ is any sentence which does not contain a free variable occurring freely in $\mathfrak{S}_l$ or in $\mathfrak{S}_j$ or in any sentence of $\mathfrak{R}_i$, then $\operatorname{dis}'_C(\operatorname{dis}_C(\mathfrak{S}_k,\mathfrak{S}_l),\mathfrak{R}_i)$ $\underset{dC}{\rightrightarrows} \operatorname{dis}_C(\operatorname{dis}_C(\mathfrak{S}_k,\mathfrak{S}_l),\mathfrak{S}_j)$, according to R' (taking $\operatorname{dis}_C(\mathfrak{S}_k,\mathfrak{S}_l)$ in the place of $\mathfrak{S}_l$). Therefore, according to the associative law for disjunction (T5-3k), $\operatorname{dis}'_C(\mathfrak{S}_k,\operatorname{dis}'_C(\mathfrak{S}_l,\mathfrak{R}_i)) \underset{C}{\rightrightarrows} \operatorname{dis}_C(\mathfrak{S}_k,\operatorname{dis}_C(\mathfrak{S}_l,\mathfrak{S}_j))$.

For an example of the transformation of R into R' see remarks on T28-10 concerning rule (11').

§ 7. General Theorems Concerning Disjunction$_C$

Some general syntactical theorems concerning disjunction$_C$ are proved. One of the results: under ordinary conditions, two signs of disjunction$_C$ are C-interchangeable (T4b).

The following theorems are proved with respect to the signs of disjunction$_C$ and negation$_C$ in PC$_1$. According to the previous discussion, they hold likewise for any other form of PC with respect to the connections$_C$ of $_C$Conn$_2^2$ (i.e. disjunction$_C$) and $_C$Conn$_3^1$ (i.e. negation$_C$), no matter whether there are connectives for these connections$_C$ or not.

T7-1. If K contains PC$_1$ and any implication$_C$ sentence with $\mathfrak{S}_m$ and $\mathfrak{S}_n$, e.g. dis$_C$(neg$_C$($\mathfrak{S}_m$),$\mathfrak{S}_n$), is C-true in K, then $\mathfrak{S}_m \underset{C}{\rightarrow} \mathfrak{S}_n$ in K. (From D3-2(5), D2-2b(5), [I] T29-81.)

+**T7-2.** Let K fulfill the conditions (A), (B), and (C) in T6-10. Then the following holds:

    a. dis$_C$($\mathfrak{S}_i$,$\mathfrak{S}_j$) is a C-implicate in K both of $\mathfrak{S}_i$ and of $\mathfrak{S}_j$. (From T5-2b, c.)

    b. If $\mathfrak{S}_i$ and $\mathfrak{S}_j$ are closed, dis$_C$($\mathfrak{S}_i$,$\mathfrak{S}_j$) is a strongest sentence in K with the property (a); that is to say, if any $\mathfrak{S}_l$ is a C-implicate both of $\mathfrak{S}_i$ and of $\mathfrak{S}_j$, then dis$_C$($\mathfrak{S}_i$,$\mathfrak{S}_j$) $\underset{C}{\rightarrow} \mathfrak{S}_l$.

Proof for (b). If the conditions mentioned are fulfilled, both dis$_C$(neg$_C$($\mathfrak{S}_i$),$\mathfrak{S}_l$) and dis$_C$(neg$_C$($\mathfrak{S}_j$),$\mathfrak{S}_l$) are C-true (T6-12). Hence the class of these two sentences is C-true ([I] T29-72), and likewise dis$_C$(neg$_C$(dis$_C$($\mathfrak{S}_i$,$\mathfrak{S}_j$)),$\mathfrak{S}_l$), because it is a C-implicate of that class (T5-3i, [I] T29-70). Therefore dis$_C$($\mathfrak{S}_i$,$\mathfrak{S}_j$) $\underset{C}{\rightarrow} \mathfrak{S}_l$ (T1).

T7-3. Let K fulfill the conditions (A), (B), and (C) in T6-10. Let $\mathfrak{S}_i$, $\mathfrak{S}_i'$, $\mathfrak{S}_j$, and $\mathfrak{S}_j'$ be any closed sentences in K such that $\mathfrak{S}_i$ is C-equivalent to $\mathfrak{S}_i'$ and likewise $\mathfrak{S}_j$ to $\mathfrak{S}_j'$. Then dis$_C$($\mathfrak{S}_i$,$\mathfrak{S}_j$) is C-equivalent to dis$_C$($\mathfrak{S}_i'$,$\mathfrak{S}_j'$).

Proof. Since $\mathfrak{S}_j$ is C-equivalent to $\mathfrak{S}_j'$, dis$_C$($\mathfrak{S}_i$,$\mathfrak{S}_j$) is C-equivalent to dis$_C$($\mathfrak{S}_i$,$\mathfrak{S}_j'$) (T6-10), to dis$_C$($\mathfrak{S}_j'$,$\mathfrak{S}_i$) (T5-3d), and further, because of the C-equivalence of $\mathfrak{S}_i$ and $\mathfrak{S}_i'$, to dis$_C$($\mathfrak{S}_j'$,$\mathfrak{S}_i'$) (T6-10) and to dis$_C$($\mathfrak{S}_i'$,$\mathfrak{S}_j'$) (T5-3d).

Condition (A) in T4, below, refers to a calculus K containing PC$_1$ twice with two signs of disjunction$_C$. This is meant in the following way. K contains two sets of rules of deduction as required in D2-2. The signs of negation$_C$ may or may not be identical. If the first set of rules (four primitive sentences and the rule of implication) refers, say, to ' $\sim$ ' and

' v ', then the second refers either to ' $\sim$ ' and ' v '' or to ' $\sim$ '' and ' v ''. In any case, according to D2-2a, the three or four connectives are general connectives (D2-1), and hence connectives of the two sets may occur within one sentence.

Condition (D) in T4 is fulfilled also by most of the non-extensional (intensional) calculi constructed so far, e.g. by Lewis' calculus of Strict Implication and the numerous similar calculi by other authors.

+**T7-4.** Conditions for K:

A. K contains PC$_1$ twice, with two different signs of disjunction$_C$, dis$_{C1}$ and dis$_{C2}$.

B and **C**, as in T6-10.

D. K is either extensional in relation to partial sentences ([I] D31-18) or, if not, every non-extensional primitive connective in K, say a_i, fulfills the following condition: if every two corresponding arguments in two full sentences $\mathfrak{S}_m$ and $\mathfrak{S}_n$ of a_i are C-equivalent, then $\mathfrak{S}_m$ and $\mathfrak{S}_n$ are C-equivalent.

a. If K fulfills the conditions (A), (B), and (C), then for any closed $\mathfrak{S}_i$ and $\mathfrak{S}_j$, dis$_{C1}(\mathfrak{S}_i,\mathfrak{S}_j)$ and dis$_{C2}(\mathfrak{S}_i,\mathfrak{S}_j)$ are C-equivalent in K.

b. If K fulfills the four conditions (A), (B), (C), and (D), then dis$_{C1}$ and dis$_{C2}$ are C-interchangeable in K ([I] D31-13).

Proof. a. Let $\mathfrak{S}_i$ and $\mathfrak{S}_j$ be any closed sentences. Then dis$_{C1}(\mathfrak{S}_i,\mathfrak{S}_j)$ is a C-implicate both of $\mathfrak{S}_i$ and of $\mathfrak{S}_j$ (T2a); and likewise dis$_{C2}(\mathfrak{S}_i,\mathfrak{S}_j)$. Therefore, the second disjunction$_C$ sentence is a C-implicate of the first (T2b), and the first of the second. Hence they are C-equivalent.

b. Since the two disjunction$_C$ sentences mentioned are C-equivalent (a), they are C-interchangeable (condition (D), [I] T31-100). But their mutual replacement in a larger sentence is the same as a mutual replacement of dis$_{C1}$ and dis$_{C2}$. Therefore these two signs are C-interchangeable.

We shall come back to T4 in a later discussion of possible

interpretations for signs of disjunction$_C$. T4 holds also for other forms of PC than PC$_1$, and even for two different forms.

§ 8. General Theorems Concerning Negation$_C$

Some general syntactical theorems concerning negation$_C$ are proved. One of the results: under ordinary conditions, two signs of negation$_C$ are C-interchangeable (T9b).

+**T8-1.** Let K fulfill the conditions (A), (B), and (C) in T6-10. Let $\mathfrak{S}_i$ be any closed sentence in K.

    a. Every sentence in K which is a C-implicate both of $\mathfrak{S}_i$ and of $neg_C(\mathfrak{S}_i)$ is C-true.

    b. $neg_C(\mathfrak{S}_i)$ is a strongest sentence which has the relation to $\mathfrak{S}_i$ stated in (a), that is to say, if $\mathfrak{S}_l$ is such that every sentence which is a C-implicate both of $\mathfrak{S}_i$ and of $\mathfrak{S}_l$ is C-true, then $neg_C(\mathfrak{S}_i) \xrightarrow{C} \mathfrak{S}_l$.

Proof. a. Let $\mathfrak{S}_j$ be a C-implicate both of $\mathfrak{S}_i$ and of $neg_C(\mathfrak{S}_i)$. Then $dis_C(\mathfrak{S}_i, neg_C(\mathfrak{S}_i)) \xrightarrow{C} \mathfrak{S}_j$ (T7-2b). Therefore, since $dis_C(\mathfrak{S}_i, neg_C(\mathfrak{S}_i))$ is C-true (T5-1a), $\mathfrak{S}_j$ is C-true ([I] T29-70).

b. Let $\mathfrak{S}_l$ fulfill the conditions stated. Then $dis_C(\mathfrak{S}_i, \mathfrak{S}_l)$, being a C-implicate both of $\mathfrak{S}_i$ and of $\mathfrak{S}_l$ (T7-2a), must be C-true. $dis_C(neg_C(neg_C(\mathfrak{S}_i)), \mathfrak{S}_l)$ is C-equivalent to $dis_C(\mathfrak{S}_i, \mathfrak{S}_l)$ (T5-3a, T7-3) and hence is likewise C-true. Therefore $neg_C(\mathfrak{S}_i) \xrightarrow{C} \mathfrak{S}_l$ (T7-1).

T8-2. Let K contain PC$_1$.

    a. If $\mathfrak{S}_i$ is C-true in K, $neg_C(\mathfrak{S}_i)$ is C-comprehensive. ([I] D30-6).

    b. If $neg_C(\mathfrak{S}_i)$ is C-true, $\mathfrak{S}_i$ is C-comprehensive.

Proof. a. Let $\mathfrak{S}_i$ be C-true. Every sentence in K is a C-implicate of $\{\mathfrak{S}_i, neg_C(\mathfrak{S}_i)\}$ (T5-2l) and hence a C-implicate of $neg_C(\mathfrak{S}_i)$ ([I] T29-81). Therefore, $neg_C(\mathfrak{S}_i)$ is C-comprehensive ([I] D30-6). — b. If $neg_C(\mathfrak{S}_i)$ is C-true, $neg_C(neg_C(\mathfrak{S}_i))$ is C-comprehensive (a), and hence $\mathfrak{S}_i$ also (T5-3a, [I] T30-49).

It is to be noted that T2, unlike T3, does not impose restricting conditions on K and $\mathfrak{S}_i$.

T8-3. Let K fulfill the conditions (A), (B), and (C) in T6-10. Let $\mathfrak{S}_i$ be any closed sentence in K.

    a. If $\mathfrak{S}_i$ is C-comprehensive, $neg_C(\mathfrak{S}_i)$ is C-true.

    b. If $neg_C(\mathfrak{S}_i)$ is C-comprehensive, $\mathfrak{S}_i$ is C-true.

Proof. a. Let $\mathfrak{S}_i$ be C-comprehensive. Then $\mathfrak{S}_i \underset{C}{\rightarrow} neg_C(\mathfrak{S}_i)$ ([I] D30-6). Further, $neg_C(\mathfrak{S}_i) \underset{C}{\rightarrow} neg_C(\mathfrak{S}_i)$ ([I] T29-32). Hence, $neg_C(\mathfrak{S}_i)$ is C-true (T1a). — b. Let $neg_C(\mathfrak{S}_i)$ be C-comprehensive. Then $neg_C(neg_C(\mathfrak{S}_i))$ is C-true (a), and hence also $\mathfrak{S}_i$ (T5-3a, [I] T29-70).

T4, below, is in a certain sense a counterpart to T1.

T8-4. Let K contain PC$_1$.

    a. Every sentence in K which C-implies both $\mathfrak{S}_i$ and $neg_C(\mathfrak{S}_i)$ is C-comprehensive.

    b. Let K, moreover, fulfill the conditions (B) and (C) in T6-10. Let $\mathfrak{S}_i$ be any closed sentence in K. Then $neg_C(\mathfrak{S}_i)$ is a weakest sentence which has the relation to $\mathfrak{S}_i$ stated in (a); that is to say, if $\mathfrak{S}_l$ is such that every sentence which C-implies both $\mathfrak{S}_i$ and $\mathfrak{S}_l$ is C-comprehensive, then $\mathfrak{S}_l \underset{C}{\rightarrow} neg_C(\mathfrak{S}_i)$.

Proof. a. If $\mathfrak{S}_j \underset{C}{\rightarrow} \mathfrak{S}_i$ and $\mathfrak{S}_j \underset{C}{\rightarrow} neg_C(\mathfrak{S}_i)$, then $\mathfrak{S}_j \underset{C}{\rightarrow} \{\mathfrak{S}_i, neg_C(\mathfrak{S}_i)\}$ and $\mathfrak{S}_j \underset{C}{\rightarrow}$ every sentence (T5-21). — b. Let $\mathfrak{S}_m$ be $neg_C(dis_C(neg_C(\mathfrak{S}_l), neg_C(\mathfrak{S}_i)))$, which is a conjunction$_C$ sentence with $\mathfrak{S}_l$ and $\mathfrak{S}_i$ (D3-2 (8)). Then $\mathfrak{S}_m$ C-implies both $\mathfrak{S}_l$ and $\mathfrak{S}_i$ (T5-2m, n). Let $\mathfrak{S}_l$ fulfill the condition stated in the theorem. Then $\mathfrak{S}_m$ is C-comprehensive. Therefore, $dis_C(neg_C(\mathfrak{S}_l), neg_C(\mathfrak{S}_i))$ is C-true (T3b). Hence, $\mathfrak{S}_l \underset{C}{\rightarrow} neg_C(\mathfrak{S}_i)$ (T7-1).

T8-6. Let K fulfill the conditions (A), (B), and (C) in T6-10.

    a. If $\mathfrak{S}_i$ is closed and $\mathfrak{S}_i \underset{C}{\rightarrow} \mathfrak{S}_j$, then $neg_C(\mathfrak{S}_j) \underset{C}{\rightarrow} neg_C(\mathfrak{S}_i)$.

b. If $\mathfrak{S}_j$ is closed and $neg_C(\mathfrak{S}_j) \underset{C}{\rightarrow} neg_C(\mathfrak{S}_i)$, then $\mathfrak{S}_i \underset{C}{\rightarrow} \mathfrak{S}_j$.

Proof. a. Under the conditions stated, $dis_C(neg_C(\mathfrak{S}_i),\mathfrak{S}_j)$ is C-true (T6-12). Hence $neg_C(\mathfrak{S}_j) \underset{C}{\rightarrow} neg_C(\mathfrak{S}_i)$ (T5-2f, [I] T29-81). — b. Under the conditions stated, $neg_C(neg_C(\mathfrak{S}_i)) \underset{C}{\rightarrow} neg_C(neg_C(\mathfrak{S}_j))$ (a). Therefore, since $\mathfrak{S}_i \underset{C}{\rightarrow} neg_C(neg_C(\mathfrak{S}_i))$ and $neg_C(neg_C(\mathfrak{S}_j)) \underset{C}{\rightarrow} \mathfrak{S}_j$ (T5-3a), $\mathfrak{S}_i \underset{C}{\rightarrow} \mathfrak{S}_j$ ([I] T29-44).

T8-7. Let K fulfill the conditions (A), (B), and (C) in T6-10. Let $\mathfrak{S}_i$ and $\mathfrak{S}_j$ be closed and C-equivalent. Then $neg_C(\mathfrak{S}_i)$ and $neg_C(\mathfrak{S}_j)$ are C-equivalent. (From T6a.)

T8-8. Let K fulfill the conditions (A), (B), and (C) in T6-10. Let $\mathfrak{S}_i$ and $\mathfrak{S}_j$ be constructed in the same way with the help of the signs of negation$_C$ and disjunction$_C$ but out of different components, those of $\mathfrak{S}_i$ being $\mathfrak{S}_{i1}, \mathfrak{S}_{i2}, \ldots \mathfrak{S}_{in}$, those of $\mathfrak{S}_j$ being $\mathfrak{S}_{j1}, \mathfrak{S}_{j2}, \ldots \mathfrak{S}_{jn}$, all these components being closed. Let any two corresponding components $\mathfrak{S}_{im}$ and $\mathfrak{S}_{jm}$ ($m = 1$ to n) be C-equivalent in K. Then $\mathfrak{S}_i$ and $\mathfrak{S}_j$ are C-equivalent. (From T7-3, T7, by inductive inference.)

The following counter-example shows that it is necessary to restrict T7 and 8 to closed components. 'P(x)' and '(x)P(x)' are C-equivalent; but '$\sim$P(x)', which is C-equivalent to '(x)($\sim$P(x))', is not C-equivalent to '$\sim$(x)P(x)'.

The following theorem, T9, requires the occurrence of two signs of negation$_C$ in K. This is to be understood in analogy to the occurrence of two signs of disjunction$_C$, as explained previously in connection with T7-4.

+**T8-9.** Conditions for K:

    A. K contains PC$_1$ twice with two different signs of negation$_C$, neg_{C1} and neg_{C2}.

    B and **C**, as in T6-10.

    D, as in T7-4.

    a. If K fulfills (A), (B), and (C), then, for any

closed $\mathfrak{S}_i$, $neg_{C1}(\mathfrak{S}_i)$ and $neg_{C2}(\mathfrak{S}_i)$ are C-equivalent in K.

b. If K fulfills (A), (B), (C), and (D), then neg_{C1} and neg_{C2} are C-interchangeable in K.

Proof. a. Let $\mathfrak{S}_i$ be closed. Then every sentence which is a C-implicate both of $\mathfrak{S}_i$ and of $neg_{C1}(\mathfrak{S}_i)$ is C-true in K (T1a); and every sentence which is a C-implicate both of $\mathfrak{S}_i$ and of $neg_{C2}(\mathfrak{S}_i)$ is C-true (T1a). Hence $neg_{C2}(\mathfrak{S}_i) \overrightarrow{_C} neg_{C1}(\mathfrak{S}_i)$ (T1b) and vice versa (T1b). Thus the two sentences are C-equivalent. — b. Proof analogous to that of T7–4b.

§ 9. General Theorems Concerning Other Connections$_C$

> Some syntactical theorems concerning connections$_C$ in general. One of the results: under ordinary conditions, two signs for the same connection$_C$ are C-interchangeable (T4b).

According to the definitions in § 4, any forms of PC correspond in a certain way to PC_1^D and hence to one another. Thus it could easily be shown that if two calculi K_m and K_n contain PC and possess the same or corresponding components, then any syntactical relation like C-implication, C-equivalence, etc., which holds for certain sentences in K_m by PC holds also for the corresponding sentences in K_n by PC. This is true even if K_m and K_n contain different forms of PC; and it is true no matter whether K_m and K_n are entirely separate calculi or are sub-calculi of one calculus K. However, it does not immediately follow from this result that any two corresponding sentences in K_m and K_n as sub-calculi of K are necessarily C-equivalent in K, not even if K_m and K_n contain the same form of PC. That this is the case has been shown above for disjunction$_C$ (T7-4a) and for negation$_C$ (T8-9a). It will now be easy to show the same for the other connections$_C$ in general, because they are expressible in terms of disjunction$_C$ and negation$_C$.

T9-1. Let K contain PC_1^D and fulfill the conditions (B) and (C) in T6-10. Let $\mathfrak{S}_i$, $\mathfrak{S}_i'$, $\mathfrak{S}_j$, and $\mathfrak{S}_j'$ be any closed sentences in K such that $\mathfrak{S}_i$ is C-equivalent to $\mathfrak{S}_i'$ and $\mathfrak{S}_j$ to $\mathfrak{S}_j'$.

> **a.** For any singulary connective $_c\mathfrak{b}_q$ ($q = 1$ to 4) in PC_1^D in K, $_c\mathfrak{b}_q(\mathfrak{S}_i)$ is C-equivalent by PC_1^D in K to $_c\mathfrak{b}_q(\mathfrak{S}_i')$.
>
> **b.** For any binary connective $_c\mathfrak{c}_r$ ($r = 1$ to 16) in PC_1^D in K, $_c\mathfrak{c}_r(\mathfrak{S}_i,\mathfrak{S}_j)$ is C-equivalent by PC_1^D in K to $_c\mathfrak{c}_r(\mathfrak{S}_i',\mathfrak{S}_j')$.

Proof for (b). Let $\mathfrak{S}_k$ be the sentence in K formed out of $_c\mathfrak{c}_r(\mathfrak{S}_i,\mathfrak{S}_j)$ by eliminating the connective $_c\mathfrak{c}_r$ with the help of its definition rule in PC_1^D (D3-6); then $\mathfrak{S}_k$ and $_c\mathfrak{c}_r(\mathfrak{S}_i,\mathfrak{S}_j)$ are C-equivalent by PC_1^D in K. Let $\mathfrak{S}_k'$ be formed analogously out of $_c\mathfrak{c}_r(\mathfrak{S}_i',\mathfrak{S}_j')$. Then these two sentences are likewise C-equivalent. $\mathfrak{S}_k$ is constructed with the help of signs of negation$_c$ and disjunction$_c$ out of $\mathfrak{S}_i$ and $\mathfrak{S}_j$ as components, and $\mathfrak{S}_k'$ is constructed in the same way out of $\mathfrak{S}_i'$ and $\mathfrak{S}_j'$ as components. (The common form of $\mathfrak{S}_k$ and $\mathfrak{S}_k'$ is that given in the table in § 3 in column (5) on the line of $_c\text{Conn}_r^2$.) Therefore, $\mathfrak{S}_k$ is C-equivalent to $\mathfrak{S}_k'$ (T8-8). Hence, $_c\mathfrak{c}_r(\mathfrak{S}_i,\mathfrak{S}_j)$ and $_c\mathfrak{c}_r(\mathfrak{S}_i',\mathfrak{S}_j')$ are likewise C-equivalent. — The proof for (a) is analogous.

T9-2. (Analogous to T8-8.) Let K contain PC_1^D and fulfill the conditions (B) and (C) in T6-10. Let $\mathfrak{S}_i$ and $\mathfrak{S}_j$ be constructed in the same way with the help of any connectives of PC_1^D but out of different components, those of $\mathfrak{S}_i$ being $\mathfrak{S}_{i1}$, $\mathfrak{S}_{i2}$, ... $\mathfrak{S}_{in}$, those of $\mathfrak{S}_j$ being $\mathfrak{S}_{j1}$, $\mathfrak{S}_{j2}$, ... $\mathfrak{S}_{jn}$, all these components being closed. Let any two corresponding components $\mathfrak{S}_{im}$ and $\mathfrak{S}_{jm}$ ($m = 1$ to n) be C-equivalent in K. Then $\mathfrak{S}_i$ and $\mathfrak{S}_j$ are C-equivalent. (From T1, by inductive inference.)

The following theorem, T3, is analogous to T7-4 and T8-9. It refers to two sub-calculi K_m and K_n of K, both containing PC_1^D. This is meant in the same way as explained previously in connection with T7-4. Thus any one of the connectives of PC_1^D in K_m may or may not be identical with the corresponding connective in K_n. The theorem holds likewise if K_m and

K_n contain any other form of PC or even two different forms of PC.

T9-3. Conditions for K:

    A. K contains two sub-calculi K_m and K_n, both containing PC_1^D.

    B and **C**, as in T6-10.

    D, as in T7-4.

Let $\mathfrak{S}_m$ be a sentence constructed with the help of connectives of PC_1^D in K_m out of closed components, and $\mathfrak{S}_n$ be a sentence constructed out of the same components in an analogous way but with the corresponding connectives of PC_1^D in K_n. Then $\mathfrak{S}_m$ and $\mathfrak{S}_n$ are C-equivalent in K.

Proof. Let $\mathfrak{S}_m'$ be the sentence formed out of $\mathfrak{S}_m$ by eliminating all defined connectives of PC_1^D occurring in it. Then $\mathfrak{S}_m'$ is C-equivalent to $\mathfrak{S}_m$ in K_m and hence in K. Let $\mathfrak{S}_n'$ be formed analogously out of $\mathfrak{S}_n$ in K_n. Then $\mathfrak{S}_n'$ is C-equivalent to $\mathfrak{S}_n$ in K_n and in K. $\mathfrak{S}_m'$ and $\mathfrak{S}_n'$ consist of the same components and have analogous forms, but $\mathfrak{S}_m'$ contains the signs of negation$_C$ and disjunction$_C$ of K_m and $\mathfrak{S}_n'$ those of K_n. Now we can transform $\mathfrak{S}_m'$ into $\mathfrak{S}_n'$ by first replacing one occurrence of the sign of disjunction$_C$ in K_m after the other by that in K_n and then doing the same with the signs of negation$_C$ in K_m and K_n. Each step in this transformation leads to a C-equivalent sentence (T7-4, T8-9); therefore $\mathfrak{S}_m'$ and $\mathfrak{S}_n'$ are C-equivalent in K, and hence also $\mathfrak{S}_m$ and $\mathfrak{S}_n$.

A corollary to T3:

+T9-4. Let K fulfill condition (A) in T3 and (B) and (C) in T6-10. Let $\mathfrak{a}_m$ be a sign of any singulary or binary connection$_C$ in PC_1^D in K_m, and $\mathfrak{a}_n$ be a sign for the same connection in K_n. Then the following holds:

    a. Two full sentences of $\mathfrak{a}_m$ and $\mathfrak{a}_n$ with the same closed component or components are C-equivalent in K.

    b. If K fulfills, moreover, condition (D) in T7-4, then $\mathfrak{a}_m$ and $\mathfrak{a}_n$ are C-interchangeable in K.

Proof. (a) is a special case of T3. The proof for (b) is analogous to that for T7-4b.

B. PROPOSITIONAL LOGIC

This chapter deals with propositional logic, i.e. the system of the propositional connections based on the normal truth-tables (NTT). It is a semantical system, in contradistinction to the syntactical system PC. Radical semantical and L-semantical concepts for the connections and for the concept of extensionality are defined.

§ 10. The Normal Truth-Tables (NTT)

The normal truth-tables (NTT) for propositional connections may be regarded as semantical rules stating the truth-conditions for the full sentences of the connectives. A table is given (p. 38) showing the four singulary and the sixteen binary extensional connections with their characteristics, which correspond to the value-columns in the truth-tables.

By the **normal truth-tables** — the system will here be called **NTT** — we mean the customary truth-tables for the singulary and binary propositional connections, regarded as semantical rules (compare [I] § 8). A truth-table for a connection of degree n lists in its first column the 2^n possible distributions of the truth-values T (truth) and F (falsity) among the n components of a full sentence of that connection; in the second column, it gives the truth-value of a full sentence for each of those distributions (see the later examples, truth-tables for negation and disjunction). We restrict ourselves, as is customary, to the singulary and binary connections; all connections of higher degrees can be expressed by negation and disjunction, as Post has shown.

In this way, the truth-table represents a function — we call it the *characteristic function* of the connection — which correlates a truth-value to each of those distributions as arguments. Thus, for instance, the characteristic function of disjunction correlates T to the distributions TT, TF, and FT, and F to FF. It is convenient to order the distributions of truth-values in the first columns of the truth-tables always in the same way; we adopt the most frequently used lexicographical order, with T preceding F (D2).

D10-2. The *t-th distribution of truth-values* for the degree n (1 or 2) $=_{Df}$ the truth-value or sequence of two truthvalues here stated:

t	t-th DISTRIBUTION for degree one	for degree two
1	T	TT
2	F	TF
3	—	FT
4	—	FF

If the order of the distributions is thus established by convention, we do not need the whole truth-table in order to describe a characteristic function. It is sufficient to state the truth-values in the order in which they occur in the second column. This sequence of truth-values for a connection is called its **characteristic** (comp. Wittgenstein [Tractatus] 4.442, [Syntax] § 57). Thus we see, for instance, from the two truth-tables below that the characteristic for negation is FT, that for disjunction is TTTF. We shall see soon (§ 12) that all extensional connections, and only these, have a truth-table and hence a characteristic function and a characteristic. The characteristics of the singulary and binary extensional connections are listed in column (5) of the subsequent table. The connections are completely characterized by their characteristics, and hence may be defined with their help. Thus a connective will be called a sign of disjunction if it possesses the characteristic TTTF.

The table that follows contains, further, the following items, to be explained later. For every connection, as defined by the characteristic in column (5), the name is given in column (2), the abbreviated name in column (1), a semantical name for the connective in column (4). The terms in columns (1), (2), and (4) correspond to those in the same columns in the table in § 3, but here they have no subscript 'C'. In this way the semantical terms of this table are distinguished from the syntactical terms of the previous table.

SEMANTICAL CONCEPTS OF PROPOSITIONAL CONNECTIONS AND CONNECTIVES IN NTT

(1)	(2)	(3)	(4)	(5)
Connections		*Connectives*		
Abbreviation	Ordinary Name	Customary Symbol	Semantical Name	Characteristic
I. The four singulary connections				
Conn_1^1	tautology		$\mathfrak{b}_1$	T T
Conn_2^1	(identity)		$\mathfrak{b}_2$	T F
Conn_3^1	negation	$\sim$	$\mathfrak{b}_3$ (neg)	F T
Conn_4^1	contradiction		$\mathfrak{b}_4$	F F
II. The sixteen binary connections				
Conn_1^2	tautology		c_1	T T T T
Conn_2^2	disjunction	$\vee$	c_2 (dis)	T T T F
Conn_3^2	(inverse implication)		c_3	T T F T
Conn_4^2	(first component)		c_4	T T F F
Conn_5^2	implication	$\supset$	c_5 (imp)	T F T T
Conn_6^2	(second component)		c_6	T F T F
Conn_7^2	equivalence	$\equiv$	c_7 (equ)	T F F T
Conn_8	conjunction	$\bullet$	c_8 (con)	T F F F
Conn_9^2	exclusion	$\mid$	c_9	F T T T
Conn_{10}^2	(non-equivalence)		c_{10}	F T T F
Conn_{11}^2	(negation of second)		c_{11}	F T F T
Conn_{12}^2	(first alone)		c_{12}	F T F F
Conn_{13}^2	(negation of first)		c_{13}	F F T T
Conn_{14}^2	(second alone)		c_{14}	F F T F
Conn_{15}^2	bi-negation		c_{15}	F F F T
Conn_{16}^2	contradiction		c_{16}	F F F F

Thus e.g. 'sign of disjunction$_c$ in K' is a syntactical concept based on the rules of deduction of PC_1 (D3-2); on the other hand, 'sign of disjunction in S' (D11-23) is a semantical concept based on the rules of NTT, i.e. the truth-tables.

As examples of rules of NTT, stated in the customary form of diagrams (truth-tables), we give here those for negation and disjunction.

TRUTH-TABLE FOR NEGATION			TRUTH-TABLE FOR DISJUNCTION			
	$\mathfrak{S}_i$	$neg(\mathfrak{S}_i)$		$\mathfrak{S}_i$	$\mathfrak{S}_j$	$dis(\mathfrak{S}_i,\mathfrak{S}_j)$
N1.	T	F	Dj1.	T	T	T
N2.	F	T	Dj2.	T	F	T
			Dj3.	F	T	T
			Dj4.	F	F	F

We may regard each line in a truth-table as a representation of a semantical rule. We designate the two semantical rules for negation, represented by the two lines of its normal truth-table, by 'N1' and 'N2', likewise the four rules for disjunction by 'Dj1' to 'Dj4', those for conjunction by 'C1' to 'C4', those for implication by 'I1' to 'I4', and those for equivalence by 'E1' to 'E4'. Formulated in words instead of diagrams, these rules are as follows.

+**Rules of NTT** for some of the connections; $\mathfrak{S}_i$ and $\mathfrak{S}_j$ are any closed sentences.

N1. If $\mathfrak{S}_i$ is true, $neg(\mathfrak{S}_i)$ is false.

N2. If $\mathfrak{S}_i$ is false, $neg(\mathfrak{S}_i)$ is true.

Dj1. If $\mathfrak{S}_i$ and $\mathfrak{S}_j$ are true, $dis(\mathfrak{S}_i,\mathfrak{S}_j)$ is true.

Dj2. If $\mathfrak{S}_i$ is true and $\mathfrak{S}_j$ is false, $dis(\mathfrak{S}_i,\mathfrak{S}_j)$ is true.

Dj3. If $\mathfrak{S}_i$ is false and $\mathfrak{S}_j$ is true, $dis(\mathfrak{S}_i,\mathfrak{S}_j)$ is true.

Dj4. If $\mathfrak{S}_i$ and $\mathfrak{S}_j$ are false, $dis(\mathfrak{S}_i,\mathfrak{S}_j)$ is false.

In shorter formulation:

N1, 2. $neg(\mathfrak{S}_i)$ is true if and only if $\mathfrak{S}_i$ is false.

Dj1 to 4. $\mathrm{dis}(\mathfrak{S}_i, \mathfrak{S}_j)$ is true if and only if at least one of the two components is true.

Further:

C1 to 4. $\mathrm{con}(\mathfrak{S}_i, \mathfrak{S}_j)$ is true if and only if both components are true.

I1 to 4. $\mathrm{imp}(\mathfrak{S}_i, \mathfrak{S}_j)$ is true if and only if $\mathfrak{S}_i$ is false or $\mathfrak{S}_j$ is true or both.

E1 to 4. $\mathrm{equ}(\mathfrak{S}_i, \mathfrak{S}_j)$ is true if and only if both components are true or both are false.

The rules of NTT for the other extensional connections can be formulated in an analogous way on the basis of their characteristics.

The following counter-examples show that it is necessary to restrict the application of the *truth-tables* to *closed sentences*. 1. Propositional logic. 'p' and '$\sim p$' are both false (this is often overlooked because of a confusion between propositional variables and propositional constants), in spite of N2. And '$p \vee \sim p$' is true, in spite of Dj4. 2. Functional logic (customary interpretation, open sentences interpreted as universal, see § 28). If there is an individual which is not P, and another one which is P and not Q, then 'P(x)' and '$\sim$P(x)' (which is L-equivalent to '(x)($\sim$P(x))') are both false, in spite of N2. Further, 'Q(x)' and 'P(x) ⊃ Q(x)' are false, in spite of I4. The necessity of the restriction is often not noticed. Sometimes the truth-tables are even explicitly formulated for open sentences, e.g. 'p', 'q', '$p \vee q$'. [It may be remarked that, in another sense, the truth-tables may be formulated for open sentences, e.g. propositional variables. While it is incorrect to formulate: "If 'p' is false and 'q' is false, then '$p \equiv q$' is true", the following is correct: "If p is false and q is false, then $p \equiv q$ is true". In the latter sentence, 'p', 'q', and '$\equiv$' are regarded as belonging to the English language. The sentence refers to the absolute concept of truth for propositions ([I] § 17), not to the semantical concept of truth for sentences. Therefore it cannot serve as a rule for a language system.]

Suppose that a semantical system S contains a binary general connective (D2-1) $\mathfrak{a}_k$. Under what conditions shall we call $\mathfrak{a}_k$ a sign of disjunction in S? We shall not require that S contain just the rules of NTT as| formulated above. S may contain rules formulated in an entirely different way, provided only that they have the same effect upon the truth-value of a full sentence $\mathfrak{a}_k(\mathfrak{S}_i, \mathfrak{S}_j)$ as the rules of NTT. Thus $\mathfrak{a}_k$ will be called a sign of disjunction in S if, for any closed components $\mathfrak{S}_i$ and $\mathfrak{S}_j$, $\mathfrak{a}_k(\mathfrak{S}_i, \mathfrak{S}_j)$ is true if and only if at least one of the components is true, in other words, if it possesses the characteristic TTTF. Here, however, two cases must be distinguished. The condition mentioned may be fulfilled either (a) by accident, so to speak, or (b) necessarily. In case (a), the situation is such that we have to use factual knowledge, namely of the truth-values of the sentences involved, in order to find out whether the condition is fulfilled. In case (b), factual knowledge is not required; the rules of S suffice for showing that the condition is fulfilled. In case (b) we shall say that $\mathfrak{a}_k$ has TTTF not only as a characteristic but also as an L-characteristic and that it is not only a sign of disjunction but also a sign of disjunction$_L$. (In case (a), we might call $\mathfrak{a}_k$ a sign of disjunction$_F$.) Analogously for the other connections. On the basis of these considerations, we shall lay down definitions for the connections.

§ 11. The Connections in NTT

The concepts for the connections can easily be defined with the help of the characteristics. Thus, for instance, $\mathfrak{a}_k$ is a sign of disjunction if it has the characteristic TTTF. We define, in addition, corresponding L-concepts. If the semantical rules suffice to show that $\mathfrak{a}_k$ has the characteristic TTTF, then this is called its L-characteristic, and $\mathfrak{a}_k$ is called a sign of disjunction$_L$. The definitions make use of the concept of L-range ([I] §§ 18 to 20).

Our task is now to formulate general definitions for 'characteristic', 'L-characteristic', '(sign for) Conn$_r^n$', and '$_L$Conn$_r^n$'

in accordance with considerations in the preceding section. These definitions and, further, those for 'extensional' and 'L-extensional' (§ 12) can best be formulated if we make use of the concept of **L-range**. It has previously been shown ([I] § 19; see the example for S_4) how the semantical rules of a system S can be formulated as rules for L-range instead of rules for truth and how the L-concepts ('L-true', etc.) and the radical semantical concepts ('true', etc.) can be defined on the basis of 'L-range' ([I] § 20). Let us briefly summarize the main features of the previous explanations and definitions. By **L-states** with respect to S we mean either completely specified possible states of affairs of the objects dealt with in S ([I] § 18), or other entities corresponding to them, e.g. state-descriptions ([I] § 19). The L-range of a sentence $\mathfrak{S}_m$ — designated by '$\mathrm{Lr}\mathfrak{S}_m$' or, in what follows, also by 'R_m' — is the class of those L-states which are admitted by $\mathfrak{S}_m$, i.e. those in which $\mathfrak{S}_m$ would be true. If the rules of S are formulated as rules of L-range, then the concept 'L-range in S' is defined by these rules, that is to say, for every $\mathfrak{S}_m$ in S, $\mathrm{Lr}\mathfrak{S}_m$ is determined by the rules. On this basis, the following concepts can be defined (as in [I] § 20). 'V_s' designates the universal L-range, i.e. the class of all L-states, 'Λ_s' the null L-range. The L-range of a sentential class $\mathfrak{R}_i$ is the product of the L-ranges of the sentences of $\mathfrak{R}_i$. (For the signs of the theory of classes, e.g. 'ϵ', '$\subset$', '$+$', '$\times$', '$-$', etc., see [I] § 6 at the end.)

D11-5. $\mathfrak{T}_i$ is **L-true** (in S) $=_{\mathrm{Df}}$ $\mathrm{Lr}\mathfrak{T}_i = V_s$.

D11-6. $\mathfrak{T}_i$ is **L-false** (in S) $=_{\mathrm{Df}}$ $\mathrm{Lr}\mathfrak{T}_i = \Lambda_s$.

D11-7. $\mathfrak{T}_i \underset{\mathrm{L}}{\rightarrow} \mathfrak{T}_j$ (in S) $=_{\mathrm{Df}}$ $\mathrm{Lr}\mathfrak{T}_i \subset \mathrm{Lr}\mathfrak{T}_j$.

D11-8. $\mathfrak{T}_i$ is **L-equivalent** to $\mathfrak{T}_j$ (in S) $=_{\mathrm{Df}}$ $\mathrm{Lr}\mathfrak{T}_i = \mathrm{Lr}\mathfrak{T}_j$.

D11-9. $\mathfrak{T}_i$ is **L-non-equivalent** to $\mathfrak{T}_j$ (in S) $=_{\mathrm{Df}}$ $\mathrm{Lr}\mathfrak{T}_i = -\mathrm{Lr}\mathfrak{T}_j$.

The definitions of radical concepts make use of '**rs**' also, which designates the real L-state. While the concept of L-range, and hence also the other L-concepts just defined, are determined by the rules of S, this is not the case for rs and the radical concepts. In order to find out which L-state is the real one, factual knowledge is required.

D11-12. $\mathfrak{T}_i$ is **true** (in S) $=_{\mathrm{Df}}$ rs ϵ Lr$\mathfrak{T}_i$.

The other radical concepts are defined on the basis of 'true' in the customary way (the definitions in [I] § 20 are like those in [I] § 9).

T11-1. The L-range of $\mathfrak{R}_i$ is the product of the L-ranges of the sentences of $\mathfrak{R}_i$. ([I] D20-1b.)

T11-6a [b]. (For 'a [b]', see remarks preceding D3-7.) Each of the following four conditions is sufficient and necessary for $\mathfrak{T}_m$ and $\mathfrak{T}_n$ to be [L-]*equivalent* in S.

1. $(R_m \times R_n) + (-R_m \times -R_n)$ contains rs [is V_s]. (From [I] D20-16, [I] T20-26 [D8].)
2. Both $R_m + (-R_n)$ and $-R_m + R_n$ (and hence also their product) contain rs [are V_s]. (From (1).)
3. $(R_m + R_n) \times (-R_m + (-R_n))$ does not contain rs [is Λ_s]. (From (1).)
4. Both $R_m \times -R_n$ and $-R_m \times R_n$ (and hence also their sum) do not contain rs [are Λ_s]. (From (3).)

T11-7a [b]. Each of the following five conditions is sufficient and necessary for $\mathfrak{T}_m$ and $\mathfrak{T}_n$ to be [L-]*nonequivalent* in S.

1. $(R_m \times -R_n) + (-R_m \times R_n)$ contains rs [is V_s]. (From [I] T9-21, [I] T20-26 [D9].)
2. Both $R_m + R_n$ and $-R_m + (-R_n)$ (and hence also their product) contain rs [are V_s]. (From (1).)

3. $(R_m + (-R_n)) \times (-R_m + R_n)$ does not contain rs [is Λ_s]. (From (1).)

4. Both $R_m \times R_n$ and $-R_m \times -R_n$ (and hence also their sum) do not contain rs [are Λ_s]. (From (3).)

5. $\mathfrak{T}_m$ and $\mathfrak{T}_n$ are [L-]disjunct and [L-]exclusive. (From (2), [I] D20-17 [9], [I] D20-18 [10].)

Now we have to formulate the rules of NTT in terms of L-range. Let us take Dj2 as an example; we call it the second rule for disjunction (or Conn_2^2) in NTT. It says: "If $\mathfrak{S}_i$ is true and $\mathfrak{S}_j$ is false, then dis$(\mathfrak{S}_i,\mathfrak{S}_j)$ is true." If, for a connective $\mathfrak{a}_k$, we find two sentences $\mathfrak{S}_i$ and $\mathfrak{S}_j$ such that $\mathfrak{S}_i$ is true, $\mathfrak{S}_j$ is false, and $\mathfrak{a}_k(\mathfrak{S}_i,\mathfrak{S}_j)$ (which we will call $\mathfrak{S}_k$) true, then we say that $\mathfrak{a}_k$ satisfies the rule Dj2 with respect to $\mathfrak{S}_i$ and $\mathfrak{S}_j$. If, on the other hand, $\mathfrak{S}_i$ is true, $\mathfrak{S}_j$ is false, but $\mathfrak{S}_k$ is false, then we say that $\mathfrak{a}_k$ violates Dj2 with respect to $\mathfrak{S}_i$ and $\mathfrak{S}_j$. If $\mathfrak{a}_k$ satisfies Dj2 with respect to any closed components, then we say simply that $\mathfrak{a}_k$ satisfies Dj2. The condition which in this case must be fulfilled for any closed $\mathfrak{S}_i$ and $\mathfrak{S}_j$ can also be stated in this way: "Either it is not the case that $\mathfrak{S}_i$ is true and $\mathfrak{S}_j$ is false, or $\mathfrak{S}_k$ is true", or: "$\mathfrak{S}_i$ is not true or $\mathfrak{S}_j$ is not false or $\mathfrak{S}_k$ is true". This is, in terms of L-range: "rs ϵ $-R_i$ or rs ϵ R_j or rs ϵ R_k", or in other words: "rs ϵ $-R_i + R_j + R_k$". If, for some $\mathfrak{S}_i$ and $\mathfrak{S}_j$, the class $-R_i + R_j + R_k$ is the universal L-range V_s, then we can know that it contains rs without knowing which L-state is rs. Thus, in this case, we know from the rules of S, without using factual knowledge, that $\mathfrak{a}_k$ satisfies Dj2 with respect to $\mathfrak{S}_i$ and $\mathfrak{S}_j$, and therefore we say that $\mathfrak{a}_k$ L-satisfies Dj2 with respect to $\mathfrak{S}_i$ and $\mathfrak{S}_j$. If this is the case for any closed $\mathfrak{S}_i$ and $\mathfrak{S}_j$, we say that $\mathfrak{a}_k$ L-satisfies Dj2. If $\mathfrak{a}_k$ satisfies all four rules Dj1 to 4, then it has TTTF as a characteristic and is called a sign of Conn_2^2 or of disjunction in S. If $\mathfrak{a}_k$ L-satisfies the four rules, then it has TTTF as an L-characteristic and is called a sign of $_L\text{Conn}_2^2$ or of disjunction$_L$ in S. On the basis of these considerations, we shall now lay down the general definitions for connections. Sometimes, when there is no danger of ambiguity, we write simply '$\mathfrak{S}_k$' for '$\mathfrak{a}_k(\mathfrak{S}_i)$' or '$\mathfrak{a}_k(\mathfrak{S}_i,\mathfrak{S}_j)$', i.e. the full sentence of $\mathfrak{a}_k$ with the component or components under consideration, and hence 'R_k' for the L-range of that full sentence.

D11-14. $\mathfrak{a}_k$ **satisfies the t-th rule** ($t = 1$ to 4) in NTT for Conn$_r^2$ ($r = 1$ to 16) *with respect to* $\mathfrak{S}_i$, $\mathfrak{S}_j$ in $S =_{Df} \mathfrak{a}_k$ is a binary general connective in S; $\mathfrak{S}_i$ and $\mathfrak{S}_j$ are closed and have the t-th distribution of truth-values (D10-2); $\mathfrak{a}_k(\mathfrak{S}_i,\mathfrak{S}_j)$ has the t-th truth-value in the characteristic of Conn$_r^2$ as given in column (6) of the table in § 10. Analogously for a singulary connective.

D11-15. $\mathfrak{a}_k$ **violates the t-th rule** ($t = 1$ to 4) in NTT for Conn$_r^2$ ($r = 1$ to 16) with respect to $\mathfrak{S}_i$, $\mathfrak{S}_j$ in $S =_{Df} \mathfrak{a}_k$ is a binary general connective in S; $\mathfrak{S}_i$ and $\mathfrak{S}_j$ are closed and have the t-th distribution of truth-values; $\mathfrak{a}_k(\mathfrak{S}_i,\mathfrak{S}_j)$ does not have the t-th truth-value in the characteristic of Conn$_r^2$. Analogously for a singulary connective.

D11-16a [b]. (Auxiliary term for D17 and D21.) $\mathfrak{a}_k$ has the **[L-]characteristic value** X (T or F) for the t-th distribution ($t = 1$ to 4) of *degree two* in $S =_{Df} \mathfrak{a}_k$ is a binary general connective in S; and if $\mathfrak{S}_i$ and $\mathfrak{S}_j$ are any closed sentences in S and $\mathfrak{S}_k$ is the full sentence $\mathfrak{a}_k(\mathfrak{S}_i,\mathfrak{S}_j)$, then the class specified below contains rs [is V_s]:

t	Value X	Class
1	T	$-R_i + (-R_j) + R_k$
1	F	$-R_i + (-R_j) + (-R_k)$
2	T	$-R_i + R_j + R_k$
2	F	$-R_i + R_j + (-R_k)$
3	T	$R_i + (-R_j) + R_k$
3	F	$R_i + (-R_j) + (-R_k)$
4	T	$R_i + R_j + R_k$
4	F	$R_i + R_j + (-R_k)$

Analogously for *degree one* ($t = 1$ or 2):

t	VALUE X	CLASS
1	T	$-R_i + R_k$
1	F	$-R_i + (-R_k)$
2	T	$R_i + R_k$
2	F	$R_i + (-R_k)$

T11-9a [b]. If a_k has the [L-]characteristic value X (T or F) for the t-th distribution of degree two in S, and $\mathfrak{S}_i$ and $\mathfrak{S}_j$ are closed sentences which have the t-th distribution of [L-]truth-values ([L-]truth or [L-]falsity), then $a_k(\mathfrak{S}_i, \mathfrak{S}_j)$ has the [L-]truth-value X. Analogously for degree one.

Proof for $t = 1$, $X = T$, $\mathfrak{S}_k = a_k(\mathfrak{S}_i, \mathfrak{S}_j)$. $-R_i + (-R_j) + R_k$ contains rs [is V_s] (D16a[b]). Since $\mathfrak{S}_i$ is [L-]true, $-R_i$ does not contain rs [is Λ_s]; likewise $-R_j$. Therefore, R_k contains rs [is V_s]. Hence, $\mathfrak{S}_k$ is [L-]true (D5). Analogously for the other values of t and X.

T11-10. a_k has the characteristic value X for the t-th distribution of degree two in S if and only if, for every closed $\mathfrak{S}_i$ and $\mathfrak{S}_j$ which have the t-th distribution of truth-values, $a_k(\mathfrak{S}_i, \mathfrak{S}_j)$ has the truth-value X. Analogously for degree one.

Proof. 1. T9a. 2. Proof for $t = 1$, $X = T$. Suppose that, for every closed $\mathfrak{S}_i$ and $\mathfrak{S}_j$ which have the first distribution and hence are true (D10-2), the full sentence $\mathfrak{S}_k$ has the value T. In other words, either $\mathfrak{S}_i$ and $\mathfrak{S}_j$ are not both true or $\mathfrak{S}_k$ is true; either $\mathfrak{S}_i$ is false or $\mathfrak{S}_j$ is false or $\mathfrak{S}_k$ is true; either rs $\epsilon -R_i$ or rs $\epsilon -R_j$ or rs ϵR_k; rs $\epsilon -R_i + (-R_j) + R_k$. Then a_k has the characteristic value T (D16a). Analogously for the other values of t and X.

D11-17a [b]. a_k [L-]**satisfies generally the t-th rule** ($t = 1$ to 4) in NTT for the binary connection Conn_r^2 ($r = 1$ to 16) in $S =_{Df} a_k$ has an [L-]characteristic value for the t-th distribution which is the same as the t-th value in the characteristic for Conn_r^2, as given in column (6) of the table in § 10. Analogously for a singulary connection ($t = 1$ and 2).

T11-11. $\mathfrak{a}_k$ satisfies generally the t-th rule ($t = 1$ to 4) for Conn_r^2 ($r = 1$ to 16) in NTT if and only if, for every closed $\mathfrak{S}_i$ and $\mathfrak{S}_j$ in S which have the t-th distribution of truth-values, $\mathfrak{a}_k(\mathfrak{S}_i,\mathfrak{S}_j)$ has the t-th truth-value in the characteristic of Conn_r^2 and hence $\mathfrak{a}_k$ satisfies the t-th rule with respect to $\mathfrak{S}_i$, $\mathfrak{S}_j$ in S. Analogously for degree one. (From D17a, T10, D14.)

D11-21a [b]. $\mathfrak{a}_k$ has $\mathfrak{R}_k$ (a sequence of four truth-values) as its **[L-]characteristic** in $S =_{\text{Df}}$ one of the following conditions is fulfilled.

1. $\mathfrak{a}_k$ is a singulary general connective and has [L-]characteristic values for the first and second distribution of degree one, and $\mathfrak{R}_k$ is the sequence of these two truth-values in this order.

2. $\mathfrak{a}_k$ is a binary general connective and has [L-]characteristic values for the first, second, third, and fourth distribution of degree two, and $\mathfrak{R}_k$ is the sequence of these truth-values in this order.

+D11-23a [b]. $\mathfrak{a}_k$ is a *sign for the connection* $_{[\text{L}]}\text{Conn}_r^n$ in $S =_{\text{Df}} \mathfrak{a}_k$ has as its [L-]characteristic the characteristic given in column (5) of the table in § 10 for Conn_r^n. Conn_1^1 is also called **tautology** (see column (2) of the table in § 10), Conn_3^1 **negation**, Conn_4^1 **contradiction**; further, Conn_1^2 **tautology**, Conn_2^2 **disjunction**, Conn_5^2 **implication**, Conn_7^2 **equivalence**, Conn_8^2 **conjunction**, Conn_9^2 **exclusion**, Conn_{15}^2 **binegation**, Conn_{16}^2 **contradiction**. Analogously, $_L\text{Conn}_3^1$ is also called negation$_L$, $_L\text{Conn}_2^2$ disjunction$_L$, etc.

It will be shown later (T12-28) that the signs for the connections $_{[\text{L}]}$ are [L-]extensional.

In some cases the term used for a connection is the same as that for a semantical relation. (In this point, our terminology at present follows the general use in spite of its disadvantages.) It is important to notice the difference between the two concepts, e.g. between the connection of implication, for which there may be a sign (e.g. '⊃ ') in the object language, and the semantical relation of implication ([I] D9-3), which is expressed in the metalanguage (e.g. by 'implies' or ' → '), and likewise between the connection of equivalence (' ≡ ') and the semantical relation of equivalence ('equivalent to'). In the case of other connections, there is much less danger of confusion because, fortunately, different terms are used. Examples: the connection of disjunction (' V ') and the semantical relation of disjunctness ([I] D9-5) ('disjunct'); the connection of negation (' ∼ ') and the corresponding semantical property of falsity ('false'). — An analogous difference must be observed in the case of L-concepts; here we put the 'L' at different places. We must distinguish between the connection (sometimes we use here the term 'connection$_L$') of implication$_L$ ('⊃ ', introduced by its truth-table) and the (L-)semantical relation of L-implication ('L-implies', ' $\underset{L}{\rightarrow}$ '); likewise between equivalence$_L$ (' ≡ ') and L-equivalence ('L-equivalent to'), between disjunction$_L$ (' V ') and L-disjunctness, between negation$_L$ (' ∼ ') and L-falsity ('L-false'). — Because of the danger of the confusion mentioned, it might be advisable to consider the use of other terms for the connections Conn_5^2 (implication) and Conn_7^2 (equivalence) (perhaps Quine's terms 'conditional' and 'biconditional'), and to reserve the terms 'implication' and 'equivalence' for the semantical relations.

We shall sometimes use ' $\mathfrak{b}_q$ ' (q = 1 to 4) (see column (4) in the table in § 10) for a sign of Conn_q^1 (in most cases, for $_L\text{Conn}_q^1$) and ' $\mathfrak{c}_r$ ' (r = 1 to 16) for a sign of Conn_r^2 (in most cases, $_L\text{Conn}_r^2$). Instead of ' $\mathfrak{b}_3$ ', we usually write **'neg'** as the semantical name of a sign of negation, and 'neg$_L$' as the name of a sign of negation$_L$; further, **'dis'**, **'imp'**, **'equ'**, **'con'** for signs of disjunction, implication, equivalence, and conjunction respectively, 'dis$_L$', 'imp$_L$', 'equ$_L$', 'con$_L$' for signs of disjunction$_L$, implication$_L$, equivalence$_L$, and conjunction$_L$ respectively. These names of connectives are mostly used for forming semantical descriptions of full sentences; 'neg$_L$($\mathfrak{S}_i$)', for instance, designates the full sentence of the sign of negation$_L$ with $\mathfrak{S}_i$ as component.

T11-12a [b]. $\mathfrak{a}_k$ is a sign for $_{[L]}\text{Conn}_q^n$ (n = 1 or 2) in

S if and only if $\mathfrak{a}_k$ [L-]satisfies generally all rules (two for $n = 1$, four for $n = 2$) for Conn_q^n in NTT. (From D23, D21, D17.)

The method here used for the definition of 'L-characteristic' (D21) and 'sign for $_L\mathrm{Conn}_r^n$' (D23) with the help of the concept of L-range, is analogous to that previously used in [Syntax] § 57 for the definition of corresponding concepts in syntax. In syntax, however, this method does not always lead to adequate concepts; this has been shown by Tarski (see "Addition 1935" at the end of § 57). Therefore the method is now transferred to L-semantics (compare [I] § 39, remarks on [Syntax] § 57).

T11-17a [b]. Let S contain $\mathfrak{a}_k$ as a singulary general connective and $\mathfrak{b}_q$ ($q = 1$ to 4) as a sign for $_{[L]}\mathrm{Conn}_q^1$. $\mathfrak{a}_k$ is also a sign for $_{[L]}\mathrm{Conn}_q^1$ if and only if, for any closed $\mathfrak{S}_i$, $\mathfrak{a}_k(\mathfrak{S}_i)$ is [L-]equivalent to $\mathfrak{b}_q(\mathfrak{S}_i)$. Analogously for a binary connective.

Proof for a[b]. $\mathfrak{b}_q$ has the [L-]characteristic for Conn_q^1 (D23), say X_1X_2. 1. If for any closed $\mathfrak{S}_i$, $\mathfrak{S}_k$ ($= \mathfrak{a}_k(\mathfrak{S}_i)$) is [L-]equivalent to $\mathfrak{S}_q$ ($= \mathfrak{b}_q(\mathfrak{S}_i)$), then both $\mathrm{R}_k + (-\mathrm{R}_q)$ and $-\mathrm{R}_k + \mathrm{R}_q$ contain rs [are $\mathrm{V_s}$] (T6 (2)). If $X_1 = \mathrm{T}$, then $-\mathrm{R}_i + \mathrm{R}_q$ contains rs [is $\mathrm{V_s}$] (D16); hence likewise $(-\mathrm{R}_i + \mathrm{R}_q) + (\mathrm{R}_k + (-\mathrm{R}_q))$, which is $-\mathrm{R}_i + \mathrm{R}_k$. Therefore, $\mathfrak{a}_k$ also has T as its [L-]characteristic value for the first distribution (D16). If $X_1 = \mathrm{F}$, then $-\mathrm{R}_i + (-\mathrm{R}_q)$ contains rs [is $\mathrm{V_s}$]; hence likewise $(-\mathrm{R}_i + (-\mathrm{R}_q)) + (-\mathrm{R}_k + \mathrm{R}_q)$, which is $-\mathrm{R}_i + (-\mathrm{R}_k)$. Therefore, $\mathfrak{a}_k$ also has F as its value for the first distribution. Analogously for the second distribution ($X_2 = \mathrm{T}$ or $X_2 = \mathrm{F}$). Thus, $\mathfrak{a}_k$ has the same two [L-]characteristic values as $\mathfrak{b}_q$, and hence the same [L-]characteristic (D21), and hence is also a sign for $_{[L]}\mathrm{Conn}_q^1$ (D23). — 2. If $\mathfrak{a}_k$ is also a sign for $_{[L]}\mathrm{Conn}_q^1$, $\mathfrak{a}_k$ has also the [L-]characteristic X_1X_2. Take for example TF. Then, for any closed $\mathfrak{S}_i$, $-\mathrm{R}_i + \mathrm{R}_q$, $\mathrm{R}_i + (-\mathrm{R}_q)$, $-\mathrm{R}_i + \mathrm{R}_k$, and $\mathrm{R}_i + (-\mathrm{R}_k)$ all contain rs [are $\mathrm{V_s}$] (D16); hence likewise $(-\mathrm{R}_i + \mathrm{R}_k) + (\mathrm{R}_i + (-\mathrm{R}_q))$, which is $\mathrm{R}_k + (-\mathrm{R}_q)$, and $(\mathrm{R}_i + (-\mathrm{R}_k)) + (-\mathrm{R}_i + \mathrm{R}_q)$, which is $-\mathrm{R}_k + \mathrm{R}_q$. Therefore, $\mathfrak{S}_k$ and $\mathfrak{S}_q$ are [L-]equivalent. Analogously for the other three characteristics (TT, FT, FF).

If, in constructing S, we lay down the rules of NTT for the four singulary and the sixteen binary connectives, then we see from these rules of S, without using factual knowledge, that those signs satisfy the rules of NTT and hence have the characteristics as given in column (6) of the table in § 10. Therefore, in this case, the signs L-satisfy the rules, have L-characteristics, and are signs for the connections$_L$. Since, however, the details of the formulation of the rules are inessential as long as they lead to the same results, we will also say that S *contains NTT* if the rules of S are formulated in any other way provided they give to the connectives the same properties as the rules of NTT would do, in other words, if they are such that they determine the same L-characteristics and hence make the connectives signs for the connections$_L$. This consideration leads to D26. For the sake of simplicity, we apply the definition only to systems whose sentences are all closed.

D11-26. S **contains NTT** $=_{Df}$ all sentences of S are closed; S contains a sign for each singulary or binary connection$_L$, i.e. four signs $_L\mathfrak{b}_q$ ($q = 1$ to 4) for $_L$Conn^1_q, and sixteen signs $_L\mathfrak{c}_r$ ($r = 1$ to 16) for $_L$Conn^2_r. These signs are called **connectives of NTT** in S.

If S contains NTT, we understand by the **ultimate components** of $\mathfrak{S}_i$ with respect to NTT those sentences out of which $\mathfrak{S}_i$ is constructed with the help of the connectives of NTT, which sentences themselves, however, are not full sentences of connectives of NTT. If $\mathfrak{S}_i$ is not a full sentence of a connective of NTT, $\mathfrak{S}_i$ is itself its only ultimate component. The ultimate components of $\mathfrak{R}_i$ are those of the sentences of $\mathfrak{R}_i$. Thus for instance, the only ultimate component of dis(neg($\mathfrak{S}_1$),$\mathfrak{S}_1$) is $\mathfrak{S}_1$. If in this example $\mathfrak{S}_1$ is replaced by any other sentence, the resulting sentence is always L-true (see below T13-25b(2)); therefore, dis(neg($\mathfrak{S}_1$), $\mathfrak{S}_1$), and likewise dis(neg($\mathfrak{S}_i$),$\mathfrak{S}_i$) for any $\mathfrak{S}_i$, is L-true by NTT. Thus this concept applies to those sentences which can be shown to be true and hence L-true by merely applying the normal truth-tables for the connectives occurring. Analogously, we shall define 'L-false by NTT', 'L-implies by NTT', and 'L-equivalent by NTT' in such a way that these concepts apply to those cases where the rules of NTT suffice to show that the corresponding radical concepts and hence the L-concepts hold. For technical reasons, we first define 'L-implies by NTT' by reference to the replacements, and then the other concepts on the basis of this concept. T25 shows that these definitions are in agreement with the previous definitions for the L-concepts (D5 to 8).

D11-29. $\mathfrak{T}_i$ **L-implies** $\mathfrak{T}_j$ **by NTT** in S $=_{Df}$ S contains NTT; $\mathfrak{T}_i'$ $\overrightarrow{L}$ $\mathfrak{T}_j'$ in S for any $\mathfrak{T}_i'$ and $\mathfrak{T}_j'$ which are constructed out of $\mathfrak{T}_i$ and $\mathfrak{T}_j$ respectively in the following way: any ultimate components of $\mathfrak{T}_i$ and of $\mathfrak{T}_j$ are replaced by any sentences in S; if a component occurs at several places in $\mathfrak{T}_i$ and $\mathfrak{T}_j$, then it must be replaced, if at all, by the same sentence at all places where it occurs in $\mathfrak{T}_i$ and $\mathfrak{T}_j$.

D11-30. $\mathfrak{T}_i$ is **L-true by NTT** in S $=_{Df}$ Λ $\overrightarrow{L}$ $\mathfrak{T}_i$ by NTT.

D11-31. $\mathfrak{T}_i$ is **L-false by NTT** in S $=_{Df}$ $\mathfrak{T}_i$ $\overrightarrow{L}$ V by NTT.

D11-32. $\mathfrak{T}_i$ is **L-equivalent** to $\mathfrak{T}_j$ **by NTT** in S $=_{Df}$ $\mathfrak{T}_i$ $\overrightarrow{L}$ $\mathfrak{T}_j$ by NTT, and $\mathfrak{T}_j$ $\overrightarrow{L}$ $\mathfrak{T}_i$ by NTT.

T11-24. If S contains NTT, then the following holds:

    a. An infinite number of sentences in S are L-true by NTT.

    b. An infinite number of sentences in S are L-false by NTT.

    c. V is L-false by NTT.

Proof. a. Given any sentence $\mathfrak{S}_m$ which is L-true by NTT (e.g. for any $\mathfrak{S}_i$, $dis_L(neg_L(\mathfrak{S}_i), \mathfrak{S}_i)$), its double negation (i.e. $neg_L(neg_L(\mathfrak{S}_m))$) is also L-true by NTT. — b. Given any sentence $\mathfrak{S}_n$ which is L-false in NTT (e.g. $con_L(\mathfrak{S}_i, neg_L(\mathfrak{S}_i))$), its double negation is also L-false in NTT. — c. From (b), [I] T14-11.

T11-25.

    a. If $\mathfrak{T}_i \underset{L}{\rightarrow} \mathfrak{T}_j$ by NTT (in S), then $\mathfrak{T}_i \underset{L}{\rightarrow} \mathfrak{T}_j$.

    b. If $\mathfrak{T}_i$ is L-true by NTT, then $\mathfrak{T}_i$ is L-true.

    c. If $\mathfrak{T}_i$ is L-false by NTT, then $\mathfrak{T}_i$ is L-false.

    d. If $\mathfrak{T}_i$ is L-equivalent to $\mathfrak{T}_j$ by NTT, then $\mathfrak{T}_i$ is L-equivalent to $\mathfrak{T}_j$.

Proof. a. From D29, with replacement of the components by themselves. — b. From (a), [I] T14-51a. — c. From (a), [I] P14-7. — d. From (a).

§ 12. Extensionality

    A connection or connective is usually called extensional (or a truth-function) if the truth-value of its full sentences depends merely upon the truth-values of the components. We also define the corresponding L-concept (with the help of the concept of L-range) in such a way that a connective is L-extensional if the semantical rules suffice to show that it is extensional. A connective is extensional if and only if it has a characteristic; L-extensional if (but not only if) it has an L-characteristic. Thus the connections listed in the table in § 10 are extensional and under certain conditions L-extensional.

The connections which have truth-tables are often called *truth-functions*, because the truth-value of a full sentence depends merely upon the truth-values of the components. Following Russell, we call connections of this kind and their connectives **extensional** and a full sentence of such a connection extensional with respect to the components. For a singulary connective $\mathfrak{a}_k$, the condition of extensionality can be formulated in the following way: if $\mathfrak{S}_i$ and $\mathfrak{S}'_i$ are any closed sentences which have the same truth-value and hence are equivalent, then $\mathfrak{a}_k(\mathfrak{S}_i)$ and $\mathfrak{a}_k(\mathfrak{S}'_i)$, which we will call $\mathfrak{S}_k$ and $\mathfrak{S}'_k$ respectively, also have the same truth-value and hence are equivalent. As in the case of many other well-known concepts, we introduce here a distinction between an L- and an F-concept dependent upon the distinction be-

tween the case where the general condition for the concept
in question, here the condition for extensionality just mentioned, is fulfilled by the contingency of the facts, and the
case where it is fulfilled necessarily, that is to say, in such a
way that we can find out that it is fulfilled on the basis of
the semantical rules of the system in question without using
factual knowledge. In order to make this distinction, we
transform the condition of extensionality in the following
way: "Either $\mathfrak{S}_i$ and $\mathfrak{S}_i'$ are not equivalent or $\mathfrak{S}_k$ and $\mathfrak{S}_k'$
are equivalent"; further, in terms of L-range (where 'R_m''
is short for '$\mathrm{Lr}\mathfrak{S}_m'$'): "Either rs ϵ (($R_i \times -R_i'$) + ($-R_i \times$
R_i')) or rs ϵ (($R_k \times R_k'$) + ($-R_k \times -R_k'$))" (T11-7a(1),
T11-6a(1)); "rs ϵ (($R_i \times -R_i'$) + ($-R_i \times R_i'$) + ($R_k \times R_k$)
+ ($-R_k \times -R_k'$))". In general, factual knowledge is re-
quired in order to find out that the last-mentioned class
contains rs. Only in the case that this class is V_s can we
know that it contains rs without knowing which L-state is
rs. In this case, we call $\mathfrak{a}_k$ **L-extensional**. If the condition
for extensionality is not fulfilled, we call the connective **non-
extensional**. [The term 'intensional' is often used in this
case. Since, however, this term is used in traditional logic
in another sense, it might be advisable not to use it here.]
If the class mentioned is null, then we know without the use
of factual knowledge that it does not contain rs and that
hence the connective is non-extensional; we call it in this
case **L-non-extensional**. These considerations lead to the
following definitions (D1 and 2); the definitions for binary
connections (D3 and 4) are analogous.

Conditions for extensionality, non-extensionality, and L-non-
extensionality which do not make use of the concept of L-range are
given in T1 and T2a,b below. It seems that a condition, and hence a
definition, for L-extensionality cannot be given in this simple way
(except in special cases where S contains certain connectives; see below, T13-31b). This is the chief reason for applying the concept of
L-range in D1b and D3b.

D12-1a [b]. A *singulary* connection (and a general connective for it) is [**L-**]**extensional** in $S =_{Df}$ if $\mathfrak{S}_i$ and $\mathfrak{S}'_i$ are closed and $\mathfrak{S}_k$ is the full sentence with $\mathfrak{S}_i$, and $\mathfrak{S}'_k$ that with $\mathfrak{S}'_i$, then $(R_i \times -R'_i) + (-R_i \times R'_i) + (R_k \times R'_k) + (-R_k \times -R'_k)$ contains rs [is V_s].

D12-2a [b]. A *singulary* connection (and a general connective for it) is [**L-**]**non-extensional** (intensional) in $S =_{Df}$ there are $\mathfrak{S}_i$, $\mathfrak{S}'_i$, $\mathfrak{S}_k$, and $\mathfrak{S}'_k$ such that $\mathfrak{S}_k$ is the full sentence with $\mathfrak{S}_i$ and $\mathfrak{S}'_k$ that with $\mathfrak{S}'_i$, and each of the following four classes (and hence also their sum) does not contain rs [is Λ_s]: $R_i \times -R'_i$, $-R_i \times R'_i$, $R_k \times R'_k$, $-R_k \times -R'_k$.

D12-3a [b]. A *binary* connection (and a general connective for it) is [**L-**]**extensional** in $S =_{Df}$ if $\mathfrak{S}_i$, $\mathfrak{S}'_i$, $\mathfrak{S}_j$, and $\mathfrak{S}'_j$ are closed and $\mathfrak{S}_k$ is the full sentence with $\mathfrak{S}_i$ and $\mathfrak{S}_j$, and $\mathfrak{S}'_k$ that with $\mathfrak{S}'_i$ and $\mathfrak{S}'_j$, then $(R_i \times -R'_i) + (-R_i \times R'_i) + (R_j \times -R'_j) + (-R_j \times R'_j) + (R_k \times R'_k) + (-R_k \times -R'_k)$ contains rs [is V_s]. The class mentioned can also b stated in the following form: $((R_i + R'_i) \times (-R_i + -R'_i)) + ((R_j + R'_j) \times (-R_j + -R'_j)) + ((R_k + -R'_k) \times (-R_k + R'_k))$.

D12-4a [b]. A *binary* connection (and a general connective for it) is [**L-**]**non-extensional** (intensional) in $S =_{Df}$ there are $\mathfrak{S}_i$, $\mathfrak{S}'_i$, $\mathfrak{S}_j$, $\mathfrak{S}'_j$, $\mathfrak{S}_k$, $\mathfrak{S}'_k$ such that $\mathfrak{S}_k$ is the full sentence with $\mathfrak{S}_i$ and $\mathfrak{S}_j$, and $\mathfrak{S}'_k$ that with $\mathfrak{S}'_i$ and $\mathfrak{S}'_j$, and each of the following six classes (and hence also their sum) does not contain rs [is Λ_s]: $R_i \times -R'_i$, $-R_i \times R'_i$, $R_j \times -R'_j$, $-R_j \times R'_j$, $R_k \times R'_k$, $-R_k \times -R'_k$.

The following theorem, T1, states the condition for extensionality in the customary form. There is no analogue to this theorem concerning L-extensionality (see, above, the remark preceding D1).

+T12-1. A singulary general connective $\mathfrak{a}_k$ is *extensional* in S if and only if the following holds. If $\mathfrak{S}_i$ and $\mathfrak{S}'_i$ are any closed equivalent sentences, then $a_k(\mathfrak{S}_i)$ is equivalent to $a_k(\mathfrak{S}_i')$. (From D1a, T11-7a(1), T11-6a(1).) Analogously for a binary connective.

T12-2a [b]. Let a_k be a singulary general connective in S. Each of the following conditions, applying to every closed $\mathfrak{S}_i$ and $\mathfrak{S}_i'$ with the full sentences $\mathfrak{S}_k$ and $\mathfrak{S}_k'$, is a sufficient and necessary condition for a_k to be [*L-*]*extensional*.

1. $-Q_i + Q_k$ contains rs [is V_s, or in other words, $Q_i \subset Q_k$]. Here, $Q_i = (R_i \times R_i') + (-R_i \times -R_i') = (R_i + (-R_i')) \times (-R_i + R_i')$; hence, $-Q_i = (R_i \times -R_i') + (-R_i \times R_i') = (R_i + R_i') \times (-R_i + (-R_i'))$; $Q_k = (R_k \times R_k') + (-R_k \times -R_k') = (R_k + (-R_k')) \times (-R_k + R_k')$.

2. Each of the following four classes, and hence also their product, contains rs [is V_s]: $R_i + R_i' + R_k + (-R_k')$, $R_i + R_i' + (-R_k) + R_k'$, $-R_i + (-R_i') + R_k + (-R_k')$, $-R_i + (-R_i') + (-R_k) + R_k'$.

T12-3a [b]. A singulary general connective a_k is [*L-*] *non-extensional* in S if and only if there are closed sentences $\mathfrak{S}_i$, $\mathfrak{S}_i'$ such that $\mathfrak{S}_i$ and $\mathfrak{S}_i'$ are [L-]equivalent, and $a_k(\mathfrak{S}_i)$ and $a_k(\mathfrak{S}_i')$ are [L-]non-equivalent. (From D2, T11-6(4), T11-7(4).) Analogously for a binary connective.

T12-4. Let a_k be a singulary general, L-extensional connective. If $\mathfrak{S}_i$ and $\mathfrak{S}_i'$ are closed and L-equivalent, $a_k(\mathfrak{S}_i)$ and $a_k(\mathfrak{S}_i')$ are L-equivalent. Analogously for a binary connective.

Proof. Let $\mathfrak{S}_k$ and $\mathfrak{S}_k'$ be the full sentences. If $\mathfrak{S}_i$ and $\mathfrak{S}_i'$ are L-equivalent, $R_i = R_i'$ (D11-8). Since a_k is L-extensional, the class mentioned in D1b is V_s, hence also $(R_k \times R_k') + (-R_k \times -R_k')$. Therefore, $R_k = R_k'$; hence $\mathfrak{S}_k$ and $\mathfrak{S}_k'$ are L-equivalent.

T12-6. If a connective a_k in S satisfies a certain rule for a connection in NTT with respect to some components and violates the same rule with respect to others, then α_k is non-extensional.

Proof. Let α_k be a singulary connective (the proof for a binary one is analogous). Let α_k satisfy the t-th rule for $Conn_q^1$ with respect to $\mathfrak{S}_i$ and violate the same rule with respect to $\mathfrak{S}_i'$. Then (D11-14 and 15) $\mathfrak{S}_i$ and $\mathfrak{S}_i'$ have the t-th distribution of truth values and hence are equivalent, while the full sentences have not the same truth-value and hence are non-equivalent. Therefore, α_k is non-extensional (T3a).

T12-12a [b]. Let S contain at least one [L-]true sentence and at least one [L-]false sentence and α_k be a singulary general connective. Then the following holds:

    1. For any t (1 or 2), α_k has at most one t-th [L-]characteristic value (D11-16).

    2. α_k has at most one [L-]characteristic.

Analogously for a binary connective.

Proof for a [b] (1). Let $\mathfrak{S}_i$ be [L-]true and $\mathfrak{S}_i'$ [L-]false in S. Let $\mathfrak{S}_k$ and $\mathfrak{S}_k'$ be the full sentences. If for $t = 1$, α_k had both T and F as an [L-]characteristic value, then $\mathfrak{S}_k$ would be both [L-]true and [L-]false, which is impossible. (More exactly, on the basis of our definitions in terms of 'L-range': both $-R_i + R_k$ and $-R_i + (-R_k)$ would contain rs [be V_s] (D11-16a[b]); since $\mathfrak{S}_i$ is [L-]true, R_i contains rs [is V_s]; hence $-R_i$ does not contain rs [is Λ_s]; hence both R_k and $-R_k$ would contain rs [be V_s], which is impossible. Analogously for $t = 2$, with $\mathfrak{S}_i'$. — a[b](2) from a[b](1).

T12-13. Let S contain at least one true and at least one false sentence and α_k be a singulary general connective. If α_k is extensional, then it has one and only one characteristic. The same holds for a binary connective.

Proof. Let $\mathfrak{S}_1$ be true and $\mathfrak{S}_2$ false in S, and α_k be extensional. Let $\mathfrak{S}_{k1}$ be $\alpha_k(\mathfrak{S}_1)$, and $\mathfrak{S}_{k2}$ $\alpha_k(\mathfrak{S}_2)$. We distinguish two cases: 1. $\mathfrak{S}_{k1}$ is true; 2. it is false. 1. For any closed $\mathfrak{S}_i$, either $\mathfrak{S}_i$ is false or $\mathfrak{S}_i$ is true and hence equivalent to $\mathfrak{S}_1$, and hence $\alpha_k(\mathfrak{S}_i)$, which we call $\mathfrak{S}_{ki}$, is equivalent to $\mathfrak{S}_{k1}$ (T1) and hence also true. Therefore, rs $\epsilon -R_i + R_{ki}$. Since this holds for any $\mathfrak{S}_i$, α_k has the characteristic value T for the first distribution of degree one (D11-16a). 2. It can be shown analogously that, if $\mathfrak{S}_{k1}$ is false, $\mathfrak{a}_k$ has the characteristic value F for the first distribution. It can be shown in an analogous way with $\mathfrak{S}_2$ that $\mathfrak{a}_k$ has T or F as its characteristic value for the second distribution. Therefore, $\mathfrak{a}_k$ has a characteristic (D11-21a) but not more than one (T12a (2)).

It is to be noted that no strict analogue to T13 holds for L-concepts. Let $\mathfrak{a}_k$ be L-extensional. Then it is extensional and hence has a characteristic (T13). It does not, however, necessarily have an L-characteristic. Since $\mathfrak{a}_k$ is L-extensional, the semantical rules without factual knowledge suffice to show that $\mathfrak{a}_k$ has one of the characteristics; but they do not necessarily suffice to find out which one. And only if they do is that characteristic an L-characteristic for $\mathfrak{a}_k$. If they do not, then $\mathfrak{a}_k$, though L-extensional, has no L-characteristic.

Example of an L-extensional connective without L-characteristic. Let $\mathfrak{a}_k$ be a singulary general connective in S. Let W be the condition that Mt. Washington is less than 4000 ft. high, and R_w be the class of those L-states in which W holds. Let the following rule of L-range be laid down for the full sentence $\mathfrak{S}_k$ of $\mathfrak{a}_k$ with any component $\mathfrak{S}_i$: $R_k = (R_i \times R_w) + (-R_i \times -R_w)$. Thus $rs \in R_k$ if and only if either $rs \in R_i$ and $rs \in R_w$, or not $rs \in R_i$ and not $rs \in R_w$. Thus $\mathfrak{S}_k$ is true if either $\mathfrak{S}_i$ is true and W holds, or $\mathfrak{S}_i$ is false and W does not hold. Hence, if $\mathfrak{S}_i$ means (designates the proposition) A, $\mathfrak{a}_k(\mathfrak{S}_i)$ means: A if and only if W. Let $\mathfrak{S}_i$ and $\mathfrak{S}_i'$ be equivalent and $\mathfrak{S}_k'$ be $\mathfrak{a}_k(\mathfrak{S}_i')$. Then either both $\mathfrak{S}_i$ and $\mathfrak{S}_i'$ have the same truth-value as W, in which case $\mathfrak{S}_k$ and $\mathfrak{S}_k'$ are both true; or both have a truth-value different from that of W, in which case $\mathfrak{S}_k$ and $\mathfrak{S}_k'$ are both false. Thus, in any case, the full sentences are equivalent. Therefore, $\mathfrak{a}_k$ is extensional (T1). Since this has been found without factual knowledge, $\mathfrak{a}_k$ is L-extensional. [This latter reasoning is rather vague. The same result is shown in the following more exact way on the basis of D1b. The rule given for R_k holds generally. Therefore, $R_k' = (R_i' \times R_w) + (-R_i' \times -R_w)$. By substituting these values for R_k and R_k' in the expression of a class in D1, after a simple transformation we find that class to be $(R_i \times -R_i') + (-R_i \times R_i') + (R_i \times R_i') + (-R_i \times -R_i')$, which is V_s. Hence, $\mathfrak{a}_k$ is L-extensional (D1b).] Without using factual knowledge, we know that a_k has a characteristic, but we do not know which one. By empirical investigation, measuring the height of Mt. Washington, we find that W does not hold. It follows that every full sentence of a_k with a true component is false, while that with a false component is true. Hence, a_k has the characteristic FT and is a sign of negation. But FT is not an L-characteristic of a_k, and a_k is not a sign of negation_L. (If we wish to use F-terms, we might say that a_k has an F-characteristic and is a sign of negation_F.)

T12-16a [b]. Let every sentence in S be [L-]true. Then for any singulary general connective a_k in S, the following holds:

1. a_k has T and not F as its [L-]characteristic value for the first distribution.
2. a_k has (vacuously) both T and F as [L-]characteristic values for the second distribution (which does not occur).
3. a_k [L-]satisfies generally the first rules for Conn_1^1 and Conn_2^1 (see the table in § 10).
4. The second rule for any singulary connection is not applicable and hence is generally [L-]satisfied by a_k.
5. a_k has both TT and TF as [L-]characteristics.
6. a_k is a sign for both $_{[L]}\text{Conn}_1^1$ and $_{[L]}\text{Conn}_2^1$.
7. S contains no sign for Conn_3^1 or Conn_4^1 (and hence none for $_L\text{Conn}_3^1$ or $_L\text{Conn}_4^1$).
8. a_k is [L-]extensional.

Proof for a [b]. 1 and 2. For any $\mathfrak{S}_i$, with the full sentence $\mathfrak{S}_k$, both $\mathfrak{S}_i$ and $\mathfrak{S}_k$ are [L-]true. Hence both R_i and R_k contain rs [are V_s], while both $-R_i$ and $-R_k$ do not contain rs [are Λ_s]. Hence, $-R_i + R_k$, $R_i + R_k$, and $R_i + (-R_k)$ contain rs [are V_s], but $-R_i + (-R_k)$ does not. Hence (D11-16a [b]), a_k has T, but not F, as its [L-]characteristic value for the first distribution and both T and F for the second. 3. From (1), D11-17a [b]. 4. From (2). 5. From (1), (2), D11-21a [b]. 6. From (5), D11-23a [b]. 7. From (1), D11-23a [b]. 8a. All sentences of S are equivalent to one another, hence also all full sentences of a_k. Hence, a_k is extensional (T1).

8b. All sentences of S are L-true and hence have the L-range V_s; hence also any full sentences $\mathfrak{S}_k$ and $\mathfrak{S}'_k$. Therefore, $R_k \times R'_k = V_s$, and hence likewise the class mentioned in D1. Therefore, $\mathfrak{a}_k$ is L-extensional (D1b).

The proofs for the following theorems, T17, 20, and 21, are analogous to that for T16.

T12-17a [b]. Let every sentence in S be [L-]true. Then for any binary general connective $\mathfrak{a}_k$ in S, the following holds:

1. $\mathfrak{a}_k$ has T and not F as its [L-]characteristic value for the first distribution.
2. $\mathfrak{a}_k$ has (vacuously) both T and F as [L-]characteristic values for the second, third, and fourth distributions (which do not occur).
3. $\mathfrak{a}_k$ [L-]satisfies generally the first rules for the eight connections Conn_1^2 to Conn_8^2 (i.e. those whose characteristic begins with T).
4. The second, third, and fourth rules for any binary connection are not applicable and hence are generally [L-]satisfied by $\mathfrak{a}_k$.
5. $\mathfrak{a}_k$ has simultaneously those eight [L-]characteristics which begin with T.
6. $\mathfrak{a}_k$ is a sign simultaneously for the eight connections $_{[L]}\mathrm{Conn}_1^2$ to $_{[L]}\mathrm{Conn}_8^2$.
7. S contains no sign for any of the connections Conn_9^2 to Conn_{16}^2 (and hence none for the corresponding connections$_L$).
8. $\mathfrak{a}_k$ is [L-]extensional.

T12-20a [b]. Let every sentence in S be [L-]false. Then for any singulary general connective $\mathfrak{a}_k$ in S the following holds:

1. $\mathfrak{a}_k$ has F and not T as [L-]characteristic value for the second distribution.
2. $\mathfrak{a}_k$ has (vacuously) both T and F as [L-]charac-

teristic values for the first distribution (which does not occur).

3. $\mathfrak{a}_k$ [L-]satisfies generally the second rules for Conn_3^1 and Conn_4^1.

4. The first rule for any singulary connection is not applicable and hence is generally [L-]satisfied by $\mathfrak{a}_k$.

5. $\mathfrak{a}_k$ has both TF and FF as [L-]characteristics.

6. $\mathfrak{a}_k$ is a sign for both $_{[L]}\mathrm{Conn}_2^1$ and $_{[L]}\mathrm{Conn}_4^1$.

7. S contains no sign for Conn_1^1 or Conn_3^1 (and hence none for the corresponding connections$_L$).

8. $\mathfrak{a}_k$ is [L-]extensional.

T12-21a [b]. Let every sentence in S be [L-]false. Then for any binary general connective $\mathfrak{a}_k$ in S the following holds:

1. $\mathfrak{a}_k$ has F and not T as its [L-]characteristic value for the fourth distribution.

2. $\mathfrak{a}_k$ has (vacuously) both T and F as [L-]characteristic values for the first, second, and third distributions (which do not occur).

3. $\mathfrak{a}_k$ [L-]satisfies generally the fourth rules for the eight connections Conn_r^2 with even r (i.e. those whose characteristic ends with F).

4. The first, second, and third rules for any binary connection are not applicable and hence are generally [L-]satisfied by $\mathfrak{a}_k$.

5. $\mathfrak{a}_k$ has simultaneously those eight [L-]characteristics which end with F.

6. $\mathfrak{a}_k$ is a sign simultaneously for the eight connections $_{[L]}\mathrm{Conn}_r^2$ with even r.

7. S contains no sign for any of the connections Conn_r^2 with odd r (and hence none for the corresponding connections$_L$).

8. $\mathfrak{a}_k$ is [L-]extensional.

+**T12-25a [b]**. If a_k is a singular or binary general connective in S and has an [L-]characteristic, then a_k is [L-]extensional.

Proof for a [b]. Let a_k be a singular general connective (the proof for a binary connective is analogous) which has an [L-]characteristic. Let $\mathfrak{S}_i$ and $\mathfrak{S}'_i$ be any closed sentences with the full sentences $\mathfrak{S}_k$ and $\mathfrak{S}'_k$ respectively. Let the four classes mentioned in T2(2) be k_1, k_2, k_3, and k_4. If the first truth-value in the [L-]characteristic of a_k is T, both $-R_i + R_k$ and $-R'_i + R'_k$ contain rs [are V_s] (D11-16a [b]), and hence both k_3 and k_4 contain rs [are V_s]. Likewise, if the first value is F, then $-R_i + (-R_k)$, $-R'_i + (-R'_k)$, k_4, and k_3 contain rs [are V_s]. If the second value is T, then $R_i + R_k$, $R'_i + R'_k$, k_1, and k_2 contain rs [are V_s]. If the second value is F, then $R_i + (-R_k)$, $R'_i + (-R'_k)$, k_2, and k_1 contain rs [are V_s]. Thus, in the case of each of the possible [L-]characteristics TT, TF, FT, and FF, each of the classes k_1 to k_4 contains rs [is V_s]. Hence a_k is [L-]extensional (T2a [b](2)).

+**T12-26**. If a_k is a singular or binary extensional connective, then a_k has a characteristic. (From T13, T16a(5), T17a(5), T20a(5), T21a(5).

This is the converse of T25a. An analogue to T26 for L-concepts, which would be the converse of T25b, does not hold (see the remark on T13 and the counter-example).

T12-28a [b]. If a_k is a sign for $_{[L]}\mathrm{Conn}^1_q$ ($q = 1$ to 4) or for $_{[L]}\mathrm{Conn}^2_r$ ($r = 1$ to 16), then a_k is [L-]extensional. (From D11-23, T25.)

§ 13. Theorems Concerning Particular Connections

Some theorems concerning negation, disjunction, conjunction, implication, equivalence, and the corresponding connectionsL (negationL, etc.) are stated. Some of these theorems state sufficient and necessary conditions for a sign to be a connective for one of these connections (T5, T13, T14); the L-ranges of full sentences (T15); relations between the connections[L] and certain radical [L-]concepts, e.g. [L-]true (T20, T25 to 28); sufficient and necessary conditions for [L-]extensionality (T31) and [L-]non-extensionality (T32).

T13-3a [b]. a_k [L-]satisfies generally the rule N1 for negation in NTT in S if and only if a_k is a singulary general connective in S, and for any closed $\mathfrak{S}_i$ with the full sentence $\mathfrak{S}_k$ the following condition (stated in three forms) is fulfilled:

    1. $-R_i + (-R_k)$ contains rs [is V_s]. (From D11-17a [b], D11-16a [b].

    2. $R_i \times R_k$ does not contain rs [is Λ_s]. (From (1).)

    3. $\mathfrak{S}_i$ and $\mathfrak{S}_k$ are [L-]exclusive. (From (1) [(2)], [I] D20-18[10].)

T13-4a [b]. a_k [L-]satisfies generally the rule N2 in NTT in S if and only if a_k is a singulary general connective in S, and for any closed $\mathfrak{S}_i$ with the full sentence $\mathfrak{S}_k$ the following condition (stated in three forms) is fulfilled:

    1. $R_i + R_k$ contains rs [is V_s]. (From D11-17a [b], D11-16a [b].)

    2. $-R_i \times -R_k$ does not contain rs [is Λ_s]. (From (1).)

    3. $\mathfrak{S}_i$ and $\mathfrak{S}_k$ are [L-]disjunct. (From (1), [I] D20-17[9].)

+T13-5a [b]. a_k is a *sign of negation*[L] in S if and only if a_k is a singulary general connective in S, and for any closed $\mathfrak{S}_i$ with the full sentence $\mathfrak{S}_k$ the following condition (stated in three forms) is fulfilled:

1. Both $R_i + R_k$ and $-R_i + (-R_k)$ (and hence also their product) contain rs [are V_s, and hence $R_k = -R_i$]. (From T11-12, T3(1), T4(1).)
2. $\mathfrak{S}_i$ and $\mathfrak{S}_k$ are [L-]disjunct and [L-]exclusive. (From T3(3), T4(3).)
3. $\mathfrak{S}_i$ and $\mathfrak{S}_k$ are [L-]non-equivalent [and hence, $R_k = -R_i$]. (From (2), T11-7(5) [and D11-9].)

T13-10a [b] (lemma). A binary general connective a_k in S [L-]satisfies generally one of the rules in NTT mentioned below (Dj1 to 4 for disjunction, C1 to 4 for conjunction, I1 to 4 for implication, E1 to 4 for equivalence) if and only if, for any closed sentences $\mathfrak{S}_i$ and $\mathfrak{S}_j$ with the full sentence $\mathfrak{S}_k$, the class specified below for that rule contains rs [is V_s]. (From D11-23, D11-21, D11-17, D11-16.)

	RULE	CLASS
1.	Dj1	$-R_i + (-R_j) + R_k$
2.	Dj2	$-R_i + R_j + R_k$
3.	Dj3	$R_i + (-R_j) + R_k$
4.	Dj4	$R_i + R_j + (-R_k)$
5.	C1	$-R_i + (-R_j) + R_k$
6.	C2	$-R_i + R_j + (-R_k)$
7.	C3	$R_i + (-R_j) + (-R_k)$
8.	C4	$R_i + R_j + (-R_k)$
9.	I1	$-R_i + (-R_j) + R_k$
10.	I2	$-R_i + R_j + (-R_k)$
11.	I3	$R_i + (-R_j) + R_k$
12.	I4	$R_i + R_j + R_k$
13.	E1	$-R_i + (-R_j) + R_k$
14.	E2	$-R_i + R_j + (-R_k)$
15.	E3	$R_i + (-R_j) + (-R_k)$
16.	E4	$R_i + R_j + R_k$

+**T13-13a [b]**. A binary general connective a_k is a sign for $_{[L]}Conn_r^2$ ($r = 2, 5, 7, 8$) in S if and only if, for every closed $\mathfrak{S}_i$ and $\mathfrak{S}_j$ with the full sentence $\mathfrak{S}_k$, the two classes specified below (and hence also their product) contain rs [are V_s, or, in other words, if and only if the condition A stated below is fulfilled]. (From T11-12, T10.)

r	CONNECTION	CLASSES	A
2	disjunction	$-(R_i + R_j) + R_k$ and $R_i + R_j + (-R_k)$	$R_k = R_i + R_j$
5	implication	$(R_i \times -R_j) + R_k$ and $-R_i + R_j + (-R_k)$	$R_k = -R_i + R_j$
7	equivalence	$(R_i \times -R_j) + (-R_i \times R_j) + R_k$ and	$R_k = (R_i \times R_j)$
		$(R_i \times R_j) + (-R_i \times -R_j) + (-R_k)$	$+ (-R_i \times -R_j)$
8	conjunction	$-(R_i \times R_j) + R_k$ and $(R_i \times R_j) + (-R_k)$	$R_k = R_i \times R_j$

+**T13-14a** [**b**]. A binary general connective $\mathfrak{a}_k$ is a sign of conjunction $_{[L]}$ in S if and only if, for every closed $\mathfrak{S}_i$ and $\mathfrak{S}_j$, $\mathfrak{a}_k(\mathfrak{S}_i,\mathfrak{S}_j)$ is [L-]equivalent to $\{\mathfrak{S}_i, \mathfrak{S}_j\}$. (From T13(8), [I] D20-1b, T11-6(2).)

The following theorem states the L-ranges of full sentences of some connections$_L$ in terms of the L-ranges of the components.

+**T13-15.** For any closed $\mathfrak{S}_i$ and $\mathfrak{S}_j$ in S, the following holds if S contains the connectives referred to:

    1. $Lr(neg_L(\mathfrak{S}_i)) = -R_i$. (From T5b(1).)

    2. $Lr(dis_L(\mathfrak{S}_i,\mathfrak{S}_j)) = R_i + R_j$. (From T13b(2).)

    3. $Lr(imp_L(\mathfrak{S}_i,\mathfrak{S}_j)) = -R_i + R_j$. (From T13b (5).)

    4. $Lr(equ_L(\mathfrak{S}_i,\mathfrak{S}_j)) = (R_i \times R_j) + (-R_i \times -R_j)$. (From T13b(7).)

    5. $Lr(con_L(\mathfrak{S}_i,\mathfrak{S}_j)) = R_i \times R_j$. (From T13b(8).)

+**T13-20a** [**b**]. For any closed $\mathfrak{S}_i$ and $\mathfrak{S}_j$ in S, the following holds if S contains the connectives referred to. [If S contains NTT, then the relations stated hold also for the L-concepts by NTT (D11-29 to 32).]

    1. $neg_{[L]}(\mathfrak{S}_i)$ is [L-]true if and only if $\mathfrak{S}_i$ is [L-]false.

    2. $neg_{[L]}(\mathfrak{S}_i)$ is [L-]false if and only if $\mathfrak{S}_i$ is [L-]true.

3. dis$_{[L]}(\mathfrak{S}_i,\mathfrak{S}_j)$ is [L-]true if and only if $\mathfrak{S}_i$ and $\mathfrak{S}_j$ are [L-]disjunct.

4. dis$_{[L]}(\mathfrak{S}_i,\mathfrak{S}_j)$ is [L-]false if and only if both $\mathfrak{S}_i$ and $\mathfrak{S}_j$ are [L-]false.

5. con$_{[L]}(\mathfrak{S}_i,\mathfrak{S}_j)$ is [L-]true if and only if both $\mathfrak{S}_i$ and $\mathfrak{S}_j$ (and hence $\{\mathfrak{S}_i,\ \mathfrak{S}_j\}$) are [L-]true.

6. con$_{[L]}(\mathfrak{S}_i,\mathfrak{S}_j)$ is [L-]false if and only if $\mathfrak{S}_i$ and $\mathfrak{S}_j$ are [L-]exclusive.

7. imp$_{[L]}(\mathfrak{S}_i,\mathfrak{S}_j)$ is [L-]true if and only if $\mathfrak{S}_i \xrightarrow{[L]} \mathfrak{S}_j$.

8. imp$_{[L]}(\mathfrak{S}_i,\mathfrak{S}_j)$ is [L-]false if and only if $\mathfrak{S}_i$ is [L-]true and $\mathfrak{S}_j$ [L-]false.

9. equ$_{[L]}(\mathfrak{S}_i,\mathfrak{S}_j)$ is [L-]true if and only if $\mathfrak{S}_i$ and $\mathfrak{S}_j$ are [L-]equivalent.

10. equ$_{[L]}(\mathfrak{S}_i,\mathfrak{S}_j)$ is [L-]false if and only if $\mathfrak{S}_i$ and $\mathfrak{S}_j$ are [L-]non-equivalent (and hence [L-]disjunct and [L-]exclusive).

Proof. (a) can easily be shown with the help of the characteristics of the connections involved, or, in other words, with the rules of NTT. — Proof for (b). Let the full sentence in each case be $\mathfrak{S}_k$. 1. $\mathfrak{S}_k$ is L-true if and only if R_k is V_s (D11-5), hence if and only if R_i is Λ_s (T5b(1)), hence if and only if $\mathfrak{S}_i$ is L-false (D11-6). 2. Likewise from D11-6, T5b(1), D11-5. 3. $\mathfrak{S}_k$ is L-true if and only if $R_k = V_s$, hence if and only if $R_i + R_j = V_s$ (T13b), hence if and only if $\mathfrak{S}_i$ and $\mathfrak{S}_j$ are L-disjunct ([I] D20-9). 4. $\mathfrak{S}_k$ is L-false if and only if $R_i + R_j = \Lambda_s$ (D11-6, T13b(2)), hence if and only if both R_i and R_j are Λ_s, hence if and only if both $\mathfrak{S}_i$ and $\mathfrak{S}_j$ are L-false. (5) from T14b. (6) from T14b, [I] D20-10. 7. $\mathfrak{S}_k$ is L-true if and only if $-R_i + R_j = V_s$ (T15(3)), hence if and only if $R_i \subset R_j$, hence if and only if $\mathfrak{S}_i \xrightarrow{L} \mathfrak{S}_j$ (D11-7). 8. $\mathfrak{S}_k$ is L-false if and only if $-R_i + R_j = \Lambda_s$ (T15(3)), hence if and only if $R_i = V_s$ and $R_j = \Lambda_s$, hence if and only if $\mathfrak{S}_i$ is L-true and $\mathfrak{S}_j$ L-false. 9. $\mathfrak{S}_k$ is L-true if and only if $(R_i \times R_j) + (-R_i \times -R_j) = V_s$ (T15(4)), hence if and only if $\mathfrak{S}_i$ and $\mathfrak{S}_j$ are L-equivalent (T11-6b(1)). 10. $\mathfrak{S}_k$ is L-false if and only if $(R_i \times R_j) + (-R_i \times -R_j) = \Lambda_s$ (T15(4)), hence if and only if $\mathfrak{S}_i$ and $\mathfrak{S}_j$ are L-non-equivalent (T11-7b(4)), and hence L-disjunct and L-exclusive (T11-7b(5)). — Since the relations hold for any components $\mathfrak{S}_i$ and $\mathfrak{S}_j$, they hold also for the L-concepts by NTT.

If S contains signs for the connections$_{[L]}$ involved, then theorem T20 gives sufficient and necessary conditions for certain radical, L-, and F-concepts, namely for (L-, F-) falsity (1), disjunctness (3), implication (7), and equivalence (9). This is the method of the so-called characteristic sentences, which has been previously explained ([I] § 22, especially T22-1 to 4) but can be exactly formulated only now that definitions for the connections have been given.

The parts (a) of the following theorems T25 to T28 are quite elementary and well-known. They can easily be proved with the help of truth-tables (i.e. on the basis of the semantical rules of NTT). Therefore we refer in the proofs to the parts (b) only.

T13-25a [b]. If S contains the connectives referred to, each of the following sentences is [L-]*true* in S for any closed $\mathfrak{S}_m$ [and, moreover, L-true by NTT, if S contains NTT]:

    1. $\text{dis}_{[L]}(\mathfrak{S}_m, \text{neg}_{[L]}(\mathfrak{S}_m))$.

    2. $\text{dis}_{[L]}(\text{neg}_{[L]}(\mathfrak{S}_m), \mathfrak{S}_m)$.

Proof for b. For each of the sentences stated, the L-range can easily be found to be V_s, with the help of T15. Therefore, the sentence is L-true (D11-5). For example, the L-range for (1) is found to be $R_m + -R_m$, which is V_s. If S contains NTT, then each of the sentences is, moreover, L-true by NTT (D11-30) because it is L-true for any $\mathfrak{S}_m$.

T13-26a [b]. If S contains the connectives referred to, then in each of the following cases $\mathfrak{T}_i$ [L-]*implies* $\mathfrak{T}_j$ for any closed $\mathfrak{S}_m$ and $\mathfrak{S}_n$ [and, moreover, $\mathfrak{T}_i$ L-implies $\mathfrak{T}_j$ by NTT if S contains NTT].

	$\mathfrak{T}_i$	$\mathfrak{T}_j$
1.	$\mathfrak{S}_m$	$\text{dis}_{[L]}(\mathfrak{S}_m, \mathfrak{S}_n)$
2.	$\mathfrak{S}_n$	$\text{dis}_{[L]}(\mathfrak{S}_m, \mathfrak{S}_n)$
3.	$\text{con}_{[L]}(\mathfrak{S}_m, \mathfrak{S}_n)$	$\mathfrak{S}_m$
4.	$\text{con}_{[L]}(\mathfrak{S}_m, \mathfrak{S}_n)$	$\mathfrak{S}_n$

Proof for b. In each case, by determining the L-ranges with the help of T15 and T11-1, it is easily found that $R_i \subset R_j$; therefore,

$\mathfrak{T}_i \overrightarrow{\underset{L}{}} \mathfrak{T}_j$ (D11-7). For instance, in (1), $R_i = R_m$, $R_j = R_m + R_n$ (T15(2)). For L-implication by NTT, see D11-29.

T13-27a [b]. If S contains the connectives referred to, then in each of the following cases $\mathfrak{T}_i$ and $\mathfrak{T}_j$ are [*L-*]*equivalent* for any closed $\mathfrak{S}_m$ and $\mathfrak{S}_n$ [and, moreover, L-equivalent by NTT if S contains NTT].

	$\mathfrak{T}_i$	$\mathfrak{T}_j$
1.	$neg_{[L]}(neg_{[L]}(\mathfrak{S}_m))$	$\mathfrak{S}_m$
2.	$imp_{[L]}(\mathfrak{S}_m, \mathfrak{S}_n)$	$dis_{[L]}(neg_{[L]}(\mathfrak{S}_m), \mathfrak{S}_n)$
3.	$con_{[L]}(\mathfrak{S}_m, \mathfrak{S}_n)$	$\{\mathfrak{S}_m, \mathfrak{S}_n\}$

Proof for b. In each case with the help of T15 and T11-1, it is found that $R_i = R_j$; therefore, $\mathfrak{T}_i$ and $\mathfrak{T}_j$ are L-equivalent (D11-8). For instance, in (1), $R_i = -(-R_m) = R_m$, $R_j = R_m$. For L-equivalence by NTT, see D11-32.

T13-28a [b]. If S contains the connectives referred to, the sentence $con_{[L]}(\mathfrak{S}_m, neg_{[L]}(\mathfrak{S}_m))$ is [*L-*]*false* for any closed $\mathfrak{S}_m$ [and, moreover, L-false by NTT if S contains NTT].

Proof for b. The L-range of the sentence is $R_m \times -R_m$, hence Λ, (T15). Therefore the sentence is L-false (D11-6). For L-falsity by NTT, see D11-31.

T13-31a [b]. Let S contain a singulary general connective α_k and signs of equivalence $_{[L]}$ and implication $_{[L]}$. Then each of the following conditions is a necessary and sufficient condition for α_k to be [*L-*]*extensional*:

1. For any closed $\mathfrak{S}_i$ and $\mathfrak{S}_i'$ with the full sentences $\mathfrak{S}_k$ and $\mathfrak{S}_k'$, $equ_{[L]}(\mathfrak{S}_i, \mathfrak{S}_i') \overrightarrow{\underset{[L]}{}} equ_{[L]}(\mathfrak{S}_k, \mathfrak{S}_k')$.

2. For any $\mathfrak{S}_i$, $\mathfrak{S}_i'$, $\mathfrak{S}_k$, and $\mathfrak{S}_k'$ as in (1), $imp_{[L]}(equ_{[L]}(\mathfrak{S}_i, \mathfrak{S}_i'), equ_{[L]}(\mathfrak{S}_k, \mathfrak{S}_k'))$ is [*L-*]true.

(1) holds analogously for a binary connective, with $\{equ_{[L]}(\mathfrak{S}_i, \mathfrak{S}_i'), equ_{[L]}(\mathfrak{S}_j, \mathfrak{S}_j')\} \overrightarrow{\underset{[L]}{}} equ_{[L]}(\mathfrak{S}_k, \mathfrak{S}_k')$.

Proof. a(1). α_k is extensional if and only if $\mathfrak{S}_i$ and $\mathfrak{S}_i'$ are not equivalent or $\mathfrak{S}_k$ and $\mathfrak{S}_k'$ are equivalent (T12-1), hence if and only

if equ($\mathfrak{S}_i,\mathfrak{S}'_i$) is false (T20a(10)) or equ($\mathfrak{S}_k,\mathfrak{S}'_k$) is true (T20a(9)),
hence if and only if equ($\mathfrak{S}_i,\mathfrak{S}'_i$) → equ($\mathfrak{S}_k,\mathfrak{S}'_k$) ([I] (D9-3)). — b(1).
$\mathfrak{a}_k$ is L-extensional if and only if (($R_i \times R'_i$) + ($-R_i \times -R'_i$)) ⊂
(($R_k \times R'_k$) + ($-R_k \times -R'_k$)) (T12-2b(1)), hence if and only if
Lr(equ$_L$($\mathfrak{S}_i,\mathfrak{S}'_i$)) ⊂ Lr(equ$_L$($\mathfrak{S}_k,\mathfrak{S}'_k$)) (T15(4)), hence if and only if
equ($\mathfrak{S}_i,\mathfrak{S}'_i$) $\underset{L}{\rightarrow}$ equ($\mathfrak{S}_k,\mathfrak{S}'_k$) (D11-7). — a[b](2) from a[b](1), T20a
[b](7).

T13-32a [b]. Let S contain a singulary general connective $\mathfrak{a}_k$ and a sign of equivalence$_{[L]}$. $\mathfrak{a}_k$ is [L-]non-extensional if and only if there are closed $\mathfrak{S}_i$ and $\mathfrak{S}'_i$, with full sentences of $\mathfrak{a}_k$ $\mathfrak{S}_k$ and $\mathfrak{S}'_k$, such that equ$_{[L]}$($\mathfrak{S}_i,\mathfrak{S}'_i$) is [L-]true and equ$_{[L]}$($\mathfrak{S}_k,\mathfrak{S}'_k$) is [L-]false. (From T12-3, T20(9) and (10).) Analogously for a binary connective.

T13-35a [b]. Let S contain a sign of negation$_{[L]}$. Then, for any closed $\mathfrak{S}_i$ and $\mathfrak{S}'_i$ with full sentences of negation$_{[L]}$ $\mathfrak{S}_k$ and $\mathfrak{S}'_k$, the following holds:

1. $\mathfrak{S}'_k \underset{[L]}{\rightarrow} \mathfrak{S}_k$ if and only if $\mathfrak{S}_i \underset{[L]}{\rightarrow} \mathfrak{S}'_i$.

2. $\mathfrak{S}_k$ and $\mathfrak{S}'_k$ are [L-]equivalent if and only if $\mathfrak{S}_i$ and $\mathfrak{S}'_i$ are [L-]equivalent.

Proof. a(1). From rules N1 and 2 in NTT, and [I] D9-3. — b(1). From T15(1), D11-7. — (2) from (1).

T13-38a [b]. Let S contain a sign of disjunction$_{[L]}$. For any closed $\mathfrak{S}_i$, $\mathfrak{S}'_i$, $\mathfrak{S}_j$ in S, if $\mathfrak{S}_i \underset{[L]}{\rightarrow} \mathfrak{S}'_i$ then dis$_{[L]}$($\mathfrak{S}_i$, $\mathfrak{S}_j$) $\underset{[L]}{\rightarrow}$ dis$_{[L]}$($\mathfrak{S}'_i,\mathfrak{S}_j$). (a. From rules Dj1 to 4 in NTT. — b. From T15(2), D11-7.)

T13-39. Let S contain a sign of disjunction$_L$. Let $\mathfrak{S}'_i$, $\mathfrak{S}_j$ and the sentences of $\mathfrak{K}_i$ be closed. Let $\mathfrak{K}_k$ be the class constructed out of $\mathfrak{K}_i$ by replacing each sentence $\mathfrak{S}_m$ in $\mathfrak{K}_i$ by dis$_L$($\mathfrak{S}_m,\mathfrak{S}_j$). If $\mathfrak{K}_i \underset{L}{\rightarrow} \mathfrak{S}'_i$, then $\mathfrak{K}_k \underset{L}{\rightarrow}$ dis$_L$($\mathfrak{S}'_i,\mathfrak{S}_j$).

Proof. R_k is the product of the classes $R_m + R_j$, one for each sentence $\mathfrak{S}_m$ in $\mathfrak{K}_i$ (T15(2)). Hence, $R_k = R_i + R_j$. If $\mathfrak{K}_i \underset{L}{\rightarrow} \mathfrak{S}'_i$, $R_i \subset R'_i$ (D11-7), hence $R_i + R_j \subset R'_i + R_j$, hence $\mathfrak{K}_k \underset{L}{\rightarrow}$ dis$_L$($\mathfrak{S}'_i,\mathfrak{S}_j$).

C. INTERPRETATIONS OF PC

The possibilities of true interpretations for PC are examined. The system NTT is an L-true interpretation for PC. It is called the normal interpretation for PC (§ 14). The analysis leads to the result that there are two kinds of true non-normal interpretations for PC (§§ 15–17). Therefore, PC is not a full formalization of propositional logic (§ 18).

§ 14. NTT as an L-true Interpretation for PC

The well-known fact that the two customary methods for dealing with the propositional connectives — PC and NTT — lead to the same results is here formulated and proved in our terminology. It is shown that, under certain conditions, a system S containing NTT is an L-true interpretation for a calculus K containing PC (T4).

In this chapter, C, we shall discuss the possible true interpretations of PC, or, more precisely, of the propositional connectives of PC. We shall leave aside here the problem of the interpretation of the propositional variables, although with respect to C-extensional calculi ([I] D31-18), which are most frequently used, it is rather simple. [For the semantics of variables in general, see [I] § 11. It is planned to discuss the problem of interpretations for propositional variables in a later volume, in connection with the discussion of extensional and non-extensional systems.] Therefore, the discussion in this chapter will refer only to calculi containing PC without propositional variables. [As we have seen in § 10, the truth-tables apply only to closed sentences and therefore not to forms of PC with propositional variables.] For the sake of simplicity, we refer in this chapter only to the forms PC_1 and PC_1^D. On the basis of the definitions in § 4, the results hold likewise for any other form of PC.

The following theorem, T1, says in effect that the definitions of other connectives on the basis of neg_C and dis_C in PC_1^D, as described in the table in § 3, are in agreement with NTT.

T14-1 (lemma). Let K contain PC_1. Let S contain the sentences of K and contain NTT (D11-26) in such a way that the signs neg_C ('$\sim$') and dis_C ('$\vee$') in K are simultaneously the signs of negation$_L$ and disjunction$_L$ in NTT in S. Let $\mathfrak{S}_q^1$ be the sentence given for $_c Conn_q^1$ ($q = 1$ to 4) in column (5) of the table of connections in § 3, and likewise $\mathfrak{S}_r^2$ that for $_c Conn_r^2$ ($r = 1$ to 16), the components $\mathfrak{S}_i$ and $\mathfrak{S}_j$ being any closed sentences in K. Then $\mathfrak{S}_q^1$ and $\mathfrak{b}_q(\mathfrak{S}_i)$ are L-equivalent by NTT in S, and likewise $\mathfrak{S}_r^2$ and $\mathfrak{c}_r(\mathfrak{S}_i, \mathfrak{S}_j)$.

This theorem is well-known. It can easily be verified by showing with the help of truth-tables that in each case the two sentences have the same L-characteristic. On the basis of our definitions, it can be shown by determining the L-ranges of the two sentences; it turns out that they are identical, and hence the sentences L-equivalent (D11-8). Thus e.g. for $r = 5$, $Lr(dis(neg(\mathfrak{S}_i), \mathfrak{S}_j)) = -R_i + R_j$ (T13-15(1) and (2)); and likewise $Lr(imp(\mathfrak{S}_i, \mathfrak{S}_j)) = -R_i + R_j$ (T13-15(3)). Since the two sentences are L-equivalent whatever the components $\mathfrak{S}_i$ and $\mathfrak{S}_j$ may be, they are L-equivalent by NTT (D11-32).

The following theorem, T2, says in effect that the rules of deduction in PC_1^D are in agreement with NTT. [It is to be noted that the conditions involve that all sentences in S be closed (C, D11-26), and hence also all sentences in K (B).]

T14-2 (lemma). Let K and S fulfill the following conditions:

A. K contains PC_1 or PC_1^D.

B. All sentences in K belong to S.

C. S contains NTT in such a way that the sign for a connection$_C$ of PC in K is simultaneously the sign for the corresponding connection$_L$ of NTT in S (i.e. $_c \mathfrak{b}_q$ in $K = \mathfrak{b}_q$ in S ($q = 1$ to 4), and $_c \mathfrak{c}_r$ in $K = \mathfrak{c}_r$ in S ($r = 1$ to 16).

Then the following holds:

a. If $\mathfrak{S}_i$ is a primitive sentence in K in virtue of (the primitive sentence schemata of) PC_1, then $\mathfrak{S}_i$ is L-true by NTT in S.

b. If $\mathfrak{R}_k \underset{dC}{\rightrightarrows} \mathfrak{S}_j$ in virtue of the rule of inference of PC_1, then $\mathfrak{R}_k \underset{L}{\rightrightarrows} \mathfrak{S}_j$ by NTT in S.

c. If $\mathfrak{S}_i \underset{dC}{\rightrightarrows} \mathfrak{S}_j$ in virtue of one of the definition rules of PC_1^D, then $\mathfrak{S}_i \underset{L}{\rightrightarrows} \mathfrak{S}_j$ by NTT in S.

The proofs are well-known. They can easily be given by an analysis of each of the rules of deduction in PC_1^D. They are usually given on the basis of the truth-tables NTT. On the basis of our definitions, they are given by determining the L-ranges with the help of T13-15(1) and (2).

a. For every primitive sentence, the L-range is V_s. — b. If $\mathfrak{R}_k \underset{dC}{\rightrightarrows} \mathfrak{S}_j$ according to D2-2b(5), then $R_k = R_i \times (-R_i + R_j)$ (T11-1) $= R_i \times R_j$; hence $R_k \subset R_j$; hence $\mathfrak{R}_k \underset{L}{\rightrightarrows} \mathfrak{S}_j$ (D11-7). — c. From T1. — The L-concepts hold by NTT (D11-30 and 29) because they hold for any components.

+T14-3. Let K and S fulfill the three conditions (A) to (C) in T2. Then the following holds:

a. If $\mathfrak{T}_i \underset{C}{\rightrightarrows} \mathfrak{T}_j$ in K by PC (i.e. either PC_1 or PC_1^D), $\mathfrak{T}_i \underset{L}{\rightrightarrows} \mathfrak{T}_j$ by NTT in S. (From T2.)

b. If $\mathfrak{T}_i$ is C-true in K by PC, $\mathfrak{T}_i$ is L-true by NTT in S. (From (a).)

+T14-4. Let K and S fulfill the following conditions:

A, B, C, as in T2.

D. K does not contain other rules of deduction than those of PC_1 or PC_1^D.

Then S is an *L-true interpretation* for K.

Proof. From T3a and [I] D34-1, because K does not contain rules of refutation (D).

+T14-5. Let K and S fulfill the following conditions:

A, B, C, as in T2.

D. K contains all sentences of S.

Let $\Re_i$ be non-empty and finite, and $\mathfrak{T}_i$ and $\mathfrak{T}_j$ be finite. Then the following holds:

    a. If $\mathfrak{S}_j$ is L-true by NTT in S, then $\mathfrak{S}_j$ is provable and hence C-true by PC (D4-2) in K.

    b. If $\Re_i \underset{L}{\rightarrow} \mathfrak{S}_j$ by NTT in S, then $\mathfrak{S}_j$ is derivable from $\Re_i$ and hence a C-implicate of $\Re_i$ by PC in K.

    c. If $\mathfrak{T}_i \underset{L}{\rightarrow} \mathfrak{T}_j$ by NTT in S, then $\mathfrak{T}_i \underset{C}{\rightarrow} \mathfrak{T}_j$ by PC in K.

Proof. **a.** As is well-known, a proof for $\mathfrak{S}_j$ in K under the conditions stated can be constructed with the help of the conjunctive normal form (see Hilbert [Logik] Kap. I, § 3). — **b.** Let $\mathfrak{S}_i$ be a sentence constructed so as to be C-equivalent to $\Re_i$ by PC in K (e.g. a conjunction$_C$ of the sentences of $\Re_i$). Then $\mathfrak{S}_i$ is L-equivalent to $\Re_i$ by NTT in S (T3a). Hence, if the condition in (b) is fulfilled, $\mathfrak{S}_i \underset{L}{\rightarrow} \mathfrak{S}_j$ by NTT. Therefore, imp$_L(\mathfrak{S}_i,\mathfrak{S}_j)$ is L-true by NTT in S (T13-20b(7)). Hence likewise dis$_L$(neg$_L(\mathfrak{S}_i),\mathfrak{S}_j)$ is L-true by NTT in S (T13-27b(2)) and C-true in K (a). It is the same sentence as dis$_C$(neg$_C(\mathfrak{S}_i),\mathfrak{S}_j)$ (C). Therefore, $\mathfrak{S}_i \underset{C}{\rightarrow} \mathfrak{S}_j$ in K (T7-1), and $\Re_i \underset{C}{\rightarrow} \mathfrak{S}_j$ in K. — **c.** If $\mathfrak{T}_i$ is a non-empty, finite $\Re_i$, and $\mathfrak{T}_j$ is $\mathfrak{S}_j$, the assertion is the same as (b). If $\mathfrak{T}_i$ is Λ, and $\mathfrak{T}_j$ is $\mathfrak{S}_j$, and $\mathfrak{T}_i \underset{L}{\rightarrow} \mathfrak{T}_j$ by NTT, then $\mathfrak{T}_j$ is L-true by NTT in S (D11-30) and hence C-true in K (a); therefore $\mathfrak{T}_i \underset{C}{\rightarrow} \mathfrak{T}_j$ in K. If $\mathfrak{T}_j$ is $\Re_j$, and $\mathfrak{T}_i \underset{L}{\rightarrow} \mathfrak{T}_j$ by NTT, then for every sentence $\mathfrak{S}_k$ of $\Re_j$, $\mathfrak{T}_i \underset{L}{\rightarrow} \mathfrak{S}_k$ by NTT, and hence $\mathfrak{T}_i \underset{C}{\rightarrow} \mathfrak{S}_k$ in K. Therefore $\mathfrak{T}_i \underset{C}{\rightarrow} \mathfrak{T}_j$ in K ([I] T29-40).

T5c shows that, under the conditions stated, K is an *L-exhaustive calculus* for S ([I] D36-3) as far as C-implication among finite $\mathfrak{T}$ is concerned (i.e. leaving aside infinite classes and L-falsity).

In the customary terminology, PC is said to be a *complete* calculus. This is sometimes meant in the sense that every sentence which is L-true by NTT ("tautology") is C-true ("provable") (T5a), sometimes in the sense that, in the form of PC with propositional variables as the only ultimate components (see § 2 at the end and § 4 at the end), every sentence is either C-true ("provable") or C-comprehen-

sive (usually called "refutable"). For proofs of completeness in the one
or the other sense, see Quine, *Journ. Symb. Log.*, vol. 3, 1938, pp. 37ff,
and his references to other authors: Post (1921), Hilbert and Ackermann (1928), Lukasiewicz (1931), Hilbert and Bernays (1934), Kalmar
(1935), Hermes and Scholz (1937). We shall see later that, in a stricter
sense of completeness, PC is not complete.

§ 15. Non-Normal Interpretations of Signs of Negation$_C$ and Disjunction$_C$

The concepts of normal and L-normal interpretations for the
connectives in a calculus are defined with the help of NTT (D1).
It is shown that, under certain conditions, if a calculus contains two signs for the same connection$_C$ and the first has a
normal or L-normal interpretation, then the second has, too
(T1 and 2). (This result might mislead us into the erroneous
assumption that non-normal interpretations are impossible.)
A non-normal interpretation of a connective would involve the
violation of a truth-table. Therefore, the consequences of supposed violations of the single rules in NTT for disjunction (Dj1
to 4, § 10) and negation (N1 and 2) are examined. Some of the
results: Dj1, 2, and 3 are generally satisfied (T4); if N1 is once
violated, then it is always violated and all sentences are true
(T5); if N2 is once violated, then the sign of negation$_C$ is non-
extensional (T7); if Dj4 is once violated, then the signs of dis-
junction$_C$ and negation$_C$ are non-extensional (T8).

We have already defined the syntactical concepts of signs
for connections$_C$ in a calculus, e.g. 'sign of disjunction$_C$ in
K', and the semantical concepts of signs for connections in
a semantical system, e.g. 'sign of disjunction (or disjunc-
tion$_L$) in *S*'. Now we shall define a related concept which —
like the concept of interpretation — refers both to a calculus
and to a semantical system and hence belongs neither to
syntax nor to semantics but to the combined field which we
have called the theory of systems (compare [I] § 5 at the end
and § 37). If, for instance, a_k is a sign of disjunction$_C$ in *K*
and simultaneously a sign of disjunction (or of disjunction$_L$)

in a true (or L-true) interpretation S for K, then we shall say that a_k has a normal (or L-normal, respectively) interpretation in S. D1 formulates this for connections in general.

+**D15-1a [b]**. The connective a_k in K has an [L-]**normal interpretation** in S $=_{Df}$ S is an [L-]true interpretation for K; a_k is a sign for $_c\text{Conn}_q^1$ or $_c\text{Conn}_r^2$ in K (D4-3) and simultaneously a sign for the corresponding connection $_{[L]}$ $_{[L]}\text{Conn}_q^1$ or $_{[L]}\text{Conn}_r^2$ in S (D11-23a [b]).

We shall now show that under certain conditions, if one sign for a certain connection in K has an [L-]normal interpretation in S, then the same holds for any other sign for the same connection in K (T1 and 2).

+**T15-1a [b]**. Let K fulfill the following conditions:

> **A**, as in T8-9 (two signs of negation$_C$, neg$_{C1}$ and neg$_{C2}$).
>
> **B** and **C**, as in T6-10.

Then the following holds: If neg$_{C1}$ has an [L-]normal interpretation in S, then also neg$_{C2}$.

Proof for a [b]. Let the conditions be fulfilled and $\mathfrak{S}_i$ be a closed sentence in K. Then neg$_{C1}(\mathfrak{S}_i)$ and neg$_{C2}(\mathfrak{S}_i)$ are C-equivalent in K (T8-9a). Since S is an [L-]true interpretation for K (D1), the two sentences are [L-]equivalent in S ([I], T33[34]-8g). Since neg$_{C1}$ has an [L-]normal interpretation, it is a sign of negation$_{[L]}$ in S (D1). Therefore, neg$_{C2}$ is also a sign of negation$_{[L]}$ in S (T11-17) and hence has an [L-]normal interpretation.

+**T15-2a [b]**. Let K fulfill the following conditions:

> **A.** K contains two sub-calculi K_m and K_n, both containing PC_1^D.
>
> **B** and **C**, as in T6-10.
>
> **D.** a_m and a_n are connectives for the same connection$_C$ of PC_1^D in K_m and K_n, respectively.

Then the following holds: If a_m in K has an [L-]normal interpretation in S, then a_n likewise. (From T9-4a, T11-17, in analogy to T1.)

We shall now study the question of the possibility of non-normal interpretations for the connectives of PC. If we try to answer this question without closer investigation, we might be tempted to guess a negative answer. It will be shown that for conjunction$_c$ a non-normal interpretation is indeed impossible. And we might perhaps believe that if a non-normal interpretation for another connection were possible, then in a calculus containing two connectives for this connection one could be interpreted normally and the other non-normally. Our previous result that this latter case cannot occur (T1 and 2) might thus lead us to the assumption that non-normal interpretations are impossible. These considerations, however, turn out to be erroneous; we shall find non-normal interpretations.

Let K contain PC_1 or PC_1^D and α_k be a sign for the connection $_c\text{Conn}_r^2$ in K. Let S be a true interpretation of K such that the following is the case (provided this is possible; that will be discussed later): α_k is not a sign for Conn_r^2 in S and hence has a *non-normal interpretation* in S (D1). Then at least one rule for Conn_r^2, represented by a line in the truth-table for this connection, will be violated by α_k in S in at least one instance, i.e. with respect to at least one pair of closed sentences as components. This violation of a normal truth-table by α_k is not necessarily such that α_k has another truth-table in S. Let us suppose that a certain rule for Conn_r^2 in NTT states the value F for the value distribution TF of the components. Then it may happen that for some instance with the values TF the full sentence of α_k is indeed false, while for another instance with the same values TF it is true. If this happens, α_k has no truth-table in S, neither the normal nor another one; the truth-value of a full sentence of α_k is not a function of the truth-values of the components; α_k is *non-extensional* (D12-2, T12-6).

In order to find possible non-normal interpretations for

signs of negation$_C$ and disjunction$_C$, we shall now study the possibilities of a violation for each of the rules for disjunction (Dj1 to 4) and negation (N1 and 2) in NTT, and analyze the consequences of these violations. It will first be shown that Dj1, 2, and 3 cannot be violated (T4). Then Dj4, N1, and N2 will be analyzed.

As has been remarked previously, we must distinguish between the concepts 'sign of negation$_C$ in K' and 'sign of negation (or negation$_L$) in S', the first being syntactical, the second and third semantical. This distinction is of especial importance in the cases now to be studied, where rules of NTT are violated. If a sign of negation$_C$ in K violates in S one of the rules N1 and N2, then it is not a sign of negation in S.

For some of the theorems in this and the following sections, we state two procedures for the proof, marked by 'I' and 'II'. Procedure I is rather simple; it is based on the formulation of the rules of NTT (e.g. Dj1 to 4) as given in § 10. Procedure II is more exact and more technical; it is based on the definitions in § 11 in terms of L-range. I applies only to radical concepts; if a theorem refers both to radical and to L-concepts (usually by 'a [b]'), then II applies to both. The results concerning non-normal interpretations will be chiefly in radical terms. Therefore a reader who is chiefly interested in those results and not in the general theory of true and L-true interpretations of PC, and who wants to travel an easy road to these results without technicalities, may skip part II in the proofs.

T15-4a [b]. Let K contain PC$_1$. Let S be any [L-]true interpretation for K. Then dis$_C$ in K [L-]satisfies generally the rules Dj1, 2, and 3 of NTT.

Proof for a [b]. Let $\mathfrak{S}_i$ and $\mathfrak{S}_j$ be any closed sentences in K, and $\mathfrak{S}_k$ be dis$_C(\mathfrak{S}_i,\mathfrak{S}_j)$. Then $\mathfrak{S}_k$ is a C-implicate in K both of $\mathfrak{S}_i$ and of $\mathfrak{S}_j$ (T5-2b, c), and hence an [L-]implicate in S both of $\mathfrak{S}_i$ and of $\mathfrak{S}_j$

([I] T33[34]-8e). I, for (a). Therefore, if $\mathfrak{S}_i$ is true in S, $\mathfrak{S}_k$ is true ([I] T9-10); thus Dj1 and Dj2 are generally satisfied (T11-11). And if $\mathfrak{S}_j$ is true, $\mathfrak{S}_k$ is true; thus Dj3 is generally satisfied. — II, for a [b]. Since $\mathfrak{S}_i \underset{[L]}{\rightrightarrows} \mathfrak{S}_k$ in S, $-R_i + R_k$ contains rs [is V_s] ([I] T20-28[10]). Likewise, $-R_j + R_k$ contains rs [is V_s]. Hence, also $-R_i + (-R_j) + R_k$, $-R_i + R_j + R_k$, and $R_i + (-R_j) + R_k$ contain rs [are V_s]. Therefore, disc has the [L-]characteristic value T for the first, second, and third distribution in S (D11-16). Since the first, second, and third values in the characteristic of disjunction are T (see column (5) in the table in § 10), disc [L-]satisfies generally Dj1, 2, and 3 (D11-17).

T15-5. Let us suppose that K and S fulfill the following conditions (without asserting that this is possible):

A. K contains PC_1.

B. S is a true interpretation for K.

C. negc in K violates the rule N1 of NTT at least once in S, say with respect to $\mathfrak{S}_1$.

Then the following holds:

a. Both $\mathfrak{S}_1$ and negc$(\mathfrak{S}_1)$ are true.

b. Every sentence of K is true in S.

c. negc always violates N1.

d. N2 is not violated by negc, nor Dj2, 3, and 4 by disc; but these rules have no instances of application.

Proof. I. a. N1 (§ 10) applied to negc says that, if $\mathfrak{S}_i$ is true in S, negc$(\mathfrak{S}_i)$ is false. Hence, the violation of N1 with respect to $\mathfrak{S}_1$ (C) means that both $\mathfrak{S}_1$ and negc$(\mathfrak{S}_1)$ are true. — b. $\{\mathfrak{S}_1, negc(\mathfrak{S}_1)\}$ is true ((a), [I] D9-1). Every sentence of K is a C-implicate of this class in K (T5-2l) and hence an implicate of it in S (B) and hence also true in S. — c. For every closed $\mathfrak{S}_i$ in K, both $\mathfrak{S}_i$ and negc$(\mathfrak{S}_i)$ are true in S (b); hence N1 is always violated. — d. From (b). — II. a. Since negc violates N1 with respect to $\mathfrak{S}_1$ (D11-15), $\mathfrak{S}_1$ has the first distribution, i.e. T (D10-2), and negc$(\mathfrak{S}_1)$ does not have the first value in the characteristic for negation, which is F; thus it too has T. — b. From (a) (as in I). — c. From (b). — d. From (b), T12-16a(4), T12-17a(4).

T15-6 (Corollary). If K contains PC_1 and S is a true interpretation for K and at least one sentence of K is false in S, then neg_C in K generally satisfies the rule N_I in S. (From T5b, T11-11.)

T15-7. Let us suppose that K and S fulfill the following conditions (without asserting that this is possible):

> **A** and **B**, as in T5.
>
> **C.** neg_C in K violates the rule N_2 of NTT at least once in S, say with respect to $\mathfrak{S}_1$; let $\mathfrak{S}_3$ be $dis_C(\mathfrak{S}_1, neg_C(\mathfrak{S}_1))$.

Then the following holds:

> **a.** Both $\mathfrak{S}_1$ and $neg_C(\mathfrak{S}_1)$ are false.
>
> **b.** neg_C in K generally satisfies N_I in S.
>
> **c.** $\mathfrak{S}_3$ is true.
>
> **d.** dis_C in K violates Dj4 with respect to $\mathfrak{S}_1$, $neg_C(\mathfrak{S}_1)$.
>
> **e.** $neg_C(\mathfrak{S}_3)$ is false.
>
> **f.** $neg_C(neg_C(\mathfrak{S}_3))$ is true.
>
> **g.** neg_C satisfies N_2 with respect to $neg_C(\mathfrak{S}_3)$.
>
> **h.** neg_C in K is non-extensional in S.
>
> **i.** If K, moreover, fulfills the conditions (B) and (C) in T6-10 and contains another sign of negation$_C$, neg'_C, then this sign too violates N_2 and is non-extensional in S.

Proof. a. From (C), in analogy to T5a. — b. From (a), T6. — c. $\mathfrak{S}_3$ is C-true in K (T5-1a), and hence true in S (B). — d. From (a), (c). — e. From (b), (c), (II: T11-11). — f. $neg_C(neg_C(\mathfrak{S}_3))$ is C-equivalent to $\mathfrak{S}_3$ in K (T5-3a), hence equivalent to it in S (B), and hence true (c). — g. From (e), (f). — h. From (g), (C), T12-6. — i. For any closed $\mathfrak{S}_i$, $neg_C(\mathfrak{S}_i)$ and $neg'_C(\mathfrak{S}_i)$ are C-equivalent in K (T8-9a) and hence equivalent in S (B). Therefore neg'_C satisfies and violates N_2 with respect to the same sentences as neg_C.

T15-8. Let us suppose that K and S fulfill the following conditions (without asserting that this is possible):

> **A** and **B**, as in T5.

    C. dis_C in K violates the rule Dj4 of NTT at least once in S, say with respect to $\mathfrak{S}_1$, $\mathfrak{S}_2$.

Then the following assertions (a) to (g) hold:

    a. Both $\mathfrak{S}_1$ and $\mathfrak{S}_2$ are false, $dis_C(\mathfrak{S}_1,\mathfrak{S}_2)$ is true.

    b. $\mathfrak{S}_1$ and $\mathfrak{S}_2$ are different.

    c. neg_C in K generally satisfies N1 in S.

    d. $neg_C(\mathfrak{S}_1)$ is false; hence, neg_C violates N2 with respect to $\mathfrak{S}_1$; the same holds for $\mathfrak{S}_2$.

    e. $dis_C(neg_C(\mathfrak{S}_1),\mathfrak{S}_2)$ is false; hence, dis_C satisfies Dj4 with respect to $neg_C(\mathfrak{S}_1)$, $\mathfrak{S}_2$; the same holds for $\mathfrak{S}_1$, $neg_C(\mathfrak{S}_2)$.

    f. dis_C in K is non-extensional in S.

    g. neg_C in K is non-extensional in S.

If K, moreover, fulfills the conditions (B) and (C) in T6-10, then, in addition, the following assertions (k) to (n) hold:

    k. If K contains another sign of $disjunction_C$, say dis'_C, then this sign, too, violates Dj4 and is non-extensional.

    l. If K contains another sign of $negation_C$, say neg'_C, this sign, too, violates N2 and is non-extensional.

    m. Every sentence $\mathfrak{S}_i$ which is a C-implicate in K both of $\mathfrak{S}_1$ and of $\mathfrak{S}_2$ is true in S.

    n. $\mathfrak{S}_2$ is not a C-implicate of $\mathfrak{S}_1$ in K; nor $\mathfrak{S}_1$ of $\mathfrak{S}_2$.

Proof. a. From (C), in analogy to T5a. — b. If $\mathfrak{S}_2$ were $\mathfrak{S}_1$, then $\mathfrak{S}_1$, being a C-implicate of $dis_C(\mathfrak{S}_1,\mathfrak{S}_1)$ in K (T5-2a), would be a C-implicate of $dis_C(\mathfrak{S}_1,\mathfrak{S}_2)$ in K and hence an implicate of this sentence in S (B), and hence true in S like this sentence (a). But $\mathfrak{S}_1$ is not true (a). Therefore $\mathfrak{S}_2$ must be different from $\mathfrak{S}_1$. — c. From (a), T6. — d. $\mathfrak{S}_2$ is a C-implicate of $\{dis_C(\mathfrak{S}_1,\mathfrak{S}_2), neg_C(\mathfrak{S}_1)\}$ in K (T5-2e) and hence an implicate of this class in S (B). $dis_C(\mathfrak{S}_1,\mathfrak{S}_2)$ is true (a); if now $neg_C(\mathfrak{S}_1)$ were true, the class mentioned would be true and hence $\mathfrak{S}_2$ too. But this is not the case (a). Therefore $neg_C(\mathfrak{S}_1)$ cannot be true and must be false. Since $\mathfrak{S}_1$ is false (a), N2 is violated. The reasoning for $neg_C(\mathfrak{S}_2)$ is analogous. — e. $\mathfrak{S}_2$ is a C-implicate of

$\{\mathrm{dis_C}(\mathfrak{S}_1,\mathfrak{S}_2), \mathrm{dis_C}(\mathrm{neg_C}(\mathfrak{S}_1),\mathfrak{S}_2)\}$ in K (T5-2h), and hence an implicate of this class in S (B). The first element of the class is true (a); if now the second were true, $\mathfrak{S}_2$ would be true; but it is not (a). Therefore, $\mathrm{dis_C}(\mathrm{neg_C}(\mathfrak{S}_1),\mathfrak{S}_2)$ must be false. Hence, Dj4 is satisfied in this case (d, a). The reasoning for $\mathrm{dis_C}(\mathfrak{S}_1,\mathrm{neg_C}(\mathfrak{S}_2))$ is analogous. — f. From (e), (C), T12-6. — g. From T7h because N2 is violated (d).

k. From (C), T7-4a (the proof is analogous to that of T7i). — l. From (d), T8-9a. — m. If $\mathfrak{S}_i$ is a C-implicate both of $\mathfrak{S}_1$ and of $\mathfrak{S}_2$, it is a C-implicate of $\mathrm{dis_C}(\mathfrak{S}_1,\mathfrak{S}_2)$ in K (T7-2b) and hence an implicate of this sentence in S (B) and hence true because $\mathrm{dis_C}(\mathfrak{S}_1,\mathfrak{S}_2)$ is true (a). — n. If $\mathfrak{S}_2$ were a C-implicate of $\mathfrak{S}_1$ in K it would be true in S (m). But it is not true (a). Analogously for $\mathfrak{S}_1$.

T15-9. Let K contain PC_1.

    a. If $\mathrm{neg_C}$ in K has a normal interpretation in S, then $\mathrm{dis_C}$ likewise.

    b. If $\mathrm{dis_C}$ in K has a normal interpretation in S and at least one sentence of K is false in S, then $\mathrm{neg_C}$ also has a normal interpretation in S.

Proof. a. Let $\mathrm{neg_C}$ have a normal interpretation in S. Then it is a sign of negation in S (D1) and hence does not violate N2 with respect to any sentence (T11-12a, T11-11). Therefore, $\mathrm{dis_C}$ does not violate Dj4 in any case (T8d) and hence generally satisfies Dj4 (T11-11). Further, $\mathrm{dis_C}$ generally satisfies Dj1 to 3 (T4). Hence, it is a sign of disjunction in S (T11-12a) and has a normal interpretation (D1). — b. Let the conditions be fulfilled. Then (in analogy to (a)) $\mathrm{dis_C}$ does not violate Dj4 in any case (D1, T11-12a, T11-11). Therefore, $\mathrm{neg_C}$ generally satisfies N2 (T7d, T11-11), and also N1 (T6). Hence, it is a sign of negation (T11-12a).

§ 16. Non-Normal Interpretations in General

The possibilities of non-normal (true) interpretations for all singular and binary connectives in PC are examined with the help of NTT (see table). It is found that the sign of conjunction$_C$ and some other less important connectives always (i.e. in any true interpretation for a calculus K containing PC$_1^D$) have a normal interpretation (T1). If the sign of negation$_C$ has a normal interpretation, then every other connective has too (T3). We distinguish two kinds of non-normal interpretations; in the first kind, every sentence (in K) is true (in S); in the second kind, at least one is false. For any case of the first kind, the following holds (T6; columns (5) to (7) of the table): the singular connectives nos. 1 and 2, and the binary nos. 1 through 8 have a normal interpretation, but the others have not; all connectives are extensional. For any case of the second kind, the following holds (T7, columns (8) to (10) of the table): the singular connectives nos. 1, 2, and 4 and the binary nos. 1, 4, 6, 8, and 16 have a normal interpretation; the others have a non-normal interpretation and are non-extensional.

So far, we have discussed the question of interpretations only for signs of negation$_C$ and disjunction$_C$. Now we shall examine other connectives in PC. In column (2), the table that follows lists again the connections$_C$ in a calculus K containing PC, as they were previously listed in the table in § 3. Column (3) here repeats column (5) of the previous table; it gives expressions for the connections$_C$ in PC$_1$, which are taken as definientia for the defined signs in PC$_1^D$ (D3-6) on the basis of neg$_C$ and dis$_C$. Column (4) repeats column (5) of the table in § 10; it gives the characteristics for the corresponding connections on the basis of the rules of NTT. Columns (5) to (10) give a survey of some of the results concerning non-normal interpretations, as stated in the subsequent theorems, especially T6 and 7.

(1)	(2)	(3)	(4)	(5)	(6)	(7)	(8)	(9)	(10)
				Non-Normal Interpretations					
				first kind (T6) (all sentences true)			*second kind* (T7) (not all sentences true)		
No.	Name of Connection$_C$ in K	Definiens for the Sign in K	Characteristic for the Sign in NTT	normal or not	which rule violated	extensional or not	normal or not	which rule violated	extensional or not
	I. The four singulary connections$_C$								
q									
1	tautology$_C$	$\mathfrak{S}_i \vee \sim \mathfrak{S}_i$	TT	n	–	e	n	–	e
2	(identity$_C$)	$\mathfrak{S}_i$	TF	n	–	e	n	–	e
3	negation$_C$	$\sim \mathfrak{S}_i$	FT	–	1	e	–	2	e
4	contradiction$_C$	$\sim(\mathfrak{S}_i \vee \sim \mathfrak{S}_i)$	FF	–	1	e	n	–	e
	II. The sixteen binary connections$_C$								
r									
1	tautology$_C$	$\mathfrak{S}_i \vee \sim \mathfrak{S}_i$	TTTT	n	–	e	n	–	e
2	disjunction$_C$	$\mathfrak{S}_i \vee \mathfrak{S}_j$	TTTF	n	–	e	–	4	–
3	(inverse implication$_C$)	$\mathfrak{S}_i \vee \sim \mathfrak{S}_j$	TTFT	n	–	e	–	4	–
4	(first component)	$\mathfrak{S}_i$	TTFF	n	–	e	n	–	e
5	implication$_C$	$\sim \mathfrak{S}_i \vee \mathfrak{S}_j$	TFTT	n	–	e	–	4	–
6	(second component)	$\mathfrak{S}_j$	TFTF	n	–	e	n	–	e
7	equivalence$_C$	$\sim(\mathfrak{S}_i \vee \sim \mathfrak{S}_j) \vee \sim(\mathfrak{S}_i \vee \mathfrak{S}_j)$	TFFT	n	–	e	–	4	–
8	conjunction$_C$	$\sim(\sim \mathfrak{S}_i \vee \sim \mathfrak{S}_j)$	TFFF	n	–	e	n	–	e
9	exclusion$_C$	$\sim \mathfrak{S}_i \vee \sim \mathfrak{S}_j$	FTTT	–	1	e	–	4	–
10	(non-equivalence$_C$)	$\sim(\sim \mathfrak{S}_i \vee \mathfrak{S}_j) \vee \sim(\mathfrak{S}_i \vee \sim \mathfrak{S}_j)$	FTTF	–	1	e	–	4	–
11	(negation$_C$ of second)	$\sim \mathfrak{S}_j$	FTFT	–	1	e	–	4	–
12	(first alone)	$\sim(\sim \mathfrak{S}_i \vee \mathfrak{S}_j)$	FTFF	–	1	e	–	2	–
13	(negation$_C$ of first)	$\sim \mathfrak{S}_i$	FFTT	–	1	e	–	4	–
14	(second alone)	$\sim(\mathfrak{S}_i \vee \sim \mathfrak{S}_j)$	FFTF	–	1	e	–	3	–
15	bi-negation$_C$	$\sim(\mathfrak{S}_i \vee \mathfrak{S}_j)$	FFFT	–	1	e	–	4	–
16	contradiction$_C$	$\sim(\mathfrak{S}_i \vee \sim \mathfrak{S}_i)$	FFFF	–	1	e	n	–	e

Conjunction$_C$ and disjunction$_C$ are often regarded as playing completely symmetrical roles in PC (the so-called duality). However, we now find (T1) that for con$_C$, in contradistinction to dis$_C$, only a normal interpretation is possible. Thus the supposed symmetry, although it is perfect within NTT, holds in PC only to a certain extent. The reason is that the rules of deduction in any of the ordinary forms of PC, in contradistinction to NTT, are in a certain sense incomplete with respect to disjunction$_C$ but not to conjunction$_C$. This will become clearer later.

+**T16-1a** [**b**]. Let K contain PC_1^D, and S be an [L-]true interpretation for K. Then each of the following connectives in K (see tables here and in § 3) is a sign for the corresponding connection$_{[L]}$ in S and hence has an [L-]normal interpretation in S:

1. Two singulary connectives: $_Cb_1$ and $_Cb_2$.
2. Four binary connectives: $_Cc_r$ for $r = 1$ (tautology$_C$), 4 (first component), 6 (second component), 8 (conjunction$_C$).

Proof for a [b]. 1. Let $\mathfrak{S}_i$ be any closed sentence in K, and $\mathfrak{S}_k$ be $_Cb_1(\mathfrak{S}_i)$. On the basis of the definition-rule for $_Cb_1$ (see D3-6), $\mathfrak{S}_k$ is C-equivalent in K to dis$_C(\mathfrak{S}_i, neg_C(\mathfrak{S}_i))$ (see column (3) of the table, line I1), and hence C-true in K like the latter sentence (T5-1a) and hence [L-]true in S. Therefore, R_k contains rs [is V_s], and hence likewise $-R_i + R_k$ and $R_i + R_k$. Therefore, $_Cb_1$ has T as the [L-] characteristic value both for the first and the second distribution (D11-16), and hence has TT as its [L-]characteristic (D11-21) and is a sign for $_{[L]}Conn_1^1$ (D11-23) and has an [L-]normal interpretation (D15-1). — Let $\mathfrak{S}_i$ be closed and $\mathfrak{S}_k$ be $_Cb_2(\mathfrak{S}_i)$. $\mathfrak{S}_k$ is C-equivalent in K (D3-6) and hence [L-]equivalent in S to $\mathfrak{S}_i$. Hence, both $-R_i + R_k$ and $R_i + (-R_k)$ contain rs [are V_s] (T11-6(2)). Therefore, $_Cb_2$ has T as the [L-]characteristic value for $t = 1$ and F for $t = 2$ (D11-16), and hence has TF as its [L-]characteristic (D11-21) and is a sign for $_{[L]}Conn_2^1$ (D11-23) and has an [L-]normal interpretation (D15-1). — 2. The proof for $_Cc_1$ is analogous to that for $_Cb_1$. The proofs for $_Cc_4$ and $_Cc_6$ are analogous to that for $_Cb_2$. — Proof for $_Cc_8$ (= con$_C$). Let

$\mathfrak{S}_i$ and $\mathfrak{S}_j$ be closed, and $\mathfrak{S}_k$ be $\text{conc}_\text{C}(\mathfrak{S}_i,\mathfrak{S}_j)$. $\mathfrak{S}_k$ and $\{\mathfrak{S}_i, \mathfrak{S}_j\}$ are C-equivalent in K (T5-3b) and hence [L-]equivalent in S. Therefore, conc_C is a sign of conjunction$_{[\text{L}]}$ in S (T13-14).

+T16-2a [b]. If K contains PC_1^D, and neg_C and dis_C in K have an [L-]normal interpretation in S, then every other connective of PC_1^D in K also has an [L-]normal interpretation in S.

Proof for $_\text{C}c_5$ ($= \text{imp}_\text{C}$); the proofs for the other connectives are similar. Let $\mathfrak{S}_i$ and $\mathfrak{S}_j$ be any closed sentences in K. Let $\mathfrak{S}_k$ be $\text{neg}_\text{C}(\mathfrak{S}_i)$, $\mathfrak{S}_k'$ be $\text{dis}_\text{C}(\mathfrak{S}_k,\mathfrak{S}_j)$, $\mathfrak{S}_p$ be $\text{imp}_\text{C}(\mathfrak{S}_i,\mathfrak{S}_j)$. (For 'I' and 'II', see remark preceding T15-4.) — I, for (a). $\mathfrak{S}_k'$ is true for the first, third, and fourth distribution, false for the second (this follows easily from the rules N1 and 2, Dj1 to 4). The same holds for $\mathfrak{S}_p$, since $\mathfrak{S}_p$ and $\mathfrak{S}_k'$ are C-equivalent in K according to the definition of imp_C (D3-6), and hence equivalent in S, which is a true interpretation for K (D15-1a). Therefore, imp_C has the characteristic TFTT and hence is a sign of implication in S and has a normal interpretation in S (D15-1a). — II, for a [b]. Each of the following classes contains rs [is V_s] (T13-5, T13-10(1) to (4)): $R_i + R_k$ (k$_1$), $-R_i + (-R_k)$ (k$_2$), $-R_k + (-R_j) + R_k'$ (k$_3$), $-R_k + R_j + R_k'$ (k$_4$), $R_k + (-R_j) + R_k'$ (k$_5$), $R_k + R_j + (-R_k')$ (k$_6$). $\mathfrak{S}_p$ and $\mathfrak{S}_k'$ are [L-]equivalent (see I); hence $R_p + (-R_k')$ (k$_7$) and $-R_p + R_k'$ (k$_8$) contain rs [are V_s] (T11-6(2)). Therefore each of the following classes also contains rs [is V_s]: $-R_i + (-R_j) + R_p$ ($= k_2 + k_5 + k_7$), $-R_i + R_j + (-R_p)$ ($= k_2 + k_6 + k_8$), $R_i + (-R_j) + R_p$ ($= k_1 + k_3 + k_7$), $R_i + R_j + R_p$ ($= k_1 + k_4 + k_7$). Hence, imp_C has the [L-]characteristic value T for $t = 1$ (D11-16), F for $t = 2$, T for $t = 3$, T for $t = 4$. Thus it has the [L-]characteristic TFTT (D11-21) and hence is a sign for $_{[\text{L}]}\text{Corr}_5^2$ ($= \text{implication}_{[\text{L}]}$) and has an [L-]normal interpretation in S (D15-1).

+T16-3. If K contains PC_1^D, and neg_C in K has a normal interpretation in S, then every other connective of PC_1^D in K also has a normal interpretation in S. (From T15-9a, T2a.)

+T16-4 (Corollary). If K contains PC_1^D, and dis_C in K has a normal interpretation in S, and at least one sentence of K is false in S, then every other connective of PC_1^D in K also has a normal interpretation in S. (From T15-9b, T3.)

On the basis of the previous discussion of non-normal interpretations for neg_C and dis_C we can now characterize in general the kinds of non-normal interpretations of connectives. There we found two kinds of cases where the rules of NTT for negation or disjunction are violated: there is either a violation of $N1$ alone (T15-5) or a simultaneous violation of $N2$ and $Dj4$ (T15-7 and 8). In a case of the first kind all sentences of K are true in S, while in a case of the second kind at least one is false. This difference yields a convenient way of defining the two kinds. Theorems T6 and 7, below, state some properties of cases of the two kinds without asserting the existence of such cases. These two kinds exhaust all possibilities for non-normal interpretations for any connective of PC in K. In columns (5) to (10) of the table, some of the results stated in T6 and 7 are listed.

+**T16-6.** Let K and S fulfill the following conditions (*non-normal interpretation of the first kind*):

    A. K contains PC_1^D.

    B. S is a true interpretation for K.

    C. All sentences of K are true in S.

Then the following holds:

    a. The following ten connectives in K do not have a normal interpretation in S: $_Cb_q$ for $q = 3$ and 4; $_Cc_r$ for $r = 9$ to 16.

    b. The other connectives in K have a normal interpretation in S: $_Cb_q$ for $q = 1$ and 2; $_Cc_r$ for $r = 1$ to 8.

    c. Every connective in K is extensional in S.
    (a. From T12-16a(7), T12-17a(7). b. Form T12-16a(6), T12-17a(6). c. From T12-16a(8), T12-17a(8).)

+**T16-7.** Let K and S fulfill the following conditions (*non-normal interpretation of the second kind*):

    A, B, as in T6.

C. At least one sentence of K is false in S.

D. At least one of the connectives of PC in K has not a normal interpretation in S.

Then the following holds:

a. An infinite number of sentences of K are false in S.

b. An infinite number of sentences of K are true in S.

c. neg_C in K violates N2, but generally satisfies N1.

d. neg_C in K is non-extensional.

e. The three other singulary connectives in K ($_C\mathfrak{b}_q$ for $q = 1, 2, 4$) have a normal interpretation in S.

f. The following eleven binary connectives $_C\mathfrak{c}_r$ in K violate a rule for Conn$_2^2$ in NTT and hence do not have a normal interpretation in S: $r = 2, 3, 5, 7, 9, 10, 11, 12, 13, 14, 15$. For $r = 2, 3, 5, 7, 9, 10, 11, 13, 15$, at least the fourth rule is violated; for $r = 12$, the second; for $r = 14$, the third.

g. The connectives of K mentioned in (f) are non-extensional in S.

h. The five other binary connectives in K ($_C\mathfrak{c}_r$ for $r = 1, 4, 6, 8, 16$) have a normal interpretation in S.

Proof. Let the conditions (A) to (D) be fulfilled. Then the following holds. — 1. neg_C generally satisfies N1 (T15-6). — 2. neg_C in K does not have a normal interpretation in S (C, T3). — 3. neg_C violates N2 at least once (1, 2), say with respect to $\mathfrak{S}_1$. — 4. $\mathfrak{S}_1$ and $neg_C(\mathfrak{S}_1)$ are false in S ((3), T15-7a). Let $\mathfrak{S}_3$ be $dis_C(\mathfrak{S}_1, neg_C(\mathfrak{S}_1))$, and $\mathfrak{S}_4$ be $dis_C(\mathfrak{S}_3, neg_C(\mathfrak{S}_3))$. — 5. $\mathfrak{S}_3$ is true (T15-7c). — 6. $neg_C(\mathfrak{S}_3)$ is false (T15-7e). — 7. $\mathfrak{S}_4$ is C-true in K (T5-1a) and hence true in S (B). — 8. $neg_C(\mathfrak{S}_4)$ is false in S (7, 1). — 9. An infinite number of sentences in K are C-equivalent to $\mathfrak{S}_1$ in K (e.g. $\mathfrak{S}_1$ with neg_C added $2n$ times),

hence equivalent to $\mathfrak{S}_1$ in S (B), hence false in S (4). This is (a). —
10. An infinite number of sentences are C-equivalent to $\mathfrak{S}_3$ in K and
hence true ((B), (5)). This is (b). — 11. (c) from (3), (1). — 12. (d)
from (3), T15-7h. — 13. For any closed sentence $\mathfrak{S}_i$ in K, $\mathrm{disc}(\mathfrak{S}_i,$
$\mathrm{neg}_C(\mathfrak{S}_i))$ is C-true in K (T5-1a) and hence true in S (B). $\mathrm{neg}_C(\mathrm{disc}(\mathfrak{S}_i,$
$\mathrm{neg}_C(\mathfrak{S}_i)))$ is false in S (1). $_C b_4(\mathfrak{S}_i)$ is C-equivalent in K and hence
equivalent in S to the sentence just mentioned (see column (3) of the
table, line I4) and hence is also false in S. Therefore, $_C b_4$ has the
characteristic value F both for $t = 1$ and $t = 2$, and hence the characteristic FF, and hence is a sign for Conn_4^1 in S (D11-23a) and has a
normal interpretation in S (D15-1a). — 14. (e) from T1a(1) and (13).
— 15. Let $_C\mathfrak{S}_r$ ($r = 1$ to 16) be $_C t_r(\mathfrak{S}_1, \mathrm{neg}_C(\mathfrak{S}_1))$. $_C\mathfrak{S}_r$ is C-equivalent
in K and hence equivalent in S to the sentence given in column (3) of
the table, but with $\mathfrak{S}_1$ instead of $\mathfrak{S}_i$ and $\mathrm{neg}_C(\mathfrak{S}_1)$ instead of $\mathfrak{S}_j$ ('$\sim$'
and '$\vee$' are neg_C and disc in K). Each of these sentences, in turn, can
easily be transformed (chiefly by virtue of T5-1 and 3) into a certain
other sentence which is C-equivalent to it in K and hence equivalent
to it in S. In this way we find (line II3 of the table) that $_C\mathfrak{S}_3$ is equiva-
lent in S to $\mathrm{disc}(\mathfrak{S}_1, \mathrm{neg}_C(\mathrm{neg}_C(\mathfrak{S}_1)))$ and further to $\mathfrak{S}_1$, and hence is
false in S (4); $_C\mathfrak{S}_5$ is equivalent to $\mathrm{neg}_C(\mathfrak{S}_1)$ and hence false (4); $_C\mathfrak{S}_7$ is
equivalent to $\mathrm{neg}_C(\mathfrak{S}_3)$ and hence false (6); $_C\mathfrak{S}_{10}$ is equivalent to $\mathfrak{S}_3$
and hence true (5); $_C\mathfrak{S}_{11}$ is equivalent to $\mathfrak{S}_1$ and hence false (4); $_C\mathfrak{S}_{13}$
is equivalent to $\mathrm{neg}_C(\mathfrak{S}_1)$ and hence false (4); $_C\mathfrak{S}_{15}$ is equivalent to
$\mathrm{neg}_C(\mathfrak{S}_3)$ and hence false (6). $\mathfrak{S}_1$ and $\mathrm{neg}_C(\mathfrak{S}_1)$ are both false (4) and
hence have the fourth distribution of values (D10-2). Therefore the
fourth characteristic value of $_C t_3$ is F (T11-10), since $_C\mathfrak{S}_3$ is false; the
same holds for $_C t_r$ with $r = 5, 7, 11, 13, 15$; but that for $_C t_{10}$ is T. —
16. The fourth value in the characteristic for Conn^2 for $r = 3, 5, 7, 11$,
13, 15 is T, that for Conn_{10}^2 is F. — 17. For $r = 3, 5, 7, 10, 11, 13, 15$,
$_C t_r$ violates the fourth rule for Conn_r^2 in S. — 18. $_C t_9(\mathfrak{S}_1, \mathfrak{S}_1)$ is equivalent to $\mathrm{neg}_C(\mathfrak{S}_1)$ (in analogy to (13)) and hence false (4). — 19. $\mathfrak{S}_1$
is false (4); hence $_C t_9$ (18) violates the fourth rule for Conn_9^2 (in analogy
to (15), (16), (17)). — 20. Let us analyze the sentences $_C t_r(\mathrm{neg}_C(\mathfrak{S}_3),$
$\mathrm{neg}_C(\mathfrak{S}_3))$, which we call $_C\mathfrak{S}_r'$. $_C\mathfrak{S}_3'$ is C-equivalent in K (in analogy
to (15)) and hence equivalent in S to $\mathfrak{S}_4$ and hence is true in S (7);
the same holds for $_C\mathfrak{S}_5'$ and $_C\mathfrak{S}_7'$; $_C\mathfrak{S}_9'$ is equivalent to $\mathfrak{S}_3$ and hence
true (5); the same holds for $_C\mathfrak{S}_{11}'$, $_C\mathfrak{S}_{13}'$, and $_C\mathfrak{S}_{15}'$; $_C\mathfrak{S}_{10}'$ is equivalent
to $\mathrm{neg}_C(\mathfrak{S}_4)$ and hence false (8). — 21. Since both components in
$_C\mathfrak{S}_r$ are false (6), they have the fourth value distribution. The fourth
value in the characteristic for Conn_r^2 for $r = 3, 5, 7, 9, 11, 13, 15$ is T,

that for $r = $ 10 is F. Thus, for $r = $ 3, 5, 7, 9, 10, 11, 13, 15, cc_r satisfies the fourth rule for Conn_r^2 with respect to the components mentioned. — 22. $cc_{12}(\mathfrak{S}_3,\mathfrak{S}_1)$ is equivalent to $\text{neg}_C(\text{dis}_C(\text{neg}_C(\mathfrak{S}_3),\mathfrak{S}_1))$ and further to $\text{neg}_C(\mathfrak{S}_1)$ and hence is false (4). — 23. Since $\mathfrak{S}_3$ is true (5) and $\mathfrak{S}_1$ is false (4), they have the second distribution. The second value in the characteristic for Conn_{12}^2 is T. Hence, cc_{12} (22) violates the second rule for Conn_{12}^2. — 24. $cc_{12}(\mathfrak{S}_3,\text{neg}_C(\mathfrak{S}_3))$ is equivalent to $\mathfrak{S}_3$ and hence is true (5). — 25. The components mentioned (24) have the second distribution. The second value in the characteristic for Conn_{12}^2 is T. Hence, cc_{12} satisfies the second rule for Conn_{12}^2 with respect to the components mentioned. — 26. $cc_{14}(\mathfrak{S}_1,\mathfrak{S}_3)$ is equivalent to $\text{neg}_C(\mathfrak{S}_1)$ and hence false (4). — 27. The third value in the characteristic for Conn_{14}^2 is T. Hence, cc_{14} violates the third rule for Conn_{14}^2 (26). — 28. $cc_{14}(\text{neg}_C(\mathfrak{S}_3),\mathfrak{S}_3)$ is equivalent to $\mathfrak{S}_3$ and hence true. (5). — 29. The third value for Conn_{14}^2 is T. Hence, cc_{14} satisfies the third rule for Conn_{14}^2 in this case (28). — 30. For each of the connectives cc_r for $r = $ 3, 5, 7, 9, 10, 11, 13, 15 in K, the fourth rule for the corresponding connection Conn_r^2 in NTT is sometimes violated (17, 19), sometimes satisfied (21). For cc_{12}, the second rule is sometimes violated (23), sometimes satisfied (25). For cc_{14}, the third rule is sometimes violated (27), sometimes satisfied (29). — 31. (f) from T15-7d (for $r = $ 2) and (30). — 32. (g): for $r = $ 2, from T15-7d and T15-8f; for the rest from (30) and T12-6. — 33. cc_{16} in K has a normal interpretation in S; the proof is analogous to that for cb_4 (13). — 34. (h) from T1a (2) and (33).

+T16-8. If K contains PC_1^D and one of the connectives cc_r for $r = $ 9 through 15 has a normal interpretation in S, then every other connective of PC_1^D in K also has a normal interpretation in S.

Proof. If one of the other connectives had a non-normal interpretation, then it would be a case either of the first or the second kind. In both cases all connectives mentioned would have a non-normal interpretation (T6a, T7f).

neg_C (T3) and the seven binary connectives mentioned in T8 are the only connectives of PC_1^D in K having the property stated in T8. Every other connective has a normal interpretation in at least one of the two kinds of non-normal interpretations (T6 and 7; compare columns (5) and (8) in the table).

§ 17. Examples of Non-Normal Interpretations

In § 16 two kinds of non-normal interpretations for the connectives in PC were studied without showing that these kinds are non-empty. This is shown here by the construction of examples for true and, moreover, L-true interpretations of both kinds.

The two kinds of non-normal interpretations for the connectives of PC which were referred to in T16-6 and 7 exhaust all possibilities of non-normal interpretations; this is seen from the conditions (C) in the two theorems. Thus there are at most these two kinds. But so far we have not seen whether there really are non-normal interpretations of these kinds. This will now be shown by examples.

For the following examples we shall take a calculus K and two semantical systems S and S' which fulfill the following conditions:

A. K contains n propositional constants, say 'A_1', 'A_2', . . . 'A_n'.

B. K contains PC_1 or PC_1^D.

C. K contains no other sentences than the molecular sentences constructed out of the propositional constants with the help of the connectives of PC (hence no variables, and only closed sentences).

D. K contains no other rules of deduction than those of PC (hence no rule of refutation; all rules of inference are extensible).

E. The sentences of S are those of K. Hence, S is an interpretation for K.

F. S' contains $n + 2$ atomic sentences, say 'A_1'', 'A_2'', . . . 'A_n'', 'A_{n+1}'' ($\mathfrak{S}_1$), 'A_{n+2}'' ($\mathfrak{S}_2$) such that the following holds: **a.** Each of the atomic sentences is L-independent of the rest (they may e.g. be full sentences of a predicate for $n + 2$ different objects). — **b.** Hence, all are factual. — **c.** $\mathfrak{S}_1$ is true, and hence F-true. — **d.** $\mathfrak{S}_2$ is false, and hence F-false. — **e.** Let $\mathfrak{S}_3$ be an L-true sentence in S' (e.g. dis($\mathfrak{S}_1$, neg($\mathfrak{S}_1$)), compare (G)). [The truth-rules for the atomic sentences in S' are supposed to be given so as to fulfill (F); in any other respect they may be chosen arbitrarily. We do not give them because their details beyond (F) are irrelevant for the nature of the interpretations in the examples.]

G. S' contains NTT. Hence the connectives of NTT in S' are signs for the connections$_L$.

H. If $\mathfrak{S}_i$ is a sentence of K and hence of S, then we designate by '$\mathfrak{S}_i'$' the corresponding sentence in S', that is to say, the sentence constructed out of $\mathfrak{S}_i$ by replacing each propositional constant that occurs, say 'A_k' ($k = 1$ to n), by the corresponding atomic sentence in S', 'A_k'', and replacing each connective that occurs by the corresponding connective in S'. [Hence, if $\mathfrak{S}_i$ is neg$_C$($\mathfrak{S}_j$), $\mathfrak{S}_i'$ is neg$_L$($\mathfrak{S}_j'$), and if $\mathfrak{S}_i$ is dis$_C$($\mathfrak{S}_j,\mathfrak{S}_k$), $\mathfrak{S}_i'$ is dis$_L$($\mathfrak{S}_j',\mathfrak{S}_k'$).] If $\mathfrak{K}_i$ is a sentential class in K and S, then we designate by '$\mathfrak{K}_i'$' the class of the corresponding sentences in S'.

In the following examples, the systems K and S' remain always the same. S differs from example to example. In each case we shall describe the system S by stating a translation of the sentences of S into some sentences of S'. The translation is meant in this way: the truth-rules in S state for the sentence $\mathfrak{S}_i$ the same truth-condition as the rules in S' state for the sentence $\mathfrak{S}_j$, into which $\mathfrak{S}_i$ is translated. Therefore, if any radical or L-concept holds for $\mathfrak{S}_j$ in S', then the same concept holds for $\mathfrak{S}_i$ in S. [If we use the concept of L-equivalence also for sentences in different systems (compare remark at the end of [I] § 16), then $\mathfrak{S}_i$ and $\mathfrak{S}_j$ are L-equivalent.] If we were to translate every sentence $\mathfrak{S}_i$ in S into the corresponding sentence $\mathfrak{S}'_i$ in S', then S would be an L-true interpretation for K, and each connective in K would have an L-normal interpretation in S. Therefore, in order to construct non-normal interpretations for the connectives in K, other translations have to be made. In each of the examples it will be shown that S is an L-true interpretation for K such that at least one connective in K has a non-normal interpretation in S. The first two examples of interpretations are rather trivial, but they suffice to show in a simple way that both kinds of non-normal interpretations previously explained are not empty.

First example: an L-true, non-normal interpretation of the first kind. We translate every sentence in S into $\mathfrak{S}_3$ (F(e)). Then the following holds: **a.** Every sentence in S is L-true. **b.** S is an L-true interpretation for K. **c.** neg$_C$ in K violates N1 in S. **d.** S is a non-normal interpretation of the first kind.

Proof. a. Every sentence in S is L-equivalent to an L-true sentence and hence L-true. — b. For every $\mathfrak{T}_i$ and $\mathfrak{T}_j$ in S, $\mathfrak{T}_i$ and $\mathfrak{T}_j$ are L-true (a), and hence $\mathfrak{T}_i \underset{L}{\rightarrow} \mathfrak{T}_j$. Thus condition (a) in [I] D34-1 is fulfilled. Condition (b) in the same definition is always fulfilled because of (D). Hence, S is an L-true interpretation for K. — c. For any $\mathfrak{S}_i$ in K, both $\mathfrak{S}_i$ and neg$_C(\mathfrak{S}_i)$ are true (a). — d. From T16-6.

Second example: an L-true, non-normal interpretation of the second kind. A sentence $\mathfrak{S}_m$ of S is translated, if it is C-true in K, into $\mathfrak{S}_3$ (which is L-true, see (F(e)), otherwise into neg($\mathfrak{S}_3$) (which is L-false). Then the following holds: **a.** S is an L-true interpretation for K. **b.** neg$_C$ in K violates N2 in S. **c.** S is a non-normal interpretation of the second kind.

Proof. a. Let the conditions be fulfilled, and $\mathfrak{S}_j$ be a direct C-implicate of $\mathfrak{R}_i$ in K. If $\mathfrak{R}_i$ is C-true in K, $\mathfrak{S}_j$ is C-true in K and is hence translated into an L-true sentence in S'; therefore, in this case, $\mathfrak{S}_j$ is L-true in S, and hence an L-implicate of $\mathfrak{R}_i$ in S. If, on the other hand,

$\Re_i$ is not C-true in K, then it contains a sentence which is not C-true in K ([I] T29-73) and which therefore is L-false in S. Hence, in this case, $\Re_i$ itself is L-false in S, and therefore $\Re_i \underset{L}{\rightarrow} \mathfrak{S}_j$. Thus S is an L-true interpretation for K. — b. Let $\mathfrak{S}_n$ be a sentence in K such that neither $\mathfrak{S}_n$ nor $neg_C(\mathfrak{S}_n)$ is C-true in K, e.g. one of the propositional constants. Then both $\mathfrak{S}_n$ and $neg_C(\mathfrak{S}_n)$ are L-false in S. Thus neg_C violates N2 with respect to $\mathfrak{S}_n$. — c. From T16-7.

Let us suppose that S', in addition to the extensional connectives of NTT, contains non-extensional connectives, e.g. signs for logical necessity and for logical (strict) implication (compare [I] §§ 16 and 17). Let us designate the full sentence of the sign of necessity with $\mathfrak{S}_i$ as component by 'nec($\mathfrak{S}_i$)'. Then we might translate every sentence $\mathfrak{S}_m$ in S into nec($\mathfrak{S}'_m$). This is essentially the same interpretation as that in the second example, because here, too, the C-true sentences in K are L-true in S, and the other sentences in K are L-false in S. $imp_C(\mathfrak{S}_i, \mathfrak{S}_j)$ is hereby translated into nec($imp_L(\mathfrak{S}'_i, \mathfrak{S}'_j)$), which is L-equivalent to (and may be taken as definiens for) the sentence of logical (strict) implication with $\mathfrak{S}'_i$ and $\mathfrak{S}'_j$ as components. Hence the chief sign of implication$_C$ in a sentence in K is here interpreted as the non-extensional connective of logical (strict) implication. This is possible because we have here no factual components.

As we have said, the two examples given are of a trivial nature. Now we shall construct examples of *non-trivial* non-normal interpretations. We shall not define the concept 'non-trivial interpretation'. The triviality meant here consists in the fact that too many sentences of K are interpreted in S as saying the same, i.e. are L-equivalent in S. Therefore it seems natural to take the following as a sufficient (though not necessary) condition for S to be a non-trivial interpretation for K: S is an interpretation for K, and for any $\mathfrak{T}_i$ and $\mathfrak{T}_j$ in K, if $\mathfrak{T}_i$ and $\mathfrak{T}_j$ are not C-equivalent in K, they are not L-equivalent in S. The following examples fulfill this condition.

Third example: an L-true, non-normal interpretation of the first kind. We translate every sentence $\mathfrak{S}_i$ in S into $\mathrm{dis_L}(\mathfrak{S}'_i, \mathfrak{S}_1)$. (For '$\mathfrak{S}'_i$', see (H); for '$\mathfrak{S}_1$', (F).) Then the following holds: **a.** Every sentence of S is true. **b.** S is an L-true interpretation for K. **c.** $\mathrm{neg_C}$ in K violates N1 in S. **d.** S is a non-normal interpretation of the first kind.

Proof. a. $\mathfrak{S}_1$ is true in S' (F(c)). Hence, for every $\mathfrak{S}_i$, $\mathrm{dis_L}(\mathfrak{S}'_i, \mathfrak{S}_1)$ is true in S' (NTT). Hence, because of the translation, $\mathfrak{S}_i$ is true in S. — b. Let $\mathfrak{S}_k$ be a primitive sentence (i.e. a direct C-implicate of Λ, see [I] D28-10) in K. Then $\mathfrak{S}'_k$ is L-true by NTT in S' (T14-2a), and hence likewise $\mathrm{dis_L}(\mathfrak{S}'_k, \mathfrak{S}_1)$ (T13-26b(1)). Therefore, because of the translation, $\mathfrak{S}_k$ is L-true in S. Let $\mathfrak{T}_m$ not be Λ, and $\mathfrak{T}_m \underset{\mathrm{dC}}{\rightarrow} \mathfrak{S}_n$ in K. Then $\mathfrak{T}'_m \underset{\mathrm{L}}{\rightarrow} \mathfrak{S}'_n$ by NTT in S' (T14-2b,c). Let $\mathfrak{T}''_m$ be that sentence or class into which $\mathfrak{T}_m$ is translated. [If $\mathfrak{T}_m$ is a class, $\mathfrak{T}''_m$ is the class constructed out of $\mathfrak{T}'_m$ by replacing every sentence $\mathfrak{S}'_m$ of $\mathfrak{T}'_m$ by $\mathrm{dis_L}(\mathfrak{S}'_m, \mathfrak{S}_1)$.] Then $\mathfrak{T}''_m \underset{\mathrm{L}}{\rightarrow} \mathrm{dis_L}(\mathfrak{S}'_n, \mathfrak{S}_1)$ in S' (T13-38b and 39). Therefore, because of the translation, $\mathfrak{T}_m \underset{\mathrm{L}}{\rightarrow} \mathfrak{S}_n$ in S. Hence, S is an L-true interpretation for K. — c and d. As in the first example.

Fourth example: an L-true, non-normal interpretation of the second kind. A sentence $\mathfrak{S}_i$ in S is translated, if it is C-true in K, into $\mathfrak{S}'_i$, and otherwise into $\mathrm{con_L}(\mathfrak{S}'_i, \mathfrak{S}_2)$. Then the following holds: **a.** If $\mathfrak{S}_k$ is a primitive sentence in K, it is L-true in S. **b.** If $\mathfrak{T}_m$ is not Λ, and $\mathfrak{T}_m \underset{\mathrm{dC}}{\rightarrow} \mathfrak{S}_n$ in K, then $\mathfrak{T}_m \underset{\mathrm{L}}{\rightarrow} \mathfrak{S}_n$ in S. **c.** S is an L-true interpretation for K. **d.** $\mathrm{neg_C}$ in K violates N2 in S. **e.** S is a non-normal interpretation of the second kind.

Proof. a. If $\mathfrak{S}_k$ is a primitive sentence in K, it is C-true in K and hence translated into $\mathfrak{S}'_k$, which is L-true in S' (T14-2a). Therefore $\mathfrak{S}_k$ is L-true in S. — b. Let $\mathfrak{T}_m$ not be Λ, and $\mathfrak{T}_m \underset{\mathrm{dC}}{\rightarrow} \mathfrak{S}_n$. Then $\mathfrak{T}'_m \underset{\mathrm{L}}{\rightarrow} \mathfrak{S}'_n$ by NTT in S' (T14-2b,c). We may assume that neither $\mathfrak{S}_n$ nor any of the sentences of $\mathfrak{T}_m$ are C-true in K; any other case can easily be reduced to a case of this kind. Then $\mathfrak{S}_n$ is translated into con($\mathfrak{S}'_n,\mathfrak{S}_2$). Let $\mathfrak{T}''_m$ be that sentence or class into which $\mathfrak{T}_m$ is translated. [If $\mathfrak{T}_m$ is a class, $\mathfrak{T}''_m$ is the class constructed out of $\mathfrak{T}'_m$ by replacing every sentence $\mathfrak{S}'_m$ of $\mathfrak{T}'_m$ by con$_L$($\mathfrak{S}'_m,\mathfrak{S}_2$).] $\mathfrak{T}''_m$ L-implies the following $\mathfrak{T}$: $\mathfrak{T}'_m$ ([I] P14-11, T13-26b(3), [I] P14-12), and hence $\mathfrak{S}'_n$ (see above, [I] P14-5), further $\mathfrak{S}_2$ (T13-26b(4)), and hence con$_L$($\mathfrak{S}'_n,\mathfrak{S}_2$) ([I] P14-12, T13-27b(3)), into which $\mathfrak{S}_n$ is translated. Therefore, $\mathfrak{T}_m \underset{L}{\overrightarrow{}} \mathfrak{S}_n$ in S. — c. From (a), (b), [I] D34-1. — d. Let $\mathfrak{S}_m$ be a sentence in K such that neither $\mathfrak{S}_m$ nor neg$_C$($\mathfrak{S}_m$) is C-true in K, e.g. one of the propositional constants. Then $\mathfrak{S}_m$ is translated into con$_L$($\mathfrak{S}'_m,\mathfrak{S}_2$). This sentence is false in S' (NTT), since $\mathfrak{S}_2$ is false in S' (F(d)). Therefore $\mathfrak{S}_m$ is false in S. neg$_C$($\mathfrak{S}_m$) is translated into con$_L$(neg$_L$($\mathfrak{S}'_m$),$\mathfrak{S}_2$), which is likewise false in S'. Therefore, neg$_C$($\mathfrak{S}_m$) is false in S. Thus neg$_C$ violates N2 with respect to $\mathfrak{S}_m$. — e. From T16-7.

§ 18. PC is not a Full Formalization of Propositional Logic

L-truth and L-implication in propositional logic, i.e. in a system containing NTT, are exhaustively represented in PC and thereby formalized. But not all logical properties of the connectives in NTT are represented in PC. If we could find a calculus K containing the connectives in such a way that every connective could only be interpreted normally (i.e. such that it would have a normal interpretation in any true interpretation of K and an L-normal interpretation in any L-true interpretation of K), then we should say that K is a full formalization of propositional logic. PC does not fulfill this requirement. The problem is whether any other calculus does.

The rules of NTT give an interpretation for the propositional connectives (more precisely, for the singulary and binary extensional connectives) and thereby constitute propositional logic. The rules PC are constructed as a calculus for propositional logic; that is to say, they have the purpose of representing the logical properties of the connectives of propositional logic as far as these properties can be represented by a calculus, i.e. by the use of the formal syntactical method.

Let us examine the question whether PC fulfills this purpose. It seems to be the generally accepted opinion that it does. And, at the first glance, there seem to be good reasons for this opinion. In order to be more concrete, let us regard a calculus K and a semantical system S fulfilling the following conditions:

A. K contains PC_1^D, and no other rules of deduction.

B. K contains only the following sentences: 1. n propositional constants; 2. the molecular sentences constructed out of them with the help of the connectives of PC.

C. The sentences of S are those of K.

D. S contains NTT in such a way that the sign for a connection$_C$ in K is simultaneously the sign for the corresponding connection$_L$ of NTT in S.

E. The truth-rules for the propositional constants in S are such that these sentences are mutually L-independent and hence factual (the further details of these truth-rules are irrelevant for the following discussion).

If a calculus is constructed as a formalization of logic within a certain region, then it is often regarded as its chief or even as its only purpose to present some or all L-true sentences of the region in question as C-true. In the case of K and S as specified, this task is fulfilled. Not only some but all L-true sentences of S are C-true in K (T14-5a), and no others (T14-3b). Thus C-truth in K is an exhaustive formalization of L-truth in S. Further, the formalization of logic, and analogously that of an empirical theory, in a certain region has a second task, which is sometimes overlooked; the calculus has to supply, in addition to suitable proofs, suitable derivations. In the case of a formalization of logic, some or all instances of L-implication have to be represented as instances of C-implication in the calculus. In our case, this second task also is fulfilled; C-implication in K has the same extension as L-implication in S (T14-5c, T14-3a). In other words, the rules PC constitute an exhaustive formalization of logical deduction by NTT. Thus the rules PC, both in proofs and in derivations, yield all those and only those results for which they are made. What else could we require of them?

The statements just made concerning PC and its relation to NTT are correct. But the conclusion which seems to be generally, though tacitly, drawn from them — namely, that PC is a complete formal representation of propositional logic, i.e. of the logical properties of the propositional connectives in NTT — is wrong. This is shown by the possibility of non-normal interpretations. Thus, for instance, it belongs to the logical properties of disjunction in propositional logic that a sentence of disjunction with two false components is false (rule Dj4 in NTT, § 10). This property is not in any way represented in PC; this is shown by examples of true (and even L-true) interpretations of a calculus containing PC, in which the rule Dj4 is violated.

A full formalization of NTT would consist in a calculus K of such a kind that any connective of PC in K would have a normal interpretation in any true interpretation for K and an L-normal interpretation in any L-true interpretation for K. The problem is whether a full formalization of NTT in this sense is possible.

Note (added 1958). The existence of non-normal interpretations of PC was pointed out already by B. A. Bernstein, though in a less exact way. This was called to my attention by Church. The problem is further discussed in Church's two papers and in his [Logic] pp. 117 f.

D. JUNCTIVES

If a full formalization of propositional logic is to be effected, new syntactical concepts must be used (§ 19). If rules of refutation are used and thereby 'C-false' is defined, the non-normal interpretations of PC of the first kind can be eliminated (§ 20). A more decisive change is made by the introduction of the junctives, i.e. of sentential classes in conjunctive and in disjunctive conception. Radical semantical concepts (§ 21) and L-concepts (§ 22) are defined for junctives. Further, junctives are applied in syntax; C-concepts are defined for them (§ 23). Their use in syntax makes possible a new kind of deductive rules, the disjunctive rules (§ 24). In this chapter, the general features of junctives and of calculi and semantical systems containing junctives are studied, leaving aside propositional logic and PC.

§ 19. Syntactical Concepts of a New Kind are Required

A calculus of the customary kind, consisting of primitive sentences and rules of inference, states conditions for C-implication (and C-truth) only. Therefore, it can formalize only those L-concepts which are definable on the basis of L-implication. 'L-true' belongs to these concepts, but 'L-exclusive' and 'L-disjunct' do not. Hence they cannot be formalized without the help of syntactical concepts of a new kind. The two concepts mentioned occur in the principles of contradiction and of the excluded middle. Therefore, these principles cannot be represented in PC. In a non-normal interpretation of the first kind, the first principle is violated; in one of the second kind, the second principle.

We found that PC does not completely fulfill its purpose; it is not a full formalization of propositional logic. This defect is by no means a particular feature of PC, however, but is based on general features of the customary method of constructing calculi. This method consists in laying down rules for C-implication. Hence, on the basis of this method, a calculus can exhibit only those syntactical properties and relations of sentences which are definable by C-implication, above all C-truth. Therefore, a calculus of this customary kind, if constructed for the purpose of formalizing the logic of a certain region, can formalize only those logical properties and relations of sentences which are definable by L-implication, among them L-truth. We shall now examine some elementary logical relations with respect to the question whether they are definable by L-implication or not.

(a)		(b)		(c)	(d)	(e)
CONDITIONAL RELATION		It is not the case that		SEMANTICAL CONCEPTS		SYNTACTICAL CONCEPTS
If $\mathfrak{S}_i$ is	then $\mathfrak{S}_j$ is	$\mathfrak{S}_i$ is	and $\mathfrak{S}_j$ is	Radical Concepts	L-Concepts	C-Concepts
1. true	true	true	false	$\mathfrak{S}_i$ implies $\mathfrak{S}_j$	L-implies	C-implies
2. true	false	true	true	$\mathfrak{S}_i$ is exclusive of $\mathfrak{S}_j$	L-exclusive	C-exclusive
3. false	true	false	false	$\mathfrak{S}_i$ is disjunct with $\mathfrak{S}_j$	L-disjunct	C-disjunct
4. false	false	false	true	$\mathfrak{S}_i$ is an implicate of $\mathfrak{S}_j$	L-implicate	C-implicate

There are four elementary relations between two sentences which can be formulated by conditional statements with respect to their truth-values (see table, column (a)), or, more exactly, by statements excluding one of the four possible distributions of truth-values (column (b)). To the radical concepts (column (c), compare [I] D9-3, 6, and 5) there are corresponding L-concepts (column (d), compare [I] § 14; for 'L-disjunct', compare remarks in [I] § 14 and [I] D20-17). There could be corresponding syntactical C-concepts (column (e)) However, with respect to a calculus of the customary kind we have only 'C-implies' and its inverse 'C-implicate', while 'C-exclusive' and 'C-disjunct' are not definable by C-implication. Therefore the concepts 'L-exclusive' and 'L-disjunct' cannot be formalized in a calculus of the customary kind. We shall see that the circumstance that these two concepts are not represented is responsible for the possibility of non-normal interpretations of the first and second kind for the propositional connectives.

If we find that a certain calculus which has been constructed with regard to certain interpretations admits also of undesired interpretations, then we have to make the calculus stronger. In a situation of this kind, one usually thinks first of adding new primitive sentences or new rules of inference. But the defect here discussed cannot be removed in this way. It is well known that the rules of PC are already complete with respect to primitive sentences and rules of inference. Therefore, a full formalization of NTT, if it is at all possible, requires syntactical concepts of a new kind.

If a form K of PC is constructed with propositional variables as the only atomic sentences, then K is complete in the following sense with respect to direct C-implication, or, in other words, with respect to primitive sentences and rules of inference. If we construct a new calculus K' out of K by declaring any sentence $\mathfrak{S}_i$ of K as an additional primitive sentence, then $\mathfrak{S}_i$ is either already C-true in K or not. In the first case the addition is superfluous, because K' is coincident with K ([I], D31-9). In the second case K' becomes rather trivial because every sentence is C-true in K', even those which are L-false in the normal interpretation. [In the customary terminology, K' is called contradictory or inconsistent in this case; but it is not C-inconsistent in our sense and still has true interpretations; see [I] D31-2 and remarks on [I] T31-31.] The same holds for the addition of a rule of inference.

If we take K and S as discussed in § 18 (fulfilling the conditions A to E), then any addition of a primitive sentence or a rule of inference would have the effect that there would be at least one $\mathfrak{S}_i$ such that it was F-true in S and C-true in K, or $\mathfrak{T}_i$ and $\mathfrak{T}_j$ such that $\mathfrak{T}_i \underset{F}{\rightarrow} \mathfrak{T}_j$ in S and $\mathfrak{T}_i \underset{C}{\not\rightarrow} \mathfrak{T}_j$ in K, in contradiction to the intention of formalizing propositional logic.

In propositional logic, the sign of negation$_L$ fulfills the following two principles (taken here in their semantical, as distinguished from their absolute, form) (T13-5b(2)).

A. *Principle of (Excluded) Contradiction.* For any closed sentence $\mathfrak{S}_i$, $\mathfrak{S}_i$ and $\text{neg}_L(\mathfrak{S}_i)$ are L-exclusive. That is to say, the two sentences cannot both be true. (This is due to the rule N1 for neg$_L$; see T13-3b(3).)

B. *Principle of Excluded Middle.* For any closed sentence $\mathfrak{S}_i$, $\mathfrak{S}_i$ and $\text{neg}_L(\mathfrak{S}_i)$ are L-disjunct. That is to say, the two sentences cannot both be false. (This is due to the rule N2 for neg$_L$; see T13-4b(3).)

Do these two principles also hold for PC? In other words, are the two properties of neg$_L$ which the principles state represented in PC? It seems to be the general belief that they are, because $\text{neg}_C(\text{con}_C(\mathfrak{S}_i,\text{neg}_C(\mathfrak{S}_i)))$ and $\text{dis}_C(\mathfrak{S}_i,\text{neg}_C(\mathfrak{S}_i))$ are C-true by PC. But the circumstance mentioned above, that 'C-exclusive' and 'C-disjunct' are not definable by 'C-implicate' and hence not definable with respect to PC, may evoke some doubt. And, in fact, the two principles do not hold for PC. Neither their validity nor their invalidity is assured by the rules of PC, because in some L-true interpretations, namely those with an L-normal interpretation of the connectives, the two principles hold, while in others they do not. In a non-normal interpretation of the first kind (T16-6), $\mathfrak{S}_i$ and $\text{neg}_C(\mathfrak{S}_i)$ are always both true; hence A is always violated, while B is always fulfilled. In a non-normal interpretation of the second kind (T16-7), $\mathfrak{S}_i$ and $\text{neg}_C(\mathfrak{S}_i)$ are sometimes — not always — both false, and always at least one of the two is false; hence B is sometimes violated, while A is always fulfilled. The C-truth of $\text{neg}_C(\text{con}_C(\mathfrak{S}_i,\text{neg}_C(\mathfrak{S}_i)))$ does not represent A; it would do so only if the L-normal interpretations of the connectives were assured by PC, which they are not; the same holds for $\text{dis}_C(\mathfrak{S}_i,\text{neg}_C(\mathfrak{S}_i))$ and B.

§ 20. C-Falsity

One new syntactical concept which might be added to those used in customary calculi is 'C-false'. It is defined on the basis of 'directly C-false', which is defined by rules of refutation. By adding a rule of this kind to PC, the non-normal interpretations of the first kind can be excluded.

Let us first discuss calculi in general and later apply the result to PC. The rules of a calculus of the customary kind determine only C-implication and thereby C-truth, but not C-falsity, which is not definable by C-implication. Therefore, if we look for new syntactical concepts, to be added to the customary ones, it seems natural to take C-falsity. We have seen previously that rules of a new kind are necessary for the introduction of this concept; we have called them rules of refutation ([I]) § 26). The rules of refutation of a calculus K define 'directly C-false in K'. On the basis of this concept, we lay down the following definition ([I] D28-3):

+D20-1. $\mathfrak{T}_i$ is C-false in K $=_{Df}$ there is a directly C-false $\mathfrak{T}_j$ which is derivable from $\mathfrak{T}_i$.

The rules of deduction of the customary kind are not sufficient for formalizing falsity. Suppose we wish to make sure that the sentence $\mathfrak{S}_1$ in K is false in every true interpretation for K. On the customary basis, we cannot reach this aim even if K contains PC. We might perhaps try to do it by taking $neg_C(\mathfrak{S}_1)$ as an additional primitive sentence. This would indeed assure that $neg_C(\mathfrak{S}_1)$ was true in every true interpretation for K. But this does not help, because, as we have seen, the rules of PC do not exclude true interpretations in which $neg_C(\mathfrak{S}_1)$ and $\mathfrak{S}_1$ are both true.

By adding a suitable rule of refutation to PC we can exclude the possibility of non-normal interpretations of the first kind and hence assure the validity of the principle of contradiction. Let us consider a system S and a calculus K

as explained in § 18 (fulfilling the conditions A to E). According to our intention to formalize the logic in S, we wish to construct a calculus K' out of K by adding a rule of refutation in such a way that all those $\mathfrak{T}$ which are L-false in S, and no others, are C-false in K'. The $\mathfrak{T}$ which are L-false in S are those which are L-comprehensive in S ([I] T14-107b), and hence those which are C-comprehensive in K ([I] D30-6) because L-implication in S coincides with C-implication in K. But it would be unnecessary to declare all C-comprehensive $\mathfrak{T}$ as directly C-false. It would suffice to take any one C-comprehensive sentence, say $\mathrm{con_c}(\mathfrak{S}_1, \mathrm{neg_c}(\mathfrak{S}_1))$, and lay down a rule in K' stating that this sentence is directly C-false; then all C-comprehensive $\mathfrak{T}$ would be C-false in K'. But even this rule would be stronger than necessary. All we have to assure is that at least one sentence of K' becomes false. This cannot be done by a rule saying "at least one sentence of K' is directly C-false", because we must have a rule of refutation *defining* 'directly C-false' before we can make an existential statement concerning this concept. The simplest way is to lay down the following rule, R1.

+**R20-1.** V (and only V) is directly C-false in K'.

Then in every true interpretation for K', V is false, and hence at least one sentence is false ([I] T9-1). Thus, rule R1 excludes non-normal interpretations of the first kind for K'.

A rule of refutation like R1 is useful in connection with many calculi. T1 shows that under certain conditions, which are also fulfilled by K and S as just discussed, the addition of R1 has the effect that L-falsity in S is exhaustively formalized in K.

+**T20-1.** Let the calculus K and the semantical system S contain the same sentences, and C-implication in K coincide with L-implication in S. Let K contain no rule of refutation, and K' be constructed out of K by adding the rule of refutation R1. Let S contain at least one L-false $\mathfrak{T}_i$. Then C-falsity in K and L-falsity in S coincide.

Proof. Let the conditions be fulfilled. Then $\mathfrak{T}_i$ is C-false in K' if and only if V is derivable from $\mathfrak{T}_i$ in K' (D1) and hence in K, hence if and only if $\mathfrak{T}_i \underset{C}{\rightarrow} V$ in K ([I] T29–54a), hence if and only if $\mathfrak{T}_i \underset{L}{\rightarrow} V$ in S, hence if and only if $\mathfrak{T}_i$ is L-comprehensive in S ([I] D14-5), hence if and only if $\mathfrak{T}_i$ is L-false in S ([I] T14-107b).

On the basis of 'C-false in K'' other concepts can be defined, among them 'C-exclusive in K'' ([I] D30-3). It can then be shown that, on the basis of rule R1, for any $\mathfrak{S}_i$, $\mathfrak{S}_i$ and $neg_C(\mathfrak{S}_i)$ are C-exclusive in K'. Thus the principle of contradiction holds for K'.

Later we shall introduce other syntactical concepts. With their help, 'C-false' will be definable on the basis of 'C-implicate' (D23-6). Therefore, the concept 'directly C-false' will no longer be necessary. Rules of refutation, as e.g. rule R1 above, will then be replaced by rules concerning 'direct C-implicate' (e.g. R24-1) and thereby become analogous to the other rules of deduction.

§ 21. Junctives in Semantics

A sentential class is usually construed in the conjunctive way, i.e. as joint assertion of its sentences. Accordingly, $\Re_i$ is regarded as true if and only if every sentence of $\Re_i$ is true. However, a disjunctive conception is likewise possible. According to it, $\Re_i$ is called true if and only if at least one sentence of $\Re_i$ is true. The customary one-sided use of the conjunctive conception only is responsible for a lack of symmetry in the ordinary structure of syntactical and of semantical concepts. We begin here using both conceptions. If $\Re_i$ is meant in the conjunctive way, it is called a conjunctive and designated by '$\Re_i^{\bullet}$'; if meant in the disjunctive way, it is called a disjunctive and designated by '$\Re_i^{\vee}$'. Conjunctives, disjunctives, and sentences are together called junctives. Definitions and theorems concerning radical concepts ('true', etc.) with respect to junctives are stated.

In accordance with the customary use, we have construed sentential classes in such a way that asserting $\Re_i$ means the same as asserting all sentences of $\Re_i$. Therefore we have called $\Re_i$ true if and only if all sentences of $\Re_i$ are true ([I] D9-1). Consequently, on the basis of NTT, a finite sentential class is L-equivalent with the conjunction$_L$ of its sentences (e.g. $\{\mathfrak{S}_1, \mathfrak{S}_2\}$ is L-equivalent with $con_L(\mathfrak{S}_1, \mathfrak{S}_2)$, T13-14b). And to say that $\mathfrak{S}_2$ logically follows from $\Re_1$ (in our terminology, that $\Re_1 \underset{L}{\rightarrow} \mathfrak{S}_2$) means that, if every sentence of $\Re_1$ is true, $\mathfrak{S}_2$ is necessarily also true.

It would obviously also be possible, although not usual, to construe sentential classes in such a way that to assert $\Re_i$ would mean the same as to assert that at least one of the sentences of $\Re_i$ holds. If we adopted this way of using sentential classes, we should call $\Re_i$ true if and only if at least one sentence of $\Re_i$ was true. And a finite class would, in this case, be L-equivalent with the disjunction$_L$ of its sentences.

The conjunctive conception of sentential classes seems

very convenient. We shall not replace it by the disjunctive conception but rather use both, distinguishing them with the help of two special signs. As previously, we shall use '$\Re$' with a subscript, e.g. '$\Re_2$', as the designation of a class of sentences. $\Re_i$ is a sentential class; it is determined, as every class is, with respect to the question of what elements (here sentences) belong to it; however, we shall regard it now as neutral with respect to the question how its assertion is to be construed. By '$\Re_i^{\bullet}$' (read "$\Re_i$-con") we designate the class $\Re_i$ as construed in the conjunctive way; by '$\Re_i^{\vee}$' (read "$\Re_i$-dis") we designate the class $\Re_i$ as construed in the disjunctive way. $\Re_i^{\bullet}$ is called a conjunctive sentential class or, briefly, a **conjunctive**, $\Re_i^{\vee}$ a disjunctive class or, briefly, a **disjunctive**. Conjunctives, disjunctives, and sentences (these we include for the sake of convenience in the formulation of definitions and theorems) are together called **junctives**. We have previously used '$\Re$' both for the neutral classes (e.g. "$\Re_1$ is a sub-class of $\Re_2$") and for the conjunctives (without this name) (e.g. "$\Re_2 \underset{L}{\rightarrow} \Re_1$"); we shall use it in the remainder of this book for the neutral classes only. We have previously used '$\mathfrak{T}$' for sentences and sentential classes; we shall use it now for junctives in general. (Hence, "if $\mathfrak{T}_i$ is false . . ." is to mean "if $\mathfrak{S}_i$ or $\Re_i^{\bullet}$ or $\Re_i^{\vee}$ is false . . .".)

It turns out that the customary tacit restriction of sentential classes to the conjunctive use is in fact the source of the lack of symmetry in the foundations of syntax and semantics, which we have often found in our previous discussions (e.g. in [I] pp. 38f, 72, 77, and 172; see, above, the remark concerning disjunction$_C$ and conjunction$_C$ at the beginning of § 16). By the use of both kinds of junctives, the foundations of semantics and likewise those of syntax will gain a perfect symmetry with respect to (L-, C-) truth and falsity, disjunction and conjunction, existential and universal sentences, etc.

The explanations above lead to the subsequent definitions for concepts applied to junctives: first their elements (D1 and 2, not often used), then truth (D3 and 4). For our purposes, it is not necessary to introduce the junctives themselves by explicit definitions. We simply assume that to every sentential class $\Re_i$ two entities are correlated, which we designate by '$\Re_i^{\bullet}$' and '$\Re_i^{\vee}$'. And we shall define semantical concepts and later syntactical concepts applied to these entities by referring to the sentential class $\Re_i$.

An explicit definition of the junctives can easily be given if we construe them as ordered pairs. $\Re_i^{\bullet}$ might be regarded as the pair whose first member is $\Re_i$ and whose second member is the connection of conjunction (hence as $\Re_i;\bullet$); analogously $\Re_i^{\vee}$ with disjunction. This procedure, however, presupposes that conjunction and disjunction are regarded as entities, say as relations between propositions; in other words, it presupposes the occurrence of (binary) connection variables in the metalanguage. But this difficulty can easily be avoided by taking any other two entities as second members of the pairs, e.g. the numbers 0 and 1, or the sentential classes V and Λ. In the latter case, $\Re_i^{\bullet} = \Re_i;V$, and $\Re_i^{\vee} = \Re_i;\Lambda$. Here, the pairs are homogeneous.

D21-1. $x \in \Re_i^{\bullet} =_{Df} x \in \Re_i$.

D21-2. $x \in \Re_i^{\vee} =_{Df} x \in \Re_i$.

+**D21-3.** $\Re_i^{\bullet}$ is *true* (in S) $=_{Df}$ every sentence of $\Re_i$ is true.

+**D21-4.** $\Re_i^{\vee}$ is *true* (in S) $=_{Df}$ at least one sentence of $\Re_i$ is true.

D1 and 2 state that the elements of a conjunctive or disjunctive are the elements of the corresponding (neutral) sentential class; hence they are sentences. D3 and 4 take the place of [I] D9-1. The other definitions in [I] § 9 (for 'false', 'implicate', 'equivalent', etc.) are maintained in their previous form. Thus all radical semantical concepts can now be applied to junctives.

Junctives of higher levels could also be used, i.e. junctives containing other junctives as elements. We may even admit inhomogeneous junctives, whose elements belong to different levels. Recursive definition for the level of a junctive:

D21-A1.

    a. The junctive $\mathfrak{T}_i$ belongs to the first level $=_{Df}$ every element of $\mathfrak{T}_i$ is a sentence.

    b. The junctive $\mathfrak{T}_i$ belongs to the level $n + 1 =_{Df}$ at least one element of $\mathfrak{T}_i$ belongs to the level n and none to a higher level.

The following definitions for 'true' (DA3 and 4) are analogous to D3 and 4. Thus the other radical concepts can also be applied analogously.

D21-A3. $\mathfrak{T}_i^{\bullet}$ is true $=_{Df}$ every element of $\mathfrak{T}_i$ is true.

D21-A4. $\mathfrak{T}_i^{\vee}$ is true $=_{Df}$ at least one element of $\mathfrak{T}_i$ is true.

In the following discussions we shall restrict ourselves to junctives of the first level.

The following theorems are based on the definitions D1 to 4. Those concerning conjunctives correspond exactly to certain theorems in the previous system ([I] § 9). Analogous theorems concerning disjunctives are added here; their proofs need not be given here, because they are analogous to the proofs for conjunctives, referring to the corresponding definitions and theorems for disjunctives.

+T21-1. $\mathfrak{K}_i^{\bullet}$ is false if and only if at least one sentence of $\mathfrak{K}_i$ is false. ([I] T9-1.)

+T21-2. $\mathfrak{K}_i^{\vee}$ is false if and only if every sentence of $\mathfrak{K}_i$ is false.

T21-5. $\mathfrak{T}_i \rightarrow \mathfrak{K}_j^{\bullet}$ if and only if $\mathfrak{T}_i$ implies every sentence of $\mathfrak{K}_j$. ([I] T9-17.)

T21-6. $\mathfrak{K}_i^{\vee} \rightarrow \mathfrak{T}_j$ if and only if every sentence of $\mathfrak{K}_i$ implies $\mathfrak{T}_j$.

The following theorems concern the null conjunctive $\Lambda^{\bullet}$, the null disjunctive $\Lambda^{\vee}$, the universal conjunctive $V^{\bullet}$, and the universal disjunctive $V^{\vee}$, with respect to a semantical system S.

T21-11. $\Lambda^\bullet$ is true. ([I] T9-32.)

T21-12. Λ^v is false. (From T2.)

T21-15. $\mathfrak{T}_i$ is true if and only if $\Lambda^\bullet \rightarrow \mathfrak{T}_i$. ([I] T9-35.)

T21-16. $\mathfrak{T}_i$ is false if and only if $\mathfrak{T}_i \rightarrow \Lambda^v$.

T21-19.

    a. $V^\bullet$ is true (in S) if and only if every sentence in S is true. ([I] T9-42a.)

    b. $V^\bullet$ is false if and only if at least one sentence in S is false. ([I] T9-43a.)

T21-20.

    a. V^v is true if and only if at least one sentence in S is true. (From D4.)

    b. V^v is false if and only if every sentence in S is false. (From T2.)

T21-23. $\Lambda^\bullet \rightarrow V^v$ if and only if at least one sentence in S is true. (From T15, T20a.)

+T21-24. $V^\bullet \rightarrow \Lambda^v$ if and only if at least one sentence in S is false. (From T16, T19b.)

§ 22. Application of L-Concepts to Junctives

The two ways explained in [I] for introducing L-concepts are here adapted to junctives. 1. Eighteen postulates (P1 to 15) are stated (corresponding to [I] P14-1 to 15), containing some of the L-concepts as primitives. A few theorems are based upon these postulates; among them: $\Lambda^\bullet$ is L-true (T22), Λ^v is L-false (T23). 2. The concept of L-range is applied to junctives (D1 and 2). On its basis, radical and L-concepts for junctives can be defined as previously (D11-5 to 8, and 12; [I] § 20). In this system, the postulates of the first system are provable.

In [I], the L-concepts were introduced in two different ways. Both of them can easily be adapted to junctives. The first way ([I] § 14) consisted in laying down fifteen postulates. Three of them ([I] P14-11 to 13) concern the relation between sentences and sentential classes; they must now be split up for conjunctives and disjunctives. The other postulates remain unchanged. Thus we come to the following system.

P22-1 to 10 ($= [\mathrm{I}]$ P14-1 to 10).
+P22-11.

    a. If $\mathfrak{S}_j \, \epsilon \, \mathfrak{R}_i$, then $\mathfrak{R}_i^{\bullet} \xrightarrow[\mathrm{L}]{} \mathfrak{S}_j$.

    b. If $\mathfrak{S}_i \, \epsilon \, \mathfrak{R}_j$, then $\mathfrak{S}_i \xrightarrow[\mathrm{L}]{} \mathfrak{R}_j^{\mathrm{v}}$.

+P22-12.

    a. If $\mathfrak{T}_i$ L-implies every sentence of $\mathfrak{R}_j$, then $\mathfrak{T}_i \xrightarrow[\mathrm{L}]{} \mathfrak{R}_j^{\bullet}$.

    b. If every sentence of $\mathfrak{R}_i$ L-implies $\mathfrak{T}_j$, then $\mathfrak{R}_i^{\mathrm{v}} \xrightarrow[\mathrm{L}]{} \mathfrak{T}_j$.

P22-13.

    a. If every sentence of $\mathfrak{R}_i$ is L-true, $\mathfrak{R}_i^{\bullet}$ is L-true.

    b. If every sentence of $\mathfrak{R}_i$ is L-false, $\mathfrak{R}_i^{\mathrm{v}}$ is L-false.

P22-14 and 15 ($= [\mathrm{I}]$ P14-14 and 15).

We give a few theorems based on these postulates. Those concerning conjunctives correspond exactly to theorems in the previous system. We add here theorems concerning disjunctives. They and their proofs are analogous to those concerning conjunctives.

    T22-1. $\mathfrak{S}_i$ and $\{\mathfrak{S}_i\}^{\bullet}$ are L-equivalent. ($[\mathrm{I}]$ T14-9.)

    T22-2. $\mathfrak{S}_i$ and $\{\mathfrak{S}_i\}^{\mathrm{v}}$ are L-equivalent.

    +T22-3. $\mathfrak{S}_i$, $\{\mathfrak{S}_i\}^{\bullet}$, and $\{\mathfrak{S}_i\}^{\mathrm{v}}$ are L-equivalent to one another. (From T1 and 2.)

    T22-6. If $\mathfrak{R}_j \subset \mathfrak{R}_i$, then $\mathfrak{R}_i^{\bullet} \xrightarrow[\mathrm{L}]{} \mathfrak{R}_j^{\bullet}$. ($[\mathrm{I}]$ T14-10.)

    T22-7. If $\mathfrak{R}_i \subset \mathfrak{R}_j$, then $\mathfrak{R}_i^{\mathrm{v}} \xrightarrow[\mathrm{L}]{} \mathfrak{R}_j^{\mathrm{v}}$.

    T22-8. If a sentence of $\mathfrak{R}_i$ is L-false, $\mathfrak{R}_i^{\bullet}$ is L-false. ($[\mathrm{I}]$ T14-11.)

    T22-9. If a sentence of $\mathfrak{R}_i$ is L-true, $\mathfrak{R}_i^{\mathrm{v}}$ is L-true. (From P11b, P6.)

T22-10. $\mathfrak{R}_i^\bullet$ is L-true if and only if every sentence of $\mathfrak{R}_i$ is L-true. ([I] T14-20.)

T22-11. $\mathfrak{R}_i^\vee$ is L-false if and only if every sentence of $\mathfrak{R}_i$ is L-false. (From P13b; P7, P11b.)

+T22-14. $\mathfrak{T}_i \underset{L}{\rightarrow} \mathfrak{R}_j^\bullet$ if and only if $\mathfrak{T}_i$ L-implies every sentence of $\mathfrak{R}_j$. ([I] T14-22.)

+T22-15. $\mathfrak{R}^\vee \underset{L}{\rightarrow} \mathfrak{T}_j$ if and only if every sentence of $\mathfrak{R}_i$ L-implies $\mathfrak{T}_j$. (From P12b; P11b, P5.)

T22-16.

    a. $\mathfrak{R}_i^\bullet \underset{L}{\rightarrow} \mathfrak{R}_i^\bullet$. (From P11a, P12a.)

    b. $\mathfrak{R}_i^\vee \underset{L}{\rightarrow} \mathfrak{R}_i^\vee$. (From P11b, P12b.)

T22-17. L-implication is reflexive; i.e., for every $\mathfrak{T}_i$, $\mathfrak{T}_i \underset{L}{\rightarrow} \mathfrak{T}_i$. (From P8, T16a,b.)

T22-18. If $\mathfrak{S}_i \underset{L}{\rightarrow} \mathfrak{S}_j$ (in S), then $\{\mathfrak{S}_i, \mathfrak{S}_k\}^\bullet \underset{L}{\rightarrow} \{\mathfrak{S}_j, \mathfrak{S}_k\}^\bullet$.

Proof. $\{\mathfrak{S}_i, \mathfrak{S}_k\}^\bullet$ L-implies $\mathfrak{S}_i$ (P11a) and hence $\mathfrak{S}_j$ (P5), and likewise $\mathfrak{S}_k$, and hence $\{\mathfrak{S}_j, \mathfrak{S}_k\}^\bullet$ (P12a).

T22-19. If $\mathfrak{S}_i \underset{L}{\rightarrow} \mathfrak{S}_j$ (in S), then $\{\mathfrak{S}_i, \mathfrak{S}_k\}^\vee \underset{L}{\rightarrow} \{\mathfrak{S}_j, \mathfrak{S}_k\}^\vee$.

Proof. $\{\mathfrak{S}_j, \mathfrak{S}_k\}^\vee$ is an L-implicate of $\mathfrak{S}_k$ (P11b) and likewise of $\mathfrak{S}_j$, and hence of $\mathfrak{S}_i$ (P5), and hence of $\{\mathfrak{S}_i, \mathfrak{S}_k\}^\vee$ (P12b).

T22-20. Every $\mathfrak{T}_i \underset{L}{\rightarrow} \Lambda^\bullet$. ([I] T14-32.)

T22-21. $\Lambda^\vee \underset{L}{\rightarrow}$ every $\mathfrak{T}_j$. (From P12b.)

+T22-22. $\Lambda^\bullet$ is L-true. ([I] T14-33.)

+T22-23. $\Lambda^\vee$ is L-false. (From P13b.)

+T22-24. $\mathfrak{T}_j$ is L-true if and only if $\Lambda^\bullet \underset{L}{\rightarrow} \mathfrak{T}_j$. ([I] T14-51a.)

+T22-25. $\mathfrak{T}_i$ is L-false if and only if $\mathfrak{T}_i \underset{L}{\rightarrow} \Lambda^\vee$. (From T23, P7; P15.)

We found previously that, within the customary framework of concepts concerning sentences and sentential classes, 'L-true' can be defined on the basis of 'L-implication' ([I] D14-B1) but 'L-false' cannot. T24 and 25 show that this asymmetry disappears if junctives are used. The same holds for the corresponding C-terms in syntax (see, below, D23-5 and 6).

T22-30. $V^{\bullet} \underset{L}{\rightarrow}$ every $\mathfrak{S}_j$ and every $\mathfrak{R}_j^{\bullet}$. ([I] T14-42.)

T22-31. Every $\mathfrak{S}_i$ and every $\mathfrak{R}_i^{v} \underset{L}{\rightarrow} V^{v}$. (From P11b, T7.)

T22-32. $V^{\bullet} \underset{L}{\rightarrow}$ every non-empty $\mathfrak{R}_j^{v}$. (From P11a, P11b, P5.)

T22-33. Every non-empty $\mathfrak{R}_i^{\bullet} \underset{L}{\rightarrow} V^{v}$. (From P11a, P11b, P5.)

The second way of the introduction of the L-concepts explained in [I] made use of the concept of *L-range* ([I] § 20; compare above § 11). This system can easily be modified so as to apply to junctives. Since we have previously based our system of propositional logic on the concept of L-range (§ 11), we shall use in our subsequent discussions of propositional logic containing junctives (§ 25) the system now to be explained. As its basis, we simply take the definition for the L-range of sentential classes (T11-1; [I] D20-1b) here applied to conjunctives (D1) and add an analogous definition for disjunctives (D2).

+**D22-1.** $\mathrm{Lr}\mathfrak{R}_i^{\bullet}$ (in S) $=_{\mathrm{Df}}$ the product of the L-ranges of the sentences of $\mathfrak{R}_i$.

+**D22-2.** $\mathrm{Lr}\mathfrak{R}_i^{v}$ (in S) $=_{\mathrm{Df}}$ the sum of the L-ranges of the sentences of $\mathfrak{R}_i$.

The previous definitions for the L-concepts based on the concept of L-range remain unchanged ([I] § 20, some of them stated above as D11-5 to 9). Further, our present system is to contain the definition of 'true' (D11-12), based on 'L-range' in connection with 'rs', and the definitions of the other radical concepts based on 'true' ([I] D20-14 to 18). The resulting concept of truth for junctives is in accordance with D21-3 and 4 (T40 and 41 below); therefore, the theorems in § 21 are valid in the present system.

T22-40. $\mathfrak{R}_i^{\bullet}$ is true if and only if every sentence of $\mathfrak{R}_i$ is true. (From D1, D11-12.)

T22-41. $\mathfrak{R}_i^{v}$ is true if and only if at least one sentence of $\mathfrak{R}_i$ is true. (From D2, D11-12.)

In [I] § 20 we have seen that the system based on the concept of L-range contains among its theorems all the postulates of the earlier system concerning L-concepts ([I] P14-1 to 15). Therefore, our present system contains as theorems those of the postulates stated above which correspond to [I] P14-1 to 15; these are P22-1 to 10, 11a, 12a, 13a, 14 and 15. But the same can easily be shown for the rest also, that is, P11b (D2, D11-7), P12b (D2, D11-7), and P13b (D2, D11-6). Thus the present system contains all postulates P22-1 to 15, and all theorems based upon them (T1, etc., above).

T22-46. (Lemma for T23-11b.) If S contains $\mathfrak{T}_i$ and $\mathfrak{T}_j$, and $\mathfrak{T}_j$ is not an L-implicate of $\mathfrak{T}_i$ in S, then there is a class $\mathfrak{M}_k$ of junctives in S which fulfills the following conditions:

  a. $\mathfrak{T}_i \,\epsilon\, \mathfrak{M}_k$.
  b. If $\mathfrak{T}_m \,\epsilon\, \mathfrak{M}_k$ and $\mathfrak{T}_m \underset{L}{\rightarrow} \mathfrak{T}_n$ in S, then $\mathfrak{T}_n \,\epsilon\, \mathfrak{M}_k$.
  c. $\mathfrak{R}_m^{\bullet} \,\epsilon\, \mathfrak{M}_k$ if and only if every sentence of $\mathfrak{R}_m \,\epsilon\, \mathfrak{M}_k$.
  d. $\mathfrak{R}_m^{v} \,\epsilon\, \mathfrak{M}_k$ if and only if at least one sentence of $\mathfrak{R}_m \,\epsilon\, \mathfrak{M}_k$.
  e. Not $\mathfrak{T}_j \,\epsilon\, \mathfrak{M}_k$.

Proof. Let $\mathfrak{T}_i$ not L-imply $\mathfrak{T}_j$. Then not $R_i \subset R_j$ (D11-7). Hence there is an s_i such that the following holds: 1. $s_i \,\epsilon\, R_i$; 2. s_i not $\epsilon\, R_j$. Let $\mathfrak{M}_k$ be the class of all junctives $\mathfrak{T}_k$ in S such that $s_i \,\epsilon\, R_k$. Then $\mathfrak{M}_k$ fulfills the conditions (a) to (e). (a) follows from (1). If $s_i \,\epsilon\, R_m$ and $R_m \subset R_n$, then $s_i \,\epsilon\, R_n$; hence (b). (c) follows from D1; (d) from D2; (e) from (2).

§ 23. Junctives in Syntax

If a conjunctive (or a sentential class) occurs as a C-implicans, we cannot eliminate it by referring to sentences only; likewise with a disjunctive as C-implicate. A rule of deduction stating a disjunctive as direct C-implicate is called a disjunctive rule. Definitions for 'C-implicate', 'C-true', 'C-false', 'C-equivalent' for junctives are given (D4 to 7). These definitions have a form quite different from that of the former definitions for C-concepts ([I] § 28). But they fulfill the requirement of adequacy; that is to say, $\mathfrak{T}_i$ is C-true in K if and only if $\mathfrak{T}_i$ is true in every true interpretation for K, and analogously for the other C-concepts (T15 to 18). And the new C-concepts are in accordance with the old ones as far as the latter go (T41).

So far we have explained the use of junctives only in semantics. But they may also be used in syntax. Here their use leads to a new kind of rules of deduction. We shall see later that, by adding rules of this new kind to PC, it will be possible to exclude all non-normal interpretations and thus to reach our aim, a full formalization of propositional logic. In this and the next sections, however, we are not concerned with PC but with the use of junctives in calculi in general.

Against the use of junctives in the construction of a calculus, the objection might perhaps be raised that it involves a fundamental change in the method of dealing with calculi. Whereas in the usual method we seem to have to do merely with sentences and therefore can carry out all operations, namely proofs and derivations, entirely within the object language, after the introduction of junctives we shall have to operate in the metalanguage. In fact, however, there is no fundamental change of this kind. A closer examination shows that, in dealing with any calculus, even one of the usual kind, we must always make use of the metalanguage.

The metalanguage is first necessary for stating primitive sentences. Simply writing them down would not do, because in this way they would be merely asserted but not specified as primitive. As to the rules of inference, it is even more obvious that the metalanguage is necessary for their formulation. Furthermore, if a derivation is to be given, it is necessary to indicate which of the sentences in the series are meant as premises. Instead of saying explicitly: "The first ten sentences of this series are taken as premises", we may, of course, use any other way of indicating the same on the basis of a suitable convention, e.g. by drawing a line under the tenth sentence. But then this line is a sign in the metalanguage, as are the assertion-sign and the signs 'Pp.', 'Dem.' in [Princ. Math.], the lines '————', '– – – –', etc., in Frege's proofs, the signs'∴' and 'q.e.d.' sometimes used in mathematical proofs, and the like. And, further, it is necessary to speak about sentential classes, not only about sentences. This fact is often concealed by the customary way of formulation, which says "derivable from such and such premises" instead of "derivable from the class of such and such premises". The sentential classes in the usual method of calculi are what we now call conjunctives. The only new feature in the new method is the use of disjunctives in addition to conjunctives. Thus there is no fundamental change in method.

The radical semantical concepts are based on the concept of truth ([I] § 9). Thus, for the application of these concepts to junctives, it suffices to define 'true' for junctives (D21-3 and 4). For the application of the syntactical concepts, an analogous procedure is not possible. First, not even analogous theorems hold. In contradistinction to D21-4, $\Re_i^v$ may be C-true, for instance by being declared directly C-true, without any sentence of $\Re_i$ being C-true. Further, 'C-true' is not a sufficient basis for the definition of the other C-terms. We have seen that in the previous system of syntax ([I], §§28 to 32) many C-terms can be defined on the basis of 'C-implicate' but some cannot (e.g. 'C-false', 'C-disjunct', 'C-exclusive', [I] §§ 28 and 30). Now we shall see that, if junctives are used, 'C-implicate' is a sufficient basis for the other terms. Therefore, we have to introduce the junctives in syntax in connection with the concept of C-implication.

In the usual method of calculi, a sentential class, corresponding to what we now call a conjunctive, is most often used as a C-implicans, i.e. as a class of premisses from which something is derived. In a case of this kind the reference to a sentential class is necessary; it cannot be replaced by a reference to sentences. Sometimes a sentential class occurs also as a C-implicate ('consequence-class', [Syntax] § 48). But in a case of this kind a reference to sentences would suffice. [Instead of saying: "$\Re_2$ (or, in the present terminology, $\Re_2^*$) is a C-implicate of $\mathfrak{T}_1$", we may say: "Every sentence of $\Re_2$ is a C-implicate of $\mathfrak{T}_1$", in analogy to T21-5.] Now we use disjunctives in addition to conjunctives. For them, the converse holds; reference to a disjunctive as C-implicans can be replaced by a reference to sentences, but reference to a disjunctive as C-implicate cannot. [Instead of saying: "$\mathfrak{T}_2$ is a C-implicate of $\Re_1^v$", we may say: "$\mathfrak{T}_2$ is a C-implicate of every sentence of $\Re_1$", in analogy to T21-6.] A rule of deduction of the form "$\Re_j^v$ is a direct C-implicate of $\mathfrak{T}_i$" cannot be expressed with the help of the usual syntactical concepts. We call a rule of deduction of this new kind, stating a disjunctive as a direct C-implicate of something, a **disjunctive rule** (of deduction).

If junctives are used, all rules of deduction of a calculus K can be stated in the same form, namely as parts of the definition for 'direct C-implicate in K'. We shall see that rules formulated in this way fulfill their purpose; that is, they have the effect that a certain intended result holds for every true interpretation of K. In order to show this, we must first define 'true interpretation' for systems containing junctives (D1a). The definition is similar to, but simpler than, [I] D33-2. The definition for 'L-true interpretation' (D1b) is analogous.

+**D23-1a [b]**. S is an [L-]**true interpretation** for K $=_{Df}$ S is an interpretation for K ([I] D33-1), and for every $\mathfrak{T}_i$ and $\mathfrak{T}_j$, if $\mathfrak{T}_i \underset{dC}{\rightarrow} \mathfrak{T}_j$ in K, $\mathfrak{T}_i \underset{[L]}{\rightarrow} \mathfrak{T}_j$ in S.

The *C-concepts for junctives*, in order to fulfill the requirement of adequacy ([I] § 28), must be defined on the basis of 'direct C-implication' in such a way that they apply in all those cases and only those in which the corresponding radical concepts apply in every true interpretation. [For instance, the definition of 'C-true' must be such that the following holds: $\mathfrak{T}_i$ is C-true in K if and only if $\mathfrak{T}_i$ is true in every true interpretation for K.] This condition of adequacy, however, uses semantical concepts and hence cannot itself be taken as a definition for the C-concepts. The task is to define these concepts in a purely syntactical way but such that the semantical condition just stated is fulfilled.

T23-1. Let S be a true interpretation for K. Let $\mathfrak{M}_k$ be the class of those junctives in K which are true in S. Then $\mathfrak{M}_k$ fulfills the following conditions:

b. If $\mathfrak{T}_i \underset{dC}{\rightarrow} \mathfrak{T}_j$ in K, then, if $\mathfrak{T}_i \,\epsilon\, \mathfrak{M}_k$, $\mathfrak{T}_j \,\epsilon\, \mathfrak{M}_k$. (From D1b, [I] T9-10).

c. $\mathfrak{K}_m^{\bullet} \,\epsilon\, \mathfrak{M}_k$ if and only if every sentence of $\mathfrak{K}_m \,\epsilon\, \mathfrak{M}_k$. (From D21-3).

d. $\mathfrak{K}_m^{\vee} \,\epsilon\, \mathfrak{M}_k$ if and only if at least one sentence of $\mathfrak{K}_m \,\epsilon\, \mathfrak{M}_k$. (From D21-4).

Our aim is to define C-implication so as to fulfill the condition of adequacy: $\mathfrak{T}_i \underset{C}{\rightarrow} \mathfrak{T}_j$ in K if and only if, in every true interpretation for K, $\mathfrak{T}_i \rightarrow \mathfrak{T}_j$, and hence, if $\mathfrak{T}_i$ is true, $\mathfrak{T}_j$ is true. Therefore we require in the following definition (D4) that for every $\mathfrak{M}_k$ fulfilling the conditions (b), (c), and (d) in T1, if $\mathfrak{T}_i \,\epsilon\, \mathfrak{M}_k$, $\mathfrak{T}_j \,\epsilon\, \mathfrak{M}_k$. It will be seen later that these conditions are in fact sufficient to make the definition adequate (T15a).

+D23-4. $\mathfrak{T}_j$ is a **C-implicate** of $\mathfrak{T}_i$ ($\mathfrak{T}_i \underset{C}{\rightarrow} \mathfrak{T}_j$) (in K) $=_{Df}$ $\mathfrak{T}_j$ belongs to every class $\mathfrak{M}_k$ of junctives which fulfills the following conditions:

a. $\mathfrak{T}_i \,\epsilon\, \mathfrak{M}_k$.

b. If $\mathfrak{T}_m \,\epsilon\, \mathfrak{M}_k$ and $\mathfrak{T}_m \xrightarrow[dC]{} \mathfrak{T}_n$, then $\mathfrak{T}_n \,\epsilon\, \mathfrak{M}_k$.

c. $\mathfrak{K}_m^{\bullet} \,\epsilon\, \mathfrak{M}_k$ if and only if every sentence of $\mathfrak{K}_m \,\epsilon\, \mathfrak{M}_k$.

d. $\mathfrak{K}_m^v \,\epsilon\, \mathfrak{M}_k$ if and only if at least one sentence of $\mathfrak{K}_m \,\epsilon\, \mathfrak{M}_k$.

T23-3. If $\mathfrak{T}_i \xrightarrow[dC]{} \mathfrak{T}_j$ in K, then $\mathfrak{T}_i \xrightarrow[C]{} \mathfrak{T}_j$ in K. (From D4a, b.)

+T23-4. C-implication is transitive, i.e. if $\mathfrak{T}_i \xrightarrow[C]{} \mathfrak{T}_j$ and $\mathfrak{T}_j \xrightarrow[C]{} \mathfrak{T}_l$, then $\mathfrak{T}_i \xrightarrow[C]{} \mathfrak{T}_l$.

Proof. Let $\mathfrak{T}_i \xrightarrow[C]{} \mathfrak{T}_j$ and $\mathfrak{T}_j \xrightarrow[C]{} \mathfrak{T}_l$. Let (a_i) be: $\mathfrak{T}_i \,\epsilon\, \mathfrak{M}_k$; (a_j): $\mathfrak{T}_j \,\epsilon\, \mathfrak{M}_k$; (a_l): $\mathfrak{T}_l \,\epsilon\, \mathfrak{M}_k$; (b), (c), (d) as in D4. From the assumptions stated, we obtain by D4 the following. If $\mathfrak{M}_k$ fulfills (a_i), (b), (c), and (d), then also (a_j); if (a_j), (b), (c), and (d), then also (a_l). Hence, if $\mathfrak{M}_k$ fulfills (a_i), (b), (c), and (d), then also (a_l). Thus $\mathfrak{T}_i \xrightarrow[C]{} \mathfrak{T}_l$ (D4).

+T23-5. C-implication is reflexive, i.e. $\mathfrak{T}_i \xrightarrow[C]{} \mathfrak{T}_i$. (From D4.)

Adequacy requires correspondence between C-concepts and radical semantical concepts. Therefore, the following definitions (D5, 6, and 7) are framed in analogy to T21-15 and 16, and [I] T9-20b. We shall see later that the concepts thus defined are indeed adequate (T16, 17, and 18).

+D23-5. $\mathfrak{T}_i$ is **C-true** (in K) $=_{Df} \Lambda^{\bullet} \xrightarrow[C]{} \mathfrak{T}_i$.

+D23-6. $\mathfrak{T}_i$ is **C-false** (in K) $=_{Df} \mathfrak{T}_i \xrightarrow[C]{} \Lambda^v$.

+D23-7. $\mathfrak{T}_i$ is **C-equivalent** to $\mathfrak{T}_j$ (in K) $=_{Df} \mathfrak{T}_i \xrightarrow[C]{} \mathfrak{T}_j$ and $\mathfrak{T}_j \xrightarrow[C]{} \mathfrak{T}_i$.

Thus here, not only 'C-true' but also 'C-false' is definable on the basis of 'C-implication'.

+T23-11a [b]. If S is an [L-]true interpretation for K and $\mathfrak{T}_i \xrightarrow[C]{} \mathfrak{T}_j$ in K, then $\mathfrak{T}_i \xrightarrow[LJ]{} \mathfrak{T}_j$ in S.

Proof for (a). Let the conditions be fulfilled, and $\mathfrak{M}_k$ be the class of the junctives in K which are true in S. Then $\mathfrak{M}_k$ fulfills the conditions D4b, c, d (T1). — 1. Let $\mathfrak{T}_i$ be false in S. Then $\mathfrak{T}_i \rightarrow \mathfrak{T}_j$ ([I] T9-12). — 2. Let $\mathfrak{T}_i$ be true in S. Then $\mathfrak{T}_i \,\epsilon\, \mathfrak{M}_k$. Hence, $\mathfrak{M}_k$ fulfills also D4a. Therefore, $\mathfrak{T}_i \, \epsilon \, \mathfrak{M}_k$ (D4); $\mathfrak{T}_j$ is true; $\mathfrak{T}_i \to \mathfrak{T}_j$ ([I] T9-13). — *Proof for* (b). Let the conditions be fulfilled. Let S' be the sub-system of S which contains the junctives of K only. Then S' is also an L-true interpretation for K. For the sake of an indirect proof, let us suppose that $\mathfrak{T}_j$ is not an L-implicate of $\mathfrak{T}_i$ in S'. Then there would be an $\mathfrak{M}_k$ which fulfills the conditions (a) to (e) in T22-46 with respect to S', $\mathfrak{T}_i$, and $\mathfrak{T}_j$. Then $\mathfrak{M}_k$ would fulfill the conditions (a), (c), and (d) in D4 with respect to $\mathfrak{T}_i$ and K. But it would also fulfill D4b; for, if $\mathfrak{T}_m \, \epsilon \, \mathfrak{M}_k$, and $\mathfrak{T}_m \underset{dC}{\to} \mathfrak{T}_n$ in K, then $\mathfrak{T}_m \underset{L}{\to} \mathfrak{T}_n$ in S' (D1b), hence $\mathfrak{T}_n \, \epsilon \, \mathfrak{M}_k$ (T22-46b). Therefore, since $\mathfrak{T}_i \underset{C}{\to} \mathfrak{T}_j$, $\mathfrak{T}_j \, \epsilon \, \mathfrak{M}_k$ (D4); but also $\mathfrak{T}_j$ not $\epsilon \, \mathfrak{M}_k$ (T22-46e). Thus our supposition is impossible. $\mathfrak{T}_i \underset{L}{\to} \mathfrak{T}_j$ in S' and hence in S.

T23-13 (lemma). Let $\mathfrak{M}_k$ be a class of junctives in S which fulfills the conditions (c) and (d) in D4.

> **a.** If every sentence in $\mathfrak{M}_k$ is true (in S), then every junctive in $\mathfrak{M}_k$ is true.
>
> **b.** If every sentence in S which does not belong to $\mathfrak{M}_k$ is false (in S), then every junctive in S which does not belong to $\mathfrak{M}_k$ is false.

Proof. a. Let the conditions be fulfilled. Let $\mathfrak{K}_i^{\bullet} \, \epsilon \, \mathfrak{M}_k$. Then every sentence of $\mathfrak{K}_i \, \epsilon \, \mathfrak{M}_k$ (c) and hence is true. Therefore, $\mathfrak{K}_i^{\bullet}$ is true (D21-3). Let $\mathfrak{K}_i^{\mathsf{v}} \, \epsilon \, \mathfrak{M}_k$. Then at least one sentence of $\mathfrak{K}_i \, \epsilon \, \mathfrak{M}_k$ (d) and hence is true. Therefore, $\mathfrak{K}_i^{\mathsf{v}}$ is true (D21-4). — b. Let the conditions be fulfilled. Let $\mathfrak{K}_j^{\bullet}$ not $\epsilon \, \mathfrak{M}_k$. Then there is a sentence $\mathfrak{S}_j$ of $\mathfrak{K}_j$ such that $\mathfrak{S}_j$ not $\epsilon \, \mathfrak{M}_k$ (c), and hence $\mathfrak{S}_j$ is false. Therefore, $\mathfrak{K}_j^{\bullet}$ is false (T21-1). Let $\mathfrak{K}_j^{\mathsf{v}}$ not $\epsilon \, \mathfrak{M}_k$. Then every sentence of $\mathfrak{K}_j$ not $\epsilon \, \mathfrak{M}_k$ (d) and hence is false. Therefore, $\mathfrak{K}_j^{\mathsf{v}}$ is false (T21-2).

T23-14 (lemma). If $\mathfrak{T}_i$ and $\mathfrak{T}_j$ are junctives in K and not $\mathfrak{T}_i \underset{C}{\to} \mathfrak{T}_j$ in K, then there is a system S such that the following holds:

> **a.** S is a true interpretation for K,
> **b.** $\mathfrak{T}_i$ is true in S,
> **c.** $\mathfrak{T}_j$ is false in S.

Proof. Let K, $\mathfrak{T}_i$, and $\mathfrak{T}_j$ fulfill the conditions. Then, according to D4, there is a class $\mathfrak{M}_k$ such that 1. $\mathfrak{M}_k$ and $\mathfrak{T}_i$ fulfill the conditions D4a, b, c, d; 2. not $\mathfrak{T}_j \, \epsilon \, \mathfrak{M}_k$. Now we construct S in the following way: 3. S contains the same sentences as K; 4. every sentence (not conjunctive or disjunctive) of $\mathfrak{M}_k$ is true in S; 5. every other sentence is false in S. [Since, in constructing a semantical system, we can freely choose the truth-conditions for the sentences, we can obtain the results (4) and (5) simply by laying down, for instance, the rules that any sentence of $\mathfrak{M}_k$ designates the L-true proposition, i.e. that it is true if and only if A or not A, and that any other sentence is true if and only if A and not A.] Then the following holds: 6. Every junctive in $\mathfrak{M}_k$ is true in S ((1), (4), T13a). 7. Every other junctive in S is false ((1), (5), T13b). 8. Let $\mathfrak{T}_m$ and $\mathfrak{T}_n$ be any junctives in K and hence in S such that $\mathfrak{T}_m \underset{dC}{\rightleftarrows} \mathfrak{T}_n$. We distinguish two cases, A and B. A. Let $\mathfrak{T}_m$ not $\epsilon \mathfrak{M}_k$. Then $\mathfrak{T}_m$ is false in S (7), and hence $\mathfrak{T}_m \rightarrow \mathfrak{T}_n$ ([I] D9-3). B. Let $\mathfrak{T}_m \epsilon \mathfrak{M}_k$. Then $\mathfrak{T}_n \epsilon \mathfrak{M}_k$ ((1), D4b) and hence is true (6). Therefore, $\mathfrak{T}_m \rightarrow \mathfrak{T}_n$. 9. (a) from D1, (3), (8). 10. $\mathfrak{T}_i \epsilon \mathfrak{M}_k$ ((1), D4a), and hence is true (6). This is (b). 11. (c) from (2), (7).

+T23-15. $\mathfrak{T}_i \underset{C}{\rightleftarrows} \mathfrak{T}_j$ in K if and only if, for every true interpretation S for K, $\mathfrak{T}_i \rightarrow \mathfrak{T}_j$ in S.

Proof. 1. From T11a. — 2. If $\mathfrak{T}_i \overrightarrow{\rightarrow} \mathfrak{T}_j$ in every true interpretation for K, then there is no true interpretation in which $\mathfrak{T}_i$ is true and $\mathfrak{T}_j$ false ([I] T9-18). Therefore, $\mathfrak{T}_i \underset{C}{\rightleftarrows} \mathfrak{T}_j$ in K (T14).

+T23-16. $\mathfrak{T}_i$ is C-true in K if and only if $\mathfrak{T}_i$ is true in every true interpretation for K. (From D5, T15, T21-15.)

+T23-17. $\mathfrak{T}_i$ is C-false in K if and only if $\mathfrak{T}_i$ is false in every true interpretation for K. (From D6, T15, T21-16.)

+T23-18. $\mathfrak{T}_i$ is C-equivalent to $\mathfrak{T}_j$ in K if and only if $\mathfrak{T}_i$ is equivalent to $\mathfrak{T}_j$ in every true interpretation for K. (From D7, T15, [I] T9-20b.)

+T23-19. If S is an L-true interpretation for K, then the following holds:

    a. If $\mathfrak{T}_i$ is C-true in K, it is L-true in S. (From D5, T11b, T22-24.)

    b. If $\mathfrak{T}_i$ is C-false in K, it is L-false in S. (From D6, T11b, T22-25.)

    c. If $\mathfrak{T}_i$ and $\mathfrak{T}_j$ are C-equivalent in K, then they are L-equivalent in S. (From D7, T11b, P22-9.)

+**T23-21.** If $\mathfrak{T}_i \underset{C}{\rightleftharpoons} \mathfrak{T}_j$ and $\mathfrak{T}_i$ is C-true, then $\mathfrak{T}_j$ is also C-true. (From D5, T4.)

+**T23-22.** If $\mathfrak{T}_i \underset{C}{\rightleftharpoons} \mathfrak{T}_j$ and $\mathfrak{T}_j$ is C-false, then $\mathfrak{T}_i$ is also C-false. (From D6, T4.)

Once the correspondence between C-concepts and radical concepts is proved (T15 to 18), further theorems concerning C-concepts in analogy to those concerning radical concepts can easily be proved (e.g. T23 to 26).

+**T23-23.** $\mathfrak{T}_i \underset{C}{\rightharpoonup} \mathfrak{K}_j^\bullet$ (in K) if and only if $\mathfrak{T}_i \underset{C}{\rightharpoonup}$ every sentence of $\mathfrak{K}_j$. (From T15, T21-5.)

+**T23-24.** $\mathfrak{K}_i^v \underset{C}{\rightharpoonup} \mathfrak{T}_j$ (in K) if and only if every sentence of $\mathfrak{K}_i \underset{C}{\rightharpoonup} \mathfrak{T}_j$. (From T15, T21-6.)

T23-25. Every $\mathfrak{T}_i \underset{C}{\rightharpoonup} \Lambda^\bullet$. (From T23.)

T23-26. $\Lambda^v \underset{C}{\rightharpoonup}$ every $\mathfrak{T}_j$. (From T24.)

T23-27. If $\mathfrak{T}_j$ is C-true, every $\mathfrak{T}_i \underset{C}{\rightharpoonup} \mathfrak{T}_j$. (From D5, T25, T4.)

T23-28. If $\mathfrak{T}_i$ is C-false, $\mathfrak{T}_i \underset{C}{\rightharpoonup}$ every $\mathfrak{T}_j$. (From D6, T26, T4.)

+**T23-30.** $\Lambda^\bullet$ is C-true. (From D5, T5.)

+**T23-31.** Λ^v is C-false. (From D6, T5.)

+**T 3-34.** $\mathfrak{T}_j$ is C-true (in K) if and only if every $\mathfrak{T}_i \underset{C}{\rightharpoonup} \mathfrak{T}_j$. (From D5, T27.)

+**T23-35.** $\mathfrak{T}_i$ is C-false (in K) if and only if $\mathfrak{T}_i \underset{C}{\rightharpoonup}$ every $\mathfrak{T}_j$. (From D6, T28.)

The definition for 'C-implication' given here (D4) for calculi containing junctives has a form quite different from the definition of the same term for calculi of the customary kind ([I] D28-4). Nevertheless, the new concept is in accordance with the old one, as far as the latter goes. This is shown by T41, based on the lemma T40.

T23-40. (Lemma.) Let the calculi K_m and K_n and the class $\mathfrak{M}_k$ fulfill the following conditions A to E.

A. K_m is a calculus of the customary kind (as described in [I] § 28), i.e. the rules of K_m refer only to sentences and sentential classes but not to junctives.

B. K_n is a calculus with junctives, containing all sentences of K_m.

C. If $\mathfrak{T}_i \underset{dC}{\rightrightarrows} \mathfrak{S}_j$ in K_m, then $\mathfrak{T}_i^{\bullet} \underset{dC}{\rightrightarrows} \mathfrak{S}_j$ in K_n. (If $\mathfrak{T}_i$ is $\mathfrak{R}_i$ or $\mathfrak{S}_i$, '$\mathfrak{T}_i^{\bullet}$' means $\mathfrak{R}_i^{\bullet}$ or $\mathfrak{S}_i$ respectively.)

D. If $\mathfrak{T}_i$ is directly C-false in K_m, $\mathfrak{T}_i^{\bullet} \underset{dC}{\rightrightarrows} \Lambda^{\vee}$ in K_n.

E. $\mathfrak{M}_k$ is any class of junctives in K_n fulfilling the conditions (b), (c), and (d) in D4.

Then the following holds:

a. If $\mathfrak{T}_j$ is derivable from $\mathfrak{T}_i$ in K_m (in the sense of [I] D28-2) and $\mathfrak{T}^{\bullet} \in \mathfrak{M}_k$, then $\mathfrak{T}_j^{\bullet} \in \mathfrak{M}_k$.

b. $\Lambda^{\vee}$ not $\in \mathfrak{M}_k$.

c. If $\mathfrak{T}_i$ is C-false in K_m, $\mathfrak{T}_i$ not $\in \mathfrak{M}_k$.

d. If $\mathfrak{T}_i \underset{C}{\rightrightarrows} \mathfrak{T}_j$ in K_m, and $\mathfrak{T}_i^{\bullet} \in \mathfrak{M}_k$, then $\mathfrak{T}_j^{\bullet} \in \mathfrak{M}_k$.

e. $\Lambda^{\bullet} \in \mathfrak{M}_k$.

f. If $\mathfrak{T}_j$ is C-true in K_m, then $\mathfrak{T}_j^{\bullet} \in \mathfrak{M}_k$.

Proof. a. Let $\mathfrak{S}_j$ be derivable from $\mathfrak{R}_i$ in K_m. Then there is a sequence of sentences $\mathfrak{R}_l$ ([I] D28-1) which fulfills the following conditions (F) and (G). F. For every sentence $\mathfrak{S}_n$ in $\mathfrak{R}_l$ not belonging to $\mathfrak{R}_i$, there is a sub-class $\mathfrak{R}_p$ of the class $\mathfrak{R}_n$ of the sentences preceding $\mathfrak{S}_n$ in $\mathfrak{R}_l$ such that $\mathfrak{R}_p \underset{dC}{\rightrightarrows} \mathfrak{S}_n$ in K_n. G. $\mathfrak{S}_j$ is the last sentence in $\mathfrak{R}_l$. Let $\mathfrak{R}_i \in \mathfrak{M}_k$. Then every sentence of $\mathfrak{R}_i$ and hence the conjunctive of every sub-class of $\mathfrak{R}_i$ belong to $\mathfrak{M}_k$ (E(c)). If $\mathfrak{S}_m$ is the first sentence of $\mathfrak{R}_l$ which does not belong to $\mathfrak{R}_i$, then $\mathfrak{S}_m$ is a direct C-implicate in K_m of a sub-class of $\mathfrak{R}_i$ (F) and hence $\mathfrak{S}_m \in \mathfrak{M}_k$ (C, E(b)). Let $\mathfrak{S}_n$ be any sentence in $\mathfrak{R}_l$ but not in $\mathfrak{R}_i$ and let $\mathfrak{R}_p$ and $\mathfrak{R}_n$ be as above (F). Then, if every sentence of $\mathfrak{R}_n$ belongs to $\mathfrak{M}_k$, $\mathfrak{R}_p^{\bullet} \in \mathfrak{M}_k$ (E(c)) and $\mathfrak{S}_n \in \mathfrak{M}_k$ (E(b)). Therefore, by induction, every sentence of $\mathfrak{R}_l$ belongs to $\mathfrak{M}_k$, hence also $\mathfrak{S}_j$ (G). Let $\mathfrak{R}_j$ be derivable from $\mathfrak{R}_i$ in K_m. Then, for every sentence $\mathfrak{S}_j$ of $\mathfrak{R}_j$, $\mathfrak{S}_j$ is derivable from $\mathfrak{R}_i$ in K_m ([I] D28-2b) and, according to the result just found, $\mathfrak{R}_i^{\bullet} \underset{C}{\rightrightarrows} \mathfrak{S}_j$ in K_n, and hence $\mathfrak{R}_i^{\bullet} \underset{C}{\rightrightarrows} \mathfrak{R}_j^{\bullet}$ in K_n (T23). The results hold likewise for $\mathfrak{S}_i$ instead of $\mathfrak{R}_i$ ([I], D28-2c). — b. From (E), D4d, since Λ has no element. — c. Let $\mathfrak{T}_i$ be C-false in K_m. Then ($[\mathrm{I}]$ D28-3) there is a directly C-false $\mathfrak{T}_p$ which is derivable from $\mathfrak{T}_i$ in K_m. If $\mathfrak{T}_i^\bullet$ were an element of $\mathfrak{M}_k$, then $\mathfrak{T}_p$ would also be one (a). Further, $\mathfrak{T}_p \xrightarrow[\mathrm{dC}]{} \Lambda^\mathsf{v}$ in K_n (D); hence (E(b)) Λ^v would be an element of $\mathfrak{M}_k$, which is impossible (b). Therefore, $\mathfrak{T}^\bullet$ not $\epsilon\,\mathfrak{M}_k$. — d. Let $\mathfrak{T}_i \xrightarrow[\mathrm{C}]{} \mathfrak{T}_j$ in K_m. Then ($[\mathrm{I}]$ D28-4) either $\mathfrak{T}_j$ is derivable from $\mathfrak{T}_i$ or $\mathfrak{T}_i$ is C-false in K_m. Let $\mathfrak{T}_i^\bullet \,\epsilon\,\mathfrak{M}_k$. Then $\mathfrak{T}_i$ cannot be C-false in K_m (c). Hence $\mathfrak{T}_j$ is derivable from $\mathfrak{T}_i$; hence $\mathfrak{T}_j^\bullet \,\epsilon\,\mathfrak{M}$. (a). — e. From (E), D4c. — f. Let $\mathfrak{T}_j$ be C-true in K_m. Then $\Lambda \xrightarrow[\mathrm{C}]{} \mathfrak{T}_j$ in K_m ($[\mathrm{I}]$ D28-5). Therefore, since $\Lambda^\bullet \,\epsilon\,\mathfrak{M}_k$ (e), $\mathfrak{T}_j^\bullet \,\epsilon\,\mathfrak{M}_k$ (d).

+T23-41. Let K_m and K_n fulfill the conditions (A), (B), (C), and (D) in T40. Then the following holds:

    a. If $\mathfrak{T}_i \xrightarrow[\mathrm{C}]{} \mathfrak{T}_j$ in K_m, then $\mathfrak{T}_i^\bullet \xrightarrow[\mathrm{C}]{} \mathfrak{T}_j^\bullet$ in K_n.

    b. If $\mathfrak{T}_j$ is C-true in K_m, $\mathfrak{T}_j^\bullet$ is C-true in K_n.

    c. If $\mathfrak{T}_i$ is C-false in K_m, $\mathfrak{T}_i^\bullet$ is C-false in K_n.

Proof. a. From T40d, D4. — b. Let $\mathfrak{T}_j$ be C-true in K_m. Then $\Lambda \xrightarrow[\mathrm{C}]{} \mathfrak{T}_j$ in K_m ($[\mathrm{I}]$ D28-5). Hence $\Lambda^\bullet \xrightarrow[\mathrm{C}]{} \mathfrak{T}_j^\bullet$ in K_n (a); hence $\mathfrak{T}_j^\bullet$ is C-true in K_n (D5). — c. Let $\mathfrak{T}_i$ be C-false in K_m. Then Λ^v belongs to every class $\mathfrak{M}_k$ which contains $\mathfrak{T}_i^\bullet$ and fulfills (b), (c), and (d) in D4, because there is no such $\mathfrak{M}_k$ (T40c). Hence $\mathfrak{T}_i^\bullet \xrightarrow[\mathrm{C}]{} \Lambda^\mathsf{v}$ (D4), and $\mathfrak{T}_i^\bullet$ is C-false (D6).

§ 24. Rules of Deduction for Junctives

In a calculus of the ordinary kind (without junctives), the statement of the primitive sentences as well as that of the rules of inference can be formulated as parts of the definition of 'direct C-implicate', while the formulation of the rules of refutation requires a new basic concept 'directly C-false' ($[\mathrm{I}]$ § 28). In a calculus with junctives, all rules of deduction can be formulated as conditions for direct C-implication. To these rules belong those just mentioned and, furthermore, several kinds of disjunctive rules. Among them, the rule "$\mathsf{V}^\bullet \xrightarrow[\mathrm{dC}]{} \Lambda^\mathsf{v}$" (R1) is of special interest. It has the effect that, in every true interpretation, at least one sentence is false (T18e).

Let us consider how rules of deduction of different kinds can be formulated in such a way that they state conditions for direct C-implication. The purpose of laying down a rule of deduction in a calculus K is to make sure that certain conditions with respect to the truth and falsity of the sentences in K are fulfilled in every true interpretation for K. It will be shown that the rules described serve this purpose.

1. Suppose we wish a certain sentence, say $\mathfrak{S}_1$, to be a *primitive sentence* in K. Our aim herein is to make sure that $\mathfrak{S}_1$ becomes true in every true interpretation for K. If we lay down the rule: "$\Lambda^{\bullet} \underset{dC}{\rightrightarrows} \mathfrak{S}_1$", this aim is reached (T1a). A similar rule is used if every sentence of a certain kind is intended to become true (T1b); there may be an infinite number of such sentences.

T24-1.

   a. If $\Lambda^{\bullet} \underset{dC}{\rightrightarrows} \mathfrak{S}_i$ in K, then in every true interpretation for K, $\mathfrak{S}_i$ is true.

   b. If $\Lambda^{\bullet} \underset{dC}{\rightrightarrows} \mathfrak{R}_i^{\bullet}$ in K, then in every true interpretation for K, $\mathfrak{R}_i^{\bullet}$ is true and hence every sentence of $\mathfrak{R}_i$ is true.

Proof. Let S be a true interpretation for K. a. Let $\Lambda^{\bullet} \underset{dC}{\rightrightarrows} \mathfrak{S}_i$ in K. Then $\Lambda^{\bullet} \rightarrow \mathfrak{S}_i$ in S (D23-1), and hence $\mathfrak{S}_i$ is true in S (T21-15). — b. Let $\Lambda^{\bullet} \underset{dC}{\rightrightarrows} \mathfrak{R}_i^{\bullet}$ in K. Then $\mathfrak{R}_i^{\bullet}$ is true in S (as in (a)), and hence every sentence of $\mathfrak{R}_i$ is true (D21-3).

2. A *rule of inference of the ordinary kind* is formulated here in the ordinary way, except that a conjunctive is taken instead of the class of premisses, e.g. "$\mathfrak{R}_1^{\bullet} \underset{dC}{\rightrightarrows} \mathfrak{S}_2$". Here it is easily seen that the purpose is fulfilled (T3a). Analogously for a class of several conclusions (T3b).

T24-3a [b]. Let $\mathfrak{R}_i^{\bullet} \underset{dC}{\rightrightarrows} \mathfrak{S}_j [\mathfrak{R}_j^{\bullet}]$. Let S be a true interpretation for K, and all sentences of $\mathfrak{R}_i$ be true in S. Then $\mathfrak{S}_j$ [every sentence of $\mathfrak{R}_j$] is true in S.

Proof for a [b]. Let the conditions be fulfilled. Then $\mathfrak{R}_i^{\bullet} \rightarrow \mathfrak{S}_j$ $[\mathfrak{R}_j^{\bullet}]$ in S (D23-1). $\mathfrak{R}_i^{\bullet}$ is true in S (D21-3). Therefore $\mathfrak{S}_j$ $[\mathfrak{R}_j^{\bullet}]$ is true ([I] T9-10) [and hence every sentence of $\mathfrak{R}_j$ (D21-3)].

3. Disjunctive rules

a. Suppose we want to ensure that, in every true interpretation for K, at least one of a given class of sentences, say $\Re_1$, is true. Then we lay down the rule: "$\Lambda^\bullet \underset{dC}{\rightrightarrows} \Re_1^v$" (T5). Here, we may call $\Re_1^v$ a *primitive disjunctive*, in analogy to the term 'primitive sentence'. If those sentences are finite in number, and each of them is known, say $\mathfrak{S}_1$, $\mathfrak{S}_2$, and $\mathfrak{S}_3$, then the rule is: "$\Lambda^\bullet \underset{dC}{\rightrightarrows} \{\mathfrak{S}_1, \mathfrak{S}_2, \mathfrak{S}_3\}^v$".

+T24-5. Let $\Lambda^\bullet \underset{dC}{\rightrightarrows} \Re_j^v$ in K, and S be a true interpretation for K. Then at least one sentence of $\Re_j$ is true in S. (From D23-1, T21-15, D21-4.)

Example of a *primitive disjunctive*. Hempel ("A Purely Topological Form of Non-Aristotelian Logic", *Journ. Symb. Logic*, vol. 2, 1937, p. 97; shorter representation in *Erkenntnis*, vol. 6, 1937, p. 436) constructs a language T of the following kind. T contains neither variables nor connectives. There are certain classes of three sentences each — we call the class of these classes $\mathfrak{M}_1$ — such that there is a true sentence in each of these classes. Hempel constructs a calculus — we call it K — for the language T. He remarks correctly that a rule of the ordinary kind determining the concept of direct consequence or consequence (i.e. direct C-implication or C-implication) does not suffice to represent the fact that there is a true sentence in every class of $\mathfrak{M}_1$. Therefore, he lays down a rule (6.6, p. 106) concerning not 'consequence' but the concept 'closed system' (in our terminology, 'C-complete, C-perfect sentential class', [I] D30-5 and 7). Although this rule is stronger than a rule of the ordinary kind, it does not suffice to ensure that, in every true interpretation for K, there is a true sentence in every class of $\mathfrak{M}_1$. (The reason for this is that there is not necessarily a state-description in S for every L-state; see [I] § 18 at the end.) This can, however, be done by the following disjunctive rule: "For every class $\Re_i$ of $\mathfrak{M}_1$, $\Re_i^v$ is a primitive disjunctive in K (i.e. $\Lambda^\bullet \underset{dC}{\rightrightarrows} \Re_i^v$)"

b. *Disjunctive rule of inference.* Suppose we want to ensure that, if $\mathfrak{T}_1$ is true in any true interpretation S for K, at least one of the sentences of a certain (finite or infinite) class $\Re_2$ is also true. We do this by the rule: "$\mathfrak{T}_1 \underset{dC}{\rightrightarrows} \Re_2^v$".

T24-7. Let $\mathfrak{T}_i \underset{dC}{\rightrightarrows} \Re_j^v$ in K. Let S be a true interpretation for K, and $\mathfrak{T}_i$ be true in S. Then at least one sentence of $\mathfrak{R}_j$ is true in S. (From D23-1, [I] T9-10, D21-4.)

c. A *rule of refutation* has the purpose of ensuring that one or several sentences are false in every true interpretation. If we want $\mathfrak{S}_1$ to become false, we lay down the rule of refutation: "$\mathfrak{S}_1 \underset{dC}{\rightarrow} \Lambda^{\vee}$". If every sentence of a given class $\mathfrak{R}_1$ is to become false, we state the rule: "$\mathfrak{R}_1^{\vee} \underset{dC}{\rightarrow} \Lambda^{\vee}$". If at least one of the sentences of $\mathfrak{R}_1$ is to become false, we state: "$\mathfrak{R}_1^{\bullet} \underset{dC}{\rightarrow} \Lambda^{\vee}$".

+**T24-9.** Let $\mathfrak{T}_i \underset{dC}{\rightarrow} \Lambda^{\vee}$ in K. Let S be a true interpretation for K. Then the following holds:
  a. $\mathfrak{T}_i$ is false in S. (From D23-1, T21-16.)
  b. If $\mathfrak{T}_i$ is $\mathfrak{R}_i^{\vee}$, then every sentence of $\mathfrak{R}_i$ is false in S. (From (a), T21-2.)
  c. If $\mathfrak{T}_i$ is $\mathfrak{R}_i^{\bullet}$, then at least one sentence of $\mathfrak{R}_i$ is false in S. (From (a), T21-1.)

The following rule R1 is a special case of a disjunctive rule of refutation (the last kind discussed above, T9c).

+**R24-1.** $V^{\bullet} \underset{dC}{\rightarrow} \Lambda^{\vee}$.

This rule does not refer to any particular form of sentences, and therefore it is possible to use it in connection with any calculus whatever. It turns out that, for many calculi, the addition of this rule is useful. This is the case if a calculus K contains sentences which, though false in the interpretation intended for K, are not C-false in K but only C-comprehensive (D1, corresponding to [I] D30-6). By adding R1, these sentences become C-false and hence false in every true interpretation (T18c, f).

D24-1. $\mathfrak{T}_i$ is **C-comprehensive** in K $=_{Df}$ $\mathfrak{T}_i \underset{C}{\rightarrow}$ every sentence in K.

T24-11. $\mathfrak{T}_i$ is C-comprehensive (in K) if and only if $\mathfrak{T}_i \underset{C}{\rightarrow} V^{\bullet}$. (From D1, T23-23.)

T24-12. If $\mathfrak{T}_i$ is C-false (in K), it is C-comprehensive. (From D1, T23-28.)

T24-13. In any calculus, the following junctives are C-comprehensive:

a. $V_{|}^{\bullet}$. (From T11, T23-5.)

b. $\Lambda^{\vee}$. (From D1, T23-26.)

T24-14. If $V^{\bullet}$ is C-false in K, then every C-comprehensive junctive in K is C-false. (From T11, T23-22.)

+**T24-18.** If K' is constructed out of K by adding the rule R1, then the assertions (a), (b), (c) hold. If, moreover, S is a true interpretation for K' containing no other sentences than K', then, in addition, the assertions (d), (e), (f) hold. (V is the universal sentential class in K, in K', and in S.)

a. $V^{\bullet} \underset{C}{\rightarrow} \Lambda^{\vee}$ in K'.

b. $V^{\bullet}$ is C-false in K'.

c. $\mathfrak{T}_i$ is C-false in K' if and only if $\mathfrak{T}_i$ is C-comprehensive in K.

d. $V^{\bullet}$ is false in S.

+**e.** There is at least one false sentence in S.

f. If $\mathfrak{T}_i$ is C-comprehensive in K, it is false in S.

Proof. a. From T23-3. — b. From (a), D23-6. — c. If $\mathfrak{T}_i$ is C-false in K', it is C-comprehensive in K' (T12) and hence in K. (The class of C-comprehensive junctives is not increased by R1, because the two junctives involved are C-comprehensive anyway; see T13 a,b.) If $\mathfrak{T}_i$ is C-comprehensive in K, it is C-comprehensive in K' and, hence, C-false in K' ((b), T14). — d. From (b), T23-17. — e. From (d), T21-19 b. — f. If $\mathfrak{T}_i$ is C-comprehensive in K, it is C-false in K' (c), and hence false in S (T23-17).

T18b and e show that the effect of R1 in a calculus with junctives is the same as that of the rule of refutation without a disjunctive: "V is directly C-false" (R20-1) in a calculus of the ordinary kind. There is, however, a difference between the two rules. R24-1 is part of the definition of 'direct C-implicate' and does not involve 'directly C-false' as an additional basic concept, as R20-1 does.

We shall apply R1 in order to supplement PC (§ 26). This will exclude one kind of non-normal interpretation of PC.

E. FULL FORMALIZATION OF PROPOSITIONAL LOGIC

The junctives introduced in the preceding chapter are here used for the construction of a new system of propositional logic (§ 25) and a new propositional calculus, called PC* (§ 26). PC*, in contradistinction to PC, is a full formalization of propositional logic (§ 27).

§ 25. Junctives in Propositional Logic

On the basis of the systems of radical and L-concepts for junctives (§§ 21 and 22), the previous system of propositional logic (§§ 11 to 13) is adapted to junctives. Among the results: a conjunction$_L$ is L-equivalent with the conjunctive of the components (T3b), a disjunction$_L$ with the disjunctive (T4b).

In the last chapter the junctives were introduced, and their use in semantics and syntax was discussed in general. Now we are coming back to propositional logic and propositional calculus, in order to find out what changes these systems undergo if junctives are used.

As a system of semantical concepts for junctives, we shall use that discussed at the end of § 22, based on D22-1 and 2. As explained in § 22, this system comprehends all theorems of § 22 (including P22-1 to 15, regarded as theorems) and of § 21; further, it comprehends the general definitions and theorems of § 11 (up to D11-12) and of [I] § 18 modified by replacing any reference to a sentential class $\Re_i$ by a reference to the corresponding conjunctive $\Re_i^*$. Then we add, as a system of propositional logic based on NTT, the pertinent definitions and theorems in § 11 (from D11-14 on), § 12, and § 13, with the same modification. On this basis, we shall state here a few more theorems concerning connectives of NTT and junctives.

+**T25-3a** [b]. If S contains a sign of conjunction $_{[L]}$, and $\mathfrak{S}_i$ and $\mathfrak{S}_j$ are closed, then $\{\mathfrak{S}_i, \mathfrak{S}_j\}^{\bullet}$ is [L-]equivalent to $\text{con}_{[L]}(\mathfrak{S}_i, \mathfrak{S}_j)$. (Corresponds to T13-14.)

+**T25-4a** [b]. If S contains a sign of disjunction $_{[L]}$, and $\mathfrak{S}_i$ and $\mathfrak{S}_j$ are closed, then $\{\mathfrak{S}_i, \mathfrak{S}_j\}^{\vee}$ is [L-]equivalent to $\text{dis}_{[L]}(\mathfrak{S}_i, \mathfrak{S}_j)$. (From T13-13(2), D22-2, T11-6(2).)

Analogous theorems hold for conjunctives and disjunctives with any finite number of elements.

T25-7a [b]. If S contains a sign of negation $_{[L]}$, then, for any closed $\mathfrak{S}_i$, $\{\mathfrak{S}_i, \text{neg}_{[L]}(\mathfrak{S}_i)\}^{\bullet}$ is [L-]false. (From T3, T13-28(1).)

T25-8a [b]. If S contains a sign of negation $_{[L]}$, then, for any closed $\mathfrak{S}_i$, $\{\mathfrak{S}_i, \text{neg}_{[L]}(\mathfrak{S}_i)\}^{\vee}$ is [L-]true. (From T4, T13-25(1).)

§ 26. The Calculus PC*

The calculus PC_1^* with junctives (D1) is constructed out of PC_1 (D2-2) by adding two rules, a disjunctive rule of inference (6) and a disjunctive rule of refutation (7). PC_1^{*D} (D2), in analogy to PC_1^D (D3-6), contains definitions for the other connectives. The general concept of forms of PC* is defined (D3).

Now we shall make use of disjunctive rules in order to supplement PC so as to exclude the possibility of non-normal interpretations for the connectives. We call the resulting calculus PC*. It will be shown (§ 27) that this calculus fulfills the purpose.

The first kind of non-normal interpretation (T16-6) is such that all sentences become true, even those which are C-comprehensive and hence L-false in the intended (L-normal) interpretation. We have seen that, if any calculus possesses this unwanted feature, it can be removed by the addition of R24-1 (see T24-18e, f). This is rule (7) in PC_1^* (D1 below).

The second kind of non-normal interpretation (T16-7) is such that rule Dj4 of NTT (§ 10) is violated. This means that PC does not exclude a true interpretation in which two closed sentences $\mathfrak{S}_i$ and $\mathfrak{S}_j$ are false but, nevertheless, their disjunction$_\text{C}$ sentence $\text{dis}_\text{C}(\mathfrak{S}_i,\mathfrak{S}_j)$ is true. On the other hand, in the system of propositional logic on the basis of NTT, if a disjunction of closed sentences is true, at least one of the two components is true, and hence their disjunctive is true; in other words, $\text{dis}(\mathfrak{S}_i,\mathfrak{S}_j) \rightarrow \{\mathfrak{S}_i, \mathfrak{S}_j\}^\text{v}$. In order to ensure that this should be the case in every true interpretation, we have merely to add a corresponding disjunctive rule: "$\text{dis}_\text{C}(\mathfrak{S}_i,\mathfrak{S}_j) \underset{\text{dC}}{\rightrightarrows} \{\mathfrak{S}_i, \mathfrak{S}_j\}^\text{v}$, for closed $\mathfrak{S}_i$ and $\mathfrak{S}_j$". This is rule (6) in PC_1^* (D1).

As an example of a form of PC, we have previously stated PC_1 (D2-2). The corresponding form PC_1^* consists of the same rules (with conjunctives instead of classes) and, in addition, the two disjunctive rules (6) and (7) just mentioned.

+D26-1. *K* **contains** PC_1^* **with** neg$_\text{C}$ **as sign of negation**$_\text{C}$ **and** dis$_\text{C}$ **as sign of disjunction**$_\text{C}$ $=_{\text{Df}}$ *K* fulfills the following conditions:

   a. neg$_\text{C}$ is a singulary and dis$_\text{C}$ a binary general connective in *K*.
   b. The relation of direct C-implication holds in the following cases for any $\mathfrak{S}_i$, $\mathfrak{S}_j$, and $\mathfrak{S}_k$ (but not necessarily only in these cases):

   1, 2, 3, 4, as in D2-2b but with '$\Lambda^\bullet$' instead of 'Λ'.
   5. $\{\mathfrak{S}_i, \text{dis}_\text{C}(\text{neg}_\text{C}(\mathfrak{S}_i),\mathfrak{S}_j)\}^\bullet \underset{\text{dC}}{\rightrightarrows} \mathfrak{S}_j$.
   6. $\text{dis}_\text{C}(\mathfrak{S}_i,\mathfrak{S}_j) \underset{\text{dC}}{\rightrightarrows} \{\mathfrak{S}_i, \mathfrak{S}_j\}^\text{v}$, where $\mathfrak{S}_i$ and $\mathfrak{S}_j$ are closed.
   7. $\text{V}^\bullet \underset{\text{dC}}{\rightrightarrows} \Lambda^\text{v}$

In analogy to 'PC_1^D' (D3-6), we define '$\text{PC}_1^{*\text{D}}$'.

+**D26-2.** K **contains** PC_1^{*D} $=_{Df}$ K contains PC_1^* and, in addition, definition rules on the basis of neg_C and dis_C for signs for all other singulary and binary connections$_C$, with definientia as given in column (5) of the table in § 3.

The general concept of forms of PC* (D3) is defined in analogy to D4-1.

D26-3. A calculus K_p **contains** (a form of) **PC*** $=_{Df}$ there are calculi K_m and K_n such that the following conditions are fulfilled:

    a. K_m contains PC_1^{*D}.

    b. K_n is a conservative sub-calculus of K_m ([I] D31-7).

    c. For every sentence $\mathfrak{S}_i$ in K_m there is a sentence $\mathfrak{S}_j$ in K_n (and K_m) which is C-equivalent to $\mathfrak{S}_i$ in K_m.

    d. K_p is isomorphic to K_n by a correlation H.

§ 27. PC* is a Full Formalization of Propositional Logic

> The interpretations for PC* are examined. It is found that the connectives neg_C and dis_C in PC_1^* have a normal interpretation in any true interpretation for PC_1^* and an L-normal interpretation in any L-true interpretation for PC_1^* (T1). The same holds for all $4 + 16$ connectives in PC_1^{*D} (T5), and likewise in any other form of PC* (T9). Thus PC* is a full formalization of propositional logic.

Now it will be shown that the connectives in PC* can only be interpreted normally.

+**T27-1a [b].** If K contains PC_1^* and S is an [L-]true interpretation for K containing only the sentences of K, then neg_C and dis_C in K have an [L-]normal interpretation in S.

Proof. Let K_m be a calculus of the ordinary kind (without rules of refutation) corresponding to K (i.e. the relation between K_m and K is that described for K_m and K_n in T23-40 A, B, C; D is fulfilled vacuously). Then, K_m contains PC_1. Therefore, analogues to all previous theorems concerning PC_1 hold for K (T23-41). — I, for (a) (see remark preceding T15-4). Let $\mathfrak{S}_i$ and $\mathfrak{S}_j$ be any closed sentences in K and S. $\mathrm{dis}_C(\mathfrak{S}_i,\mathfrak{S}_j) \overrightarrow{_{dC}} \{\mathfrak{S}_i, \mathfrak{S}_j\}^\vee$ in K (D26-1b(6)); therefore $\mathrm{dis}_C(\mathfrak{S}_i,\mathfrak{S}_j) \to \{\mathfrak{S}_i, \mathfrak{S}_j\}^\vee$ in S (D23-1a). Hence, if $\mathrm{dis}_C(\mathfrak{S}_i,\mathfrak{S}_j)$ is true in S, $\{\mathfrak{S}_i, \mathfrak{S}_j\}^\vee$ is also true, and at least one of the two sentences is true (D21-4). In other words, if both sentences are false, $\mathrm{dis}_C(\mathfrak{S}_i,\mathfrak{S}_j)$ is false. Thus dis_C generally satisfies rule Dj4 in NTT. Further, dis_C generally satisfies Dj1 to 3 (T15-4a). Hence, dis_C is a sign of disjunction in S (T11-12a) and has a normal interpretation (D15-1a). neg_C in K cannot violate N2 in S because otherwise dis_C would violate Dj4 (T15-7d). In consequence of rule (7) (D26-1b(7)), at least one sentence in S is false (T24-18e). Therefore, neg_C generally satisfies N1 (T15-6), is a sign of negation in S, and has a normal interpretation. — II, for a [b]. Let $\mathfrak{S}_k$ be $\mathrm{dis}_C(\mathfrak{S}_i,\mathfrak{S}_j)$. Because of rule (6), $\mathfrak{S}_k \overrightarrow{_{[L]}} \{\mathfrak{S}_i, \mathfrak{S}_j\}^\vee$ in S (D23-1). Therefore, $-R_k + R_i + R_j$ contains rs (D22-2, [I] T20-28) [is V_s (D22-2, [I] T20-10)]. Hence, dis_C generally [L-]satisfies Dj4 (T13-10(4)), and likewise Dj1, 2, and 3 (T15-4). Hence, dis_C is a sign of disjunction$_{[L]}$ in S (T11-12). Let $\mathfrak{S}_n$ be $\mathrm{neg}_C(\mathfrak{S}_i)$, and $\mathfrak{S}_p$ be $\mathrm{dis}_C(\mathfrak{S}_i,\mathfrak{S}_n)$. Then, because of rule (6) as above, $-R_p + R_i + R_n$ contains rs [is V_s]. $\mathfrak{S}_p$ is C-true in K (T5-1a), and hence [L-]true in S (T23-16 [T23-19a]). Hence R_p contains rs [is V_s]. Therefore, $R_i + R_n$ contains rs [is V_s]. Let $\mathfrak{K}_m^\bullet$ be $\{\mathfrak{S}_i, \mathfrak{S}_n\}^\bullet$. $\mathfrak{K}_m^\bullet \overrightarrow{_{C^\bullet}}V^\bullet$ in K (T5-2l, T23-23); hence $\mathfrak{K}_m^\bullet \overrightarrow{_{[L]}} V^\bullet$ in S (T23-11). Because of rule (7), $V^\bullet$ is [L-]false in S (T24-18d [T22-25]). Therefore, $\mathfrak{K}_m^\bullet$ is [L-]false ([I] T9-11 [P22-7]). Hence, $R_i \times R_n$ does not contain rs [is Λ_s] (D22-1); hence, $-R_i + (-R_n)$ contains rs [is V_s]. We found previously the same for $R_i + R_n$. Therefore, neg_C is a sign of negation$_{[L]}$ in S (T13-5).

Note on T1. If K contains two sub-calculi of the form PC_1^*, and S is an [L-]true interpretation for K, then obviously, according to T1, both signs of negation$_C$ and both signs of disjunction$_C$ have an [L-]normal interpretation in S. But the same result is obtained if only one of the sub-calculi has the form PC_1^* while the other has the ordinary form PC_1 without disjunctive rules, provided that K fulfills the conditions (B) and (C) in T6-10. This follows from T15-1 and 2.

+T27-5a [b]. If K contains PC_1^{*D} and S is an [L-]true interpretation for K containing only the sentences of K, then all connectives of PC_1^{*D} in K have an [L-]normal interpretation in S. (From T1, T16-2. Analogues to previous theorems concerning PC_1^D hold here; see proof for T1.)

+**T27-9a [b]**. Let K contain any form of PC*. If S is an [L-]true interpretation for K containing only the sentences of K, then every connective of PC* in K has an [L-]normal interpretation in S.

Proof for a [b]. Let the conditions be fulfilled, and K_p be K. Then there are calculi K_m and K_n fulfilling the conditions (a) to (d) in D26-3. Let us further make the following assumptions. (They do not restrict the generality, except that we refer only to a binary connective; the consideration for a singulary connective would be analogous.) **A.** Let S_p be S; hence S_p is an [L-]true interpretation for K_p. **B.** Let $\mathfrak{a}_n$ be a sign in K_n and hence in K_m, and let it be the sign for $cConn_r^2$ in PC_1^{*D} in K_m. **C.** Let $\mathfrak{S}_n$ and $\mathfrak{S}_n'$ be any closed sentences in K_n. **D.** Let $\mathfrak{a}_p$, $\mathfrak{S}_p$, and $\mathfrak{S}_p'$ be the H-correlates (according to D26-3d) in K_p to $\mathfrak{a}_n$, $\mathfrak{S}_n$, and $\mathfrak{S}_n'$ respectively. **E.** Let the system S_n be constructed in such a way that the following conditions (a) and (b) hold; then (c) holds too. **a.** S_n contains the same sentences as K_n. **b.** The truth-condition stated by the rules of S_n for any sentence in K_n is the same as that stated by the rules of S_p for the H-correlate of that sentence in K_p. **c.** Any sentence in S_n is equivalent and even L-equivalent to its H-correlate in S_p. (Concerning the application of semantical relations to items in different systems, see remarks at the end of [I] § 12 and of [I] § 16.) **F.** Let the system S_m be constructed in such a way that the following conditions hold: **a.** S_m contains the same sentences as K_m. **b.** For any sentence in S_m which belongs also to S_n, the same truth-condition is laid down in S_m as in S_n. **c.** For any sentence in S_m which does not belong to S_n, the same truth-condition is laid down in S_m as for a sentence in S_n which we choose arbitrarily among those which are C-equivalent to it in K_m (D26-3c); hence the two sentences are L-equivalent in S_m.

On the basis of these assumptions, the following holds:

1. $\mathfrak{a}_p$ is a sign for $cConn_r^2$ in K_p. (From B, D, D4-3.) — 2. S_n is an [L-]true interpretation for K_n. (From A, D26-3d, E.) — 3. If a sentence in K_m is C-equivalent in K_m to each of several sentences in K_n, then these sentences are C-equivalent to one another in K_m and hence also in K_n (D26-3b), and [L-]equivalent to one another in S_n

(2) and hence also in S_m (F(b)). — 4. If a sentence $\mathfrak{S}_i$ in K_m which does not belong to K_n is C-equivalent in K_m to a sentence $\mathfrak{S}_j$ in K_n, then there is a sentence $\mathfrak{S}_k$ in K_n (namely, that chosen according to F(c)) which is [L-]equivalent to $\mathfrak{S}_i$ (F(c)) and to $\mathfrak{S}_j$ in S_m (3); hence $\mathfrak{S}_i$ is [L-]equivalent to $\mathfrak{S}_j$ in S_m. — 5. If $\mathfrak{T}_i \underset{C}{\overrightarrow{}} \mathfrak{T}_j$ in K_m, then $\mathfrak{T}_i \underset{[L]}{\overrightarrow{}} \mathfrak{T}_j$ in S_m. (Proof. There are $\mathfrak{T}_k$ and $\mathfrak{T}_l$ in K_n such that $\mathfrak{T}_i$ is C-equivalent to $\mathfrak{T}_k$ in K_m (D26-3c) and likewise $\mathfrak{T}_j$ to $\mathfrak{T}_l$. Then $\mathfrak{T}_i$ is [L-]equivalent to $\mathfrak{T}_k$ in S_m (4), and likewise $\mathfrak{T}_j$ to $\mathfrak{T}_l$. Since $\mathfrak{T}_i \underset{C}{\overrightarrow{}} \mathfrak{T}_j$ in K_m, $\mathfrak{T}_k \underset{C}{\overrightarrow{}} \mathfrak{T}_l$ in K_m (T23-4), and hence also in K_n (D26-3b). Therefore $\mathfrak{T}_k \underset{[L]}{\overrightarrow{}} \mathfrak{T}_l$ in S_n (2); hence $\mathfrak{T}_i \underset{[L]}{\overrightarrow{}} \mathfrak{T}_j$ in S_m ([I] T9-14b [P22-5]).) — 6. S_m is an [L-]true interpretation for K_m. (From D23-1, T23-3, (5).) — 7. $\mathfrak{a}_n$ is a sign for $_{[L]}\mathrm{Conn}_r^2$ in S_m (from D26-3a, F(a), (6), B), and hence in S_n (F(b)). — 8. $\mathfrak{a}_n(\mathfrak{S}_n, \mathfrak{S}'_n)$ in S_n is [L-]equivalent to $\mathfrak{a}_p(\mathfrak{S}_p, \mathfrak{S}'_p)$ in S_p. (From D, E(c).) — 9. $\mathfrak{a}_p$ has the same [L-]characteristic in S_p as $\mathfrak{a}_n$ in S_n. (From E(c), (8).) — 10. $\mathfrak{a}_p$ is a sign for $_{[L]}\mathrm{Conn}_r^2$ in S_p. (From (9), (7).) — 11. $\mathfrak{a}_p$ in K_p (= K) has an [L-]normal interpretation in S_p (= S). (From D15-1, (1), (10).)

It has previously been explained (at the end of § 18) under what condition a calculus may be called a *full formalization of propositional logic* as represented by the rules NTT. T1, 5, and 9 show that any calculus containing the special forms PC_1^* or PC_1^{*D} or in general any form of PC* fulfills that condition.

We have formerly seen (§ 19 at the end) that the following two principles hold in the propositional logic, but that their validity is not assured by PC:

A. *Principle of (Excluded) Contradiction.* A sentence and its negation cannot both be true.

B. *Principle of Excluded Middle.* A sentence and its negation cannot both be false.

It follows from the preceding results that the validity of both principles is assured by PC*; that is to say, the principles hold in any true interpretation of a calculus containing PC* with respect to neg_C in PC*. In the case of PC_1^*, this can easily be seen directly on the basis of the rules (see D26-1).

Let K contain PC_1^* and hence PC_1. Let S be a true interpretation for K, and $\mathfrak{S}_i$ be any closed sentence in K. Then every sentence, and hence also V, is a C-implicate of $\{\mathfrak{S}_i, \text{neg}_C(\mathfrak{S}_i)\}$ in PC_1 (T5-2l). Therefore, $\text{V}^\bullet$, and hence, according to rule (7) (D26-1), Λ^v is a C-implicate of $\{\mathfrak{S}_i, \text{neg}_C(\mathfrak{S}_i)\}^\bullet$ in K. Hence, this conjunctive is false in S (T23-11a, T21-16), and at least one of the two sentences $\mathfrak{S}_i$ and $\text{neg}_C(\mathfrak{S}_i)$ is false in S (T21-1). This is A. Further, $\text{dis}_C(\mathfrak{S}_i, \text{neg}_C(\mathfrak{S}_i))$ is C-true in K (T5-1a). Hence, according to rule (6), $\{\mathfrak{S}_i, \text{neg}_C(\mathfrak{S}_i)\}^\text{v}$ is C-true in K and true in S. Therefore at least one of the sentences $\mathfrak{S}_i$ and $\text{neg}_C(\mathfrak{S}_i)$ is true in S (D21-4). This is B.

F. FULL FORMALIZATION OF FUNCTIONAL LOGIC

The problem of the possibility of a full formalization of functional logic (with respect to predicates of first level only) is discussed. The ordinary form FC_1 of the (lower) functional calculus is not sufficient for this purpose (§ 28). With the help of transfinite junctives (§ 29), the calculus FC_1^* is constructed (§ 30). This calculus is a full formalization of functional logic (§ 31). Finally, an alternative to the use of junctives is explained, based on a concept called 'involution'; with its help, a calculus FC_1^{**} is constructed, which is likewise a full formalization of functional logic (§ 32).

§ 28. The Functional Calculus (FC)

As logic of functions, we take a system with predicates of first level and a denumerable set of individuals, all of them designated by individual constants. The rules of a special form (FC_1) of the ordinary lower functional calculus (FC) are laid down (D1 and 2). The concepts of normal interpretations for the universal and the existential operators are defined (D6 and 7). A true interpretation of FC_1 is indicated in which the operators have a non-normal interpretation. Therefore, FC is not a full formalization of functional logic. — The result of substituting an individual constant for a free individual variable in $\mathfrak{S}_i$ is called an instance of $\mathfrak{S}_i$ (D3).

In the previous chapters we have studied the ordinary propositional calculus PC. By using junctives, we have transformed it into a new calculus PC*, which is a full formalization of propositional logic. Analogously, we shall now study the ordinary functional calculus FC, and transform it into a new calculus FC*, which is a full formalization of functional logic. Here the use of transfinite junctives will be necessary.

For the sake of simplicity and brevity we shall restrict the following investigation in several respects. We shall analyze only the lower functional calculus (containing predicates of the first level only). We shall discuss only one form of it; we shall call it FC_1 because it is analogous to the form PC_1 of PC (D2-2). As in the case of PC, the results found for FC_1 hold in an analogous way for the other forms of FC also.

The form FC_1 to be explained below is, in its essential features, the form constructed by Hilbert and Bernays; see Hilbert and Ackermann [Logik], Kap. III, and Hilbert and Bernays [Grundl. Math. I], § 4. We simplify this form here by using individual variables as the only variables. We discard propositional variables (see § 2) and predicate variables; instead of Hilbert's primitive sentences we have then to use primitive sentential schemata (as in PC_1; see § 2). The inclusion of these two kinds of variables would not, however, cause any difficulty in establishing a full formalization.

We presuppose a system of functional logic; the task will be to give a formalization, and if possible a full formalization, of this functional logic. We suppose that the realm of individuals, i.e. the realm of values for the individual variables, is denumerable (i.e. there is a one-one correlation between the individuals and the natural numbers). Further, we presuppose that every individual is designated by an individual constant in the system (e.g. 'a', 'b', . . .). [Instead of individual constants, individual expressions might be used, as e.g. the so-called accented expressions 'o', 'o'', 'o''', etc., as used by Hilbert in another system, and in [Syntax] in languages I and II; see [Syntax] § 3.]

The calculus FC is a calculus of the ordinary kind; that is to say, we deal here not with junctives but with sentences and sentential classes only. Later we shall again make use of junctives.

The Calculus FC₁

1. Classification of signs

a. Sign of negation (neg_C), sign of disjunction (dis_C), parentheses, comma (as in PC_1).

b. Individual constants.

c. Individual variables (i).

(b) and (c) are called individual signs (in).

d. Any number of predicates of any degree.

(pr^n is the class of predicates of degree n.)

e. The existential sign '$\exists$' (its name in the metalanguage is also '$\exists$').

2. Rules of formation

+D28-1. An expression in FC_1 is a *sentence* in FC_1 $=_{Df}$ it has one of the following forms (a) to (e).

a. $pr^n(in_{k1}, in_{k2}, in_{k3}, \ldots in_{kn})$ (an atomic sentence consisting of a predicate of degree n with n individual signs as arguments).

b. $neg_C(\mathfrak{S}_i)$.

c. $dis_C(\mathfrak{S}_i, \mathfrak{S}_j)$.

d. $(i_k)(\mathfrak{S}_i)$.

e. $(\exists i_k)(\mathfrak{S}_i)$.

3. Rules of deduction

+D28-2. Direct C-implication in FC₁ holds in the following cases (1) to (5), (8) to (13), and only in these.

1 to 5, as in PC_1; see $D2\text{-}2$.

8. $\Lambda \xrightarrow[dC]{} dis_C(neg_C((i_k)(\mathfrak{S}_i)), \mathfrak{S}_i)$.

9. $\Lambda \xrightarrow[dC]{} dis_C(neg_C(\mathfrak{S}_i), (\exists i_k)(\mathfrak{S}_i))$.

10. $\mathfrak{S}_i \xrightarrow[dC]{} \mathfrak{S}_i \binom{i_k}{in_m}$, where in_m is not a variable which would be bound at one of the places of substitution after the substitution.

11. $\mathrm{dis_C}(\mathfrak{S}_i, \mathfrak{S}_j) \underset{\mathrm{dC}}{\rightarrow} \mathrm{dis_C}(\mathfrak{S}_i, (\mathfrak{i}_m)(\mathfrak{S}_j))$, provided $\mathfrak{i}_m$ does not occur as a free variable in $\mathfrak{S}_i$.

12. $\mathrm{dis_C}(\mathrm{neg_C}(\mathfrak{S}_i), \mathfrak{S}_j) \underset{\mathrm{dC}}{\rightarrow} \mathrm{dis_C}(\mathrm{neg_C}((\exists \mathfrak{i}_m)(\mathfrak{S}_i)), \mathfrak{S}_j)$, provided $\mathfrak{i}_m$ does not occur as a free variable in $\mathfrak{S}_j$.

13. $\mathfrak{S}_i \underset{\mathrm{dC}}{\rightarrow} \mathfrak{S}_j$ where $\mathfrak{S}_i$ contains as part a sentence $\mathfrak{S}_k$ of the form $(\mathfrak{i}_m)(\mathfrak{S}_p)$ or $(\exists \mathfrak{i}_m)(\mathfrak{S}_p)$, and $\mathfrak{S}_j$ is constructed out of $\mathfrak{S}_i$ by replacing $\mathfrak{S}_k$ with $(\mathfrak{i}_n)\left(\mathfrak{S}_p\binom{\mathfrak{i}_m}{\mathfrak{i}_n}\right)$ or $(\exists \mathfrak{i}_n)\left(\mathfrak{S}_p\binom{\mathfrak{i}_m}{\mathfrak{i}_n}\right)$ respectively; here, $\mathfrak{i}_n$ may be any variable not occurring in $\mathfrak{S}_p$.

Explanation. (8) and (9) correspond to the following two primitive sentences in Hilbert's system, written with a predicate variable 'F' and with '$\supset$' as a defined sign of implication$_C$: '$(x)(F(x)) \supset F(x)$' and '$F(x) \supset (\exists x)(F(x))$'. (10) is the rule of substitution. $\mathfrak{S}_i\binom{\mathfrak{i}_k}{\mathfrak{in}_m}$ is the sentence constructed out of $\mathfrak{S}_i$ by substituting $\mathfrak{in}_m$ for $\mathfrak{i}_k$ at all places where $\mathfrak{i}_k$ occurs as a free variable in $\mathfrak{S}_i$. (11) and (12) are the rules of insertion for the universal and the existential operator. (13) is the rule for replacing one bound variable by another.

D28-3. $\mathfrak{S}_j$ is an **instance** of $\mathfrak{S}_i$ with respect to $\mathfrak{i}_k$ in $\mathrm{FC_1}$ (or in $\mathrm{FC_1^*}$, § 30) $=_{\mathrm{Df}}$ $\mathfrak{S}_j$ has the form $\mathfrak{S}_i\binom{\mathfrak{i}_k}{\mathfrak{in}_m}$ where $\mathfrak{in}_m$ is an individual constant.

Examples. 'P(a)', 'P(b)', etc., are instances of 'P(x)' with respect to 'x'. Of 'P(x) ∨ Q(y)', 'P(a) ∨ Q(y)' is an instance with respect to 'x', 'P(x) ∨ Q(a)' with respect to 'y'. If $\mathfrak{i}_k$ does not occur as a free variable in $\mathfrak{S}_i$ (e.g. 'x' in 'R(a,b)', 'R(a,y)', '(x)R(a,x)'), then $\mathfrak{S}_i$ itself is the only instance of $\mathfrak{S}_i$.

D28-4. $\{\mathfrak{S}_i\binom{\mathfrak{i}_k}{}\}$ (in $\mathrm{FC_1}$ or $\mathrm{FC_1^*}$) $=_{\mathrm{Df}}$ the class of the instances of $\mathfrak{S}_i$ with respect to $\mathfrak{i}_k$.

In T4, we list some examples for C-implication in $\mathrm{FC_1}$, for reference in subsequent proofs.

T28-4. In each of the following cases, $\mathfrak{S}_j$ is a *C-implicate* of $\mathfrak{S}_i$ in $\mathrm{FC_1}$.

	$\mathfrak{S}_i$ is:	$\mathfrak{S}_j$ is:
a.	$(\mathfrak{i}_k)(\mathfrak{S}_p)$	$\mathfrak{S}_p\!\begin{pmatrix}\mathfrak{i}_k\\ \mathfrak{in}_m\end{pmatrix}$
b.	$\mathfrak{S}_p$	$(\mathfrak{i}_k)(\mathfrak{S}_p)$
c.	$\mathfrak{S}_p\!\begin{pmatrix}\mathfrak{i}_k\\ \mathfrak{in}_m\end{pmatrix}$	$(\exists\mathfrak{i}_k)(\mathfrak{S}_p)$
d.	$(\exists\mathfrak{i}_k)(\mathfrak{S}_p)$	$neg_C((\mathfrak{i}_k)(neg_C(\mathfrak{S}_p)))$
e.	(d) in inverse order	
f.	$(\mathfrak{i}_k)(\mathfrak{S}_p)$	$neg_C((\exists\mathfrak{i}_k)(neg_C(\mathfrak{S}_p)))$
g.	(f) in inverse order	

Proofs. In each of the cases described, $dis_C(neg_C(\mathfrak{S}_i),\mathfrak{S}_j)$ is known to be provable in FC_1 (see e.g. Hilbert [Logik], Kap. iii, § 6, or, for a slightly different calculus, Whitehead and Russell [Princ. Math.], vol. I, *10), and is hence C-true in FC_1 ([I] T29-100). Therefore, since FC_1 contains PC_1, $\mathfrak{S}_i \underset{C}{\rightarrow} \mathfrak{S}_j$ (T7-1).

Let S be a semantical system containing individual variables and individual constants; S may, for instance, contain the signs and sentences of FC_1. The values ([I] § 11) of the individual variables are called the **individuals** in S. We presuppose here that all individual constants in S are value expressions for the individual variables. Therefore, the designata of the individual constants in S belong to the individuals; we call them *directly designated individuals*. (Other individuals in S may either be designated by complex individual expressions, e.g. full expressions of functors, or not be designated at all in S.) Analogously, we call those attributes which are designated by predicates in S *directly designated attributes* in S.

By the normal interpretation of FC we mean that which is ordinarily used. According to it, '$(x)(P(x))$' means 'for every x, x is P (i.e. x has the property P)', and '$(\exists x)(P(x))$' means 'for at least one x, x is P'. Hence, if the operators have a normal interpretation in S, then '$(x)(P(x))$' is true in S if and only if every individual in S has the property determined ([I] § 11) by the sentential function '$P(x)$'; and

'$(\exists x)(P(x))$' is true if and only if at least one individual has that property. This consideration leads to the following definitions D6 and 7.

+**D28-6.** The **universal operator** in FC_1 has a **normal interpretation** in S =$_{Df}$ S is a true interpretation for FC_1, and any closed sentence of the form $(i_k)(\mathfrak{S}_p)$ is true in S if and only if every individual in S has the property determined by $\mathfrak{S}_p$.

+**D28-7.** The **existential operator** in FC_1 has a **normal interpretation** in S =$_{Df}$ S is a true interpretation for FC_1, and any closed sentence of the form $(\exists i_k)(\mathfrak{S}_p)$ is true in S if and only if at least one individual in S has the property determined by $\mathfrak{S}_p$.

It is easy to see that there are true interpretations for FC_1 in which the operators have a non-normal interpretation, even if the connectives have a normal interpretation. Thus, e.g., S_1 may be a true interpretation of such a kind that the connectives have a normal interpretation in S_1, while '$(x)P(x)$' is interpreted in S_1 as "every individual is P, and b is Q", and '$(\exists x)P(x)$' as "at least one individual is P, or b is not Q". (For this example, see [Syntax] § 62.) Therefore FC_1 is not a full formalization of the logic of functions.

The rest of this section is of less importance; the results will not be used in the subsequent sections. T10 shows that some of the previous theorems which contain the condition of extensibility (D6-1) hold also for FC_1 and hence for many other calculi constructed on the basis of FC_1.

T28-10. The rules of inference in FC_1 (D2(5), (10) to (13)) are extensible.

Proof. For (5): T6-5. — The proof for (10) is analogous to that for T6-3a. — For (11). From $dis_C(\mathfrak{S}_k, dis_C(\mathfrak{S}_i, \mathfrak{S}_j))$, C-implication leads, step for step, to the following sentences, under the conditions required for i_m (in rule (11)) and for $\mathfrak{S}_k$ (in D6-1): $dis_C(dis_C(\mathfrak{S}_k, \mathfrak{S}_i), \mathfrak{S}_j)$ (T5-3k); $dis_C(dis_C(\mathfrak{S}_k, \mathfrak{S}_i),\ (i_m)(\mathfrak{S}_j))$ (rule (11)); $dis_C(\mathfrak{S}_k, dis_C(\mathfrak{S}_i,(i_m)(\mathfrak{S}_j)))$

(T5-3k). — For (12). From $\text{dis}_C(\mathfrak{S}_k, \text{dis}_C(\text{neg}_C(\mathfrak{S}_i), \mathfrak{S}_j))$, C-implication leads to the following sentences, under the conditions required for i_m and $\mathfrak{S}_k$: $\text{dis}_C(\text{neg}_C(\mathfrak{S}_i), \text{dis}_C(\mathfrak{S}_k, \mathfrak{S}_j))$ (T5-3j); $\text{dis}_C(\text{neg}_C((\exists i_m)(\mathfrak{S}_i)),$ $\text{dis}_C(\mathfrak{S}_k, \mathfrak{S}_j))$ (rule (12)); $\text{dis}_C(\mathfrak{S}_k, \text{dis}_C(\text{neg}_C((\exists i_m)(\mathfrak{S}_i)), \mathfrak{S}_j))$ (T5-3j). — For (13). Between the disjunction$_C$ sentences, direct C-implication holds, by rule (13) itself.

If K contains a form of FC with predicate variables and contains a rule of simple substitution for predicate variables and a rule of substitution with arguments for predicate variables, then these rules can easily be shown to be extensible. The proof is analogous to that for T6-3a.

Let us consider a calculus K containing the following rule (11′), which is simpler but weaker than (11). Rule (11′): $\mathfrak{S}_j \underset{dC}{\rightarrow} (i_m)(\mathfrak{S}_j)$. This rule is not necessarily extensible. It is so if K permits the operation known as "shifting the universal operator", i.e. if $(i_m)(\text{dis}_C(\mathfrak{S}_i,$ $\mathfrak{S}_j)) \underset{C}{\rightarrow} \text{dis}_C(\mathfrak{S}_i, (i_m)(\mathfrak{S}_j))$ in K provided that i_m does not occur as a free variable in $\mathfrak{S}_i$. This is, for instance, the case in the calculus called language II in [Syntax], because of PS II 19 ([Syntax] § 30). Therefore the rule R II 2 ([Syntax] § 31), which corresponds to rule (11′) above, is extensible, as is shown by [Syntax] Theorem 32.2a. Hence T10 holds also for language II.

The reason for the restriction with respect to free variables in the definition for 'extensible' (D6-1) can now be explained by an example in FC. If we take the rule (11′) just mentioned, then '$P(x)$' $\underset{dC}{\rightarrow}$ '$(x)P(x)$'. On the other hand, '$\sim P(x) \vee (x)P(x)$' ($\mathfrak{S}_2$) is certainly not a C-implicate of '$\sim P(x) \vee P(x)$' ($\mathfrak{S}_1$), because $\mathfrak{S}_1$ is C-true while $\mathfrak{S}_2$ is C-equivalent to '$(x)(\sim P(x) \vee (x)P(x))$' and hence to '$(x)(\sim P(x))$ $\vee (x)P(x)$' and is therefore C-indeterminate. (In the normal interpretation, $\mathfrak{S}_2$ is false if some individuals are P and some are not.) This shows that the restriction in D6-1 is necessary. On the other hand, it can be shown that the restriction is strong enough. It suffices to require that any free variables in $\mathfrak{S}_k$, i.e. the component added, do not occur freely in the rest, without requiring that $\mathfrak{S}_k$ be closed; because '$P(y) \vee Q(x)$' (where '$P(y)$' takes the place of $\mathfrak{S}_k$) is C-equivalent to '$(y)(P(y)) \vee Q(x)$'.

Earlier (at the end of § 6), a procedure was indicated for transforming a non-extensible rule into an extensible one. As an example, let us suppose that a calculus K contains rule (11′) in such a way that (11′) is not extensible, e.g. by containing only the rules of deduction of FC_1 (D2) but with (11′) instead of (11). Then the procedure described earlier would transform (11′) into the extensible rule (11).

+**T28-11.** If K contains FC_1 and there are no other rules of inference in K than those of FC_1 (D2(5),(10) to (13)), then the assertions (a) and (b) in T6-14 hold for K. (From T10, T6-10, T6-12.)

T11 may be called the *deduction theorem for* FC_1 (see remark on T6-12). T10 holds also for the other forms of FC and for the customary forms of the higher functional calculus. Therefore T11 holds for very many calculi in practical use. Many postulate systems are constructed on the basis of the (lower or higher) functional calculus; the postulates (axioms) are additional primitive sentences (see [Foundations] § 16); in most cases there are no additional rules of inference.

§ 29. Transfinite Junctives

If the rules of deduction defining the concept of direct C-implication (or direct derivability) are such that in any given case we can find out by a finite number of steps whether or not that concept holds, then that concept and those rules are called definite; otherwise, indefinite. An indefinite rule usually refers to a transfinite junctive. This is, in the cases of indefinite rules used by logicians so far, a transfinite sentential class (or conjunctive) as C-implicans. But it is also possible to use a disjunctive rule with a transfinite disjunctive as C-implicate. The use of indefinite rules referring to transfinite junctives will be necessary for solving the task of a full formalization of functional logic.

In this section we shall discuss indefinite rules and transfinite junctives because we shall later find them necessary for the construction of a calculus which is to be a full formalization of functional logic (§ 30).

A concept is called **definite** (or effective) if its definition provides a so-called method of decision (*Entscheidungsverfahren*), i.e. a method by whose application we can decide in any given case in a finite number of steps whether or not the concept holds ([Syntax] § 15). If a concept is not definite, it is called **indefinite**. If one of the basic concepts defined by the rules of a calculus K (usually 'sentence' and 'directly derivable', including 'primitive sentence'; sometimes also 'directly C-false') is definite, we call the rules defining that concept definite. If all rules (rules of formation and rules of deduction) of K are definite, we call K a **definite calculus**; otherwise, an **indefinite calculus**. All calculi of the customary kind are definite. But indefinite calculi seem to be admissible and convenient and even necessary for certain purposes.

The above remark concerning the concept 'definite' is meant as a rough explanation only. Within an arithmetized syntax (Gödel's method, see [Syntax] § 19) an exact definition can be given. In this method, expressions are correlated with natural numbers; therefore properties and relations of expressions, e.g. the basic concepts of a calculus mentioned above, are correlated with functions of natural numbers. A syntactical concept is definite if the correlated arithmetical function has a certain property for which several exact definitions have been given which have been shown to coincide with one another: 'λ-definable function' (Church and Kleene), 'general recursive function' (Herbrand and Gödel), 'computable function' (Turing; see *Journ. Symb. Log.*, vol. 2, 1937, p. 153).

Concerning indefinite rules which have been used by logicians, see, below, the comment on D30-3 (14). Concerning the question whether indefinite rules are admissible, see [Syntax] §§ 43 and 45. An example of a task which cannot be solved without the use of indefinite rules is that of constructing an L-exhaustive calculus ([I] D36-3) for arithmetic (see [Syntax] §§ 14 and 34a, [Foundations] § 10 at the end).

If indefinite rules of deduction for calculi are admitted, then the rules may refer not only to sentences or finite sentential classes but also to transfinite sentential classes. We call a rule of deduction which refers to a transfinite sentential class or junctive a **transfinite rule.**

All indefinite rules of deduction which logicians have used

so far seem to be transfinite. Most, if not all, are rules of inference (i.e. of the form " $\mathfrak{T}_j$ is directly derivable from $\mathfrak{T}_i$") of such a kind that the C-implicans ($\mathfrak{T}_i$) is a transfinite class while the C-implicate ($\mathfrak{T}_j$) is a single sentence. The reason for this fact is that the sentential classes have always been taken in the sense which we call now conjunctive, and that the use of a conjunctive is essential only as a C-implicans, not as a C-implicate (§ 23). Now we also use disjunctives; and their occurrence is essential if they are used as C-implicates. Therefore it is now possible to extend the scope of the deductive method still more, by using transfinite rules of a new kind, with a transfinite disjunctive as C-implicate.

Incidentally, in (interpreted, not formalized) logic as represented in L-semantics there are analogous possibilities for the extension of the scope of logical deduction by using a transfinite conjunctive as L-implicans and a transfinite disjunctive as L-implicate.

§ 30. The Calculus FC*

We construct the calculus FC_1^* (D3), which is similar to FC_1; the difference is that FC_1^* is a calculus with junctives and contains three more rules of deduction. These are the two disjunctive rules which PC_1^* contains in distinction to PC_1 (D26-1(6) and (7)), and a rule (D3(14)) stating that $\mathfrak{S}_i$ is a direct C-implicate of the transfinite conjunctive of the instances of $\mathfrak{S}_i$. In FC_1^*, a universal sentence is C-equivalent to the conjunctive of the instances of its operand (T2c); an existential sentence is C-equivalent to their disjunctive (T3c).

With the help of junctives, a calculus FC* can be constructed out of FC such that FC* represents a full formalization of functional logic. For the sake of brevity, we shall restrict our discussion to the form FC_1^* corresponding to FC_1. The classification of signs and the rules of formation of FC_1^* are the same as those of FC_1 (D28-1). The rules of deduction of FC_1^* (see D3, below) contain those of FC_1 (D28-2), with conjunctives instead of sentential classes; further, three rules (6), (7), and (14) are added. The rules (6) and (7) are those which we added earlier to PC_1 in order to construct PC_1^* (see D26-1b(6) and (7)). (14) is a new rule for the universal operator, with a transfinite conjunctive as C-implicans (see D28-4). It will be seen later (§ 31) that, on the basis of these rules, not only the universal operator but also the existential operator has a normal interpretation in any true interpretation for FC_1^*.

Rules of deduction for FC_1^*

+D30-3. Direct C-implication in FC_1^* holds in the following cases (1) to (14), and only in these.

  1 to 7 as in PC_1^*, see D26-1b.

  8 to 13 as in FC_1, see D28-2, but with '$\Lambda^{\bullet}$' instead of 'Λ' in (8) and (9).

  14. $\{\mathfrak{S}_i\binom{\mathfrak{i}_k}{}\}^{\bullet} \underset{dC}{\rightarrow} \mathfrak{S}_i.$

Rule (14) refers to a transfinite conjunctive. Therefore, a rule of this kind can be established without the use of junctives by reference to a transfinite sentential class. In this way a transfinite rule corresponding to (14) was first proposed by Tarski (1927) and Hilbert (1931); see references in [Syntax] § 48, and further Tarski, *Journ. Symb. Log.*, vol. 4, 1939, p. 105. I have used a corresponding rule for language I ([Syntax] § 14, rule DC2) and made more extensive use of transfinite rules also for variables of higher levels (rules of consequence for language II, [Syntax] § 34a–d, f); see also Rosser, *Journ. Symb. Log.*, vol. 2, 1937, p. 129.

The following syntactical theorems (T1, 2, 3) will be used later for showing that, in every [L-]true interpretation for FC_1^*, the operators have an [L-]normal interpretation (T31-1 and 2).

  T30-1.

    a. If $\mathfrak{S}_i$ (or $\mathfrak{K}_i$) $\underset{C}{\rightarrow} \mathfrak{S}_j$ in FC_1, then $\mathfrak{S}_i$ (or $\mathfrak{K}_i^{\bullet}$, respectively) $\underset{C}{\rightarrow} \mathfrak{S}_j$ in FC_1^*. (From T23-41a.)

b. If $\mathfrak{S}_i$ is C-true in FC_1, it is C-true in FC_1^*. (From T23-41b.)

+T30-2. For any $\mathfrak{S}_i$ and $\mathfrak{i}_p$, with $\mathfrak{R}_i = \{\mathfrak{S}_i\binom{\mathfrak{i}_p}{}\}$, the following holds in FC_1^*:

    a. $(\mathfrak{i}_p)(\mathfrak{S}_i) \underset{C}{\rightarrow} \mathfrak{R}_i^{\bullet}$.

    b. $\mathfrak{R}_i^{\bullet} \underset{C}{\rightarrow} (\mathfrak{i}_p)(\mathfrak{S}_i)$.

    c. $(\mathfrak{i}_p)(\mathfrak{S}_i)$ and $\mathfrak{R}_i^{\bullet}$ are C-equivalent.

Proof. a. $(\mathfrak{i}_p)(\mathfrak{S}_i)$ C-implies every element of $\mathfrak{R}_i$ (T28-4a, T1a), and therefore $\mathfrak{R}_i^{\bullet}$ (T23-23). — b. $\mathfrak{R}_i^{\bullet} \underset{dC}{\rightarrow} \mathfrak{S}_i$ (D3(14)). Therefore, $\mathfrak{R}_i^{\bullet} \underset{C}{\rightarrow} (\mathfrak{i}_p)(\mathfrak{S}_i)$ (T28-4b, T1a, T23-3, T23-4). — c. From (a), (b).

+T30-3. Let $\mathfrak{i}_p$ be the only free variable in $\mathfrak{S}_i$, and let $\mathfrak{R}_i$ be $\{\mathfrak{S}_i\binom{\mathfrak{i}_p}{}\}$. Then the following holds in FC_1^*:

    a. $\mathfrak{R}_i^{\vee} \underset{C}{\rightarrow} (\exists\mathfrak{i}_p)(\mathfrak{S}_i)$.

    b. $(\exists\mathfrak{i}_p)(\mathfrak{S}_i) \underset{C}{\rightarrow} \mathfrak{R}_i^{\vee}$.

    c. $(\exists\mathfrak{i}_p)(\mathfrak{S}_i)$ and $\mathfrak{R}_i^{\vee}$ are C-equivalent.

Proof. a. Let $\mathfrak{M}_k$ be any class of junctives such that $\mathfrak{R}_i^{\vee} \in \mathfrak{M}_k$ and that the conditions (b), (c), and (d) in D23-4 are fulfilled. We have to show that $(\exists\mathfrak{i}_p)(\mathfrak{S}_i) \in \mathfrak{M}_k$. Since $\mathfrak{R}_i^{\vee} \in \mathfrak{M}_k$, at least one element of $\mathfrak{R}_i \in \mathfrak{M}_k$ (d); thus there is an $\mathfrak{in}_m$ such that $\mathfrak{S}_i\binom{\mathfrak{i}_p}{\mathfrak{in}_m} \in \mathfrak{M}_k$. $\mathfrak{S}_i\binom{\mathfrak{i}_p}{\mathfrak{in}_m} \underset{C}{\rightarrow} (\exists\mathfrak{i}_p)(\mathfrak{S}_i)$ in FC_1 (T28-4c). Hence, $(\exists\mathfrak{i}_p)(\mathfrak{S}_i) \in \mathfrak{M}_k$ (T23-40d). — b. Let $\mathfrak{M}_k$ be any class of junctives such that $(\exists\mathfrak{i}_p)(\mathfrak{S}_i) \in \mathfrak{M}_k$ and that the conditions (b), (c), and (d) in D23-4 are fulfilled. We have to show that $\mathfrak{R}_i^{\vee} \in \mathfrak{M}_k$. Let $\mathfrak{S}_m$ be any closed sentence, and $\mathfrak{S}_n$ be $\text{dis}_C(\mathfrak{S}_m, \text{neg}_C(\mathfrak{S}_m))$. Then $\mathfrak{S}_n$ is C-true in PC_1 (T5-1a), hence in FC_1 (D28-2), hence $\mathfrak{S}_n \in \mathfrak{M}_k$ (T23-40f). $\mathfrak{S}_n \underset{dC}{\rightarrow} \{\mathfrak{S}_m, \text{neg}_C(\mathfrak{S}_m)\}^{\vee}$ (D3(6)); hence this disjunctive belongs to $\mathfrak{M}_k$ (condition (b) for $\mathfrak{M}_k$). Therefore, for any closed $\mathfrak{S}_m$, either $\mathfrak{S}_m$ or $\text{neg}_C(\mathfrak{S}_m) \in \mathfrak{M}_k$ (condition (d)). Now we shall show that at least one sentence of $\mathfrak{R}_i$ belongs to $\mathfrak{M}_k$. For the purpose of an indirect proof, let us suppose that no sentence of $\mathfrak{R}_i$ belonged to $\mathfrak{M}_k$. Then, according to the result just found, for every sentence $\mathfrak{S}_l$ in $\mathfrak{R}_i$, $\text{neg}_C(\mathfrak{S}_l)$ would belong to $\mathfrak{M}_k$, since $\mathfrak{S}_l$ is closed. Let $\mathfrak{R}_l$ be the class of these negations$_C$ of the sentences of $\mathfrak{R}_i$. Then $\mathfrak{R}_l^{\bullet}$ would belong to $\mathfrak{M}_k$ (condition (c)). Let $\mathfrak{S}_j$ be $(\mathfrak{i}_p)(\text{neg}_C(\mathfrak{S}_i))$. Then $\mathfrak{R}_l^{\bullet} \underset{dC}{\rightarrow} \mathfrak{S}_j$ (D3(14)); hence $\mathfrak{S}_j$ would belong to $\mathfrak{M}_k$ (condition (b)). On the other hand, $(\exists \mathfrak{i}_p)(\mathfrak{S}_i) \underset{C}{\rightarrow} \mathrm{neg}_C(\mathfrak{S}_j)$ in FC_1 (T28-4d). Therefore, $\mathrm{neg}_C(\mathfrak{S}_j) \, \epsilon \, \mathfrak{M}_k$ (T23-40d). Hence, $\{\mathfrak{S}_j, \mathrm{neg}_C(\mathfrak{S}_j)\}^\bullet$ would belong to $\mathfrak{M}_k$ (condition (c)). Every sentence is a C-implicate of $\{\mathfrak{S}_j, \mathrm{neg}_C(\mathfrak{S}_j)\}$ in PC_1 (T5-2l) and hence in FC_1 and, hence, would belong to $\mathfrak{M}_k$ (T23-40d) in contradiction to our supposition that no sentence of $\mathfrak{R}_i$ belongs to $\mathfrak{M}_k$. Therefore this supposition is false; at least one sentence of $\mathfrak{R}_i \, \epsilon \, \mathfrak{M}_k$. Hence $\mathfrak{R}_i^{\mathrm{v}} \, \epsilon \, \mathfrak{M}_k$ (condition (d)). — c. From (a), (b).

T3b is especially noteworthy: an existential sentence C-implies the disjunctive of the instances of its operand. Thus we find a transfinite disjunctive as a C-implicate in FC_1^*, although the two disjunctive rules in PC_1^* refer only to finite disjunctives (with two and no elements respectively; see D26-1, rules 6 and 7) and no new disjunctive rule is added in FC_1^* (D3). This is brought about by the particular form of the definition of C-implication for junctives (D23-4).

Instead of the transfinite conjunctive rule for the universal operator in FC_1^* (D3, rule 14), we could use the following transfinite disjunctive rule for the existential operator.

Rule 14′. $(\exists \mathfrak{i}_k)(\mathfrak{S}_i) \underset{dC}{\rightrightarrows} \{\mathfrak{S}_i\binom{\mathfrak{i}_k}{\ }\}$ where $\mathfrak{i}_k$ is the only free variable in $\mathfrak{S}_i$. (As to the reason for the restricting condition, see, below, remark on D31-2.)

Rule (14′) leads to the same results as rule (14) (that is to say, FC_1^* and the calculus containing (14′) instead of (14) are coincident calculi [I] D31-9).

§ 31. FC$_1^*$ is a Full Formalization of Functional Logic

> In any [L-]true interpretation for FC$_1^*$, the universal opera-
> tor has an [L-]normal interpretation (T1); that is to say, a
> universal sentence is [L-]equivalent to the conjunctive of the
> instances of its operand (D1). Likewise, in any [L-]true in-
> terpretation for FC$_1^*$, the existential operator has an [L-]normal
> interpretation (T2); that is to say, an existential sentence is
> [L-]equivalent to the disjunctive of the instances of its operand
> (D2). Hence, FC$_1^*$ is a full formalization of functional logic.

As we have said earlier (§ 28), we presuppose a system of
functional logic of such a kind that every individual in it is
directly designated. Therefore, a universal sentence $(i_k)(\mathfrak{S}_i)$
is true if and only if every instance of $\mathfrak{S}_i$ is true. Hence, if
we use junctives, the universal sentence is true if and only
if the conjunctive of the instances of $\mathfrak{S}_i$ is true; both are
L-equivalent to one another. Analogously, the existential
sentence $(\mathfrak{I}i_k)(\mathfrak{S}_i)$ (if it is closed) is true if and only if at
least one instance of $\mathfrak{S}_i$ is true; it is therefore L-equivalent to
the disjunctive of the instances. On the basis of these considerations, we can define the concepts of normal interpretations of the operators (D1a, D2a) with respect to FC$_1^*$. These
definitions are simpler than the former ones with respect to
FC$_1$ (D28-6 and 7). It is easy to see (with the help of D21-3
and 4) that the new concepts are in accordance with the
previous ones. Further, the concepts of L-normal interpretations are here easily definable (D1b, D2b).

+**D31-1a** [b]. The **universal operator** in a calculus K
(containing a form of FC or FC* with junctives) has an
[**L-**]**normal interpretation** in $S =_{Df} S$ is an [L-]true interpretation for K, and for every $\mathfrak{S}_i$ and i_k in K such that
i_k is the only free variable in $\mathfrak{S}_i$, $(i_k)(\mathfrak{S}_i)$ is [L-]equivalent to
$\{\mathfrak{S}_i(^{i_k})\}^{\bullet}$ in S.

+**D31-2a** [b]. The **existential operator** in a calculus K

(containing a form of FC or FC* with junctives) has an
[L-]**normal interpretation** in S =$_{\text{Df}}$ S is an [L-]true interpretation for K, and for every $\mathfrak{S}_i$ and $\mathfrak{i}_k$ in K such that
$\mathfrak{i}_k$ is the only free variable in $\mathfrak{S}_i$, $(\exists\mathfrak{i}_k)(\mathfrak{S}_i)$ is [L-]equivalent to
$\{\mathfrak{S}_i\binom{\mathfrak{i}_k}{}\}^\vee$ in S.

The following counter-example shows that the condition that $\mathfrak{i}_k$ is
the only free variable in $\mathfrak{S}_i$ is essential for D2. In functional logic,
'$(\exists x)R(x,y)$' is not L-equivalent to the disjunctive of the instances
'$R(a,y)$', '$R(b,y)$', etc. The existential sentence is L-equivalent to
'$(y)(\exists x)R(x,y)$', while the instances are L-equivalent to '$(y)R(a,y)$',
'$(y)R(b,y)$', etc., respectively, and hence their disjunctive is L-equivalent to '$(\exists x)(y)R(x,y)$'. This sentence is stronger than '$(y)(\exists x)$
$R(x,y)$'.

The same condition in D1 is not essential (the proof for T1 makes
no use of it) but has been added merely for the sake of analogy.

+**T31-1a [b]**. If S is an [L-]true interpretation for FC$_1^*$,
then the universal operator in FC$_1^*$ has an [L-]normal interpretation in S.

Proof for a [b]. Let S be an [L-]true interpretation for FC$_1^*$. Then,
for any $\mathfrak{S}_i$ and $\mathfrak{i}_k$ in FC$_1^*$, $(\mathfrak{i}_k)(\mathfrak{S}_i)$ and $\{\mathfrak{S}_i\binom{\mathfrak{i}_k}{}\}^\bullet$ are C-equivalent in
FC$_1^*$ (T30-2c) and hence [L-]equivalent in S (T23-18 [19c]). Thus
the universal operator has an [L-]normal interpretation in S (D1).

It is easy to see that a transfinite rule is necessary in order
to assure the [L-]normal interpretation of the operators in a
calculus K containing FC$_1$. $(\mathfrak{i}_k)(\mathfrak{S}_i)$ and $\{\mathfrak{S}_i\binom{\mathfrak{i}_k}{}\}^\bullet$ must be
C-equivalent in K. The rules of FC$_1$ suffice to make every
instance of $\mathfrak{S}_i$, and hence also their conjunctive, a C-implicate of $(\mathfrak{i}_k)(\mathfrak{S}_i)$. The problem is how to make the universal
sentence a C-implicate of the conjunctive of instances. The
universal sentence is not an L-implicate of any proper sub-
class of the conjunctive, since from the fact that some individuals have a certain property we cannot infer that all
have it; still less is it an L-implicate of any finite sub-class.
Here, therefore, a transfinite rule is necessary which makes

use of the whole transfinite class of instances, as rule (14) in FC_1^* (D30-3) does and the alternative rule (14') mentioned above.

+T31-2a [b]. If S is an [L-]true interpretation for FC_1^*, then the existential operator in FC_1^* has an [L-]normal interpretation in S.

Proof for a [b]. Let S be an [L-]true interpretation for FC_1^*. For any $\mathfrak{S}_i$ and $\mathfrak{i}_k$ in FC_1^* such that $\mathfrak{i}_k$ is the only free variable in $\mathfrak{S}_i$, $(\exists \mathfrak{i}_k)(\mathfrak{S}_i)$ and $\{\mathfrak{S}_i(^{\mathfrak{i}_k})\}^\vee$ are C-equivalent in FC_1^* (T30-3c) and hence [L-]equivalent in S (T23-18 [19c]). Thus the existential operator has an [L-]normal interpretation in S (D2).

T1 and 2 show that FC_1^* is a *full formalization of functional logic*.

An existential sentence can be transformed in FC_1 into a C-equivalent sentence with a universal operator and two signs of negation$_C$ (T28-4d, e). Therefore, if the universal operator and the sign of negation$_C$ have an [L-]normal in-terpretation, then the same holds for the existential operator. On the other hand, a universal sentence can be transformed into a C-equivalent sentence with an existential operator and two signs of negation$_C$ (T28-4f, g). Therefore, if the existen-tial operator and the sign of negation$_C$ have an [L-]normal interpretation, then the same holds for the universal operator. Thus we have seen that in FC_1^* (D30-3), where neg$_C$ has always an [L-]normal interpretation because of the sub-calculus PC_1^* (T27-1), the rule (14) for the universal operator suffices to assure the [L-]normal interpretation not only for this operator (T1) but also for the existential operator (T2). Likewise, the rule (14') for the existential operator (see § 30 at the end), taken instead of (14), would suffice to assure the [L-]normal interpretation for both operators.

§ 32. Involution

An alternative to the use of junctives is outlined. It consists in the introduction of the concept of involution (D1) and the corresponding L- and C-concepts (D2 and 6). A calculus FC$_1^{**}$ is given in the form of a definition for 'direct C-involution' (D12). This calculus corresponds to FC$_1^*$; however, it refers not to junctives but only to sentences and sentential classes. FC$_1^{**}$ is, like FC$_1^*$, a full formalization for functional logic.

An alternative to the use of junctives will briefly be explained here, a semantical and syntactical terminology which allows the formulation of the same things we have formulated above in terms of junctives.

We have previously introduced junctives in syntax in connection with the concept of C-implication (§ 23). We have seen that the reference to a conjunctive $\Re_i$ is essential only when it occurs as a C-implicans, while its occurrence as a C-implicate can always be avoided by a reference to the sentences of $\Re_i$. On the other hand, the reference to a disjunctive $\Re_i^v$ is essential only when it occurs as a C-implicate. This suggests the introduction of a term, say 'C-involution', for the special case of the relation of C-implication between a conjunctive and a disjunctive. Therefore, we shall introduce **'involution'** (D1) in such a way that '$\Re_i$ involves $\Re_j$' means the same as previously '$\Re_i$ implies $\Re_j^v$'; the terms 'L-involves', 'F-involves', and 'C-involves' will be used in an analogous way. However, 'involves' will not be defined in terms of junctives. We shall use it in a metalanguage which does not refer to junctives but only to sentences and neutral sentential classes. These classes are neutral in the sense that they are construed neither conjunctively nor disjunctively. Therefore, the concept of truth is not applied to sentential classes but only to sentences. This concept is taken here as basic (in D1); the other radical concepts may be defined as previously ([I] § 9) but with respect to sentences only.

D32-1. $\Re_i$ **involves** $\Re_j$ ($\Re_j$ is an involute of $\Re_i$; $\Re_i \dashv \Re_j$) (in S) $=_{\mathrm{Df}}$ at least one sentence of $\Re_i$ is not true or at least one sentence of $\Re_j$ is true.

We define this and the following concepts with respect to sentential classes only. We make the general convention that the application of one of these concepts to a sentence $\mathfrak{S}_i$ is an abbreviation for its application to $\{\mathfrak{S}_i\}$.

T32-1. $\mathfrak{S}_i \dashv \mathfrak{S}_j$ if and only if $\mathfrak{S}_i \to \mathfrak{S}_j$.

Proof. $\mathfrak{S}_i \dashv \mathfrak{S}_j$ if and only if $\{\mathfrak{S}_i\} \dashv \{\mathfrak{S}_j\}$ (convention), hence if and only if $\mathfrak{S}_i$ is false or $\mathfrak{S}_j$ is true (D1), hence if and only if $\mathfrak{S}_i \to \mathfrak{S}_j$ ([I]D9-3).

On the basis of D1 and T1, 'involution' can now be applied to $\mathfrak{T}$, i.e. to members which are either sentences or (neutral) sentential classes.

The concept of L-involution could be introduced either by a reformulation of the postulates for L-concepts (§ 22, [I] § 14) or on the basis of the concept of the L-range of a sentence (Lr$\mathfrak{S}_i$, §§ 11 and 22, [I] § 20). We shall indicate here the second way. L-implication corresponds to inclusion of L-ranges (D11-7); hence $\Re_i \underset{L}{\dashv} \Re_j^{\mathrm{v}}$ if and only if the product of the L-ranges of the sentences of $\Re_i$ is contained in the sum of the L-ranges of the sentences of $\Re_j$ (D22-1 and 2). This leads to D2.

D32-2. $\Re_i$ **L-involves** $\Re_j$ ($\Re_j$ is an L-involute of $\Re_i$; $\Re_i \underset{L}{\dashv} \Re_j$) (in S) $=_{\mathrm{Df}}$ the product of the L-ranges of the sentences of $\Re_i$ is contained in the sum of the L-ranges of the sentences of $\Re_j$.

In the syntax of junctives, the rules of deduction of a calculus K are formulated as a definition of 'direct C-implication in K' (§ 23). On the basis of this concept, C-implication (D23-4) and the other C-concepts are defined in such a way that they fulfill the requirement of adequacy, i.e. that they hold in all those cases, and only those, in which the corresponding radical concepts hold in every true interpretation for K. An analogous procedure can be applied for the introduction of 'C-involution'. Here, the rules of deduction define '**direct C-involution**' ('$\underset{dC}{\dashv}$'). We have to begin with a definition of 'true interpretation', analogous to D23-1.

D32-5a [b]. S is an [L-]true interpretation for K $=_{Df}$ S is an interpretation for K ([I] D33-1), and for every $\mathfrak{T}_i$ and $\mathfrak{T}_j$, if $\mathfrak{T}_i \underset{dC}{\dashv} \mathfrak{T}_j$ in K, $\mathfrak{T}_i \underset{[L]}{\dashv} \mathfrak{T}_j$ in S.

The definition of 'C-involution' is analogous to D23-4 but simpler.

D32-6. $\mathfrak{K}_i$ **C-involves** $\mathfrak{K}_j$ ($\mathfrak{K}_j$ is a C-involute of $\mathfrak{K}_i$; $\mathfrak{K}_i \underset{C}{\dashv} \mathfrak{K}_j$) (in K) $=_{Df}$ every class $\mathfrak{K}_k$ which fulfills the following conditions, (a) and (b), contains at least one sentence of $\mathfrak{K}_j$.

    a. $\mathfrak{K}_i \subset \mathfrak{K}_k$.

    b. For every $\mathfrak{K}_m$ and $\mathfrak{K}_n$, if $\mathfrak{K}_m \subset \mathfrak{K}_k$ and $\mathfrak{K}_m \underset{dC}{\dashv} \mathfrak{K}_n$, then at least one sentence of $\mathfrak{K}_n \in \mathfrak{K}_k$.

$\mathfrak{K}_k$ in D6 corresponds to $\mathfrak{M}_k$ in D23-4. In analogy to T23-1, it can here easily be seen that, if $\mathfrak{K}_k$ is the class of the sentences in K which are true in a true interpretation S for K, then $\mathfrak{K}_k$ fulfills the condition (b) in D6. Further, in analogy to T23-11: If S is an [L-]true interpretation for K and $\mathfrak{T}_i \underset{C}{\dashv} \mathfrak{T}_j$ in K, then $\mathfrak{T}_i \underset{[L]}{\dashv} \mathfrak{T}_j$ in S. Hence D6 fulfills the requirement of adequacy. The same holds for D7 and 8.

D32-7. $\mathfrak{S}_i$ is **C-true** (in K) $=_{Df}$ $\Lambda \underset{C}{\dashv} \mathfrak{S}_i$.

D32-8. $\mathfrak{S}_i$ is **C-false** (in K) $=_{Df}$ $\mathfrak{S}_i \underset{C}{\dashv} \Lambda$.

Any sentence or rule in the metalanguage (semantics or syntax) formulated in terms of junctives can easily be translated into a sentence or rule formulated in terms of involution. For instance, a sentence stating the relation of implication (or L-implication, or C-implication, respectively) between two junctives is translated into a sentence stating the relation of involution (or L-involution, or C-involution, respectively) in the following way. '$\mathfrak{S}_i$' remains unchanged; '$\mathfrak{K}_i^{\bullet}$' as (L-, C-) implicans and '$\mathfrak{K}_i^{\vee}$' as (L-, C-) implicate are replaced by '$\mathfrak{K}_i$'; '$\mathfrak{K}_i^{\bullet}$' as (L-, C-) implicate and '$\mathfrak{K}_i^{\vee}$' as (L-, C-) implicans are replaced by 'every sentence of $\mathfrak{K}_i$'.

As an example of the formulation of the rules of deduction of a calculus K as a definition for 'direct C-involution in K', we shall state the rules for the calculus FC_1^{**}. This calculus corresponds to FC_1^{*} (D30-3) in the sense that its rules result if we translate the rules of FC_1^{*} from the syntax language of junctives into the syntax language of involution in the way just indicated. Therefore the calculus FC_1^{**} is likewise *a full formalization of functional logic*.

D32-12. Direct C-involution in FC_1^{**} holds in the following cases, (1) to (14), and only in these.

> **1 to 5** as in D2-2b but with '$\underset{dC}{\dashv}$' instead of '$\underset{dC}{\rightarrow}$'.
>
> **6.** $\mathrm{dis}_C(\mathfrak{S}_i, \mathfrak{S}_j) \underset{dC}{\dashv} \{\mathfrak{S}_i, \mathfrak{S}_j\}$, where $\mathfrak{S}_i$ and $\mathfrak{S}_j$ are closed.
>
> **7.** $\mathrm{V} \underset{dC}{\dashv} \Lambda$.
>
> **8 to 13**, as in D28-2, but with '$\underset{dC}{\dashv}$' instead of '$\underset{dC}{\rightarrow}$'.
>
> **14.** $\{\mathfrak{S}_i\binom{i_k}{}\} \underset{dC}{\dashv} \mathfrak{S}_i$.

BIBLIOGRAPHY

The abbreviated titles in square brackets are used in citations in this book. The titles marked by an asterisk have been added in 1958.

Bernstein, B. A. *(Review of Whitehead and Russell [Princ. Math.]), *Bulletin of the American Mathematical Society,* 32 (1926), 711–713.

—— *"The Relation of Whitehead and Russell's Theory of Deduction to the Boolean Logic of Propositions", *ibid.,* vol. 38 (1932).

Carnap, R. [Syntax] *Logical Syntax of Language.* (Orig., Vienna, 1934) London and New York, 1937.

—— [Foundations] "Foundations of Logic and Mathematics", *International Encyclopedia of Unified Science,* vol. I, no. 3, Chicago, 1939.

—— [I] *Introduction to Semantics.* Cambridge, Mass., 1942. (Included in the present volume.)

Church, A. *(Review of Carnap, *Formalization of Logic*), *Philosophical Review,* 53 (1944), 493–498.

—— *"Non-normal Truth-tables for the Propositional Calculus", *Boletin Soc. Mat. Mexicana,* 10 (1953), 41–52.

—— *[Logic] *Introduction to Mathematical Logic,* vol. I. Princeton, 1956.

Hilbert, D., and Ackermann, W. [Logik] *Grundzüge der theoretischen Logik.* Berlin (1928), 3rd ed. 1949. English translation: *Principles of Mathematical Logic.* New York, 1950.

—— and Bernays, P. [Grundl. Math. I] *Grundlagen der Mathematik,* vol. I. Berlin, 1934.

Lukasiewicz, J., and Tarski, A. [Untersuchungen] "Untersuchungen über den Aussagenkalkül", *C. R. Soc. Sci. Lett. Varsovie,* Classe III, vol. 23, 1930, 30–50. English translation in A. Tarski, *Logic, Semantics, Metamathematics.* Oxford, 1956. Chapter IV.

Post, E. L. [Introduction] "Introduction to a General Theory of Elementary Functions", *American Journal of Mathematics,* 43 (1921), 163–185.

Whitehead, A. N., and Russell, B. [Princ. Math.] *Principia Mathematica.* 3 vols. Cambridge, 1910–13; 2nd ed., 1925–27.

Wittgenstein, L. [Tractatus] *Tractatus Logico-Philosophicus.* London, 1922.

INDEX

The numbers refer to pages. The most important passages are indicated by bold-face type.

a[b], 15
ACKERMANN, W., 73, 136
Adequacy of C-terms, 116
Application of semantics, xiii f.
ARISTOTLE, viii ff., 6

b_q, **38**, 48; cb_q, 12, **14**, 17
BERNAYS, P., xiii, 8, 26, 73, 136
Binary connective, 8
Bi-negation, 47
BOOLE, G., x

C1 to C4, **39f.**
C-comprehensive, 125
C-false, **101**
C-implication by PC₁, **15**; by PC, **17**
C-involution, 153
C-terms, **7**, **116f.**
cb_q, 12, **14**, 17
cc_r, 12, **14**, 17
Characteristic, **37f.**, 41, 47, 57, 61
Characteristic function, 36; sentence, 66; value, 45
CHURCH, A., 143
Completeness, xi, **72f.**, 99
con, **38**, 48; con꜀, 12, **14**; conₗ, 48
Conjunction, **38**, **47**, 64; conjunction꜀, 12, 13; conjunctionₗ, 47
Conjunctive, **105**
Conn$_r^n$, **47**; ꜀Conn , 12, **13f.**, 17; ₗConn$_r$, **47**
Connections, **38**, **47**; connections꜀, 11, 12; connectionsₗ, 47
Connective, **8**, **12**, **38**; of NTT, 50
Contradiction, 47
c_r, **38**, 48

Deduction theorem, 26, 142
Definite, **142f.**
Definitions of connectives, 15
Degree, **8**

dis, **38**, **48**; dis꜀, **9**, 12, 14; disₗ, 48
Disjunction, **38**, **47**, 64; disjunction꜀, **9**, 12f., 28f.; disjunctionₗ, **47**
Disjunctive, **105**
Disjunctive rule, **115**, **124f.**
Distribution of truth-values, 37
Dj1 to Dj4, **39f.**

E1 to E4, **39f.**
Effective, see Definite
equ, **38**, **48**; equ꜀, 12, **14**; equₗ, 48
Equivalence, **38**, **47f.**; equivalence꜀, 12; equivalenceₗ, **47**
Exclusion, 47
Extensible rule, **22f.**, **140f.**
Extensional, **52**, **54f.**, 67

FC, **135**; FC₁, **136f.**; FC*, **144f.**; FC$_1^*$, **144f.**; FC$_1^{**}$, 154
Formal, 6
Formalization, **3**; of logic, vii, **4ff.**, 95f.
FREGE, G., x, 6, 18, 114
Full formalization: of propositional logic, **95**, **133**; of functional logic, **150**, 154
Functional calculus, **135ff.**
Functional logic, 136

General connective, **8**
GÖDEL, K., xi f., 143

HEMPEL, C. G., **124**
HERBRAND, J., 143
HERMES, H., 73
HILBERT, D., x, xiii, 8, 20, 26, 72, 73, 136, 138, 139, **145**

I1 to I4, **39f.**
imp, **38**, **48**; imp꜀, 12, **14**; impₗ, 48
Implication, **38**, **47f.**, 64; implication꜀, 12f.; implicationₗ, 48

Indefinite, 143
Individual, 136, **139**
Instance, 138
Intensional, *see* non-extensional
Interpretation for PC, 69ff.; *see* Normal, L-normal, Non-normal
Involution, 151f.

Junctive, **105f.**; C-concepts, 116f.; L-concepts, 109, 111; radical concepts, 106

KALMAR, L., 73
KLEENE, S. C., 143

L-, **42**
L-characteristic, 41, **47**, 49
L-exhaustive calculus, 72
L-extensional, **53ff.**, 67
L-implication by NTT, 51
L-involution, 152
L-non-extensional, **53ff.**, 68
L-normal interpretation, **74, 148ff.**
L-range, **42**, 111
L-satisfying, 46
L-state, **42**
L-terms, **42**; by NTT, 51
LEIBNIZ, G. W., 6
LEWIS, C. I., xiv, 29
Logical analysis, xiii
Lr, **42**
LUKASIEWICZ, J., 11, 73

Matrix, 11
Methodology of science, xiii f.
Modal logic, xiv

N1, N2, **39**
neg, 38, 48; negC, 9, 12, 14; negL, 48
Negation, 38, **47**, 62; negationC, 9, 13, 30ff.; negationL, 47, 62
NICOD, J., 18
Non-extensional, **53ff.**, 68
Non-normal interpretation: for connectives, **75, 82, 85, 91ff.**; for operators, 140
Normal interpretation: for connectives, **74**; for operators, **139f., 148ff.**

Normal truth-table, 36
NTT, 36, **39, 50**

PC, **8, 17**; PC$_1$, 9, 20f.; PC$_1^D$, **15**; PC$_2$ to PC$_5$, 18; PC*, 128, 130; PC$_1^*$, 129; PC$_1^{*D}$, 130
Philosophy, xiiif.
Primitive disjunctive, 124
POST, E. L., 4, 36, 73
Principle: of contradiction, **100**, 133; of excluded middle, **100**, 133
Propositional calculus, **8**, 10
Propositional logic, 10, 36
Propositional variable, 9f., 18, 69

QUINE, W. V., 18, 48, **73**

R$_m$, 42
Real L-state, 43
ROSSER, J. B., 145
rs 43
Rule: disjunctive, 115, 124f.; of implication, 9f., **24**; of refutation, 101f., 125; of substitution, 9f., 137f.; transfinite, 143ff.
RUSSELL, B., xiii, 8, 52, 114, 139

Satisfiable, **xi**
Satisfying a rule, 45f.
SCHOLZ, H., 73
Semantical tendency, ix
Set-theoretic logic, xiii
SHEFFER, H. M., **18**
SINGER, M. B., **x**
Singulary connective, 8
Symmetry, lack of, 83, 105, 111
Syntactical tendency, ix

Tables: of connectionsC, 12; of connections, 38; of non-normal interpr., 82
TARSKI, A., x, xii, 11, 49, **145**
Tautology, 47
Terminology of connections, 47f.
Transfinite rule, 143ff., 149
True interpretation, 115
Truth, **43**
Truth-function, 52
Truth-table, **36, 39f.**

Truth-value, 39
TURING, A.M., 143

Ultimate component, 50
Universally valid, xi

Violating a rule, 45, 76ff., 82

WARSAW SCHOOL, x
WHITEHEAD, A. N., 139
WITTGENSTEIN, L., 37

SYMBOLS

$\sim$, $\vee$, 8
$\cdot$, $\supset$, $\equiv$, $|$, 12, 38
$\dashv$, 152
$\exists$, 137
Λ_s, V_s, 42
$\mathfrak{R}^{\bullet}$, $\mathfrak{R}^{\mathsf{Y}}$, 105
$\mathfrak{S}_i(i_k)$, 138